# Eden Within Eden

# Eden Within Eden

## OREGON'S UTOPIAN HERITAGE

James J. Kopp

Oregon State University Press

Corvallis

The paper in this book meets the guidelines for permanence and durability of the Committee on Production Guidelines for Book Longevity of the Council on Library Resources and the minimum requirements of the American National Standard for Permanence of Paper for Printed Library Materials Z39.48-1984.

**Library of Congress Cataloging-in-Publication Data**
Kopp, James J.
  Eden within Eden : Oregon's utopian heritage / James J. Kopp.
     p. cm.
  Includes bibliographical references and index.
  ISBN 978-0-87071-424-5 (alk. paper)
  1. Collective settlements--Oregon--History. 2. Aurora Colony (Marion County, Or.)--History. 3. Utopias--United States--History. I. Title.
  HX655.O7K67 2009
  307.7709795--dc22

                              2008043489

First published in 2009 by Oregon State University Press
Printed in the United States of America

**Oregon State University Press**
121 The Valley Library
Corvallis OR 97331-4501
541-737-3166 • fax 541-737-3170
http://oregonstate.edu/dept/press

*Dedicated to all who sought,*

*and perhaps found,*

*some part of Eden in Oregon.*

*Oregon is insanely green. It is the thin light left over from Eden.*

William Stafford (1914-1993)
17 October 1975


Engraved on basalt column in Foothills Park, Lake Oswego, Oregon

# Contents

# Preface

I have been seeking utopia in Oregon for over three decades, at least in a scholarly manner. I may have been seeking utopia in Oregon for years prior to that growing up on the eastern side of the Cascade Mountains and then as an undergraduate student at a time when there was a revival of interest in finding Eden, Nirvana, or whatever name one chose to identify their place of perfection. As a native Oregonian I came to feel that there was something special about this land of the empire builders that drew others to this place to seek their own dreams. I became a student of utopianism in both its literary and communal manifestations and, although I took my studies in different directions over the years, I constantly was thinking about how utopia was an important aspect in Oregon's history.

When I finally decided to focus my research on Oregon's utopian heritage, I initiated a three-phased approach to exploring those attempts to establish Eden within Oregon. The initial phase centered on identifying and documenting communal experiments in Oregon. With support from a research grant from the Oregon Council for the Humanities, and with assistance from libraries across the United States, particularly the Special Collections at the University of Oregon Libraries and the Oregon Historical Society Research Library, I was able to track down information not only on the known utopian endeavors in Oregon, such as the Aurora Colony where I spent considerable time going through the files of the Aurora Colony Historical Society, but also in many new and yet undocumented communal groups.

The second phase was to engage in public presentations on the topic and, again with support from the Oregon Council for the Humanities—in particular OCH's Chautauqua program for which I was selected to participate—my presentation, "Eden Within Eden: Exploring Oregon's Utopian Heritage," was offered over thirty times across the state, from Yachats to Enterprise, and from St. Helens to Glendale, from 2003 to 2006. These events were important not only for sharing information about this project but for obtaining information on communal groups and experiments made in the state, particularly since the 1960s, as individuals attending these sessions would often bring to my attention groups that I had not yet identified. As a result of these first two components of my efforts to study Oregon's utopian heritage I identified nearly three hundred communal experiments attempted, or at least planned in some fashion, since the Aurora Colony was established in 1856. The largest segment of these experiments took place in the revival of communal groups in the 1960s and after, but the roots of a number of these communities can be traced to earlier attempts in Oregon and elsewhere. Many of these groups shared the basic belief that the place to attempt these experiments was in Oregon, a place that long had been viewed and described as Eden, or at least resembling elements of what were perceived to be aspects of this paradise known as the Garden of Eden.

The third phase of this study is to present these findings in a narrative survey on Oregon's utopian heritage as well as provide a resource guide on these communal experiments. The document in hand is the result. What follows is an attempt to place Oregon's utopian heritage in several contexts. First is that there is a longstanding view of Oregon as "Eden" and this created an environment, or at least the impressions of one, that would be receptive to utopian experiments. Another important, and often overlooked, context of Oregon's utopian heritage is within the broader history of utopianism in American history, from the religious and philosophical roots of the early settlements and the founding of the country, to the outburst of utopian communal societies that were formed in the United States in the mid-nineteenth century and again in the 1960s and later period. There also is the sense that as Oregon commemorates its sesquicentennial that there still exists a spirit of the ideal that served as the basis for not just communal societies within the state but nurtured broader utopian ideas and attitudes.

The resource guide that appears as the Appendix is intended to provide the most complete information compiled to date on Oregon's utopian heritage. But like the text, the intent of this resource guide is as a starting place for continued exploration and discovery of communal groups within Oregon. The resource guide, although extensive, is not complete, not only for the communities listed, but also for many more groups that have yet to be identified and documented. It is largely for this reason that this project was undertaken—to initiate further research and writing on Oregon's utopian heritage.

Several aspects of this project were in themselves of a utopian nature. One of these was the documentation project itself, which I discussed in a "research files" piece in the *Oregon Historical Quarterly*.[1] Another challenge—both in the presentation phase and in preparing this manuscript—centered on the balance of presenting a work rooted in scholarly methodologies but that would also be of interest to a broader readership. The plethora of notes as well as the resource directory in the Appendix highlight the scholarly intent of the book but, hopefully, this does not get in the way of presenting the story of Oregon's utopian heritage in a way of interest to the lay reader as well. Some of my approach was based on the Chautauqua presentation on this topic that I gave throughout Oregon where I tried to balance the type of information presented. As noted, this was a utopian challenge and I suspect that the ideal was not achieved but the intent was there.

Similarly, finding the balance between conveying information on fairly well-known experiences in Oregon while presenting information on lesser-known communities and offering totally new information on others was a challenging task. I opted for limiting the information in the narrative on some of the more substantial experiments—the Aurora Colony at one end of the utopian spectrum and Rajneeshpuram at the other—while including more text on some of the other communities. In part, this was done because the Aurora and Rajneeshee stories have been told elsewhere—and the sections of these communities in the Appendix demonstrate this—but also because the lesser-known or even unknown stories present views that highlight the breadth of communal undertakings attempted in this Eden called Oregon. Again, that balance is an ideal and undoubtedly does not meet everyone's perception of the perfect presentation.

As noted throughout this study, a key aspect of communal groups is cooperation and community, and this also is vital in the compilation of a work such as this. I am grateful for the cooperation I received from numerous individuals and institutions, and the sense of community that evolved from those who came together in the quest to bring together this study. Having worked in libraries for three decades, I already am well aware of the cooperative and collaborative nature of those who "live" in that community. Many libraries and individuals within them have supported my research efforts, most of them behind the scene in providing valuable resources. Several warrant particular acknowledgments, including James Fox and Linda Long of Special Collections at the University of Oregon, Jenny Bornstein, Doug Erickson, Jeremy Skinner, and Paul Merchant of the Watzek Library at Lewis & Clark College, and MaryAnn Campbell, Lisa Walker, and Lucy Berkley of the Oregon Historical Society Research Library. In addition to libraries around the country, I also found important resources in bookshops—both the physical and online versions—and I want to acknowledge some of these of particular value in my research, including Bolerium Books of San Francisco, Great Northwest Books of Portland, and Wessel & Lieberman Booksellers of Seattle.

Many individuals came forward with information on communal groups in the state that was very valuable and often led to other sources of information. Several of these had attended one or more of my Chautauqua presentations or had learned of my project from someone who had. Included among these were members of a number of the communal groups and I am extremely grateful for their willingness to share their thoughts and experiences with me. However, because of the nature and extent of this survey, I was unable to contact as many of these past and present members of some of Oregon's communes and intentional communities as I would have liked. But the hope is that this project is just a beginning and the opportunity will be there to follow up on this study with more in-depth conversations and discussions with yesterday's, today's, and tomorrow's communards.

As is evident in several chapters of this book, particularly dealing with late twentieth-century groups, I owe much to the critical work that Timothy Miller undertook on the 1960s-era communes. Tim, along with Deborah Altus and others, did much of the initial digging to uncover many of Oregon's communal groups from 1965 to 1975, and highlight that the state was a beacon for these "new pioneers." Similarly, I appreciate the studies undertaken by others on Oregon's utopian roots, including a large number of papers, theses, and dissertations on elements of this heritage, from the Aurora Colony to the feminist and lesbian communities that still exist.

Several individuals provided support in reading drafts of chapters and in other ways. Special thanks for their thoughts and suggestions to Evan Berry, Carol Ginter, Alan Guggenheim, Patrick Harris, Jane Kirkpatrick, Peter Kopp, and Jim Proctor. Also very supportive were Charles LeWarne, who early on suggested that a book on Oregon's utopian heritage was needed, and to Carol Hickman and Marianne Keddington-Lang, who both on several occasions patiently listened to my musings on one communal group or another. Also, in the patiently listening (or not) category were students in several classes I taught at Lewis & Clark College on America's utopian experience where we engaged in many topics relevant to points examined in this book. I also must acknowledge the support (and indulgence) of my colleagues at Lewis & Clark College who have allowed me to pursue this activity.

Grateful thanks are due to the good folks at the Oregon State University Press who saw potential in a study of this kind. Mary Braun heard me speak on Oregon's utopias at a Pacific Northwest History conference and approached me about publishing possibilities. She has been a consistent source of encouragement and guidance in bringing this project to completion. Jo Alexander performed her outstanding skills in editing to tighten up the text and making this a much stronger work, while offering helpful insights into the presentation and content. Tom Booth and Micki Reaman also have assisted in the communal process of bringing this book out. And I also want to thank David Drummond who designed a cover that captures the spirit and scope of this study.

Most importantly, I wish to acknowledge the support, patience, good humor, and camaraderie of my immediate community—my family, who have let me pursue this utopian quest and others. My thanks and love to Sue, Lucy, Ryan, Peter, Sarah, Joe, and Harry for making my good place close to the ideal.

# *Oregon as Eden*

*Yes, ho, for the West! For the*
*blest land of promise,*
*Where mountains, all green,*
*bathe their brows in the sky,*
*While down the great snow peaks*
*the torrents come dashing,*
*And eagles scream out from their*
*eyries on high.*

Abigail Scott Duniway
*Oregon: Land of Promise (1907)*[1]

This last stanza from a poem that Abigail Scott Duniway wrote in 1872 captures the spirit of many who came to Oregon before her, as well as many since. Oregon was a land of promise, of new beginnings, and, for many, a land that conjured up images of the Garden of Eden. Duniway herself used the Eden metaphor in describing two sections of the state in her novel, *From the West to the West: Across the Plains to Oregon.* She first used it to describe the Grande Ronde Valley in Eastern Oregon: her travelers move "through a veritable Eden of untamed verdure."[2] Later some of her characters described "the Willamette valley as the 'Garden of Eden' and gave glowing accounts of the soil, climate, scenery, and plenty with which the western part of the great Oregon country abounded."[3] Duniway is not alone in using the Edenic metaphor for Oregon. In *Pioneer Days of Oregon History* (1905), S. A. Clarke in describing the Grande Ronde Valley encountered by the Jason Lee party notes, "that was as lovely as the Garden of Eden could have been, as it lay in Nature's most exquisite loveliness, cradled among the Blue Mountain ranges."[4] Many other writers have found similar Edenic qualities in the Oregon landscape.

Malcolm Clark, Jr. explores this theme in his *Eden Seekers: The Settlement of Oregon, 1818-1862*:

*The motivation which urged men west were very often personal and*
*never after reduced to paper, or perhaps even to thought, and so are*
*buried beyond discovery. But there was one which was held in common*
*and so has come down to us. It was the vision of a fair land whose fat*
*earth was fed by sweet waters and whose trees moved lazily to blessed*

1

*breezes which blew warm from whatever quarter. Its name was Eden and it was the major apparition of the American Dream.*[5]

Although Eden was apparition, it was also, as Clark notes, aspiration. And he continues, "The image of Eden was capable of endless variations, each nicely calculated to please the mind's eye of the beholder, but none approximated reality."[6] Reality and the dream of Eden are a constant tension in the study of utopia, and this is explored later in this study.

Whether the Oregon country was Eden or something quite different has been a matter of debate almost since the first American set foot on the soil. Some writers note that Eden may have existed prior to the arrival of the Euro-Americans. As William Robbins notes, "One people's Eden ... was another's tragedy; and some would say that the consequences of the newcomer's heroic odyssey was to despoil Eden itself."[7] Native Americans, other ethnic groups, and even the environment itself suffered as the result of a Euro-American view of Eden in Oregon—as they did elsewhere in the history of the United States.

It does not appear that Lewis and Clark or any other member of the Corps of Discovery viewed the land that would become Oregon as Eden, although Meriwether Lewis's joy at sighting the Pacific was close to an Edenic moment. But clearly the trials of the winter the expedition spent at Fort Clatsop were not viewed as living in paradise. Frederick Merk illustrates the varying views of the Oregon country: "The opinions ventured ran the gamut, from the rhapsodies of Benton and Floyd, according to whom the country was a Garden of Eden, to the strident judgment expressed in a New York journal that the country was fit only for the seat of a penal colony."[8] Another assessment from the 1820s notes, "Tracy of New York had met people who had been at the mouth of the Columbia, and so knew that, instead of an Eden there was an inhospitable wilderness; climate black and humid, so that crops could hardly be raised and hardly any place fit for settlement. East of the Cascades was only a waste of sand and gravel."[9] Land that was seen fit for a penal colony or "a waste of sand and gravel" hardly conjures up images of Eden.

Clearly Oregon was not *the* Garden of Eden but the impression that it had certain Edenic qualities was an important factor in how many early settlers saw the territory and how residents described it. William Lang suggests that the reasons for coming to Oregon were numerous but a large number of the fifty-three thousand individuals who emigrated to the Oregon country between 1840 and 1860 were certainly moving *from* something *to* something more promising, perhaps even to "a latter-day Eden." "The image of Oregon carried more than just a symbolic physical resemblance to Eden; it also suggested a community that had a regenerative quality, one that could restore damaged lives."[10] Another author notes, "There is evidence that Oregon held for many minds a mystic attraction as a land of social regeneration."[11]

Advertisements for the Oregon Land Company in the late 1880s would go one step beyond this in their boosterism. Under the large banner of "OREGON IS GOD'S COUNTRY!!," the ad states that "The Willamette Valley has been fitly termed the "GARDEN OF OREGON." Eden had now, in fact, become Oregon. Calling Oregon "THE HEALTHIEST STATE IN THE UNION," the ad further states, "The Willamette valley has the most healthful and pleasant climate of any locality within the state of Oregon." Comparing the Willamette Valley to states to the north and south, the ad unabashedly states, "It is a stranger to the harsh and cheerless fogs of Puget sound, and the hot, dry, dusty days of drought-ridden California."[12] The Willamette Valley certainly is presented as Eden.

That is not to say that other parts of the state do not warrant that description—and the Grande Ronde Valley has already been noted as such—but the Willamette Valley most often is mentioned in these terms, from the early 1800s to freeway signs at the end of the twentieth century proclaiming "The Eden at the End of the Trail."[13] The views of the Willamette Valley as Eden, the impact this had on the Native Americans residing there, and the continuing debate about how to use and preserve the natural resources of the environment were explored in a long-running exhibit at the Oregon Historical Society aptly titled "Willamette Valley – Visions of Eden." As the publicity for the exhibit noted:

> *It was a vision of paradise. An enormous valley rich with woodlands and pastures, temperate, and amply watered by the great river that would share its name. When the first Europeans arrived and began to settle the Willamette Valley, it seemed a place untouched by humans. But American Indians had lived here for years before, altering the land in accord with their own needs, and deeply held beliefs. It was a study in contrasting cultures, differing perspectives on the relationship between people and nature, and the beginning of an ongoing Oregon debate on how best to use the valley and its resources.*[14]

Beyond the Willamette Valley the sense of Eden can be identified in other parts of the state. In fact, there were at least two Edens in the state. The earliest was a post office in Wallowa County established October 2, 1907, but, perhaps in somewhat Edenic fashion, it never materialized and the appointment of B. E. Puller as postmaster was rescinded six months later. This Eden was to have been a few miles south of Troy on the Grande Ronde River in an area known as Eden Ridge.[15] Eden Ridge also was the source of the name for a post office "in the extreme southwest part of Coos County,

3

in the very rough, mountainous country on West Fork Cow Creek," which was established on July 21, 1914, and discontinued January 14, 1922. As Lewis A. McArthur notes in *Oregon Geographic Names*, "The ridge and post office apparently were named by people fond of isolation and pioneer living."[16]

Beyond Eden, other place names suggest the sense of promise and opportunity felt by early settlers. Several of these were in the far northeastern corner of the state. McArthur observes: "Wallowa County has had more than its share of post offices with names showing that its settlers seemed to be pleased with the prospects. Among these names have been: Paradise, Promise, Joy, Arcadia, Utopia, Eureka, and Enterprise."[17] A post office in Wallowa County was named by a homesteader and school teacher, Charles N. Walker, who "was so impressed with the surrounding country that he named the post office for Sir Thomas More's imaginary paradise on earth." The Utopia post office ran from 1905 to 1911 and, McArthur adds, "The place was on Middle Point between Wallupa and Wildcat creeks about two miles southeast of Promise, and the name of the post office in Promise may have suggested the name Utopia."[18] Of all these place names reflecting some aspect of hope, promise, and other Edenic qualities, Enterprise is the only one still in existence, serving as the county seat for Wallowa County. The spirit of the ideal is still reflected in the city's web site which proclaims: "Enterprise Oregon is in one of the most beautiful settings on the planet. Wide open grassy meadows surround the town, pine forests to the north and the incredible Wallowa Mountains to the south. It's an outdoor paradise."[19] All these were not just place names but also ideas that capture the sense of the ideal for early settlers and homesteaders in the state, and for some a continuing sense of the possibilities and promise offered in Oregon.

Oregon is not the only state with place names that reflect Edenic ideals. From Eden, New York, to Utopia, Texas, and from Promise, Tennessee, to Paradise, California, many settlers adopted names throughout the country that captured that sense of promise and possibility. Similarly, many states and regions have been viewed as some reflection of Eden.[20] The last two states added to the union, Alaska and Hawaii, have had their share of references to Eden or utopia, for very different reasons. Alaska was even labeled "Utopia" in one of the "Road" shows of Bing Crosby, Bob Hope, and Dorothy Lamour with the *Road to Utopia* (1946) centered on the gold rush in Alaska and the promises associated with striking it rich. Hawaii and Eden are linked in a multitude of ways but most commonly due to the tropical paradise nature of the islands.

While Oregon is not unique in being viewed as Eden, that sense of a special place, both for its natural beauty and as "a community that had a regenerative quality" continued through the twentieth century and still can be seen today, although that tension of reality and idealism persists as well.[21] Some of that became more visible during the governorship of Tom McCall, from 1967 to 1975, and it is not surprising that the name of Eden was invoked in Brent Walth's *Fire at Eden's Gate: Tom McCall and the Oregon Story* (1994). Walth examines this important period in the struggle to preserve many of the Edenic qualities of Oregon while also illustrating the utopian aspects of doing so. From the famous sign on Interstate 5 north of the California border ("Welcome to Oregon. We Hope You Enjoy Your Visit") to the less than idealistic aspects of McCall's personal life, Walth captures the problematic nature of living in paradise.[22] Other scholars and writers have utilized the Eden metaphor to examine aspects of Oregon's history, heritage, and culture. Craig Wollner did so in his *Electrifying Eden: Portland General Electric 1889-1965* (1990) as did Patricia Brandt and Lillian A. Pereya in *Adapting in Eden: Oregon's Catholic Minority 1838-1986* (2002).[23] There are also studies on "Cooking in Eden: Inventing Regional Cuisine in the Pacific Northwest" and "Preserving Eden: The Culture on Conservation in Oregon, 1960-1980."[24] Eden also has been tied to the literature of Oregon in such works as Cobie de Lespinasse's *Second Eden: A Romance* (1951), which is a thinly guised account of the Aurora Colony, and Richard S. Wheeler's *The Fields of Eden* (2001), a historical novel about Oregon pioneer days.[25] Although Malcolm Clark suggests that "Modern-minded literalists . . . are inclined to distrust the lure of Eden, and a few even deny its existence altogether," as the twenty-first century progresses there are still many that view Oregon as Eden, if even in just a historical or literary sense.

Upon this backdrop of Oregon as Eden in various connotations, it is not surprising that the state also became an attractive place for individuals or groups seeking their own forms of an ideal life or perfection in some manner. The same features of the land and the environment that drew early pioneers and homesteaders also were factors for those seeking to create their own Eden within the broader Eden of the natural beauty and regeneration quality that Oregon provided. Since the establishment of the Aurora Colony on the banks of the Pudding River in 1856, there have been nearly three hundred attempts to achieve some type of communal Eden within the borders of Oregon. The vast majority of these were not in the days of the pioneers but took place after 1965 in conjunction initially with the hippie movement but also embracing such growing movements as environmentalism and feminism. Many religious-based communities also sought to create their own heaven in various parts of the Oregon landscape. Most of these endeavors were short-lived and some never actually made it past the planning stages, but collectively they provide an important, and often overlooked, aspect of the heritage of the state. This study seeks to initiate the telling of the story with

5

the hope that others will continue to explore and add to the narrative and the resources available for further research.

Although there have been some historical accounts of Oregon's utopian endeavors, even those on the well-known communities such as the Aurora Colony are incomplete and a general survey is needed. Robert V. Hine's *California's Utopian Colonies* (1953) is one of the benchmark studies on communal groups within a state.[26] Charles Pierce LeWarne examined the *Utopias on Puget Sound 1885-1915* (1975), another classic in the study of communal groups on the West Coast.[27] Two works on utopian communities in British Columbia also have been published – Justine Brown's *All Possible Worlds: Utopian Experiments in British Columbia* (1995) and Andrew Scott's *Promise of Paradise: Utopian Communities in B. C.* (1997).[28] The absence of a comprehensive work for Oregon, with its rich utopian heritage, is noticeable and this work seeks to remedy that.[29]

Prior to examining the specific attempts to achieve the better life in Oregon over the past one hundred fifty years, it is important to provide some definitions for terms often used in communal and utopian studies (including Eden, utopia, and communal), to present some background on the utopian tradition, and to establish some boundaries for the broader study at hand. These issues are discussed in the next chapter, followed by a survey of the utopian tradition in America, as the Oregon experience is deeply rooted in this history. Chapter 3 begins the study of utopian experiments in Oregon with the most widely known and longest-lasting community of the nineteenth century, the Aurora Colony. Several late-nineteenth-century communal experiments in Oregon are examined in Chapter 4, from a Jewish agricultural colony in Douglas County to a colony in Lincoln County named for the author of two utopian novels, Edward Bellamy. Two proposed, but unrealized, communities or schemes are explored in Chapter 5. Chapter 6 examines two other unrealized communities but ones based on a growing movement of cooperative endeavors taking place early in the twentieth century. A shift from cooperation to survival is discussed in Chapter 7, reflecting broader economic, political, and global developments of the mid-twentieth century. These developments lead in part to the revitalization of the communal spirit during the 1960s, which is presented in Chapter 8, followed by the expansion of this spirit from the 1970s to the present in Chapter 9. Two infamous and notorious communal efforts are the focus of Chapter 10. The Conclusion looks at other ways in which Oregon has been linked to utopian ideals, from literary endeavors to city planning. The Appendix includes a resource directory for further information on Oregon communities, although the mere number of communal efforts in Oregon since the 1850s precludes an in-depth analysis of these within the narrative.

This is viewed as a starting place for further exploration of Oregon's utopian heritage.

Abigail Scott Duniway saw Oregon as a land of promise with physical attributes that reflected to her the image of the Garden of Eden. In doing so, she captured a spirit that perfection could perhaps be achieved in Oregon that also prompted many others to seek such perfection. A utopian quest? No doubt, but one that is an integral part of the heritage of Oregon.

# Eden and Utopia:
# Background and Boundaries

When Oregonians are asked what ideas come to mind when they think of Eden, words like paradise, perfection, ideal, innocence, beauty, and immortality come to mind. For some, the initial association is with apples, nudity, sin, and snakes. And for still others, words like expulsion and unachievable are mentioned.[1] All of these ideas in one way or another relate to the Western concept of Eden. Although there is an extensive literature on Eden and utopias, it is important to present here some background on these concepts and to suggest how these relate to the boundaries, and terminology, of Eden and utopia used in this study.

## Eden

The concept of Eden, of course, is rooted in the first book of the Old Testament in the Bible, Genesis, specifically in Chapters 2 and 3. However, very little detail is provided about this place and there is some uncertainty about the meanings or derivation of the word "Eden." It is used to designate a region in southern Mesopotamia and the word may come from the Hebrew, by way of Akkadian and Sumerian words meaning "plain" or "steppe." So the "garden of Eden" may have just been located in this plain in a general sense, as Genesis states "the Lord God planted a garden in Eden, in the east" (Genesis 2:8). Another Hebrew word from which Eden may derive means "to be fertile, luxuriant" and a third suggests a "garden of fertile luxurance"; both of these are tied more into the modern concept of Eden.[2]

Many specifics of the Garden, however, are not provided in Genesis. The text states that "the Lord God made to grow every tree that is pleasant to the sight and good for food," not to mention the "tree of the knowledge of good and evil" that would play prominently later in the story and the "tree of life" (Genesis 2:9).[3] Later, "the Lord God formed every animal of the field and every bird of the air" to keep the man in the Garden company (Genesis 2:19). Seeing that this was not enough, the Lord God then created woman as "his partner" and the two "were both naked, and were not ashamed" (Genesis 2:20-25). Beyond this, few specifics of the Garden of Eden are provided. Chapter 3 of Genesis includes the story of the temptation of the woman (who is not named Eve until later—Genesis 3:20), eating fruit from the tree of the knowledge of good and evil (and it was not yet called an apple), and the punishment bestowed by the Lord God upon Eve and the man, who has not yet been given a name.[4] That punishment included banishment "from the garden of Eden" (Genesis 3:23), and God settled them "east of the garden of Eden," posting "the cherubim, and a sword flaming" to protect the Garden, particularly the tree of life (Genesis 3:24).

Thus very few details about the Garden of Eden come from the original source. The concepts that are associated with it came from later theologians, writers, scholars, poets, artists, and, perhaps more importantly, traditions.[5] Frank E. Manuel and Fritzie P. Manuel note that "In the first century of the Christian era the Garden of Eden was subject to a form of interpretation that came to be sanctioned by both Judaism and Christianity."[6] As this symbolic interpretation became accepted, or at least presented, more details were added to the Eden story. Dante Alighieri's description of the earthly paradise in his *Purgatorio* from the early fourteenth-century *Divine Comedy* was important for the development of the idea and visualization of Eden. More interpretation took place up to the seventeeth century, leading to John Milton's *Paradise Lost* (1667), from which many modern views of Eden derive.[7]

Although Milton sought to be true to the text of Genesis, he extrapolated from this to create many other dimensions of the story, not only of the Garden of Eden but of elements such as the fall of the angels and the creation of Hell. In doing so, he brought in facets of many early views of the Eden story, including those of early Christian poets who Joseph Duncan notes "were converting classical rhetoric to the sensuous pictures of paradise and to the sensitive portrayals of Adam and Eve." Milton also may have incorporated other earlier developments such as the medieval gardens that sought to create "gardens of delight."[8] And the Renaissance painters who began to present their artistic interpretations of the Garden of Eden also influenced Milton's ideas.[9]

It was these developments, and more since, that established modern views of the nature of the Garden of Eden. Although some of the modern concepts of Eden are based on a long, and sometimes conflicting, development of the idea of the Garden of Eden as place, the critical aspect of this luxurious spot created for humans by God is that the original tenants were sentenced to a list of punishments, most significantly the banishment from Eden. Getting back to Eden is central to many Western religions, and, more directly relevant to this study, these developing interpretations of Eden were taking place at the same time as the exploration and early settlements in the Americas.[10] For many, the new world on the horizon fit well into the concept of returning to Eden.

## Utopia

The story of Eden has a long history but so too does the concept of utopia. The idea of utopia has perhaps existed since humans began to envision something better than their existing condition, but it certainly has roots in ancient writings and traditions. Joyce Hertzler posits that the prophets were "forerunners of the utopians." Plato's *Republic*, written in the fourth century BCE, is often cited as the earliest recorded attempt to present a utopian scheme, with the ideal city he developed as an example of such a place of perfection.[11] But Plato was not alone nor was he in fact the earliest. As the Manuels state, "The Greeks were endowed with the gift of utopian fantasy," and there were many elements of their beliefs and writings that centered on utopian themes, including the myth of a golden age and the fanciful daydreams of the comic poets of the fifth century BCE.[12]

The Romans, as the Manuels suggest, were too practical and "except for occasional glosses on the works of their Hellenistic predecessors, were singularly devoid of interest in such unrealistic manifestations of the human spirit."[13] But an event occurred during the Romans' watch of Western civilization that changed not only the history of this world but, for many, the next. That was the birth, life, and perhaps most significantly, the death of Jesus Christ. As Lewis Mumford states, even though it seemed that utopia "dropt [sic] out of literature, it did not drop out of men's minds; and the utopia of the first fifteen hundred years after Christ is transplanted to the skies, and called the Kingdom of Heaven."[14] This is very significant in the examination of utopia *and* Eden, particularly in a Christian-centric view that is key to this study, as here was the means by which the return to Eden could be realized. The writings of the New Testament, especially the Book of Revelation, set forth the idea of Christ's second coming, spawning millennial  beliefs that for two millennia have served as the basis for numerous utopian schemes.[15] Apocalyptic writers were not limited to those in the New Testament but these served as the core inspiration of many utopian activities for centuries, including many in the United States.[16] Other important developments of utopian thought include St. Augustine's *City of God* from the fifth century CE and such myths as the Land of Cokayne in the medieval era, but the most significant development took place early in the sixteenth century through the writing of an English scholar, lawyer, writer, statesman, and, ultimately, saint.[17]

Thomas More's *Utopia* was published in 1516 in Belgium.[18] Written in Latin, the work most likely was intended for a small audience of scholars and intellectuals, many of whom were in the group known as the Renaissance Humanists, including Desiderius Erasmus and Peter Giles.[19] The text of *Utopia* is presented in two books. Book One includes a critique of early–sixteenth-century society as viewed by characters representing many actual individuals, including More himself. Entering the discussion is a fictitious traveler by the name of Raphael Hythloday, who supposedly had been on three of the four voyages of Amerigo Vespucci, including the last, where he and several others became stranded on an island known as Utopia. Book Two then presents Hythloday's sometimes detailed, sometimes vague description of the land, people, and customs of this supposedly ideal place. The nature of those descriptions is not vital for the study at hand but what is significant is the work itself and, in particular, the name More gave to this island nation.

More built on Greek roots to generate comical, fanciful, or satirical terms for proper names in his text. Raphael Hythloday, for instance, derives from Greek words that make him "the teller of nonsense." For the name of the island, More used the Greek roots *ou* meaning "no" and *topos* (or *topia*) meaning "place." Thus *utopia* is "no place." This is consistent with the ideal nature of the island and most likely the intent of the work as a fanciful, satirical jest. It is a place of perfection that cannot possibly exist. Yet, in the spirit of some Humanistic pun, More may also have been suggesting the Greek root *eu* meaning "good" with *topos*, so that *utopia* is a "good place." The riddle, almost five hundred years old, continues to be discussed and debated, very likely to Thomas More's amusement. Most importantly, by creating a new word for his island nation, More provided a word for attempts to describe an ideal society.

*Utopia* appeared in other editions in 1517 and 1518 and a map of the island was added to the text, although its precise location in relation to other lands was never provided.[20] The book was not translated into English until 1551, sixteen years after More's execution for his objection to the divorce by Henry VIII of his first wife, Catherine of Aragon.[21] The work continued to be published and translated into other languages in the seventeenth century and up to the present. It has become the benchmark for the examination of utopian literature.[22]

For this study, it is important to understand the historical and intellectual framework related to the appearance of More's *Utopia* and how it tied into that age-old quest of finding the ideal. The work appeared just twenty-four years after the initial voyage of Christopher Columbus. Although we now know that Columbus' voyages were more of rediscovery, they and those of other explorers in the next two decades, including Amerigo Vespucci, fueled the interest in this "new land." As Robert M. Adams points out:

> *Europeans knew very little about the new land beyond the ocean, and what information they got from the first explorers was sparse, ill-written, and, worst of all, not very interesting, especially when it was accurate. Just at this time More appeared with a finished and elegant*

*literary production, describing some enchanting people who, in addition to all the "natural" virtues like innocence, simplicity, and native honor, had some very sophisticated institutions perfectly suited to comment on the most notorious abuses of contemporary Europe.*[23]

For Europeans there was now a work that offered what the explorers did not. Maybe "no place" was "some place." Perhaps this America was that Edenic land they were seeking. As Adams continues, "Naïve folk of the early sixteenth century swallowed More's account of Utopia as a fair description of the New World; tougher and more practical men still tended, when they came to America, to see the natives as potential Utopians or ex-Utopians." The idea of America as Utopia is explored more fully in the following chapter but here it is important to note not just the literary contributions of More's *Utopia*, and his creation of the word to describe such places, but also the thought that perhaps there was a perfect place, an Eden, yet to be found. Adams suggests, "The book is thus of special interest to Americans, North and South; it helped to make us what we are today by determining, nor our immediate institutions, but the level of our expectations."[24]

The notion that Eden, paradise, or utopia might be an actual location on Earth was not initiated with the appearance of Thomas More's work. In fact, there is a long history of attempts to locate paradise in a physical place. Alessandro Scafi explores this in detail, tracking many efforts to locate paradise in space and time, as well as efforts to place paradise on the map. In doing so he notes, "A map that shows paradise as part of the world involves a leap of the imagination."[25] This is reflected in the oft-quoted comment of Oscar Wilde that "A map of the world that does not include Utopia is not worth even glancing at" because, as he continues in his 1891 essay, "The Soul of Man Under Socialism," "it leaves out the one country in which Humanity is always landing."[26] The leap of which Scafi speaks did not seem to hinder a variety of attempts to place paradise, or Eden, on the map. From the eighth century to the early sixteenth century, Scafi documents what he calls the "Heyday of Paradise on Maps" with efforts to illustrate where paradise might exist on Earth. Many of these maps highlighted the apocalyptic nature of belief that the location was tied to the end of the world and finding paradise was the last accomplishment to be made on this world.

Thus far this summary of utopianism has presented mostly literary and mythical representations of utopian ideals. However, *Eden Within Eden* primarily focuses on the actual attempts to put these utopian ideals into practice, commonly called communal societies, but the roots of these attempts to achieve perfection are largely founded in the utopian ideals represented in the literary heritage.

13

## *Boundaries of Utopia*

The boundaries of utopia are by nature vague.[27] When Thomas More coined the word "utopia" to describe the ideal island, he was not only providing a dichotomous meaning of "good place" or "no place" but he was in many ways providing a geographic riddle of where utopia ends or begins. That same uncertainty surrounds the attempt to put parameters around the efforts to establish some types of perfected societies. Most studies of these attempts include a statement similar to that of James H. Sweetland: "The first problem confronting anyone dealing with communal groups is the definition."[28] But the problem goes deeper; even the definitions and connotations of words (e.g., "communal") used in the terms to describe these endeavors pose problems.

The terminology used to describe such groups over the past century have included the adjectives communal, collective, cooperative, communistic, communitarian, egalitarian, mutualistic, and socialistic, to name but a few, as well as the nouns communes, cooperatives, collectives, and, perhaps the most accepted term at the beginning of the twenty-first century, intentional communities. The shifting vocabulary is in itself problematic but the implied connotations of many of the words to describe utopian endeavors became even more troublesome during the twentieth century, when words such as communist, socialist, and collective became increasingly linked with political and socio-economic agendas and ideological conflicts. It is important to understand how some of these words have been used and the impact they have had on these communities in Oregon and the efforts to study them.

The earliest examination of communal or cooperative communities is considered to be Mary Hennell's 1844 study, which includes some American communities and interestingly identifies the North American Indians among these groups, primarily based on their shared sense of property within a tribe.[29] The first work published in the United States on American communities is that of John Humphrey Noyes, founder of the Oneida Community, one of the most successful and controversial utopian experiments in the nineteenth century.[30] His 1870 book, *History of American Socialisms*, provides a glimpse of a number of American communities from the Shakers to his own community at Oneida. In his Preface, he notes, "This country has been from the beginning, and especially for the last forty years, a laboratory in which Socialisms of all kinds have been experimenting."[31] He uses the word "socialism," but the socialisms of which he speaks are broader than the more specific sense of the word as commonly viewed today. The nature of many of these groups predated the rise of scientific socialism as it came to be known from the works of Karl Marx and Friedrich Engels and reflected aspects of what is considered classical socialism, as well as the various types of "utopian socialism" developed in the nineteenth century by Charles Fourier and others.

The tag of "socialism" with such communities would carry forward into the twentieth century and, while there were indeed communities that adopted Socialist philosophies in the twentieth-century sense, the view that all communal groups are of this nature is inaccurate. The significance of the impact of the word "socialism" upon the American mindset in the mid-twentieth century can perhaps be illustrated with the 1966 republication of Noyes' work with two separate titles—one was *History of American Socialisms*, as originally published, but the second was *Strange Cults & Utopias of 19th-Century America*. Just why this alternative title was used can be only speculative but seems to be an effort to remove the baggage of "socialism" in the title, and the more sensational "Strange Cults & Utopias" offers a different message (and highlights another word, "cults," that comes into play in dealing with communal groups). Although the title page notes parenthetically "Formerly titled: History of American Socialisms," it is clear that a different message was trying to be conveyed.[32]

## Communism

The next major survey of communities, by Charles Nordhoff, published in 1875, treated many of the same groups as Noyes, but Nordhoff used the label "communistic" in his title instead of "socialisms."[33] However, as with Noyes, the intent of the descriptor was not to suggest a socio-political affiliation or agenda. The word "communistic" or "communist" can be applied to many groups, including early Christian sects, long before the words took on different connotations from the late nineteenth century to the present. The problem with the word is illustrated in relation to Oregon's first utopian community group, the Aurora Colony. Henry C. Finck, writing to his son, Henry T., on December 13, 1877, tells of Wilhelm Keil, leader of the colony, who has taken ill; Finck remarks, "The paper will now be filled with a lot of nonsense about the death of the communist leader, but in his heart he never was a communist any more than was Ben Holladay."[34] More recently, Franklin H. Littell captured the gist of this problem when he wrote in a prefatory essay to the 1965 printing of Nordhoff's work:

*A book about "communistic" communities must today inevitably run up against a kind of logophobia in the American reading public. "Communism" has come to signify Marxism, more precisely the ideology known as dialectical materialism. Granted the shaping of the public mind by superficial images, "communism" means "Russia" and "individualism" means "America." ... To defame the socialist and communist societies here described because their religion called them to practice of an intensive and disciplined common life is as ridiculous as condemnation of St. Peter because he and his friends practiced the common life (Acts 2:44, 4:32).*[35]

15

But these words have continued to present obstacles in the assessment of these idealistic endeavors, even those of a strongly religious nature.

Included among these was the Aurora Colony in Oregon, which Nordhoff's work was the first to include. Ted Carlson, writing on the Aurora Colony in a 1966 article in the *Eugene Register-Guard*, echoes some of the same sentiments expressed by Littell: "Back before Communism became a dirty word, a dedicated group of German immigrants followed a whiskey-filled coffin for 2,000 miles and set up a model communal society in the Willamette Valley."[36] Many other writers used the same term to describe Aurora and its predecessor, Bethel in Missouri. Stewart Holbrook wrote of "Aurora Communists" in 1948 and John E. Simon examined "William Keil and Communistic Societies" in 1935.[37] These descriptors are accurate but they continue to be problematic for colony descendants and others who link them with the Communism of Marx, Lenin, Stalin, and other twentieth-century ideological movements. Eugene Snyder urged caution in the use of "communists," stating, "This word needs to be used with care in relation to the Aurora Colony."[38] Holbrook tried to alleviate some of these concerns: "These first communists to cross the plans were not followers of Karl Marx ... . They were mostly disgruntled Rappists whom Keil had persuaded to follow the special brand of Christian communism which he himself had invented."[39]

Franklin Littell noted in his introduction to the Nordhoff reprint that this problem had existed even before the rise of communistic states in the twentieth century.

> *Even in the last century the polarization of public opinion had reached the point where Hinds in his American Communities, could only describe the language problem by reference to another period: "Communism is another unfortunate word, whose history has been similar to that of republicanism." Of course, when we think of it, in the days when intelligent men were still defending the divine rights of kings "republicanism" was a word which conjured up the most unfortunate connotations.*[400]

By bringing William Alfred Hinds into the discussion, Littell introduces the third major work on American communal groups published in the 1870s. Hinds, long associated with the Oneida Community, built on the work of both Noyes and Nordhoff, and two expanded editions of Hinds' study were completed early in the twentieth century.[41] Hinds avoided the problem of "socialisms" and "communistic" by dropping the terms altogether, at least in his title, *American Communities*, but the issues of how these words fit into the study and definition of these communities was still an issue.

## Socialism

As problematic as the word "communist" is in the examination of utopian communities, "socialism" presents more complexities. In 1893, William Graham suggested in his study of *Socialism: New and Old* that "it is impossible to give a single definition that would find general acceptance," and this statement holds true today.[42] But Graham does propose some definitions for what he feels are the "three different senses" of socialism as viewed in the late nineteenth century. In many ways, these definitions still work well in understanding its usage in communal enterprises, particularly those in the nineteenth century when they were most often applied.

Graham offers for his initial definition the following:

*In the widest sense of the word, Socialism is any scheme of social relations which has in view a more equal distribution of wealth, or the preventing too great inequality, in whatever way this be effected, whether by State action, the voluntary efforts of individuals directed towards that end, Church action, philanthropy, or any other means; in which wide sense of the word Socialism embraces many social phenomena and movements, both in the present and in the past.*[43]

He then offers that "in the present it would embrace co-operative production, the communistic experiments in the United States and elsewhere, Christian Socialism, contemporary legislation to ameliorate the condition of small tenant farmers and the working classes generally, and even, if we set aside the means to be employed, contemporary anarchists' final aims." And he also suggests that this broadest definition of socialism would include "ancient laws and customs aiming at the prevention of poverty or of great inequality, the various risings of the people for the same ends in England, in France, and in Germany, together with the ideas, and sentiments that prompted them."[44] This broad definition might be labeled classical socialism for it has its roots, as Graham points out, in "ancient laws and customs" and can be found not only in action by the state but in a number of other ways, including the Church (and others would suggest that even prior to the formation of the "Church" in a Christian sense that the earliest Christians themselves practiced socialism in this manner). Graham's definition includes many utopian communities that were established as early as the seventeenth century.

Graham's second definition (or "sense") of socialism is one that "covers only a portion of the above field of meaning" and that is when it "is applied only to the aim and endeavour of the State to secure, by laws or institutions, a greater equality of conditions, or to prevent too great inequality." He suggests the English Poor Law would thus be socialistic, as would the

17

Convention during the French Revolution. It is Graham's third "sense" of socialism that is conjured up in most minds in the present day after a century of various attempts to achieve this goal. In this sense, "Socialism is that system economic and political, in which the production of wealth is carried on solely by the State, as the collective owner of the land and instruments of production, instead of by private-capitalist employers or companies." He continues, "This, the only true Socialism according to its adherents, is now generally called Collectivism, to denote the collective ownership or ownership by the State, as the representative of all, of the land and instruments of production." It is also important to note, from Graham's perspective, that this "distinguishes itself from Communism, inasmuch as it admits of private property in articles of consumption, and to a certain limited extent, of inequality of shares, accumulations, and inheritance."[45]

An example of an advocate of "the only true Socialism" is Morris Hillquit, an early scholar of modern socialism, who offers this more concise explanation: "The political social movement of our day is primarily a movement of the working class, and has for its object the reconstruction of the present-day system of industry on the basis of collective ownership of the tools of production." He maintains that "the modern socialist movement has nothing in common with the utopias of Plato, Campanella and More, or with the prehistoric tribal institutions, early Christian practices or the various sectarian communities of the Middle Ages."[46] Hillquit, like many other earlier Socialist writers, most notably Karl Marx and Friedrich Engels, saw the attempts in the early nineteenth century by such individuals as Robert Owen and Charles Fourier as "utopian socialists," for their ideals could not be achieved; their movements were, in his opinion, humanitarian rather than political. He suggests, "The early socialists saw only the evils of the new system of production; they did not penetrate into its historical significance and tendencies."[47]

So what definition is applicable in the examination of Oregon's utopian heritage? The answer is simply none of them and all of them. Different groups had different aspects of socialistic tendencies, from the "classical" to the "utopian" to the "scientific," although most of these were practiced on such a small scale that they were hardly an impact on any movement. But there were indeed Marxists among communities that were formed in Oregon and some scholars include the abbeys at Mount Angel and Lafayette among "socialistic" groups in Oregon, at least in terms of some aspects of their monasticism.[48] Perhaps what is most significant in terms of the issue of socialism as practiced in communal groups, in Oregon and elsewhere, is the fundamental issue that Hillquit identified early in his study – "Socialism and individualism are the two main contending principles underlying all modern social theories and movements."[49] This contention, whether formal socialism is practiced in communal groups or not, is at the core of the success and failure of many of these endeavors.

## *Cooperation*

One of the ways to address this contention was in the spirit of cooperation, another important term in the examination of utopian experiments in Oregon. Not as complex as the issue of communism and socialism, the concept of cooperation still has some complexities (not to mention how one treats the word—it will be seen as cooperation, co-operation, coöperation). There is a whole movement of cooperation but it is another word that can be helpful or get in the way in the examination of communal societies.

Early in the twentieth century, the Rev. Alexander Kent put forth some classifications of what he called "cooperative communities," and is so doing made some distinctions between "communistic" and "socialistic" practices of these communities, while also adding "cooperative" to the mix. He laid out this scheme for categorizing these cooperative endeavors:

> *Cooperative communities in the United States may be classified according to their aims rather than their achievements. They are of three kinds: (1) Communistic; (2) Socialistic; (3) partially cooperative. The communistic are those which aim at the widest possible community of goods, and which seek to have both labor and income equally distributed among the members.*
>
> *The socialistic are those which aim at collective ownership of all the means of production, and at equitable rather than equal distribution. Averse to private capital, they are not averse to private property. Opposed to exploitation, they are not opposed to honest thrifts. They would encourage industry and skill and discourage laziness and inefficiency.*
>
> *The partially cooperative communities are those which favor collective ownership and action in others, but wish for a larger degree of cooperation than is yet engaged by the community at large.*[50]

Even with these guidelines, Kent notes that the differences may not be so distinct, and various combinations might come into play among different communities and even within the same community over time. He applies this scheme to a number of communities, from the Shakers to several smaller cooperative endeavors, including the Nehalem Valley Cooperative Colony and the Union Mill Company, both in Oregon (to be discussed in Chapter Four). Later writers supplied their own categorizations with some common characteristics within these communal groups, but they are also quick to point out that such an effort is far from consistent or complete.[51] Although the terminology of what to call these entities is fluid and often interchangeable, some other generalizations can be suggested.

One common method of categorization at a higher level breaks the communal history of the United States into general chronological categories, with those communities begun prior to 1800 largely being religious in nature and, more specifically, millennial focused in one form or another. From around 1800 to the Civil War era many of the communities were influenced by one of the several "utopian socialist" leaders, including Robert Owen, Charles Fourier, and Etienne Cabet. That is not to say that the earlier type did not also continue; one only has to look at the Shakers, who continued through several time periods, and some of the earlier communities spun off other communities that would last for years.

From the end of the Civil War to the early twentieth century, there were an increasing number of sectarian communities and ones specifically devoted to certain reforms of the period, from health reform to political reform. Fogarty suggests that there were three categories of communal societies prominent during this era: "co-operative colonizers," "charismatic perfectionists," and "political pragmatists." The co-operative colonizers "believe that secular salvation could be attained by establishing groups of people in new settlements and that by collectively assuming financial responsibility for their communities the colonists would improve their economic and moral condition." The charismatic perfectionists were charismatic "either based on the potential personal sanctity of the membership as a whole and/or based on the potential sanctity, special gifts or power of a forceful leader" and their perfectionism is centered on the promise "that the 'perfected life' could be led within the confines of a community."[52] The political pragmatists were "political and social radicals who were seeking an arena to test and publicize their principles in action." But, again, some communities did not fit neatly into one or any of these categories and others may have started out as one type and changed to another.

In the late nineteenth century and into the early twentieth century there was widespread "colonization" in America—and in Oregon—by a large influx of immigrants. Most of these "colonies" fall outside the general boundaries of utopia, for, as Lisa Walker notes, these groups "could better be described as ethnic enclaves based on individuals and families, rather than communal societies based on shared ideology and communal living."[53] But some of these colonies, such as the Jewish agricultural colony in Douglas County and a colony of Norwegian settlers in Lincoln County, do fall within the boundaries based on aspects of communal organization within the group.

The first half of the twentieth century saw further changes in the communal landscape that Timothy Miller calls "an evolving phenomenon of American history." There was more widespread adoption of cooperative principles as well as other "changes in the pattern of community," as Miller suggests. Once more, however, many of these cooperative undertakings would not fall within the boundaries of communal utopian enterprises but for those that did, there were some common elements. These include smaller size, a "decline of personal, centralized leadership," leading to new structures, new economic profiles, and new patterns of ownership. There also were "lower demands for commitment by members," lower profiles for most of the communities, and overall less of a distinction between many of the communities and the larger American culture.[54] Many of the same characteristics can be applied to the communal groups that came into existence from the 1960s to the present, although aspects of these communities evolved, including their names. These latter groups are often viewed as the generic "commune," but that term applies only to a small number of the groups in this period and reflects just one type of community. Communes gave way to intentional communities, and there were still cooperatives and collectives as well. And other new forms of communal groups, from ecovillages to cohousing, have continued to make the landscape, and the terminology, of communal societies a challenging one to navigate and understand.

Miller adopted a set of criteria for inclusion of groups in his two studies of twentieth-century communities and these generally have been adopted here. These are:

> *A sense of common purpose and of separation from the dominant society.*
> *Some form and level of self-denial, of voluntary suppression of individual choice for the good of the group.*
> *Geographic proximity.*
> *Personal interaction.*
> *Economic sharing.*
> *Real existence.*
> *Critical mass.*[55]

The one exception in the study at hand is where "real existence" is set aside as a criterion to explore the sense of "no place" in Oregon. But then, in a Thomas More sense, all of these attempts to achieve utopia in Oregon may have been a "no place." Yet it is the quest to find utopia, even if it is a no place, that is at the core of this study and of Oregon's utopian heritage. The boundaries of the territory may not always be clear, but the intent is generally the same—to find Eden, or even just a small part of it.

# The American Utopian Tradition

◈ ◈ ◈

When Christopher Columbus set sail in 1492 his destination was not Eden, but after encountering the "new world" by accident he thought he might have found it. As Louis B. Wright notes: " If Columbus did not realize that he had discovered a new continent, he did believe that he had found the terrestrial paradise. On his third voyage, in 1498, he sailed along the coast of Venezuela and became convinced that the country inland from the Gulf of Paria was verily the site of Eden."[1] Wright offers the view that America and Eden were closely linked, at least in the minds of certain individuals, since the earliest explorations in the late fifteenth century. This idea would manifest itself in various ways over the next centuries, economically, religiously, politically, and culturally.[2] In the study of Oregon's utopian experiences it is important to understand these earlier views of America as Eden or utopia, as that heritage was the basis for much of what would develop in Oregon.[3]

## America As Eden

As we know, Columbus not only was incorrect in his assessment that he had reached the East but he was also in error about having discovered Eden. But for many, the newly discovered land offered numerous possibilities, including economic wealth. One of these possibilities was closely tied with the legend of El Dorado, a place rich in gold and precious stones. The legend was primarily centered on what would become South America, but had impacts further north as well; the promise of these limitless riches spurred the exploration and exploitation of the continent. El Dorado did not exist, but the myth fanned the flames of other possibilities.[4]

For the European of the seventeenth and eighteenth centuries these dreams were part of what Harold V. Rhodes labeled *outward* utopias, or "the belief utopia exists now—somewhere—but not here" (Rhodes also recognized *upward* utopias, discussed below). In an outward utopia, "A better world is open to man if he will physically move from here to there." Rhodes presents three prerequisites for the realization of this utopia: "First, man must reject his present condition. Then, he must be able to move. And finally, there must be a utopia to which he can move."[5] This utopian drive can be seen not only in the draw of Europeans to America in the colonial period but also in the westward movement that would bring immigrants to Oregon. In fact, Rhodes suggests that the outward utopia concept is central to the frontier thesis of Frederick Jackson Turner, and he quotes from Ray Allen Billington to support his position: "In the west, according to the frontier myth, a veritable Garden of the World awaited to transform newcomers into superior beings. There, where nature's abundance stifled the competitive instinct, men lived together in peace and contentment, freed of the jealousies and meanness inevitable in the crowded East."[6] That notion of utopia being "out there" is central in American history from the earliest settlement period and even to the present.

The dreams of prosperity were matched, if not exceeded, in early American history by dreams of salvation and the thought of returning to Eden as reflected by Columbus and others. Even the supposed quest of Juan Ponce de León—for the Fountain of Youth that promised immortality—is linked with the notion of Eden, for the loss of immortality was key to the banishment from Eden. The discovery voyages created a renewed sense of a paradise re-found. Joel Nydahl addresses this by noting that "the European mind ... was ready in the sixteenth century to believe that a New Eden (perhaps the old one recreated or rediscovered) existed and that a new chance for man on earth could be had merely by going from here to there."[7] Nydahl draws on Rhodes' work in his inclusion of outward and upward utopias. Rhodes defines an *upward* utopia as "an other-worldly concept of utopia, and it underlies the whole Judaic-Christian tradition [that] rests upon an assumption that utopia awaits man in a life after death." Rhodes notes that "The upward concept of utopia is one of the earliest to make its appearance in American social thought," being "formulated in almost classical terms in the writings of the American Puritans."[8] The Puritans, in fact, are one of the earliest examples in American history of the coming together of the outward and upward senses of utopia, and this perhaps is most often exemplified in John Winthrop's "city upon a hill" comments in his sermon, "A Modell of Christian Charity."[9]

The "other-worldly concept" of utopia also would be seen early in American history in the number of individuals who came from Europe to await the Second Coming. As Nydahl suggests, "Utopia Americana lies at the confluence of two historically important streams flowing westward from the Old World to the New: Paradisiacal Dreams and Millennial Expectations." Not only was America seen possibly as Eden but also as the place to be when the Second Coming arrived: "America became associated in men's minds with both the beginning and the end of time."[10] Many of the earliest, identifiable, utopian communal groups in what would become the United States were of a millennial nature.

To the economic and religious aspects of utopian roots in America must be added those of a political nature. Although many of these would develop later due to the nature of colonization, they would manifest themselves in

23

the founding ideals and documents of the United States. Such ideals grew out of the economic and religious aspects of utopian thought in America and also drew on the literary presentations of utopia, by Thomas More and later writers.[11] *Utopia* appeared at a time when there was an increased interest in the discoveries taking place in the Americas. More's work emphasized the possibilities of the New World, removed from the problems of European society. But even for those who had not read *Utopia*—and that would be most until translations became more readily available in the early seventeenth century—the explorations of the Americas presented utopian ideals. In a chapter titled "Seeking Utopia in America" in 1900, E. Sparks suggests, "The discovery of a new world created many hopes that these dreams might at last be realized on soil untainted by the greed and tyranny of past civilization. ... Poets sang of a Utopia in a land untrammeled by the conventionalities of old-world life."[12] V. F. Calverton offers similar views: "Men could escape the heavy hand of old-world authority, translate principles into practice, beliefs into realities, initiate enterprises, inaugurate plans and projects, which would have been inconceivable in the old world. ... Never before had men discovered such a rare and rich opportunity to test their hopes, explore their potentialities, realize their aspirations."

## The New World and Utopian Visions

More's *Utopia* was not the only utopian work to influence views of America, or even the development of the United States itself. In the early seventeenth century many more utopian works began to appear. Most notable are Giovanni Campanella's *La Città del Sole* (*City of the Sun*) published in 1602 with later versions appearing in 1623 (as *Civitas Solis*) and 1627; Johann Valentin Andreae's *Christianopolis* (1619); and Francis Bacon's unfinished work, *The New Atlantis*, published posthumously in 1627. Other works that stirred the utopian imagination of early seventeenth century Europeans included Joseph Hall's satirical *Mundus Alter et Idem* (1605, translated as *The Discovery of A New World or A Description of the South Indies, Hitherto Unknowne*), John Salkeld's *A Treatise of Paradise* (1617), and even William Shakespeare's *The Tempest* (1611), which is set on the island of Bermuda.[14]

Perhaps the most influential utopian work during the colonial period was an antiroyalist book published in 1656. James Harrington's *The Commonwealth of Oceana* offered some idealistic views of how a better society might be established. Unlike More's work, which can be seen as more fanciful (i.e., "no place"), Harrington's work was written with a more purposeful intent of suggesting how changes, particularly in government, might alter the course of England in the troubled period of the mid-seventeenth century. Couched as a "political romance," the work includes some specific practices such as a written constitution, a government divided into three functional areas with a system of checks and balances, religious liberty, and many other facets of what Harrington believed to be necessary steps for England to take. These ideas were received with interest by some in England but also resonated with individuals across the Atlantic, where several colonies had already formed and more would come into existence.

H. F. Russell Smith notes that "No one who has studied Harrington's writings can help being struck by the resemblance between the political ideas expressed there and those that have been successfully put into practice in America." The influence that Harrington's work might have had in America was not only due to the nature of the work itself but, as Smith suggests, was because "Many of the early settlers had breathed the same political atmosphere as Harrington, had gone to the same university, and had read the books he had read."[15] Smith observes that Harrington's *Oceana* was read in two critical periods of early American history, the developmental colonial period and the revolutionary period, and he suggests that John Adams "was one of the most fervent devotees that Harrington ever had."[16]

How broadly Harrington was read among the founders is unknown but it is likely that this and other utopian works were among the readings of Thomas Jefferson, James Madison, and other crafters of the founding documents of the United States. There also was a broader spirit of utopianism tied to the republican beliefs inherent in the move toward independence.[17] "The American Revolution qualifies as a utopian project," claim Pamela Neville-Sington and David Sington. It is not difficult to see utopian ideals inherent in the statement that "all men are created equal" and with the right to life, liberty, and the pursuit of happiness. The same authors point out that "Jefferson was drawing upon a utopian tradition instituted by Thomas More and followed by many of his imitators, notably Campanella."[18]

## *Early American Communal Utopias*

The utopian possibilities for America were tied to more than just literary imaginings or philosophical ideals. Several practical attempts were initiated to create "heavens on earth," as Mark Holloway titled his study of American communal utopias.[19] Prior to the grand utopian scheme of the United States itself, there were a number of attempts to find utopia in the colonies of the New World. The settlement at Jamestown and that of the Puritans at Plymouth can be viewed in some manner as utopian endeavors, but the earliest recognized communal utopia in America is that of Zwaanendael (or Swanendael, meaning Valley of the Swan), also known as Horekill, founded near present-day Lewes, Delaware in 1663. Led by Pieter Cornelisz Plockhoy, this was a group of forty Mennonites from Holland who sought to live in a communistic manner similar to the early Christians. Like many of

25

the religious communities of the colonial era, they were fleeing persecution and intolerance in Europe, achieving some freedoms of a religious nature. But the commune was established during the rivalry of the English and Dutch over economic control of the colonies, and with the defeat of the Dutch in 1664 and the takeover of New Netherland to the north, the small settlement in Delaware was destroyed with several members killed and others enslaved. Plockhoy later returned to the area but the communal society never revived.[20]

It was twenty years before the next known utopian settlement was attempted, a community of over one hundred individuals who were the followers of Jean de Labadie, a former Jesuit priest in France who left the Catholic Church to preach his own mystical theology based on millennial beliefs. Prior to his death in 1674 he had established a communal settlement outside Amsterdam, having been driven out of France. His followers, called Labadists, thought the best place to settle would be in America and under the direction of Peter Sluyter and Jaspar Dankaerts a community called Bohemia Manor was established in 1683 in what is now Cecil County, Maryland. The community lived very simply under strict discipline and practiced equality between the sexes. The community prospered but after five years the communistic aspects were questioned and a proposal was made to divide the property among members. Although this did not happen until 1698, the initial cohesion of the community was never as strong, and after 1698 many members left the group, perhaps in part due to the behavior of Sluyter, who became ruthless in his dealings. The colony formally dissolved in 1727.[21]

One of the more intriguing communal groups of the colonial period was that led by Johannes Kelpius, a scholar turned hermit, who took over a group of forty men who planned to settle in America under the direction of Johann Jacob Zimmerman, a German Pietist and astronomer (or, more accurately, an astrologist). Zimmerman had calculated that the end of the world would happen in the autumn of 1694 and he sought to lead this group to the wilderness of America to prepare for this event. He died shortly before the scheduled departure and Kelpius assumed the leadership of the group. They set sail on February 13, 1694, and encountered severe storms that ran the ship aground on a sand bar, where the captain assumed they all would perish. Kelpius claimed this would not happen and the ship miraculously broke free and completed its voyage. The group eventually settled on land on the Wissahickon Creek, near Germantown, Pennsylvania. They initially named their community "The Contended of the God-Loving Soul" but it soon came to be known as the Society of The Woman in the Wilderness (Das Weiß in der Wuste) in reference to a passage in the Book of Revelation in which a woman is to announce the millennium. There they awaited this event, which did not occur as Zimmerman had predicted. Several reasons were suggested, including the fact that the group had not had exactly forty members at the time of the predicted event, so additional members were recruited. Meanwhile the colonists built a central building although Kelpius lived in a cave nearby. After more members were recruited and some revisions were made to the predicted date of the millennium, which also passed, the community eventually moved away not only from its millennial views but also its celibate lifestyle. Some members left, including Henry Bernhard Köster, who had an argument with Kelpius and decided to establish a separate community called Irenia nearby. Irenia existed only from 1696 to 1699 and, although The Woman in the Wilderness would last until 1720, it would never have the intense focus of its early years.[22]

Many more communal societies were established in the eighteenth century, including the long-lasting Moravian communities of Bethelem and Nazareth in Pennsylvania, but only two will be discussed here in any length.[23] Both were utopian societies that lasted into the twentieth century to various degrees and, as such, were the longest lasting of any communal settlements in America. The first is the Ephrata community in Pennsylvania, founded by Joseph Conrad Beissel in 1732. With roots in the Church of the Brethren (commonly known as Dunkards or Dunkers), the Ephratans were German Seventh-day Baptists, a sect Beisell founded. Beissel had intended to join The Woman in the Wilderness group but, finding it had dissolved when he arrived in Pennsylvania, he lived for several years with the Brethren in Germantown. But his belief in keeping the seventh day as Sabbath was at odds with Brethren beliefs, so in the late 1720s he began plans to establish his own sect and community. He studied Bohemia Manor to learn of its successes and failures and then set out to form a colony on the Cocalico River that he initially called Economy but soon changed to Ephrata, in reference to a biblical name for Bethlehem, and became known as the Ephrata Cloister.

Like several of the communal societies during the colonial era, Ephrata practiced celibacy although, unlike The Woman in the Wilderness, the membership, which probably peaked around 350 in the early 1750s, comprised both men and women. Beissel held tight reins over the community and members dressed in a monastic habit, lived in stark conditions generally, and ate simply and sparingly. As would be seen in many later communal societies, tensions grew within the community, particularly centered on the beliefs and actions of the increasingly mystic Beissel. The disputes were spiritual and economic, and the colony was in constant turmoil from the mid-1740s until Beissel's death in 1768. His passing brought some relief to the community but it already had shifted in many ways from the initial intent. Several communities spun off from Ephrata and in the 1780s the land

27

went into a trusteeship.[24] The colony became less communistic, although the Ephrata Cloister continued until 1814, when the Society of Seventh-day Baptists was incorporated. And many individuals remained at the colony site well into the twentieth century. The Seventh-day Baptists denomination dissolved in 1934 and with it the last vestige of Ephrata.[25]

## *The Shakers*

Without question, the longest-lasting utopian society in America and the most widely known is that of the United Society of Believers in Christ's Second Appearing, or the Shakers. The Society was formed in England in the 1740s as a spinoff from the Quakers and acquired the more popular name, originally intended as a derogatory remark, because of the violent quivering and shaking that characterized members in their religious meetings. Thus they became "Shaking Quakers," or Shakers. The fate of the movement changed dramatically in 1758 when a convert named Ann Lee joined the society. Over the next several years—that included her marriage to a blacksmith and bearing four children, who died soon after birth—Lee's religious zeal intensified and she was repeatedly imprisoned for her beliefs and preaching. During one of these periods of incarceration she had visions that convinced her that she herself was the Second Coming of Christ in human form and that the original sin of Adam and Eve was not eating of the tree of life but having sexual intercourse. Another vision led her to take her beliefs and her message to America. So on the eve of the American Revolution, in 1774, she brought a small group to New York to form a colony on the Hudson River that was called Niskeyuna, and later would be known as Watervliet, the first of nearly thirty Shaker communities established in the United States over the next four decades.

Others joined Mother Ann, as she was now being called, and buildings were erected at Niskeyuna and preaching was done there and elsewhere. As the Shakers were pacifists, a stance that gained them notoriety not just in the Revolutionary War but during the Civil War and other armed conflicts, Mother Ann was imprisoned for treason in 1780. Later she began to preach more broadly and was persecuted as much as she was praised. As a result of the persecutions—including being stoned—and general weakness due to her travels and stringent habits, she died in 1784 at the age of forty-eight.

Mother Ann's death marked the end of the first phase of Shaker history but it also signaled the beginning of the expansion of the movement. Over the next two decades, led by both a man and woman—for the Shakers believed that God is both man and woman—many of the features of the Shaker beliefs evolved. Joseph Meacham and Lucy Wright were mostly responsible for these developments, and after Meacham's death in 1796 Wright assumed leadership of the group through some important and tumultuous times.

During Wright's leadership some of the first publications by members of the society appeared, including Benjamin S. Youngs' *The Testimony of Christ's Second Appearing* (1808), and she was instrumental in establishing schools within the society and for development of the ritual of rhythmic motions that accompanied Shaker music.[26]

In the early 1800s, during the Second Great Awakening in the United States, when a revival of religious interest was widespread and the American frontier was moving west, the Shakers expanded to communities in Ohio, Indiana, and Kentucky.[27] After Lucy Wright's death in 1821 and into the 1830s the Shakers moved more into spiritualism, leading to a period of manifestations called Mother Ann's Work in the late 1830s and 1840s, when young girls experienced visions in which Mother Ann and other figures of American history spoke to them. It was during this period that the membership in the Shakers reached its peak of around six thousand, although the precise number is difficult to determine. Many individuals came and went within the Shakers, including a group affectionately called "Winter Shakers," who came to spend the cold winter months within a Shaker community but left in the spring.

Beginning in the late 1840s a steady period of decline started and the first Shaker community closed in 1875. Although many communities lasted well into the twentieth century, the number steadily decreased as members died or, particularly in the case of men, were drawn into outside society for various reasons. By the late nineteenth century the Shakers were seen predominantly as a women's sect. In the first three decades of the twentieth century, community after community closed but a small core of women maintained the remaining communities until the end of the century. At the beginning of the twenty-first century only a handful of Shakers remained, all women, in one community; for all intents and purposes the Shakers died out with the end of the twentieth century.

The history of the Shakers is extensive and well documented.[28] The summary here is given to present some of the key aspects of this utopian society and its contributions to society at large and to American's utopian tradition. The Shakers believed in strict celibacy, and the separation of men and women was demonstrated in many aspects of their life, including not just in living quarters but in separate doorways and stairwells for the brothers and sisters. They practiced simplicity and this is reflected in their architecture and other arts and crafts. Living simply was one of Mother Ann's tenets and the Shakers strongly believed, as reflected in the Shaker song "Simple Gifts," written by Elder Joseph Brackett in 1848, that "'Tis is a gift to be simple." They were known for their music and elements of this influence can be seen in such works as Aaron Copland's *Appalachian Spring* in which "Simple Gifts" is incorporated.[29]

29

The Shakers also were successful farmers and operated efficient commercial enterprises for most of the nineteenth century, including one of the leading seed businesses. They were inventors with a number of contributions to their credit, including the circular saw (1813), a "hair cap" for brethren who were bald (1816), a "truss for hernia" (1836), and the washing machine or "wash mill (1852).[30] Their success as a utopian community was based not only on their religious zeal and strict organizational structure but also on their economic success and acceptance into broader society. They epitomized that outward and upward sense of utopia that had drawn them to America and allowed them to be one of the most successful communal experiments in American history. They were even more successful in what Harold Rhodes calls the "third expression of the utopian impulse," which is the inward sense. As he states, "The basic presupposition of the inward utopian is that the better life must be carved from out of the existing human condition." That is, "Existing society must be transformed for man to live the good life." The Shakers were highly successful in this often most difficult aspect of utopianism, for, as Rhodes suggests, "the inward utopia depicts a society at order within itself."[31] This sense of order is very challenging but it is the basis on which the Shakers were founded and it characterized their success. And their success in part can be seen in the rise of other utopian communities in the first half of the nineteenth century, many of which the Shakers interacted with in one way or another.[32]

The large number of Shaker communities established in the 1790s and the early 1800s dominated the total number of utopian societies in that period but other types of communal groups were also making an appearance. Most of these, like the Shakers, were religious in nature and many were millennial in at least some part of their beliefs. Among others were the vegetarian Dorrillites that lasted a little more than a year in Massachusetts in the late 1790s and an early cooperative venture near Potsdam, New York, known as The Union that existed from 1804 to 1810.[33]

## Nineteenth-Century Communal Societies

By the 1820s more secular communities would be established, many tied into various reform movements of the time. Central to many of these were the efforts of Robert Owen (1771-1858) whose short-lived New Harmony community in Indiana influenced not just communal societies but also other aspects of American society, from education to astronomy. Owen had successfully transformed an industrial city in Scotland—New Lanark—into a model city through improvements in education, health, and generally providing an environment more conducive to the well-being of the workers and their families. He based these changes on communitarian ideals that he saw as the foundation for broader improvements in society. He then sought to transplant these ideas to the United States and purchased property in Indiana that had been the site of an earlier utopian community, as discussed below, and sought to create a utopian environment by bringing in educators, scientists, and other intellectuals to achieve this model community. New Harmony lasted less than three years but it served as the basis for many other communities over the next two decades. As Donald Pitzer notes, "New Harmony became the first of no fewer than nineteen communities its adherents attempted in America, ten avowedly Owenite and the others strongly influenced by Owenite ideas."[34] As noted in the previous chapter, Owen was one of the primary utopian socialists. "The concepts he experimented with on the banks of the Wabash," Robert Sutton states, " ... all laid the foundation for the growth of utopian socialism throughout the remainder of the nineteenth century."[35]

The 1830s witnessed another religious revival and this spawned several new utopian communal societies. Chief among these were the Mormon United Order settlements at Kirkland, Ohio, and the United Order of Enoch in Independence, Missouri, Nauvoo, Illinois, and elsewhere. Joseph Smith and his followers of the Church of Jesus Christ of Latter Day Saints often are viewed as a utopian experiment, with many of the same characteristics as those of other such groups.[36] Another community initiated in the 1830s was Equity, in Ohio, established by Josiah Warren as the first of three anarchist communities he founded to attempt to put into practice the idea that the cost of goods should be based solely on the cost of materials and time involved in selling the item.[37]

All this activity in the early nineteenth century, however, was just a prelude to the outburst of utopian experiments that were attempted in the 1840s. Most sources include at least sixty known utopian communities initiated in this decade and many view this as a conservative reflection on the number of such groups and the broader utopian spirit of that time. This heretofore unprecedented eruption of communal efforts was fueled by the expanding American frontier, by the broader changes in society due to industrialization and technological developments, and perhaps most significantly by the adoption of the philosophies and schemes of such individuals as Charles Fourier (1772-1837).

Fourier based his utopian ideas on the concept of a cooperative community of a limited size that he called a phalanx—his name for the association that farms a rural area. Although Fourier died before his ideas were adopted in the United States, one of his disciples, Albert Brisbane (1809-1890), took his ideals and revamped his model for implementation in America. His *Social Destiny of Man* (1840) helped spread the word about Fourier in America, as did a series of articles he wrote for the *New York Tribune* in 1842 and 1843. Over half of the communal societies established in the 1840s were Fourierist

31

communities, for at least part of their existence. The Social Reform Unity established in 1842 at Goose Pond, Pennsylvania, is considered the earliest Fourierist commune in the United States. The North American Phalanx in New Jersey was the most successful of the Fourierist experiments, lasting from 1843 to 1856. The most widely known is probably Brook Farm in Massachusetts, famous for its years as a haven for transcendentalists, but which adopted Fourierism in 1845, only to have its unfinished phalanstery building—the main building within a phalanx—burn in March 1846, effectively ending its period as a phalanx although the community did not disband until the following year.[38]

One of the most famous, and infamous, communities of the mid-nineteenth century was the Oneida community in New York, established in the 1840s by John Humphrey Noyes (1811-1883). Noyes was influenced by the religious revival of the early 1830s and then spent much of the rest of the decade seeking and defining his views on religion and sexual relations. He essentially tied the two together and proposed, as Lawrence Foster notes, that "in the holy community of Christians, love, including sexual love, would be expressed freely among all God's saints."[39] This view of "free love" did not sit well with his contemporaries, including many of his supporters, so he further developed his ideas to suggest that because the Second Coming had already taken place humans were already living in a state of millennial perfection, and that he essentially was free from sin and thus perfect. Noyes argued that the Second Coming of Christ had occurred in 70 CE with the fall of the temple of Jerusalem, that humans were now in an initial state literally of "heaven on earth," and that a second resurrection was imminent that would take all to the non-corporeal heaven. In such a state, he declared, conventions such as traditional marriage had no place, and he developed the concept of complex marriage whereby individuals were free to mate with whomever they chose, although in practice the selection of mates was not as freely exercised in Oneida as individuals could be intentionally paired with others.

The intent of complex marriage was not solely sexual, although this was significant, but Noyes saw the monogamous marriage structure as presenting too much individualism and believed that it would hinder the broader goals of the community. Essentially he was changing the rules to create his own utopian environment. This he did initially in his hometown of Putney, Vermont. The Putney Corporation was established in the early 1840s to serve as the basis of the Perfectionists, as Noyes' followers were called. But his views of complex marriage were not well accepted in Vermont and he fled from the state in 1847 as charges of adultery were brought up against him and several of his followers who had been putting into practice the concept of complex marriage.

Noyes and a small group of followers then settled on land at Oneida Creek, some twenty miles from Syracuse, New York, in 1848. Unabashed by the experience in Vermont, Noyes continued to develop his views on complex marriage as well as the practice of male continence, or *coitus reservatus,* in which males of the community trained themselves to not reach a climax, or the "propagative" state, during sexual intercourse. The reasons for this practice range from Noyes' concern over the difficulties of childbirth to another method of social—and in this case, population—control. He also advocated the practice of mutual criticism, in which an individual would receive criticism from a group (sometimes the entire community) in a public manner. The intent was a spiritual cleansing but the practice also served as a mechanism of social control for Noyes. Later in the history of the community, the group also practiced stirpiculture, a selective breeding program. This can also be seen as another form of control by Noyes and a small group of leaders of the community.

At Oneida the Perfectionists slowly grew in number and achieved many levels of success in their communal efforts. A branch community was established in Wallingford, Connecticut in 1851 and it lasted for the duration of the Perfectionist experiment. Other smaller branches initiated in Brooklyn, New York, Newark, New Jersey, Cambridge, Vermont, and Manlius, New York were discontinued in the mid-1850s to allow for a concentration on the two larger communities. Despite attacks by clergy and others on the "free love" colony, the Oneidans became generally accepted and, similar to the Shakers, combined their religious beliefs with efficient and effective commercial activities, including the making of traps, silks, and later spoons. They were successful farmers and became largely self-sufficient in their needs. They also placed an emphasis on education and publishing. Noyes edited several publications, and, as noted earlier, his *History of American Socialisms* (1870) was the first American study of communal societies in the United States.

By the 1870s the Oneida Community had grown to over three hundred individuals and Wallingford's population had peaked at eighty-five. But tensions both internally and externally were taking their toll on the two communities. There were many external assaults on the practice of complex marriage, some of which were reported in one of the longer-lasting publications of the Oneida Community, *The American Socialist.* Individuals who had adopted the practice of complex marriage in the late 1840s were now in their fifties or older and the younger members of the community were less tied in with the spiritual background that formed the basis for these practices. Feeling this pressure, particularly from within the community, Noyes stepped down as the leader in 1877 and turned over the reins to his son, Theodore. Two years later the practice of complex marriage

33

was abandoned. Without the elder Noyes' leadership and without the mechanisms of social control that he placed on the community, the Oneida Community did not survive, and was legally dissolved in 1881. A joint stock company was formed to continue the commercial operations, including the manufacturing of spoons and other flatware, a business that continues to the present. Noyes fled to Canada, where he died at Niagara Falls in 1886. Many individuals remained at Oneida, including William Hinds, whose studies of American communities were noted earlier and will be again, but the community of Perfectionists ceased to exist.[40]

In many respects, the particulars of the Oneida community are not critical for the study of Oregon's utopian heritage, although there are some connections to at least one important player in a utopian experiment in Oregon, and possibly with others. More significant is that the Oneida community, apart from the Shakers and the Mormons, was perhaps the most successful utopian communal society of the nineteenth century and exemplified the utilization of a number of common characteristics of successful communal endeavors, such as a charismatic leader, mechanisms for social controls (Rhodes' "inward utopia" concept), and a balance of religious fervor ("upward utopia") with commercial vitality and acceptance by the broader community.

These same characteristics would be demonstrated in Oregon's most famous and successful utopian experiment of the nineteenth century, the Aurora Colony (discussed in Chapter Three). It is also of note that, when the years of Wilhelm Keil's earlier communal effort in Bethel, Missouri, are included, both the Keilite and the Oneida experiments began in the mid-1840s and dissolved in the early 1880s. Other similarities between the two communities—from attitudes and practices towards marriage and the interactions between the sexes to the practical products that both communities became known for—have yet to be fully explored and may be nothing more than coincidence.

## The Harmonists

The utopian communal society that had the most direct connection with the Aurora Colony and the dawn of utopianism in Oregon was one of the earliest founded in the nineteenth century. It was not just one colony but three, as the group moved twice during its existence, starting in Pennsylvania, moving to Indiana, and returning to Pennsylvania. It was a society rooted in religious and millennial beliefs and with connections to German Pietism. And for most of its years of existence, it followed one spiritual and communal leader, George Rapp.

Rapp was born in the village of Iptingen, Germany in 1757 and appeared destined to live the life of a weaver. By 1783 he had married and had two children. But there was more stirring in Rapp's mind than the weaving of cloth for he had begun to question many aspects of the Evangelical Lutheran Church in which he was raised. He broke with the church in 1785 and began to preach that participation in what essentially was the state church was in itself sinful. Of course, this did not sit well with the church or government leaders and when Rapp declared in 1791 that, "I am a prophet, and I am called to no one," he had more than crossed over the line. He was imprisoned and threatened with exile, as were some of his followers. Undaunted, Rapp continued to pursue his Separatist agenda based on Pietist ideals, which, as Karl J. R. Arndt notes, "stressed heartfelt conversion from sin, personal communication with God, and the pursuit of Christian perfection."[41] A summary of his beliefs was presented in *Articles of Faith*, prepared in 1798 at the request of the Reform Legislature. In addition to the tenets of Separatism included in this volume, Rapp also believed in celibacy, which he and his wife had adopted in 1785, and in the imminent Second Coming of Christ. By the beginning of the nineteenth century, over ten thousand individuals had joined the Separatist movement with Rapp as its leader.[42]

The expanding size of the following, along with the risky beliefs of the Separatists and their increasing adoption of millennialism, was a threat to the ruling government and the church and a confrontation, possibly even a violent one, seemed imminent. Realizing this, and using a passage from Revelation similar to that of The Woman in the Wilderness group, Rapp sought to lead his group "into the wilderness" and left for America in the summer of 1803. He originally hoped to settle on government land in Ohio, but his wish was thwarted by early-nineteenth-century bureaucracy, even though Rapp took his request directly to President Thomas Jefferson. As a result, when the first group of Rapp's followers arrived in the summer of 1804 they did not have land on which to settle. Late that year Rapp acquired land thirty miles from Pittsburgh on the Connoquenessing Creek. The following spring the reassembled followers of George Rapp moved to the settlement of Harmony (or Harmonie), after the Harmony Society was officially formed with five hundred charter members in February 1805.[43]

The history of the Harmony Society (whose members were called Harmonists and Rappites) is well documented, but several aspects of the community should be noted.[44] From the beginning of the American experience of the Harmony Society there were dissenters from some of the beliefs and practices of Father Rapp, as he became known. The nature of the dissent for some centered on the practice of celibacy, the millennial beliefs, and the adoption of a communal lifestyle that were supplemental to the core tenets of the Separatists. Even the initial group that arrived in the summer of 1804 included individuals who did not join Rapp at Harmony. Later dissenters would split the group further.

35

Harmony did adopt communal practices, including the sharing of community goods, more out of necessity than from some pre-defined plan. The practice of celibacy was officially adopted in 1807, partly in response to a religious revival among the Harmonists that prompted a stronger millennial belief, leading to the belief that marriage and procreation were unnecessary. Celibacy and its inconsistent practice, including by Rapp himself, as some suggested, remained a problematic issue for the Harmonists throughout their history. Similarly, the spirit of millennialism was difficult to maintain through the years of the society and the various moves that were made by Rapp may, in part, have been related to keeping the millennial spirit revitalized.

The first move took place in 1814 and largely was a result of Rapp's dissatisfaction with the site of Harmony. It was not, as noted, his first choice of land and as the colony grew, not only in size but in agrarian and commercial production, the lack of an adequate waterway became a pressing issue. A location along such a waterway was found in the Indiana Territory on the Wabash River and some thirty thousand acres were acquired. Although the swampy land led to widespread malaria for the early settlers there—over one hundred died from the disease—the Harmonists persevered, draining swamps and improving the living conditions for their new home, which they called New Harmony.

The Harmonists prospered and produced high-quality materials, including leather goods, linens, and whiskey, much of which was sold under the trademark of the golden rose, a millennial reference. Although the residents of New Harmony still held to their millennial and celibate beliefs, their commercial success and the construction of several fine buildings, including a tavern and a mansion for Father Rapp, suggests that the religious zeal that had prompted the enterprise initially had been tempered. This is also evident to some degree in the fact that Rapp performed some marriages at New Harmony to appease a growing faction of dissenters on marriage and celibacy. Other tensions were evident also and perhaps in part as a result Rapp decided once more to move the colony in 1824.

Often viewed as prompted by the persistent threat of malaria, the reasons for the move from New Harmony were many, from a renewed millennial forecast to the desire to be closer to Eastern markets. Rapp sold New Harmony to Robert Owen and, as noted earlier, this became the center of the Owenite movement in America. To relocate the Harmonists, Rapp chose land on the Ohio River ten miles north of Pittsburgh and here the colony of Economy was established. At Economy the Harmonists assumed their success not only in commercial ventures but also in educational and cultural activities, including music and publishing, that had been initiated at New Harmony.[45] But along with these successes, tensions and dissent continued, centered on the practice of celibacy to some degree but also increasingly on the power and control of Father Rapp. Further tensions related to Rapp's prediction that the millennium would take place on September 15, 1829. When that date came and went, there was great relief, until a letter was received on September 24, written by the "Lion of Judah," that appeared to many to be the sign of the Second Coming. The author of the letter was one Bernhard Mueller, who wrote from Germany and who would become a catalyst for the biggest rift among the Harmonists and, interestingly for the study at hand, had a connection with several individuals who would eventually settle at the Bethel Colony in Missouri and the Aurora Colony in Oregon.

Even Father Rapp believed for a time that the "Lion of Judah" might be the Anointed One to herald the new age, and there was much anticipation of the arrival of this individual. This did not take place until the autumn of 1831 and when he was introduced to the Harmony Society he was identified as Count Maximilian de Leon. Rapp's assessment of Mueller (aka the Count) as the one to lead them to a new age quickly faded and he grew uneasy with the presence of the charismatic Count. On the other hand, others found in the Count a way to focus their growing dissent and saw him as a way to separate from Rapp. The result was a schism, with one third of the members seceding to follow the Count. An agreement was drawn up and the 175-180 followers of Mueller agreed to leave Economy and to accept a $105,000 settlement for the rights to any claims they had upon the Harmony Society.

The group moved to Phillipsburg, ten miles from Economy, and established the New Philadelphia Society in 1832. The Count, who claimed to have found the Philosopher's Stone, practiced other forms of alchemy while mismanaging the resources of the new colony and it dissolved the next year. Still with enough sway to convince some to follow him, the Count established a new colony, Grand Ecore, in Louisiana in 1834. That colony lasted two years, after which a cholera epidemic killed Mueller and several others. Some of the Count's followers from Economy and others from Germany then established the colony of Germantown in Louisiana, which lasted until 1871.

While all of these events were taking place, Economy continued, but it never fully recovered from the 1832 schism and Rapp's leadership was losing its grasp as he entered his late seventies. Tragedy struck in 1834 when his adopted son and heir apparent as leader of the community, Frederick Rapp, was killed in an accident. When George Rapp died in 1847, the community adopted a new governance structure and, without some of the limitations of the Rapp era, actually entered the most productive phase in its history as a commercial entity. Much of the religious zeal had gone but the community still adhered to the practice of celibacy, resulting in gradually dwindling numbers. As the older members died, the communal properties were sold. Steps were initiated in 1906 to dissolve Economy and the Harmony Society officially dissolved in 1916.

George Rapp and the Harmonists contributed a great deal to the communal history of the United States and to the growing country itself. They also contributed to Oregon's utopian heritage as some of the Harmonists who had followed the Count to Phillipsburg would later find another charismatic German mystic with a vision of heaven on earth to follow. This would be Wilhelm (William) Keil and with that individual comes the dawn of utopianism in Oregon.

## CHAPTER THREE

# The Dawn of Utopia in Oregon:
# The Aurora Colony

*Before reaching Oregon City, the town of Aurora may properly claim
the attention of the tourist. Here was located, a number of years ago,
an experimental German colony. Just upon what basis it was founded,
I am unable to say, nor does it particularly matter. The colony system
had been virtually abandoned, but in the orchards and vineyards with
which these industrious and thrifty men have converted a wilderness to
a garden, can be found an instructive hint as to the vast possibilities of
the magnificent country through which the tourist has traveled thus far.*[1]

In this fashion A. T. Hawley described the small village of Aurora in 1888.
Hawley's description does not provide many details of Aurora but these few
lines capture some important aspects of this settlement along the Pudding
River that separates Marion and Clackamas counties. One is that the history
of this "experimental German colony" was unknown beyond a few basic
facts even in the same decade as the dissolution of the colony in the early
1880s. But even in the mid-1870s, when the colony was still thriving under
the leadership of its founder Wilhelm Keil, there was a lack of knowledge
and understanding of this communal society. Charles Nordoff, in one of the
earliest published accounts of the Aurora Colony in the broader context of
American communal settlements, captured a similar perspective. Early in his
report of his visit to Aurora, he offers this anecdotal example of how Aurora
was perceived:

> *When I mentioned to an acquaintance in Portland my purpose to spend
> some days at Aurora, he replied, "Oh, yes—Dutchtown; you'll feed
> better there than any where else in the state;" and on further inquiry I
> found that I might expect to see there also the best orchards of Oregon,
> the ingenious expedients for drying fruits, and an excellent system of
> agriculture. Beyond these practical points, and the further statement
> that "these Dutch are a queer people," information about them is not
> general among Oregonians.*[2]

In the 1930s, John Simon echoed these earlier observations, noting:
"Aurora hides volumes of the most singular and interesting history. It is to
be regretted however that so very little of it has been preserved to posterity."[3]

39

In the early twenty-first century, little has changed in terms of knowledge of Aurora's history and contributions to Oregon's general history, not to mention its role as the first communal utopian settlement in the state. In fact, most Oregonians would likely not be able to locate or identify Aurora at all.[4]

Although Hawley dismissed the colony nature of Aurora, his description captures the sense of the Willamette Valley as Eden and "the vast possibilities of the magnificent country." The Aurora colonists saw these possibilities and developed perhaps the most successful utopian experiment west of the Rocky Mountains in the nineteenth century. Moreover, the Aurora Colony played an important role in several ways in the development and history of the Willamette Valley. One could argue that there were utopian elements in various aspects of Oregon's history prior to the establishment of Aurora in 1856, including the missionary work of Jason Lee and others. But the followers of Wilhelm Keil who migrated with him from the earlier colony in Bethel, Missouri, by way of Willapa in Washington Territory, were clearly in the utopian tradition. In fact, the Aurora Colony has many links to other utopian experiences of the nineteenth century and very likely with earlier ones as well.

The roots of the Aurora Colony can be traced back to some of the same geographic areas and religious and intellectual influences from which some of the earliest communal groups in America sprang. These include the impacts of the Reformation in Europe  and the rise of several separatist religious groups among the Germanic people. Similar to George Rapp and the Harmonists are the influences of German Pietism.[5] Some of the other influences that may have shaped the development of the ideals that manifested themselves in the establishment of the Bethel and Aurora colonies include millennialism and various mystic beliefs popular in the eighteenth and early nineteenth centuries. And one common element throughout these early utopian experiments that also was central to the establishment of Bethel and Aurora was that the place to undertake such experiments was in the new land of the United States.

The individual who was the carrier of these past influences and other beliefs and traditions was Wilhelm Keil (1812-1877).[6] Keil arrived in the United States in the 1830s at a time when a religious revival was again taking hold, the western movement was gathering steam, and, related to both, there was also an increase in utopian communal experiments.[7] Keil spent some time in New York before ending up in Pittsburgh, where he took up the apothecary trade, one of many "professions" he would practice in his life. In the late 1830s Keil went through a series of religious transformations, first being influenced by the Methodist missionary work of Wilhelm Nast and converting to the Methodist Episcopal church, where he became an influential preacher. Almost as quickly as he had converted to this branch of Methodism he split from it, and then was briefly affiliated with the Protestant Methodist church before separating from that. He then denounced all sects and organized church groups and by the early 1840s had largely settled on the "church of Keil" as his theological base—not a formal denomination but an act that would be consistent with his positions on many issues for the rest of his life.[8] Aspects of his beliefs also were tied to mysticism, such as that espoused by Jacob Boehme, the seventeenth-century German mystic, and his followers.[9] The combination of fundamental Christianity, mysticism, along with an early inclination to the stage and an "indomitable will and bull-dog tenacity," as William Bek suggests, made Keil a charismatic preacher and a potential leader of souls who were seeking a means to live a simple and pure life in anticipation of the millennium, which was again on people's minds.[10]

Such a group of individuals who were seeking to live in a Christian communistic manner were located in relative proximity to Pittsburgh where Keil was living. These included the Harmonists still living at Economy and, perhaps more importantly, the remnants of the Harmony separatists who had followed Count de Leon to Phillipsburg. Just when and how Keil connected with these people is unclear. As Coralie Stanton noted in her 1963 study of Aurora, "There is no agreement, even among the descendants of Keil's followers, as to exactly when Keil first organized his adherents."[11] That some of those adherents were part of the Harmonist group at Phillipsburg is known through the appearance of eventual Bethel and Aurora citizens in the listing of residents of Phillipsburg in 1833.[12] Keil's contact or interaction with George Rapp is unclear and how much influence Rapp and the Harmonists directly had upon Keil, if any, is another matter for speculation and debate.[13] Certainly Keil was aware of Rapp and the history of the Harmonists, but they were only one among a growing number of groups at the time seeking to establish their own heaven on earth.[14]

However Keil came to believe in a communal society, he saw the opportunity to do this and in early 1844 sent three of his lieutenants west to look for land for a possible community. They chose a site on the North River in Shelby County, Missouri, and later that year Keil and his family, along with a small group of disciples, moved to the land. They were joined the following spring by other colonists from Pennsylvania and elsewhere who were drawn by Keil's vision of a righteous Christian community devoted to the Golden Rule. The name they chose for the settlement was Bethel, an apt Biblical name meaning the "House of God" or "A Place of Worship."[15]

Many factors aligned well for the Bethel community to achieve success in several ways, despite harsh winters and the scourge of disease that periodically swept through the area, as well as the defection of some colonists

41

who were at odds with Keil's authoritarian ways. Perhaps foremost was their devotion to their Christian ideals, and secondarily their allegiance to Keil as the leader of this Christian communistic experiment. But the nature of the individuals themselves was also a strong factor in their success. As William Bek notes, "Many of the Germans whom Keil gathered around him and especially the former adherents of Rapp and Leon were skilled artisans."[16] The industriousness of the German folk in the community was seen in the manner they built a church, homes, and several buildings to support the industries developed at Bethel, from a tannery and sewing shop to a sawmill and gristmill. Perhaps most widely known was the distillery where Golden Rule whiskey was made. The items produced at Bethel, including the whiskey, were primarily for use within the community but they also were in high demand by the growing tide of immigrants settling in Missouri and heading further west in the late 1840s and early 1850s. Products including wagons, plows, and gloves were highly sought by these individuals on the westward migration trails. Because of this, the community prospered and grew, with over six hundred colonists in the early-1850s and with a branch community started at Nineveh in Adair County in 1850 and other small satellite settlements at Mamri and Hebron.[17]

The community also prospered from its German heritage in being known for its food and for its music, as the Bethel band and choir were famous in the area. Music served to draw outsiders to the colony, as several festivals were held in which music was a key attraction. For the German immigrants at Bethel, and later at Aurora, music became a catalyst for community cohesiveness and identity, as well as providing a connection for them to their homes and relatives in Europe.[18]

This dichotomy of prospering because of their isolation and German identity but also because of the income produced by the selling of their products and services to outsiders highlights the nature of a paradoxical situation that would exist at Bethel and later be transported to Oregon. In fact, this came to the fore when Keil felt in the early 1850s that civilization was descending on eastern Missouri too rapidly and a more isolated location was needed for his communistic society. He obviously made the choice knowing that it was encroaching civilization—indeed, those taking society further west—that was the bread and butter of Bethel's economic good fortunes. But he was also fearful of the potential contamination of his community by external influences and control of the community is more easily maintained when such external influences are minimized. As Patrick Harris notes, "A prosperous economy, the opportunity to educate their children beyond the community's borders, and the tumult of Missouri politics were luring Keil's followers into the ways of the outside world." And, as Harris continues,

"Keil's solution was to seek a refuge on the frontier where his followers' godly ideals could be preserved in relative isolation."[19]

Keil sent out a group in 1853 to scout for a new location for the colony. Among this group of ten was Emma Wagner Giesy, the young wife of Christian Giesy and the only woman on the scout party. The group found land in the Willapa Valley of Washington Territory and took out a Donation Land Claim, the result of an act in 1850 that was the precursor of the Homestead Act.[20] Several members of the party returned to Bethel in 1854 to report to Keil while the rest, including Emma Giesy, stayed to begin work on the newly acquired land. Here Giesy gave birth to the first member of the Keil movement to be born near the land that was expected to be the new Eden of the transplanted followers of Keil. Events, however, would prove otherwise.

The long-anticipated move west began somberly as, prior to the departure of Keil and some one hundred seventy-five colonists from Bethel, Keil's oldest son, Willie, died of malaria. Rather than a joyful trip west, the caravan became a four and a half month funeral procession from Missouri to Washington Territory with the makeshift, metal-lined, whiskey-filled coffin of nineteen-year-old Willie Keil in the lead wagon, fulfilling Keil's promise to his son that he could ride at the head of the group moving west. When the party arrived at Willapa Keil quickly expressed his dissatisfaction with the site selected for the new colony, but he chose to bury Willie there, which they did on December 26, 1855.[21] Keil chose not to remain at Willapa and he and some hundred of the other Bethelites who had journeyed west wintered in Portland, where they found homes and employment. While in Portland Keil learned of property south of the city and, after investigating it, he purchased two sections of land on Deer Creek where it joins the Pudding River. He named the site Aurora, for his daughter. As there had been a mill at the creek, it also became known as Aurora Mills. The question of whether Aurora was to be the permanent home of the colony was raised years later when a letter dated January 1, 1878 on "The Late Dr. Keil" appeared in the January 5, 1878, edition of *The Oregonian*. The letter writer, identified only as "S," noted that Keil founded Aurora "where he established what he then thought a temporary home for his colony." But, as the brief account continues, "After a temporary home was established at Aurora, there were additions from time to time from his people in Missouri, who began to permanently improve the place until he, with the balance, abandoned the idea of removing to a place better adapted for a colony."[22]

Much of that permanent growth of the colony did not take place until a second large wave of immigrants from Bethel arrived in 1863, including many of the craftsmen and artisans of the community. The arrival of nearly

43

three hundred colonists from Missouri marked a new beginning for Aurora but it followed another tragic experience: a smallpox epidemic in the fall of 1862 struck Aurora and nearby communities with many deaths, including four of Keil's children—Aurora being one. Despite this setback, the Aurora Colony continued to grow, with more colonists arriving through the 1860s, and to prosper as the orchards and other agricultural products, as well as the same goods produced at Bethel, including whiskey, were popular among individuals up and down the Willamette Valley. Eugene Snyder labels the period from 1863 to 1870 as Aurora's "Golden Age."[23] The industriousness and inventive characteristics of the colonists, as well as the experience of having done it before, were instrumental in the success of the colony. Homes were built along with other buildings, eventually including a church and a hotel, which became an attraction for tourists, who came to Aurora to partake of the excellent food and to hear the Aurora colony bands (there was more than one), as music continued to be a significant part of the colony life.

Keil maintained tight control at Aurora, and sought to do so also through lieutenants at Bethel but the distance likely diminished his influence in practice.[24] Although the colonists in Aurora were spread out over two adjacent counties, there was still a strong sense of community tied to their German heritage and their devotion to "Father Keil." But the death of his children and his own advancing age led Keil to draw up an agreement in April 1866 that would transfer control of the colony and its properties to a group of "trustees and aldermen of the Aurora community or co-operative association." In turn, these seven men drafted "Articles of Agreement" between themselves and the members of the colony outlining the relation of the membership to the trustees. These two documents essentially became the Aurora Constitution.[25]

Nonetheless Keil remained the power figure at Aurora, while taking less of a public role. His influence was still strong within and outside the community, and he was instrumental in the arrival of the Oregon & California Railroad in Aurora in October 1870, which further bolstered Aurora's appeal to travelers from Portland and elsewhere. By its fifteenth anniversary in 1871, Aurora was a successful community in the Willamette Valley, still retaining its "queer German" character but also integrating more with the broader community in the area. The year 1872 would see another personal setback to Keil as his sole remaining daughter, Amelia, died at the age of twenty-two. Perhaps due in part to that event as well as contemplating his own passing, Keil transferred ownership of over four thousand acres of colony land to the households of many of the Aurora colonists, with the intent to transfer more at a later date. This did not occur before Keil's sudden death on December 30, 1877. Without an heir apparent, there was no leader to assume the role

*The Aurora Colony Band at the Oregon State Fair*
*(Aurora Colony Historical Society)*

in which he had served at both Bethel and Aurora. However, because of the agreements established in 1866, there was some order to the eventual dissolution of both colonies, although it would take until 1883 before the final step in the process was completed. Overseen by Judge Matthew P. Deady, three decrees were involved in the dissolution—the first occurred on July 27, 1881, the second on September 19, 1881, and the third on January 22, 1883, which "declared to be a just and final settlement of the affairs of such community."[26]

This is the basic history of the Aurora Colony although many more details could be told, including its contributions to architecture, music, agriculture, and other aspects of Oregon's history and culture.[27] Aurora became a colony three years before Oregon was admitted as the thirty-third state in the Union. The colony spanned the transformation of the Willamette Valley from its late pioneer days to the early stages of train travel in the valley. It weathered major epidemics and other traumas at the personal and communal level. And it did this under the leadership of an individual who was called "Father Keil" by some, "King Keil" by others, and likely many other names, both of reverence and aspersion.

Many of the inconsistencies, contradictions, and even mysteries related to the history of the Aurora Colony center on its leader, Wilhelm Keil. He was, in effect, a paradox himself, showing contradictory or inconsistent qualities that led to various interpretations of his actions and even more widely varying diverse views of his person and persona. Much of this likely is due to the fabric of history by which he is viewed and who was stitching together the quilted story of Wilhelm Keil. Continuing the quilting analogy—and

45

the quilts of the Aurora Colony tell their own story[28]—there are relatively few contemporary "blocks" of information on Keil from which a complete design can be constructed, particularly in the early stages, when he was formulating his utopian ideals but also in his later life. And there is a wide variance in the few contemporary accounts of Keil that are available and serve as the basis of the history and analysis of the Aurora Colony.

As David Nelson Duke notes, "most traditional descriptions of the religion of Keil's community have depended heavily on an antagonist's eyewitness account." Generally the same can be said of many aspects of the early history of the Aurora Colony and of Keil himself. Carl Koch's *Lebenserfahrungen* (1871) is one of the most often-cited works on Keil and the communities he founded. Duke continues: "[Koch] is an invaluable resource, for much of his chronology, identification of persons, and description of events can be verified at least in part by other sources. Still, the reader must be cautious of Koch's interpretation."[29] Koch, a preacher within Keil's community, had grown wary of the leader's ways and had left the community with little good to say about him. This is reflected in his work and it indeed needs to be taken with the cautionary note that Duke presents. However, dismissing his criticisms may be premature, as there likely are some truths behind the attacks by Koch. H. S. Lyman, writing in one of the earliest twentieth-century studies of Aurora, suggests that "it would seem upon investigation that the most of the criticism was without foundation," but he offers only one example that perhaps refutes Koch's assertions and that is itself based on inconsistent and inconclusive evidence.[30] John E. Simon provides a different viewpoint, noting: "Koch's testimony is in the main reliable. He was well informed of the events at Aurora and Bethel and was capable of fairly correct judgments."[31]

William G. Bek, whose four-part study of Bethel and Aurora appeared in 1909 and 1910, used Koch in his compilation of the history of these communities and their leader, but he also balanced this with other sources. He states:

> *I base my account of Keil's life on: 1. a mass of letters written by himself to members of the society at Bethel; 2. statements of trustworthy persons at Bethel, Missouri, and Aurora, Oregon—not only of those who praise Keil, but also of those who defame him; and 3. brief accounts found in the various histories of communistic life in this country, but especially on the account of the early years of Keil's life as found in a rare and odd book by a clergyman, Carl G. Koch, who at one time was an adherent to Keil's views."*[32]

46

Particularly with the use of Keil's own letters, Bek may present one of the more evenly balanced presentations on Keil, but that he calls Koch's work an "odd book" still suggests some bias.

As previously noted, a commonly cited work and the basis for many later studies is the report on Aurora by Charles Nordhoff, which is based on a personal visit to Aurora. As Mark Holloway notes in the Introduction to a 1966 reprint of Nordhoff's work, "The eye-witness value of Nordhoff's book is great because of the trust we can place in him as an unprejudiced and capable observer."[33] Some caution, however, should also be used in viewing this nineteen-page report as most of the information came from Keil directly and Nordhoff's brief visit took place very late in the history of the colony.

Another visitor to Aurora who reported on his experience was Theodor Kirchhoff, whose two-volume *Reisebilder und Skizzen aus Amerika* (*Stories and Sketches of Travel in America*) (1875-76) includes his "Visit to the King of Aurora." Kirchhoff visited Aurora and Keil in September 1871 and his report includes facts on the colony at the time and, depending on the translation examined, some varying views on Keil himself. This highlights another complexity in assessing the history of the community and of its leader—the translation of the few texts available from the colony period. Kirchhoff's report apparently was first published in a German magazine in 1872 and then translated by Elizabeth Sill for the January 1873 issue of *Lippincott's Magazine of Popular Literature and Science*, a full two years before the publication of the first volume of Kirchhoff's complete work.[34] Perhaps because of the nature of the readership of the magazine or due to the source for her translation—it is not clear from which text she was working—Sill's translation is less critical than the translation that appears in the other translation into English, which did not appear until 1987.

In this work, which was edited and translated by Frederic Trautmann, only those writings from Kirchhoff's two-volume travel sketches dealing with Oregon are presented, but the translation is from the book. Trautmann notes that Sill's "version is incomplete and otherwise differs in minor ways from the one here."[35] Sill's translation omits six paragraphs at the close of the sketch that present a harsh assessment by Kirchhoff on the prospects for the Aurora Colony and, most significantly, on the character of Wilhelm Keil. It is very possible these paragraphs were added after the time when Sill undertook her translation. In this section Kirchhoff questions the viability of the colony after Keil's death—with a fairly accurate projection of what transpired—and states "Keil's claim of financial well-being is untenable." But to Kirchhoff, "Most remarkable is the fact that a man so ill-bred has been able to keep his colony together so long." He is puzzled why the members "do not try to throw off that yoke" and "readily accept regimentation from that boor—the clearest proof of how low they must stand on the ladder of cultural development." But Kirchhoff is not finished—he states that listening to one of Keil's sermons leads to "an earful of crudeness" and that "ignorant expressions fly out of his mouth every minute."[36]

47

Kirchhoff also notes Keil has likely seen the report in the original German and the Sill translation, remarking that Keil "has often complained that, in gratitude for his hospitality, I defamed him to the world in German and English" and that Keil was angry about the title of "The King of Aurora." Then Kirchhoff, wondering whether he was fair, states, "I refer the reader to Charles Nordhoff's book."[37] This is a potentially revealing statement, not only about Kirchhoff's writing but also about this translation. In his notes Trautmann states: "Nordhoff's and Kirchhoff's views of Keil and Aurora practically coincide. Kirchhoff paraphrases from Nordhoff a long and generous discussion of Bethel and Aurora, which has not been included here."[38] This raises at least two questions: How much of Kirchhoff's writing was gleaned from Nordhoff? And, if Sill's work was noted as incomplete, why was this segment removed from Trautmann's translation? The inclusion of it may have presented a better sense of the nature and true extent of Kirchhoff's "visit to the King of Aurora."

Further contradictions and incompleteness of the historical records relate to the settlement in Oregon. From the outset the Aurora Colony was beset by paradoxes and problems that were unanticipated by Keil when seeking a new location for his communal society and these impacted both the short-term and longer-term nature of the Oregon settlement. Keil's dissatisfaction with the site selected by the scouts at Willapa was one of the first problems. When he chose not to remain there and to move his colony south, several members decided to stay, causing a small tear in the fabric of the community. The decision to move also highlighted another dilemma that Keil had not anticipated in the move west. As Patrick Harris notes, "Keil chose adaptation rather than isolation by moving his colony to Aurora" because the site was in proximity to two existing settlements, Champoeg and Oregon City. It was evident that other settlers were going to respond to the draw of the Edenic aspects of the Willamette Valley. Harris continues, "Keil had declared that he left Missouri because of outside temptations to his people, yet he settled the new colony in a region guaranteed to attract thousands of people."[39] External influences and the fact that some members did not all reside within the "village" of Aurora detracted from the influence of "King Keil."

48

Some have suggested that Keil's zeal for the communal life, at least as he originally projected it, was tempered by the loss of his oldest son. Similarly, the death of four more of his children, including Aurora, in late 1862 from smallpox also seemed to affect his role as the charismatic leader of a religious, communal settlement. It was soon thereafter that the constitution for Aurora was drafted, and unlike the "constitution" of Bethel, which emphasized uniting "into a Christian society" that "must not rest on anything else than the love of God," the Aurora Constitution primarily deals with the conveyance and transfer of Keil's "real and personal estates." In fact, the Aurora Constitution and accompanying Articles of Agreement make no mention of a "Christian society" nor is there any specific reference to God.[40] Keil is still recognized as the "beloved leader and protector," and would be by most until his death in December 1877, but the nature of the community that he led had transformed significantly in the ten years since Aurora was established. It would continue to do so, largely due to Keil's emphasis on "adaptation," as Patrick Harris suggests.

Although adaptations were taking place at Aurora, the spirit of community was a strong factor in keeping the colony together as long as it did, even with the allegiance to the "beloved leader and protector," and this has raised some paradoxical issues. Nordhoff commented on this on his brief visit to Aurora: "What puzzled me was to find a considerable number of people in the United States satisfied with so little." But he continues: "What they have secured is neighbors, sufficient food probably of a better kind than is enjoyed by the ordinary Oregon farmer, and a distinct and certain provision for their old age, or for helplessness. The last seemed, in all their minds, a source of great comfort." He goes on to suggest why this is so: "It is probable, however, that in the minds of most of them, the value of united actions, the value to each of the example of the others, and the security against absolute poverty and helplessness in the first years of hard struggle, as well as the comfort of social ties, has counted for a great deal."[41]

That sense of community was captured over eighty years later among the descendants of those colonists that Nordhoff had encountered. The lasting impact of the communal spirit of community was noted by Stanton in her study of the Aurora Colony in 1963, who stated that she "was inspired by ... the survivors' unselfish concern for each other's comfort and welfare." Witnessing this at "an Oregon Centennial year celebration at Champoeg Park in 1959," she observed: "Although there were many Oregon pioneer descendants present and participating in the program, the Aurora people seemed to convey an impression of unusual and distinctive personality."[42] The "unusual and distinctive personality" was a vital element in Aurora's success as a communal society and in its heritage. Yet not all was milk and honey at Aurora (or sausage and beer). There is evidence of some underlying tensions among the community but that spirit of "united action" and "unselfish concern for each other's comforts and welfare" has kept much of that history from being told, or even speculated about. But there have been times when such perspectives have surfaced with a wide range of reactions among descendants and historians.

Some of these perspectives on the history of Aurora have been presented in the form of historical fiction. A novel written by Cobie de Lespinasse, published in 1951, seems to be the earliest attempt to bring the story of Keil

49

and his followers into the public view through a fictionalized approach. *Second Eden: A Romance* is a thinly veiled story of the Aurora experience that captures some of the historical nature of the community but intertwines a subplot of sexual overtones that caused considerable concern when it was published. More recently the story of the Aurora Colony has been the focus of three works included in Jane Kirkpatrick's "Change and Cherish Historical Series." The three novels are presented in the first person of Emma Wagner Giesy (1833-1916), the only woman on the scout party sent west in 1853 by Keil. The trilogy commences at the Bethel Colony in Missouri and covers the trip west and the settlement at Willapa, and ends with the heroine at the Aurora Colony. Kirkpatrick does not include the same level of sensationalism as did Lespinasse, but the perspective of a woman involved in the colony offers a different view of the nature of Keil's leadership. Like Lespinasse, Kirkpatrick relied a great deal on the available historical record and even uncovered previously unknown documents in researching her stories.[43]

As these novels suggest—both in the stories they tell and the historical record each author utilized and uncovered in their research—there is still much to be explored about the Aurora Colony. Although there have been numerous articles, theses, and books written about Wilhelm Keil and his followers at Bethel and Aurora, a definitive history has yet to be written. But even without such a comprehensive study it is clear that the Aurora Colony was rooted in utopian traditions and that the successes it achieved and the contributions it made to Oregon's history were closely intertwined with its communal nature. As such, it is the fitting place to commence an examination of Oregon's utopian and communal heritage.

## CHAPTER FOUR

# Seeking the Ideal Community in Oregon in the 1880s and 1890s

◈ ◈ ◈

In the quarter century from the founding of the Aurora Colony in 1856 to its dissolution, there are no known successful attempts at establishing communal societies in Oregon. The years prior to, during, and immediately following the Civil War were a time of diminished activity in communal experiments nationally, particularly compared to the large number of such ventures in the 1840s, considered the heyday of communal settlements in the United States until the late 1960s.[1] Numerous factors are attributed to these shifts, most significantly the Civil War, but other factors such as economic conditions, availability of lands, advancements in transportation and other technologies, and a broad range of social, political, and other influences also play a role. Consistent with the dichotomous nature of utopian endeavors, such influences can be seen as deterrents to communal experiments or as the impetus for these endeavors. Overall, however, the enthusiasm for utopian societies dissipated after mid-century and would only see a modest spike again as the new century approached.

The newly established state of Oregon (1859) followed this general pattern and would not see any successful attempt at a communal settlement, other than Aurora, until the 1880s. A small and diverse array of communities was attempted prior to the end of the century. None of these would last as long as the Aurora Colony, nor have the broader impact of Wilhelm Keil and his followers, but they are an important part of the story of Oregon's utopian heritage.

## Aiming at the Stars in Douglas County

The first documented successful attempt to establish a utopian colony in Oregon in the 1880s had some distinctive qualities that would be unmatched in Oregon's utopian heritage. Although it lasted less than five years, outside of the Aurora Colony it is one of the most documented of Oregon's utopian endeavors. This is largely because of the nature of the colony and the various ties it had with other communal experiments and reform activities in the United States and elsewhere. The community is the New Odessa Colony in Douglas County.

The roots of this experiment lie in tsarist Russia, particularly during the initial year of the reign of Alexander III, who had risen to power following

51

the assassination of his father, Alexander II, on March 13, 1881. Soon after Alexander II's death, anti-Jewish pogroms began to take place, in part due to the actual and perceived involvement of Jews in the assassination plot, but also as part of a broader wave of anti-Semitism that developed in parts of Europe following the economic depression of the 1870s. In response to these pogroms, several radical elements among Jewish students and intellectuals formed groups seeking broader reforms and even revolution. Some sought to remain in Russia and push for the revolution that would topple the tsarist regime. Others thought that revolution was futile and sought emigration as the solution. Among the latter, two distinct movements evolved—one that saw their destination as Palestine, called BILU (*"Beir Ya'ako Leku Ve-neklja*," meaning "Let the house of Jacob go," from Isaiah 2:5), and a second group that looked to America as their destination and destiny. This group was called Am Olam (meaning "the eternal people" in Hebrew), a term inspired by an article by that title written by Peretz Smotenskin and published in 1872 in the Hebrew publication *Hashahar (The Dawn)*.[2]

The Am Olam movement was located in several Russian towns and cities but the largest concentration seems to have been in Odessa, a major port city on the Black Sea, where the movement was organized by Moyshe (Moses) Herder and Monye Bokal. The motto of Am Olam was "Jewish colonization," and "their ultimate goal," as Abraham Menes notes, "was the establishment of a home for the Jewish people in free America and some of them even toyed with the idea of establishing an autonomous Jewish state or 'canon' in the United States." Menes goes on to state that, "Their immediate task was the normalization of Jewish economic life" and this normalization "entailed eschewing 'unproductive callings' such as business and the intermediary occupations, and engaging in agriculture exclusively."[3] The emblem chosen to represent their goals and Jewish ties was the plow and the Ten Commandments.

The members of Am Olam were not the only Jewish immigrants seeking to form agrarian communities at this time. A wide range of groups was engaged in similar efforts, many of whom had been part of the large Jewish migration from Russia. The 1880s would see a number of agrarian colonies formed, from Louisiana—with the Sicily Island colony of Russian Jews being the first in October 1881—to North Dakota, and from Connecticut to Oregon.[4] There had been earlier attempts at Jewish agrarian colonies in the United States; the first was the settlement of Sholom in Ulster County, New York, in 1837, but it lasted only until 1842.

An initial group of over sixty members of Am Olam departed Odessa for New York, arriving in the United States in January 1882. The group lived in a cooperative in New York City for several months, studying English and learning as much as they could about their adopted nation. Several sought employment that might prepare them for the rigors of the farming life they envisioned, as few had been engaged in manual labor in Russia. Some found such positions in Connecticut and Indiana. In the next several months scouting parties were sent out to investigate suitable locations for establishing a colony.

The Am Olam scouting parties sent to the Midwest and Southwest were unimpressed with the prospects for a colony in these arid climates. The group that went to the Pacific Northwest reported more favorably about the potential and a decision was made to target Oregon for their colony. Just where in Oregon was determined by a set of circumstances that would prove of immediate value but, in the long term, was a factor in the brief duration of the colony.

While in New York the Am Olam immigrants were befriended by Michael Heilprin, a noted Polish-born Jewish author and editor, who had migrated to the United States in the 1850s and was a strong advocate of colonization.[5] Heilprin soon became a mentor to the group and through him the prospective colonists made connections with a number of groups and individuals, including those in the Relief Organization for Russian Jews that later provided funds for the colonists. Another of Heilprin's contacts was Henry Villard, who then was building his railroad interests including the Oregon and California Railroad. Villard was instrumental in directing the scout party that went to the Pacific Northwest to land between Roseburg and Ashland where the Oregon and California was then building an extension. As Helen Blumenthal notes, "Villard told Heilprin that in addition to working the land, which was partly cleared and on which crops could easily be grown, the colonists would be able to clear additional land and sell the timber to the railroad for ties and fuel."[6] After the scout party visited the land outside present day Glendale they brought back the recommendation that this should be the site of their colony. How much influence Villard had in that decision is not known, but that he arranged for transportation of the colonists at twenty dollars per person suggests that he had some interest in this venture.[7]

Another significant aspect of Heilprin's connection with the scout party is that one member of this group was not part of the Am Olam movement but a Russian immigrant named William Frey, a seasoned veteran of communal experiences in America. Frey was born Vladimir Konstantinovich Geinz in Russia in 1839. He came from an aristocratic family—his father was a Russian general. He studied astronomy and taught mathematics in the Military Academy at St. Petersburg. He was not Jewish, and had become an avid disciple of August Comte's positivism, two significant differences from the members of the Am Olam group. But he did share many of their socialist views and had come to America in 1868 believing that this was the place that "communism," as he saw it in the utopian sense, could be achieved.[8]

53

Even while in Russia, Frey had become fascinated with the utopian socialistic reform ideas of Charles Fourier, Robert Owen, Saint-Simon, and Etienne Cabet, all of whom were influential in the American utopian communal developments of the 1820s, 1830s, and 1840s. He also was involved in several secret societies in Russia, including the "Land of Liberty" movement of the 1860s, a short-lived effort to seek an overthrow of the aristocratic government, reminiscent of many such attempts in France earlier in the century. Following an emotional crisis in 1866 that led him to the brink of suicide, Frey refocused his energies on the idea of establishing a Russian colony in the United States, possibly on the model of the Oneida community of John Humphrey Noyes, which he had read about in excerpts from William H. Dixon's *New America*, published in translation in a Russian gazette. Following his marriage on February 12, 1868, to Maria Slavinskaya, a woman eight years younger than Frey, who saw the opportunities for women in America as an impetus, the two sailed for the United States, arriving in mid-April at which time they adopted the names of William and Mary Frey.[9]

The Am Olam members may have seen Frey as a valuable member of the scout party because of his Russian heritage but perhaps more because soon after his arrival in America he had become immersed in a series of communal experiments, most of them in Kansas.[10] Initially he had hoped to join the Oneida community, even writing directly to John Humphrey Noyes in early 1869, but, as Edward Spencer Beesly observed in his eulogy of Frey, "their Christianity proved an obstacle."[11] Instead he was drawn to the Reunion Colony in Missouri, a Fourierist community, established in 1868 by Alexander Longley, that also was known as the True Family. William and Mary Frey, along with their baby daughter Isabella, born in late 1869, arrived at the Reunion Colony in April 1870. They were pleased with the life of the community based on the principle of common work and common property. However, they also found that a majority of the colony was adopting the doctrine of free love and this caused a rift not only within the community but also between the community and its neighbors. Although William Frey was intrigued by the concept of complex marriage as practiced at Oneida, the nature of the free love movement at Reunion did not sit well, nor did some of the leadership methods of Longley. For this reason and others, Frey joined some others from the Reunion Colony to establish a new colony and they chose land near Cedar Vale, Kansas, where in January 1871 they established the Progressive Community.[12]

Initially home to primarily Russian settlers, the colony expanded to include many Americans, mainly spiritualists. Frey was increasingly uneasy with the spiritualist contingent and in 1875 he withdrew from the Progressive Community and established another colony nearby on land ceded by the

Progressive Community that he called Investigating Community. Another significant development at Progressive was one of a domestic nature, as William and Mary grew apart, perhaps due to his adoption of practices borrowed from the Oneida community such as mutual criticism and male continence, which in turn may have driven Mary to two affairs with other Russian immigrants. She left Progressive with the second, Vladimir Muromtzen, in the spring of 1875. However, several weeks later following Muromtzen's return to Russia, Mary returned to Progressive, pregnant with Muromtzen's child, but Frey vowed to treat the child as his own.[13] Within months of Mary's return, Frey and his family—which now included Vladimir, the son of Mary and Muromtzen—resettled at the Investigating Community.

Times were difficult at the Investigating Community, and only three adults joined the Frey family. The colony was close to collapse when its members were invited to join another nearby, the Cedarvale Community, which had been formed by a group of Russians known as the "God-men," followers of Alexander Kapitonovich Malikov. Malikov had been a revolutionist in Russia but in dramatic fashion he gave up the revolutionary cause and found a new one in healing society through spiritual enlightenment. He led a group to the United States in 1874, who, learning of Frey's various activities in communes, headed for Kansas to establish their own agricultural commune. From the outset the "God-men" were in disarray and late in 1875 they invited Frey to join their community to provide some experience and bring order to the group. Frey and the few others at the Investigating Community joined the Cedarvale Community but the "God-men" were not ready for the regimental structure Frey imposed on the community or the various health reform practices Frey had adopted, from vegetarianism to hydropathy. He also imported some of the practices from Oneida that he saw of value, including mutual criticism and a dislike for monogamous marriages, which would lead to divisiveness in the community. Added to this was the despair of many of the recent Russia immigrants about the bleak conditions in Kansas and their longing for their home country. The colony existed in a constant state of turmoil for two years when it finally collapsed. Some of the "God-men" returned to Russia while others joined Shaker communities in Kentucky and New York.[14]

Following the collapse of the Cedarville Community, Frey remained in Kansas with Mary and the two children. The marriage had not healed and Mary was depressed and distraught much of the time. Matters had grown more complicated: Frey had had an affair with one of the women in the colony, Lydia Eichoff, and she was pregnant with their child at the time of the colony's collapse. She chose not to return to Russia with some of the others, even though Frey showed very little affection for her, and went to the

Shaker community in South Union, Kentucky, where she had a miscarriage. She returned to Kansas and lived with the Freys in his developing version of a "complex family," adopted from Noyes.

Frey continued his interest in and studies of communal experiences. He wrote an article, "Conditions of Successful Communism," which appeared in the January 1878 issue of the Oneida community's publication, *American Socialist*. He communicated with individuals in France and the United States about the philosophy of Etienne Cabet and the Icarians, and he was invited to settle in Icaria, the community in Corning, Iowa, but did not do so. He did seek to join the Oneida community during this time but received a letter in February 1879 from William Hinds (noted earlier and later for his studies in American communities) saying that they were not accepting members at the time. Frey remained in Kansas until late 1879 and then moved to Clermont, Iowa, in the spring of 1880 with Mary, the two Frey children, and Lydia Eichoff and her infant son by Frey, born in February of that year. Here the "complex family" would live until mid-1881 when they moved to New York City. During this time Frey had adopted the principles of August Comte's positivism and the Religion of Humanity, which he now saw as the means to achieve the utopia he was seeking.[15]

It was with this background that William Frey was asked to participate in the scouting party for the Am Olam colonists. It is important to understand the history of Frey's activities and beliefs for not only did the immigrants seek his aid in finding a location for their proposed colony but they would also persuade him to join them as their leader after they settled in Oregon. Like many other aspects of this venture, this proved valuable but also divisive.

Following the decision to settle on the land in Douglas County, Heilprin led the efforts to raise funds from supporters in America and Germany. Chief among the supporters, and an ally of Heilprin, was Dr. Julius B. Goldman, a lawyer and like Heilprin a strong advocate of Jewish colonization activities. Goldman had traveled to the West to investigate the opportunities for agricultural settlements and his report to the newly formed Hebrew Emigrant Aid Society was in favor of such settlements but, as Gustav Pollak notes, "the Hebrew Emigrant Society was oppressed by the weight of its daily duties and the care of a motley mass of refugees clamoring for bread." Rather, it was another society established by Heilprin that provided the necessary support for the Am Olam immigrants. Originally known as the New Odessa Fund, the society's name was changed to the Montefiore Agricultural Aid Society in March 1882, with Heilprin as secretary, Goldman as controller, and M. S. Isaacs as treasurer.[16] "The rule of the Montefiore Society," Pollak states, "was to select for agriculturists only earnest young men and small families, and to help only those able to help themselves." The society's focus was on agricultural endeavors but it did not specify where such endeavors would be undertaken nor did it require settlers to agree to any binding commitment to a colony.[17] Over the next several months, Heilprin was able to raise several thousand dollars that would be used not only for the establishment of a colony in Oregon but for several other Jewish colonies as well, some associated with Am Olamites.

In July 1882, twenty-six Am Olam members departed for Portland.[18] They traveled by steamer to Panama, crossed the Isthmus, and took two more steamers before reaching Portland. A Roseburg, Oregon, newspaper was one of the first public acknowledgments of the arrival of these prospective colonists in Portland:

> *By the* California *arrived a colony of Russian Jews from Odessa, consisting of 28 men and some half dozen women. They have rented a building back of East Portland, where they are located for the present. The men are mostly young, only 2 or 3 being married. Several of them are well educated and are druggists, engineers, etc. by profession. They are comfortable in circumstances and it is their express intention to secure a tract of land and settle in a body as tillers of the soil.*[19]

Soon thereafter a subset of this group left on foot for Glendale to secure that land, which they now called New Odessa, and make preparations for the arrival of the remainder of this initial group and others expected in the spring.[20] The rest remained in Portland to earn money, some of which was sent to those who had gone south, to improve their English, and to learn more of Oregon.[21]

The group in Oregon, as well as those still in various locations in the East and Midwest, were aware that they needed someone to lead their efforts at New Odessa. They turned to William Frey, who was reluctant to move to New Odessa even though he had been part of the scouting party that had chosen the location. As Avraham Yarmolinsky notes in his biography of Frey, "He warned the pioneers that they would not find him an agreeable companion," but the Am Olamites persisted and Frey finally agreed to join them.[22] Lydia Eichoff and her child were part of the first group of Am Olamites from elsewhere in the United States to join the initial settlers at New Odessa early in 1883 with William, Mary, and the other two children to follow later. At New Odessa the "complex family" would continue to live together but Lydia was introduced to and viewed by the other colonists as Frey's sister-in-law.

March 1883 was a critical month for the colony. "[O]ld deeds show that the property was sold to Simon Krimont, one of the colonists, by Samuel Marks, Hyman Wollenberg, and his wife, Julia." The date was March 8, 1883, and the price was $4800, with an initial payment of $2000.[23] It was also in March that the group in Portland moved to New Odessa, although

Group photo of the New Odessa colonists
*(William Frey Papers, Manuscripts and Archives Division, The New York
Public Library, Astor, Lenox and Tilden Foundations)*

a few remained behind, having found promising employment. The colonists
from New York and other locations also started to arrive and work began
on planting crops and clearing the forest.

Early in the summer William Frey and his family arrived at New Odessa.
A correspondent records the sentiments felt with the arrival of their leader:

> *The most important events of recent days are the general assembly of
> all brothers and sisters of the colony, the successful conclusion of our
> undertaking, and the arrival of the Frey family. These three events form
> a milestone in the history of our "commune." Our long wanderings
> over the vast lands of America have come to an end and a new life
> begins for us, which enables us to turn in earnest to our spiritual,
> moral, and physical development.*

58  The letter goes on to provide some details of life at the colony early in its
existence:

> *As soon as we assembled, we threw ourselves heart and soul into our
> work, which, in spite of the meager food we received and the general
> unfavorable circumstances of our life, was crowned with a measure of
> success. Our food consisted of bread, potatoes, peas, beans, and a little*

*milk. We suffered greatly from the cold, for we were short of quilts. Nevertheless, we industriously wielded ax, hammer, and saw.*[24]

A second correspondent, writing on August 2, 1883, presents a different version of the colony life after the arrival of William Frey:

*With their arrival a new regimen was established. We undertook the study of mathematics under the instructorship of Frey, and the study of English, under Marusia [Mary] and Lydia, the wife and sister-in-law of William, respectively. This is our daily schedule. We work from six o'clock in the morning till half-past eight in the morning. From half-past eight to three-quarters of nine we have breakfast. Work is resumed at ten o'clock and continued to four o'clock in the afternoon. Between four and five o'clock is dinner followed by a rest period and intellectual activity. Monday, Tuesday, Thursday, and Friday are devoted to the study of mathematics, English, and to Frey's lecture on the philosophy of positivism. On Wednesday, current matters are discussed and on Saturday, the problems of the "commune." On Sunday we rise at six o'clock and immediately a lively discussion begins on the subject of equal rights for women. ... Thus the time passes till breakfast. This meal consists of rice, oatmeal, baked and raw apples, beans, potatoes, break and milk. (The members of the "commune" are vegetarians.) After breakfast, one member goes to survey the farm, another reads a newspaper or a book, the rest sing, shout, and dance. At four o'clock dinner is served. Two men wash the dishes, the choir sings, the organ plays. ... At seven o'clock in the evening begins a session of mutual criticism; then the work for the week is assigned.*[25]

The nature of this "new regime" reflects some of the warning Frey had given the settlers about not finding him "an agreeable companion," but for the first several months of the colony this regime and its leader were viewed as necessary.

For the remainder of 1883 the colony cleared more land, harvested their initial crops, and furnished wood to the Oregon and California Railroad, which they had contracted to provide at two and a half dollars per cord. As one colonist wrote, "we industriously wielded ax, hammer, and saw, and by the end of the month, we managed to furnish 125 cords of wood ... and were thus convinced that we would meet our obligations."[26] The initial obligation was two thousand cords of wood, but during the productive time of the colony they produced four thousand cords and the railroad was willing to contract for more.

The author of the August 2, 1883 letter quoted above provides these details of the colony living arrangements:

*The farm, as reported in the New York Sun, has three buildings, hardly deserving of that name for they afford no protection from rain or cold. Two of these buildings are about the height of a man, comprising two rooms each. One of these buildings contain[s] the shop at present. The third house, which has only recently been vacated by its owner, is better than the other two and contains five rooms. Since these accommodations are insufficient for the colonists, they have decided to add to this building another story and a half. The ground floor will house the kitchen and the dining room and the upper stories will be turned into bedrooms. ... One bedroom they have set aside for visitors, who frequently remain overnight.*[27]

The letter also noted, "The colony consists of thirty-six males (four of them married), seven women and four children." Thus the large majority of the colonists were unmarried men, most likely in their early twenties. This demographic later would be seen as one of the reasons for the collapse of the colony.

The colonists adopted a constitution based on the following principles:

*1. No colonist could have work outside the colony. 2. No colonist could engage in any form of commerce except the sale of the colony's products. 3. A special fund was to be set aside to aid new colonists. 4. Each family had full autonomy in the management of its internal affairs. 5. The work in the colony was to be distributed according to individual abilities. 6. Men and women were to enjoy equal rights. 7. Any member of the colony who attained his eighteenth birthday was eligible to vote, and anyone reaching the seventeenth birthday was eligible to take part in the deliberations of the commune. 8. New members had to pass a probationary period of one year. 9. Upon his failure to pass the probationary period, the new member was required to leave the colony, and his share in the crop was given to him. 10. All problems pertaining to the colony were to be settled by the meeting of the membership of the colony.*[28]

These elements reflect various influences, from reform movements of the period to Frey's views and ideas from other utopian colonies. How closely these rules were followed, or whether such aspects as the probationary period were practiced, is not evident in the documentation available.

What is known is that more colonists continued to arrive at New Odessa and at its peak, probably some time in late 1883 or early 1884, there were sixty-five members.[29] At this time the colony was viewed as a viable possibility and stories of it were published in the New York *Sun* and a number of Jewish newspapers including the *American Israelite*. Colony members made recruiting trips, including one to New York in May 1884 by Paul Kaplan, the leader of the Jewish members of New Odessa.[30] From such efforts other colonists arrived at New Odessa and many visitors came to the colony to see this experiment. As Abraham Menes remarks, they "were unanimous in their praise of its cleanliness, industry, order, and discipline."[31] The strict efforts of William Frey appeared to be accepted and working in the colony.

One visitor who was not so impressed with the situation at New Odessa was Rabbi Judah Wechsler of St. Paul, Minnesota, who visited the colony in mid-1884. Wechsler was involved in establishing a colony in North Dakota for Russian immigrants, Painted Wood, and his visit to New Odessa was in part to compare the colonies. While he was impressed with many aspects of the colony, including "the beautiful situation of the large and extensive farm upon which the settlers are located" and the substantial library that had been accumulated in one of the buildings, he was "sadly disappointed" in their "religious views and practices." There appeared to be no observance of the Sabbath or Jewish holidays. And while he found that "they live together in the greatest harmony," he also regretted "that this otherwise intelligent community ... are led astray by many views which sooner or later will be an obstacle in their way to promote their welfare."[32]

By the time of Wechsler's visit, tensions already were increasing among the colonists. Several of them, including Paul Kaplan, grew weary of Frey's proselytizing and there are reports that Kaplan "sat and grinned daggers" when listening to Frey's Positivist sermons.[33] Others, as Rabbi Wechsler anticipated, were concerned about the lack of Jewish observances. The young, unmarried men grew increasingly dissatisfied with the "scarcity of women."[34] Abraham Cahan, noted Jewish activist and writer, observed in his memoirs, "In Oregon, their enthusiasm beat every day upon hard reality like a ship being battered on the cruel rocks." Cahan also states, "quietly, the dissatisfaction grew and spread and blossomed into misunderstandings, intrigues, and bitter jokes." He suggests that "there were jealousies that resulted from sex relations" with "love entanglements and some free love."[35] Perhaps the "complex family" situation of William Frey, his wife, and Lydia Eichoff had come to light.

Robert Rosenbluth, whose parents lived at New Odessa and whose older brother and sister were born at the colony, recalls in a letter to Thomas Vaughan at the Oregon Historical Society that he had heard that "the commune was torn by countless and endless debates, which made many unfit for work the next day." He also adds that "newly cleared land was then supposed to be malarial" so the health of the colonists was a concern.[36] Elsewhere Rosenbluth suggests that the use of Chinese laborers by the railroad put the colonists out of work in providing wood and ties to the railroad.[37] Even if the import of Chinese laborers was not an issue, the

61

profitable contract with the railroad became problematic as the amount of effort needed to meet this supply drew away from other tasks. One of these activities was marketing their own products and produce, which suffered from a lack of experience or leadership in this area. Philip Cowen recalls "a letter from one of them telling of the quantities of large, luscious strawberries they raised, but were compelled to consume themselves for lack of transportation."[38] The diet put in place by Frey also led to discontent, earlier suggested in one of the letters of the colonists. In an interesting report on the colony one of the criticisms is of the "bean soup and hard baked biscuits of unbolted flour called after the name of that wretched dyspeptic Graham."[39]

From bean soup to the lack of women, discontent was growing at the New Odessa Colony, but it was the increasing rift between the pro-Frey contingent and the pro-Kaplan contingent that signaled the beginning of the end. The details of many aspects of this increasing chasm in the colony have not been recorded but the differences in philosophies and styles of Frey and Kaplan were central to this split. Frey continued to push his Positivist agenda and he lectured on the Fourth of July 1884 on the topic at a community picnic. Soon thereafter, Frey wrote to a colleague "that his success in teaching positivism at New Odessa exceeded all his expectation."[40] Frey may have indeed thought this was the case but it is more representative of his idealism than actual fact.[41]

Frey perhaps recognized this himself and saw the divisiveness that was taking place in the colony. His earlier experiences in Missouri and Kansas demonstrated the difficulty of keeping a colony together and, in his initial hesitation to join the Am Olam colonists, he had had doubts that this endeavor in Oregon would fare better. For these reasons, and undoubtedly others, he chose to leave New Odessa. Although the exact date is unknown, it is evident that Frey was in London with his family in early 1885. When he left the colony in late 1884 or early 1885, some fifteen other colonists left with him. One who did not was Lydia Eichoff, who had married another member of the colony, reportedly with Frey presiding at the wedding, and Frey's "sister-in-law" remained, at least for some time, at New Odessa.[42]

The departure of Frey was not necessarily embraced as a victory of any sort for Paul Kaplan and the remaining colonists. The reports suggest the separation was a cordial one and "tears fell like rain" because of the close ties that had been made among the colonists. Even those who did not adhere to Frey's philosophy did appreciate what he had done early on in the establishment of the colony. Rather than revel in Frey's departure, if anything they feared that event seemed to suggest the imminent failure of the colony. These feelings were only strengthened when early in 1885 the community building that housed the library burned down. Following this disaster, others started leaving the colony individually and in larger groups. And those who remained seemed to have lost the industrious spirit that had impressed earlier visitors. Helen Blumenthal interviewed a member of the family who bought the land where the colony was located and he recalled stories of how after the fire in 1885 the colonists "were remembered primarily for lying around all day, sleeping, reading, and discussing."[43]

By the fall of 1885 there was only a fraction of the population left from the sixty-five colonists of two years earlier. Paul Kaplan also left the colony and returned to New York where he and others who had established the "Commune" when they first arrived in the United States resurrected this concept in a tenement house on the East Side of Manhattan. Davidson and Goodwin even go as far as to state, "The Commune of New Odessa was simply transferred to Essex and Suffolk Streets," although this is an overstatement of the actual situation.[44] The members of the Commune opened a cooperative laundry that they called New Odessa Cooperative Laundry but it, like the colony, failed after little more than two years.

Technically the colony still existed in 1886 but it was a mere shadow of what had existed just a little over two years earlier. Although support was offered from Jews in Oregon and elsewhere to keep the experiment alive, there was no longer a driving force to make this happen. A bankruptcy suit was filed on October 18, 1887, and notices of foreclosure were published in the *Roseburg Review*. In February 1888 the foreclosure proceedings were recorded.[45] Nine months later, on November 5, 1888, William Frey died in London at the age of forty-nine. The utopian visions of New Odessa and its spiritual leader both expired the same year.

New Odessa was seen as a failure by most but it was the longest lasting of any of the Am Olam colonies. It left no lasting legacy as a place on Oregon's physical landscape but it did carve a niche in Oregon's utopian heritage. For New Odessa was based on utopian ideals and the various players in its brief history, from William Frey to the Am Olamites, captured elements of a variety of utopian schemes in the nineteenth century. And, returning again to Thomas More's sense of "utopia," it continued to be a utopia even after it failed. In fact, Leo Shpall sums up the New Odessa experience in that way by stating, "The entire project remained a utopia."[46] Gabriel Davidson offers a similar assessment when he observes, "These dreamers aimed at the stars, and the stars seemed to move further away."[47]

63

## *"The Nehalem cranks and dynamiters"*

About the same time as the New Odessa colony was headed towards its demise, another utopian experiment was forming in the northern Coast Range in Oregon, in the Nehalem Valley, a few miles from the settlement of Mist. Organized initially as the Columbia Cooperative Colony on

December 5, 1886, the group changed its name to the Nehalem Valley Cooperative Colony in September 1888, when it was incorporated in the State of Oregon. Although not included in William Hinds' 1902 edition of *American Communities*, the colony is noted in the Rev. Alexander Kent's study of "Cooperative Communities in the United States." Kent provides this brief entry:

> Its principal object was "homes and employment for members," with "justice for all." It was socialistic in aim, and held property collectively. The membership fee was $500 in money or material. It had about fifty members, of various nationalities, representing many laboring trades, but engaged chiefly in lumbering. Men worked eight hours a day, and showed no disposition to shirk or lean. Sex relations were normal. The causes given for dissension and withdrawals were "inexperience" and "other interests."[48]

Kent provides no explanation of how he compiled information on this community or the many others in his study, but the nature of the description, plus the use of quoted material, suggest that some method of compilation was undertaken, such as a survey or questionnaire to former members of the community. However the data were gathered, Kent's description of the Colony became the basis for inclusion in many subsequent compilations of communal settlements in the United States.[49]

Despite the absence of information on the source of Kent's description, and more importantly of any apparent records of the Colony, it is possible to piece together additional elements of the history of the community and the individuals involved. Most of this information comes from publications of other utopian colonies in California and Washington, as well as a newspaper of a movement based on a utopian novel of the period. The source of much of this information is one H. E. Girard, who was Secretary of the Colony and as part of his secretarial duties was spreading the word of the Nehalem Valley Cooperative Colony.

The earliest reference of this kind appears in the *Kaweah Commonwealth*, a publication of the Kaweah Co-operative Commonwealth in California.[50] The Kaweah colony was founded in 1885 by Burnette G. Haskell (1857-1907), a labor organizer from San Francisco, and was based on the ideas put forth in Laurence Grönlund's *The Coöperative Commonwealth in Its Outlines. An Exposition of Modern Socialism* (1884). Haskell, who had organized the International Workingmen's Association, found in Grönlund's work a model for developing a practical commonwealth on the banks of the Kaweah River in Tulare County.[51] Haskell edited two publications associated with the Kaweah colony—the *Commonwealth*, a monthly journal printed in San Francisco in 1888 and 1889, and the *Kaweah Commonwealth*, a weekly that began in 1890 and ran until 1892.

It is in the *Kaweah Commonwealth* that some of the more detailed information on the Nehalem Valley Cooperative Colony comes to light. The March 8, 1890 issue contains a lengthy letter from Girard, sent from Mist and dated "Dec. 15, 1889," which provides this background on the development of the colony:

> *We started this colony three years ago, seven or eight of us, under the leadership of Daniel Cronen. I say leadership, because he was the promoter of the colony and having entire confidence in the man, we were willing to join lots with him in anything to advance the downtrodden labor. After his having selected a location in the Nehalem Valley for a site for the colony, and having collected about $60 to buy provisions with and equip himself, Cronen left Portland in midwinter with his wife and six children to lay the foundation of what will be in the near future one of the institutions for which we are all, who believe in the principles of co-operation, striving, or in other words, advancing the principles of Socialism by practically illustrating to the world that it is not merely an idea or a hobby, but a solid fact which can be felt and handled.*[52]

Girard then provides details on some of the early struggles as well as the promise of the proposed colony:

> *Well, after having arrived on the ground of the future colony, and erected a shanty on the side of a fallen tree, with plenty of air all around and all of their furniture and most of their clothes and bedding thirty miles away, with not a sign of a prospect of getting them before spring, the situation looked rather discouraging to an ordinary man. But such men and women as Mr. Cronen and his wife, who had felt the stings of competition so long, were resolved to put up with all sorts of hardships sooner than return into that same world of competition, and they stuck, and here they will stick as long as they live. After having looked about them a short while, work seemed the proper thing to do, and at it they went, felling trees and boring logs in order to clear away a small patch of ground to let in the sunshine and avoid being crushed by falling trees which were very plentiful. In the meantime, two or three members came down to see the elephant, and were so delighted with the prospect that they also went to work, and in a few months the place was looking very different.*[53]

65

The early development of the colony and the connections to Kaweah are then presented by Girard:

*All this time we were working a sort of goody-goody concern of "you trust me and I'll trust you," and did so for two years, increasing our membership very slowly, owing to our limited facilities for publishing to the outside world our enterprise. Last September one year [September 1888] we organized under the name of the Nehalem Valley Co-operative Colony, and incorporated under the laws of the State of Oregon into a stock company, the only form under which we could organize, with a membership of thirty, several of whom have withdrawn since, leaving us to-day with a membership of twenty-six. Our constitution is in a great measure similar to that of the Kaweah colony, having taken their constitution for a guide, and now, little by little, we are working into a proper business system. We have now about fourteen or fifteen resident members, and are busy building a sawmill and dam, which will be our chief industry at present, as we have plenty of flue timber and a ready market for it as soon as manufactured. The capacity of our mill will be ten to twelve thousand feet per day, and we expect to have it in full operation about the middle of February.*[54]

Next Girard notes the efforts to increase membership and the target groups for recruitment:

*As I said before, we have gotten along very slowly on account of a small membership and consequently a limited amount of capital to carry on the work faster; but what we have done is permanent. Daniel Cronen started on the 5th of December for Minnesota, with money earned himself this summer (independent of the colony) to recruit members, and the prospects are that he will be successful to a great extent, having recommendations from several labor organizations in Portland, and being in himself a man who can represent the labor problem in all is details, and a good speaker. We feel sanguine that our population will be somewhat augmented.*[55]

In the penultimate paragraph of his lengthy missive, Girard offers some descriptions of the environment, laced with some boosterism.

*A thing I should not forget to tell you is that we possess all the natural resources which are so beneficial to communities. We can engage in almost all sorts of manufacturing, having facilities for obtaining material, a climate surpassed nowhere, and a soil that will produce whatever we plant, congenial to this latitude. The surface of the country is hilly, with bottoms here and there traversed by innumerable small creeks.*[56]

The letter concludes with some information connecting the Nehalem Colony with their comrades at the Kaweah colony:

*We had the visit for five or six weeks this fall, of a member of the Kaweah Colony, Mr. Geo. Speed, who left us well pleased to see the progress we were making in the reform movement, and who also was of some service to us in the way of advice on questions in which we were inexperienced and they had solved. He expressed a desire to see our mill in operation before returning to California.*[57]

This correspondence presents some of the most detailed information available on the colony at Mist but it would not be Girard's only contribution to the documentation of the Nehalem Valley Cooperative Colony. Nor would it be the only evidence of links, at least in intent, with the Kaweah colony. One of the more intriguing examples of these links appears in the pages of *The Weekly Nationalist,* published in Los Angeles as one of several organs in California in support of the Nationalist movement inspired by the plan for a new order presented in Edward Bellamy's utopian novel, *Looking Backward 2000-1887.*[58] Among the ads included in *The Weekly Nationalist* throughout 1890 is one for "The Nehalem Valley Cooperative Colony," which reads:

*Situated in the Nehalem Valley, Columbia County, Oregon; incorporated September 10, 1888.*
*This Colony is on the broad road to success, fully illustrating the principles of Co-operation as advanced in Edward Bellamy's "Looking Backward," and Laurence Grönlund's "Co-operative Commonwealth." For full particulars, address*
*H. E. Girard, Sec'y.*[59]

Here Girard notes not only the influence of Grönlund, who had also been an inspiration for Haskell in the establishment of Kaweah, but also of that of Bellamy's novel, which had been published in early 1888. Bellamy's work also was seen as further inspiration for Kaweah.[60] The ad for the Kaweah Co-Operative Colony that appears just above the one for the Nehalem Valley Cooperative Colony in many issues of *The Weekly Nationalist* reads:

*A practical democratic Co-operative Commonwealth, founded upon the principles of Laurence Grönlund's "Co-operative Commonwealth" and Edward Bellamy's "Looking Backward." Founded in 1886. Located in the Giant Forest and on the North Fork of the Kaweah River, Tulare County, California. P. O. address care of J. J. Martin, Sec'y, P.O. Box 427, Visalia, Cal.*[61]

67

The similarities in these ads further suggest common elements of the Kaweah colony and the Nehalem Valley Cooperative Colony, at least in terms of intent and inspirational basis. And it explains to some degree why Girard's report appeared in the publication of the Kaweah colony.

The influence of Edward Bellamy upon the Nehalem Valley Cooperative Colony was not just because of its commonalities with the Kaweah group but was part of a broader interest in Bellamy that developed in Columbia County. *The Nationalist,* the principal publication of the Bellamy-inspired Nationalist movement based in Boston, carried reports of club activities across the country and the August and September issues for 1890 included reports of groups forming in such locations in Columbia County as Beaver Creek, Natal, Vernonia, Pittsburgh, and "at Briggs school-house."[62] That Girard and others at the Nehalem Valley colony found inspiration in the writing of Edward Bellamy was part of widespread discontent over economic conditions in Columbia County at the time. The nature of this discontent is suggested in a history of the county: "The owners of the timber and the logging operators and mill owners were hostage to the weather and the roads, the availability of orders, boxcars, and river shipping, and the fluctuations of the market."[63] It is not clear just how the Nehalem Valley Cooperative Colony was "fully illustrating the principles" of either Grönlund's or Bellamy's work but it is significant to note that they, like their comrades at the Kaweah colony, turned to these works for inspiration.

Girard again took up his pen in the summer of 1890 to provide an update on the Nehalem Valley Cooperative Colony to the readers of the *Kaweah Commonwealth.* In a letter dated August 19, and published in the August 30 issue of that publication he writes:

> *We are getting along very well in spite of many disadvantages. We have done a great deal of work and are within a couple of months of being self-supporting. We should have been in a very prosperous condition at present but for the actions of a member whom we thought was honest and a co-operator, but who has proven himself quite the reverse, drawing out with an improved claim worth at present $1,500 or $2,000 and not content with that, has done everything in his power to injure our colony. The colony has sustained through him since March 1st, a loss of $1,000 per month at the least, owing to the inability of running our sawmill when he had charge of constructing.*[64]

Details of the member who presented this problem for the colony are unknown but, despite these setbacks, Girard presents an upbeat prognosis for the colony. Girard's optimism is common among such endeavors, particularly when sharing information with other communities. Girard suggests that they "are receiving communications from all over the world,"

68

but there is little evidence to substantiate that word about the community is being disseminated broadly. Perhaps ads for the colony, such as the one in the Kaweah publication, were more widespread than now known but it seems unlikely that the small endeavor in the Oregon Coast Range would be getting much publicity.

Girard goes on to offer more concrete, if wishful, projections of the colony's situation:

> *And now as to our ultimate prospects. As I have said before, we are only waiting for the rainy season to run our mill (it being a water mill), the capacity of which is 12,000 feet per day. We calculate having ready for sale next spring half or three quarter of a million feet of clear cedar which will net us $20 per thousand, besides fir at $8, which we will sell locally. We will raise enough for our own consumption, which will then make us independent of outside members. We number at present 26 members, with the prospects of a large increase before long.*[65]

In the next sentences, Girard foreshadows the future of the colony— "Comrade Cronen and family are in Portland at present, preparing to go down to the Nehalem Bay, where he has taken a homestead for the colony, a place which will eventually be of considerable value to us." He then provides some of the only known information on several members of the community when he reports, "Comrade Sharp is still with us, and a solid one he is. Fowler, too, Gaylord also, and Mrs. Steele is mother to us all. Our President, Fousbee, is from Tennessee and is a good man." Girard ends his second report: "Extend the congratulations of the Nehalem cranks and dynamiters to the cranks and dynamiters of Kaweah, and, as you say, let us come a little closer together. We are doing the same work and should be in a manner related to each other."[66]

H. E. Girard's reports in the *Kaweah Commonwealth* provide some insights into the community and offer some of the names of the members of the colony. Full membership rosters, however, are lacking and detailed information on the individuals identified by Girard is scarce. The *Oregon Mist* newspaper, published in St. Helens, includes occasional references to J. W. Foushee, identified as the president of the colony in Girard's report, but there is little information of note in these items. One report from September 1891 states: "J. W. Foushee, of the Colony, was seen on our streets this week about free from his limping gait caused by rheumatism. He spent two months or more at Portland trying the effects of electricity, but the disease had hold of a good man and let go with great reluctance."[67] Later that month, the paper includes this one line notice: "J. W. Foushee of the colony was over on Monday."[68] Other than these brief notices, the local papers did not seem to carry much news about the colony or its members, suggesting that any notoriety such as that Girard mentions was from further afield.

Some information on another member of the colony, A. J. Gaylord, appeared several years later in the organ of a utopian colony in the Pacific Northwest, the Burley Colony on the southern Puget Sound. Established in 1897, the Burley Colony, or the Co-operative Brotherhood Colony, also had some connections to Edward Bellamy but was more directly tied to socialist agendas of the period.[69] In the December 29, 1900, issue of *The Co-operator,* the publication of the Burley Colony, appears a lengthy letter "sent in connection with an application for membership from Brother A. J. Gaylord of Lowden's Ranch, Calif."[70] Gaylord's letter begins with his background in cooperative activities: "I have spent seven years as a resident member of Co-operative Associations—The Nehalem Valley Co-operative Colony of Mist, Columbia Co., Oregon, and the Nehalem Bay Union Mill Co., of Nehalem, Tillamook Co., Oregon—having served in both as a director, and in the latter as secretary." He goes on to suggest that these experiences have assisted him in understanding the situation of such colonies: "I think I realize to some extent what the pioneers of such an enterprise have to encounter, and as a non-resident member of your Brotherhood (if accepted) I will try to lighten the greatest hardship of all, namely, want of money, to the best of my ability. If conditions remain with me as they are at present I shall remit from $10 to $25 per month until my part is paid in full."[71] The remainder of the letter, in addition to suggesting that paying dues upfront would benefit the organization better than a dues schedule spread out over years, said that members of the Brotherhood, either resident or non-resident, must act together instead of just paying their dues.[72] Gaylord's letter struck a chord with others, as subsequent issues include several responses to his suggestions.

In a second letter Gaylord adds a more impassioned statement:

*Brothers, you may think I am a crank. I may be, but let me say a word in your ear. I have stood for years on the headlands of universal brotherhood of man. I have seen the truest of the true sink before the gale into nameless graves, but not unforgotten. I have seen a little band of motherless children, who by association were as dear to me as my own could have been, scattered to the four winds of the world. One of them, as bright a boy as the one you are so proud of, sleeps at Manila, a victim of that same cruel greed that is searching after that boy of yours. Others sleep, God knows where.*

*If that and much more has made me a crank, I had rather become two cranks with two men on each handle than to see the same fate overtake Burley. And as a crank is something to go around, I think each one will get his share; and should the friction reduce my motion, will each one be kind enough to give me an extra turn?*[73]

If some of Gaylord's "years on the headlands of universal brotherhood of man" were those at the Nehalem Valley Cooperative Colony and the successor colony at Nehalem Bay, these glimpses of his views may be reflective of other members of these colonies in Oregon.

Information on a few other members of the colony is found in various other documents, including the incorporation paper of the Nehalem Valley Cooperative Colony filed in the Oregon State Archives. The signatories of this document were Daniel Cronen, H. E. Girard, and L. H. Botts.[74] We are also told that William J. Haycox was a member of the community. As reported by his son, Ernest J. Haycox, "My father was a member of a co-operative colony that bought a large track of land four miles from Mist. There was a heavy stand of timber on most of the land owned by the colony. Tom Nordby, purser of the [steamboat *G. W.] Shaver*, acted as business agent and sales manager for the colony."[75]

Other details of the Nehalem Valley Cooperative Colony are scarce, including its demise around 1892. Otohiko Okugawa notes in the entry in his compilation that, "As late as 1892, the Nehalem Valley Co-operative Colony was listed in the directory as owner of a sawmill."[76] Several possible reasons for the failure of the colony are suggested by compilers of works on communities and by descendants of colony members. Alexander Kent notes, "The colony is said to have failed because of 'surrounding opposition and lack of funds'."[77] Most later sources offer similar reasons for its collapse. Ernest Haycox, Jr., on reflecting on the colony of which his grandfather was a member, cites several reasons common in the failure of such endeavors: "Utopian communities were arguably uncertain affairs, in that some conscripts were naïve in their expectations as a result of reading hopefully optimistic tracts about communal living while others weren't prepared for the hard labor that this new world entailed." But he also offers an interesting perspective, and one of the few instances when women are mentioned: "In this case, the failure also reflected domestic concerns. My father was told that the women rebelled when advised by their governors that they would be required to prepare meals in a communal kitchen." And he sums up some of the practical versus idealist struggles of this colony and others:

71

*Economically, the Nehalem Valley Cooperative Colony made little sense. Significant markets were distant; lumber from the mill had to be hauled in wagons over a difficult road to Clatskanie on the Columbia River. Every step of the way, of course, it was shaded by standing timber that was cheaper to haul to market than theirs. To be sure, they had gotten away from the world. That is a theme of several memoirs of early Nehalem Valley settlement; immigrants are described as being uncertain why they came for any reason more substantial than a love of solitude.*[78]

There is no question that the Nehalem Valley Cooperative Colony dissolved as a colony some time in or around 1892, at least as a cooperative enterprise. Haycox notes that his grandfather, William, kept his homestead on the site of the colony after it failed, at least for a few years. What transpired with other colony members has been largely lost or, at best, speculated.

## Union Mill Company

The information on the Union Mill Company is even more sparse then that of the Nehalem Valley Cooperative, although the early sources are essentially the same. Alexander Kent includes this entry for what he labeled "The Unions Mill Company":

> *The Unions Mill Company was organized in 1892, at Nehalem, Tillamook County, Oreg. It was socialistic in aim, but made all workers equal in regard to salary. All property outside of stock was held in common. Stock was $100 per share, and only stockholders could be members. The principal industry was lumbering, carried on cooperatively under the eight-hour rule. There was no infringement on the family life.*[79]

Later works largely echo the information presented here. Okugawa's list adds some important information by noting, "In 1891, Daniel Cronen and his wife Catherine filed the deed to the Union Mill Company." His entry ends, "While this community appears to resemble the Nehalem Valley Cooperative Colony... established earlier in the adjacent county, it is not clear if they were connected."[80] This uncertainty is raised in most of the other descriptions of the colony.

The ending date of the Nehalem Valley Cooperative Colony in 1892 and the starting date of the Union Mill Company, either 1891 or 1892, suggests some possible ties. So too does the fact that both were centered on lumbering and generally followed socialistic principles, although these characteristics could be found in other colonies on the West Coast. But the correspondence from H. E. Girard and A. J. Gaylord, published in organs of some of those other colonies, demonstrates that there are some definite connections between the two. In fact, the colony on the Nehalem Bay on the coast most likely was a successor to the one some fifty miles away in the Coast Range.

As noted earlier, one of Girard's letters, written in the late summer of 1890, to the *Kaweah Commonwealth* included the information that Comrade

Cronen was going to Nehalem Bay, looking for a new location, or possibly a second location, for the work of the Nehalem Valley Cooperative Colony.[81] As Okugawa notes, Cronen and his wife filed the deed to the Union Mill Company the following year. Whether this was part of a broader strategy of moving the colony out of the mountains down to the coast is yet unclear, but it definitely shows a likely connection between the two colonies.

Further evidence of such a connection is suggested in the letter of A. J. Gaylord to *The Co-operator*, where he refers to having been a member of both colonies. This infers a possible connection, although individuals certainly moved from one colony to another with some regularity. However, that he also "served in both as a director, and in the latter as secretary" could indicate a strong connection between the two.[82] Without substantial documentation, which has yet to be uncovered, these possible connections are still speculative but there does seem to be more evidence than earlier identified that such a connection is likely.

There are still numerous questions and unknowns about the Union Mill Company, including the size of its membership and the names of other members.[83] That Gaylord notes that he was secretary raises the question of what happened to Girard, who served in that capacity at the Nehalem Valley Cooperative Colony. And the few names associated with the former colony have yet to surface at the later colony.

There are no details of colony life and little information on its demise. Kent reports that "Failure is attributed to 'a stringency in the money market,' " likely a reflection of the economic downturn of the Panic of 1893 when the railroads, banks, and many mills failed and unemployment was widespread.[84] If this is the case, it could be very likely that the Union Mill Company had barely got off the ground before tough financial times struck. Okugawa notes that "The sheriff's deed of 1897 attests to the seizure of all the right to the company's property," but chances are the colony had dissolved prior to this formal end of its existence on paper in 1897.[85]

The Nehalem Valley Cooperative Colony and the Union Mill Company were small undertakings with limited, if any, successes but they are important elements of the utopian heritage story of Oregon. These were attempts to establish ideal settlements in response to what were perceived as growing evils of an industrialized and increasingly monopolistic society. As such, they were different than earlier communal experiments in Oregon and are noteworthy for that. That the Nehalem Valley Cooperative Colony, at least, found inspiration in the writings of Edward Bellamy and Laurence Grönlund is also significant. Bellamy, Grönlund, and Julius A. Wayland (founder of the Ruskin Cooperative Association in Tennessee and founder and editor of the influential *The Coming Nation*) were important individuals in what has been called the "revival of communitarianism," largely in part to "their distinctly American ideology."[86] The Nehalem Colony was thus part of this revival activity. It is also of note that this small colony in the Oregon Coast Range found inspiration in Bellamy, as most of his followers and advocates were in industrialized cities or in traditional farmlands, not in remote lumbering country. And the heretofore unrecognized links with the Kaweah Colony in California are important in understanding not only the impetus for certain aspects of the Nehalem Valley Cooperative Colony (and possibly the Union Mill Company) but also in demonstrating inter-colony communication and interests about utopian experiments in various parts of the country.

## *"The mysterious religious colony on Poole Slough"*

As the Columbia Cooperative Colony was being formed in the northern Coast Range, further south a small group of individuals was embarking on an effort to establish their own colony on land near Newport in what was then part of Benton County (now in Lincoln County). Their land was near where Wright Creek enters Poole Slough on the south side of Yaquina Bay. Details of the colony are sketchy at best but there is information available on some of the members of the community, primarily culled from reports of two daughters of colony members. The earliest of these reports, by Monica St. Romain, centers on the recollections of Anne Jane Brooks, one of two daughters of Louis Kassuth Brooks and Mary Miller Brooks, who was just two years old when the family moved to the forming colony in 1886.[87] A second report draws upon this account but also adds some reflections of Alice Elinor Lambert, daughter of Charles Edward Lambert, who likely was the founder or co-founder of the colony on Poole Slough.[88]

It is Charles Edward Lambert who seems the hub of this communal effort. Born in Ireland in 1841, he came to the United States just as the Civil War was breaking out and he joined the Union Army in Kansas. After the war he attended Baker University in Baldwin City, Kansas, followed by further study at Northwestern University; he graduated from Northwestern in 1875, then took seminary training at Garrett Biblical Institute to become a Methodist minister. He moved in 1876 to Indiana, where he married Ella Amelia "Nellie" Lathrop. In 1879 Lambert and his family moved to Salem, Oregon, perhaps having been called by Willamette University, then a Methodist institution. Shortly after arriving he was named president of Willamette, although he only served one year (1879-1880), and then was succeeded by a Phi Gamma Delta fraternity brother from Northwestern, Thomas Van Scoy, who served as Willamette's president from 1880 to 1891. In 1882, Lambert and his family moved to Eugene, where he joined the faculty at the University of Oregon, but then he decided to leave the university in 1886 and to settle on the land along Poole Slough.[89]

The nature and extent of the colony is unclear. It was believed to be religious in nature although there is no evidence that it was tied to any Methodist group. It may have been called Iona, although that is only speculative.[90] If so, the learned Lambert may have been making a connection with the island off Scotland that became an important religious place and the burial ground for Irish, Scottish, and Norwegian royalty.[91]

There is information on several of the members of the colony. In addition to the Lambert family, there was the Brooks family, who had moved from Foster, Oregon. A Reverend Wilson Wright is believed to have co-founded the colony with Lambert and may have been its head. St. Romain reports on nearby residents on Poole Slough who remember the Wright children but no lasting record of the families or the colony seems to exist. St. Romain also states, "The families built a large two-story colony house, started a school for their children, and probably established a post office," but there is no record of such a post office and the two-story house burned some time in the 1920s after being struck by lightning.[92]

The Brooks family appears to have been the first to leave, moving to Toledo, where Louis Brooks taught until 1898 when the family moved to Yakima, Washington. Charles Lambert obtained a teaching position in a boys' school several miles from the colony and his family eventually moved off the colony land. In 1893 they moved again when Lambert became the president of a small academy where he reportedly taught "reforestation, animal husbandry, and agricultural sciences." In the late 1890s the Lambert family, now numbering seven children, moved to Tacoma and later to Seattle. Charles Lambert died in 1932, without providing any records or personal history of what St. Romain describes as "the mysterious religious colony on Pooles [sic] Slough."[93]

## *"Two New Utopias"*

As the Union Mill Company and the religious colony on Poole Slough were in their downswing, other visions of utopian settlements were developing in Oregon although we likely have record of only a very small percentage of these. *The Oregonian* offered a glimpse of two of a very diverse nature in its February 18, 1894 issue under the headline "The Two New Utopias," with the subheading, "One of Them in Eastern Oregon, the Other in the Dark Continent." Before describing these distinctively different endeavors, the paper offers these observations on the climate for such activities:

*Among the queer developments of these adamantine times in Oregon and Washington is a threatening reversal of the course of empire's star.*

*Popular discontent, parent of emigration, has brought forth a couple of projects whose common aim is partial depopulation of this city [Portland]. With this aim, however, their similitude ends, as one of them seeks to land its followers in far-off Africa, while the other one proposes to plant its devotees in the northeastern part of this state. Neither of them was born in Portland, but both have advocated here and [been] received with favor by the people who are most keenly feeling the prosperity-crushing effects of the "change" inaugurated with the present national administration.*[94]

The colony in Eastern Oregon, according to *The Oregonian*, had its start when a cooperative union was organized in Spokane some two months before by "idle tradesmen." An elderly farmer named A.E. Jewett, owner of a 340-acre farm on the banks of the Columbia comprising 10 acres of vineyard, 40 acres of nursery ground, and a 25-acre orchard, promised to give the farm to the union. Fifteen or twenty men from Spokane had signed on at the time of the article, and were planning to move to the farm in a matter of weeks.

The newspaper then offered some details on the proposed colony:

*The conditions of admission to the colony are simple but inflexible. The applicant must possess good health, industrious habits, strict morality, a peaceable disposition, a good reputation for honesty and fair-dealing, and $100 in cash. He must also promise to conform to the rules of the society as adopted by the majority. A Spokane paper says that the direction of all work on the farm is to be intrusted to a board of directors elected by the colonists. All the men in the colony agree to work at anything as these may direct. Next month some will be set to plowing, others to clearing woodland, and a third band will put up the sawmill and begin cutting lumber for the new houses that must be built. Each man will have his own home, built to order, ready to receive his family when midsummer comes.*[95]

Each worker was to receive equal pay in "coupon orders on the community store." Goods that could not be made at the colony would be bought with money from the sale of surplus fruit and other products. Very little else has been recorded of this effort.

The second "new utopia" reported by *The Oregonian* is not for a settlement in Oregon but is nonetheless noteworthy. Several young men from Astoria were planning a colony "in what is now supposed to be the new El Dorado, in the Transvaal, South Africa." The newspaper focused its story on the region's economic opportunities and drawbacks.

The *Oregonian* reporter is skeptical about this adventure, but it would not be the only direction citizens of Astoria would take to seek utopian ideals. A number of the Finnish community that had settled in Astoria were enticed to move to British Columbia a few years later to one of several utopian settlements established in this Canadian province.

The most famous, and infamous, of these was the Sointula community on Malcolm Island. Over two thousand Finns from all over the world were reported to have been drawn to this community by its charismatic leader, Matti Kurikka. Kurikka had already led a small group to Australia in an unsuccessful attempt at establishing a utopian community there when he was invited to British Columbia to organize a communal society. As a way to recruit members and supporters, he lectured throughout Canada and the United States, including in Astoria, "where it was noted that the number of women in each audience grew as word of the speaker's 'glowing good looks' spread through the community." Kurikka's vision included equal pay and the right to vote for women, which was a major draw for women of the time; "Kurikka's physical appearance may have drawn the women to the meetings, but it was his stirring oratory and innovative ideas that convinced them to go home and pack their families' possessions."[96] It is not known how many women, and men, from Astoria were drawn to Malcolm Island by the promises of Kurikka's utopia, but there were some who followed his enticing message and hopeful ideas. But in a story that is typical of many such endeavors, the charismatic leadership of Kurikka did not make up for his lack of business sense and experience and the colony suffered for it. Significant, and perhaps warranted, accusations of Sointula as a "free love" colony also were detrimental to the community, as was a tragic fire in 1901 that killed eleven. Although the colony under Kurikka's control lasted until 1905, it already was on the decline well before that.[97]

From South Africa to British Columbia, some of the citizens of Astoria were drawn to a utopian dream outside Oregon. Undoubtedly there were other schemes that drew individuals away from the state but the documentation of these is even more difficult to trace than for the communal societies formed in Oregon.

## "This embryo communistic experiment named after the great author, Edward Bellamy"

While some of the Finnish residents of Astoria were seeking a better life outside the state and the country, another group of mostly Norwegian immigrants sought to find their utopia on land on Depot Creek, about four miles north of Toledo in Lincoln County, in late 1897. The colony lasted less than two years but is noteworthy because of the nature of the group that settled there and the name they chose for their community—Bellamy. While the Nehalem Valley Cooperative Colony may have found inspiration in the writings of Edward Bellamy, the small group of individuals, who, as one descendant noted, "found a measure of prosperity and the freedom" denied in their native Norway, named their settlement for the author of the utopian novels, *Looking Backward 2000-1887* and *Equality*, the latter published just months prior to the colony's formation.[98]

The roots of the Bellamy Colony are traced to Minnesota where economic conditions, labor unrest, and a particular sense of homesickness seemed to ignite a spark in a few Norwegians that a better life could be achieved in a cooperative colony in a place other than the American Midwest. One of the instigators for such action was Olaf Anders Tveitmoe, a native of Valdres, Norway, who had migrated to the United States in 1882.[99] In 1891 Tveitmoe first became active in the Farmers' Alliance, a reform movement that grew out of the discontent of farmers throughout the country in the 1870s.[100] The Farmers' Alliance recommended the reading of Bellamy's *Looking Backward*, believing that it presented a possible solution for the ills of society at the time, including those of the farming community. The Nationalist Movement that grew out of interest in Bellamy's work and the ideal society described in the novel was one of interest to Alliance members.[101] Tveitmoe may have been influenced by Bellamy through the Farmers' Alliance or Nationalist Movement or even by reading *Looking Backward* in his native language, as it was translated into Norwegian in the early 1890s.[102] However Tveitmoe came to discover Bellamy, he saw in the notion of an ideal society a potential model for a cooperative venture. He also clearly was influenced by other socialist schemes of the time, including the Ruskin Colony in Tennessee, founded by Julius Wayland.[103]

The earliest evidence of Tveitmoe's evolving plan for a cooperative colony is an article he wrote in the Norwegian-language newspaper, *Rodhuggeren*, published in Fergus Falls, Minnesota. In the June 1897 issue Tveitmoe presented his ideas, based on the principles of Wayland's Ruskin Cooperative Association in Tennessee, suggesting that each prospective member would invest $500 in the venture to go along with a $3000 base fund. His proposal generated some interest among the Norwegian communities in Minnesota and Wisconsin but also some opposition. *The Reform*, a Norwegian newspaper in Eau Claire, Wisconsin, published several exchanges through the summer and fall of 1897 between Tveitmoe and one Waldemar Ager, with the latter accusing Tveitmoe of a checkered past and ill-conceived plans.[104] A third correspondent, Sondre Romtvedt of Westbrook, Minnesota, then entered the exchange and provided additional information on the proposed colony. He argued that the controversy was only preventing improvements in society and that such debates should stop.

He identified himself as president of Tveitmoe's cooperative enterprise and stated that Tveitmoe would be removed as secretary of that organization pending a review of Ager's accusations.[105] It is not clear whether such a review was conducted as Tveitmoe continued to be active in the colony scheme and, despite Romtvedt's title as president, appeared to be the leader and spokesperson.

The next that is known about the colony is when Sondre Romtvedt, his wife Aasne, and four of their nine children arrived by train in Oregon, together with John Allen, who owned the property that was being made available to the Norwegian colonists.[106] Allen is described by Fred Romtvedt, Sondre's son, in his memoirs as "a Swedish bachelor ... who was about 85 years old."[107] The land being leased or sold was "a 160 acre farm on Depot Slough three and one-half miles north of Toledo on the Siletz road."[108] It had been the homestead of one Si Copeland, and was then owned by Al Waugh before being purchased by Allen in late 1896 or early 1897. It is not clear if Allen was directly involved in the colony scheme but later events suggest that he most likely was not.

Olaf Tveitmoe also arrived in Oregon some time in December 1897 along with his pregnant wife and three children; a fourth child was born on December 31.[109] In February 1898 Nils Matre of Moody County, South Dakota and B. Tonder joined the colony.[110] Both were bachelors. Little information is available on Tonder or on Oscar Pederson who also became a member of the colony along with his wife and two sons. Another family that became part of the colony was that of Oliver Johnson, who came with his wife and son. Mrs. Johnson was sickly and died a few months after their arrival and just two months after the birth of their second son, leaving the infant and a four-year-old son.[111] Thus the colony in the first few months of its existence had seen two births and one death among its small group of four families and two bachelors. The time of joy and grief would characterize the short-lived colony's history, in many respects.

The *Lincoln County Leader* is one of the principal sources of information on the activities of the colony. In the spring of 1898 the paper reported that the colonists had built two houses, cleared land, and sowed five acres of wheat.[112] The June 17, 1898 issue reports that a post office had been established at the colony and "is to be known as Bellamy, in honor of the great labor writer of that name."[113] This was just weeks after Edward Bellamy had died in Massachusetts on May 22. Little is reported on the colony in the summer of 1898, except for the death of Mrs. Johnson, and all seemed to be going satisfactorily for the Bellamy colonists. A report later that year reveals that this was not the case and subsequent reports in this paper and elsewhere indicate that all was not well at Bellamy.

Under the headline, "The Bellamy Land Case," the December 23, 1898 issue of the Toledo paper reported on the case of John O. Allen against the Bellamy colony, noting that "The evidence is very voluminous and will cover 200 type written pages" and "More evidence was necessary and court was continued till some future day prior to the time of our circuit court." The case centered on these details: "According to the contract Mr. Allen sold his land to the colony for $2,800, payable $100 per year without interest. Mr. Allen is 78 years of age and claims he never signed the contract, but that it is a case of forgery or fraud. The other parties claim it to be only an open business transaction, without fraud or anything wrong."[114] The newspaper would carry periodic updates on the case over the next several months until a decision was rendered in April 1899.

In the meantime, evidence of other problems for the colony came to light. As occurred with other nineteenth-century utopian societies in Oregon, important information on the Bellamy Colony appeared in the publication of a colony outside Oregon. In this case, a piece by O. A. Tveitmoe was published in the newsletter of the Equality Colony on the Puget Sound in Washington. Equality was named for Edward Bellamy's second novel, centered on an ideal society in the year 2000, which included more details than *Looking Backward* and had been written in part to address concerns about and shortcomings of the earlier novel.[115] It is not surprising then that "Bellamy Beamings," as Tveitmoe's article is titled, appeared in this organ of a brother colony.

Tveitmoe begins his report by providing some geographic information about the colony:

> *Bellamy is not found on the map, but if you at any time happen to be in Toledo, Lincoln Co., Oregon, you will certainly find Bellamy, providing you are looking for it. This embryo communistic experiment named after the great author, Edward Bellamy, is located on the Depai [sic] Creek 4 miles north of the countyseat [sic] of Lincoln Co., Ore.*
>
> *The distance along the county road to Newport, "the city by the sea," is 10 miles; by water it is 20 miles.*[116]

After noting that "Bellamy is but 10 months old and is organized on a similar plan to Ruskin, Tennessee," Tveitmoe offers some sharp attacks on unnamed individuals while highlighting accomplishments of the "embryonic communistic experiment":

> *Owing to the furious and ignoble attacks of the enuemy [sic] and still more so the infernal machinations of cowardly traitors, Bellamy's growth during its short period of existence has been greatly retarded. However, in spite of this sad fact, the association has already*

*demonstrated a marvelous capacity in the way of accumulating property. Taking the invoice of January 2d '99, it shows $1,500 assets over and above all liabilities. This $1,500 is the product of 10 months hard work cheerfully rendered by a few selfsacrificing [sic] men and women. In view of the seemingly unsurmountable [sic] difficulties and disadvantages, which have harrassed [sic] our work, this showing is truly amazing, and one can but vaguely surmise, what could have been accomplished, if the association had been left unmolested to work out its own success. Still another fact of far greater importance, which Bellamy already has demonstrated, is the unyielding power and moral strenght [sic] of an organized brotherhood. And today the members of Bellamy are more determined than ever, and they will succeed, though the arch-traitor Judas Iscariot with all the hounds of hell are trying to hunt them down![117]*

These accusations suggest some internal dissension but his next paragraph, after describing the post office and how provisions, clothing, and dry goods are obtained, points to some issue with external players as well. "And another thing," he states, "we do not know how long the wholesalers will sell us at wholesale rates, as we understand, the retailers have already treatened [sic] to boycott the houses trading with us and some petty peanut dealers even atempt [sic] a more nefarious warfare scandalizing, libeling and throwing slurs on the association with certain houses and jobbers." Despite these difficulties, he uses these examples as a means to highlight the very reasons why the cooperative goals of colonies such as the Bellamy Cooperative Association and the Equality Colony must be achieved:

*These colonies ought in a few years, through practical arrangement and a sensible policy to be one self-sustaining, self-producing communistic brotherhood without having to cater or trade but nominally with the outside world. In order to derive all the benefit of and facilitate such an inter-colonial-trade or exchange of products the brotherhood must own and operate its own means of transportation, and fortunately enough in this respect—nearly all these colonies have been wisely located, having an outlet and access to the God-given highway not yet monopolized by human greed—the mighty Pacific Ocean!*
*The Brotherhood must have its own line of steamers![118]*

Tveitmoe goes on to offer advice, including some seemingly based on his experience at the Bellamy Colony. He advises cooperation rather than competition between colonies, adding:

81

*The first years of a colony's life is the trying time. Disappointments
will come. Malcontents and crackers are omnipresent and "driftwood"
is found in the finest stream. There is a class of people who never can
feel at home in heaven, and they always prefer hell; and even if they
perchance have drifted into the wrong quarter, they will in time find
their right place.*[119]

He then presents some practical reflections on the notion of utopia and the
inherent conflict with practical goals:

*We are trying to reform the world; but let us not forget the fact that we
are yet a part of it and that the reformation must begin at home! Away
with all vague notions and chimerical dreams! Mushroom utopias are
well enough for the romancers, but they will never do for living men
and women of the nineteenth or twentieth century. Nothing but hard
rational practical work with brain and muscles will ever solved this
question!*[120]

In his concluding remarks, he stands high on his socialistic soapbox:

*The age of talking belongs to the past—ours is the age of action.
Practice the golden rule—tolerate and forbear—"do as you would
be done by." Let every socialist wherever he is and whatever he may
be who believes in the justice for our cause, let him fight with every
legitimate weapon like the Spartans of Old, and if we fall let us fall like
the heroes at Thermopylae—but we shall not fall, and we will not fall,
until the last son of toil is emancipated from the shackles of capitalistic
slavery.*[121]

Tveitmoe clearly was targeting his audience at Equality Colony but it is
unclear how much of his message reflected the views of others at Bellamy.

It also is not evident when Tveitmoe wrote this text but, by the time it
appeared, other significant developments had taken place at the Bellamy
Colony. The January 13, 1899 issue of the *Lincoln County Leader* carried
this item in its "Of Interest to Everybody" column: "Ye editor visited
Bellamy colony Monday. He found a beautiful tract of land there and a
coterie of men who are good farmers, energetic workers and will succeed.
Everything is cared for about the place. Two new houses have been erected
and time only is needed to make this place a beautiful home."[122] But by the
following week the newspaper ran the first of a series of reports that suggest
that all was not quite so "beautiful" at the colony: the announcement of
a stockholders' meeting "to be held on Monday, January 30, 1899 10
o'clock a.m. at Bellamy, Lincoln County, Oregon." This notice would not
be too significant it if it were not presented by "O. A. Tveitmoe, Secretary"

82

*Sondre Romtvedt family prior to moving to Bellamy Colony
(Carol Romtvedt Ginter)*

and "Nils J. Matre, Acting President." With Matre as acting president, a position previously held by Sondre Romtvedt, clearly something was amiss in Bellamy.[123] This was confirmed in the following week's edition of the paper when a second notice of the forthcoming meeting appeared under a brief notice that read: "Notice is hereby given that the undersigned no longer has any connection with the Bellamy Co-Operative Association and will be responsible for none of its obligations. S. Romtvedt. Dated Toledo, Or., Jan 27, 1899."[124] Romtvedt was leaving the colony, but why?

Although there is no evidence to support a claim that Sondre Romtvedt was the target of Tveitmoe's barbs against "arch-traitor, Judas Iscariot," nor is there any evidence that Romtvedt would warrant such accusations, the fact that Romtvedt severed his ties with the colony at this time might be viewed as linked to Tvietmoe's discontent with someone within the colony. Perhaps the reason for Romtvedt's departure included some lingering feelings, and possible feud, from the positions of Tveitmoe and Romtvedt in Minnesota, and Romtvedt's assertion that Tveitmoe would be removed as secretary of the colony. Perhaps it was a power struggle between the two men that led to Tveitmoe's remarks and Romtvedt's departure. The one colony descendant who has left any personal record of his reflections of the colony, Fred Romtvedt, noted in an interview in 1966 that Tveitmoe "was very authoritative" and "was partly responsible for the break-up of

83

the colony."[125] It is also possible that Sondre Romtvedt saw in the court case against the colony some similarities to Tveitmoe's problems back in Minnesota.

Whatever the nature of Romtvedt's discontent with the Bellamy Cooperative Association, he moved his family from the colony in early 1899. The *Lincoln County Leader*'s report on the stockholders' meeting stated that "Two new members were admitted, and the resignation of one member accepted." Although no names are provided for either the new members or the member that resigned, the latter had to be Romtvedt. The paper also notes, "Financially the Association has made a very creditable showing the last year, and it starts out on its second year with renewed determination to succeed—and it will succeed."[126] However, by the middle of April the colony had folded and the colonists scattered to various locations.

The cause of this rapid collapse was the suit against the colony by John Allen, very likely one of the targets of Tveitmoe's criticism. The *Lincoln County Leader* reports on the decision in this case in the April 14, 1899 edition: "Our readers will regret to hear that by the result of the suit decided against the Bellamy Colony, that association has divided its property and gone out of business." Some the members would leave, while others would stay nearby." A separate item in the same edition of the paper notes, "O. A. Tveitmoe and Nils Matre will leave on the next steamer for San Francisco," also adding, "We regret their departure as this county has none too many industrious settlers."[127] Fred Romtvedt recalls that the Pedersons moved to Coos Bay and the Johnsons to Chitwood.[128] With the departure of postmaster Tveitmoe and with most of the colonists leaving the area, the Bellamy post office officially closed on June 15, 1899, thus ending this brief, but revealing, history of the Bellamy Colony.

There are some interesting postscripts to this story, however. One is that Sondre Romtvedt moved back to the land occupied by the colony in 1900 and bought it from John Allen. The Romtvedts lived on the property through the 1930s. After Sondre Romtvedt passed away in 1912, his son Fred bought out the other heirs. He and his wife, Mary Whitney, raised six daughters on the former colony land, including Carol Romtvedt Ginter, who along with Rosa Claridge, was instrumental in gathering information on the Bellamy Colony and keeping the history alive.[129]

The story of Olaf Tveitmoe after his departure from the Bellamy Colony is a remarkable and infamous one. He became a labor leader in San Francisco and assisted in establishing the Building Trades Council in 1901, editing its newspaper, *Organized Labor*. He also was president of the Asiatic Exclusion League and unsuccessfully ran for mayor of San Francisco on a labor platform. After moving to Los Angeles he was implicated in the October 1910 bombing of the *Los Angeles Times* building in which twenty-one lives were lost and, although two unionists confessed to the crime, he along with many others was convicted in 1912. In 1914 the U. S. Court of Appeals reversed the decision against Tveitmoe and, as no evidence was brought forward for a new trial against him, charges were dropped. He subsequently was involved with the Industrial Workers of the World (IWW) and the Socialist Party of California, but he suffered a stroke in 1917 from which he never fully recovered. Olaf Tveitmoe died on March 29, 1923.[130]

The Bellamy Colony is little more than a footnote in the life of Olaf Tveitmoe and was largely a lost piece of Oregon history until Claridge's study in the 1960s. But the short-lived colony is another important part of the utopian landscape of Oregon because of the socialistic nature of the community, the Norwegian settlers that were at the core of the colony, and even the involvement of Olaf Tveitmoe in this "embryo communistic experiment named after the great author, Edward Bellamy."

◙ ◙ ◙

Edward Bellamy is also believed to be one of the inspirations for another settlement in Oregon in the late 1890s that may or may not have adopted communal practices. Socialist Valley was in Polk County and the principal source of information on this community is in McArthur's *Oregon Geographic Names*, which states:

> *It appears in the late 1890s a small communal or socialist hamlet was started in the valley by a group who operated their own sawmill in Falls City. Like the residents of Bellamy nearby in Lincoln County, they were inspired by Edward Bellamy's utopian book,* Looking Backward. *Unlike some similar groups, they had no formal organization and were able to maintain an amicable community until the early 1920s. In 1917, the valley, in a time of anti-Communist feeling, was renamed Reynolds Dell after a local resident. The community vanished, but in the 1960s the name was restored to the original Socialist Valley Road.*[131]

Another community that has left a puzzling history not only to its communal elements but also its name is New Era. Again, the name implies some utopian ideals but documentation is lacking to substantiate this aspect of a settlement along the Willamette River between Oregon City and Canby. As early as 1926 Lewis McArthur suggested two explanations for the name of New Era, one centered on the fact that railroad construction had reached the mouth of Parrott Creek in Clackamas County, thus signaling a "new era" in transportation, and the second based on the fact "that a local family were spiritualists and devoted to a publication called the *New Era* and named the place for that account."[132] McArthur also notes that the post office of New Era operated from 1876 to 1940. While McArthur claims that the first reason "has the earmarks of truth," and some indeed may have deemed this a "new era of transportation," the second reason is closer to the mark in terms of the naming of the settlement. The workers of the Writers' Program of the Work Projects Administration also picked up on this second reason; the entry for New Era states it "is the scene of the annual summer camp-meetings of the Spiritualist Society of the Pacific Northwest. ...The community was founded by Joseph Parrot, who named it for a visionary publication of the day."[133]

There were, in fact, two New Eras. One was the settlement that had the post office but not far away, up Parrott Creek, was a camp founded by the New Era Spiritualist Society. The camp assumed the name New Era Spiritual Camp after it was established in 1873, three years before the post office opened at the nearby settlement. As the WPA compilation suggests, the "local family" mentioned by McArthur likely was that of Joseph Parrott, for whom the creek is named, as he is believed to been a follower of spiritualism. The camp drew visitors from many areas to its activities and a hotel was built in 1887 to accommodate these visitors. As David Johnson notes in an article that places New Era within "Oregon's utopian tradition," "Spiritualists held regular séances, lectures, and discussions in huge tents, and visitors were charged a dollar a day at the New Era Hotel or fifty cents to a dollar for a week's use of a private tent."[134] In 1967, the camp was still going strong, and Roy and Lillian Parmenter of Canby reflected on their life-long membership in the camp noting, "At one time the New Era Spiritualists were the largest denomination in the Oregon City area. More people went to the church than any other."[135]

The nature of the camp, however, was itinerant and the camp season was about a month, usually beginning in early July. Although some individuals or families may have lived year-round on the grounds, there is no evidence that there were communal practices common to other utopian endeavors in Oregon and elsewhere. And the nearby settlement close to the Willamette seems to have drawn its name from the spiritualist camp and was likely not a communal settlement either.

The incomplete information on Socialist Valley and New Era makes it unclear if, or how, they fit into Oregon's utopian heritage. Undoubtedly there were more attempts to find some type of ideal communal life in Oregon in the late nineteenth century, but documentation on these has yet to be discovered. There was, on the other hand, another movement that took place in the late nineteenth century for which there is considerable documentation but how this movement fits into the boundaries of utopia is questionable. It does reflect the concept of Oregon as Eden, however, even if just in the promotional literature used to entice groups of settlers to move to the state.

From the mid-1870s through the next several decades, the Oregon Immigration Board and later the Pacific Northwest Immigration Board published numerous documents extolling the virtues of Oregon in language filled with superlatives and promises. The earliest publications provided facts on climate, agricultural data, commerce, and industry, but by the late 1880s the tone of the publications shifted to one with more boosterism.[136] H. N. Maguire, in a letter published in *The Universal Republic* on the "Colony Matters—the Place for Homes," states, "If there is anywhere between Alaska and the equator a more favorable section for colonization enterprise or the investment of capital I know not where it is."[137] Many publications carried ads for the Oregon Immigration Board as well as for other companies, such as H. N. Maguire's in Portland, that sought individuals for colonization efforts.

The result of these efforts was a broad range of "colonists" making their way to Oregon. The newspapers from the early 1890s through the first decade of the twentieth century are filled with reports of colonies being formed or planned all over the state. Some of these, such as the Bellamy Colony of mostly Norwegian immigrants, can be considered utopian communities, but most are of a broader nature of colonization. Yet their intent to come to Oregon often was based on the promise of Edenic proportion that was offered here, whether real or imagined.

# No Place

In addition to many attempts to establish utopian settlements in Oregon in the late nineteenth century that met with varying degrees of success, there were some that got little further than the planning stages. Many of these unrealized efforts have little, if any, record of their ideas and plans; they may have been nothing more than a scheme discussed around a dinner table, in a public forum that was unrecorded or lost, or even in the personal musings of an individual who saw their ideal world as a potential model for society. These plans are mostly lost, or deeply embedded in personal diaries or journals, yet to be harvested as part of the utopian heritage story of Oregon.[1] There are, however, a few notable recorded attempts at creating a good place that ended up being, in one of Thomas More's senses of the meaning of utopia, a no place. This chapter explores two very different attempts to create an ideal place within Oregon that left us only dreams.

## A Christian Utopia

The influx of settlers to the Oregon Territory in the late 1840s and 1850s created many opportunities but also some significant challenges. One such challenge was how to minister to the growing congregation of souls that were making their way by land and by sea to the Oregon country, particularly along the Willamette River. The number of ministers necessary to meet the demands of the faithful and the sinners was not keeping abreast of these souls. In response to this critical need, Bishop Thomas F. Scott of the Episcopal Diocese of the Oregon Territory made an urgent plea to clergymen in the East who could move west and meet these demands. The call reached Grahamsville, South Carolina, where it was heard by two brothers, James R. W. Sellwood and the Rev. John Sellwood. James was a father of two and a lay brother in the parish of St. Luke's in Grahamsville, where John was the pastor. On March 31, 1856, the two Sellwood brothers along with James' wife and sons boarded a steamer for Charleston, where James was ordained. Then the party took another steamer to New York, where they in turn took passage on the *Illinois* to the Panama isthmus via Havana and Aspinwall (Colón), a Caribbean seaport. While they were awaiting a train to carry them across the isthmus, a riot occurred that separated John Sellwood from the rest of his family in the melee. He was beaten and shot and the mob trashed the belongings of the travelers. James finally located his brother and the family sought assistance from the American Consul and were put up in a hotel for two weeks while John convalesced. They then set sail for San Francisco and eventually reached Oregon.[2]

Upon their arrival in the Oregon Territory, James was given charge of St. Paul's parish in Salem, where he remained for nine years, followed by two years at St. John's parish in Milwaukie, and then East Portland. His son, who was also named John, was ordained and served as pastor in churches in Oregon City and Butteville. The elder John Sellwood first was assigned by Bishop Scott to the Trinity parish in Portland where he served three years, then moved to St. Stephen Chapel, assisting Bishop Scott, for ten years while also preaching in the State Penitentiary in Portland. In 1870 he was appointed rector at St. John's Episcopal Church in Milwaukie, a position he held until his death in August 1892.[3]

The dramatic adventure of the Rev. John Sellwood perhaps influenced his thoughts on the ultimate mission he was to undertake in Oregon. It certainly left permanent scars on his forehead and on both hands. Another impact of the Panama incident was that he received a land grant of 320 acres as compensation for his injuries and personal losses. He saw this as an opportunity to make a lasting contribution to society and a reflection of his Christian ideals. These ideals centered very much on his own lifestyle, which has been described as "almost monastic" and as an "evangelistic ascetic."[4] The Rev. William H. Stoy in eulogizing John Sellwood offers a more extensive description: "To people in general, who knew nothing of his inner thoughts, habits, and motives, he was always an enigma; he was so different from other men, even from those of his own sacred profession, that he seemed strange and eccentric, although all paid him deference and respect."[5] From this monastic, if not strange and eccentric, individual came a plan for a Christian utopia on the banks of the Willamette River. In the late 1870s, John Sellwood developed criteria for this endeavor that he called Hopeland.

"Rules to be Observed by All the Residents of Hopeland, Oregon" is a 351-word document that lays out in some detail the expectations of prospective residents of this Christian utopia.[6] Most of the rules begin with "No" and reflect Sellwood's strict adherence to his personal Christian ideals of self-restraint and abstinence. Even before providing a brief description of what the community was to be he presents one of the apparently strongest criteria in a line separate from the body of the text: "No divorced persons nor married persons who cannot agree to live together as husband and wife are wanted at Hopeland." He then offers the closest thing to a statement of the nature of his proposed community: "It is to be distinctly understood that Hopeland is intended to be a Christian Settlement. It is expected therefore that all the Residents be persons of good moral character and conduct themselves in every respect as Christians ought to behave." The next several lines of the document lay out some specifics on how good Christians ought to conduct themselves, several of which echo some of the Ten Commandments: "No quarrelling.—No improper language.—No taking the name of God in vain.—No swearing.—No evil speaking, lying or slandering.—That they regularly attend Divine Worship in Hope Church—and keep holy the whole of the Lord's Day." The list continues with increased reflections on personal and societal concerns of the time: "That they abstain from the use of opium in every shape and form.—No gambling.—No lascivious conduct.—Nothing tending to drunkenness.—No theft of any kind.—No trespassing on the property of others." And then the Rev. Sellwood lays out additional specific limitations on the citizens of the proposed Christian utopia:

*No dancing parties.—No theatrical representations.—No serenading of newly married persons.—No bathing in the river on Sunday nor at any time without having first put on in private a decent bathing suit.—No opium, intoxicating drinks or tobacco to be sold or bartered or kept or exposed for sale.—No horses, cattle, swine, goats or poultry of any kind to run at large. Pigeons to be confined within wire netting.*

Following these restrictions, Sellwood provides the overarching guiding principles of Hopeland:

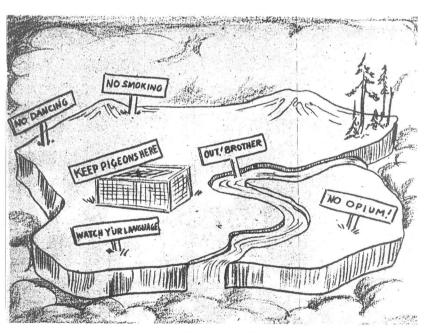

90

*Artist's conception of Hopeland from 1953 article in*
Enterprise-Courier *magazine*

*It is the earnest wish of the founder of this settlement, that all of its inhabitants would keep in remembrance and practice the words of our Blessed Saviour: "Whatsoever ye would that men should do to you do ye even so to them," and also the words of the Apostle Paul: "Whether ye eat or drink or whatsoever ye do, do all to the glory of God."*

The result of all this is posited in the next portion of the document: "In such case, peace and harmony and love would reign among them, and they could confidently expect to enjoy the favor, the protection, and the blessing of Almighty God." The document concludes with a pledge to be signed by prospective residents of Hopeland.

Although there were undoubtedly some individuals attracted to the ideas and ideals in Sellwood's plan, there is no evidence that any signed on for this Christian utopia. Perhaps even in a time of calls for temperance and other reforms, the rules of Hopeland were too much for Oregonians of the era. A cartoon drawn in 1953 to accompany an article on Hopeland captures the spirit from some seventy-five years earlier.[7] Or one can turn to the eulogy of Sellwood offered by the Rev. William H. Stoy in 1892 to sum up the efforts and impact of this dream of John Sellwood.

*[H]e deeply and seriously entertained and tried hard to perfect a far more extensive and permanent design of aiding and benefiting men temporally, who were willing to accept a rule and live religiously in the conception of what he was pleased to call his "Hopeland"! The design was without a doubt eutopian, and—in this hurrying, selfish, and irreligious age—impracticable; but it is none the less creditable to his Christian faith and to his pious desire to benefit his fellow-men in a heavenward and holy way. His design did not take form nor assume being, because men could not be found to accept it. It is accepted of God all the same, and will be part of his crown of rejoicing in the eternal world.*[8]

Although the plans for Hopeland had dissolved long before John Sellwood's death on August 27, 1892, with his passing that mortal dream also was gone. Hopeland was no place although one man's vivid good place.

## *"The convent in the woods"*

The idealism that serves as the impetus for thoughts and plans for utopian endeavors often leads to a reality of aborted dreams and "almosts." One particular colony planned in Oregon presented an opportunity for the mid-Willamette Valley to be a gathering place and showcase for America's developing Arts and Crafts Movement in the first decade of the twentieth

91

century. Unfortunately, as so often happens in utopian experiments, human nature intervened and what might have been a thriving artist colony near Alsea was dissolved before it took shape.

Ralph Radcliffe Whitehead was born in 1854 in Yorkshire, England, the only son and sole surviving child of Francis Frederick Whitehead and Isabella (Dalglish) Whitehead. His father, along with three uncles, owned and operated the Royal George Mills, manufacturer of piano felts. The Whiteheads were part of the booming textile-manufacturing segment of the mid-nineteenth century and Ralph would inherit a wealth that would permit him not to work a day in his life. As one of his long-time acquaintances and collaborators, Bolton Brown, noted years later, "He inherited a water faucet that flowed money whenever he turned it on."[9] Ralph's interests, and destiny, however, were beyond the manufacturing heritage of his family and work would become a key interest of his.

When Whitehead entered Balliol College at Oxford in 1873 he perhaps had already been influenced by the works of John Ruskin and his disciple, William Morris. At Oxford he would become the student of Ruskin, who was the Slade Professor of Fine Art and who already had established his vision "for a company of men and women dedicated to oppose modernism by their refined beauty of manner and thought, their order and precision."[10] This vision, as Ruskin's biographer notes, was based on the thought that "If men would, each in his place, carry out the rudiments of justice and social morality—doing good work well, helping others, harming none, and showing themselves law-worthy—if such-minded men and women would withdraw from the struggle for success in the world and set the example of better things in a wholesome country life; that, he felt would really effect a change."[11] This concept, combined with Ruskin's Socialist views, made a significant impression on Whitehead, so much so that he returned home during his second year at Oxford and proposed that the family mill be turned into a cooperative enterprise based on Ruskin's model. This, of course, did not sit well with his father and uncles and the young Whitehead was sent to Paris to be removed from Ruskin's influence. While in Paris he apprenticed with a carpenter and gained experience working with his hands, a time he would recall as being some of the best of his life.[12] The quarrel with his family eventually abated and he returned to Oxford, but his admiration for Ruskin was as strong as ever. In 1876 Whitehead traveled to Italy with Ruskin where his own views on beauty, life, and society were further developed. He returned to Oxford and completed his master's degree in 1880.

Details of the following decade in Whitehead's life are largely unknown and, at times, speculative, perhaps even fabricated. He may have tried to start one or two communes in Europe.[13] Alf Evers notes:

*His life there [in Europe] gave rise to a mingling of fact, fancy, and ill-founded assumption. He bought and restored a castle at Syria, where he shut himself up with a learned German professor who guided the excursion of his wide-ranging mind. He lived a fashionable and gay life in an Italian palazzo, designed an extraordinary garden in Avignon, married a princess, a duchess, an American, a barmaid, a ballet dancer.*[14]

What is known is that Whitehead did marry an Austrian woman, Marie, about whom little is known, and they may indeed have attempted a colony of some sort in Austria at Styria.[15] It is clear that his wealth was allowing Whitehead to live a substantial existence but it became increasingly apparent that his life was less fulfilling than he would have liked. He subsequently would call the 1880s "ten years of wasted life," and lament that "I was dead to all that had moved me before."[16] In the early 1890s Whitehead's life would change in many respects and his drive to better society took the fore. The Ralph Whitehead that reemerged at this time was later described as "a Socialist, a radical, an idealist, and he remained so to the day of his death."[17]

While in Florence in April 1891 Whitehead penned an essay titled "Work" that laid out many of his ideas about the establishment of a colony, or a "convent" as he terms it. "Work" reflected the impacts of Ruskin and Morris on his thought as well as a new influence, that of the American poet Walt Whitman, who Whitehead quotes extensively in another essay, "Art and Life."[18] In the opening lines of "Work" Whitehead writes:

*You may smile, but our "convent" shall not be a mere Château d'Espagne. I know not whether Fortune will allow that these four who talked on the hill shall ever join its foundation; perhaps even this may be possible, the future is in the hands of God; but one thing I know, that you and I, before many years are past, shall start some rational life of our own, and through that life we shall form around us a community, it may be only of two or three, and those not under the same roof, whose lives shall be happy and reasonable because of the reason and happiness of our own.*[19]

Whitehead sees the following as the driving elements in forming such a "convent":

*Two things are obvious: first, that man cannot live alone, that there is strength in unity and that in place of the form of so-called "society," which we despise, we shall require some human intercourse; the second is that man cannot run fast enough to catch happiness by pursuing*

93

*it, happiness must come as the bloom comes on a peach; he must,
therefore, have an occupation for his time, and in the satisfaction of
doing his work well earn a good digestion and a smiling countenance.*[20]

The work he describes centers on arts and crafts, including painting,
sculpture, music, literature, carpentry and cabinet-making, wood-carving,
leather-work and book-binding, hand-work in brass and iron, pottery,
spinning and weaving, as well as farming, gardening, and forestry.[21]
Whitehead suggests that the New World might well be the best place for
such a community while also acknowledging that "Our aim must not be, at
the first, to found an ideal republic."[22]

The essay goes on to provide several specifics about the proposed
community, including the existence of a common house, "to form a
nucleus," that would include sleeping rooms, "a refectory, a meeting-room
for quiet with books, and one for amusement with a piano and an organ."
He provides two restrictions related to marriage among the members of the
community: "they must be able to support children before producing them,
and they must not marry if afflicted by serious hereditary disease."[23] Other
specifics include "simple and expansive" rules and condition of membership,
cost of living ("£85 a year"), expulsion of members, religion, and education.
The end result of this enterprise he sums up in this manner:

> *Consider, too, how the health of the race might improve when men
> and women, who are now run to seed from a too nervous life, and
> the pursuit of a low form of intellectual cleverness, at the cost of all
> vigour and freshness, should regain their balance, and a healthy body
> should once more be the house for a reasonable soul. We shall thus be
> healthier, and, as a whole, richer, and with the increase of health and
> reason we may trust to the maintenance of a better balance then is now
> possible between the number of the population and the country which
> has to support it.*[24]

For a variety of reasons, the writing of this essay marked a new direction in
Whitehead's life. It demonstrated the influences of Ruskin and Morris while
also illustrating the development of Whitehead's own ideals. His suggestion
that this endeavor might be undertaken in the New World is prophetic in
its eventual realization. Perhaps most significant, in many respects, is the
immediate audience referred to in the initial lines of the essay, which are
directed to Jane Byrd McCall, an American artist who had been studying in
Italy and who was spending an increasing amount of time with Whitehead.
She would become his second wife and his collaborator for most of the next
four decades.

94

Jane Byrd McCall (1871-1955) came from an affluent and influential Philadelphia family. Little is known of her early life but she was drawn to the arts and in her twenties was traveling through Europe making the acquaintance of many prominent artists, and studying with several, including Ruskin. It was during one of these excursions that she likely met Whitehead, as early as 1885.[25] As Whitehead was married, the relationship between him and McCall developed slowly, but by 1890 they were communicating with each other through letters and meeting at various locations. With her interests in art and sharing some of the same influences, such as Ruskin, the two grew increasingly close in spirit and ideals. As Nancy E. Green notes, McCall began "to 'Dream of Somewhere',", perhaps a planned community.[26] Their increasing closeness is also evident in her correspondence with Whitehead, such as her April 1891 letter to him where she comments, "All one wants to be armed with is a little love, a little health, a little philosophy, and a good deal of nature out of doors."[27]

There was, of course, the matter of Whitehead's marriage to Marie, but by the time "Works" was being written he was already planning to address this. With an English divorce difficult to obtain, Whitehead moved to Germany to obtain German citizenship in February 1892 and in March he was granted a divorce from Marie. The following month he traveled to New York and in August he and Jane were married in Portsmouth, New Hampshire. The two then spent a year in Europe. Upon their return to the United States, they purchased land outside Santa Barbara, California, and built a villa they named Arcady, reflecting their interests and experience in Italy. As a colleague later noted:

> *Italy had been his mistress since his youth, and this landscape offered a medium for all that he had gathered. An Italian villa, an Italian terraced garden, with olive trees and Florentine roses against the sea. Even the live oaks that dotted the meadow slopes seemed Italian, and the blue beyond the barley fields might be Mediterranean or Adriatic.*[28]

The villa became a hub for musicians, artists, and others with similar interests as the Whiteheads, but, as Green notes, "both of the Whiteheads became restless with its aimlessness."[29]

Ralph Whitehead addressed this restlessness by taking up his pen to produce some essays that appeared as an infrequent series titled *Arrows of the Dawn*.[30] He also spent much time away from home with a group of artists and, more significantly at least in terms of his relationship with Jane, in a brief affair with a Louise Hart. The couple overcame this problem and in May 1896 they had their first child, a son, who lived just one day.[31] Later that year the two set out to travel to heal their sorrow, to renew their trust in each other, and to rekindle their interest in art and social reform.

95

This trip, and subsequent trips he took without Jane in 1897, proved to be critical in the further development of the ideas Whitehead had put forth in his "Work" essay five years earlier. He visited a number of communal groups, including Ruskin Colony in Tennessee and Summerbrook, a Fabian experiment in the Adirondacks in New York, where he met Charlotte Perkins Stetson.[32] Later that year, en route back to California, Whitehead stopped in Chicago where he had been advised by Stetson to meet with Hervey White, a bohemian writer and friend of Stetson.[33] A colleague would later describe White as "very much the poet—long hair, whiskers, no hat, red necktie, and strong for radicalism in every form."[34] White writes of this encounter with Whitehead: "A friend had written me from a Socialist colony in the Adirondacks. (I was then a librarian with a salary.) 'I am sending you a Yankeeized Englishman who is to spend a few days in Chicago. His name is Whitehead. Be nice to him, you may find him interesting'." White goes on to provide further details of this first encounter: "Mr. Whitehead explained that he was in Chicago to investigate certain Spiritualist mediums for the Society of Psychical Research, and asked me to accompany him when convenient. In this way we came somewhat acquainted." White did indeed find Whitehead interesting and, as he notes, "In the three years that followed, he stopped to see me as he passed through Chicago."[35] White ended up visiting the Whiteheads at Arcady and during these visits the concept of the "convent" again began to unfold, in this case with a more serious intent on Whitehead's part.

At one of these visit in early 1900 White recalls,

*Mr. Whitehead was now tired of his California ambitions, he could see no results that would influence the future, and he longed for a larger venture in a new country that he would own, which would be entirely in his control, a place where his children could grow up among people who earned their living by the making of beautiful things, far away from all superintendents and boards of directors.*[36]

This concept was Whitehead's utopian dream and, as White recorded in his unpublished autobiography, "Mr. Whitehead has been urging me to go in with him to buy some land and start an Art and Craft Colony. He especially wanted to make furniture, and I had agreed to go with him to Oregon where he knew of a situation he thought favorable."[37] When White asked Whitehead why the situation in Oregon might be favorable, the response was "Oregon had beautiful trees."[38]

There is no evidence to suggest that Ralph Whitehead had visited Oregon previously. His knowledge of and interest in Oregon stems from information he obtained from a violinist, June Reed, in his small chamber ensemble that he brought to his estate in Arcady from Los Angeles.[39] In 1899 Reed had informed Whitehead that her brother, Ole Reed, owned a small clearing near Alsea in the Oregon Coast Range that he had obtained from the Oregon & California Railroad. Whitehead was intrigued by this possibility and he began to make arrangements to visit the land and to procure it for his proposed colony. He also made arrangements with the musician's brother who was living on the land with his mother and available to offer assistance to Whitehead. According to White, "Mr. Whitehead sent money to build a dining room and log cabin studio, with five frame shacks for bedrooms for musicians."[40] The plan was to have Ole Reed build the original structures and for three musicians to move to Oregon several weeks before he and White would come to see the land and its development.

The musicians were sent ahead so the two men could "have some Beethoven trios to accompany them" and, as White notes, "trees are not enough for our enjoyment." In addition to June Reed, whom White describes as "a lady of brilliant talent," there was Louise Tolles, the pianist, "also a lady of genius and charm," and Mr. Opid, the cellist, "who was really a great musician, a nephew of Madame Modjeska."[41] Opid was married and had small children. Louise Tolles apparently also was married at the time the group left for Oregon while June Reed was single. This ensemble set out for Oregon in early June 1900 and arrangements were made for a grand piano to be rented in Portland and shipped to Alsea.

The trip by Whitehead and White is chronicled in several letters Whitehead wrote to his wife while in Oregon and in the reminiscences of White.[42] Whitehead's initial impression of Oregon are favorable, particularly the people and the Douglas firs, which were one of the principal reasons for his interest in Oregon. In his first letter, dated July 1, 1900, and written at McKenzie Bridge, he tells Jane "of beautiful mountain country, with Douglas firs covering the slopes, and greenery enough with them to satisfy anyone coming from a parched country."[43] Two days later later he observes, "The change of air is certainly very delightful & the healthier more active less worry & worn out people make a pleasanter human environment than we have."[44]

On July 4, 1900, Whitehead and White are in Portland and Whitehead takes times to write an eight-page letter to Jane with many observations about the city and the people, noting: "You would not like Portland, it is very western, altho' different to California. The people are healthier up here and not so blatantly impertinent as in California, even the storekeepers are pleasant!"[45] He also checks to make sure Jane has sent a violin to Alsea and notes they will be heading up the Columbia and then up to a hotel high on the side of Mt. Hood. Later Whitehead would pen two long letters to Jane from the Cloud Cap Inn. In his reminiscences of Whitehead, White recalls "excursions to forests and mountains, including a week of Alpine climbing at

Mt. Hood, and a Fourth of July celebration in showery Portland." Thus the two men took their time getting to the site of the colony, supposedly under construction and awaiting their arrival. As White recalls, "the wheels had already been set in motion, and all we had to do was to bide our time."[46]

The two men finally arrived at Alsea on July 15, as Whitehead reported to his wife in a letter that day: "We have got to Alsea. It is a long, rough but very beautiful drive from Corvallis, 25 miles, 7 of which are a bad mountain road with chuckholes deeper than the axles."[47] Upon reaching the land, this is what the two men found, according to White's recollection:

> *The clearing contained not more than three acres; a rivulet trilled along through its meadow. On each side red hills standing thick with high hardwood, and rising out of these, an occasional Douglas fir towering above the hardwoods like palm trees ... four hundred feet high they were, and then you approached one, you saw nothing of its foliage or branches, a huge trunk simply big as a house rising, disappearing in the foliage of the hardwoods; no hint of light or sky—a deep submarine dimness all around. You could picture tropic fish swimming past it.*[48]

Whitehead offered his own brief assessment of the place in his letter to Jane: "The air is very delightful, & I am in hopes that it will be summer while I stay here." But the following day Whitehead offered a somewhat tempered assessment when he wrote to Jane: "One cannot have the scenery of this forest country & the luxury of Italian nights. ... The forest country is magnificent and the days are beautiful, like June days in New England, but there are no Italian nights. The nights are damp."[49] After one damp night in the woods Whitehead already seemed to sense that this utopia was not to be realized. However, he was not revealing to Jane that it was not just because there were no Italian nights at Alsea, for there was other trouble in the attempt at paradise.

Whitehead and White arrived at Alsea intending to listen to Beethoven trios, but there was no music to be heard. White offers this assessment of the situation upon arrival at Alsea: "The musicians had quarreled from the beginning, and not a single trio had been rehearsed. We found the studio, the grand piano on the platform, unopened, untouched."[50] Elsewhere White provides an expanded version of these troubles in paradise:

98

> *In the first place, the pianist lady was divorced. And the cellist could not introduce her to his wife or allow her to sully the innocence of his children. Result, the pianist could not speak to the cellist. In the second place, the pianist had started a little love affair with the violinist's attractive brother, and the pleasant riding parties of three had been broken up, and the violinist was not speaking with the pianist.*

*In the third place, the violinist had an argument about democracy in America with the Polish cellist and had called him a pig-headed foreigner, so the cellist was not speaking to the violinist.*

There was no music to be played and Whitehead realized that this was not to be the place for his "convent." But, as White notes, "Mr. Whitehead saw the humor of the situation." He goes on to explain, "He was so interested in letting the lady pianist know that he didn't know of her liaison with the young brother that he played the comedy for a fortnight without music, and we all had a charming picnic in the woods and mountains, visiting the members separately, of course."[51]

Whitehead refrained from sharing the details of the situation with his wife, but his disappointment can be noticed in some of the correspondence with Jane. On July 21 he wrote to her: "I wish you were here to see the magnificence of this forest country. You would love these woods, & the greenery of them. But the life is pretty rough, about what we had in that hut at Glenmore. It is certainly the best place we have found on our trip."[52] But the best place was not going to work and after they "played about, riding horses," the two men left Alsea to return to California. Before he departed, however, White recalls that Whitehead "bought a few hundred acres of land, which probably went finally to the young brother."[53] The land, in fact, remained in Whitehead's name until his death in 1929.

The quest to find the best spot did not end at Alsea as White, the Whiteheads, and a new player, Bolton Brown, continued to seek for an appropriate location for their Arts and Crafts "convent." They found it in the hills outside Woodstock, New York, where the Byrdcliffe Colony was established in 1903, becoming a hub of the American Arts and Crafts Movement in the early twentieth century.[54]

Ralph Radcliffe Whitehead passed away on February 23, 1929, officially from pneumonia, although his health had been declining since the loss of his son, Ralph, Jr., several months earlier. The younger Ralph was aboard the *S. S. Vestris* when it sank during a heavy storm on November 12, 1928, sailing from New York to South America.[55]

Because of the success of Byrdcliffe, the history of the Alsea experience is usually delegated to little more than footnote status. But in the exploration of Oregon's utopian heritage, it is a significant example of what might have been, but ended up being a no place.

## CHAPTER SIX

# Cooperation in Oregon in the Early Twentieth Century

◈ ◈ ◈

The ideal "convent" of Ralph Radcliffe Whitehead, discussed in the previous chapter, was one man's concept of what might be developed on some land in the Oregon Coast Range, and aspects of his plan for an Arts and Crafts colony were very detailed. But they pale in comparison to the plans for what was perhaps Oregon's most significant attempt at a utopian settlement and much more, but which also ended up as a no place. This scheme was centered on the increased emphasis on cooperative endeavors that became more popular at the end of the nineteenth century and the beginning of the twentieth.

## History of Cooperatives

In principle, cooperation is a mainstay of communal activity and has a lengthy history. John Curl states, "The first Americans to practice collectivity, cooperation, and communalism were of course Indians." As he suggests, "In the same household, sharing a common store of provisions and tools; groups of families were organized into larger cooperative units, and the collection of these made up the tribe." Curl also points out that the early settlers, such as the Pilgrims, "formed and worked communally" and, in fact, "Plymouth was a commune."[1] Wayne D. Rasmussen offers a similar assessment: "Cooperatives have been part of American life since the continent was first inhabited by humans. The first cooperatives, those of the American Indians and the first European settlers, were informal, a way of survival."[2] And E. Sparks also speaks of "Coöperation from necessity, such as marked the first Virginia colony."[3] All three writers see the communal activities of the seventeenth and eighteenth centuries leading up to a more refined movement of cooperation, with a renewed focus appearing in the mid-nineteenth century with the rise of industrialization.

100     This outgrowth of industrialization spurred a cooperative movement based on an economic model that appeared with the efforts of the Rochdale Society of Equitable Pioneers in 1844. Rochdale was a small city in England that, like many others during this period, experienced dramatic changes in the textile industry that served as the hub of the town. Industrialization was displacing the traditional textile workers and a means was sought to provide for these workers' survival. Drawing upon earlier reform efforts, including

those of Robert Owen, the Rochdale Pioneers, as they were called, laid out several principles that would serve as the basis for a cooperative enterprise, and these were applied to a shop where subscribers could get their food and supplies.[4] In time, the cooperative venture expanded to housing and other services for its members. E. G. Nourse suggests that three fundamentals served as the basis of the success of the Rochdale Pioneers:

> 1. *Increased efficiency or reduced costs of service: no credit, no solicitation, and gratuitous or nominally paid service by members.*
> 2. *Popular distribution of savings or profits: minimum interest paid to invested capital, any surplus to go as patronage and wage dividends.*
> 3. *Democratic control, each member voting as an individual.*[5]

Several U. S. endeavors in the nineteenth century adopted elements of the Rochdale model, but not as quickly as in Europe, reflecting the ongoing tension between capitalism and the welfare of not only industrial workers but also increasingly farmers. But by the beginning of the twentieth century, the United States cooperative movement had begun to pick up steam.[6]

In the late nineteenth century "cooperative commonwealth" became a descriptor for cooperative ventures, largely due to the writings of Laurence Grönlund whose *Coöperative Commonwealth* (1884) has been noted for its influence in some of Oregon's utopian experiments. While some ambiguity exists in the word "cooperation," there was a similar vagueness in "cooperative commonwealth." In his study of a family that would be involved in a cooperative endeavor in Oregon, Ross E. Paulson offers this explanation on the various meanings of the latter term:

> *The phrase "cooperative commonwealth" had beguiled American radicals since it had been given currency by Laurence Gronlund in 1884. Its ambiguity made it mean all things to all kinds of radicals. To the orthodox Socialist it was a synonym for the Socialist state. To the moderate Socialist it conveyed the image of an Americanized utopia, a nonviolent society of equality. To those who believed in replacing the raw Darwinian competition of capitalism with some form of fraternal cooperation, the phrase frequently was identified with the colony idea. In the chaos in reform and radical circles that characterized the turn of the century, two separate tendencies—the cooperative colony movement and the "people's" educational ventures—frequently were combined under the rubric of the cooperative ideal.[7]*

101

From whatever perspective one took, multiple types of cooperative activities were undertaken at the beginning of the twentieth century. Two of these efforts in Oregon have received little examination to date. The most significant effort to achieve a cooperative utopia in Oregon was covered in the Oregon press for most of the first decade of the twentieth century, had significant financial backing from investors, issued a constitution and by-laws and at least two prospectuses, and changed the name of one of the towns in the Willamette Valley to Christadelphia.

## Co-operative Christian Federation

The front-page headline of the *Oregon Daily Journal* on June 26, 1905 proclaimed in large print: "OREGON TO BE HOME OF WORLD'S GREATEST COOPERATIVE SCHEME." A sidebar to the lengthy main article states:

> *The Cooperative Christian Federation, organized with a plan to solve the problem of profit-sharing between labor and capital, will build a great manufacturing and residential city in the upper Willamette valley, develop a million acres of land in central Oregon and establish the greatest cooperative empire in the history of the world. Two corporations—the Title Guarantee & Trust company of New York and the Trust Company of America—have perfected plans for financing it, and that their representatives will arrive in Portland within a few days to go over the ground preparatory to the marketing of a bond issue of $50,000 50-year 5 per cent bonds upon which the enterprise is to be launched. The exact location will soon be announced.*[8]

The article notes that the Federation "is the result of several years of work by" the Rev. H. S. Wallace, the head of the movement, and that a number of influential men had been accepted by the New York trust companies as the nucleus for a board that would eventually total fifty, "among them many of the leading financiers and business men of the country." In addition to the financial support, the Federation would be "backed by the moral influence of the American Institute of Social Service."[9] Wallace reportedly had conferences with such reformers of the period as Josiah Strong, founder of the Social Gospel movement, and J. M. Buckley, editor of the *Christian Advocate*.

The *Oregonian* followed up two days later with a much shorter article, but it provides more information on some aspects of the Federation, including some on its founder, H. S. Wallace, "formerly of Junction City, for some years past a resident of Portland," whom the newspaper praises for his unanticipated success in this venture. "One of the financial authorities in New York said to Mr. Wallace just before his departure for home, expressing well the new departure it embodies: 'This enterprise has three supports: First, the good will and endorsement of the churches; second, approval of the business leaders whose support is promised; and third, the enthusiasm and personality of the founder, whose life is given to its success.'" In addition to the prospective board members listed in the *Journal* article, this piece identifies H. D. Staley as secretary and F. S. Gotshall as treasurer. The article notes that no specific site has yet been determined.[10]

An editorial response on the following day notes, "The homes of the workers will be in factory and residence towns in Western and Eastern Oregon, where beauty and healthfulness of location nearness to factory and store, garden, field and orchard will remove from factory life the huge drawback common now." As to why Oregon was "chosen for this great and far-reaching experiment," the editorial suggests, "The capitalist's money is safe when resting on property of incerasing [sic], even of multiplying, value."[11] The editorial writer encourages Oregonians to support the venture.

While the *Journal* had only noted that the Federation "is the result of several years work by Mr. Wallace," *The Oregonian*'s editorial presents this assessment: "It seems to have taken Mr. H. S. Wallace eight years of continuous effort to frame, to modify, and to secure recognition for his ideas, which in their present shape are indorsed by many leading authorities in the labor world. It was a long apprenticeship of struggle and disappointment."[12] Very few details of this "long apprenticeship of struggle and disappointment" have yet been uncovered, but there are earlier documents that provide glimpses into the development of the Co-operative Christian Federation.

Interestingly, one of the earliest public reports of the Federation appeared in an unlikely source. The *Appleton's Annual Cyclopædia and Register of Important Events of 1899* included this report within the section for Oregon:

> A co-operative colony has brought 8,000 acres at Monroe, Benton County, in the Willamette valley. It is called the Co-operative Christian Federation, No. 1, and the intention is that, while nonsectarian, the colony shall make the teachings of Jesus the rule of action in all its affairs. The charter members are mostly from Oregon and Washington, though some have come in from other States. To be accepted as a member of the community, the applicant must be in good health and of sound moral character. Membership in the federation gives free schools, free doctors and nurses, and free homes. Free schools include music and art and manual training in your chosen trade or profession, and when you, from any cause, can no longer labor, your home remains the same, your food and clothing the same, your medicine, doctor, and nurse the same. And if you die, your children have the same home, schools, food and clothing, and medical service until eighteen years of age.[13]

103

That the notice of the Federation was included in *Appleton's* is quite remarkable as it generally published routine statistics or prominent happenings for each state. The appearance of this brief account of the Cooperative Christian Federation suggests that someone may have had some strong connections to get this published.

Another interesting and early mention of the Co-operative Christian Federation appeared in the newspaper of the Burley Colony on the Puget Sound in Washington, *The Co-operator*. A brief announcement appeared in the February 23, 1901 issue, noting that the Federation was looking for the services of a competent civil engineer "to assume the responsibility of surveyor and civil engineer of the railroad and canal to be constructed by and for the federation."[14]

The next document of note on the Federation comes as part of a package sent to an individual already noted several times earlier in this study for his efforts in compiling information on American communities. On March 7, 1902, H. D. Staley, Secretary of the Federation, transmitted it to "Mr. Wm. A. Hinds, Kenwood, N.Y." with an accompanying note typed on Federation letterhead, at the top of which is "Our Motto": "We pray the very God of Peace to sanctify wholly, and the whole Spirit, Soul and BODY be preserved blameless, in the life that NOW is, and in that life that is to come." According to the note, Hinds had asked for information on the Federation, and Staley sent what he termed their "Prospectus" that included "all general information regarding our Colony; its objects, aims and benefits—Christian Socialism."[15]

The document is titled the *Constitution, By-Laws and Prospectus of the Co-Operative Christian Federation Incorporated Under the Laws of the State of Oregon*, issued at Christadelphia, Oregon, in Benton County and also with a Post Office address in Portland. The ninety-two-page document itself is undated but is presumed to have been developed in 1901 or early 1902, perhaps in response to the request from William Hinds for inclusion in his compilation of communal societies. As noted earlier, Hinds provided one of the first studies of communal groups in America and, at the time of this correspondence, was working on a second edition that would be published in 1902. He developed a survey form with twenty-four questions ranging from the "Name of the communistic or cooperative society" and where the society had started to such details as "What are the hours of work?" and "What is their attitude toward the relation of the sexes?"[16] The transmission of the information by Staley to Hinds in March 1902 appears to be a response to this questionnaire. However, it also appears that the documentation was received too late to be included or it did not meet specific criteria for it was not included in either the 1902 edition, or the second revised 1908 edition. The 1902 edition includes a list of projected communities but the Federation is not among them. Nonetheless, the "Prospectus" sent to Hinds offers a glimpse into the principles and philosophy of the Federation at this time.

The "Introduction" is a twenty-five-page discourse that is more sermon than prospectus. Although no authorship is given, it is presumed to be the work of Rev. H. S. Wallace. The document is undated but reference is made to the assassination of President McKinley and to President Roosevelt so it was penned some time after September 1901.[17] The opening statement notes that the Federation "is founded on the Bible, and makes the ethics of Jesus Christ the supreme law." The rationale for the organization is offered two paragraphs later in prose that is typical of this lengthy Introduction:

*The promoters of the Federation are laboring to restore that Christian brotherhood that prevailed in the Penticostal [sic] days of Christianity and practiced by primitive Christians, believing such a brotherhood to be a fundamental principle of Christianity; in fact, Christianity itself, and the only solution offered that will, or can, solve the problems of a just and equitable distribution of the laborers of the world, as well as the products of the world's labor, thus appeasing the anger and suppressing the fierce quarrels now raging between man and man and called the fight between capital and labor, meaning the stubborn struggle between laborers and capitalists over the division of the products of labor. This perpetual struggle of man with his brother for the products of each other's labor is the inevitable and necessary results of unregenerate human nature, manifest through unrestricted human selfishness—HUMAN GREED—or, expressed in the popular phrase, the "Love of the almighty dollar.[18]*

In this vein, the Introduction goes on for twenty more pages with a focus on brotherhood and how fraternities and social groups take better care of those in need than do churches.

The author presents several examples of unnamed preachers ignoring pleas for assistance while groups such as the Odd Fellows, Masons, and other fraternal orders answer that call. The following offers a poignant example of the author's concern:

*As I walked through the streets of Eugene, Oregon, about 10 o'clock one night, I passed the door of the Odd Fellows' hall just as the pastor of the Humphrey Memorial Methodist church in company with his presiding elder came down out of the hall. I stopped and said, "Brethren, how do you explain to your brethren (especially those who are so opposed to secret societies) the fact of your spending time and money and being out at this hour of the night once each week?" The presiding elder replied: "I have preached in the church all my life, and I have not one month's provision ahead now, and if I or my family get*

105

*sick the church has made no provision whatever for my care. Some of the individual members may, as Christians, take up the case for awhile and make me an object of charity; so would the county. They would tell how poor and needy their pastor was and portray my poverty to the world—not the church only—and beg for me as a pauper, while my lodge will send to my house the cash every week and brethren to nurse me; and if I die I am decently buried in a decently kept cemetery, and my wife and children are cared for and educated. The church does no such thing, and in the sight of God I feel justified.*[19]

Beyond caring for others, the Introduction also speaks to the prevalence of armed conflict among humans as another sign of the failure to love one's neighbor. The cause of all this is "selfishness—greed." Over eight pages of citations and stories from the New Testament follow in support of the author's intent. And the Introduction concludes with the statement, "The above quoted and cited Scripture are relied on to support the 'Co-operative Christian Federation'."[20]

The emphasis on restoring "that Christian brotherhood that prevailed in the Penticostal [sic] days of Christianity, and practiced by primitive Christians," is key to understanding some of the principles of the Federation outlined in the eight-page Constitution that follows the Introduction and the more detailed twenty-three-page By-Laws.

The Federation is located at Christadelphia, as the title pages notes, a city not located on most, if any, maps of Oregon. The Introduction notes that the Federation was incorporated in Monroe, in Benton County, which the Federation has renamed Christadelphia or "Christian Brotherhood." The Prospectus goes on to state, "Nature has rarely wrought out a more beautiful and inspiring picture than is framed in the heaven and earth at Christadelphia."[21]

The first two Articles of the Constitution reflect the nature of this focus on Christ and the Scriptures. Labeled "Supreme Law," Article I states:

*The ETHICS of JESUS CHRIST and HIS APOSTLES, as found in the NEW TESTAMENT, SHALL FOREVER BE THE SUPREME LAW OF THE CO-OPERATIVE CHRISTIAN FEDERATION,* 106 *AND SHALL GOVERN THE MEMBERS IN ALL THEY SAY OR DO, AND THIS SECTION (1 OF ARTICLE I) SHALL NEVER BE REPEALED, AMENDED ABRIDGED OR IN ANY WAY SUSPENDED, CONTRAVENED OR CHANGED.*[22]

Article II then ties in these basic principles with the intent of the Federation: "The object and desire of the founders of the Co-operative Christian Federation is to organize and perpetuate forever a Christian brotherhood the members of which shall practice the ethics of Jesus Christ as written IN THE NEW TESTAMENT OF THE HOLY SCRIPTURES." Membership is covered in Article III, which states that "members of the Co-operative Christian Federation shall be men and women who accept the Holy Scriptures as the inspired word of God and Jesus Christ as their personal Savior, and the ethics of Jesus Christ as their SUPREME LAW and obey, practice and teach the same forever."[23]

Common Property, Equal Wage, Cooperative Labor, and a Spiritual Department are covered in the next four articles. Article VIII echoes some of the same rules as those for Hopeland as presented by Rev. John Sellwood, but with a little leniency included.

*The use, manufacture, sale and giving away of any malt, spirituous or vinous liquors or of narcotics, opiates, anaesthetics and all harmful and injurious drugs by any member of the Federation is hereby absolutely and forever prohibited, except that a reasonable and sufficient supply of such liquor and drugs may be authorized by the Board of Directors to practice on the property of the Federation, and the further exception that persons who are addicted to the use of tobacco at the time of becoming members of the Federation may continue to use the same, but shall not use it on the public ways, streets or offices, factories, shops, stores, mills, halls, auditoriums, or any public building, parks or pleasure grounds, hotels or any public gathering. And no member not addicted to the use of tobacco when admitted to the Federation shall use or acquire the habit of using tobacco after becoming a member of the Federation.[24]*

Articles IX through XIV deal with more practical matters and amendments to the Constitution, "excepting Articles I, VII, X, and XI, which shall never be repealed, amended, abridged, suspended, contravened or changed in any way whatsoever."[25]

The By-Laws provide in more detail the structure and intent of the Federation. Membership criteria are explained, including "a satisfactory medical certificate to the effect that the applicant is in good health." Membership is open to the wives of members as long as they meet the eligibility qualifications and that they can supply the admission fee ($200 for charter members) with earnings from work in the Federation. Children over eighteen also may become members. A non-resident category of membership is possible for those who do not wish to live or work within the colony. Details of meetings of members and the board of directors are described, as are the composition and duties of the board. Here is another indication of the date of the Constitution and By-Laws, as board members are to serve three-year terms and it is noted, "the first Board of Directors, which shall be appointed by H. S. Wallace, who shall appoint three directors to serve until the first Monday in January, 1903, three to serve until the first Monday, 1904, and three to serve until the first Monday in January, 1905.[26] Thus the By-Laws appear to have been drafted some time between 1900 and early 1902, when the document was sent to Hinds.

Specific articles in the By-Laws address "Church and Religion" and the "Lord's Day." The latter prohibits "labor of every kind, whether for profit or for pleasure ... except labor required for acts of necessity or mercy." It also includes a ban on "fishing, hunting, or in any games which tend to embarrass, disturb or bring reproach upon the church." Article XXI provides details on "Work and Wages," while Articles XXII and XXIII echo some of the rules of Hopeland with more elaborate restrictions. The former forbids "Cursing, swearing, or the use of vulgar or obscene language, or the repeating or telling vulgar or obscene stories, anecdotes or the circulating or showing vulgar or obscene pictures or literature." It also bans "Complaining, grumbling, quarrelling, angry disputing, backbiting, evil speaking, repeating scandal or any thing that is a reproach upon or derogatory to the character of any man." Article XXIII stipulates "Dancing, gambling, horse racing and all other questionable amusements violating the statutes and laws of the state, visiting saloons and all houses or places of immoral or sinful practices is forbidden." Other articles address expulsion of members, "Religious Discussion," and "Politics." The final three articles cover "Homes, Schools, Doctors, Medicines, Nurses, Hospitals, Colleges, Funeral, Cemetery, and Care of Widows and Orpphans [sic]." These sections describe in some detail the free services offered by the Federation to its members, and the spirit of Christian Brotherhood often neglected by regular churches, as noted in the Introduction. The final Article on "Widows and Orpphans" concludes by stating "if no member of the family be able to labor or render any service whatever, the family shall have the same care, home, food, clothing and education, including a diploma from the state agricultural college at Corvallis, or from the University of Oregon at Eugene, or some other college."[27]

The next section of the document provides detailed information on the seemingly most tangible aspects of the organization, "Description of Federation Property." Twelve tracts of land and other properties are presented in this thirteen-page section. For the farmlands, acreage under cultivation is provided, as are gross receipts from crops and a detailed valuation by appraisers. And the proximity to Monroe or Junction City is noted, along with information regarding roads and railroads passing through or near the property. The farm properties are listed, with an associated name and acreage.[28]

In addition, the flour mill at Monroe is listed and described in some detail, including the "Sampson, Lafell water wheel" and "40 acres of ground on

Front street, valuable property." The last properties listed are the "Junction City Hotel Company's buildings," which include the two story hotel and opera house. Although no specific intent is provided for any of these properties, it can be assumed that the founders of the Federation sought to illustrate the local backing they had for their enterprise.

The next section is an excerpt from a letter written by C. C. Hogue titled "A New Colony," in which Hogue presents a detailed description of the land and the climate of the Willamette Valley, leading up to a discussion of the colony:

> *Some years ago a minister, Rev. H. S. Wallace, was converted to socialism, and his constant thought since has been to found a Christian colony. Last year he learned of what he considered a fine opportunity to secure a site and at once set to work to work the matter up. His labors culminated in securing options on several thousand acres of this land near Monroe, which lies on the Willamette River near but below the head of navigation. The option includes a number of houses, barns, a store and the stock of goods if desired, flour mills, 100 acres of prune trees, gardens, orchards and pasture; also a very fine water power. There is good clay for brick and fine building stone, and it is thought there is limestone or cement near at hand. Water power is to be had at slight expense in every direction, and near at hand. The intention of those who have joined Mr. Wallace in this work is to found a Christian colony.*[29]

Hogue includes a call for members and suggests "several thousand can be accommodated after the colony gets in working order."[30]

The following seventeen pages contain "Anticipated Questions Answered." These may be based on the twenty-four questions included in the Hinds questionnaire, as some of the same information is provided, but there are sixty-three formal questions and answers, along with a "bonus" question at the end offering information on what hotel one should stop at while visiting the Federation office in Portland.[31] Many of the other questions echo information in the Constitution, By-Laws, and description of property, with some further explanation provided. In response to the question, "What other industries will the Federation engage in?":

109

> *The manufacturing of flour and feed, manufacturing lumber, shingles, doors and sash, operating woolen mills, canneries, creameries, fruit dryers, brick and tile factory, manufacturing shoes, can salmon, work stone quarries, dispensatory, a general store, do a banking business and build and operate the Corvallis & Southern railroad.*[32]

Other questions center on fees, wages, labor, and such issues as "Suppose a man is lazy and will not work?"—the response, quoting II Thes., 3:10, "Then he shall not eat."[33] And perhaps most telling in terms of the initial founders and their interest is question LX, "Who is doing all this?"

> *The whole plan was organized by one man. He organized the Corvallis & Southern Railroad Company that he might present the thing to the financial world. The Corvallis & Southern Railroad Company is composed of the best and most successful business men along the line. The president is G. C. Millet, the owner of the Millet tract of land described and stock in the hotel described in list of our property; also one of the directors. The vice-president is A. Wilhelm, of whom the Federation bought the mill, about 2300 acres and nearly all the townsite of Monroe. He is worth a quarter of a million. The treasurer is Hon. C. W. Washburne, of Junction City, Or. He is the largest individual taxpayer in Lane county, a gentleman of large means and varied interests, including immense tracts of land, mills, city property in different cities, bank stock and hotels, etc. Another is Mr. J. S. Bushnell, president of the local bank. The secretary and general manager is H. S. Wallace, the originator of the entire proposition. Wallace represents the railroad company in New York to arrange for the sale of the bonds. All of these gentlemen are much interested in the Federation.*[34]

The document concludes with the form, CERTIFICATE OF ELECTION AND RECEIPT OF EARNEST FEE IN CO-OPERATIVE CHRISTIAN FEDERATION, NO. 1.[35]

Although this document was sent to Hinds in March 1902, there is little public evidence of activity by the Federation until the outburst of press coverage beginning in June 1905. Possible reasons for this might be that the scheme was too vast and all the parts were not yet in place. Such key parts may have been the necessary financial backing required even though the properties "held" by the Federation were extensive. This could substantiate the "long apprenticeship of struggle and disappointment" encountered by H. S. Wallace and noted in the June 28, 1905 editorial in *The Oregonian*, when he sought "to frame, to modify, and to secure recognition for his ideas." Some of that reframing and modifying may have been to some of the more rigid requirements of membership in the Federation that, like those of Hopeland, interested parties probably had difficulty in swallowing whole. Whatever the reason for the three-year absence of any noticeable efforts by the Federation, Wallace's ability to secure the backing of the New York trusts marked a critical turning point in the endeavor.

Throughout the summer of 1905 the Portland papers repeatedly reported on the Federation. On July 16, 1905, *The Oregonian* carried a two-column article, subheaded "Christian Co-Operative Colony Seems Assured," which reports on a conversation with Wallace:

> *That Mr. Wallace is not altogether a dreamer is proved by his industry. For nine years since he left his Methodist pulpit at Junction City, in Oregon, he has, with a confidence born of inspiration, been working day after day, in season and out, to bring his theories to fruition.*
>
> *A typical parson of the Wesley persuasion, he is poor and has always been so. He has walked when others rode, gone hungry while others were fed, ragged while others were well clothed. He has journeyed up and down and across this big country of John D. Rockefeller's for nine years, asking the ear of listeners, explaining, beseeching, imploring.*
>
> *Now he says that his devotion to the great one idea has brought him to the verge of success.*[36]

The curtain did indeed seem to be going up on the "gigantic enterprise" of the Co-Operative Christian Federation.

Two weeks later *The Oregonian* reported on a sermon given by Rev. Wallace at the Central Baptist Church, at the close of which he spoke about the Federation and distributed information.[37] The religious focus of the enterprise was still evident but the financial aspects were getting equal attention, as the following day *The Oregonian* reported, "Contracts were signed in Portland last night for the sale of the French-Glenn ranch of Harney County, comprising 164,000 acres to the Federation." The Federation, represented by eight members of its executive board, agreed to pay $1.8 million for the ranch, with the first installment to be paid within thirty days. The article noted that the Federation had outbid the Mormon Church for the land, which would accommodate "homes for 10,000 people" with a railroad line built to connect the area with the main lines.[38] Key to these plans was the work of Rev. David Lippert of Ontario who claimed, "This is not a paternal scheme, it is a fraternal one, far removed from the ideas of the Mormons or of any known plan now in existence." He also notes, "I am glad to be able to say that the people of Ontario and vicinity are heartily in favor of the plan as proposed by the Federation."[39] Other reports in August 1905 state the Federation "proposed to secure 800,000 acres of land from the owners of the old grant made years ago by the Government to the Willamette Valley and Cascade Mountain Wagon Road," which would "provide homes and employment for 40,000 inhabitants."[40]

This flurry of news about the Federation faded with the coming of fall 1905 and it is not until mid-November that the next significant report can be found, which would initiate a series of reports over the next fourteen months that were increasingly repetitious. The November 13, 1905, *Oregonian* carries an article with the headlines, "Plans to Succeed" and "Capital is

111

Forthcoming" and discusses board member Wallis Nash's three-week trip "East in the interest of the Federation."[41] The same trip is reported again three months later.[42] Three days after that, *The Oregonian* reported that Rev. Wallace is optimistic about raising the necessary funds to realize the planned Federation.[43] And a March 1, 1906, article presents a similar report and notes "The faith of the men who are associated with the federation is unshaken and they firmly believe in its ultimate success."[44]

There is an increased emphasis on building railroads and "ultimate success" is projected in five years; this suggests a new focus of the Federation. The emphasis on Christian Brotherhood, although still evident to some degree, has been overshadowed by the industrial aspects, the concept of the "model city," and the building of railroads. Interestingly, it was these announcements in February and March that were picked up by early historians of Oregon's railroads as the point of incorporation of the Federation. These are some of the few mentions of the Co-operative Christian Federation found in later historical reports.[45]

Reports diminish again until late in 1906 when another flurry of newspaper articles appears. This coincides with the issuance of a seven-page pamphlet on the Federation that provides a much-distilled version of the document prepared some six years earlier and sent to Hinds. Consistent with the newspaper accounts of the previous two years, there is less emphasis on the Christian elements of the enterprise; in fact, there is not a single Scriptural reference. The Federation is simply described as "An Association of persons who, by character and capabilities, meet the requirements of the Constitution of the Federation." Its aim is "To afford to such persons the right to share in the profits of co-operative labor, under conditions favorable to pleasant and cultivated social life, in model towns and settlements in Oregon, where morality, and fraternity, shall prevail, and Christian ethics shall be the governing spirit." And "Its Sphere" is described as "Co-operative industries of many kinds, ranging from the operation of railroads, and filling all positions in factory and industrial life, to the minor industries dependent on the life of city, town, and settlement."[46]

The reports in the December papers carry the same message as earlier articles—"Its Affairs Taking Shape" (December 6, 1906) and "Plans Are Ready—Co-operative Christian Federation About to Begin Work" (December 22, 1906). The latter report notes that the Federation was incorporated in Portland in July 1905, which neglects the Christadelphia period.[47] Two articles early in January 1907 report on meetings held in Ontario and Vale, where Mr. Nash "found nothing but the heartiest indorsement of the plans of the federation." It also is noted that federation officers are planning to visit Harney County next and that a request had come from Weiser, Idaho, to visit there. In addition, "A delegation from Dead Ox Flat called on the federation officers at Ontario and asked for water and a chance to subscribe for bonds."[48]

Two other events are significant for the Federation in 1907 and mark a further shift in focus and, most likely, signaled the beginning of the end of the grand scheme. The next item in *The Oregonian* appeared in the March 2, 1907, issue under the headline, "Must Change Its Plans." The article discusses another visit by Nash to New York, where he once again was meeting with financiers, and reports "that in the purchase of the Harriman interest in the Corvallis & Eastern Railroad one of the important plans of the Federation has been defeated." The report continues, "As a result, it has been decided by the Federation to obtain from the Clackamas River the necessary power for the operation of an electric line from this city into Clackamas County to a point about 20 miles from this city, where a townsite will be located." Nash added, "The enterprise has been so seriously disturbed by the reported sale of the Corvallis & Eastern Railroad property ... that it will necessitate getting out a new prospectus, in which the railway scheme will be made of secondary consideration, the industrial feature of the enterprise taking precedent." And, as usual, "The Federation is satisfied that it will be able to make a sufficiently satisfactory showing to insure the ready issuance of bonds with which to finance the scheme."[49] The actual sale of the Corvallis & Eastern Railroad to E. H. Harriman was not completed until December 1907, and it was then conveyed to Southern Pacific.[50]

The new prospectus anticipated by Nash appeared later that year. Like the pamphlet issued in December 1906, this document moves away from the focus on Christian Brotherhood and takes a more practical, if still idealistic, approach to its aim. This is captured in the initial line of the revised prospectus: "The central idea of the 'Co-operative Christian Federation' is the 'City of Happy Homes, supported by co-operative industries'." Moreover, the nature and location of the proposed "Garden City" has changed, as implied in Nash's report in *The Oregonian*. The new prospectus states, "The first of such cities is to be placed on a large tract of fertile land, now occupied by prosperous farms, in Clackamas County, Oregon, about fifteen miles from the City of Portland."[51] The building of a dam on the Clackamas for water power is planned, as is an "electric road from Portland," as Nash had suggested in his earlier report.

The prospectus identifies specific industries to be established for the proposed Garden City and estimates of skilled and unskilled workers to be employed are presented in a table. The list of industries is comparable to earlier versions of the scheme: woolen mills, clothing factory, creamery and cheese factory are included along with a slaughter and packing house, furniture factory, stone quarry, and a co-operative store along with others. New to the list is a Street Car Service although no workers are listed for this

113

item. In total, the projected employment would be 1,139 workers and total capital invested in the project would be above $1,040,000.[52] A minimum of eight hundred families is calculated as necessary for Garden City No. 1 or a population not less than four thousand. Specific information is given on the types of house to be provided to members of the Federation.

It is only on page 10 that a brief mention is made of the Constitution and that it requires that "churches and other buildings for Divine worship" are to be made available to members. This is the only reference to the "Christian" nature of the scheme, a major change from the initial prospectus. The transformed focus of the intent of the Federation is captured in the penultimate paragraph of the document: "No one who has watched the marvelous development of the industrial life of Oregon during the last five years can fail to appreciate the certainty of progress at a still greater ratio during the coming years."[53]

The shift to the notion of the Garden City is an interesting development and one that reflects other utopian roots for this scheme. The Garden City Movement evolved from the ideas and ideals of Ebenezer Howard, an Englishman who himself had been influenced by the utopian schemes of Edward Bellamy's *Looking Backward 2000-1887*. As early as 1892, Howard had developed his idea of an ideal city, or Garden City, that would be "a tightly organized urban center for 30,000 inhabitants, surrounded by a perpetual 'green belt' of farms and parks. Within the city there would be both quiet residential neighborhoods and facilities for a full range of commercial, industrial, and cultural activities."[54] He presented his idea in a book published in 1898 as *To-morrow: A Peaceful Path to Real Reform* and re-issued in 1902 as *Garden Cities of To-morrow*. These works served as the basis for the rise of the Garden City Movement in England and the United States, and the coincidental timeframe for the development of some of the ideas of the Co-operative Christian Federation suggests there may have been some influence on the development of that scheme, particularly after the need to issue a revised prospectus but perhaps even earlier.[55]

Despite this new prospectus and the "certainty of progress" suggested within it, the momentum of the Christian Co-operative Federation was seeping away. Prior to a full-page article by Wallis Nash that appeared in the November 3, 1907 *Oregonian*, only one other brief report on the Federation appeared in that paper in June of that year. Like several earlier reports, this one highlighted the fact that the Federation was ready to begin work on a central Oregon colonization project.[56] Nash's extensive piece in November appears to have been the last hurrah for public awareness and interest in the endeavor. Nash reiterates many of the same topics explored in earlier reports and in the two prospectuses. In typical fashion, Nash notes that "There must be a dawn before day breaks. Now is the Federation dawn."[57]

But, in truth, it was the Federation's sunset, or perhaps more accurately the dawn that never happened. There are no further reports on the Federation in *The Oregonian* or in other papers and it is assumed that those who backed the project finally realized that it was the dream that was not to be. The purchase of the Corvallis & Eastern Railroad by Harriman clearly marked an important point in the direction of the Federation, but the repeated attempts to show that financing was available and bonds were soon to be issued highlight the continuing struggle to get the needed support for the scheme. In the end, the "long apprentice of struggle and disappointment" experienced by H. S. Wallace in the formative years continued for five more years until the project dissolved altogether.

## Another Cooperative Dream

The Co-operative Christian Federation was a grand utopian scheme that did not materialize but it was not the only such attempt undertaken in Oregon during the initial decade of the twentieth century. A less elaborate scheme, but one with significant connections on the East Coast and roots in other utopian endeavors, was introduced in late 1906. There are some similarities between these two proposed cooperative experiments although they do not seem to have been related. The second, reported first in *The Oregonian* of December 29, 1906, under the headline, "Co-Workers Will Build Model City," suggests in its subheadings "Boston Fraternity Plans to Establish a Co-operative Colony in Oregon" that will "Reclaim the Wilderness." And a fourth heading declares, "Rev. Hiram Vrooman Outlines Purpose of Association of which He Is President—Make Poor Families Homebuilders." Details of this venture are presented at the outset of this article:

> *Rev. Hiram Vrooman, Ph.D., president of the Co-Workers' Fraternity, of Boston, Mass., who has made his home in Portland for the past year, has drawn plans for the building of a "co-operative city with an industrial college and university," to be located on a large tract of yet undeveloped land, to be acquired by purchase in Oregon. The object is to make it possible for families to become home builders, and afford their children opportunities for industrial and literary education. It is a project modeled largely after the California Home Extension Association organized in 1904 , of which J. S. Clark is the author.*[58]

115

Quoting an interview with Vrooman, the article presents an outline of the plan and reports that "the parent company proposes to issue common and preferred stock." The report also includes information on the Co-Workers' Fraternity of Boston that is backing the scheme. It lists the members of the Fraternity, many of whom have a significant role in reform activities of the late nineteenth and early twentieth centuries.[59]

The idea for this endeavor was appropriately a cooperative one between Rev. Vrooman, his brothers Carl and Harry, and Bradford Peck. As Robert S. Fogarty notes, "The Vrooman family had been involved in varied phases of reform activity since before the Civil War and was particularly active in labor and cooperative circles in the 1880s."[60] These activities continued into the 1890s, including the Union for Practical Progress, spearheaded by Benjamin Flower in an effort in which "small groups of enlightened, self-sacrificing lovers of humanity" would "direct local efforts in cooperation with the policies and plans laid down by a national advisory board."[61] The Rev. Hiram Vrooman presented his views and support of this initiative in an article in which he states:

*Men holding all shades of religious belief and unbelief have agreed to bury their differences and work shoulder to shoulder against the common enemy. They have decided to separate all matters of common public concern from theological and sectarian interests, and to quiet denominational turmoil in a united effort to help those whose lives are made all but unbearable by criminal and destructive social conditions.*[62]

During this same time, Peck was developing his own views on social reform with a particularly strong emphasis on cooperation. He was influenced by Henry George's *Progress and Poverty* (1879) and even more by Edward Bellamy's *Looking Backward 2000-1887* (1888). He crafted his own utopian vision, which he published himself in 1900 as *The World A Department Store: A Twentieth Century Utopia*.[63] The Co-operative Association of America was founded in late 1899 in Lewiston, Maine, with the intent "to teach the principles of cooperation to the local townspeople, especially the businessmen." The Association received a charter in the state in January 1900 and a system of membership was set up with each member, as Wallace Evan Davies notes, receiving "certificates bearing photographs of Bellamy and George, as well as an etching of 'Christ as the Good Shepherd'." Several hundred individuals subscribed and with these membership funds, along with sales of the novel, the Co-operative Association of America took hold, first applying its principles in a grocery store in Lewiston and in Peck's own Grand Department Store.[64]

116

While Peck was establishing this association, Hiram Vrooman was forming the Co-Workers Fraternity as "a holding company which planned to use the dividends from the enterprises it controlled to start a university with strong labor sympathies."[65] Vrooman also started a Workers Co-operation Association in Boston at this time and it was at a meeting of this group in January 1901 that Peck and Vrooman met. The two men agreed to join forces, with each becoming an officer in the organization established by the other and the Co-Workers Fraternity of Peck acquired ninety percent of the Association's stock.[66]

Over the next five years the two men and their intertwined organizations continued to advocate for cooperative endeavors, bringing other reformers and businessmen together to develop their plans. Hiram Vrooman wrote several articles; the first of these, "Government Can Employ the Unemployed," proposed the establishment of a Coöperative Commonwealth with an industrial army of one hundred thousand in Nevada.[67] The second item is a summary of the "Co-operative Association of America."[68] The June 1902 issue of *The Arena* included Vrooman's announcement of "A National Co-operative Conference" to be held that month in Lewiston, Maine.[69]

In 1903 Vrooman published a book titled *The Federation of Religions*, which also was the name of another organization he founded and served as president. The purpose of this group was "to bring into co-operative relationship as many persons as possible, from any or every religion, who are truly open minded and loyal hearted to truth."[70] Peck also continued to write on cooperation, including a small volume titled *The Spirit of Co-operation*, which was published by the Co-operation Association of America in 1905. That same year Hiram Vrooman moved to Portland to initiate his "investigation" for the next major activity of the Co-Workers Fraternity, the establishment of a cooperative colony. Land also was bought in Florida and Massachusetts for similar efforts.[71]

After the initial announcement of this activity in late 1906, the next steps in the venture were identified in *The Oregonian* of February 18, 1907. The article reports on Vrooman's work to form a "Co-operative City Club" in Oregon and it notes that a prospectus was sent out. One of the subheadings of the article declares, "Promoters Have Received Offers to Locate Utopian Town From Ten Different Parts of the State." Specifics from the prospectus are presented, excluding the location of the proposed site as "utmost secrecy must be maintained" on that matter.[72] The tone of the scheme, and even some elements of it, are very similar to the Co-operative Christian Federation. Unlike the efforts of H. S. Wallace and others, however, the plans for the co-operative colony of Hiram Vrooman went no place much more quickly.

There are very few reports on that proposed "utopian city" after early 1907 and the plans for the cooperative enterprise were soon laid to rest, at least in Oregon. There is speculation that some of the backers, perhaps even Bradford Peck, were losing interest or were moving on to other projects. Although several supporters still were behind the effort, the Co-operative Association of America steadily lost steam over the next several years and by mid-1912 had dissolved completely while the Co-Workers Fraternity had exhausted its resources.[73]

Hiram Vrooman still pursued his cooperative path with an increased focus on the religious perspective. *The New York Times* of August 18, 1912, reported on a "New Religious Body to Clean Up Corrupt Colorado" with the Rev. Hiram Vrooman as head of the Liberal Congregation of Denver. The article states that Vrooman "believes Colorado is the most promising field for the realization of all he had hoped for." He is quoted, "I am starting the Liberal Congregation of Denver with the purpose of making such contributions as may be in my power toward supplying this, as I conceive it, the greatest need of the hour, namely, genuine spirituality within the ranks of the world's social reformers."[74] This objective, laudable as it is, apparently was not enough for Vrooman, as three years later *The New York Times* reported on a "Utopia for Colorado," which is a plan by "Hiram Vrooman and others" to establish "Industrial City near Walden, Colo., in North Park where … each man will receive the full product of his toil." This "will be the scene of one of the most interesting socialogical [sic] experiments in the history of the world, according to the Rev. Hiram Vrooman, formerly of New York City."[75] It does not appear that this dream was realized either.

## CHAPTER SEVEN

# From Cooperation to Survival in the Twentieth Century

◈ ◈ ◈

While communal efforts did not disappear nationally in the first half of the twentieth century, there were some shifts in the pattern of such communities and there was an overall decline in number of new undertakings.[1] But many communities founded earlier were still active at the beginning of the twentieth century. These included such groups as the Hutterites and the Shakers, with their long traditions of communal living. Many other groups, such as the colonies near Puget Sound, had started in the 1890s and carried forward into the new century. And a number of other colonies were initiated in the first two decades of the twentieth century, such as the art colonies like Byrdcliffe, as well as several religious, ethnic, and secular communities.[2] But among the standard compilations of communal groups, only Foster Stockwell includes an Oregon communal group in the first thirty years of the twentieth century—a short-lived community of Russian Molokans that settled on a thousand acres in the Willamette Valley in 1912. They were one of several Molokan settlements established between 1912 and 1924 but the Oregon group, called the Freedom Colony, lost their land due to the manner in which they drew up the legal papers for the land.[3]

The causes for the decrease in communal activities in general, and in Oregon specifically, are many and, as Michael Barkun suggests, may be part of the general cyclical nature of such experiments.[4] Numerous suggestions have been offered, ranging from the "closing of the frontier," as Frederick Jackson Turner declared in his famous 1893 study, to broad-ranging shifts in society due to rapid developments in science, technology, and medicine.[5] Steven Kesselman even suggests links between Turner's frontier thesis and the Great Depression, noting that there were other "frontiers" impacted by changes in the early twentieth century, including what he calls the technology frontier, the production frontier, the organizational frontier, and the population frontier. At the end of the nineteenth century these "frontiers" were seen as limitless and as leading to expansive progress in society. But the events of the early twentieth century leading up to the Depression impacted these frontiers, just as Turner suggested the closing of the frontier impacted society as a whole. For many, Kesselman posits:

*Basically, the idea was that the American way of life had reached the end of its road, that America's uniqueness was fast disappearing. World*

119

*War I not only killed progressivism as a political and social movement, it destroyed the notion of the inevitable progress of mankind towards a better life. The effect was delayed in America by the shaky prosperity of the 1920's, which kept alive the hope that the old order of capitalism and free enterprise were leading America toward a utopian existence free from poverty and want.*[6]

The utopian hope of the 1920s ended with the Crash of 1929, and the Depression that followed brought about a different reality.

These and other negative results of the rise of industrialization and technology were at the core of another shift in the realm of utopian thought, which may have been a factor in the decrease of communal experimentation. With the advent of the twentieth century there grew uneasiness with where all these changes were taking society. The writings of the muckrakers, particularly Upton Sinclair's *The Jungle* (1906), vividly represented a bleak side of the impact of industrialization and technology upon society. There also developed a new element of literature that looked at the dark side of utopia, or how utopian ideals can turn bad or are even bad in themselves. These works, labeled dystopias ("bad place"), increasingly came to reflect attitudes about the twentieth century, especially following the series of events beginning with the outbreak of World War I and the Russian Revolution.[7] For some, the twentieth century represented a shift from "utopia to dystopia" or, as Chad Walsh states in his aptly titled 1962 study, *From Utopia to Nightmare*: "The wars and revolutionary upheavals of the past half-century have erased many names from the map. ... In the midst of old countries disappearing and new ones coming to birth, few men have paused to notice that a familiar and cherished nation, unique in offering citizenship to all humanity, is in danger of quietly fading from the map. That country is Utopia."[8] The upheavals that Walsh suggests include not only the economic crisis of the Great Depression but World War II and the Cold War with its specter of nuclear annihilation fueling dystopian thoughts.[9] It was upon this backdrop that the nature and intent of communal societies struggled to survive and redefine themselves in the first several decades of the twentieth century.

One of the ways to address these concerns, and for many the means to survive in the twentieth century, was through cooperative methods. As discussed in Chapter Six, cooperation became a focal point of utopian and communal endeavors at the end of the nineteenth and the beginning of the twentieth century. Cooperative activities had also expanded to non-communal ventures in the nineteenth century, including consumer cooperatives such as stores and exchanges. Oregon had a few attempts at consumer cooperatives in the nineteenth century, including those attempted by the state and local granges, but most of these were unsuccessful.[10] Efforts continued in the early twentieth century and by the 1920s cooperative ventures were appearing in several parts of Oregon.

A United States Bureau of Labor Statistics Bulletin in 1927 lists twenty-two "consumer societies" in Oregon, such as cooperative stores in Bandon, Dayton, Hood River, and at Reed College. Also listed were the Consumers Co-operative Association in Astoria, the Calapooia Cooperative Exchange in Halsey, the Wichita Co-operative Water Association in Milwaukie, and the Huntington Cooperative Company in Huntington. Several cooperatives existed in the fishing industry, and although the listing is suppose to be "other than agricultural," such groups as the Lebanon Farmers' Cooperative Exchange in Lebanon, the Polk County Farmers' Cooperative Co. in Rickreall, and the Azalea Cooperative Broccoli Association in Riddle are included.[11]

The publication's intent to exclude agricultural cooperatives was because they were so numerous; agricultural cooperatives were one of the fastest-growing and needed types of organization. E. G. Nourse, in his examination of "The Economic Philosophy of Co-operation" points out: "It is in … agriculture, that the attempt to apply the coöperative form of organization to modern economic needs and problems has been by all odds the most important in America." But he is very quick to point out that, "Agricultural coöperation, of course, does not mean coöperative farming," adding, "This latter is a sickly growth found only in the hothouse atmosphere of a few fanatic colonies." And he explains further, "Agricultural coöperation means the association of farmers, stockmen, orchardists, or the like for the joint performance of certain parts of their business which cannot be satisfactorily carried on alone."[12]

While Nourse wrote this in the early 1920s, the next ten years witnessed a dramatic shift, first in the state of the nation's agricultural stability during the 1920s and then with the major economic crisis of the Great Depression. The impact was that the "sickly growth" of cooperative farming, "found only in the hothouse atmosphere of a few fanatic colonies," not only became more widespread and accepted but it became the utopian dream of survival for many. But this was not a new dream as Joseph W. Eaton suggests in his 1943 book, which explores "co-operative group farming as a method of rural rehabilitation," "the co-operative corporation farms of the Farm Security Administration," and "other co-operative group farms." In this last section he devotes a chapter to "Utopian co-operative group farms of the past," where he suggests that there is a significant heritage from earlier utopian ventures of importance to the present situation:

121

*Co-operative group farming is indigenous to America. Although today it is practiced more widely in Russia, Mexico and Palestine, America was the principal location of its early development. The existing projects are similar in nature to their utopian predecessors. Although many conclusions based on such a belief have little foundation in fact, the experiences of these early American co-operative rural settlements are not without present significance.*[13]

In a separate study on a similar topic, Eaton and Saul M. Katz identify "more than two hundred co-operative group farms or communities which existed in the United States up to the first World War." Among these is the Aurora Colony, which Eaton and Katz present as a nineteenth-century example of a group farming community and a precursor to such entities in the twentieth century.[14]

In addition to a heritage of cooperative group farming, there also arose early in the century a "back-to-the-land" movement that had utopian underpinnings. A writer in 1912 noted, "In return for small income and hard labor the man who goes back to the land recovers his independence and secures a chance to work irrespective of hard times and strikes."[15] But that sense of the frontier spirit was tempered by the changing economic and social condition of the increasingly industrial society. H. L. Davis reflected on this utopian ideal countered by the reality of the times in a piece he wrote in 1912. The final line in this essay captures some of the spirit of the good place and no place of these homesteaders: "We used to hear them when they moved out, passing the cattle-ranch in the night, arguing to make their wives stop crying, and explaining that there was still a new section of country a couple of hundred miles farther on, where a man stood a chance."[16] Finding a place where "a man stood a chance" was not just a utopian dream but, as the twentieth century progressed, a matter of survival. The return of soldiers from active duty in World War I created an unprecedented demand for a solution and one that rose to the top was to settle these doughboys on farmland.[17] This was a concern in Oregon as the *Oregon Voter* for September 6, 1919, includes an article that endorses the Mondell Bill then being considered in Congress for a half-billion-dollar National Soldiers settlement proposal.[18]

During the Depression finding a place where men and women stood a chance became an issue not only for soldiers but for large numbers of individuals and families displaced by the economic downturn as well as droughts and disasters, natural and otherwise. As R. W. Murchie wrote, "In all times of economic stress and industrial disruption the cry of 'back to the land' is certain to be heard." Although he noted the futility of earlier utopian experiments in America, Murchie suggests that there is something to be gained from the knowledge of these endeavors, from Oneida to the Llano Cooperative Colony, adding, "At the present time scarcely a week goes by that some political leader or prominent business man does not enunciate a new scheme or an adaptation of an old one for moving the unemployed back to the farm, either as a permanent or as a temporary measure for unemployment relief."[19] In short, America was looking for "The Happy Valley," as Alvin Johnson suggested in an essay in the 1933 *Yale Review*.[20]

Part of Franklin Delano Roosevelt's New Deal initiatives, the Resettlement Administration was created by Executive Order 7027 on May 1, 1935 to assist in the resettlement of displaced farm families and to plan for new communities, which became known as greenbelt towns.[21] The Resettlement Administration was headed by Rexford Guy Tugwell (1891-1979), an academic from Columbia University, who became part of the "Brain Trust" involved in FDR's campaign. Tugwell brought to the Resettlement Administration a strong sense of reform and idealism that was labeled utopian by both his supporters and his dissenters.[22] He had definite ideas about utopias himself but not as a panacea to look back to a simpler, pastoral time.[23] He saw the Resettlement Administration as one means to take "the clay of to-day" to mold hope for tomorrow for many displaced by the Depression.

The efforts of the Resettlement Administration were described by Jonathan Mitchell in 1935 as the promise of "Low-Cost Paradise." The ideal promise of these "new suburban communities" prompted Mitchell to ask, "How does the citizen go about obtaining a home in one of the government-built suburban Edens?" Besides the Edenic new communities planned by the Resettlement Administration, Mitchell notes some sixty-five projects in twenty-two states that were part of the agency's plans to resettle "about 350,000 families in economically dead areas where government has pledged itself to reestablish in new occupations or new homes or both."[24]

The list of existing or proposed projects does not include any from Oregon, and the Longview Homesteads project in Washington is the sole project listed for the Pacific Northwest. But Oregon was included in the promotional literature of the Resettlement Administration, such as the fourteen-page brochure issued on June 30, 1936. Only a few of the elements of these programs were initiated in Oregon but the utopian ideals were clearly present.[25]

123

Another development during the Depression that would have some direct impact in Oregon was the outgrowth of what was called cooperative living from the cooperative group farming experiences, including those sponsored by the New Deal initiatives. In 1938 John Hyde Preston wrote, "The reader familiar with history will know that the idea [of collective living] is as old as civilization, that it was an animating principle of early Christian communities, that collective living was widespread in the Middle Ages." He prefaces these remarks, however, by noting: "The idea of collective living gives most American an emotional fright. It suggests a cross between a college reunion and a summer camp, held together by a concept lifted out of the agricultural program of the Soviet Union."[26] Four years later, Edward A. Norman elaborated on this point:

> *At the present time, of course, to most Americans, thinking as they are, not in terms of the conditions that probably will confront them, but instead in terms of the world as they have known it, the idea of cooperative living must seem repellent. Privacy is one of the chief desires of most people. However, cooperative living need not necessarily be unpleasant, especially if the alternatives are either starvation, circumscription of their lives by a system of centralized control, or hard, unproductive work and suffering alone. Properly organized, a cooperative farm community can be a very pleasant place in which to live, especially if the group is made up of congenial people. The careful choosing of one's association for this sort of thing is one of the basic essentials of success.[27]*

In addition to cooperatives and cooperative farming, a movement toward cooperative living was also developing in the 1930s and would continue to gain momentum in the next two decades, and was in many respects the framework for a more intense movement that would take place in the 1960s.[28]

Although the efforts of the Resettlement Administration had few direct effects in Oregon, the rise of cooperatives and cooperative group farming both did have impacts in the state. These activities are discussed here as a reflection of broader examples of reform and cooperation that characterized much of the 1930s and Oregon was part of this spirit of cooperation and survival evident throughout the country. Furthermore, they present a foreshadowing of events that would take place later in the century with a major resurgence of communal living. Two small, but noteworthy, examples illustrated how this manifested itself in Oregon during the Depression.

## *Co-operative Farm*

124

One of the few recognized attempts to establish a communal group in Oregon in the first half of the twentieth century took place outside Eugene when a group of present and former University of Oregon students organized the Co-operative Farm on August 1, 1931. Established prior to the initiatives of FDR's New Deal, the Co-operative Farm reflected many of the characteristics and concerns of other cooperative endeavors of the period. However, it also captured the elements of a communal enterprise, in intent, organization, and, apparently, in its short-lived nature. Interestingly, these elements created some indirect links with the Aurora Colony, at least in terms of the information we have on the farm.

One of the first news items about the Co-operative Farm appeared in the *Sunday Oregonian* on February 28, 1932, in an editorial titled "The Aurora Experiment." How the Aurora Colony gets linked to this cooperative endeavor is an intriguing example of the way that utopian experiments become intertwined in history, or at least in association. The piece begins: "Nine men and women, organized into a co-operative society, purchased 85 acres of land near Eugene last fall for a farm, and secured 100 acres in addition by lease. This spring they hopefully will sow their first seeds." The author offers some views on this communal experiment and others in general: "We sincerely desire otherwise, but fear that much will grow besides wheat and kale. The crop—if past experiences counts for anything—will include dissension and ultimate defeat." And then the Aurora connection is provided:

> *None of the American co-operative societies—or communistic societies, if it is preferred to call them—have prospered permanently unless they were buoyed with religious enthusiasm, and even most of the religious groups have broken up because of the assertiveness of the members. Our best known Oregon experiment, that of Aurora, brought to the state some of its finest citizens, but it could not survive the death of its dominant figure, Dr. William Keil.[29]*

It is interesting to note that the Aurora Colony was serving as a benchmark for communal attempts some fifty years after the colony disbanded.

The connection to Aurora does not end with this editorial, however, for much of the extant information on the Co-operative Farm appears in Robert J. Hendricks' *Bethel and Aurora*, published in 1933. Hendricks examines other communal attempts, such as Amana in Iowa, the Llano Cooperative Colony in California and its successor in Louisiana—New Llano, and the Doukhobors in Canada, along with the Co-operative Farm outside Eugene. Exactly what Hendricks seeks to suggest by including these various groups is somewhat vague although, as the subtitle to his works suggests, he is presenting accounts of "past and present ventures in collective living," particularly as experiments "in communism as practical Christianity." But it is curious that he chose the Co-operative Farm as one of the examples, perhaps primarily as it was located nearby.[30]

Hendricks based most of his comments on the Co-operative Farm on a series of articles in the *Eugene Register-Guard* in January 1933. These reports by Roy Craft sought to provide information on this group, which was causing some concern in the Eugene area. An "Editor's Note" at the

125

beginning of the series states: "Controversy over the real nature of the Cooperative Farm, near Coburg, has led *The Register-Guard* to inquire into the nature of the experiment, the kind of people taking part in it, their views and ideals, their mode of life. Mr. Craft visited the farm, talked at length with all members." The first report begins, "If the depression has done nothing else, it has at least turned the everyday American into an economist and a student of sociology." Of those who looked for a solution to the economic strife of the Depression was a group of nine individuals, "most of them University of Oregon students and ex-students who had become interested in the cooperative movement as discussed at the campus Y. M. C. A. open forum."[31] They patterned their organization "after a plan originated in England," likely the Rochdale model.

Craft provides general information on the group's scheme and then specific information on the fourteen members then living at the farm, five original members and nine who had since joined, including two "associate members" who could achieve full membership when they turned twenty-one. Of the original nine members, six were men and three women, including three married couples. All were in their twenties at the outset of the experiment. Craft notes that at least three of the original members were Danes, and that one of them returned to Denmark after his wife died and the other Danish couple moved to Salem, "where they have jobs and can make enough money to send to the 'old country'."[32]

Typical of the information Craft provides for the members in January 1933 is that for A. Bristol and his wife (who is only identified as "Mrs. A. Bristol") and their infant daughter:

> *A. Bristol—One of original Oregon students who formed cooperative farm. For the past several years employed at the university and at present on a leave of absence because of ill health. He is secretary at the farm and pools his university salary. Is a native born American of English ancestry. Registered as an independent in the last election and voted as a socialist. Attends Congregational church.*
>
> *Mrs. A. Bristol—One of original founders. Attended University high school and later University of Oregon. Native American raised in Hawaiian Islands. Voted same as husband; attends Congregational church. Helps with laundry and does baking for stall in public market.*
>
> *Baby La Verne Bristol—Age 18 months. Was born two days before farm was formed so is not original farm baby.*

Other members listed are Paul Blazer, Charles Blazer, Dorman Blazer, Helen Blazer Wright, Eugene Wright, Mrs. Anna Devries, Herman Devries, Elsa Mehlmann, Isaiah Domas, Mrs. Ann Domas, Edgar Hupp, Zadie Hupp, John Creager [visitor, not member], Clifford Creager, [small son of John, also a visitor], Newton [another visitor]. The backgrounds of the group were diverse: Herman Devries was a civil engineer and his wife, Anna, "an accomplished pianist and professional instructor." Ann Domas was a concert pianist and several members were experienced farmers, including the Blazer family from Hillsboro. Devries and Elsa Mehlmann had both spent time in Russia and Isaiah Domas worked for two years at the Henry Street Settlement in New York City.[33]

In his second article, Craft explained the workings of the farm, noting the communal aspects of the group—eating at a common table, receiving a monthly allowance, purchasing of clothes and other personal items by the secretary. New members turn over their property or money to the group, and if a member leaves they can withdraw their money. Craft explains that the "group is developing a diversified truck garden, specializing in berries," and have constructed an irrigation system for the crops. They also grew grain and used this to make and sell baked items in Eugene's public market, where they also sold produce grown on the Farm. They raised swine for market and also had a number of dairy cows.[34]

The third article in the series examines rumors of dissent within the community and the general unease among some external groups about the Farm's intent and activities. Some of this uneasiness is likely due to the fact that socialism was a key element of the group. As Craft notes, "Naturally, the members believe in socialism and no one not in complete sympathy with the movement would be welcome." As for dissent within the community, one member is quoted as saying, "the home is conducted in complete harmony and every one of the 14 members is enjoying life here." Visitors were welcome and, as Craft suggests "are always received cordially at the farm."[35]

The third report also states that the "farm publishes a mimeographed bulletin each month which is sent out each month to other co-operative farms in the United States, and others interested." The article includes several examples of the personal items, new stories, business affairs, and social events included in the publication. The *Bulletin* also served as a source for Hendricks' discussions of the Co-operative Farm. The intent of the group, as reflected in their *Bulletin*, was "to serve as a living example of a larger way of life than our capitalistic system; to assure its members the necessities of life, and to allow its members an opportunity to live in an unselfish way, practicing the ethical principles of Jesus and living the socialistic, co-operative life."[36] As such, the Co-operative Farm carried forth the spirit of earlier communal efforts, particularly those tied to Christian Socialism, as well as the intent of the unrealized Co-operative Christian Federation. There were a number of similar groups throughout the United States during the Depression and the social and economic environment seemed to make such

127

efforts appear a little more than radical efforts to change society. However, the fate of these cooperative communal efforts was very similar to those of their nineteenth-century precursors and the words of *The Oregonian* editorial would eventually ring true—"The crop ... will include dissension and ultimate defeat."

Although it is not clear how much dissension was a factor in the dissolution of the Co-operative Farm, by mid-1933, less than two years after its founding, much of the energy and most of its members had departed. The June 1933 *Bulletin* reported on a May 10 meeting in which the work program was to be arranged but, in so doing, it was discovered that only two members chose to remain. The absence of later reports suggests that the Farm dissolved altogether soon after.[37]

The Co-operative Farm is noteworthy for its efforts as a nongovernmental community during the Depression as well as its roots in communal experiments of the nineteenth century (and the curious links with the Aurora Colony implied through published accounts). Perhaps most interesting from a twenty-first-century perspective is its position as a harbinger of the outburst of communal spirit and activity in Oregon that would take place in the late 1960s and after.

## Coöperative Subsistence Colony

A second type of communal effort was initiated in Oregon during the Depression when a group of workers from Portland formed a colony on twelve hundred acres of land outside Dallas, Oregon, in 1933. Information on this group comes from a front-page report in the December 7, 1933, issue of the *Christian Science Monitor*:

> DALLAS, Ore.—*Believing that they can better provide for themselves as a group during these difficult times, a number of unemployed skilled artisans of Oregon have banded themselves together in a novel organization known as the Oregon Coöperative Subsistence Colony, or "Oco-op" for short. The colony is located near here on the site of the old Black Rock lumber mill.*[38]

The group had a board of directors of nine members and, as reported by Mr. H. I. Cummings, vice-chairman of the board, "its members are men, chiefly artisans, who have been out of work for months, and are now pooling their resources in an attempt to set themselves up as a self-sustaining cooperative unit."[39] Houses were being built and plans were being made for gardens the following year. The plight of this group, however, is unclear.

## *Student Cooperatives*

Other cooperative activities were undertaken in the 1930s and into the early 1940s that serve as predecessors to communal endeavors in the 1960s and later. Like the Co-operative Farm, the impetus for several of these took place on college campuses. In her history of "distributive and service cooperation in the United States," Florence E. Parker includes "student 'living' associations" as a type of cooperative venture that had roots in the 1920s but, as she notes, "it was not until the Great Depression that the student houses began to develop." She offers these positive aspects of these cooperatives:

*Aside from the chief benefit of bringing down the cost of room and board, the student organizations have several important values: They provide practical training in household operation and management and the collateral activities, as well as business training in thrift, buying, bookkeeping, making reports, and direction of others; they promote high scholastic standards; they tend to develop a spirit of independence, resourcefulness, and self-help, and to make the individual adaptable and tolerant of others' views; and they provide lessons in democracy and citizenship.*

She also notes that, "By 1941, the 150-odd 'living associations' had an estimated membership of nearly 10,000 students."[40]

One of these cooperatives was formed in 1935 by a group of students at the University of Oregon who were inspired by the master's thesis of a UO student named Wallace J. Campbell. Campbell wrote on "Depression Cooperatives" and the students chose to name their cooperative after him.[41] The Campbell Club became the hub of the Students Co-operative Association, which has expanded to two other residences and is still active. The Students Cooperative at the University of Oregon is one of the oldest student co-op associations in the United States and in terms of longevity of communal groups in Oregon it should be considered the longest lasting and still active organization.[42]

Students at Oregon State College in Corvallis also experimented with a student cooperative in the 1930s. During the 1936-37 academic year, a house that had served as the Beta Kappa Fraternity from 1928 became the Beaver cooperative. Although the house reverted to overflow housing for women's dormitories the following year, in 1964 the house again became a cooperative when an interdenominational non-profit group based in Salem, Bible Teaching, Incorporated, purchased the house and Varsity House was founded. It has served since as a co-op for Christian men attending the Oregon State College (later University) and Linn Benton Community College.[43]

129

Another type of cooperative that grew out of the 1930s and served students from American colleges and universities was summer work camps. Based on models of such camps in Europe in the 1920s, the American Friends Service Committee initiated the first private work camp in the United States in 1934. As Kenneth Holland notes, "By the fall of 1940 about 1,300 persons had participated in work camp programs for college students in this country." And another organization, Work Camps for America, began to offer camps not just for college students but for "rural youth, and youth from worker families."[44] Although not strictly communal in nature, some of the goals of these work camps were reflective of other cooperative undertakings and also foreshadowed later developments. A more immediate development, however, affected the summer work camps and other cooperative endeavors—the entry of the United States into World War II in December 1941.

## World War II and "New Associations"

The war would create a halt or at least a hiatus in many of the cooperative activities of the 1930s. But the war also spurred some broader considerations of cooperation among the population at large due to rationing and other aspects of working toward the common good. As Florence Parker suggests in her history of cooperation, "new associations" were brought on by the war. Two are of particular interest as she notes, "World War II also produced two transitory types of cooperatives—those of Japanese Americans in the War Relocation Camps and of conscientious objectors in the Civilian Public Service camps."[45] Although these camps could hardly be called utopian, they did, as Parker suggests, include aspects of cooperation that were based on survival. And some of them, including the Civilian Public Service (CPS) camps in Oregon, did create a community that achieved several successes that would carry on beyond the years of internment during and after the war.

These communities, however, were truly unintentional in terms of the residents; there was some choice involved for the conscientious objectors, but little choice was available to the Japanese Americans in the internment camps. Although there was not a Japanese American internment camp physically in Oregon, these camps did impact Oregonians and it is important to note these "transitory types of cooperatives," as Parker labels them, in the examination of cooperation in the twentieth century.[46] Parker includes these because, as she states rather generously, "All the needs of the camp residents were supplied through cooperatives promoted and encouraged by the War Relocation Authority." There were one hundred nine such cooperatives in place by 1943, serving the ten internment camps in the United States.[47]

Parker's focus on the CPS camps was mainly on their cooperative ventures, such as the stores, but many of the CPS camps adopted features that resembled aspects of earlier communal groups and a sense of community evolved into some broader cooperative activities of note.[48] Of the four CPS camps in Oregon—#21 in Wyeth/Cascade Locks, #56 in Waldport, #59 in Elton, and #60 in La Pine, the Waldport camp has been recognized for the development of a fine arts community with activities in music, theater, painting, and publishing.[49] The Fine Arts Group at Waldport resembled a communal undertaking in many ways, even including the objections of neighboring individuals, and that sense of community carried beyond the internment at the camp after the war. Several members of Camp #56 at Waldport went on to be influential in the San Francisco Renaissance during the late 1940s and into the 1950s.[50]

World War II brought about some of the same conditions that prompted concerns related to resettlement of those returning from conflict, but on even a broader scale than after World War I. Early in the war Edward Norman saw this as another opportunity for the development of the cooperative farm. As he wrote in the Preface to the Eaton and Katz research guide:

*Indications are accumulating that when the war ends there will be a tendency of the American population to migrate from the cities to the country. To state the matter in another way, many people may be seeking to shift their occupations from industry, commerce, and the professions to agriculture. Moreover, this tendency eventually may evidence itself in a form novel to the contemporary American scene, the cooperative group farm.[51]*

But President Roosevelt and Congress wanted to avoid the problems associated with the displacement of veterans following World War I and in June 1944 the Servicemen's Readjustment Act, commonly known as the GI Bill, was signed into law. Although it was controversial and did not resolve all issues associated with returning military personnel, the GI Bill did aid in the transition of veterans to life after the war, particularly through its educational and home loan provisions. Norman's vision of a large rise of cooperative farms did not materialize, and even though cooperative endeavors continued to exist in several aspects of society in the post-World War II years there never arose the same level of widespread interest as seen in the 1930s.

131

## Postwar Dreams and Realities

America became engaged in a whole new world in the late 1940s and the 1950s. For some this was the era of the realization of some type of utopian ideals, perhaps exemplified in the rise of suburbia as the fulfillment of the American dream.[52] Beneath this façade of utopianism, however, there was a darker side that appeared not only in the writings of George Orwell and other dystopian writers, but also was increasingly apparent in the novels and films of popular culture.[53] Others saw the 1950s as a bleak time where, as Daniel Bell suggests in his *The End of Ideology* (1960), utopia itself was exhausted.[54] Although the value and potential of cooperative enterprises continued to be seen during these years, it no longer seemed to be the means for survival for most. In fact, due to the increased distance in ideologies evident during the Cold War, the nature of cooperative activities came under even closer scrutiny in post-World War II America. Along with words like communism, socialism, and collectivism, which already had grown to become linked with anti-American values, even cooperation became increasingly suspect.

Yet cooperation was an important part of survival for many during much of the first half of the twentieth century, and it would see a significant revival later in the century. While Oregon did not have a substantial number of communal experiments in the first sixty years of the twentieth century, there were a broad range of cooperative activities that were still part of the utopian heritage from earlier years. These cooperative endeavors shared many of the same characteristics and intents as the outburst of utopian experimentation that took place in the state in the last half of the 1960s and that have continued to the present day.

## CHAPTER EIGHT

# Rediscovering Utopia:
# The New Pioneers of the Late 1960s

⧉ ⧉ ⧉

In a very perceptive and moving letter printed in the third issue of *Communities* in 1973, Margaret Ford, then in her seventies, provided some history, some hope, and some advice for those involved in the rebirth of communal groups in the late 1960s and early 1970s.

> *I knew that sooner or later it had to come, the forming of communities. I am so happy! This is the way, the only way to go. I knew the young folks would lead the people of this land out of the complexity of metal and paper built up by the power mad generations before them. I saw you and I knew you while you were yet babes, and I knew. You knew me too. As your mother wheeled you past in your little cart you saw me and recognized me, and smiled. You answered me with your intelligent eyes. This was a new kind of people, I said.*
>
> *Colonization is not a new thing; it is the concept upon which this nation was founded. But in this century we lost it somewhere along the way. They say there are no more pioneers. Well, I think there are. And you are the new pioneers.*
>
> *I am 73, I am daughter [sic] of American pioneers. I lived at the beginning of this century in a community. They tell me that the idea has never quite been lost and the people of Oregon where I lived are still aware of it.*
>
> *I have time to observe and experience and read and question and study. I see nothing great about a Nation dedicated to constant murder, robbery, corruption and the breaking of all 10 commandments. But I do see a Nation made up of the worth of people, the minds and talents of people expressed in worthwhile endeavor toward the welfare of all. We can come back to that because we are a majority. You can. All I can add is the result of my having lived here. This I gladly bequeath to you. The economy of this Nation will collapse as it did in the early '30s. The circumstances will vary but the effects will be the same. A few of us are still around that can remember the great depression. We would like to see you prepared to meet it better than we were. So, lose no time, establish your communities quickly. And build again. You are the new pioneers.*[1]

133

Although Margaret Ford's views were unlikely to have been shared by many of her generation in this period of social and political turmoil, she provides an insightful glimpse into the spirit of the revival of communal living that began to emerge in American society, and in Oregon, in the mid-1960s.[2] And the utopian nature of that revival was identified by Elinor Lander Horwitz, who wrote:

> Utopia—the land that cannot be found on any map of the world—continues to excite the imagination of dreamers and explorers. Man is good but society is evil, today's utopians are saying, as utopians have said through the ages. If man discovers an ideal society in which to live he can shake off faulty social teachings and the corruption of today's world, say the new utopians—as did the old. Can man free himself of the shackles of class and materialism and the sins of competitive ruthlessness and greed? Can man—in short—achieve perfection in a world of his own devising? Yes, cry the new utopians, as did their forebears. Yes. Yes. Yes.[3]

The manner in which these new pioneer utopians sought to achieve their goals, however, was different in many respects from that of "their forbears." Joseph Olexa suggested one difference:

> The most fascinating aspect of the current development toward a new utopian orientation is its kaleidoscopic nature. Instead of springing forth full-blown like Plato's Republic or More's Utopia, it is being developed in bits and pieces by many individuals who are more concerned with changing society not at the system level . . . , but in the realm of their own individual lives.[4]

The six decades prior to the mid-1960s saw some communal development throughout the country but not much in Oregon. This would change dramatically in the second half of the 1960s and into the 1970s as Oregon became a hotbed of communal activity and seemed to rediscover its utopian heritage in the process. In Timothy Miller's landmark study of the 1960s-era communal experience, he offers these observations of why "No part of the United States had a stronger communal presence in the 1960s era than did the Northwest":

134

> If the communes of the 1960s era could be counted accurately, the largest number of them would probably turn out to have been in the area from San Francisco northward to the Canadian border and from the Pacific inland perhaps a hundred miles. The relatively mild Northwest climate provided a congenial place to settle in communes that often lacked modern amenities, and the epicenter of the countercultural population was there as well.[5]

The appendix in Miller's work includes a listing of over fourteen hundred communities, of which one hundred and seven are in Oregon. Building upon the number of communities identified in Miller's study, augmenting the list for the decade he examines, and expanding the study from 1975 to the present, the current study has increased the number of intentional communities in Oregon since 1965 to over two hundred fifty. This chapter and the next explore these communities in a broad manner, identifying the types of communities established or planned in Oregon, the nature of these communities and their location, as well as discussing additional reasons why Oregon was, and continues to be, attractive for formation of such groups.

Oregon's embryonic communal experience burst upon the national scene in mid-July 1969 but few realized that what they were seeing and reading was about a commune on 240 acres of rural land in southern Oregon near Sunny Valley. The July 18, 1969, issue of *Life* magazine carried a cover photo of five adults and three young girls looking like a pioneer family from the nineteenth century except for the beads, flowers in the hair, and the shoes that most of them were wearing. The lead story, with several full-page color photographs, was on the subject of youthful communes.[6]

*The Family of Mystic Arts on cover of* Life *magazine, July 18, 1969*

135

The featured commune was called the Family of Mystic Arts but the interviews with the commune members by John Stickney and the photos by John Olson were allowed only on the condition of anonymity and a promise not to reveal the location.[7] Privacy was important to the Family of Mystic Arts. *Alternatives*, one of the early publications of the commune movement, published the post office box for the Family in its Commune Directory, and received this request:

> *Dear Brothers and Sisters—*
> *The Lord bless you and fill you with his light. We wish our name and address to be immediately deleted from your magazine.*
> *This is our home, not a tourist vacation spa. We are trying to gain, spread, promulgate the love of Jesus the Christ and find it necessary to control the number of brothers and sisters who share here with us. We also seek more subtle methods of soul-mating than computerizing. We appreciate your inclusion of our address and now would appreciate your exclusion of same. Kindly R.S.V.P. that this has been done.*
> *Love and Peace*
> *El Twig, secretary*[8]

As this letter illustrates, the Family of Mystic Arts not only cherished their privacy but they also were very religious in nature. Richard Fairfield, who received the letter above, notes that the founders of the commune "were devout fundamentalists [sic] Christians—believers in the Literal words of the Bible." As such, the group harked back to several earlier communal groups that sought removal from society to practice what they believed were the ways of the early Christians. Like these earlier groups, the members of the Family sought to achieve this in a simplistic manner. As the *Life* magazine article notes, "The youthful pioneers, unlike the earlier Americans who went into the wilderness to seek their fortunes, are refugees from affluence." The idealistic nature of their experiment is reflected in these words of one member of the Family: "We are entering the time of the tribal dance ... as we go to live in tepees, celebrate our joys together, and learn to survive. We go to a virgin forest with no need for the previously expensive media of electric technology. The energy we perceive within ourselves is beyond electric; it is atomic, it is cosmic, it is bliss." The credo of the commune also reflects this pioneer spirit and the idealism inherent in their objectives: "Getting out of the cities isn't hard, only concrete is. Get it together. This means on your own, all alone or with a few of your friends. Buy land. Don't rent. Money manifests. Trust. Plant a garden, create a center. Come together."[9]

The struggle with idealism and the balance between individual and community also is brought out in the *Life* article:

*The commune has its share of everyday squabbling, and a little incident can bring the loftiest ideals abruptly back to earth. During a recent three-day fast by the group, one member whose spirit was weakened walked seven miles to a gas station to buy a candy bar. When the others spotted the empty wrapper sticking out of his back pocket, they laughed—and then everyone continued the fast.*[10]

Bob Carey, founder of the Family of Mystic Arts, speaks to another aspect of this in an interview:

*One of the things that is noticeable here is that when we first came out here, we had the idea that by coming here, by dropping out, by making this move, we'd all drop all our hang-ups; but everyone brought all their little things with them, their little things. So the first thing was to bust the bubble of how we imagined it would all be and then go back to working things out for real. There is nothing here to blame your hang-ups on. You can't say it's society, because it's your society here.*[11]

Bob Carey provides a connection to what might be considered one of Oregon's earliest communes in the post-1965 era, that of Ken Kesey's Merry Pranksters. This famous group migrated to Oregon in late 1967 and early 1968 after Kesey settled on his brother's farm outside Springfield, Oregon, following a period of imprisonment for marijuana possession.[12] The Merry Pranksters' communal existence in Oregon was short-lived as Kesey grew weary of the communal scene after several years. Kesey's assessment, as quoted in *Rolling Stone*, was: "We were all lying to each other, saying that what we were doin' was righteous when we didn't really feel it." As the story goes, he had fellow Prankster and friend Ken Babbs take a busload of Pranksters to the Woodstock Festival in the summer of 1969 with instructions not to return.[13] Thus the Merry Pranksters as a communal group drove off into the sunrise but remnants of them can be found among other communal experiments in Oregon, including the Family of Mystic Arts.

Carey was involved in Kesey's psychedelic bus rides and through his involvement with the Pranksters had experimented with LSD and other drugs, as had other members of the Family. But after Carey found the land that would be home to the Family, the use of LSD and other drugs was not totally forbidden but it was frowned upon within the commune.[14] Instead, working the land, living with nature, and focusing on Biblical teachings became the basis for the spiritual lives of members of the community.

Even though the identity of the Family of Mystic Arts was shielded in the *Life* article, the images of the commune became a symbol of the movement taking place not only in Oregon and the United States, but elsewhere.[15] The identity of the commune became known fairly soon after the article appeared

137

and, according to Timothy Miller, "hippies by the hundreds swarmed to and over the idyllic locale, undoubtedly hastening its decline."[16] The commune became a magnet for the curious and the original intent and focus of the members of the Family were diminished. Over time the community changed its name to the Family of Living Arts and the initial phase of the commune had declined by the mid-1970s, though some individuals still live on the land. Reunions of former members were held in the summers up through the 1990s.[17]

In the frequent vagueness of communal history it is difficult to identify the first "new pioneer" communal experiment in 1960s Oregon. At least twenty other communal experiments were begun between 1965 and 1970 in the state. With limited documentation on some of these communities, identifying the exact date when they were established is problematic and for some there is only a general sense of when they were formed and the word "formed" is perhaps too specific. The formation of a group may have taken a period of time, even years, and some might be considered almost in a permanent state of formation. Others perhaps never quite achieved a state where they could be considered established—another problematic word—but even those are included in this study as they reflect the interest and spirit of communal experimentation and they also could possibly lead to additional information on their development. Many groups may have formed without a specific name (e.g., "the farm") or organizational structure. The Appendix includes dozens of references to announcements and advertisements for individuals or groups seeking to find or establish a community, yet at this time there is no evidence that such groups were formed.

The earliest group of new pioneers in Oregon may have been those who appeared on the coast in Newport in late 1965 when, as Timothy Miller notes, "a group of protohippies rented a big house."[18] Little is known about this commune named The Zoo, including its duration. The Mountain Grove community near Glendale is another early communal group with one source giving its formation as 1966.[19] This was a spiritual and educational center with a background in the teachings of Jiddu Krishnamurti (1895-1986). Mountain Grove continued into the late 1990s with fluctuating membership. Other communes established in the last five years of the 1960s include three formed in 1967—the Great Pumpkin Commune in Tillamook, Fort Mudge in Dexter, and The Human Dance Company in Ashland. Of these, the most is known of The Human Dance Company, which, as its name implies, was a group of individuals who used dance to communicate their views and passion about life. Andre Carpenter wrote of the troupe's attitudes towards family, sex, and marriage, the theme of the November/December 1975 issue of *Communities* magazine:

138

*Essentially, all the members of the company are individually oriented towards "androgynous consciousness." We don't know what is really the difference between males and females—if it's biological or cultural or both—or maybe the difference is so slight, actually, that it isn't even worth thinking about, and therefore shouldn't affect sexual behavior. Most of us find it almost insulting or simply boring to be liked or disliked simply because of having a male or female body. We've also observed that sexual attraction based on gender tends to perpetuate the alienation and misunderstanding between the genders and therefore within ourselves.[20]*

An earlier call for members suggests the type of individual sought to join the community: "We are looking for: individuals with an adventurous consciousness and heart; especially those with a strong and supple body, whoever has resources and skills, or abilities and talents—latent or awakened—and is willing to put them at the service of humanness, and more precisely, of the Human Dance Company."[21] The community published a newsletter, *For Humans Only*, and in the mid-1970s toured the West Coast performing "Becoming Human" and also presenting workshops on movement.

As Miller notes: "The latter months of 1967 through the first few years of the 1970s saw a frenzy of commune-founding that dwarfed what had gone before."[22] This national phenomenon was also mirrored in Oregon's communal scene. The years 1968 and 1969 saw increasing numbers of groups formed in Oregon with a wide range in the type and nature of these communities. Though they are often referred to as "hippie communes," this generalization is overused. Miller states elsewhere, "The most common mistake is the presumption that a stereotype called the 'hippie communes' accurately represents the historical reality of the day."[23] A relatively small portion of the communities founded in the late 1960s and early 1970s were genuinely hippie communes, but they certainly were the ones receiving the publicity.

Although not even a majority of the communes in this period could be considered hippie communes, the influence of the San Francisco Bay area and the countercultural activity centered there did have an influence on Oregon's communal experience, albeit in a range of ways. One of the communes established in the late 1960s with significant hippie overtones was High Ridge Ranch in southern Oregon, which for reasons based on protection of privacy was identified as both Magic Farm and Saddle Ridge Farm in early reports and studies.[24] Elaine Sundancer, herself a commune member, uses Saddle Ridge Farm in her book. Early in her report, Sundancer

139

writes: "The story of Saddle Ridge Farm begins in Berkeley, in the winter and spring of 1968. Some people who wanted to find a new way of living had formed a discussion group. It used to meet on Wednesday nights, each week at a different member's house, so we called it the Wednesday Night Group."[25] These meetings were the brainchild of Richard Fairfield, the editor of the *Modern Utopian*, who had brought his interest and beliefs in alternative lifestyles to Berkeley in 1966 from Boston. Gardner states, "These discussions, which lasted about a year, were the genesis of at least three subgroups which eventually set out to put theory into practice and become actual communes themselves."[26] Not just one but two of the groups settled on land in southwestern Oregon.

The more successful of the Oregon communes that evolved from the Wednesday Night Group was High Ridge Farm, founded in September 1968 on the Illinois River, which would become the location of several hippie-era communes. While the early residents of High Ridge Farm did not adopt group marriage, their lifestyle was based, as Gardner points out, on "personal freedom rather than group commitment."[27] People came and went and amazingly without much, if any, formal structure things got done although in a slow and somewhat chaotic fashion. By the latter part of 1969, there was a mass exodus. In many respects, this aided in the longevity of High Ridge Farm for some structure was begrudgingly adopted in the next year or two. When Robert Houriet visited the commune in 1971 he noted that, "The commune has only one schedule, a recent one at that—a chart of who cooks the evening meal." He also offered this assessment of the structure of the commune:

> *Without the aid of committees, chairmen, quotas, policy or timeclocks, the household chores eventually got done, just as they get done in any other American household—except that the eleven adults and six children of the farm are not a family in the traditional sense. Unrelated by blood, they function like a family, though I'm not sure yet how or why.*[28]

Although structure was at a minimum, the residents of High Ridge Farm adopted group-encounter techniques to address communal issues. These activities probably accounted for some measure of durability of the commune even with significant turnover in its early years. Even amid the free spirit attitude of High Ridge Farm, there was a growing acceptance of adapting to the outside world. They were one of the few communes in the area that had electricity and they sent their children to public schools. Elaine Sundancer reflects on this: "I wonder how our children feel, shifting every day between this orderly, well-equipped, stuffy room, and the mud and chaotic, liveliness of the farm. I don't know. I always said I'd never send my child to public school, but I'm learning that life isn't as easily manageable as I thought."[29]

Another commune formed from the Wednesday Night Group was Talsalsan Farm, also on the Illinois River. (Talsalsan means "the river.") Founded in April 1968, Talsalsan started out as a group-marriage commune, like another Wednesday Night Group in the Bay Area—Harrad West, but this lasted only a year before some of the frequent aspects of human nature intervened. As Gardner reports, from the only member who remained at the commune after eighteen months, "the failure of the early attempt was attributable to not being honest with each other, not having meetings for mutual feedback, unclear and ulterior motives on the part of some individuals which only later became apparent, and hang-ups about jobs and jealousy, which were all the more deeply ingrained because of the ages of the founders." In 1969 the property went into a trust agreement and the initial phase of the community ended. But, as would happen in other communes, Talsalsan saw a revival in the early 1970s, and became part of the Jesus People movement although that too was fleeting.[30]

Also founded in 1968 in the same general area was the Sunnyridge commune, which was initially settled by a group who had come together at New Paltz State College in New York (now the State University of New York at New Paltz). They purchased a mining claim and converted a small cabin and sheds into living space for about a dozen people. Stan Kahn, who would join the commune later, recalls, "Sunnyridge was born of a positive need to create a new way of living in tandem with feeling propelled out of the sorry state of the American city as it existed back in the 1960's."[31] Despite being novices at living off the land, the group survived the first, harsh winter and the community grew to about thirty-five individuals after two years. As Kahn notes: "In the beginning the fervor of creation kept the commune going but within about six years the novelty had worn off and the necessity of living with a large number of people made life a decided chore."[32]

Another commune founded in 1968 that reflected a struggle with its identity, or at least the nature of the community, was the CRO Research Organization, also known as CRO Farm (or just Cro or Crow), located near Veneta, west of Eugene. CRO was established as "a radical new experiment in 'total involvement' living," according to its prospectus, and "Its overriding goal is to create a total immersion community in a rural environment that combines creatively the advantage of farm living with those usually associated with the urban setting."[33] As such, as one Crofarmer noted in Eugene's *The Augur* newspaper, it had a hybrid environment that distinguished itself "from the urban commune and the primitive [sic] commune often portrayed in *Life* magazine." The same article noted,

141

"Of course, life at CRO is not an utopian dream," but ends by stating: "The adults are free to learn, to work at what they want. Idealistic as it may sound, CRO farm is alive and doing well."[34] Several of CRO farm's members continued to work full- or part-time outside the community to pay for expenses, but as membership declined, particularly among those who were bringing in cash, times became tough through the first winter. But new members and a new focus on agricultural services and logging helped to solidify the economic foundation of the community so that additional property, including buildings, was purchased along with a herd of cattle.

But beneath the surface there were many tensions within the community. Some of these centered on a mix of practices and beliefs on marriage and sexual activity. The farm was considered by Fairfield as a group-marriage commune, but the reality is that there was a mix of monogamous couples with others who practiced the open sexuality of group marriage. In such an environment, there are bound to be rifts and at CRO, as Fairfield notes, this manifested in the two groups living in separate houses. In effect, he suggests, "There were two separate communes, eating together and sometimes working together, but essentially distinct—one living in the large brown house, the other in the small white house."[35] In such a situation the nature of organization and communication can be problematic and this seemed to be the case at CRO.

Another problem at CRO, as in many of the early communes throughout the United States, was the male-dominating nature of the organizations and the communities. Although there were groups that practiced, or at least preached, gender equality, most of the communes of the 1960s followed more traditional male-female roles with male domination in the family and in the community as a whole. Vivian Estellachild, at one time a member of the CRO community, reported on this problem at several "Hippie Communes" including CRO Farm. Her observations, although admittedly biased, were frank and hostile to the CRO environment, at least the males within the commune. "The major problems of the commune," she states, "were male chauvinism, insensitivity, and stagnation." Innovation was frowned upon and ridiculed, and mental and physical abuse of women was observed. Her overall assessment of CRO was negative and she notes: "If Crow Farm sounds repulsive I assure you that it was. The only good thing that came out of it was my beginning awareness of women's problems and focusing on them." She also relates a story about action taken after she left the commune:

*Shortly after I left, the Crow men took my car (which I had donated to the commune and used only once), crashed it, ran over it with the caterpillar, and pushed it into the dump heap. I am sure it was a cathartic experience. Probably gave them a hard-on. Somehow they never could subdue me and the car was second best.*[36]

Another woman who lived at CRO for two years, Cindi Smith, presents a different assessment of her time there—"It was a remarkable experience to have lived in, to have experienced." In response to a question about why she left, however, she does identify some level of stress within the commune: "I saw no other outlet than to leave, and ... two years is a long time to live in that kind of a tense environment." But she also notes more generally, "Two years is a long time for someone to stay in a commune."[37]

A commune established in 1968 reflected the influence of the Beatles as it was named Yellow Submarine. Located in Eugene, Yellow Submarine was one of the earliest communes within the metropolitan area of an Oregon city. As Richard Fairfield noted after a visit to the commune in the summer of 1970, "it is one of thousands of typical urban-suburban residential houses being used as something more than a college co-op, and something less than a revolutionary commune."[38] The group had as many as twenty-five members in the summer of 1969 and in September of that year, as Kay Teeter notes, "the commune was incorporated and the name was changed to Rivendell, after the home of the King of the Elves in J. R. R. Tolkien's *Lord of the Rings*." Teeters identifies the commune "as a religious organization with two purposes: first, to recognize the brotherhood of man; and second, to engage in social research to extend man's utopian vision."[39] In an earlier report on the commune in *The Augur*, the spelling is given as Rivendale and the goals are given as "to provide a large family unit in which all members work for a common good" and "a move toward self-sufficiency."[40]

Another commune named for the landscape in Tolkien's Middle Earth was Ithilien, founded in 1969 near Willamina. Besides the Tolkien connection, and more significantly, Ithilien grew out of the nonviolence movement of the late 1960s, particularly that centered in the Bay Area in California. Some of the earliest reports of the efforts to establish Ithilien appeared in *Kaliflower*, one of the first intercommunal periodicals, appearing in April 1969.[41] The September 1, 1969, issue includes an article on Ithilien in its formative stage and gives an Oakland address as the hub of "a bunch of Gandhi-type nonviolence freaks" and notes that they "are seeking land in southern Oregon."[42] The address was that of Peter Bergel, a founder of Ithilien, who reflects on the intent and the nature of the commune in a 2007 communication:

143

*The goal that drove me to found Ithilien was a desire to create a School of Nonviolent Living to which city dwellers could repair to get in touch with the earth and the country in order then to return to political struggle in urban environments. While at Ithilien, people would learn to actually live out the principles of Gandhian nonviolence. The reality fell somewhat short of these idealistic goals, I must admit, though.*[43]

The group looked for land in southern Oregon near Cave Junction, site of several early communes in Oregon. Instead, seventy-three acres of land was located on Doane Creek Road south of Willamina.[44] As Rudy Berg, a friend of the group, notes, "It took a while for everyone to make it up to the land, which initially had no buildings, thus the reference to Ithilien North during this transition period."[45]

Ithilien was incorporated as a church in the state and all members including children at the time of incorporation were considered elders. Few details of the early years are currently available but Herb Seal in his study of communes and intentional communities offers these observations:

*One Sunday I was part of a group that visited the Ithilien Commune in Oregon and was proudly shown the new pond that had been bulldozed that week. Everyone was excited about it because it meant not only water for irrigation but also a place to swim in summer. Good feelings were running high. I don't know what the Ithiliens' problems have been in the past, but I do know that the commune seemed very together on my visit, so much so that all of us who visited that day felt positive about living in such a place.*[46]

Ithilien did have problems, including the typical interpersonal ones but also some of a more central and physical nature. These are captured in the entry for the commune in the 1975 Community Directory published in *Communities* magazine:

*Into farming and being a family, with origins in the non-violence and potentials movement. 14 members (11 adults, 3 children). Becoming self-sufficient along with becoming integrated into the community. Work voluntarily through consensus. Not looking for members, and presently no visitors as our main house burned down after a superb Hallowe'en party. Ithilien resembles every other country commune—the joys and failures, continual learning, outside construction jobs, private cabins, ego hassles, auto junkyard, many projects, crafts, martyrs, prophets, cynics, angels, and people.*[47]

144

The commune phased out in the late 1970s but the land is retained by the community with the intent "to keep the land from ever being brought back into the real estate market."[48] One member and his wife have lived on the land since the 1980s. Former members of the commune held a reunion in 1991 and continue to communicate with each other.[49]

Other communes started in the late 1960s included the Ferry Street Sisters (or Ferry Street Home) in Eugene; Alta, with the only location given as Northern Oregon; and Temple Tribe in Portland. Of these, very little is known. A commune identified as Sunny Valley, in Sunny Valley, that began in 1968 was featured in one of the earliest documentaries on communes, titled *Year of the Communes* (1971), narrated by actor Rod Steiger.[50] The Crook's Creek commune was another of the many groups in Sunny Valley inspired by the publication in *Life* of the story of the Family of Mystic Arts and was one of the thirteen communes examined in detail in Hugh Gardner's *The Children of Prosperity* (1978).[51]

The first of many communes associated with the Jesus People movement were established in Oregon in 1968-69, including the House of Joy in Portland, and Christ Brotherhood and House of the Risen Son, both in Eugene.[52] The largest network of communal groups of the Jesus People movement, within Oregon and throughout the country, was one that came to be centered near Eugene. The Shiloh Youth Revival Centers, as they were called, had their beginnings in early 1968 in California, where John Higgins, Jr., a recent convert to Christianity, sought to share his zeal and enthusiasm about the Bible and the teachings and life of Jesus Christ. He rented a house in Costa Mesa in May 1968 that came to be known as the "House of Miracles," which became a magnet for youth interested in converting to Christianity and in spreading the word. The following spring several of these individuals moved to land outside Eugene and sought to construct their own commune and center for their evangelical mission. They chose Shiloh as the name for their organization from Genesis, and the property came to be known as The Land. As Joe V. Peterson notes, "It was their 'Garden of Eden,' a focal point of the community's history to the very end."[53] From this beginning, Shiloh Houses or Shiloh Youth Revival Centers sprang up throughout Oregon and the United States with about one hundred seventy communal houses existing in the height of the movement in the mid-1970s and over thirty of these in Oregon.

Although communal in nature, the Shiloh organization shared little else with other communal groups established at the same time. With a fundamentalist, Pentecostal Christianity as a common element, the focus and intent of these groups, as Peterson notes, was different from those of the hippie and other communes: "Shiloh's main motivation was not communal living, but rather Christian mission and evangelism." He continues, "It was not an earthly utopia its members sought, but a 'city of refuge' until the Rapture into the Kingdom 'built without hands'."[54] In many ways, Shiloh reflected some of the earliest communal experiments in America with a focus on Christian doctrine, eternal salvation, and a sense of millennial anticipation, as well as some of the same patterns of organization, with an authoritarian and patriarchal structure that did not mesh with the rising movements of the time, particularly among women. These aspects of Shiloh have been explored by Lynne Isaacson and others.[55] Shiloh, in fact, has prompted a wide range of studies, from organizational methods to reasons for leaving the community.[56]

Shiloh would lose membership in the late 1970s and essentially fade out by the end of the decade, but, in almost Biblical fashion, it had a second coming during the 1980s before financial and organizational issues led to its demise by 1989. Peterson suggests that an estimated one hundred thousand individuals experienced Shiloh in its twenty-year history, which undoubtedly makes it one of the most influential communal movements of the late twentieth century.[57] But Peterson also notes that those who experienced Shiloh saw it as both the "best" and "worst" experience and, although it may not have been intended as "an earthly utopia," the overall experience is one that presents a vivid example of the "good place" and "no place" dichotomy of utopia.

The discussion thus far has been primarily on those communities known to have been founded in the years 1965-1969. Others may have been established within this time frame but specific data on those dates are lacking. And there is no magical aspect of the change from 1969 to 1970 except to note that beginning in 1970 the number of communities in Oregon would increase substantially.[58] What is known, however, is that more than one hundred thirty communal utopian groups were initiated in Oregon from 1970 through 1979, and that total does not include those communities started earlier that continued to exist or were restructured in some fashion in the 1970s. As such, it is impractical, if not impossible, to treat each of the endeavors individually in this study but in the following chapter an effort is made to examine some important groupings of communities and to highlight a few selected communities as representative of types of communities that present an interesting perspective on Oregon's utopian heritage.[59]

# The Dream Continues: From the 1970s to the Twenty-first Century

*Looking out from the window*
*top of the barn—*
*The wet, burnished green*
*and empty fields—*
*The summer days come back*
*in a flush—*
    *work week, its color and climate of talk—*

*I quietly return to the*
*Indian corn*
*the working men*
    *the women's voices drifting up—*

*Together we are bringing in the sheaves*
*the music and mysticism of the work*
    *concealed in our hearts*

"The Farm" by David Kherdian[1]

An article in the August 29, 1971, *Eugene Register-Guard* highlights the outburst of communal activity then apparent in the rural areas of Lane County:

> *Ever since communes became a blossoming phenomenon in America during the 1960s, the rural countryside in and around Lane County has shown an obvious attraction for young adults seeking to carve out new lives on the land.*
>
> *The evidence is there, for those who drive the back roads and look for it.*
>
> *Painted on rural mailboxes or emblazoned on front porch signs, the unusual names of many of these communal groups are gaily displayed for the world to see.*
>
> *To list a few, there's "Hog Farm" near Marcola, "Christian Farm" near Brownsville and "Earth Rising" near Monroe. And there's "Church of the Creative" near Creswell, "Lynx Hollow Farm" near*

147

*Cottage Grove and "Footbridge" and "Indian Creek" farms near Swisshome.*
*And there's a "Hungry Hill Farm," "Live Wood Farm," "Rainbow Farm," and an "Organic Mud Farm," too.*
*They're among the several dozen small colonies, cooperatives and affinity groups—most commonly called communes—which dot the area's landscape.[2]*

A key criterion for groups is "low-cost land of marginal agricultural value, sometimes priced as low as $250 an acre." Such land in 1971 was getting hard to locate and costs were reaching $1000 an acre or more. The article also provides other criteria of communes seeking land: "The typical group has five requirements. The property must be secluded, it must be picturesque, it should have running water, it should be within an hour's drive of Eugene and it should have a livable structure ... or at least a temporary shelter where the group can live while building a livable structure."[3]

The concentration of communes near Eugene and elsewhere in Lane County is typical of how rural communes developed in Oregon, often in clusters. This presents one of the paradoxes of communal activity, already noted in relation to some early societies—they sought isolation but also connections with similar-minded groups and individuals, and some link with the outside community, particularly for commerce reasons. The outburst of communal activity ranged from the California border to the south and the Washington border to the north, but was primarily west of the Cascade Mountains, with just a handful of groups identified east of this geographic divide. Within this strip from the Cascades to the Pacific Ocean there were concentrations of communities in several areas. The area around Eugene has been noted and extended to Creswell and Cottage Grove to the south. West of Eugene, several groups settled in the Deadwood and Swisshome area. As seen with the Family of Mystic Arts, there was a draw to the Sunny Valley area in Josephine County and further to the north and west the Wolf Creek area became a hub for a large number of communities. Further south in Josephine County, just north of the California border, the land around Takilma and Cave Junction attracted several groups and the land between Williams and Grants Pass also became home to a number of communal groups. Across the county line in Jackson County, communities formed in Applegate, Medford, Central Point, Jacksonville, and Ashland. There were other smaller pockets of communities in the state and the Portland metropolitan area was home to numerous communal groups from the 1960s to the present. However, the significant number of communal groups situated in the southwestern corner of the states presents its own paradox as this area has been politically and culturally one of the most conservative in the state. Yet here was the home of perhaps the largest concentration of communes and intentional communities in the state and possibly even in the nation.

Efforts have been made to categorize these communities by social structure and types of communes. Herb Seal suggests that there were three most popular structures—open, co-op, and extended family. He also presents four predominant types of groups—agrarian, religious, political, and urban, and within the last offers three subgroups—student communes, "hippie crash-pads," and professional communes (i.e., for professionally employed individuals).[4] The categorization of these groups is in many respects a utopian task itself as the focus and intent of these groups often is not clear or consistent, changing with membership or over time. There are clearly religious types, such as the Jesus People groups as at Shiloh, but there is a broad range of "spiritual" groups, many of which do not fall within any organized religious group. Timothy Miller uses the catchall phrase "Secular Visionaries" to attempt to categorize a range of secular communities, many with social reform agendas. He also presents other types that are fairly broad and fuzzy enough around the edges to not be too limiting. Among these are group-marriage communes—some of which have already been noted—"communities of art and culture," "urban middle-class communes," environmental communes, and gay and lesbian communes.[5] Oregon had several of each type of these groups in the 1970s, plus others, but the immediate focus here will be on examples of one of these types that is particularly noteworthy in Oregon's communal history and utopian heritage.

Some of the most distinctive and lasting of these "new pioneer" communities in Oregon are lesbian communal groups, first established in the 1970s. Sandia Bear thinks that "Oregon might well have been the matrix out of which the movement sprang."[6] Miller agrees: "Oregon seems to have had had the largest concentration of lesbian communes and to have kept that distinction since."[7] The Web site of the Association of Lesbian Intentional Communities in 2007 includes ten communities, more than in any other state.[8] Most of these communities are located in southwestern Oregon in areas, as noted, also home to many other communal activities of the late 1960s and early 1970s, but there are others in the state, most notably the We'Moon Land near Estacada, which was the earliest organized women's land in 1973.[9] The development of numerous lesbian communal groups in Oregon was part of a broader movement for the establishment of women-only communities or women's land.

A confluence of various forces gave rise to the development of women's land in Oregon and throughout the country. The back-to-the-land movement that served as the basis for much of the communal activity and the broader

149

countercultural movement in general set the larger context. Building on this was the women's liberation movement in the late 1960s and early 1970s; as noted earlier and by a number of female commentators, sexism remained even within the communal groups of the period. One result, as noted by Ni Aódagain, who lived on the land for two decades, was "women began to break away from male-dominated communal arrangements and demand women-only space."[10] This separatism was vital for the achievement of freedom, independence, and power, which should have a familiar ring to it.[11] The separatist identity these women sought is rooted in the same utopian tendencies that are inherent in the founding of the United States and in most communal societies, from the earliest attempts in the Americas to those of the new pioneers of the 1960s and 1970s. That this concentration of feminist and lesbian communities would take place in Oregon possibly reflects that draw of the Edenic qualities of the state, but in this case Eve returned to the garden herself, along with her sisters. Thus the nature and success of this community of women in Oregon are continuing elements of the state's utopian heritage.

The herstory of women's land in Oregon provides rich documentation resources for these experiences, much of it coming from the voices of the women of the communities as they expressed themselves in numerous ways—stories, poetry, art, photography, and in writing their own herstory.[12] Many of the communities offered writing workshops and the collective activity that brought out *WomanSpirit* magazine from 1974 to 1984 is characteristic of the creative energy inherent in the movement. Ní Aódagaín explored this energy in a 1992 article:

> *This large southern Oregon women's community has over the years, developed and nurtured the belief that each woman is capable of creating; each woman is the daughter of the Muse. This community's herstory, its strength and longevity, its warmth and vitality, all stem from the honoring of this basic belief. The women of this community, in loving this belief and sustaining each other in it, have created a nurturing, caring environment where any woman can find support and encouragement on her journey as a creative woman.*[13]

150 Besides the support within and among individual communities, groups such as the Southern Oregon Writer's Group, Gourmet Eating Society and Chorus was also an impetus for women to express themselves.

One of the daughters of the Muses who captured the energy and existence of the women's land through photography, art, and writing was Tee Corinne (1943-2006), who was drawn to women's land in Oregon by this creative energy.[14] Other women were drawn to Oregon's land by the efforts of Jean and Ruth Mountaingrove, who began *WomanSpirit*, which

*Ruth and Jean Mountaingrove with two-woman saw (Ruth Mountaingrove Papers, University of Oregon)*

for ten years became a beacon for women on land throughout the United States and abroad, as well as an important draw for other feminist and lesbian publications, as many were sent on exchange with *WomanSpirit*. Jean and Ruth accumulated hundreds of titles from across the United States and over thirty countries. Three dozen titles were from Oregon and provide important, and often obscure, information and perspectives on women's land in the state. Such titles as *Women's Press*, *Woman's Place Newsletter*, and *Rag Times* were newsletters of the 1970s and 1980s that often include reports and news from these women's communities.[15] Other women have documented their experiences on the land in Oregon in published works, the earliest being the collective work that tells the story of the WomanShare Collective, first published in 1976 with a second printing in 1980 that includes a brief postscript with updates on the women involved in the community near Grants Pass.[16] WomanShare also was featured in a 1985 compilation titled *Lesbian Land*, which includes pieces on Golden and Rootworks.[17] In 2000 two works were published that focused on Oregon women's land—one focusing on Fly Away Home, and the other including discussion of many of the Southern Oregon communities and the success and challenges of these women on the land.[18] There also have been dissertations and theses written on Oregon's lesbian communities.[19]

This herstoriographical interlude illustrates that the experiences of the lesbian communities in Oregon are likely some of the best documented of the communal groups in the state and have been the subject of serious research, but in a typical utopian paradoxical way they are also the least known. Some of this is due to the success of these communities in their separatist intent but it also is due to their alternative sexual preference and rejection of patriarchal institutions. However, as noted earlier, it is these elements that highlight these communities as excellent examples of Oregon's utopian heritage.

The success of the lesbian communes can be attributed to the separatism and spiritualism inherent in the early communal efforts of the 1970s and the evolution to the concept of sanctuary, which Ní Aódagaín describes as "offering a physical space and an ideological constraint that encourages and supports women to become their most capable, creative and authentic selves."[20] Overarching all of these, perhaps, is the broader sense of community that brought these women together and manifested itself in such ways as the establishment of the Oregon Women's Land Trust (OWLT) in late 1975.[21] The first meeting of interested women was held in Eugene in mid-September and, in what can be considered unusual speed, the Articles of Incorporation of Oregon Women's Land were filed in December 1975. The purposes of the nonprofit entity were listed as:

*(1) To acquire, administer, and hold in perpetuity land and other assets in trust for the benefit of women, particularly for women who would otherwise be denied such access.*

*(2) To promote, explore, develop, and maintain the spiritual, physical, and cultural well-being of women by*

>*(a) providing women access to land*

>*(b) encouraging self-sufficiency and the means to attain it*

>*(c) fostering and exploring new patterns of human relations, and*

>*(d) providing other experiences to promote the well-being of women.*

*(3) To encourage thereby the development of harmonious and ecologically sound land-based communities*

*(4) To preserve land and protect it from speculation and over-development, and to foster the recognition of land as a sacred heritage and resource belonging to all, and*

>*(5) To serve as a resource for individuals and groups of women with interests in any of the above.*[22]

In May 1976, the third state conference of the Trust decided to purchase 147 acres near Canyonville and this became Oregon Women Land Farm, or OWL Farm (also known as Open Womyn's Land Farm). A year later in a report in *WomanSpirit*, the ideological background for OWLT was offered:

*The Oregon Women's Land Trust is a unique organization with little precedent. After studying land trusts in the past we realized that the land trust we developed would bear little resemblance to the traditional form. We are not nuclear families who are leasing land from a trust for private use; rather we are an ever-changing, mobile family circle who dream of seeing the land accessible to all women, and especially to those women who lack the connections and money to live on land individually. We are a grass-roots organization, not a high-financed conglomerate. We do not envision nor encourage small landowners who wish to homestead and work the land for farming, building or other use. We believe the land exists by her own right; we claim no ownership; our purpose is to be sensitive to the land's needs, to carry out a long range program to protect, revitalize, and restore land in the name of nature and ecology.*[24]

But the article adds, "if you have heard rumors that all is not idyllic on our 'open collective' land, we hasten to admit they may not be unfounded." OWLT, although unique in some respects, was like many other organizations in going through growing (or perhaps birth) pains. As the report continues, "In less than a year we have been besieged by contradiction and conflicts which are perpetually demanding to be resolved."[25] Such is life on the utopian frontier, but the Trust offered a venue to air out these grievances and attempt to address concerns, although issues continued to persist. In October 1978 another report on the Trust noted: "We need more unity among women. There is a sense of isolation among women living in the country and women living in the city. There is anger and pain about class privilege and racial inequalities."[26] The Oregon Women's Land Trust would continue to be a work in progress but its continued existence highlights the broader aspects of community that was part of the woman's land movement in Oregon, and that this network also included women in urban areas illustrates the expansion of this community.

The networking aspect of the Oregon women's community also was evident in the establishment of the Older Women Network (OWN), also known as the Older Women's Rural Community. A letter in the August 1975 issue of *Women's Press*, outlines concerns of older women in community:

> *As an older woman, it has been difficult at times to understand and accept the attitude of some younger women toward the concept of work; to "hang loose" and "flow with it," when I've come out of a generation where the work ethic and a sense of responsibility (born out of guilt) was so predominant. . . . Though older women are few in number in these feminist communities, they are on the increase. For us, it takes a certain amount of courage to move into this kind of life-style. Once we've made the decision to change our situation, we are faced with the question of how radical a change we dare make.*[27]

Others shared the writer's concerns and, following a workshop in October 1975 for older women, the Older Women Network was established, based in Wolf Creek. It would take over a year for the group to get organized, but

153

*Older women's gathering at Golden, 1978 (Ruth Mountaingrove Papers, University of Oregon)*

a report in March 1977 noted that they were looking for land in Oregon and northern California.[28] The land had been purchased by summer 1978, when a report in a special "Women's Issue" of *Communities* notes a workshop was being held to "establish a structure of our OWN ... as well as constructing a solar greenhouse on OWN's 60 acre farm/forest land in southern Oregon."[29]

Women had been living on the land in Oregon prior to the establishment of the Trust and OWN but these developments highlight the degree that the earlier efforts had evolved into a broader movement and a broader community. As noted earlier, the land outside Estacada that became known as WHO Farm may be considered the earliest of the Oregon communal groups designated as women's land in 1973, although Cabbage Lane at Wolf Creek, which later became a lesbian commune, was established in 1972 as a mixed community of gay men and lesbians. "The transformation," as Ní Aódagaín calls it, "from 'hippie sister' to 'lesbian land'" took place in 1974.[30] That year the WomanShare Collective was formed near Grants Pass and Golden was founded at Wolf Creek, although it too started out as a mixed community of gay men and lesbians.[31] It was at Golden that Jean and Ruth Mountaingrove started *WomanSpirit* before moving the operation to their own land at Rootworks in 1978. Between 1974 and 1979 several other lesbian communities were established in southwestern Oregon, including, as previously noted, OWL farm, as well as Rainbow's End, Fly Away Home, Steppingwoods, and Rainbow's Other End.

154

The sentiment of the women settling the land often was similar to that expressed by Bethroot Gwynn regarding Fly Away Home: "The first day I walked the land that was to become Fly Away Home, I knew it was perfectly designed to be a place where women would gather in sacred ceremony and where we could create new forms of ritual theater."[32] And it was typical of the creative expression that was part of this movement that some of the herstory of these communities was captured in verse, such as Valerie Sonnenberg's reflection on Rainbow's End and Rainbow's Other End on the sixth anniversary of the settling of the former:

> *Rainbow's End has an Other end*
> *A Family of seven womoon*
> *A collective of five*
> *A collective of two*
> *seven sisters collected on the hillside.*
>
> *Rainbow's End has 47 acres*
> *attached to the earth,*
> *praise the deeper 'truth'*
> *the earth's all one.*
> *We have a parcel to hold.*
>
> *The Other end is 2.85 more acres*
> *attached to Rainbow's End*
> *around the bend*
> *attached to the earth*
> *the whole earth.*[33]

As Catriona Sandilands notes, "By the late 1970s, these 'core' southern Oregon lesbian communities had been joined by other communities and properties ... to the extent that the I-5 corridor between Eugene and the California border came to be known as the 'Amazon Trail'."[34]

The rise of women's land in Oregon in the 1970s was just a small part of the communal outburst in that decade, albeit one of the most concentrated and cohesive. Over one hundred other attempts at communal utopias were attempted during the decade, though many lasted only a short time. And, as noted earlier, the estimate of the number of communities in existence or attempted may be considerably conservative. Although Kay Teeters wrote her honors thesis at the University of Oregon at the very beginning of this period (1970), her observations on the challenges of gathering data on these groups is applicable to later communal groups as well:

> *[I]t is rather difficult to get accurate information (or any information at all, for that matter) about many of these current utopian experiments. For one thing, their members tend to be highly mobile and often rather restless; many are students and swell the population during the summer months. Also, many of these communes have encouraged some degree of hostility from the local people. They discourage the casual visitor or sightseer and do not appreciate being treated as guinea pigs by social scientists. Very few of the communes make any effort to publicize their groups, fearing it may draw more hostility or tourists.*[35]

155

*Women gathering at OWL*
*(Ruth Mountaingrove Papers, University of Oregon)*

The inaugural issues of *Communities* magazine in December 1972 included a Community Directory, the first of many published by the magazine. Only eight communities in Oregon were listed, of which three were groups started in the 1960s (and previously discussed). The newer communities listed included The Eater Family in Coquille, a former theater group; Mu Farm in Yoncalla, which had been listed in *Alternatives* and *Communitas*, precursors to *Communities*; the Portland Group, which had land in Washington state; Rainbow Family of Living Light in Eugene, which started in Dunes City and would evolve into the Rainbow Tribe; and Vonu Life in Cave Junction.[36]

Religious groups continued to be numerous with an increasing number of these appearing in cities, such as the Manifest Sons and Prince of Peace communities in Portland, Orchard Street Church in Eugene with several communal households, and the Gospel Outreach ministries with locations in Grants Pass and Silverton. Shekinah in Logsden, in the north Coast Range, was connected with the Mennonite church, and Jesuit Volunteer Corps, which was started in the early 1950s, established a presence in Portland in the late 1970s as a communal group. Faith also was central to such groups as Artopia in Forest Grove that described itself as "not like other intenstional [sic] communities." The entry in the November/December 1976 issue of *Communities* continues: "Artopians know how to meditate, but do not wish to follow any religion or leader, because they realize they were born with perfectly good genius of their own. We wish to build and maintain a place for these 'known-to-themselves' artists who wish to pursue an individual dream."[37]

Other groups sought harmony with the Earth and with others, such as the Crack of Dawn community in the Cascades east of Ashland, Four Winds Farm outside Hood River, and Two Rivers Farm near Aurora, inspired by the work of the Sufi-influenced G. I. Gurdjieff.[38] The Terrasquirma group in Portland, formed by a chapter of the Movement for a New Society (MNS) called the Main Street Gathering, introduced recycling in the early 1970s as part of their environmentally conscious effort of alternative living.[39] And many other types of communal groups with variations of lifestyles, philosophies, and agendas were established, disappeared, and often revitalized in a different place, with a different name, and a different mix of individuals seeking to find or create their own Eden within Oregon.

Various movements centered in the San Francisco Bay area continued to influence communities in Oregon. One such movement was that of polyfidelity that came out of a group calling themselves The Purple Submarine, which based their practices on the concept of Kerista, developed in the mid-1950s by John Presmont, later known as Brother Jud. In the early 1960s the Keristans, as they became known, were prototypes of many aspects of what later would be viewed as hippie culture or, as Timothy Miller suggests, "the first of the 'Do It!' people."[40] Central to their beliefs was the concept of polyfidelity, described by one of their founders as a "group of best friends, highly compatible, who live together as a family unit, with sexual intimacy occurring equally between all members of the opposite sex, no sexual involvement outside the group, an intention of life-time involvement, and the intention to raise children together with multiple parenting."[41] Such Kerista groups as these were known as Best Friend Identity Clusters (or B-FIC), which evolved from the initial Living School Residence Group (LSR), later identified as a superfamily, and then as polyfidelitous closed group (PCG).[42] Polyfidelity, as the name implies, was more than just "free love"; it was based on "the feeling in the late sixties and early seventies that commonplace monogamous marriage and the nuclear family had failed as an institution," as David Harrington of the Crabapple community north

157

of Florence on the Oregon Coast describes the ideals behind the experiment.[43]

Although only a small number of communes in the Bay Area adopted polyfidelity as a practice, the ideals of the Keristans were presented in a number of ways, from posters to publications. The publication, *Kaliflower*, already noted, carried frequent items on the Keristans. It also included several articles on John Humphrey Noyes and the Oneida Community as that nineteenth century

CRABAPPLE
(503) 997-2781

POLYFIDELITOUS
HOMESTEADERS

We'd like to expand our family with more good people who want the benefits of an expanded family plus homesteading.

CRABAPPLE
Owen Harrington & Shirley Reeves
P.O. Box 1302
Florence, Oregon 97439

communal group was seen as a possible model for the ideals of polyfidelity.[44] Getting the word out on their vision also led the Keristans to publish their own newspaper, *Storefront Classroom*, in 1973 with articles, a directory of stores and other resources in the Bay Area, and "Far Out West," a comic strip drawn by Even Eve. This was followed in 1975 by the appearance of *Utopian Eyes*, published by the Performing Arts Social Society (PASS), which became the non-profit organization of the Keristans and was part of a broader activity called the Utopian Society. *Utopian Eyes* was published on a quarterly basis and included articles on utopian philosophy, histories of communal groups including Oneida, poems, songs, and "Far Out West" comics. It also published news of the Utopian Society.[45] Beginning with the Summer 1976 issue, a "Communal Living Directory" was published in the magazine; the only Oregon community listed was Cerro Gordo Ranch.[46] Cerro Gordo also was listed in the next issue (Fall 1976), as was a listing for Crabapple under David Harrington's name. The entry reads:

> *Crabapple is a polyfidelitous group of 3 seeking to expand to 6 to 10 people. They live on a farm where they raise their own food and are striving towards self-sufficiency. They are looking for rational, intelligent people who enjoy discussing ideas and have no conversational taboos. In David's words, they want to "rationally construct a comfortable family circle in which to grow joyously old."*[47]

The next issue also carried a listing for Crabapple as well as entries for Lichen at Wolf Creek, ECOS at Cave Junction, and individuals in Oregon seeking others to join groups in Blodgett, Selma, and Eugene. Besides the listing for Crabapple, only the Eugene listing mentions a polyfidelitous connection.[48] But no additional information is provided on this endeavor.

Crabapple, on the other hand, appears regularly within the pages of *Utopian Eyes*, including in advertisements beginning in 1979. Crabapple did not start out as a polyfidelitous community when it was established in 1975 but, as with many communities during this period, there was a shift in focus and intent after an initial effort failed to take hold. As Harrington recalls:

*Lifestyle Design*

at Cerro Gordo

Lynn, Allan, & Joey of the Homestead Neighborhood at Cerro Gordo are interested in creating a polyfidelitous family (or cluster of families) within Cerro Gordo.

People interested in polyfidelity, community design, & equality in a rural lifestyle, write:

Lynn Coody
Allan Jenson
Joey White
1142 Chestnut St.
Cottage Grove, OR.
9 7 4 2 4

*It was only after the breakup and failure of our first attempt that my then wife and I heard about and contacted the Keristans—mostly for moral support and possible help with recruiting new members. There ensued a great deal of contact between the rump of Crabapple and the Purple Submarine over the next couple of years, with both entities trying to keep their dreams alive. We visited the Haight-Ashbury digs of Kerista, and many of their people—mostly their rejectees— found their way up to visit us—even the leader-guru Judd [sic] himself, at one point.[49]*

The visit by Brother Jud and "the Travelling Gestalt Caravan of Kerista Village" took place in the summer of 1978 leading to a report in the Autumn 1978 issue of *Utopian Eyes*.[50]

As reported in the "Communal Living Directory" in *Utopian Eyes*, Crabapple was not the only Oregon community to attempt, at least in part, a polyfidelitous experiment. Cerro Gordo briefly was the home of a polyfidelitous group; this is often overlooked, but both Crabapple and Cerro Gordo were considered centers of the polyfidelity movement in the United States. The report of the 1978 visit to Cerro Gordo includes this information on polyfidelity at the community:

*The polyfidelity contingent at Cerro Gordo is held down by Allan, Lynn, and Joey. Cerro Gordo is a community now forming which encompasses quite a variety of lifestyles. Within Cerro Gordo is a group of people called the Homestead Neighborhood. Within the Homestead Neighborhood are Allan, Lynn, and Joey who are building a polyfidelitous center within the neighborhood. Lynn and Allan have been in a group together for about one year. The name of their group is Hedera and they want to communicate with anyone interested in combining polyfidelity, Utopian ideals, and the virtues of the simple life in a homestead setting.[51]*

Following this report was a map of the United States with five polyfidelity centers identified, including those in Florence and Cottage Grove. Others are in Seattle, Washington, and Sturgeon Bay, Wisconsin, as well as San Francisco. Advertisements for the Cerro Gordo polyfidelity group, like Crabapple, would appear in *Utopian Eyes*. Polyfidelity at Cerro Gordo seemed to fade from the scene but Crabapple continued to seek its polyfidelitous utopia into the early 1980s before, as Harrington notes, "things fell apart, as most such experiments have done over the years." Like several other communities

159

from the 1970s, the land is still owned by a member of the community but rented out. Harrington notes that the current resident, "a nice conservative lady from Michigan who had nothing to do with the former 'commune'" still was drawn to the land in the 1990s as she found it " 'edenseque' after having searched over much of America."[52]

The polyfidelity communities in Oregon were a small portion of the communal activity in the 1970s but they were an interesting twist and represented a significant portion of these communities in the United States at the time. Another group that sits on the fringes of communal utopian settlements was one that was involved with a cooperative project of reforestation in Oregon and other western states, from New Mexico to Alaska. A worker-owned cooperative, Hoedads, Inc., did not meet the criterion for communal living in the same fashion as other groups as there was no central community and the work crews were mobile. As Miller asks, "Can you be communal without a single permanent location, as in the case of the Hoedad groups that spent most of the year on the road in communal tree-planting projects?"[53] But Miller does include the Hoedads among the list of groups founded between 1965 and 1975, and others also list the Hoedads as a distinct utopian experiment.[54]

The concept for the Hoedads grew out of an earlier collaboration among three former University of Oregon students who became involved in tree planting in 1970. The three—Jerry Rust, John Sundquist, and John Corbin—called themselves the Triads and took on tree planting jobs in the Oregon Coast Range. In 1971 they were offered a job that required more help so others became partners in this venture, which now needed a new name and they agreed upon Hoedads, adopted from a tool used for planting trees. The expanding group received new contracts and established an organizational structure with Rust as president and the home of Jerry and his wife, Sidney, became the hub of the Hoedads operation.[55] In the next few years the Hoedads received more contracts and expanded their operation in other states throughout the West. Many of the work crews took on an identity of their own and adopted such names as Cougar Mountain Crew (the original Hoedads crew), Cheap Thrills, Comets, J-Roots, and Full Moon Rising, which was the first all-woman crew of tree planters.[56]

160 The Hoedads work crews lived communally while on jobs and the entire operation adhered to collective activities. The crews often were characterized as "tribal."[57] In many ways the Hoedads resembled the cooperative undertakings of the 1930s and can be considered a frontrunner in the revitalization of these practices in the 1970s. The organization, based in Eugene, published *Together,* which appeared every few months and included news of the organization, meeting agendas, information on finances and insurance, as well as stories, poems, photographs, and drawings. An item

in the second issue of *Together* in July 1974, titled "Business As Unusual," captures some of the spirit of the Hoedads:

> *Now we have it. Our work, our co-op is a lifestyle chosen by all of us. You are involved as you wish to be. There is no feeling of hopelessness and lonlineess [sic] at work; oh no, there is an overwhelming feeling of love and hope in the Hoedads. The glowing eyes and gleaming smiles of people who* know *that they are doing something new and right. Got our shit together.*[58]

As with any organization, even one with "an overwhelming feeling of love and hope," problems were bound to occur. They had a brief run-in with members of another communal group, Crow Farm, who were bothered by the manner in which the Hoedads had been given a contract.[59] The September 1975 issue of *Together* reports on the subpoena issued by the State of Oregon Unemployment Division, one of several encounters with state officials regarding business practices.[60] The matter of how crews were paid for their work also raised concerns not just between the crews and the organization but within the crews themselves. The all-woman crew of Full Moon Rising resigned from the Hoedads in 1979 over the method of payment but there also was dissent within the crew, resulting in a split. A second crew, called Half & Half, was set up and reestablished a link with the Hoedads, continuing as a crew into the 1980s.[61]

Membership in the Hoedads peaked at over five hundred in 1978, although estimates of the number of individuals who had been part of the Hoedads organization range from close to two thousand up to three thousand.[62] With changes in the lumber industry in Oregon and a general economic downtown in the state in the early 1980s, the Hoedads saw a period of decline. The organization underwent some restructuring to meet these changing conditions, but never regained its stature as during the heyday of activity in the 1970s. The Hoedads came to be viewed as a significant contributor to the development of worker cooperatives and "the prototype forest workers co-op."[63] The Hoedads were successful for many years in a different type of communal experiment and offered fuel for study on cooperative activities in the late twentieth century.

Three other communities established in the 1970s proved to have what it takes for a lasting existence, although all three went through fluctuations and often difficult times. These are the A, B, and C of Oregon's communal experience of the 1970s and beyond—Alpha Farm, Breitenbush, and Cerro Gordo. A summary of each of these groups provides further insights into the breadth of the communal scene in Oregon in the 1970s and the qualities, or at least learning experiences, that are necessary to make a community last more than a year or two, which more often was the case.

161

While the Family of Mystic Arts may have been the initial icon for the commune movement in America, and in Oregon when its location became known, Alpha Farm on Deadwood Creek Road outside Deadwood in western Lane County has become one of the lasting icons of Oregon's new pioneer era of communal groups. Pictured on the dust jacket of the oversized volume of Joel Sternfeld's 2006 photo essay, *Sweet Earth: Experimental Utopias in America*, is a scene from Alpha Farm in 2004 with one of the members of the community at the time and his son (and Chaos the cat on the roof).[64] Other than the more modern bicycle and some other small hints of more recent history, the photo might have been taken when Alpha Farm was founded in 1972. This was not the first time Alpha had been featured in a photo essay on America's communal groups—the Summer 1996 issue of *Aperture* included a piece on the farm.[65] A few years earlier, Alpha Farm had been included in an article in *Life* magazine.[66] And a photo on the cover of the September/October 1978 issue of *Communities* shows members of Alpha Farm helping neighbors bring in the hay, with an article that discusses the then six-year-old community (described as "mature") and its relationship with neighbors.[67] For over three decades Alpha Farm has been a symbol of Oregon's communal experience in the post-1965 era.

In addition to being the subject of photographic essays, Alpha Farm has been written about consistently through its existence, with some of the Oregon newspapers seemingly rediscovering the community periodically for a feature story. One of the first articles on Alpha appeared in the first issue of *Communitas* in which Glenn Hovemann, one of the founding members, relates the genesis of the idea for the community—which took place in a small inn in Massachusetts in spring 1971—through to the purchase of the land in late 1971 and the settlement there in early 1972 by thirteen individuals. As Hovemann describes the property, it was "a farm which comprised an entire small finger valley in Oregon's Coast Range of mountains, west of Eugene." He also notes: "Old maps of the place dating back to the stagecoach era name it Alpha. We could not have come up with a more suitable name: Alpha, the beginning."[68] Elsewhere in the same issue of *Communitas*, the following description is given: "Alpha is beginning. Thirteen adults and children, multiracial, multigenerational, 280 acres, a finger valley in the hills and forests of Oregon. Deeply pacifistic. Quaker heritage, socially conscious group."[69]

Hovemann presents some of the working assumptions of the founding group, including social, economic, political, and spiritual values. He also presents the initial ideas of the group related to money, occupations, growth, outward-directedness, and living arrangements: "Alpha was conceived not as a commune, with the psychological pressure-cooker that 'commune' sometimes implies, but as an intentional community where a

162

balance is achieved between individual and group lives."[70] Hovemann also lists the members of Alpha in 1972 with brief background information on each. Two listed are Caroline E. and James E., who are Caroline Estes and James Estes, co-founders of Alpha Farm, who would be involved with the community from its inception into the twenty-first century.[71] As Leah Yanoff notes in her 2006 examination of Alpha Farm, based largely on interviews of community members including Caroline and Jim Estes, "In many respects Alpha Farm still survives today because of Caroline's leadership and unrelenting dedication to the community and its ideals."[72]

With this continuity of leadership, and the strong adherence to the ideals of extended family and the application of consensus in the decision-making process, Alpha Farm has remained a successful, practicing community since 1972, and, with the addition of the Alpha-Bit bookstore and café in nearby Mapleton, it has had some commercial success as well, another frequent element of a lasting communal organization.[73] As with other long-lasting intentional communities, it has had its swings in membership and finances, but it remains a living icon of Oregon's new pioneers. The mission of Alpha Farm continues to reflect the ideas established by a group of individuals in the early 1970s: "Our purpose is to create a holistic community with each other and the earth, sharing along the way with the wider community and society."[74]

Another community started in the 1970s that continues three decades later with a mission very consistent with its original intent is Breitenbush, or Breitenbush Hot Springs Retreat and Conference Center, located near the town of Detroit, Oregon. Alex Beamer bought the land in 1977 to establish an intentional community and develop a retreat center at the natural hot springs in the picturesque setting in the Mount Jefferson area of the Oregon Cascades. A visitor to the community provided these observations and history: "Long before we arrived there, we had heard of its legendary qualities. Located about 60 miles east of Salem, Breitenbush Hot Springs used to be a traditional healing place for Native Americans. It became a commercial hot springs for the white community early this century but went out of business in the 1950's."[75] The efforts to rebuild the resort were substantial and coupled with these was a years-long struggle with the U. S. Forest Service regarding the logging of the old-growth timber around the springs. But by 1980 Breitenbush was hosting such events as the North Oregon Healing Gathering, a Sufi Camp, and their annual Come Unity Gathering. By the mid-1980s, Breitenbush was known as a meditation center and for its holistic health classes and workshops.[76]

The retreat and conference center operates as a worker-owned cooperative, as it has from the beginning, and the worker-owners live at the community. From its early history, the community utilized consensus building as core to

163

their mission. As the entry in the *Communities Directory 2007* notes: "The community lives across the river from the retreat center in an Ecovillage setting. We have regular community sharings, and three times a year we close for a four-day community renewal where we join together for training, fun, and community building."[77] Although the lifestyle of the community is welcoming and supportive, the work associated with the operation of the retreat and conference center is demanding and turnover is common.[78] But Breitenbush continues as a community and a worker-owned cooperative consistent with its initial vision.

The entry for the Cerro Gordo Ecovillage in the *2007 Communities Directory* states that "Our goal is a symbiosis of village, farm, and forest for up to 2500 people on 1200 acres—a whole valley on the north shore of Dorena Lake, near Eugene, Oregon. ... We're planning a self-supporting settlement, with organic agriculture, sustainable forestry, and a wide range of small businesses on-site."[79] The entry for the Cerro Gordo Community in the 1977 Community Directory in *Communities* magazine states, "Future residents are planning a care-free, do-it-yourselves village for 2,000-2,500 people with individually owned homes on commonly owned land clustered in a natural setting, 1200 acres on Dorena Lake."[80] Three decades separate the statements but the similarities in the listing, particularly with the emphasis on "planning," tell much of the story of Cerro Gordo over the years, as it has been in a constant state of planning for over thirty-five years. Although the goal has been a community of two thousand or more people, the 1977 entry states that there were "currently 100-plus members" or "potential future residents" while the entry for 2007 lists the population at forty-two. Cerro Gordo is a good place in concept that has gone no place in many respects in its long and challenging history.

The promise of an ideal city originated in the 1960s with Cerro Gordo founder, Chris Canfield, who as a teenager became enthralled with the lifestyle and beliefs of the Hopi Indians, particularly as related to the Earth and humans' relationship to the natural environment. Canfield and others started a group in 1970 called Pahana—"a Hopi term meaning 'one across the water, the lost white brother'," as Louis C. Androes notes. What became known as the Pahana Town Forum was based in Santa Barbara, California, and group discussions were held in several cities and letters of support were solicited. Androes continues, "In 1971, with approximately 100 families and pledges of $250,000 as a base, the group incorporated and Chris and his wife, Sherry, began a search in earnest for land suitable to their plans for an ideal city." Several potential sites for land were explored, including property near Grants Pass and Cave Junction in Oregon, near other communal sites. With assistance from an Oregon State University professor, Charles (Chuck) DeDeurwarder, land near Cottage Grove called the Cerro Gordo Ranch was selected as the site for the community and a land package was prepared.[81] In January 1974 fourteen hundred acres of land were purchased. A few months later, the lead article in the March/April 1974 issue of *Communities* was on "The New New Towns," and Pahana, as it was still being called, was included in this report with the author noting, "Pahana thus far seems to be the most 'successful' of the alternative new town projects."[82] The "successes" of the plan, however, soon turned into problems.

A report in the April 10, 1974 *Eugene Register-Guard* announced that the Lane County Planning Commission delayed a decision on whether to "allow a new utopian community to be built near Dorena Reservoir at Cottage Grove."[83] Again in late May, the Planning Commission delayed a decision on the proposed "demonstration community."[84] And in the June 12, 1974 edition of the paper it is reported, "The Lane County Planning Commission put up a barricade on the road to Utopia Tuesday night," under a large headline, "Cerro Gordo plan rejected; appeal pledged."[85] This would be the start of a steady stream of setbacks for Chris Canfield and the Cerro Gordo Project. In December of that year Canfield was "accused of violating Oregon securities law in raising money for the venture," and a cease and desist was issued.[86] For the next several years the headlines from the *Eugene Register-Guard* tell the on-again, off-again fate of the Cerro Gordo project.[87]

Thus went the first several years of the Cerro Gordo experiment. Reports in *Communities* and elsewhere put a positive spin on the potential for the community. Chris Canfield contributed a lengthy essay and description of the project to a 1981 book titled *Resettling America: Energy, Ecology & Community*.[88] This was part of the "tenacity" that Louis Androes addressed in his article in the Summer/Fall 1986 issue of *Communities*, which highlighted the continuing efforts to make Cerro Gordo a reality: "One of the major strengths of Cerro Gordo is the number of original settlers who have managed to hang on and are still striving for community. If nothing else, this has served as an impenetrable armour plate for Canfield, protecting and supporting when most needed."[89]

The long-running setbacks, from zoning issues to accusations of illegal practices, did take their toll and there was increasing tension between Canfield and some of his previous supporters.[90] The uncertainty carried into the 1990s. The dream of the ecovillage of Cerro Gordo was a sound one, and in its early stages it could have been a frontrunner of such ideal cities. However, the realities of achieving this dream have made Cerro Gordo a decades-long example of an unrealized utopian undertaking.

Alpha Farm, Breitenbush, and Cerro Gordo all were started in the 1970s and carried forward through the 1980s, 1990s, and into the twenty-first century with varying degrees of success. Most communities begun in the

165

1970s did not last beyond that decade, as there was a general shift away from the communal ideal in the ensuing decades. The utopian ideal still existed but in a different way and with different results. The number of new communal groups established in Oregon in the 1980s dropped considerably from the outburst of activity in the previous decade. Less than two dozen new communities were founded in Oregon from 1980 through 1989, over a hundred less than in the 1970s. The economic, political, and social climate was not as conducive to the same level of activity and the counterculture movement that had been a major catalyst for earlier communities had slipped by the wayside. A few of the same types of groups were established, included gay and lesbian communities as well as several religious groups. There also was a continuing interest in polyfidelity groups, spearheaded by the Polyfidelitous Educational Productions, Inc. (PEP), a non-profit organization based in Eugene that was linked to such groups as the Alternative Relationship Center and the Liberty Cluster, a group tied to the earlier attempt to establish a polyfidelitous cluster at Cerro Gordo.[91]

Two groups initiated in the 1980s that reflect a broader move to educational missions among many communal groups were the Aprovecho Institute (Research Center) in Cottage Grove and the Lost Valley Educational Center in Dexter. Aprovecho (from the Spanish for "I make the best use of") had its beginnings in the mid-1970s when individuals from several countries united "to help people in developing countries handle the changes that came with dwindling resources."[92] It became a non-profit organization and in 1981 bought land outside Cottage Grove to serve as the base for the service and educational mission of the organization. End of the Road is the community that was developed to be the home for those individuals operating the Research Center and to serve itself as a model of sustainability. Aprovecho offered courses, workshops, and internships in many areas of permaculture, sustainability, and appropriate technology. As the entry for Aprovecho states in the 2007 *Communities Directory*, "Our initial mission has expanded somewhat to emphasize sustainable forestry, food production, and related skills as well as appropriate technology, but the spirit of our work remains unchanged: to learn how to live together sustainably and ecologically and to help others to do the same in this and other countries."[93]

166

Reminiscent of the manner in which Robert Owen acquired the property of the Harmonists at New Harmony in the mid-1820s, the Lost Valley Educational Center acquired land in 1989 that formerly had been part of the Shiloh Youth Revival operation in Dexter. Like Aprovecho, the intent of Lost Valley is as an educational center, but it is also a community where the individuals involved in the activities of the center live in cabins, yurts, and a six-plex building. It is a practicing ecovillage, and many of the courses it offered, and continues to offer, are centered on sustainability, permaculture, and such concepts as Naka-Ima—living in the present through the practice of honesty—which also is central to the community at Lost Valley.[94] Perhaps more than any other communal group in Oregon, Lost Valley has taken an aggressive approach in advertising and sharing information about the educational opportunities offered and the community itself. *Talking Leaves*, the magazine of the community, is available on its Web site, and ads for Lost Valley appear regularly in such publications as *Communities* and *The Permaculture Activist*.[95] The community has had some challenges, including financial ones as well as organizational and interpersonal ones common to communal living, but it has maintained well as it approaches its twentieth anniversary.[96] Lost Valley, like Aprovecho, is a successful communal experience combined with an education center that reflects an ongoing shift in communal groups from the 1980s into the twenty-first century.

From 1990 to 2008 there was an increase in communal activity with at least thirty groups formed (or "forming") in Oregon from 1990 through 1999 and more than forty identified in some stage of formation from 2000 to 2007. The definitions of former/forming and even the existence of some of these groups become more problematic, but it does appear that there has been a steady increase in communal activity in the past two decades.[97] There are several reasons for this apparent increase. One of the most obvious is the growth in cohousing groups. An outgrowth of a Danish communal activity with origins in the 1960s, the concept of cohousing was introduced in the United States in the early 1980s by architects Kathryn McCarmant and Charles Durrett.[98] As the Web site of the Cohousing Association of the United States notes, cohousing is a link with the past with an "old-fashioned sense of neighborhood." The site also provides the "six defining characteristics of cohousing": Participatory process; Neighborhood design; Common facilities; Resident management; Non-hierarchical structure and decision-making; and no shared community economy.[99] These characteristics are very similar to those of earlier communal experiences with the lack of shared community economy presenting the most significant difference, although the cohousing spirit of "neighborhood" has a more suburban feel to it than many earlier communal groups. Cohousing caught on in Oregon early in the 1990s and over twenty such communities have formed or are forming.[100]

Another type of community accounting for new interest in communal living in the past two decades is the ecovillage, or groups involved in Earth activism. These groups are not on as large a scale as that attempted at Cerro Gordo, with several resembling more the communes of the late 1960s and early 1970s, and a number of them also are in urban settings, such as Maitreya Ecovillage in Eugene and Try/on Life Community in Portland, which serves as co-stewards of the land with Cedar Moon. Part

167

of the mission of these newer eco-conscious communities is an educational one, and other types of educational communities have also been established since 1990. These include the Association for Education, Research, and Integration of Occult and Universal Studies (or Aerious) at Deadwood, with a focus on metaphysics, and the Titanic Lifeboat Academy in Astoria, the name of which is a metaphor for keeping afloat in a postcarbon society, meaning that the Academy focuses on sustainable living.[101] The last two decades also continued to see the formation, and reformation, of some of the same types of groups as in the 1970s and 1980s, with the exception of fewer new religious groups established.

Although it has been impossible here to present more than a capsule view of Oregon's communal activity from the mid-1960s to the early years of the twenty-first century, what is clear is that the state continues to be a place where individuals and groups are drawn to seek a better life.

## CHAPTER TEN

# The Dark Side of Utopia

Anyone familiar with Oregon's past, communal or otherwise, may note the omission from previous discussions of two communities that have left a lasting mark on the utopian heritage landscape of the state. One of these likely is more widely known as it dominated the news of much of the mid-1980s in Oregon and elsewhere. This was the Rajneeshpuram settlement in north Central Oregon, also known as Rancho Rajneesh and by other names. The second is lesser known and much smaller than the Rajneeshees but also significant in exploring Oregon as a place for seeking perfection in one manner or another. This group existed early in the twentieth century and was popularly known as the Holy Rollers but also the Brides of Christ, followers of an individual named Franz Edmund Creffield.

## Cults

These two groups fall at the edges of the utopian communal experience in Oregon in a territory often referred to as cults. But "cult" is another word in the study of utopias and communal societies that is highly charged and problematic. Like commune, communists, and collective, cult is another "c" word that is often cast in a light that suggests the dark side of utopia. There are a number of reasons for this. Tim Miller addresses several of these in an essay that appears in several editions of the *Communities Directory*. As he notes: "For better or worse, intentional communities are often drawn into the 'cult' controversy. Communities, after all, in many cases do have features that many consider cultic." Miller suggests that the "'cult' scene is, by and large, seriously overblown." He also provides several common elements used to identify cults, including:

*a strong dominant leader*
*zealousness in attracting new members*
*preoccupations with getting money*
*suppression of questioning and doubt*
*indoctrination techniques to get people involved*
*major lifestyle restrictions on members*
*severing ties with families and friends*
*strong commitment of time to the group*[1]

169

Many, if not most, of these criteria can be applied to a variety of groups, including communities previously examined here, but also to a broad range of religious groups, as well as political groups and businesses. However, cults do exist and Miller counsels for "eternal vigilance" and offers several suggestions for evaluating intentional communities and religious groups.

Many "true" cults have had histories and outcomes that have highlighted their danger. But too frequently other groups are broadly generalized as cults based on incomplete information and the lack of a thorough understanding of their nature and intent. For example, the boundaries get blurred when we try to distinguish between *Sects, Cults, and Spiritual Communities,* as in this 1998 study. Included among the nine "nontraditional groups" in this "sociological analysis" are Heaven's Gate, Jesus People USA, The Farm (in Tennessee), Love Family, Amish women, and Scientology, a broad range of examples that by inference are categorized as cultic although they more aptly may be considered sects or spiritual communities.[2] The shifting landscape of what is defined as a cult has only enhanced fear and uncertainties about not only cults but other groups, such as sects and spiritual communities— and intentional communities in general—that get placed within the same sweeping categorization.

The "cult scare" in the last quarter of the twentieth century was based on three very vivid and tragic episodes—the Jonestown suicides and massacre in Guyana in 1978, the Branch Davidian tragedy in Waco, Texas, in 1993, and the deaths associated with the Heaven's Gate group in 1997. Each of these events has been studied and recorded extensively, including the Oregon connections with Heaven's Gate.[3] Other layers of the cult scare have also shaded views of intentional communities, and this was true not only in the late twentieth century but likely as long as there has been any movement of a communal society separate from the main society. As Miller suggests, many of the early and historical utopian communal societies in America have been viewed as cults, including the Shakers, the Harmony Society, and the Mormons. What made these groups stand out was, as Miller notes, "They were 'different,' and therefore obviously evil."[4] One could extend this argument back through history and see how many other groups would fall within these same parameters, from the followers of a Jewish carpenter's son put to death for his "difference," to too many cases of mass genocide associated with cleansing of the human race. In recent times, the term "cult" has been applied to such a range of groups as Jehovah's Witnesses and the Hell's Angels.[5] Thus the boundaries of "cults" can get as blurred as those of utopia, and for some the two blend into each other.

Much of the problem lies in the word "cult" itself. In his introduction to a cult-themed issue of *Communities,* Miller suggests: "The fundamental problem here is that the word 'cult,' as it is popularly used in the United States, no longer has any descriptive value. It doesn't communicate any clear, focused concept, but rather simply indicates a prejudgment or disapproval."[6] He points out that in certain fields, such as sociology, as well as in other countries the word does have some specific meanings, most related to religious worship, but the American popular usage has lost its sense of true value. Interestingly, many who use the word in its common derogatory manner would be surprised to learn that the root of the word is from the Latin *cultus*, meaning to worship, and early usage was for "reverential homage rendered to a divine being or beings," a meaning now obsolete.[7] The word does still refer to particular forms or systems of religious worship but the connotation often is derogatory, such as the quote attributed to "Wiley's Dictionary" in the popular comic strip *BC* by Johnny Hart—"Cult: The church down the street from mine."[8] Cult also has come to mean "devotion or homage to a particular person or thing," such as a cult following of a rock star, and a specific type of film has come to be known as a "cult film." For many though, the OED definition of "a relatively small group of people having religious beliefs or practices regarded by others as strange or sinister" applies to intentional communities. This negative view is not new.

## *The Holy Rollers*

The idea of cults not only has raised many fears for years but it also has captured the American imagination for decades, if not centuries. In his *Cults of America* (1964), Maurice Beam played to the curious and presented a book that, as the rear cover notes, provides "the authentic, colorful story of these cults, and of the men who founded them to satisfy their personal desire for sex, money, or power." Among the groups he examines are those promoting free love, nudism, polygamy, and voodoo. Included in this exposé is a chapter titled "Crazy after Women," in which he describes the "naked necromancer of the Oregon wilderness, [who] has become the archetype of the hell-raising breed of religious wise man." The man was Franz Edmund Creffield, who envisioned himself as the new Joshua. Beam minces few words in his description of Creffield:

> He was the most obnoxious person imaginable, yet women yearned for him and proved it by surrendering all they held most precious—their reputations, their marriages, even their children. He was mean, vicious, and conniving. Yet he was one of the saddest of human characters, for his life from beginning to end was tortured by painful desires, half quenched at times, but ever persistent, goading and relentless.[9]

The fascination, that would turn to horror, of Creffield became evident soon after he arrived in Corvallis in 1903 and a following of mostly young women formed to heed the call of the Second Joshua, as Creffield came to call himself. Over the next three years as the incredible story unfolded

171

of Joshua and the Holy Rollers, as his followers were popularly known, in a continuing sequence of bizarre twists, the newspapers of Oregon and elsewhere printed hundreds of reports of these events.[10] Prior to talking movies, radio, theater, and television, the saga of Creffield and the Holy Rollers made for unbelievable drama.

That interest would fade in time but it also reappeared periodically throughout the twentieth century and in interesting ways. One of the first to "rediscover" Edmund Creffield was journalist and historian Stewart Holbrook (1893-1964), who was often fascinated by what biographer Brian Booth calls "the lowbrow history of the region," as well as its offbeat history.[11] Holbrook wrote of "Oregon's Secret Love Cult" in the February 1937 issue of *American Mercury*, included Creffield and his followers in a collection of essays on crime, and also wrote about the group under two pseudonyms in two 1930s pulp magazines.[12] The attraction of this bizarre and sensational story to readers of pulp detective magazines also is evident in the story by Lewis Thompson published in the March 1951 issue of *Startling Detective* with the provocative title of "Nemesis of the Nudist High Priest," with accompanying suggestive illustrations.[13]

So what was this provocative story of Creffield and the Holy Rollers? The strange history of this group first formed in Corvallis can only be summarized here as the details are too numerous, and often unbelievable.[14] The story centers on Creffield, who as already noted has been labeled "the seducing prophet," "the sex-crazed prophet," and the "nudist high priest," but also would be called "the man who put the hex on San Francisco" and a guru.[15] Little is known of Creffield's early life, and his date of birth has been given from 1864 to 1873. It is known that he was German and in 1899 arrived in Portland, where he became an officer in the Salvation Army. Over the next two years he was stationed in several Oregon cities for brief periods.[16] He also wrote an essay on "Holiness" that appeared in the September 8, 1901 issue of the Salvation Army's *War Cry*. Soon thereafter he resigned from the Army to pursue his own brand of Christianity. He attempted to put this into practice in an effort called the Peniel Mission in The Dalles but, failing to find a following there, he moved on and became an itinerant preacher for a year or so.[17]

He reappears in late 1902 or early 1903 in Corvallis and was no longer Franz Edmund Creffield but Joshua the Second, a self-proclaimed prophet and leader of what he called the Church of the Brides of Christ. After preaching at various locations, including the Salvation Army headquarters in Corvallis, he obtained a following of about two dozen men and women, mostly younger women. The fledgling church met in homes of the members, centering on the home of Victor Hurt, his wife and two daughters. Here the lavish ceremony that would give the followers its named was practiced. Stewart Holbrook described this experience:

172

> *Pulling down all the blinds of the meeting place ... Joshua began a chant, swaying to its rhythm, waving his arms, and calling upon what he addressed rather familiarly as the Full Spirit to descend upon the meeting.*
>
> *The girls and women soon began to sway. They chanted; they moaned; they "spoke in tongues" and cried aloud while the prophet seemed to gain in stature and his normally calm eyes sank deep into his head, where they glowed like two pits of fire. The swaying and the chanting went on.*
>
> *Suddenly, like a thunderbolt, the prophet's voice boomed out: "Vile clothes, begone!" The whiskered fellow then disrobed and, without urging on his part, many of the women present did likewise. There was nothing coy about it, no sense of shame. They threw off their peekaboo waists, their skirts, and their multitude of petticoats; they tore wildly at their whalebone corsets, meanwhile moaning like all get-out.*
>
> *"Roll, ye sinners, roll!" thundered Joshua; and roll they did, some in chemises, some without, all over the bare floor, with Joshua and Brother Brooks rolling happily among them.*[18]

This demonstration was just part of the ritual, for Joshua also preached that he had been commanded by heavenly authority to find the next mother of God on earth. He took this command very seriously, as did many of the female followers, and, as Holbrook delicately describes, Joshua went about this "in a thorough and searching manner, which manner was obviously of the empirical school."[19] This move to sexual license, if not predatoriness, was too much for many of the married women in the group and they left, most with their daughters in tow. Some of the young women were sent to one of the asylums in the state to keep them from returning to these rituals of Joshua. The practices also created some conflicts within the Hurt family and the Holy Rollers were asked to quit using the Hurt home as their place of worship. Joshua and his followers then ended up on an island in the middle of the Willamette River where they built a wigwam and continued with their ritualistic practices through the summer of 1903.[20]

The Holy Rollers had remained largely out of the public view at first, but the move to the island along with the word getting out about their practices increased awareness of their existence and their activities. Those activities were often loud and Holbrook notes, "the vast workings of the Spirit could be heard on either shored of the mainland."[21] Public outcry became stronger throughout the summer and into the fall. When the weather turned in the fall, the group abandoned the island camp and returned to the Hurt house, where they resumed their public and private rituals. The front page headlines on *The Oregonian* for, perhaps appropriately, October 31, 1903, cry out: "BURN UP GOODS—Fanatics' Antics Excite Corvallis—Cats and Dogs

173

in Flames—Holy Rollers Destroy Everything in 'Carnal' Hands—Terrible Noise at Worship—Rolling on the Floor, Adherents Give Way to Shrieks, Shouts and Groans, Indicating Great Mental Anguish."[22] Victor Hurt grew increasingly annoyed with the group, particularly because Creffield and his principal disciple, Brother Brooks, had moved into the Hurt house when they returned from the island. *The Oregonian* for November 24, 1903, under the headline "Rollers Turned Out," reports: "Apostles Creffield and Brooks have been ordered out of the hospitable home which has given them such comfortable shelter for the past several weeks and they are thrown upon the cold and unappreciative world to shift for themselves as best they can."[23] Even though Creffield and Brooks were ordered from the Hurt home, the group still continued to congregate there leading others to take matters into their own hands. After nude photographs of the Holy Rollers were circulated, a group of vigilantes, known as the White Caps, arrived at the Hurt House on the evening of January 4, 1904, where they bound Joshua and three of his followers and led them away. They were taken outside of town where Joshua and Brother Brooks were tarred and feathered.[24]

This action would seem to suggest the end of the Holy Rollers and their charismatic leader but the story only gets started here. Although terrified by the action of the White Caps, Joshua did not flee—as did Brooks—but instead agreed to marry one of his followers, Maud Hurt. The ceremony took place in the Albany courthouse, using his given name. Although the marriage appeased some, the White Caps were alarmed that Joshua had returned to Corvallis and sought to capture him again, but he fled. He

*Edmund Creffield in prison
attire (Oregonian)*

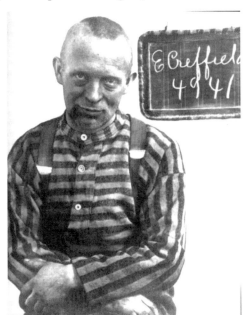

174

ended up in Portland where he resumed his practice of seeking out the next mother of Christ with a former disciple who was now married. Her husband discovered the two and filed charges for Joshua's arrest for adultery. However, Joshua once again vanished and, after several weeks of no sightings, it was again thought that the Holy Rollers episode was over.

That was until Joshua was discovered hiding, in the nude, under the Hurt house in Corvallis, where he apparently had been since escaping the outraged husband nearly three months earlier. Several of his followers were feeding him through the floorboards but his other needs were left unattended. Holbrook describes his appearance as told to him by one of the police officers on the scene when Joshua was apprehended: "Naked as to clothes, and dirty as a hog, the prophet was hairy all over as a water spaniel, and most wonderfully endowed by Mother Nature withal. His beard grew down to his stomach and was bushy as a clump of black alder. But he was as thin as a fence rail. He was weak, too, and could scarcely stand."[25] Joshua was taken to Portland and tried for adultery; the jury quickly found him guilty. Throughout the trial, Joshua was unrepentant. He was sentenced to two years in the Oregon State Penitentiary but he was released in December 1905 after seventeen months for good behavior.[26]

Again, the story might have ended, but it continued to get more complex. While Joshua was in the penitentiary Maud had obtained a divorce under pressure from her father. Also, Joshua had continued his discussions with the Almighty during which it had been revealed to him that he was not just to beget the new Christ on Earth but that he himself was the new Christ. With this new development, he left prison and went to Seattle where he beckoned Maud to join him, which she did. They were remarried in April 1906. That same month he put a curse on the "modern Sodoms of Seattle, of Portland, of San Francisco, of Corvallis itself." A few days later San Francisco was devastated by an earthquake and subsequent fires.[27] The coincidence of these events no doubt impacted the call issued earlier for the Brides of Christ to gather on land near the Yachats River on the Oregon Coast and many hastened to get to the site, which Holbrook describes as "a true Garden of Eden in which the flock could live in a manner best suited to them and their beliefs, free from the profane gaze of scoffers."[28] Joshua and Maud headed south to join them. As they were boarding a ferry to cross Yaquina Bay, the husband and father of two women who were rejoining the Brides of Christ attempted to kill the prophet but his revolver misfired five times, a sign for some of Joshua's invincibility. But subsequent events would prove otherwise.

After accompanying the group along the coast, Joshua informed his followers that he was going north to find a better location for their new Eden. He and Maud took separate paths back to Seattle; hers took her through Albany, where others learned of her plan to meet with Joshua in Seattle. One of these was George Mitchell, the brother of one of the most devoted disciples of Joshua, Esther Mitchell, who vowed to kill the man who had taken advantage of his sister. Mitchell traveled to Seattle and on May 7, 1906, found Maud and Joshua in the retail district of Seattle, where he shot and killed the prophet with a single bullet to the head.

Even with Joshua dead, the story continued in a series of strange events. First, the Brides of Christ who were waiting for Joshua's return did not initially hear of his death and, when they did, they believed he would rise from the dead to be among them. Eventually, after many tried to flee from authorities, they were rounded up and returned to their homes, still reluctant to give up on Joshua's prophecies. In July 1906 George Mitchell was tried for the murder of Creffield and was acquitted, which was a popular decision. However, as he was preparing to return to Oregon from the trial in Seattle, he was gunned down on the railroad platform by his sister, Esther. She had avenged the death of her prophet and was subsequently committed to an asylum as she was considered too insane to even be brought to trial.

Thus ended the amazing story of Joshua the Second and the Holy Rollers, but the impact of these events was felt for some time. Although the communal aspects of this group were never fully explored amid all the sensationalism associated with their beliefs and activities, the group did have an impact on the longer-term views of cults in Oregon. As more than one writer has noted, any time a group outside the norm gains some publicity in the state, the Brides of Christ resurface yet again. During the 1980s there was another renewal of fascination with Creffield, perhaps because public attention was riveted on another strange cult in the state.[29]

## Rajneeshpuram

The more well-known and infamous of Oregon's cult communities was established in north central Oregon in the early 1980s and became a national and international focal point of media during its existence and of study since its collapse. As such, it became the most documented communal experiment in Oregon's history with additional information still being identified and researched. To present an exhaustive discussion of Rajneeshpuram is beyond the scope of this study but it is examined here in the broader sense of a communal utopian experiment that went bad.

The Bhagwan Shree Rajneesh arrived in Oregon in late 1981 after having already established a worldwide following based on the ancient Indian tradition of sannyas. He was born Chandra Mohan in December 1931 in the Indian state of Madhya Pradesh. He achieved the state of enlightenment in March 1953 but did not share this publicly for many years until he adopted the title "Bhagwan," meaning "Enlightened One," in 1971. Well educated, with degrees from the University of Saugar, he was a professor of philosophy at the University of Jabalpar in the early 1960s, but he saw his life work not in the classroom but as a spiritual leader, or Acharya. His views on Indian politics, sexual practices, and organized religion, as presented in several lectures and presentation, alienated many among Hindu leaders, but he was attracting disciples.

As his following grew in the late 1960s and early 1970s, Rajneesh started meditation centers that eventually led to a broader organization called the Neo-Sannyas International Movement. By the mid-1970s, centers existed in fifteen countries, including the United States, and Rajneesh had adopted the title "Shree," meaning "Sir." The organization based in Poona (now Pune), India, at the Shree Rajneesh Ashram grew quickly with a university, publication operations, and meditation centers. Much of the management of the organization was under the control of his first female administrative assistant, Ma Yoga Laxmi. The rapid growth of the organization along with violence and sexual practices among his disciples created tensions in India and in 1980 efforts were undertaken to locate a new center for the organization. That same year Rajneesh began a period of silence in which he made no public appearances and worked only through his closest assistants.[30]

It was at this point that a woman named Sheela Silverman, later Ma Anand Sheela, came into the picture, assuming the role of principal assistant to Rajneesh and displacing Laxmi in the role of business manager of the organization. She first bought a mansion in Montclair, New Jersey, for a meditation center named Chidvilas, where Rajneesh joined her and several disciples in 1981. In the meantime, Sheela also acquired sixty-four thousand acres of land in Eastern Oregon that had been the Big Muddy Ranch, located outside Antelope, a small town in Wasco County. Plans were soon underway to convert the ranch to a center for the Rajneesh sannyasins, a community that would be called Rajneeshpuram. From the outset there were tensions and conflicts between the Rajneeshees, as they became known, and several individuals and groups—county commissioners, land-use boards, and the U.S. Immigration and Naturalization Service, among others. If nothing else, this increasing opposition intensified the resolve of Sheela and other Rajneeshee leaders to transform the former ranch into a community that would accommodate up to seven thousand residents and many more visitors.[31]

177

Events moved quickly in the story of Oregon's largest cult experience; by 1982 the community was growing rapidly and tensions with external parties were also increasing. Commercial efforts by the Rajneeshees heightened controversy. Politically, the growing number of sannyasins impacted the balance of power and the result was that the city council of Antelope was taken over by the followers of Rajneesh, assisted by the resignation of some council members who refused to sit at the table with the elected Rajneeshees. By November 1982 Antelope was renamed the "City of Rajneesh." Over the next two years a number of facilities were completed at the community, including a large hotel, but this growth was countered by poor policy decisions that harmed efforts to incorporate Rajneeshpuram itself. Efforts were initiated to deport Rajneesh on grounds of visa irregularities but these were rescinded. Several church and state issues were raised; Oregon Attorney General David Frohnmayer became involved, as did U. S. Senators Mark Hatfield and Robert Packwood, who saw the actions of the sannyasins as an attempt to take control of the county with larger objectives in mind. Such fears were supported when in the spring of 1984 the Rajneeshees brought in thousands of homeless individuals to bolster their ranks for a county election. This was one of Sheela's plans and was called the Share-A-Home Program. Following the election the homeless were distributed in other areas.

The climax of these efforts to gain control of Wasco County came in September 1984 when Sheela's directive to place salmonella in the salad bars at several restaurants in the county resulted in the sickening of over seven hundred fifty people. This act of bioterrorism, which was merely a test to see how it would impact the electorate, was only discovered after some of the conspirators came forward with information.[32] But this desperate act was a sign that the wheels were coming off the Rajneeshee wagon. Many of the faithful followers of Rajneesh were disillusioned by the tactics of Sheela and others and an exodus from Rajneeshpuram began in late 1984 and early 1985. Before details of the poisoning, as well as stockpiling of weapons, wiretapping, and other crimes, became known, Sheela and a few other leaders fled the country in mid-September 1985, after which Rajneesh broke his five-year period of silence to accuse Sheela and others. An investigation by federal and state offices, including the discovery of salmonella cultures, confirmed the many charges made against Sheela and other members of the community. Rajneesh himself was not indicted but as Rajneesh tried to leave the country, he and those accompanying him were detained in North Carolina on October 27, 1985. The following day FBI agents arrested Sheela and two others in West Germany, and they were extradited to Portland where they were tried on multiple counts. As part of an agreement, Sheela and the other leaders were given prison sentences and Rajneesh was allowed to leave the country. Sheela served two and a half years in prison in California and then was released for good behavior and deported to West Germany. Bhagwan Shree Rajneesh, or Osho as he became known in 1988, returned to Poona where he died in January 1990.[33] The community of Rajneeshpuram quickly dissolved after the events of 1985 and the fleet of ninety-three Rolls-Royces that Rajneesh had accumulated, and which became a symbol of his lifestyle, were sold.

As with the Holy Rollers, this is just the outline of the story of this cult activity in Oregon. The dimensions of the Rajneeshpuram episode are much greater than those of Joshua and his followers, with elements covering a multitude of interests and investigations. There have been studies, reports, interviews, documentaries, and other types of examinations and portrayals of Rajneeshpuram. From religion and philosophy to politics and economics, and from sociology and psychology to gender studies and family studies, there is continuing analysis of this cult activity.[34]

The cult aspects of Rajneeshpuram are evident but questions are often raised as to its utopian nature. If one can get past the classic case of power corrupting, as it was for Sheela and other leaders, the roots of utopianism are evident in the basic beliefs of Rajneesh. Even in the concept of the community in Oregon, there were familiar utopian elements in Rajneeshpuram. Susan J. Palmer, who has written on many aspects of the community, notes that the Rajneesh movement was "based on utopian principles of communalism, free love, absolute birth control, work as 'worship,' ecological harmony, and women's rule."[35] Some or all of these elements could be found in many utopian experiments from the Shakers and the Oneida Community to communes and intentional communities in Oregon in the 1960s to the present. The tension arises when, as Kirk Braun notes, there is a clash not only of cultures but a clash of "utopias." The "utopia" of the residents of Antelope and surrounding areas was disrupted by this "other" utopian scheme, particularly one that fell within the broader framework of a cult.[36]

The place of Rajneeshpuram in the broader context of the American communal utopian experience was explored in the mid-1980s, just as the community started its meltdown, in two very different studies. Marie Daly Price presented *Rajneeshpuram and the American Utopian Tradition* as a discussion paper published by the Department of Geography of Syracuse University in April 1985.[37] The following year Frances FitzGerald included Rajneeshpuram as one case study of several in *Cities on A Hill: A Journey Through Contemporary American Cultures*. That she uses as her title the phrase John Winthrop used to describe his Puritan vision of a new life in America seems fitting in this brief examination of cults. For were the Puritans a cult? And was America established on cultist ideals?

# Oregon As Utopia

In a 1943 letter to his literary agent accompanying the manuscript for a utopian novel he was submitting for her consideration, Ellis F. Lawrence (1879-1946), founding Dean of the School of Architecture and Allied (Fine) Arts and campus architect at the University of Oregon, wrote: "I feel the times call for some positive idealism to renew faith—perhaps another 'News from Nowhere'—'The Great Good Place,' or 'Utopia'."[1] Although Lawrence's manuscript, titled "The City of Good Will," was never published, the fact that he sought to create a "dream world," as he called it, is reflective of an attitude about how to deal with issues confronting not only society as it was in the middle of a world war but also those confronting him personally. That he alludes to earlier works by William Morris, Henry James, and Thomas More suggests his awareness of these examples of utopian literature but also reveals that he saw this means of expression as presenting some "positive idealism" that was much needed.

Lawrence's "City of Good Will" is just one of a number of examples of attempts by individuals and groups in Oregon to create some positive idealism for themselves and the world around them. Most of these attempts were in the form of communal societies, as previously examined, but others, like Lawrence's, were of a literary nature. Lawrence's fantasy "city," in fact, combined the two by writing of an attempt to establish an ideal place along the Oregon coast. Beyond the Edenic nature of its landscape and the regenerative qualities that drew settlers from the nineteenth century to the present, and beyond the nearly three hundred known attempts to establish a communal Eden within the state, Oregon has been home to other utopian undertakings, from literary efforts to practical applications such as city planning.

## Portland As Utopia

One of the more intriguing of these came from the pen of Portland author Jeff W. Hayes (1853-1917).[2] In 1913 two identical compilations of stories by Hayes were published, both including a forty-page utopian story— "Portland, A.D. 1999"—that projects what Portland would be like at the end of the twentieth century.[3] Using a convention common to many utopian authors of the late nineteenth and early twentieth century, Hayes presents a mysterious eighty-six-year-old woman who has the ability to see into the future. She begins her prophecy, as do many other prognosticators in the utopian literature, by noting changes in transportation. The locomotive and trolley car have become too slow and have been replaced by "aerial" cars, fueled by "electricity, gasoline, compressed air, or perhaps still another potent agent, at present undeveloped, which will usurp the place of all others, be cheaper, safer, and more reliable than any known energy." The vehicle will travel "at a height of 500 feet" and those riding "will look down and express a feeling of sympathy for those who must brave the dangers besetting life on the surface of this mundane sphere." She also points out that "The death dealing automobile will be a thing of the past and even the merry motor cycle will have gone the way of the equine." Hayes' perception of the possibility of alternative fuel is noteworthy, as is his assessment of the safety of the automobile. [4]

Wooden homes have been replaced by "warm concrete dwellings" and in lieu of bridges across the Willamette River there are now 75–foot-wide tubes across the water. Without automobiles the need for hard surface pavements was eliminated and these were removed "so that the city of Portland is one perpetual system of parks, where the youngster may play to his heart's content." All the hills within and around Portland, except for Council Crest, have been leveled, giving "a vast area to West Portland which is vital to its business supremacy." While some of these prophecies seem outrageous, the accuracy of others is intriguing. Hayes' seer notes, "Portland embraces the entire county of Multnomah and a portion of other adjacent counties and extends in an unbroken line from Oregon City to the South to the delta of the Columbia river on the North, East to the foot of Mt. Hood and West to Hillsboro." [5]

Women play a more critical role in government, and "the name of Abigail Scott Duniway is held in much reverence by these women officials." Many laws in support of women's rights have been enacted, including what the prophetess sees as a major one that allows a woman to retain her own name after marriage. Due in part to the increased role of women in government, the city has a higher moral code with "less roistering, riotousness and lawlessness than existed earlier in the century." As in many other literary utopian schemes, prisons and jails have been done away with and "a more Christian form of dealing with the socalled [sic] lawless element has been inaugurated and the fruits became immediately apparent." The government is a mix of "the best ideas of all parties" and "Much of the good in Socialism has been incorporated ... and the objectionable part of the doctrines were eschewed." [6]

181

Portland still celebrates the Rose Festival in 1999, as well as the Fourth of July; fireworks are no longer used but the "music from 50,000 phonographs was listened to." Such festivities, however, were without alcohol, not because of a universal acceptance of temperance or prohibition but because in 1950 "it became quite observable that corn, wheat, rye, and other cereal entering into the production of alcohol had lost the power to ferment and to be converted into beer, wine, and whiskey," but the existing breweries, including Weinhard's, were still profitable "selling a splendid substitute for alcoholic beverages."[7]

The styles of dress have changed, with the women "in more of an Oriental style which is very becoming and which allows them more individuality of design." The men and boys "have gone back to the old Knickerbocker style of dress and they look very natty in their new attire." And while the women have adopted an Oriental style, the sprinkling of Chinese and Japanese of the city, who "have long since passed the stage of 'undesirables'," have taken on "the American style of dress, even to the knee pants." There is "now one universal language" with a "dictionary containing less than 8,000 words but it is capable of expressing every idea that the human mind may evolve."[8]

It is the technological developments that seem most startling, including "a huge air bag with a rubber hose attached" that "is allowed to rise to a height of about 1,000 feet and water from the Willamette river is pumped up into it" and then used to sprinkle the streets and parks. Also addressed is the means of lighting the city as "one immense electric light suspended in the air at a height of several thousand feet which illumines the city as bright as the brightest day."[9] But "the greatest of all the world's inventions" was introduced in 1925 and "consisted of an apparatus which may be applied to a balloon or other object suspended in midair, which, when properly adjusted and at a certain height from the earth, will shake off or cast off the gravitation of the earth allowing it to suspend in space as an independent planet." The intent of this was that instead of traveling, you could simply wait for your destination to come to you. For example, since "the earth moves from west to east, so that it will take a little more than 20 hours at this latitude to have New York roll around to you, but if you are in New York it would take but four hours to come to Portland, provided they are in exactly the same latitude." Of course, there are flaws in this great invention but the possibilities in Hayes' Portland of 1999 seem limitless.[10]

Other technological developments rely on natural resources and suggest something of a true sense of prophesy by Hayes. The ocean's waves have been harnessed to produce electricity. Water is obtained from the ice packs of Mt. St. Helens and Mt. Hood, although the latter erupted in the mid-1970s cutting off water supply for some period. Enhancements also were seen in health and medicine and in many other aspects of life on the cusp of the twenty-first century.[11]

## Oregon and Utopian Literature

Hayes' short utopian story was one of many published in the late nineteenth and early twentieth century but it is the only one known to have focused on Oregon, and Portland specifically, for the location of its perfected society. There were other utopian works written by Oregon authors or published in Oregon during this period but their subject and focus were broader. The earliest might be the serialized novel "'Bijah's Surprises" by Abigail Scott Duniway that appeared in the weekly *The Pacific Empire* from April through December 1896. Set in Idaho's Lost River Valley, where Duniway lived briefly, the story tells of the establishment of a utopian community that reflects the ideals of the author.[12] Not long after, Charles Cole wrote a utopian novel set on Mars, where strict vegetarianism is practiced, including no cooking, and free love and sexual equality are elements of the Martian society.[13] Mars is also the setting for a 32-page self-published work by Ira S. Bunker, which presents a Christian Science utopia with an emphasis on technological advancements.[14] Francis H. Clarke wrote a story in which the Rockefeller estate is willed to the government and becomes the basis of a paternalistic brotherhood.[15] Two of the stories in Dr. Charles Ellsworth Linton's 1920 collection include utopian themes, technological advancements, telepathy and the absence of sin.[16] There were likely other works written by Oregon authors or published in Oregon but many of these works have been lost or discarded. In the late twentieth century, the utopian literary landscape was redefined in many ways by Oregon author Ursula K. Le Guin. Her novel, *The Dispossessed* (1974), was subtitled *An Ambiguous Utopia* and her *Always Coming Home* (1985) also centered on utopian themes, as do several of her other writings.[17]

## Ecotopia and Utopian Planning

Also later in the century Oregon was included as part of the secessionist country of Ecotopia presented in Ernest Callenbach's novel of that name in 1975.[18] Callenbach captured some of the environmental consciousness already evident in the state by the mid-1970s. Oregon had pioneered some key environmentally friendly legislation, most notably the Oregon Bottle Bill of 1971, championed by Richard Chambers as a way to eliminate litter on Oregon's road and in its wilderness. The Terrasquirma community in Portland spearheaded early recycling efforts. As seen in the rise of ecovillages among communal groups in the late twentieth and early twenty-first centuries, the spirit of Ecotopia continues to be present in Oregon.

183

Portland was once more viewed as utopia by Jeff Kuechle in a 1989 article in the *Pacific Northwest* magazine.[19] And almost a decade later Bradshaw Hovey examined Portland's recent past to illustrate "how good planning, effective citizen participation, and regional growth management can produce what is commonly referred to as a good 'quality of life'."[20] Hovey's study was not published in a city planning journal but in the journal of the Society for Utopian Studies, for he was demonstrating what he called "Portland's Implicit Utopian Project."

He begins his essay by noting, "Among American urban planners, Portland, Oregon, is increasingly celebrated as a kind of planning utopia," explaining "Portland is widely recognized as a leader in downtown redevelopment, neighborhood revitalization, historic preservation, urban design control, mass transit development, and regional growth management." He characterizes these developments as "utopian" as they are "the product of no less than 30 years of cumulative work toward a widely-shared and continuously discussed vision of what life in Portland could and should be." Basing his assessment on what he labels as "downtown planning," "the neighborhood revolution," and "planning the region," Hovey argues that certain actions, including design, preservation, and organization or institutional development "have not only advanced the utopian vision of a more livable Portland, they have created the condition for the further pursuit of the vision."[21] Specifically he uses the removal of the Harbor Freeway on the west side of the Willamette and replacing it with the Tom McCall Park as one example of community-based action in leading toward a more livable urban environment. He also notes the development of Pioneer Courthouse Square in downtown Portland and the light rail system as models of this vision, as well as the cessation of the proposed Mt. Hood Freeway. His suggestion that these earlier developments "created the condition for the further pursuit of the vision" seems to have been justified as in the decade since he wrote this article the city of Portland has seen a continuation of many of those elements he identified as aspects of this utopian vision and has continued to garner praise as a livable—if not perhaps entirely utopian—city.[22]

## Eden and Utopia in the Twenty-first Century

Where are Eden and utopia in the early twenty-first century? Environmental historian and ecofeminist philosopher Carolyn Merchant posits that "Today's incarnations of Eden are the suburb, the mall, the clone, and the World Wide Web" and, for some, "The shopping mall, the 'new main street,' the gated community, and the Internet are the latest visions of a reinvented Eden."[23] Merchant's study of the modern reinvention of Eden is important for addressing the various changes in what constitutes the concept of an ideal place in the early twenty-first century, including the virtual place of the Internet and the Web. In fact, the virtual environment has taken on many aspects of community through social networking sites and the proliferation of blogs and other means of interacting. But is this Eden?

More clearly tied with an Edenic concept, and with a sense of achieving an ideal place, are some of the other types of modern Edens Merchant identifies, including suburbs and gated communities. Suburbs, as noted earlier, were an outgrowth of the new town and greenbelt movements in the first half of the twentieth century. But even by the late 1960s, the utopian aspects of the suburbs were turning dark.[24] Since then several efforts to escape from suburbs have led to other utopian schemes, including the many communal groups from the 1960s to the present. As Merchant suggests, one of these reinvented Edens is the gated community.

In many respects gated communities—and to a lesser degree home owners' associations—are neo-communal entities. There is a definite intent of separatism that historically is common to communal societies and for many there are forms of governing reflective of communal groups, ranging from consensus building to an occasional charismatic leader. As Edward T. Blakely and Mary Gail Snyder title their chapter on lifestyle communities—retirement communities, golf and leisure communities, and gated new towns—these are intended as "Gates to Paradise." However, the impact of such communities is evident in the title of their 1997 study—*Fortress America*.[25] The gates, of course, are to keep "others" out (and reflect back to the Genesis account of Adam and Eve's banishment from the Garden), which brings up the always-present question of utopia for whom.

Oregon not only has a rich history of communal experiments but the state has been home to these other types of communities with utopian underpinnings—from suburbs to gated communities. Consistent with its utopian heritage, Oregon is at the forefront of this clash over the competing ideals of "perfection" as represented in these and other types of communities, and the broader issues of how land in this Eden is utilized. The highly controversial land use ballot passed in Oregon in 2004 (Ballot Measure 37) is one of the most recent examples of these varying views of what Eden and utopia mean within the state.[26] In fact, Oregonians' penchant for the ballot measure as a means to modify their "Eden" has been a constant since it was first implemented as the Oregon System in 1902. For many, the capability to make such decisions at the ballot box is viewed as an ideal aspect of living in the state; for others, it raises the basic question of "whose utopia is it?" That is a question Oregonians will continue to pursue, but most feel that they are in the right place to achieve utopia, whatever it is for them.

That is the beauty, and frustration, of utopia, for it may be a good place for some and a no place (or even a bad place) for others, or both a good place and a no place at the same time for any group or individual. Thomas

185

More likely would be pleased that we are still grappling with this issue nearly five hundred years after he gave us the word. But although he most likely intended his fictitious island to be a "no place," the message (the "More-al"?) is that it is important to continue to strive to realize the good place.

This survey of Oregon's utopian heritage has sought to show that there continues to be that seeking of perfection within the state, even when the dark side of utopia appears now and then. Early pioneers saw Oregon as Eden, and efforts continue to achieve that paradise.

# From Abba's Way to The Zoo:
## A Resource Guide to Oregon's Utopian Heritage

Presented here are works used in this study as well as a broad range of printed and other resources related to Oregon's communal history not discussed in any detail in the survey. The intent is to document what is available but also to provide a starting point for further information and research on these communities. Following an introductory section on general works on utopian and communal studies that serve as the background for this study, the resources are organized by the name of a community (real or planned) in alphabetical order. Information on location, dates, inclusion in directories, and publications or Web sites is provided for most communities. The final "Miscellaneous" section includes a variety of advertisements or announcements in publications related to individuals or groups that were seeking to form new communities or to join existing communities. For groups with extensive listings, resources are presented in the format in which they exist (e.g., journal/ magazine articles, monographs, theses, newspaper reports, videos).

### General Works on the American Utopian and Communal Experience

Ald, Roy. *The Youth Communes*. New York: Tower Publications, 1970.

Albertson, Ralph. *A Survey of Mutualistic Communities in America*. Reprinted from *Iowa Journal of History and Politics*, 34 (1936). New York: AMS Press, 1973.

Atcheson, Richard. *The Bearded Lady: Going on the Commune Trip and Beyond*. New York: John Day Company, 1971.

Berry, Brian J. L. *America's Utopian Experiments: Communal Havens from Long-Wave Crises*. Hanover, NH: Darmouth College, 1992.

Bestor, Arthur, Jr., *Backwoods Utopias: The Sectarian Origins and the Owenite Phase of Communitarian Socialism in America, 1663-1829*. Philadelphia: University of Pennsylvania Press, 1950.

Bouvard, Marguerite. *The Intentional Community Movement: Building a New Moral World*. Port Washington, NY: Kennikat Press, 1975.

Braunstein, Peter, and Michael William Doyle, eds. *Imagine Nation: The American Counterculture of the 1960s and '70s*. New York and London: Routledge, 2002.

Calverton, V. F. *Where Angels Dared to Tread*. Indianapolis and New York: Bobbs-Merrill Company, 1945.

Case, John, and Rosemary Taylor. *Co-ops, Communes and Collectives: Experiments in Social Change in the 1960s and 1970s*. New York: Pantheon Books, 1979.

Clark, Elmer T. *The Small Sects in America*. New York: Abingdon-Cokesbury, 1949.

Cohen, Daniel. *Not of the World: A History of the Commune in America.* Chicago: Follett Publishing Company, 1973.

*Communities Directory: A Guide to Cooperative Living. 1995 Edition (revised for 1996).* Rutledge, MO: Fellowship for Intentional Community, 1996.

Dare, Philip N. *American Communes to 1860: A Bibliography.* Bibliographies on Sects and Cults in America, Vol. 12. New York & London: Garland Publishing, 1990.

Eaton, Joseph W., and Saul M. Katz. *Research Guide on Cooperative Group Farming.* New York: H. W. Wilson Company, 1942.

Ebert, Donald Drew, and Stow Persons. *Socialism and American Life.* Princeton, NJ: Princeton University Press, 1952.

Egerton, John. *Visions of Utopia.* Knoxville: University of Tennessee Press, 1977.

Fairfield, Richard. *Communes USA: A Personal Tour.* Baltimore, MD: Penguin Books, 1972.

Fogarty, Robert S. *All Things New: American Communes and Utopian Movements, 1860-1914.* Chicago and London: The University of Chicago Press, 1990.

Fogarty, Robert S. *Dictionary of American Communal and Utopian History.* Westport, CT.: Greenwood Press, 1980.

Fogarty, Robert S., comp. *American Utopianism.* Itasca, IL: F. E. Peacock Publishers, 1972.

Forsey, Helen, ed. *Circles of Strength: Community Alternatives to Alienation.* Gabriola Island, BC, Canada: New Society Publishers, 1993.

Friesen, John W. and Virginia Lyons Friesen. *The Palgrave Companion to North American Utopias.* New York: Palgrave Macmillan, 2004.

Gardner, Hugh. *The Children of Prosperity: Thirteen Modern American Communes.* New York: St. Martin's Press, 1978.

Gide, Charles. *Communist and Co-operative Colonies.* Translated by Ernest F. Row. New York: Thomas Y. Crowell Company, [1930].

Guarneri, Carl J. *The Utopian Alternative: Fourierism in Nineteenth-Century America.* Ithaca, NY: Cornell University Press, 1991.

Hall, John R. *The Ways Out: Utopian Communal Groups in an Age of Babylon.* London, UK: Routledge & Kegan Paul, 1978.

Hayden, Dolores. *Seven American Utopias: The Architecture of Communitarian Socialism, 1790-1975.* Cambridge, MA: MIT Press, 1976.

Hedgepeth, William. *The Alternative: Communal Life in New America.* New York: Macmillan, 1970.

Herscher, Uri D. *Jewish Agricultural Communes in America, 1880-1910.* Detroit, MI: Wayne State University Press, 1981.

Hertzler, Joyce Oramel. *The History of Utopian Thought.* New York: Macmillan, 1923.

Hinds, William Alfred. *American Communities: Brief Sketches of Economy, Zoar, Bethel, Aurora, Amana, Icaria, The Shakers, Oneida, Wallingford, and the Brotherhood of the New Life.* Oneida, NY: Office of the American Socialist, 1878.

Hinds, William Alfred. *American Communities. Revised Edition. Enlarged to Include Additional Societies, New and Old, Communistic, Semi-Communistic and Co-operative.* Chicago: Charles H. Kerr & Company, 1902.

Hinds, William Alfred. *American Communities and Co-operative Colonies.* Second Revision. Chicago: Charles H. Kerr & Company, 1908.

Hine, Robert V. *California's Utopia Colonies.* San Marino, CA: Huntington Library, 1953.

Hine, Robert V. *California Utopianism: Contemplations of Eden.* San Francisco, CA: Boyd & Fraser, 1981.

Holloway, Mark. *Heavens on Earth: Utopian Communities in America, 1680-1880.* New York: Library Publishers, 1951.

Horton, Lucy. *Country Commune Cooking.* New York: Coward, McCann and Geoghehan, 1972.

Houriet, Robert. *Getting Back Together.* New York: Coward, McCann & Geoghegan, 1971.

Jackson, Dave. *Coming Together.* Minneapolis, MN: Bethany Fellowship, 1978.

Jackson, Hildur, and Karen Svensson. *Ecovillage Living: Restoring the Earth and Her People.* Foxhole, Dartington, Devon, UK: Green Books; Holte, Denmark: Gaia Trust, 2002.

Janzen, David. *Fire, Salt, and Peace: Intentional Christian Communities Alive in North America.* Evanston, IL: Shalom Mission Communities, 1996.

Jerome, Judson. *Families of Eden: Communes and the New Anarchism.* New York: Seabury Press, 1974.

Jones, Helen Dudenbostel, comp. *Communal Settlements in the United States: A Selected List of References.* Washington, DC: Library of Congress General Reference and Bibliography Division, 1947.

Kagan, Paul. *New World Utopias: A Photographic History of the Search for Community.* New York: Penguin Books, 1975.

Kantar, Rosabeth Moss. *Commitment and Community: Communes and Utopias in Sociological Perspective.* Cambridge, MA: Harvard University Press, 1972.

Kantar, Rosabeth Moss, ed. *Communes: Creating and Managing the Collective Life.* New York: Harper & Row, 1973.

LeWarne, Charles Pierce. *Utopias on Puget Sound, 1885-1915.* Seattle and London: University of Washington Press, 1975.

Manuel, Frank E., and Fritzie P. Manuel. *Utopian Thought in the Western World.* Cambridge, MA: Belknap Press of Harvard University Press, 1979.

McCamant, Kathryn, Charles Durrett, and Ellen Hertzman. *Cohousing: A Contemporary Approach to Housing Ourselves.* Berkleley, CA: Ten Speed Press, 1994.

McLaughlin, Corinne, and Gordon Davidson. *Builders of the Dawn: Community Lifestyles in a Changing World.* Walpole, NH: Stillpoint Pub., 1985.

Mercer, John. *Communes: A Social History and Guide.* Dorchester, UK: Prism Press, 1984.

Miller, Timothy. *American Communes, 1860-1960: A Bibliography.* New York & London: Garland Publishing, 1990.

Miller, Timothy. *The Quest for Utopia in Twentieth-Century America. Volume I: 1900-1960.* Syracuse, NY: Syracuse University Press, 1998.

Miller, Timothy. *The 60s Communes: Hippies and Beyond.* Syracuse, NY: Syracuse University Press, 1999.

*Modern Man in Search of Utopia [The Modern Utopian].* San Francisco: Alternatives Foundation, 1971.

Moment, Gairdner B., and Otto F. Kraushaar, eds. *Utopias: The American Experience.* Metuchen, NJ, and London: Scarecrow Press, 1980.

Morgan, Arthur E. *Nowhere Was Somewhere: How History Makes Utopias and How Utopias Make History.* Chapel Hill: University of North Carolina Press, 1946.

Morris, James M., and Andrea L. Kross. *Historical Dictionary of Utopianism.* Lanham, MD: Scarecrow Press, 2004.

Mumford, Lewis. *The Story of Utopias.* New York: Boni and Liveright, 1922.

Negley, Glenn. *Utopian Literature: A Bibliography with A Supplementary Listing of Works Influential in Utopian Thought.* Lawrence: Regents Press of Kansas, 1977.

Negley, Glenn, and J. Max Patrick, eds. *The Quest for Utopia: An Anthology of Imaginary Societies.* New York: Henry Schuman, 1952.

Neville-Sington, Pamela, and David Sington, *Paradise Dreamed: How Utopian Thinkers Have Changed the Modern World.* London: Bloomsbury, 1993.

Nordhoff, Charles. *The Communistic Societies of the United States; From Personal Visit and Observation: Including Detailed Accounts of the Economists, Zoarites, Shakers, The Amana, Oneida, Bethel, Aurora, Icarian, and Other Existing Societies, Their Religious Creeds, Social Practices, Numbers, Industries, and Present Condition.* New York: Harper & Brothers, 1875.

Noyes, John Humphrey Noyes. *History of American Socialisms.* Philadelphia, PA: J. B. Lippincott & Co., 1870.

Oved, Yaacov. *Two Hundred Years of American Communes.* New Brunswick, NJ, and Oxford, UK: Transactions Books, 1988.

Pease, William H., and Jane H. Pease. *Black Utopia: Negro Communal Experiments in America.* Madison: State Historical Society of Wisconsin, 1963.

Pitzer, Donald E., ed. *America's Communal Utopias.* Chapel Hill, NC, and London: The University of North Carolina Press, 1997.

Popenoe, Oliver, and Chris Popenoe. *Seeds of Tomorrow: New Age Communities That Work.* San Francisco, CA: Harper & Row, 1984.

Rexroth, Kenneth. *Communalism: From Its Origins to the Twentieth Century.* New York: Seabury Press, 1974.

Roemer, Kenneth M., ed. *America as Utopia.* New York: Burt Franklin & Company, 1981.

Rhodes, Harold V. *Utopia in American Political Thought.* Tucson: University of Arizona Press, 1967.

Roskind, Robert. *Memoirs of an Ex-Hippie: Seven Years in the Counterculture.* Blowing Rock, NC: One Love Press, 1971.

Sargent, Lyman Tower. *British and American Utopian Literature, 1516-1985: An Annotated, Chronological Bibliography.* New York and London: Garland Publishing, 1988.

Schehr, Robert C. *Dynamic Utopia: Establishing Intentional Communities As A New Social Movement.* Westport, CT: Bergin & Garvey, 1997.

Seal, Herb. *Alternative Life Styles.* Singapore: Printed for CCS, Inc. by FEP International, 1974.

Selth, Jefferson P. *Alternative Lifestyles: A Guide to Research Collections on Intentional Communities, Nudism, and Sexual Freedom.* Westport, CT: Greenwood Press, 1985.

Shugar, Dana R. *Separatism and Women's Community.* Lincoln, NE, and London: University of Nebraska Press, 1995.

Skinner, Charles M. *American Communes: Practical Socialism in the United States.* Brooklyn, NY: Brooklyn Daily Eagle, 1901.

Solis, Miguel J. *American Utopias (1683-1900): Evolution versus Revolution: A Descriptive and Bibliographic Dictionary.* Bloomington, IN: The Author, 1984.

Sternfeld, Joel. *Sweet Earth: Experimental Utopias in America.* Göttingen, Germany: Steidl, 2006.

Stobbart, Lorainne. *Utopia, Fact or Fiction? The Evidence from the Americas.* Stroud, Gloucestershire, UK: Sutton Publishing Ltd., 1992.

Stockwell, Foster. *Encyclopedia of American Communes, 1663-1963.* Jefferson, NC: McFarland & Co., 1998.

Summerhawk, Barbara, and La Verne Gagehabib. *Circles of Power: Shifting Dynamics in a Lesbian-Centered Community*. Norwich, VT: New Victoria Publishers, 2000.

Sutton, Robert P. *Communal Utopias and the American Experience: Religious Communities, 1732-2000*. Westport, CT: Praeger, 2003.

Sutton, Robert P. *Communal Utopias and the American Experience: Secular Communities, 1824-2000*. Westport, CT: Praeger, 2004.

Sutton, Robert P. *Modern American Communes: A Dictionary*. Westport, CT, and London: Greenwood Press, 2005.

Todd, Douglas, ed. *Cascadia—The Elusive Utopia: Exploring the Spirit of the Pacific Northwest*. Vancouver, BC: Ronsdale Press, 2008.

Ward, Hiley H. *The Far-Out Saints of the Jesus Community: A Firsthand Report and Interpretation of the Jesus People Movement*. New York: Association Press, 1972.

Webber, Everett. *Escape to Utopia: The Communal Movement in America*. New York: Hastings House, 1959.

Weisbrod, Carol. *The Boundaries of Utopia*. New York: Pantheon Books, 1980.

Wooster, Ernest S. *Communities of the Past and Present*. Newllano, LA: Llano Colonist, 1924.

Zicklin, Gilbert. *Countercultural Communes: A Sociological Perspective*. Westport, CT, and London: Greenwood Press, 1983.

## Community Listings

The following information may be presented; if the specific information is unknown, it is not listed:

**Place:** If known, as specific a location as possible is given. In many cases, this may be the nearest town or post office.

**Dates/Formed/Forming:** For nineteenth-century and early twentieth-century communities, inclusive dates are given. For later groups, the best date known when the group was "formed" is given. For some, the term "Forming" is given when evidence of a date of establishment is lacking.

**Directories:** Included here are sources that include directories to communal groups that include the specific community. Brief title information is given for the following sources:

Ald, Roy. *The Youth Communes*. New York: Tower Publications, 1970.

Association of Lesbian Intentional Communities (online http://www.alapine. com/pages/ALICdirectory.htm)

Cohousing Directory (online http://www.cohousing.org/directory)

*Communities* magazine (various issues that include directory information)

*Communities Directory* (editions for 1996, 2000, 2005, and 2007). Fellowship for Intentional Community.

Communities Directory (online http://directory.ic.org/)

*Directory of Collectives* 1985. West Coast. USA. Canada. Berkeley, CA: The Intercollective, [1985].

*Directory of Intentional Communities: A Guide to Cooperative Living. 1990/91 Edition.* Evansville, IN: Fellowship for Intentional Community and Stelle, IN: Communities Publications Cooperative, 1990.

*Directory of Intentional Communities: A Guide to Cooperative Living. 1992 Edition.* Evansville, IN: Fellowship for Intentional Community and Rutledge, MO: Communities Publications Cooperative, 1992.

Jackson, Dave. *Coming Together*. Minneapolis, MN: Bethany Fellowship, 1978.

Mercer, John. *Communes: A Social History and Guide*. Dorchester, UK: Prism Press, 1984.

Miller, Timothy. *The 60s Communes: Hippies and Beyond*. Syracuse, NY: Syracuse University Press, 1999.

*Shewolf's Directory of Wimmin's Land. Fifth Edition, 2007-2010.* [Melrose, FL: JRB, 2007].

**Formerly:** This includes any previous name for a community.

**Also see:** Reference to alternate name.

**Note:** This includes additional information about a community such as subsequent name(s) or locations, and other descriptive information.

**Publications:** If the community produces a publication on a regular basis, this is noted here when known.

**Web:** If a Web site exists for the community, it is noted here.

**Archives/Manuscripts/Oral Histories/Photographic Collections:** If there are any special collections or archival resource available for a community, this is noted here.

For some more recent communities (e.g., Aprovecho, Lost Valley), numerous listings for calendar events and other activities are included to reflect the nature and extent of educational offerings and commerce activities.

## Abba's Way
Formed:       1970s
Directories:  Miller, *The 60s Communes*: 253.

Duin, Julia. "Authority & Submission in Christian Community." *Communities* 92 (Fall 1996): 52.

## Aerious/Yewwood
Place:        Deadwood, 93640 Deadwood Cr. Rd.
Formed:       1992
Directories:  *Communities Directory* (2000): 196.
Publications: *Aerious: Journal of Metaphysics*
Note:         Association for Education, Research, and Integration of Occult and Universal Studies
Web:          http://www.aerious.org/

## Agape Inn
Place:        Eugene, 745 W. 10th Ave.
Formed:       1970
Directories:  Miller, *The 60s Communes*: 253.

Baker, Ann. "Young Converts Join Hands as Christian Household." *Eugene Register-Guard* (March 6, 1971): 2A.

## Agate Acres
Place:        Central Point
Forming:      2001

[Communities Forming – Agate Acres, Central Point, Oregon]. *Communities* 110 (Spring 2001): 76.
[Communities Forming – Agate Acres, Central Point, Oregon]. *Communities* 111 (Summer 2001): 75.
[Communities Forming – Agate Acres, Central Point, Oregon]. *Communities* 112 (Fall 2001): 67.
[Communities Forming – Agate Acres, Central Point, Oregon]. *Communities* 113 (Winter 2001): 75.

## Alcyone
Place:        Ashland
Formed:       1979

McLaughlin, Corinne, and Gordon Davidson. *Builders of the Dawn: Community Lifestyles in a Changing World* (Walpole, NH: Stillpoint Pub., 1985), 350.

## Alpha Farm
Place:        Deadwood, 92819 Deadwood Cr. Rd.
Formed:       1972
Directories:  "Commune Directory" (*Communities* 7): 29.
              "1975 Community Directory" (*Communities* 12): 24.
              "Directory 1977" (*Communities* 24): 5.
              "Directory of Intentional Communities 1978" (*Communities* 30): 33.
              *A Guide to Cooperative Alternatives*, 1979 (*Communities* 38): 164.
              "1981 Directory of Intentional Communities and Resources" (*Communities* 46): 32.

193

"1983 Directory" (*Communities* 56): 57-58.
"1985 Directory of Intentional Communities" (*Communities* 66): 43.
Mercer, *Communes: A Social History and Guide*: 128.
*Directory of Collectives*, 1985: 73
*Directory of Intentional Communities*, 1990: 169.
*Communities Directory*, 1996: 214.
*Communities Directory*, 2000: 199.
*Communities Directory*, 2005: 94-95.
*Communities Directory*, 2007: 128.

Web:       www.pioneer.net/~alpha/

[Ad – Building Strong Organizations Through Consensus – Alpha Institute].
    *Communities* 127 (Summer 2005): 66.
[Ad – Consensus Decision Making and Meeting Facilitation, a workshop with
    master facilitator Caroline Estes – Alpha Institute]. *Communities* 89 (Winter
    1995): 71.
[Ad – Consensus Decision Making and Meeting Facilitation, a workshop with
    master facilitator Caroline Estes – Alpha Institute]. *Communities* 90 (Spring
    1996): 63.
"Age-old Lifestyle, Pure Environment Still Draw People to Alpha Farm." *Salem
    Statesman Journal* (May 30, 1987): 4b, 5b.
"Alpha Farm" in Robert P. Sutton, *Modern American Communes: A Dictionary*
    (Westport, CT and London: Greenwood Press, 2005): 6.
Altongy, Janine. "Alpha Farm, Deadwood Creek, Oregon." Photographs by
    Eugene Richards. *Aperture* 144 (Summer 1996): 60-73.
Bjerklie, Steve, and Diana Leafe Christian. "How Are Communities Preparing [for
    Y2K]?" *Communities* 101 (Winter 1998): 36-39.
Boyce-Abel, Olivia. "Preserving Community Land: Conservation Easements &
    Other Tools." *Communities* 110 (Spring 2001): 24-29.
Brumann, Christoph. "The Dominance of One and Its Perils: Charismatic
    Leadership and Branch Structures in Utopian Communities." *Journal of
    Anthropological Research* 56(4) (Winter 2000): 425-51.
Colt, George Howe. "For the Foreseeable Future (The American Family, Part Six)."
    Photographic Essay by Eugene Richards. *Life* 14 (December 1991): 76-87.
"Communal Quest Alpha Farm Sets Example, Proves That It Is Possible to Live in
    Harmony with Self, Others and the Environment." *The Oregonian* (August 30,
    1987).
[Communities with Openings]. *Communities* 89 (Winter 1995): 69.
[Communities with Openings]. *Communities* 90 (Spring 1996): 70.
[Communities with Openings]. *Communities* 91 (Summer 1996): 72.
[Communities with Openings]. *Communities* 92 (Fall 1996): 70.
[Community Calendar – May 10-15 – Consensus Decision Making and Meeting
    Facilitation, with Caroline Estes]. *Communities* 90 (Spring 1996): 68.
[Community Calendar – Oct 4-9 – Consensus Decision Making and Meeting
    Facilitation, with Caroline Estes]. *Communities* 91 (Summer 1996): 71.
[Community Grapevine]. *Communities* 96 (Fall 1997): 8.
[Community Grapevine]. *Communities* 97 (Winter 1997): 8-9.
[Community Grapevine]. *Communities* 103 (Summer 1999): 11-12.
"Cooperative Independence: A Mix of Personalities Populate Alpha Farm, a
    Holistic Community in the Coast Range." *The Oregonian* (December 9, 2001).
[Cover photo]. *Communities* 34 (September/October 1978).
Estes, Caroline. "Consensus Ingredients" in *Directory of Intentional Communities:
    A Guide to Cooperative Living. 1992 Edition.* (Evansville, IN: Fellowship

for Intentional Community and Rutledge, MO: Communities Publications Cooperative, 1992): 78-81.

Estes, Caroline. "Sometimes the Magic Works: Alpha Farm Ten Years Later." *Rain* (June 1982): 8-9.

Greenbaum, Sarah. "48 Hours on Another Planet: Work Ethics & Anarchism on a Cooperative Farm – Alpha Farm, Deadwood, Oregon." *BootsnAll Travel* http://www.bootsnall.com/travelstories/na/feb02alpha1.shtml

Harkovitch, Mitch. "Alpha-Bit: Charmingly, Disarmingly Nice." *The Siuslaw News* (Spring 1991): 21-22.

Hovemann, Glenn. "Alpha." *Communitas* 1 (July 1972): 20-23.

Johnson, David. "Greener Grass: A Short History of Oregon's Utopia Tradition," *Oregon Heritage* 1 (Winter/Spring 1995): 17.

Keith. [Letter – Communities Seeking Elders]. *Communities* 113 (Winter 2001): 4.

Kelly, Marcia, and Jack Kelly. *The Whole Heaven Catalog: A Resource Guide to Products, Services, Arts, Crafts, and Festivals of Religious, Spiritual, and Cooperative Communities* (New York: Bell Tower/One Spirit, 1998): 210.

Kozeny, Geoph. "Good Neighbors: Cults, Communities, and Neighborhood Relations." *Communities* 83 (Summer 1994): 8-9.

Layva, Cathy. "Community Prospers Through Respect for Life, Work Ethic." *The Siuslaw News* (September 28, 1994): 1.

McLaughlin, Corinne, and Gordon Davidson. "Alpha Farm: Cooperative Corporation with Farm and Businesses" in *Builders of the Dawn: Community Lifestyles in a Changing World* (Walpole, NH: Stillpoint Pub., 1985): 121-24, also 350 and throughout text.

Miller, Timothy. *The 60s Communes: Hippies and Beyond* (Syracuse, NY: Syracuse University Press, 1999): 75-77, 158, 169, 233.

Mitchell, Jann. "Communal Quest – Alpha Farm Sets Example, Proves That It Is Possible to Live in Harmony with Self, Others and the Environment." *The Oregonian* (August 20, 1987): B1.

[More Grapevine]. *Communitas* 1 (July 1972): 51.

Newell, Frances. "I Didn't Know You Were a Warrior." *Communities* 45 (October/November 1980): 38-43.

Owen, Wendy. "Cooperative Independence." *The Oregonian* (December 9, 2001): A17.

Plagge, Dick. "Alpha – Nothing Half-Baked." *Willamette Week* 4:12 (January 24, 1978): 4-5.

Ross, Paula. "Warmth and Caring Guide Alpha-Bit On." *Willamette Valley Observer* (October 9, 1980).

Schehr, Robert C. *Dynamic Utopia: Establishing Intentional Communities As A New Social Movement.* (Westport, CT: Bergin & Garvey, 1997): 47.

"Small Rural Communities." *Communities* 83 (Summer 1994): 35-38.

Sternfeld, Joel. "Alpha Farm, Deadwood, Oregon, August 2004" in *Sweet Earth: Experimental Utopias in America* (Göttingen, Germany: Steidl, 2006): 10-11.

Sutton, Robert P. "Alpha Farm" in *Modern American Communes: A Dictionary* (Westport, CT: Greenwood Press, 2005): 6.

Thoele, Mike. "Alpha." *Eugene Register-Guard* (January 11, 1976): 1D-3D.

Thoele, Michael. "Alpha Farm." *Communities* 34 (September/October 1978): 14-19.

Tristram, Pierre. "American Impressions, Chapter 48: Oregon – The Commune." http://www.pierretristam.com/Bobst/americanimp/48oregon.htm; also as "American Impressions; Oregon – The Commune." *The Ledger* (December 6, 1999) http://www.theledger.com/static/americanimp/1206_oregon.html

Vanneman, Brian Robert. "Alpha Farm: An Intentional Community and Extended Family" in "Searching For Paradise in the Rain: Oregon's Communes and Intentional Communities of the 1960s and 1970s." (Honors thesis, University of Oregon, 1997): 39-51.

Williams, Kate. [Grapevine – Alpha]. *Communitas* 2 (September 1972): 48-49.

Wilner, Joseph Bear. "All My Sisters and Brothers: Redefinitions of Family in Oregon Intentional Communities During the Late Twentieth Century." (M. A. thesis, University of Oregon, 2000): 42-46.

"Women's Wisdom: Voices of Experience." *Communities* 82 (Spring 1994): 48-52.

Yanoff, Leah. "Communing to Work: Practical Idealism at Alpha Farm, A Back-to-the-Land Intentional Community." Senior thesis, Lewis & Clark College, 2006.

Zuckerman, Seth. "Stretching the Bonds: Can a Communal Farm Accommodate the Nuclear Family?" *Natural Life* 61 (May/June 1998): 6.

## Alsea Art Colony

Brown, Bolton. "Early Days of Woodstock." *Publications of the Woodstock Historical Society* 13 (Aug.-Sept. 1937): 3-14.

Edward, Robert. "The Utopias of Ralph Radcliffe Whitehead." *The Magazine Antiques* 127 (185): 260-76.

Evans, Heidi Nasstrom. "Jane Byrd McCall Whitehead: Cofounder of the Byrdcliffe Art School" in Nancy E. Green, ed. *Byrdcliffe: An American Arts and Crafts Colony* (Ithaca, NY: Herbert F. Johnson Museum of Art, 2004): 56-73.

Evers, Alf. *The Catskills: From Wilderness to Woodstock*. Garden City, NY: Doubleday & Company, 1972.

Evers, Alf. *Woodstock: History of an American Town*. Woodstock, NY: Overlook Press, 1987.

Green, Nancy E. "The Reality of Beauty: Ralph Whitehead and the Seeds of Utopia in John Ruskin, William Morris, and Victorian England" in Nancy E. Green, ed. *Byrdcliffe: An American Arts and Crafts Colony* (Ithaca, NY: Herbert F. Johnson Museum of Art, 2004): 36-55.

Green, Nancy E., ed. *Byrdcliffe: An American Arts and Crafts Colony*. Ithaca, NY: Herbert F. Johnson Museum of Art, 2004.

Joseph Downs Collection of Manuscripts and Printed Ephemera. Winterthur Library, Winterthur, DE.

Kreisman, Lawrence, and Glenn Mason. *The Arts and Crafts Movement in the Pacific Northwest* (Portland, OR: Timber Press, 2007): 23.

Miller, Timothy. "Artists' Colonies as Communal Societies in the Arts and Crafts Era." *Communal Societies* 16 (1996): 43- 70.

White, Hervey. "Autobiography." University of Iowa Libraries.

White, Hervey. "Ralph Radcliffe Whitehead." *Publications of the Woodstock Historical Society* 10 (July 1933): 14-29.

Whitehead, Ralph Radcliffe. *Grass of the Desert*. London, UK: Chiswick Press, 1892.

[Whitehead, Ralph Whitehead]. "The Unemployed." *Arrows of the Dawn* no. 1 (1895).

## Alta

Place:         Northern Oregon
Formed:        Ca. late 1960s
Directories:   Ayd, *The Youth Communes*: 166.
               Miller, *The 60s Communes*: 253.

## Alternative Relationship Center

Place:      Eugene
Formed:     1984

[Reach – Groups Looking]. *Communities* 62 (Spring 1984): 53.

## Appletree/Appletree Co-op

Place:       Eugene, Cottage Grove [originally in Boulder, Colorado]
Formed:      1974
Directories: Miller, *The 60s Communes*: 254.
             "1981 Directory of Intentional Communities and Resources"
             (*Communities* 46): 33
             "1983 Directory" (*Communities* 56): 58-59.
             *Directory of Collectives*, 1985: 71.
             "1985 Directory of Intentional Communities" (*Communities* 66): 43.
             *Directory of Intentional Communities*, 1990: 169.

"Federation of Egalitarian Communities." *Communities* 70 (Spring 1986): 51.
McLaughlin, Corinne, and Gordon Davidson. *Builders of the Dawn: Community Lifestyles in a Changing World* (Walpole, NH: Stillpoint Pub., 1985): 339, 350.
Miller, Timothy. *The 60s Communes: Hippies and Beyond* (Syracuse, NY: Syracuse University Press, 1999): 90.
[Reach – Groups Looking]. *Communities* 54 (June/July 1982): 62.
[Reach – Groups Looking]. *Communities* 60 (October/November 1983): 64.
[Reach – Groups Looking]. *Communities* 61 (Winter 1983/84): 52-53.
[Reach – Groups Looking]. *Communities* 66 (Spring 1985): 93.

## Aprovecho Research Center

Place:        Cottage Grove, 80574 Hazelton Rd
Formed:       1976
Directories:  *Communities Directory*, 1996: 214.
              *Communities Directory*, 2000: 200-201.
              *Communities Directory*, 2005: 97.
              *Communities Directory*, 2007: 131.
Publications: *Skipping Stones*
Web:          http://www.aprovecho.net/

[Allied Groups]. *The Permaculture Activist* I(2) (Fall 1985): 14.
Aprovecho Institute. *Fuel-Saving Cookstoves*. Braunschweig/Wiesbaden, Germany: Vieweg & Sohn, 1984.
[Calendar – February 5-17, 1991 – Guatemala Sustainable Agriculture Study Tour]. *The Permaculture Activist* VI(3) (Autumn 1990): 40.
[Calendar – October 22-30 – Permaculture for Homesteaders]. *The Permaculture Activist* IV(3) (August 1988): 32.
[Calendar – March 18-19 – Tree Crops & Permaculture]. *The Permaculture Activist* V(1) (February 1989): 16.
[Calendar – May 13-21 – Permaculture for Homesteaders]. *The Permaculture Activist* V(1) (February 1989): 16.
[Calendar – May 13-21 – Permaculture for Homesteaders]. *The Permaculture Activist* V(2) (May 1989): 24.
[Calendar – June 17-July 2 – Permaculture for the Third World]. *The Permaculture Activist* V(1) February 1989): 16.
[Calendar – June 17-July 2 – Permaculture for the Third World]. *The Permaculture Activist* V(2) May 1989): 24.

197

[Calendar – Mid-July – Rural Self Reliance]. *The Permaculture Activist* V(1) (February 1989): 16.

[Calendar – Mid-July – Rural Self Reliance]. *The Permaculture Activist* V(2) (May 1989): 24.

[Calendar – Sept 30-Oct 7 – Design Techniques for Permaculturists]. *The Permaculture Activist* V(1) (February 1989): 16.

[Calendar – Sept 30-Oct 7 – Design Techniques for Permaculturists]. *The Permaculture Activist* V(2) (May 1989): 24.

[Calendar – Sept 30-Oct 7 – Design Techniques for Permaculturists]. *The Permaculture Activist* V(3) (August 1989): 24.

[Calendar – May-June 1990 – Guatemala Permaculture Study Tour]. *The Permaculture Activist* VI(2) (Summer 1990): 32.

[Calendar – July 19-August 1 – Permaculture Design Course]. *The Permaculture Activist* 64 (May 2007): 57.

[Calendar – Sept. 27-29 – Permaculture Teachers Gathering]. *The Permaculture Activist* V(3) (August 1989): 24.

[Calendar – June 15-30, 1990, Oregon; July 15-30, 1990, Mexico – Sustainable Development for the Third World—Sixth Annual Linked Courses]. *The Permaculture Activist* VI(2) (Summer 1990): 32.

[Calendar – August 3-17 – Sustainable Development for the Third World]. *The Permaculture Activist* VII(1) (Spring 1991): 40.

[Calendar – June 28-July 5 – Sustainable Development for the Third World]. *The Permaculture Activist* IX(1) (February 1993): 52.

[Calendar of Events – June 18-July 3, 1988 – Permaculture in the Third World]. *The Permaculture Activist* IV(2) May 1988): 31.

[Calendar – August 15-17 – Permaculture Design Course]. *The Permaculture Activist* 69 (August 2008): 62.

Childers, Laurie F. "Balancing Justice and Mercy at Aprovecho." *Communities* 85 (Winter 1994): 38-40, 50.

[Classes, Workshops, Work Study]. *Communities* 90 (Spring 1996): 69.

[Classifieds – Books and Publications – *Skipping Stones*]. *The Permaculture Activist* VIII(1) (May 1992): 50.

[Classifieds – Feed & Seed – Aprovecho Select 1988 Fava Bean Seed]. *The Permaculture Activist* V(1) (February 1989): 15.

[Classifieds – Feed & Seed – Aprovecho Select 1988 Fava Bean Seed]. *The Permaculture Activist* V(2) (May 1989): 23.

[Classifieds – Feed & Seed – Aprovecho Select 1988 Fava Bean Seed]. *The Permaculture Activist* V(3) (August 1989): 23.

[Classifieds – Feed & Seed – Aprovecho Select 1988 Fava Bean Seed]. *The Permaculture Activist* V(4) (November 1989): 23.

[Classifieds – Help Wanted – Aprovecho Institute staff and intern openings for evolving small community education center]. *The Permaculture Activist* VI(4) (Winter 1990): 47.

[Classifieds – Internships]. *The Permaculture Activist* VII(3) (Winter 1991-92): 40.

[Classifieds – Work Opportunities – Builder/Maintenance person]. *The Permaculture Activist* VIII(1) (May 1982): 51.

[Classifieds – Work Opportunities – Head gardener to manage 1-1/2 acre organic garden]. *The Permaculture Activist* VIII(1) (May 1992): 51.

[Community Calendar – Mar 1 – Aprovecho Internship Program, also June 1]. *Communities* 90 (Spring 1996): 68.

[Community Grapevine]. *Communities* 97 (Winter 1997): 10.

Estes, Jim. "Home or Activist Community" in *Directory of Intentional Communities: A Guide to Cooperative Living. 1992 Edition.* (Evansville,

IN: Fellowship for Intentional Community and Rutledge, MO: Communities Publications Cooperative, 1992): 67.

Evans, Ianto. "A Second Point of View" in Caroline Estes, "Consensus Ingredients" in *Directory of Intentional Communities: A Guide to Cooperative Living. 1992 Edition.* (Evansville, IN: Fellowship for Intentional Community and Rutledge, MO: Communities Publications Cooperative, 1992): 81.

Evans, Ianto. "Practical Permacultural: Year-Round Eating Means 12-Month Harvesting." *The Permaculture Activist* III(3) (August 1987): 12-13.

[Events – Permaculture Design Course]. *The Permaculture Activist* 64 (May 2007): 51.

[Events – Permaculture Design Course]. *The Permaculture Activist* 69 (August 2008): 56.

[Help Wanted/Offered – Work with Aprovecho Institute]. *The Permaculture Activist* III(2) (June 1987): 23.

[Help Wanted/Offered – Work with Aprovecho Institute]. *The Permaculture Activist* III(3) (August 1987): 22.

[Help Wanted/Offered – Work with Aprovecho Institute]. *The Permaculture Activist* III(4) (November 1987): 30.

[Help Wanted/Offered – Work with Aprovecho Institute]. *The Permaculture Activist* IV(1) (February 1988): 30.

[Help Wanted/Offered – Work with Aprovecho Institute]. *The Permaculture Activist* IV(2) (May 1988): 30

Help Wanted/Offered – Work with Aprovecho Institute]. *The Permaculture Activist* IV(3) (August 1988): 31.

[Help Wanted/Offered – Work needed on Aprovecho's journal, *News from Aprovecho*]. *The Permaculture Activist* IV(4) (November 1988): 23.

[Help Wanted – Aprovecho Research Center, in spectacular scenery, teaches Permaculture, investigates sustainable lifestyles & agriculture]. *The Permaculture Activist* V(3) (August 1989): 23.

[Help Wanted – Aprovecho Research Center, in spectacular scenery, teaches Permaculture, investigates sustainable lifestyles & agriculture]. *The Permaculture Activist* V(4) (November 1989): 23.

[Internships/Work Study]. *Communities* 84 (Fall 1994): 70.

Johnson, David. "Greener Grass: A Short History of Oregon's Utopia Tradition," *Oregon Heritage* 1 (Winter/Spring 1995): 17.

Mallery, Stephen A. "Aprovecho Institute." *The Permaculture Activist* III(3) (August 1987): 4-5.

Mallery, Stephen, and Ianto Evans. "Aprovecho Institute and the End of the Road Community." *Communities* 74 (Summer 1987): 34-36.

McLaughlin, Corinne, and Gordon Davidson. *Builders of the Dawn: Community Lifestyles in a Changing World* (Walpole, NH: Stillpoint Pub., 1985): 27, 53.

[Networks & Resources – Aprovecho Research Center Offers Internships]. *The Permaculture Activist* 37 (September 1997): 55.

O'Neill, Elizabeth. "Simple Treasures: Aprovecho Takes Low-Tech Design and Sustainable Living on the Road." *Eugene Weekly* (April 20, 2000): 12.

"Other Programs at the Aprovecho Institute." *The Permaculture Activist* III(2) (June 1987): 7.

[Permaculture Education – Aprovecho Institute Sustainable Development for the Third World 1993 Courses]. *The Permaculture Activist* IX(1) (February 1993): 40.

[Permaculture Educational Programs – Permaculture in the Third World]. *The Permaculture Activist* IV(2) (May 1988): 26.

199

[Permaculture Educational Programs – Aprovecho Institute – 1989 Workshop Calendar]. *The Permaculture Activist* V(2) (May 1989): 18.

[Permaculture Educational Programs – Aprovecho Institute Sponsors Sixth Annual Linked Courses – Sustainable Development for the Third World=Desarrollo Sostenible para el Tercer Mundo]. *The Permaculture Activist* VI(2) (Summer 1990): 26.

[Permaculture Educational Programs – Aprovecho Institute – Upcoming Workshops]. *The Permaculture Activist* V(3) (August 1989): 18.

[Permaculture Education Programs – Aprovecho Institute – Upcoming Workshops]. *The Permaculture Activist* V(4) (November 1989): 18.

[Permaculture Educational Programs – Aprovecho Fall Workshops]. *The Permaculture Activist* VI(3) (Autumn 1990): 33.

[Permaculture Educational Programs – Aprovecho Intern Program]. *The Permaculture Activist* VII(3) (Winter 1991-92): 31.

[Permaculture Educational Programs – Guatemala Permaculture Study Tour]. *The Permaculture Activist* VI(2) (Summer 1990): 27.

[Permaculture Educational Programs – Guatemala Sustainable Development Study Tour, Traditional Mtn. Agriculture]. *The Permaculture Activist* VI(3) (Autumn 1990): 35.

[Permaculture Educational Programs – Sustainable Development for the Third World, 7th Annual Paired Courses]. *The Permaculture Activist* VII(1) (Spring 1991): 32.

[Permaculture Learning – Aprovecho Institute Sustainable Development for the Third World]. *The Permaculture Activist* 29-30 (July 1993): 64.

[Reach – Groups Looking]. *Communities* 75 (Summer 1988): 54.

[Reports from Regional Groups – Publications Coordinator Needed At Aprovecho]. *The Permaculture Activist* VI(3) (Autumn 1990): 30.

[Reports from Regional Permaculture Groups – Aprovecho Announces Two Openings]. *The Permaculture Activist* VI(4) (Winter 1990): 41.

[Resource Guide – Organizations] in Susan Campbell, *Earth Community: Living Experiments in Cultural Transformation* (San Francisco: Evolutionary Press, 1983): 218.

[Resources – Appropriate Technology]. *Communities* 61 (Winter 1983/84): 48.

Roth, Chris. "The Haybox Cooker: Why Every Community Needs One." *Communities* 115 (Summer 2002): 48-50.

Roth, Jeremy. "A Day in the Life at Aprovecho Research Center." *Talking Leaves* (Late Summer/Fall 2004).

Sternfeld, Joel. "A Rocket Stove development workshop, Aprovecho Research Center, Cottage Grove, Oregon, August 2004" in *Sweet Earth: Experimental Utopias in America* (Göttingen, Germany: Steidl, 2006): 88-89.

Still, Dean. "Straw Bales in a Wet Climate: Field Report from Aprovecho's Strawbale Dormitory." *The Permaculture Activist* 44 (November 2000): 47-48.

Still, Dean. "Correcting a Correction [letter]." *The Permaculture Activist* 46 (July 2001): 65.

Still, Dean, and Jim Kness. *Capturing Heat: Five Earth-Friendly Cooking Technologies and How to Build Them.* Cottage Grove: Aprovecho Research Center, [1996].

Ward, Tom. "The Answer Game." *The Permaculture Activist* V(4) (November 1989): 7.

Ward, Tom. "The Answer Game." *The Permaculture Activist* VII(2) (Autumn 1991): 9.

Ward, Tom. "Sheep Pond Spring Development at Aprovecho Institute." *The Permaculture Activist* V(4) (November 1989): 6-7.

Wilner, Joseph Bear. "All My Sisters and Brothers: Redefinitions of Family in Oregon Intentional Communities During the Late Twentieth Century." (M. A. thesis, University of Oregon, 2000): 51-52.

## Aquarius

| | |
|---|---|
| Place: | Detroit |
| Forming: | 2006 |
| Directories: | Communities Directory (online) |
| | *Communities Directory*, 2007: 296. |

## Art Springs

| | |
|---|---|
| Place: | Gaston |
| Directories: | Association of Lesbian Intentional Communities online map |
| | *Shewolf's Directory of Wimmin's Land*, Fifth Edition. |

## Artopia

| | |
|---|---|
| Place: | Forest Grove |
| Formed: | 1976 |

[Reach – Artopia]. *Communities* 23 (November/December 1976): 51.

## Aspen Ridge Ranch

| | |
|---|---|
| Place: | Chiloquin |
| Forming: | 2007 |
| Directories: | Communities Directory (online) |
| Web: | www.OutsideTheBoxx.net |

## Atlantis

| | |
|---|---|
| Formed: | Early 1970s |
| Directories: | Miller, *The 60s Communes*: 255. |

Horton, Lucy. *Country Commune Cooking* (New York: Coward, McCann and Geoghehan, 1972): 50.

Miller, Timothy. *The 60s Communes: Hippies and Beyond* (Syracuse, NY: Syracuse University Press, 1999): 215-16.

## Aurora Colony

| | |
|---|---|
| Place: | Aurora |
| Dates: | 1856-1883 |

**Archives/Manuscripts/Oral Histories/Photographic Collections**
Aurora Colony Archives. Aurora Colony Historical Society.
Aurora Colony. Oregon Historical Society Manuscript Collections.
Aurora Colony. Oregon Historical Society Research Library Vertical Files.
Aurora Colony. Oregon Historical Society Oral History Collections.
Aurora Colony. Papers 1855-1885. Oregon Historical Society Library. [Microfilm from originals at Oregon State Archives.]
Aurora Colony. Oregon Historical Society Photographic Collections.
Baehart, Michael et al. vs. Phillip Miller et al. Dissolution of the Aurora, Oregon and Bethel, Missouri Communities. U.S. District Court, Oregon. File 752, Judgment Docket 663, 1881-83. (Oregon State Archives, Salem. Film 11, item 1.)

201

Barker, Burt Brown (1873-1969). Oregon Historical Society Oral History Collections. Recordings made in 1962 and 1965. 6 tapes.

Clark Moor Will Papers. Special Collections & University Archives. University of Oregon Libraries.

Hendricks, Robert J. "Miscellaneous Papers Relating to the Aurora Community." Oregon State Archives Microfilm.

Will, Sarah Elizabeth Naftzger (1910-1982). Oregon Historical Society Oral History Collections. Recorded January 28, 1981. Interview by Linda S. P. Brody. 1 cassette.

## Unpublished Works

Boone, Darrell. "[William Keil]." Paper submitted at the University of Oregon, 1957. Clark Moor Will Papers. Special Collections & University Archives, University of Oregon Libraries.

Burckhardt, J. Fred. "A Historical Narrative of the Old Bethel Colony." Oregon Historical Society microfilm.

Freeman, James. "Aurora Colony." Results of Research Done in Oregon State Archives for Credit in Northwest History Research – Willamette University, Salem, Oregon. January 1954. 24p.

Hendricks, Robert J. "Keil Colony: A Success Over All Others." Typed manuscript. [1935]. Oregon Historical Society Research Library Vertical Files.

Keeler, Betty. "The Cultural Landscape of Aurora, A German Communal Society Settlement, 1856-1881." Paper prepared for Geog 493, Oregon State University, June 21, 1974. Clark Moor Will Papers. Special Collections & University Archives, University of Oregon Libraries.

Love, Thomas F. "The Growth of Music in Oregon: The Early Years." Paper for Music V1015y, Columbia University, October 13, 1971. Clark Moor Will Papers. Special Collections & University Archives, University of Oregon Libraries.

Peters, Victor. "The German Pietists; Spiritual Mentors of the German Communal Settlements in America." Paper presented to the National Historical Communal Societies Association, Aurora, Oregon, October 20, 1977. Oregon Historical Society Research Library Vertical Files.

Walker, Lisa. "A Selected Bibliography of Sources on Communal Societies in Oregon and Washington Available at the Oregon Historical Society." (March 15, 1992): 5-17.

## Dissertations and Theses

Buhl, Audrey Ann. "Clothing and Textiles at Aurora, Oregon, 1857-1877," M.S. thesis, Oregon State University, 1971.

Harkness, Ione. "Certain Community Settlements of Oregon," M.A. thesis, University of Southern California, 1925.

Hennes, Teresa Lynn. "The Aurora Colony, Oregon: Structure of a Utopia." B. A. thesis, Reed College, May 1979.

Krauchi, Christian. "The Swiss Settlement of the Willapa Valley, Washington, 1853-1930," M.A. thesis, University of Washington, 1984.

Kraus, George. "Dr. Wilhelm Keil, Founder of the Bethel, Missouri – Aurora, Oregon Christian Commune (1844-1883): A Study of Religious and Cultural Influences." M. A. thesis, Emmanuel School of Religions (Johnson City, TN), 1901.

McCarl, Robert S., Jr. "Aurora Colony Furniture: A Model for the Folkloristic Interpretation of Museum Artifacts." M.A. thesis, University of Oregon, 1974.

Parks, Bonnie Wehle. "'Aurora Blue': Paint Research in an Oregon Utopian Society, Ca. 1870." M. S. thesis, University of Oregon, 1986.

Peterson, Mark Frederic. "Ox Barn Museum, Aurora" in "Burt Brown Barker: His Role in Historic Preservation in Oregon" M.A. thesis, Portland State University, 1983: 95-114.

Simon, John E. "William Keil, Founder of Aurora." M.A. thesis, University of Oregon, 1935.

Solomon, Mark Isaiah. "Communal Experiments in Nineteenth Century America: Causes of Their Relative Success." Ph.D. dissertation, University of Oregon, 1975. p. 519-22, passim.

Stanton, Coralie Cassell. "The Aurora Colony, Oregon." M. A. thesis, Oregon State University, 1963.

Weddle, John Walter. "Early Bands of the Mid-Willamette Valley, 1850-1920." D.M.A. dissertation, University of Oregon, 1989. p. 110-24; plates 9-19 (p. 144-55).

Williams, Julia Elizabeth. "An Analytical Tabulation of the North American Utopian Communities By Type, Longevity and Location." (M. A. thesis, Department of Sociology, University of South Dakota, 1939): 7.

## Journal/Magazine Articles

Albertson, Ralph. "The Bethel-Aurora Communities" in "A Survey of Mutualistic Communities in America." *Iowa Journal of History and Politics* 34 (1936): 387.

"The Aurora Colony Band: the Puget Sound-Victoria Trip, April 20 to May 5, 1869: Notes from the Journal of George A. Wolfer, Bass Horn Player for this Jaunt." *Sou'wester* 9 (Autumn 1974): 43-47.

Bek, William G. "The Community at Bethel, Missouri, and its Offspring at Aurora, Oregon." *The German American Annals*, n. s. 7 (1909): 257-76, 306-28; n. s. 8 (1910): 15-44, 305-30.

Bek, William G. "From Bethel, Missouri to Aurora, Oregon: Letters of William Keil, 1855-1870." *Missouri Historical Review* 48 (1953): 23-41; 48 (1954): 141-53.

Bek, William Godfrey. "A German Communistic Society in Missouri." *Missouri Historical Review* 3 (October 1908): 52-74, 99-125.

Brumann, Christoph. "The Dominance of One and Its Perils: Charismatic Leadership and Branch Structures in Utopian Communities." *Journal of Anthropological Research* 56(4) (Winter 2000): 425-51.

Bushee, Frederick A. "Communistic Societies in the United States." *Political Science Quarterly* 20 (December 1905): 657, 663.

Buell, Huldamay. "The Giesy Family Cemetery." *Sou'wester* 21 (Summer 1986): 38-44.

Dailey, Harold. "The Old Communistic Colony at Bethel." *The Pennsylvania Magazine of History and Biography* 52 (1928): 162-67.

Dole, Philip. "Aurora Colony Architecture: Building in a Nineteenth-Century Cooperative Society." *Oregon Historical Quarterly* 92 (Winter 1992): 377-416.

Duke, David Nelson. "The Evolution of Religion in Wilhelm Keil's Community: A New Reading of Old Testimony." *Communal Societies* 13 (1993): 84-98.

Duke, David Nelson. "A Profile of Religion in the Bethel-Aurora Colonies." *Oregon Historical Quarterly* 92 (Winter 1992): 346-59.

[Final Exhibit – Photo of Clark Moor Will playing E Solo Trumpet]. *Marion County History* 12 (1977-78): 72.

Gooch, John O. "William Keil, A Strange Communal Leader." *Methodist History* 5 (1967): 36-41.

203

Grant, H. Roger. "Missouri's Utopian Communities." *Missouri Historical Review* 66 (October 1971): 20-48.

Grant, H. Roger. "The Society of Bethel: A Visitor's Account." *Missouri Historical Review* 68 (1974): 223 31.

Heming, Carol Piper. "'Temples Stand, Temples Fall': The Utopian Vision of Wilhelm Keil." *Missouri Historical Review* 85 (October 1990): 21-39.

"Historic Community Profile: Aurora and Bethel." *Communiqué: The Communal Studies Association Newsletter* 31(1) (Winter 2006): Insert (p.1-4).

"Historic Communal Sites to Visit." *Communities* 71/72 (Summer/Fall 1986): 10-16.

"Historical Time Line of Communities." *Communities* 74 (Summer 1987): 42-43.

Holbrook, Stewart H. "Aurora Communists." *American Mercury* 67 (July 1948): 54-59. Reprinted in Brian Booth, ed., *Wildmen, Wobblies & Whistle Punks* (Corvallis: Oregon State University Press, 1992), 254-62.

Horn, Lisa, and Laurel Wilson. "Textile Production in the Communalistic German Colony at Bethel, Missouri: 1844-1879." *Clothing and Textile Research Journal* 12 (1993): 43-50.

Horner, John B. "Activities of Philomath College." *Oregon Historical Quarterly* 30 (December 1929): 344-45.

Johnson, David. "Greener Grass: A Short History of Oregon's Utopia Tradition." *Oregon Heritage* 1 (Winter/Spring 1995): 14, 16.

"The Kirsh Family of Forks Prairie (Edited WPA Interview)." *Sou'wester* 21 (Autumn 1986): 53-55.

Kopp, James J. "Aurora." The Oregon Encyclopedia (http://www.oregonencyclopedia.org/entry/view/aurora/)

Kopp, James J. "Documenting Utopia in Oregon: The Challenges of Tracking the Quest for Perfection." *Oregon Historical Quarterly* 105 (2004): 308-19.

"The Letters of Dr. William Keil." *Sou'wester* 28 (Winter 1993): 3-20.

LeWarne, Charles P. "Introduction [Special Issue on Aurora Colony]." *Oregon Historical Quarterly* 92 (Winter 1991-92): 341-45.

Lyman, H. S. "The Aurora Community." *Quarterly of the Oregon Historical Society* 2 (March 1901): 78-93.

Lyman, H.S. "The Aurora Community." *Northwest Legacy: Magazine of Northwest History* 3 (April 1978): 205-20. Reprinted from *Quarterly of the Oregon Historical Society* (March 1901).

McArthur, Lewis A. "Earliest Oregon Post Offices As Recorded in Washington." *Oregon Historical Quarterly* 41 (March 1940): 53-71[71].

McArthur, Lewis A. "Oregon Geographic Names." *Quarterly of the Oregon Historical Society* 26 (December 1925): 309-423[325-26].

[News and Comments – Miscellaneous – Razing of the Old Hotel at Aurora]. *Oregon Historical Quarterly* 35 (June 1934): 187.

Olson, Deborah. "The Schellenbaum: A Communal Society's Symbol of Allegiance." *Oregon Historical Quarterly* 92 (Winter 1992): 360-76.

Olson, Deborah M., and Clark M. Will. "Musical Heritage of the Aurora Colony." *Oregon Historical Quarter* 79 (Fall 1978): 233-67.

Parrish, Philip H. [Review of *Bethel and Aurora* by Robert J. Hendricks]. *Oregon Historical Quarterly* 34 (December 1933): 374.

Peters, Victor. "The German Pietists: Spiritual Mentors of the German Communal Settlements in America." *Communal Societies* 1 (Autumn 1981): 55-66.

Powers, Alfred and Mary-Jane Finke. "Survey of First Half-Century of Oregon Hotels." *Oregon Historical Quarterly* 43 (September 1942): 232-81[243].

Ross, Marion D. "Architecture in Oregon, 1845-1895." *Oregon Historical Quarterly* 57 (March 1956): 32-64[39-40].

Shoemaker, Floyd C. "Shelby County, Home of Experimentation, Progress, and Good Citizenship." *Missouri Historical Review* 50 (1956): 256-63.

Simon, John E. "William Keil and Communist Societies." *Oregon Historical Quarterly* 36 (June 1935): 119-53.

Stephan, Karen H., and G. Edward Stephan. "Religion and the Survival of Utopian Communities." *Journal of the Scientific Study of Religion* 12 (March 1973): 89-100[95].

Swanson, Kimberley. "'The Young People Became Restless': Marriage Patterns Before and After Dissolution of the Aurora Colony." *Oregon Historical Quarterly* 92 (Winter 1992): 417-31.

Talabere, Annie. "The Unusual Dr. William Keil." *Real West* 20(150) (March 1977): 36-39.

"Trek of Keil Colony to Willapa Valley [*The Raymond Herald*, Friday, April 29, 1949]." *Sou'wester* 28 (Winter 1993): 20-21.

White, John G. "Bethel: A Town Awakened." *Missouri Life* (Sept.-Oct. 1978): 11-20.

Will, Clark Moor. "Aurora Colonists Ascend Mount Hood in 1870." *Marion County History* 11 (1972-76): 34-37.

Will, Clark Moor. "Aurora Colony Church Bells." *Oregon Historical Quarterly* 67 (1966): 273-76.

Will, Clark Moor. "The Aurora Story." *Marion County History* 1 (1958): 11-15.

Will, Clark Moor. "Early Oregon Orchardist." *Marion County History* 12 (1977-78): 14-16.

Will, Clark Moor. "The Harris Anvil [Letter to the Editor]." *Oregon Historical Quarterly* 69 (March 1968): 57-59.

Will, Clark Moor. "The Burial of Willie Keil." *Sou'Wester* 3(4) (Winter 1968): 63-65.

Will, Clark Moor. "Prelude to the Burial." *Sou'Wester* 3(4) (Winter 1968): 63.

Will, Clark Moor. [Sketches]. *Marion County History* 12 (1977-78): 17-21.

Will, Clark Moor. "To the Editor [letter]." *Oregon Historical Quarterly* 67 (September 1966): 273-76.

Will, Clark Moor. "Willapa Valley Has Willie – and This." *Sou'Wester* 2 (Summer 1967): 23-26.

"The Willie Keil Story: From a Willapa Bay History." *Cowlitz County Historical Quarterly* 3 (November 1961): 13-14.

Woodward, W. C. "The Rise and Early History of Political Parties in Oregon. V." *Oregon Historical Society Quarterly* 12 (1911): 301-50[331].

Wright, Sue Marie. "Women and the Charismatic Community: Defining the Attraction." *Sociological Analysis* 53 (1992 Supplement): S35-S49.

Zieglschmid, A. J. F. "Dr. Wilhelm Keil's Communal Enterprises: Bethel, Missouri and Aurora, Oregon." *The American-German Review* (December 1947): 28-31.

## Newspaper Articles

There were many contemporary newpapers articles on the Aurora Colony and these are not represented here. The articles below are representative of retrospective views of Aurora since the dissolution of the colony.

Amsden, Elizabeth. "Communes Rooted in Oregon History." *The Oregonian* (October 11, 1984): C6.

Apsler, Alfred. "The Pious Communists of Aurora Colony." *The Sunday Oregonian Magazine* (July 5, 1953): 2-3.

"Aurora Colonists Sought Equality, Were Devoted to Arts, Sciences." *The Oregonian* (December 26, 1978): D5.

"Aurora, Site of Communal Colony, to Observe Centennial." *The Oregonian* (July 15, 1968): 39.

Bogue, Lucille. "Colony House in Aurora." *North Willamette News* (Aurora, Oregon, 1965).

Campbell, Polly. "Museum Celebrates Aurora Colony." *The Oregonian* (April 6, 2006).

Carlson, Ted. "How Communism Came to Oregon." *Eugene Register-Guard* (February 27, 1966).

Carter, Katlyn. "Aurora Colony Music Digitized." *The Oregonian* (July 17, 2008).

Colby, Richard. "Dig at Aurora Brings to Light Clues to Colony Life." *The Oregonian* (September 13, 1979): C8.

"Communism Was A Success at Aurora." *Oregon Statesman* (March 28, 1926).

Edward, Herman. "Aurora Residents Recall Early Days." *The Oregonian* (July 15, 1956): 38.

Furey, John. "Keeping Promise Creates Longest Funeral Procession in History." *The Oregonian* (April 16, 1993): C5.

Haught, Nancy. "Utopia in Oregon." *The Oregonian* (June 24, 2006): C1.

"History of Aurora." *Champoeg Pioneer* 1 (July 1956): 1.

Holbrook, Stewart. "Oregon's Faded Aurora Has Unique Story." *The Oregonian* (June 2, 1958): 18.

Johnson, Steve, and Dick Plagge. "Aurora – Our First Commune." *Willamette Week* 4:12 (January 24, 1978): 6.

Lockley, Fred. [Dr. William Keil]. *Oregon Journal* (June 10, 1927).

Lockley, Fred. "Impressions and Observations of the Journal Man." *Oregon Journal* (April 11, 1922).

Macqueen, Joseph. "Founding of Town of Aurora, Or. By Dr. Keil Recalled." *The Oregonian* (July 1, 1934): 4.

Mahar, Ted. "History With a Future." *The Oregonian* (June 30, 1994): 1.

Nielsen, Rebecca. "Community of the Dawn." *The Oregonian* (September 1, 1991): T4.

"The Pious Communists of Aurora Colony." *The Oregonian* (July 5, 1953): 2.

Pollard, Lancaster. "Aurora Society Century Ago Based on Communal Life." *The Oregonian* (January 25, 1959): 23.

Pollard, Lancaster. "Satchmo's Visit Recalls Aurora Group." *The Oregonian* (October 7, 1956): 37.

Reed, Ione. "This is Aurora 110 Years Later." *Eugene Register-Guard* (February 27, 1966).

Snyder, Eugene Edmund. "Aurorans Practiced Faith a World Apart." *The Oregonian* (October 23, 2005): B11.

Stabler, David. "The Aurora Colony Pioneer Band to Be Recreated—100 Years Later." *The Oregonian* (August 19, 1988): F4.

Terry, John. "One Long, Strange Trip Brought Willie Keil to Northwest Graves." *The Oregonian* (June 22, 1997): C4.

Terry, John. "Oregon Trails: A Circuitous Route to Aurora Colony." *The Oregonian* (June 27, 2004): A15.

Terry, John. "Oregon Trails: Differing Accounts Depict Life in Aurora Colony." *The Oregonian* (July 4, 2004): A13.

Terry, John. "Small-Town Brass Spread Sound of Music, And Doc Was High Notes." *The Oregonian* (July 26, 1998): D4.

"Trek of Keil Colony to Willapa Valley." *The Raymond Herald* (April 29, 1949).

"Wear of Century Yielding in Aurora Keil House," *Portland Reporter* (May 5, 1961) Sec B, p. 1, col 1-2, and p.2. col. 1.

## Monographs

Bogue, Lucile (comp.). *Colony House in Aurora, Oregon*. Compiled by Lucile Bogue. Assisted by Mary Ann Campbell. Aurora: The Author, 1965.

Dole, Philip, and Judith Rees. *Aurora Colony: Historic Resources Inventory*. [Salem]: Oregon State Historic Preservation Office, 1988.

Hendricks, Robert J. *Bethel and Aurora: An Experiment in Communism As Practical Christianity With Some Account of Past and Present Ventures in Collective Living*. New York: Press of the Pioneers, 1933.

Kirkpatrick, Jane. *Aurora: An American Experience in Quilt, Community and Craft*. Colorado Springs, CO: Waterbrook Multnomah Publishing Group, a Division of Random House, 2008.

Koch, Carl. *Lebenserfahrungen von Carl G. Koch, Prediger des Evangeliums*. Cleveland, OH: Verlagshaus der Evangelischen Gemeinschaft, 1871.

Minor, Rick, Linda K. Jacobs, and Theresa M. Tilton. *The Stauffer-Will Farmstead: Historical Archeology at an Aurora Colony Farm. University of Oregon Anthropological Papers No. 24.*[Eugene: University of Oregon], 1981.

Parks, Bonnie Wehle. *Aurora Blue: Identifying and Analyzing Interior Paint in an Oregon Utopia, ca. 1870*. Eugene: Historic Preservation Program, School of Architecture & Allied Arts, University of Oregon, 1986.

Schroeder, Adolph E. *Bethel Germany Colony, 1844-1883: "Viele Hande Machen Bald Ein Ende" Many Hands Make Quick Work*. Bethel: Bethel Germany Colony, n.d.

Schroeder, Adolph E., ed. *Bethel Germany Colony, 1844-1879: Religious Beliefs and Practices*. Bethel, MO: Historical Bethel Germany Colony, 1966.

Snyder, Eugene Edmund. *Aurora, Their Last Utopia: Oregon's Christian Commune, 1856-1883*. Portland, OR: Binford & Mort, 1993.

Will, Clark Moor. *The Story of Old Aurora in Picture and Prose, 1856-1883: An Information Hand Book to fill the need for a brief record of the historic Oregon experiment in communal living*.[Salem, OR]: C. M. Will, 1972.

## Sections in Monographs/General Works

Adams, Raymond. "Bethel and Aurora" in *A Booklist of American Communities, A Collection of Books in the Library of Raymond Adams* (Chapel Hill, NC: The Author, 1935): 3.

Albertson, Ralph. "The Bethel-Aurora Communities" in *A Survey of Mutualistic Communities in America*. Reprinted from *Iowa Journal of History and Politics*, 34 (1936). (New York: AMS Press, 1973): 387.

Arndt, Karl J. R. *George Rapp's Harmony Society 1785-1847*. Revised Edition. (Rutherford: Fairleigh Dickinson University Press, 1972): p. 539, 541.

Arndt, Karl J. R. "George Rapp's Harmony Society" in Donald E. Pitzer, ed. *America's Communal Utopias* (Chapel Hill: University of North Carolina Press, 1997): 78.

Bates, Elizabeth Bidwell, and Jonathan L. Fairbanks. "Bench – Aurora Colony, Oregon, c. 1860" in *American Furniture: 1620 to the Present* (New York: Richard Marek Publishers, 1981): 433.

Blankenship, Russell. "William Keil and Aurora" in *And There Were Men* (New York: Alfred A. Knopf, 1942): 95-120.

Bliss, William D. P., and Rudolph M. Binder, eds. *The New Encyclopedia of Social Reform*. New Edition (New York and London: Funk & Wagnalls, 1908): 111, 265.

Burkholder, Arthur. "The Aurora Colony" in Victoria Case (comp. and ed.). *This I Remember: Personal Pioneer Experiences* ([Portland]: Rose Villa, Inc., 1972): 90-91.

207

Calverton, V. F. "Bethel and Aurora" in *Where Angels Dared to Tread* (Indianapolis and New York: Bobbs-Merrill Company, 1945): 86-96.

Carey, Charles Henry. *A General History of Oregon Prior to 1961.* Volume II (Portland: Metropolitan Press, 1935): 664-65.

Cohen, Daniel. *Not of the World: A History of the Commune in America* (Chicago: Follett Publishing Company, 1973): 100-103, 158.

Deady, Matthew P. *Pharisee Among Philistines: The Diary of Judge Matthew P. Deady, 1871-1892.* Edited with an Introduction by Malcolm Clark. Jr. (Portland: Oregon Historical Society, 1975): 21, 31,48, 136, 146-47, 159, 193, 214, 340, 342, 377.

Eaton, Joseph W., and Saul M. Katz. *Research Guide on Cooperative Group Farming* (New York: H. W. Wilson Company, 1942): 35, 41.

Finck, Henry T. *My Adventures in the Golden Age of Music* (New York: Funk and Wagnalls, 1926): 12-60.

Florin, Lambert. "Aurora, Oregon" in *Ghost Towns of The West* (New York: Promontory Press, 1993): 694-96.

Fogarty, Robert S. "Keil, William," "Bethel-Aurora Colonies" in *Dictionary of American Communal and Utopian History* (Westport, CT: Greenwood Press, 1980): 60-61, 130-31. Also "Bethel Community" (190), "Nineveh" (195), and "Aurora Community" (200) in Appendix.

Friedman, Ralph. *This Side of Oregon.* (Caldwell, ID: Caxton Printers, 1985): 27, 51.

Friesen, John W., and Virginia Lyons Friesen. "Bethel, Missouri, 1844-1879," "Aurora, Oregon, 1856-1883" in *The Palgrave Companion to North American Utopias* (New York: Palgrave Macmillan, 2004): 160-68.

Gulick, Bill. *Roadside History of Oregon.* (Missoula, MT: Mountain Press Publishing Company, 1991): 158-64.

Gutek, Gerald, and Patricia Gutek. "Wilhelm Keil's Keilites" in *Visiting Utopian Communities: A Guide to the Shakers, Moravians, and Others* (Columbia: University of South Carolina Press, 1998): 151-58.

Harris, Patrick. "William Keil and the Aurora Colony: A Communal Society Crosses the Oregon Trail" in Carl Guarnieri and David Alvarez, eds., *Religion and Society in the American West: Historical Essays* (Lanham, MD: University Press of America, 1987): 425-47.

Hinds, William Alfred. "Aurora Community" in *American Communities: Brief Sketches of Economy, Zoar, Bethel, Aurora, Amana, Icaria, The Shakers, Oneida, Wallingford, and the Brotherhood of the New Life* (Oneida, NY: Office of the American Socialist, 1878): 46-48.

Hinds, William Alfred. "The Bethel-Aurora Communities" in *American Communities. Revised Edition. Enlarged to Include Additional Societies, new and Old, Communistic, Semi-Communistic and Co-operative* (Chicago: Charles H. Kerr & Company, 1902): 287-99.

Hinds, William Alfred. "The Bethel-Aurora Communities" in *American Communities and Co-operative Colonies.* Second Revision (Chicago: Charles H. Kerr & Company, 1908): 326-39.

Holbrook, Stewart. *Far Corner: A Personal View of the Pacific Northwest* (New York: Macmillan, 1952): 60-69.

Holloway, Mark. *Heavens on Earth: Utopian Communities in America, 1680-1880* (New York: Library Publishers, 1951): 20, 160, 162-65, 222, 224, 227.

"Keil House (Aurora)" in *Social and Humanitarian Movements. The National Survey of Historic Sites and Buildings: Theme XXII* (Washington, D.C.: National Park Service, 1965): 151-52 and photo.

Kirchhoff, Theodor. *Oregon East, Oregon West: Travels and Memoirs by Theodor Kirchoff, 1863-1872.* Edited and Translated and with an Introduction by Frederic Trautmann (Portland: Oregon Historical Press, 1987): 115-25.

Kirchhoff, Theodor. *Reisebilder und skizzen aus Amerika* (Alton, CT: Schulter; New York: E. Steigler, 1875-76).

Leifmann, Robert. *Die kommunistischen Gemeinden in Nordamerika* (Jena, Germany: Gustav Fischer, 1922): 17.

Lockley, Fred. "Dr. William Keil—Founder of the Aurora Colony" in *Visionaries, Mountain Men & Empire Builders* (Eugene: Rainy Day Press, 1982): 196-205. Originally published in the *Oregon Journal* (April 11, 1922).

Nordhoff, Charles. "The Aurora and Bethel Communes" in *The Communistic Societies of the United States; from Personal Visit and Observation* (New York: Harper & Brothers, 1875): 305-30.

Olsen, Deborah M. "Aurora Colony Historical Society" in D. W. Krummel, Jean Geil, Doris J. Dyen, and Deane L. Root, eds. *Resources of American Music History: A Directory of Source Materials from Colonial Times to World War II* (Urbana: University of Illinois Press, 1981): 302-3.

*Oregon: End of the Trail.* Compiled by Workers of the Writers' Program of the Work Projects Administration in the State of Oregon. Revised Edition with added material by Howard McKinley Corning (Portland: Binfords & Mort,[1951]): 306-9.

Oved, Yaacov. "Beth El and Aurora" in *Two Hundred Years of American Communes* (New Brunswick, NJ, and Oxford, UK: Transactions Books, 1988): 95-99.

Pitzer, Donald E., ed. *America's Communal Utopias* (Chapel Hill: University of North Carolina Press, 1997): 78, 463, 473.

Reps, John W. "Zoar, Bethel and Aurora, and Amana" in *The Making of Urban America: A History of City Planning in the United States* (Princeton, NJ: Princeton University Press, 1965): 456-63.

Rexroth, Kenneth. *Communalism: From Its Origins to the Twentieth Century* (New York: Seabury Press, 1974): 183-85.

Scofield, W. M. "Aurora" in *Oregon's Historical Markers* (Pleasant Hill, OR: Souvenir Publishing Co., 1966): 77.

Scott, Harvey W. *History of the Oregon Country.* Compiled by Leslie M. Scott (Cambridge, MA: Riverside Press, 1924): II, 59, 206, 324, 348; III, 188; IV, 39, 40.

Semler, Heinrich. "Die Bethelgemeinde" (103-8), "Die Auroragemeinde" (108-13) in *Geschichte des Socialismus und Communismus in Nordamerika* (Leipzig, Germany: F. A. Broadhaus, 1880). Reprinted as *Geschichte des Socialismus und Communismus in Nordamerika. Mit einer Einleitung von Helmut Reinicke Sozialismus und Kommunismus als Kooperativebewegung in der bürgerlichen Gesellschaft* (Glashütten im Taunus, Germany: Detlev Auvermann, 1973).

Skiff, Frederick W. *Adventures in Americana: Recollections of Forty Years Collecting Books, Furniture, China, Guns and Glass* (Portland: Metropolitan Press, 1935): 200-223.

Smith, Phyllis, and Jim Smith. "Aurora" in *Historic Homes of Oregon: Sketches by Emily* (Anchorage, AK: White Stone Press, 2006): 38-39.

Solis, Miguel J. "Aurora Colony"; "Will, Clark Moor" in *American Utopias (1683-1900): Evolution versus Revolution: A Descriptive and Bibliographic Dictionary* (Bloomington, IN: The Author, 1984): 23.

Stockwell, Foster. "Aurora," "Bethel" in *Encyclopedia of American Communes, 1663-1963* (Jefferson, NC: McFarland & Co., 1998): 23-24, 28-29.

Sutton, Robert P. "Bethel/Aurora" in *Communal Utopias and the American Experience: Religious Communities, 1732-2000* (Westport, CT: Praeger, 2003): 46-48.

Trahair, Richard C. S. "Beth El" and "Keil, William" in *Utopias and Utopians: An Historical Dictionary* (Westport, CT: Greenwood Press, 1999): 37, 212-13.

Tyler, Alice Felt. "Bethel and Aurora" in *Freedom's Ferment: Phases of American Social History to 1860* (Minneapolis: University of Minnesota Press, 1944): 125-28.

Wooster, Ernest S. "The Bethel-Aurora Communities" in *Communities of the Past and Present* (Newllano, LA: Llano Colonist, 1924): 60-61.

Wright, Sue Marie. "Women and the Charismatic Community: Defining the Attraction" in William H. Swatos, Jr., ed. *Gender and Religion* (New Brunswick, NJ: Transaction Publishers, 1994): 143-57.

**Videos**

Epp, Allen. *God Provides a Way Around a Mountain.* KOAP-TV; Allen Epp, producer/writer, 1976. 29 min.

Epp, Allen. *The Pennsylvania Dutch Corner of Oregon.* KOAP-TV; Allen Epp, producer writer, 1976. 29 min.

Epp, Allen. *A Vision Pursued.* KOAP-TV; Allen Epp, producer/writer, 1976. 29 min.

Orr, Glenn, and McCarthy, Nancy W. *Aurora: A Colony Remembered.* 1975. 14 min.

**Pamphlets**

Jangenbach, John J. *The Journey of Willie Keil: Commemorating the 100th Anniversary of the Settling of the Willapa Valley.* Raymond, WA: The Author, 1955.

*100 Years of Growth and Development in Oregon's Great Willamette Valley: Aurora Colony Centennial Celebration Pamphlet.* West Linn, OR: Clint Mansfield, 1956.

**Literary Works**

Kirkpatrick, Jane. *A Clearing in the Wild: A Novel.* Colorado Springs: Waterbrook Press, 2006.

Kirkpatrick, Jane. *A Tendering in the Storm: A Novel.* Colorado Springs: Waterbrook Press, 2007.

Kirkpatrick, Jane. *A Mending at the Edge: A Novel.* Colorado Springs: Waterbrook Press, 2008.

Lespinasse, Cobie de. *Second Eden: A Romance.* Boston: Christopher Publishing House, 1951.

## Bag-End Community

Place:    Medford
210    Formed:    1976

[Reach – Groups forming – Bag-End Community]. *Communities* 20 (May/June 1976): 43.

## Bear Grass Village

Place:    Ashland
Formed:    2002
Directories:  Cohousing Directory (online)
           Communities Directory (online)

Web:        www.ashlandcoho.com
Formerly:   Fordyce Street Cohousing

## Beaver Lodge Incorporated [The Lodge]
Place:       Corvallis
Formed:      1940
Directories: *Communities Directory*, 2000: 206.
             *Communities Directory*, 2007: 136.
Web:         http://beaverlodge.org/

## Bee Farm
Place:       Ashland, 2255 Ashland Mine Rd.
Formed:      1974
Directories: "1975 Community Directory" (*Communities* 12): 24.
             Mercer, *Communes: A Social History and Guide*: 129.
             Miller, *The 60s Communes*: 255.

[Communes Looking for People]. *Communities* 10 (November 1974): 56.
[Reach – Communes Looking for People]. *Communities* 14 (May/June 1975): 57.

## Bellamy Colony
Place:       Depot Slough, Lincoln County
Dates:       1897-1899

Claridge, Rosa. "Lincoln County's Bellamy Colony," prepared for the Lincoln
    County Historical Society and the Sons of Norway. Typescript, 1965-66.
Ginter, Carol Romtvedt. "Looking Backward ... at the Bellamy Colony." *The
    Bayfront* 9 (June 1999).
Ginter, Carol. "Romtvedt Reunion This Weekend." *South Lincoln County News*
    (July 26, 1995): 4.
Jacobsen, Bernhardt Selvig. "Viking Roots: The Story of the Family of Roy and
    Sophia [Romtvedt] Jacobsen." Typescript, 1963.
Kopp, James J. "Documenting Utopia in Oregon: The Challenges of Tracking the
    Quest for Perfection." *Oregon Historical Quarterly* 105 (2004): 308-19.
Kopp, James J. "Looking Backward at Edward Bellamy's Impact in Oregon."
    *Oregon Historical Quarterly* 104 (Spring 2003): 62-95.
Kopp, James J., and Carol Ginter. "Seeking Prosperity and Freedom on the Oregon
    Coast: The Bellamy Colony, Lincoln County, Oregon (1897-1899)." *Communal
    Societies* (2005): 57-74.
Lustvedt, Lloyd. "O. A. Tveitmoe: Labor Leader." *Norwegian-American Studies*.
    Volume 30 (Northfield, MN: Norwegian-American Historical Association,
    1985): 3-54.
McArthur, Lewis A. *Oregon Geographic Names*. 7th Edition. Revised and enlarged
    by Lewis L. McArthur. (Portland: Oregon Historical Society, 2003): 68-69.
*Reform* (July 6, 1897; August 24, 1897; September 7, 1897; October 12, 1897).
Romtvedt, Fred. "Fred Romtvedt: His Life & Loves, 1890-[1983]." Written by
    Himself, June 1981. Typed with Errors by Carol Ginter (typescript).
St. Romain, Monica. "County Saw Another Try at Religious Colony Plan."
    *Newport News-Times* (June 26, 1969): Sec. 3, p. 4.
Tveitmoe, O. A. "Bellamy Beamings." *Industrial Freedom* (Feb. 4, 1899): 2.

211

## Beth El

Formed:     1970s
Directories:   Miller, *The 60s Communes*: 255.

Duin, Julia. "Authority & Submission in Christian Community." *Communities* 92 (Fall 1996): 52.

## Bethlehem Covenant Community

Place:      Portland
Formed:     1980s

Peterson, Joe V. "Jesus People: Christ, Communes, and the Counterculture of the Late Twentieth Century in the Pacific Northwest and a Brief Review of the Shiloh Youth Revival Centers, Inc., The Highway Missionary Society/Servant Community, and the House of Elijah." (M.A. thesis, Northwest Christian College, 1990): 31.

## Bienvenida House

Place:      Portland
Formed:     1990s

Wilner, Joseph Bear. "All My Sisters and Brothers: Redefinitions of Family in Oregon Intentional Communities During the Late Twentieth Century." (M. A. thesis, University of Oregon, 2000): 102-3.

## Blocks Farm

Place:      Cottage Grove
Formed:     ca. 1970
Directories:   Miller, *The 60s Communes*: 256.

## Blue Star

Place:      Deadwood
Formed:     1970s
Directories:   Miller, *The 60s Communes*: 256.

## Boggs' Homestead

Place:      Coquille
Formed:     1989
See:        Mountain Homestead

## Breitenbush Community

Place:      Detroit
Formed:     1977
Directories:   "1983 Directory" (*Communities* 56): 60.
                *Directory of Collectives*, 1985: 71
                "1985 Directory of Intentional Communities" (*Communities* 66): 44.
                *Directory of Intentional Communities*, 1990: 173.
                *Communities Directory*, 1996: 221-222.
                *Communities Directory*, 2000: 209.
                *Communities Directory*, 2005: 107.
                *Communities Directory*, 2007: 140-41.
Web:       http://www.breitenbush.com/

"A Great Escape for the Holistic at Heart – Breitenbush." *The Oregonian* (November 13, 1988): L1.

[Calendar – September 23-25 – Landscaping in Nature's Footsteps]. *The Permaculture Activist* IV(3) (August 1988): 32.

[Calendar – June 8-10 – Plants for Sustainable Landscaping, Three-day Workshop]. *The Permaculture Activist* VI(2) (Summer 1990): 32.

[Classifieds – Breitenbush Community has resident openings]. *Communities* 75 (Summer 1988): 64.

[Communities Directory Summer '99 Update]. *Communities* 103 (Summer 1999): 66.

[Communities with Openings]. *Communities* 92 (Fall 1996): 70.
[Communities with Openings]. *Communities* 94 (Spring 1997): 70.
[Communities with Openings]. *Communities* 98 (Spring 1998): 67.
[Communities with Openings]. *Communities* 99 (Summer 1998): 72.
[Communities with Openings]. *Communities* 100 (Fall 1998): 72.
[Communities with Openings]. *Communities* 101 (Winter 1998): 72.
[Communities with Openings]. *Communities* 102 (Spring 1999): 71.
[Communities with Openings]. *Communities* 103 (Summer 1999): 72.
[Communities with Openings]. *Communities* 104 (Fall 1999): 71.
[Communities with Openings]. *Communities* 107 (Summer 2000): 67.
[Communities with Openings]. *Communities* 108 (Fall 2000): 70.
[Communities with Openings]. *Communities* 109 (Winter 2000): 70.
[Communities with Openings]. *Communities* 110 (Spring 2001): 73.
[Communities with Openings]. *Communities* 111 (Summer 2001): 71.
[Communities with Openings]. *Communities* 112 (Fall 2001): 64-65.
[Communities with Openings]. *Communities* 113 (Winter 2001): 70-71.
[Communities with Openings]. *Communities* 114 (Spring 2002): 69.
[Communities with Openings]. *Communities* 115 (Summer 2002): 69.
[Communities with Openings]. *Communities* 116 (Fall 2002): 70-71.
[Communities with Openings]. *Communities* 117 (Spring 2003): 69.
[Communities with Openings]. *Communities* 118 (Summer 2003): 66.
[Classifieds with Openings]. *Communities* 119 (Fall 2003): 58.
[Communities with Openings]. *Communities* 121 (Winter 2003): 62-63.
[Communities with Openings]. *Communities* 122 (Spring 2004): 71.
[Communities with Openings]. *Communities* 123 (Summer 2004): 70-71.
[Communities with Openings]. *Communities* 124 (Fall 2004): 64-65.
[Communities with Openings]. *Communities* 125 (Winter 2004): 62.
[Communities with Openings]. *Communities* 126 (Spring 2005): 68.
[Communities with Openings]. *Communities* 135 (Summer 2007): 66.
[Communities with Openings]. *Communities* 136 (Fall 2007): 65.
[Communities with Openings]. *Communities* 137 (Winter 2007): 68.
[Communities with Openings]. *Communities* 138 (Spring 2008): 63.
[Communities with Openings]. *Communities* 139 (Summer 2008): 69.

[Community Calendar – Dec 12-15 – A Gathering of the Clans: Celebrating the Culture of Community]. *Communities* 89 (Winter 1995): 67.

[Community Calendar – Apr 8-13 – Spring Service Week]. *Communities* 110 (Spring 2001): 69.

[Community Employment]. *Communities* 98 (Spring 1998): 64.
[Community Employment]. *Communities* 100 (Fall 1998): 71.
[Community Employment, Internships]. *Communities* 99 (Summer 1998): 70
[Community Grapevine]. *Communities* 85 (Summer 1997): 8.
[Community Grapevine]. *Communities* 115 (Summer 2002): 9.

213

[Internships and Work Opportunities – Breitenbush Hot Springs, Detroit, Oregon]. *Communities* 107 (Summer 2000): 73.

John, Michael, comp. *The Rainbow Nation 1982 Cooperative Community Guide V. A Peoples Guide to the Liberation of Earth* (McCall, ID: [Rainbow Nation], 1982): 60.

Johnson, David. "Greener Grass: A Short History of Oregon's Utopia Tradition." *Oregon Heritage* 1 (Winter/Spring 1995): 17.

Kelly, Marcia, and Jack Kelly. *The Whole Heaven Catalog: A Resource Guide to Products, Services, Arts, Crafts, and Festivals of Religious, Spiritual, and Cooperative Communities* (New York: Bell Tower/One Spirit, 1998): 212.

Kozeny, Geoph. "Community Spirit, Community 'Glue'." *Communities* 107 (Summer 2000): 49-51.

McLaughlin, Corinne, and Gordon Davidson. *Builders of the Dawn: Community Lifestyles in a Changing World* (Walpole, NH: Stillpoint Pub., 1985): 47, 351.

[Natural Building Calendar – September 7-12 – Advanced Cob]. *The Permaculture Activist* 41 (May 1999): 81.

Newell, Frances. "I Didn't Know You Were a Warrior." *Communities* 45 (October/November 1980): 38-43.

"Permaculture Educational Programs – Plants for Sustainable Landscaping – Three-day workshop." *The Permaculture Activist* VI(1) (Spring 1990): 26.

[Reach – June 27-29 – Northern Oregon Healing Gathering]. *Communities* 44 (June/July 1980): 55.

[Reach – August 9-16 – Sufi Camp]. *Communities* 44 (June/July 1980): 55.

[Reach – August 27-Sept. 3 – 2nd annual Come Unity Gathering at Breitenbush, OR]. *Communities* 44 (June/July 1980): 55.

[Reach – Spring Equinox Peace Gathering, March 21-24]. *Communities* 65 (Winter 1984/5): 51.

[Reach – Calendar of Events]. *Communities* 70 (Spring 1986): 60.

Sandhill, Laird. "Snapshop of a Moving Target: The Communities Movement." *Communities* 97 (Winter 1997): 5-7.

"Traditional Sweat Lodge Ceremony Cleanses Visitors to Breitenbush." *The Oregonian* (August 16, 1998): T4.

Vanneman, Brian Robert. "Searching For Paradise in the Rain: Oregon's Communes and Intentional Communities of the 1960s and 1970s." (Honors thesis, University of Oregon, 1997): 18.

Wasserman, Stuart. "Breitenbush Mixes Business With Pleasure." *The Oregonian* (June 16, 1991): T4.

Wilner, Joseph Bear. "All My Sisters and Brothers: Redefinitions of Family in Oregon Intentional Communities During the Late Twentieth Century." (M. A. thesis, University of Oregon, 2000): 46-48.

**Videos**

*Visions of Utopia: Experiments in Sustainable Culture*. Produced and directed by Geoph Kozeny. San Francisco: Community Catalyst Project, 2002.

214

## Brides of Christ Church (Holy Rollers)

**Place:**     Corvallis/Waldport
**Dates:**     1903-1906

Baldasty, Gerald J. *Vigilante Newspapers: A Tale of Sex, Religion, and Murder in the Northwest*. Seattle and London: University of Washington Press, 2005.

Beam, Maurice. "Crazy After Women" in *Cults of America* (New York: MacFadden-Bartell, 1964): 35-58.

"Creffield, Franz Edmund" in Robert P. Sutton, *Modern American Communes: A Dictionary* (Westport, CT, and London: Greenwood Press, 2005): 37.

Crew, Linda. *Brides of Eden: A True Story Imagined*. New York: Harpers Collins, 2001.

Gartner, Rosemary, and Jim Phillips. "The Creffield-Mitchell Case, Seattle 1906: The Unwritten Law in the Pacific Northwest." *Pacific Northwest Quarterly* 94 (Spring 2003): 69-82.

[Holbrook, Stewart H.]. "Blonde Esther and the Seducing Prophet" by S. Underwood (pseud.) *True Detective Mysteries* 27 (March 1937): 10-15; 92-94.

Holbrook, Stewart H. "Death and Times of a Prophet." In Stewart H. Holbrook, ed. *Murder Out Yonder: An Informal History of Certain Classic Crimes in Back-Country America* (New York: Macmillan, 1941): 1-21, 221-22.

Holbrook, Stewart H. "Death and Times of a Prophet." In Brian Booth, ed., *Wildmen, Wobblies and Whistle Punks* (Corvallis: Oregon State University Press, 1992), 41-60.

[Holbrook, Stewart H.]. "The Enigma of the Sex-Crazed Prophet" by C. K. Stanton (pseud.). *Front Page Detective* (January 1938): 4-9; 108-10.

Holbrook, Stewart H. "Murder Without Tears" (4 parts). *The Sunday Oregonian* (February 8, 15 and 22; March 1, 1953).

Holbrook, Stewart H. "Oregon's Secret Love Cult." *American Mercury* 40 (February 1937): 167-74.

Holbrook, Stewart H. "Oregon Secret Love Cult." In Alexander Klein, ed., *Grand Deception: The World's Most Spectacular and Successful Hoaxes, Impostures, Ruses and Frauds* (Philadelphia, PA: Lippincott, 1955): 16-23.

Holy Rollers. Oregon Historical Society Research Library Scrapbooks (SB 57).

Hynd, Alan. "Prophet Joshua and His Holy Rollers." In Alan Hynd, *Murder, Mayhem and Mystery: An Album of American Crime* (New York: Barnes, 1950): 265-73.

Johnson, David. "Greener Grass: A Short History of Oregon's Utopia Tradition." *Oregon Heritage* 1 (Winter/Spring 1995):16.

Mathison, Richard R. "Franz Creffield: Naked Reformer" (Chapter 41) in *Faiths, Cults and Sects of America: From Atheism to Zen* (Indianapolis: Bobbs-Merrill Company, 1960): 301-5.

McCracken, T[eresa], and Robert B. Blodgett. *Holy Rollers: Murder and Madness in Oregon's Love Cult*. Caldwell, ID: Caxton Press, 2002.

Miller, Timothy. "Bride of Christ" in *The Quest for Utopia in Twentieth-Century America. Volume I: 1900-1960* (Syracuse, NY: Syracuse University Press, 1998): 113-14.

Miller, Timothy, "Brides of Christ Church" in *American Communes, 1860-1960: A Bibliography* (New York & London: Garland Publishing, 1990): 45-46.

Morris, James M., and Andrea L. Kross, "Bride of Christ" in *Historical Dictionary of Utopianism* (Lanham, MD: Scarecrow Press, 2004): 46-47.

Nash, Jay Robert. *Murder America: Homicide in the United States from the Revolution to the Present*. (New York: Simon and Schuster, 1980): 182-84.

Parrot-Holden, Jan. "Joshua the Second: The Man Who Put the Hex on San Francisco." *Columbia* 11 (Winter 1997-98): 35-37.

Phillips, Jim, and Rosemary Gartner. *Murdering Holiness: The Trials of Franz Creffield and George Mitchell*. Vancouver, BC, Canada: UBC Press, 2003.

Phillips, Jim, Rosemary Gartner, and Kelly DeLuca. "Incarcerating Holiness: Religious Enthusiasm and the Law in Oregon, 1904." In Jonathan Swainger and Constance Backhouse, eds. *People and Place: Historical Influences on Legal Culture* (Vancouver and Toronto, Canada: UBC Press, 2003): 170-97.

215

Pintarich, Dick. "The Gospel According to Edmond Creffield." *Oregon Magazine* (March 1983): 44-46.

Pintarich, Dick. "The Gospel According to Edmond Creffield." In Win McCormack and Dick Pintarich, eds. *Great Moments in Oregon History: A Collection of Articles from the Oregon Magazine* (Portland: New Oregon Publishers, 1987): 105-10.

Pintarich, Dick, and J. Kingston Pierce. "The Strange Saga of Oregon's Other Guru." *The Oregonian* (January 7, 1986): C1-C2.

Thompson, Lewis. "Nemesis of the Nudist High Priest." *Startling Detective* 42 (March 1951): 5-11.

Walker, Lisa. "A Selected Bibliography of Sources on Communal Societies in Oregon and Washington Available at the Oregon Historical Society" (March 15, 1992): 29-30.

## Brush Brook Family

Formed:        Early 1970s
Directories:   Miller, *The 60s Communes*: 256.

## Butler Hill

Place:         Monroe
Directories:   Miller, *The 60s Communes*: 257.

## Butternut Farm

Place:         Western Oregon
Formed:        Early 1970s
Directories:   Miller, *The 60s Communes*: 257.

## Cabbage Lane

Place:         Wolf Creek
Formed:        1972
Directories:   Miller, *The 60s Communes*: 257.
               Association of Lesbian Intentional Communities online
               *Shewolf's Directory of Wimmin's Land*, Fifth Edition
Publication:   *Cabbage Lane* [newsletter]
Archives/Manuscripts:

Ruth Mountaingrove Papers. Special Collections & University Archives, University of Oregon Libraries.

Ruth Mountaingrove Videotape Autobiography Collection, 1988-1997. Special Collections & University Archives, University of Oregon Libraries.

SO CLAP! (Southern Oregon Country Lesbian Archival Project) Collection, 1974-1999, Special Collections & University Archives, University of Oregon Libraries

Tee A. Corinne Papers, 1966-2003. Special Collections & University Archives, University of Oregon Libraries.

Association of Lesbian Intentional Communities. "Come to Oregon Women's Lands." http://alicinfo.com/pages/oregon.htm.

Carroll, Fran. "Cabbage Lane." *Maize* 48 (1996): 37-40.

"History of Cabbage Lane As Recalled by Nelly in 1991" in Tee Corinne, ed., "Community Histories: Living in Southern Oregon." SO CLAP! Files, Special Collections & University Archives, University of Oregon Libraries.

Kaufer, Nelly. "The Story of Cabbage Lane." SO CLAP! Files, Special Collections & University Archives, University of Oregon Libraries.

Kleiner, Catherine B. "Doin' It For Themselves: Lesbian Land Communities in Southern Oregon, 1970-1995." (Ph.D. dissertation, University of New Mexico, 2003): 100-104 .

Miller, Timothy. *The 60s Communes: Hippies and Beyond* (Syracuse, NY: Syracuse University Press, 1999): 139.

Ní Aódagaín, H. "Empowerment through Community: From Separatism to Sanctuary." Paper presented at the 26th Annual Gender Studies Symposium, Lewis & Clark College, March 8, 2007.

Sandia Bear, "Lesbians on Land: A Tribe of Womyn." In Lynn Witt, Sherry Thomas, and Eric Marcus, eds. *Out in All Directions: The Almanac of Gay and Lesbian America* (New York: Warner Books, 1995): 323-26.

Sandilands, Catriona. "Lesbian Separatist Communities and the Experience of Nature: A Queer Ecology." *Organization & Environment* 15 (June 2002): 131-63.

Sandilands, Catriona. "Rainbow's End? Lesbian Separatism and the Ongoing Politics of Ecotopia." In Margrit Eichler, June Larkin, and Sheila Neysmith, eds. *Feminist Utopias: Re-Visioning Our Future* (Toronto, Canada: Inanna Publications and Education, 2002): 37-50.

Summerhawk, Barbara, and La Verne Gagehabib. *Circles of Power: Shifting Dynamics in a Lesbian-Centered Community* (Norwich, VT: New Victoria Publishers, 2000): 40-44.

Wilner, Joseph Bear. "All My Sisters and Brothers: Redefinitions of Family in Oregon Intentional Communities During the Late Twentieth Century." (M. A. thesis, University of Oregon, 2000): 61-63.

## Cape Foulweather Religious Community
Place:          Otter Rock
Formed:         1975
Publications: *The Graceful Wave*

[Grapevine – Excerpts from *The Graceful Wave*]. *Communities* 18 (January/February 1976): 46.

[Resources – Support Groups – Cape Foulweather Religious Community] in *A Guide to Cooperative Alternatives* (New Haven, CT and Louisa, VA: Community Publications Cooperative, 1979): 90.

## Caring Rapid Healing Center
Place:          Otter Rock
Formed:         1996
Formerly:       Vision Foundation
Directories:  [Communities Directory Summer '96 Update – Index of Listings] (*Communities* 91): 67.

## Cascadia Commons
Place:          Portland, 4377 S. W. 94th Ave.
Formed:         1992
Directories:  Communities Directory (online)
              *Communities Directory*, 2005: 113-14.
              *Communities Directory*, 2007: 146.
              Cohousing Directory (online)

Web:          http://www.cascadiacommons.com/
[Ad – Cascadia Commons]. *Communities* 117 (Spring 2003): 71.
[Ad – Cascadia Commons]. *Communities* 118 (Summer 2003): 16.
[Ad – Cascadia Commons]. *Communities* 119 (Fall 2003): 16.
[Ad – Cascadia Commons]. *Communities* 121 (Winter 2003): 22.
[Ad – Cascadia Commons]. *Communities* 122 (Spring 2004): 72.
[Community Houses and Property for Sale or Rent – Cascadia Commons
    Cohousing, Portland, Oregon]. *Communities* 117 (Spring 2003): 73.
Fawcett, Elaine Marshall. "It Takes a Village to Raise a Mother," in David
    Wann, ed., *Reinventing Community: Stories from the Walkways of Cohousing*
    (Golden, CO: Fulcrum Publishing, 2005): 240-46.

## Cat's Cradle
Directories:   Miller, *The 60s Communes*: 257.

## CaveCampKids Commune
Place:         Williams
Directories:   Miller, *The 60s Communes*: 257.

## Cedar Moon
Place:         Portland, 11640 SW Boones Ferry Rd.
Formed:        2003
Directories:   Communities Directory (online)
               *Communities Directory*, 2007: 146-47.
Note:          Co-stewards with Try/on Life Community Farm

Dvorak, Laura, and J. Brush. "Let's Do Greywater First! Could the City of
    Portland Become … Ecotopia?" *Communities* 137 (Winter 2007): 44-47.

## CedarSanctum
Place:         Portland, 3508 NE Simpson
Formed:        2000
Directories:   Communities Directory (online)
               *Communities Directory*, 2005: 115.
               *Communities Directory*, 2007: 305.
Web:           http://www.cedarsanctum.net/

## Center for Well Being
Place:         Creswell, 82644 House Land
Formed:        1990
Directories:   *Directory of Intentional Communities*, 1990: 177.

## Cerro Gordo
Place:         Cottage Grove
Formed:        1973
Directories:   Miller, *The 60s Communes*: 257.
               "Directory 1977" (*Communities* 24): 47.
               "Directory of Intentional Communities 1978" (*Communities* 30):
                   34-35.
               *A Guide to Cooperative Alternatives*, 1979 (*Communities* 38): 166.
               "1981 Directory of Intentional Communities and Resources"
                   (*Communities* 46): 35.

"1983 Directory" (*Communities 56*): 60.
Mercer, *Communes: A Social History and Guide*: 130.
*Directory of Intentional Communities*, 1990: 177.
*Communities Directory*, 1996: 227.
*Communities Directory*, 2000: 218.
*Communities Directory*, 2005: 116.
*Communities Directory*, 2007: 147-48.
Communities Directory (online)
Web:      http://www.cerro-gordo.org/

[Ad – *The Open Forum*]. *Communities* 83 (Summer 1994): 17.
[Ad – *The Open Forum*]. *Communities* 84 (Fall 1994): 15.
Androes, Louis C. "Cerro Gordo: A Study in Tenacity." *Communities* 71/72 (Summer/Fall 1986): 18-24.
Androes, Louis C. "Cerro Gordo" [letter]. *Communities* 75 (Summer 1988): 4.
Arnold, Dave. "The Best of Intentions." *Eugene Register-Guard* (September 30, 1979): 1E-2E.
Bates, Doug. "Developer Blasts R-G Investigation." *Eugene Register-Guard* (April 15, 1979): 2C.
Bates, Doug. "Is Chris Canfield a Saint or a Fake?" *Eugene Register-Guard* (April 14, 1979): 2A.
Bishoff, Don. "Cerro Gordo Plan Rejected; Appeal Pledged." *Eugene Register-Guard* (June 12, 1974): 1C.
Bishop, Bill. "State Files Lawsuit Against Eco-Village." *Eugene Register-Guard* (June 27, 1997): 1B, 5B.
Canfield, Christopher. "Cerro Gordo: Future Residents Organize to Plan and Build an Ecological Village Community" in Gary J. Coates, ed., *Resettling America: Energy, Ecology, & Community* (Andover, MA: Brick House Publishing Co., 1981): 186-213.
Canfield, Chris. [Letter]. *Communities* 80/81 (Spring/Summer 1993): 8.
"Cerro Gordo." *Communities* 30 (February 1978): 54.
"Cerro Gordo – Letters." *Communities* 74 (Summer 1987): 17-22.
"Cerro Gordo" in Robert P. Sutton, *Modern American Communes: A Dictionary* (Westport, CT and London: Greenwood Press, 2005): 28.
"Cerro Gordo Dream Still Alive, but Barely." *Eugene Register-Guard* (February 26, 1976): 1C.
"Cerro Gordo Edict Surprises Developer." *Eugene Register-Guard* (December 19, 1974): 2C.
[Book Reviews – *Cerro Gordo Experiment*]. *Communities* 16 (September-October 1975): 60.
[Community Grapevine]. *Communities* 100 (Fall 1998): 10.
"Couple Typical of Those with Cerro Gordo Dream." *Eugene Register-Guard* (June 9, 1974): 1B.
Curl, John. *History of Work Cooperation in America: Cooperatives, Cooperative Movements, Collectivity, and Communalism from Early America to the Present* (Berkeley: Homeward Press, 1980): 48.
[Directory]. *Utopian Eyes* 2 (Summer 1976): 39.
[Directory]. *Utopian Eyes* 2 (Autumn 1976):[33].
[Grapevine – Cerro Gordo]. *Communities* 14 (May/June 1975): 51.
[Grapevine -- Excerpts from *The Community Association Newsletter*]. *Communities* 18 (January/February 1976): 45-46.
[Grapevine – Cerro Gordo]. "Directory of Intentional Communities 1978" (*Communities 30*): 54.

219

Hemenway, Toby. "Cerro Gordo's Long Road to Community." *The Permaculture Activist* 35 (November 1996): 14-16.

Kelly, Marcia, and Jack Kelly. *The Whole Heaven Catalog: A Resource Guide to Products, Services, Arts, Crafts, and Festivals of Religious, Spiritual, and Cooperative Communities* (New York: Bell Tower/One Spirit, 1998): 213.

Koser, Barbara. [Letter]. *Communities* 80/81 (Spring/Summer 1993): 8.

Luta, Larry. "Board Approves Subarea Plan: Doesn't Condone Cerro Gordo." *Eugene Register Guard* (June 16, 1977): 3B.

McNamer, Deirdre. "Building a Dream." *Eugene Register-Guard* (January 16, 1977): 1F-2F.

Miller, Timothy. *The 60s Communes: Hippies and Beyond* (Syracuse: Syracuse University, 1999): 140-141.

Morrow, Michael. "Cerro Gordo Project: A Large Scale Alternative Moves Into Tomorrow." *Communities* 32 (May/June 1978): 20-25.

Mowat, John. "Energy Production at Cerro Gordo." *Communities* 16 (September/October 1975): 34-39.

Nelson, Don. "Cerro Gordo Ranch—What Will Be Its Fate?" *Eugene Register-Guard* (June 9, 1974): 1B.

[Networks & Resources – Cerro Gordo: A New Eco-Town in Oregon]. *The Permaculture Activist* 34 (June 1996): 58.

"Plan Ahead." *Communities* 11 (December 1974): 36-38.

[Reach -- Communes Forming]. *Communities* 13 (March/April 1975): 56.

[Reach – The Cerro Gordo Center for Creative Community]. *Communities* 26 (May/June 1977): 58.

[Reach – Conferences]. *Communities* 43 (April-May 1980): 53-54.

[Reach – Groups Looking]. *Communities* 25 (March/April 1977): 52.

[Reach – Groups Looking]. *Communities* 54 (June/July 1982): 56, 59-60.

[Reach – People Looking for Groups]. *Communities* 28 (September/October 1977): 58.

[Resources – The Cerro Gordo Experiment]. *Communities* 16 (September/October 1975): 58-60.

[Resources – Land Planning and Appropriate Technology – The Cerro Gordo Experiment]. *Communities* 57 (February/March 1983): 46.

Rodale, Robert. "Some Seekers of Utopia Hope for a New Depression." *Eugene Register-Guard Emerald Empire* (July 14, 1974): 11.

Sutton, Robert P. "Cerro Gordo" in *Modern American Communes: A Dictionary* (Westport, CT: Greenwood Press, 2005): 28.

Thompson, John. "Long-delayed Cerro Gordo Project Started." *Eugene Register-Guard* (November 15, 1977): 1A-2A.

Tims, Marvin. "Planners Delay Action on Cerro Gordo Complex." *Eugene Register-Guard* (May 30, 1974): 2B.

Tims, Marvin. "Planners Delay 'Utopian' Village Decision." *Eugene Register-Guard* (April 10, 1974): 2B.

Urhammer, Jerry. "Cerro Gordo CETA Funds Investigated: Public Funds Went to Artisans Guild in Community and to Solar Project Planned for Sale." *Eugene Register-Guard* (April 19, 1979): 1C-2C.

Urhammer, Jerry. "Lane County Sues Cerro Gordo For CETA Funds." *Eugene Register-Guard* (September 26, 1979): 3C.

Urhammer, Jerry. "Repayment Demanded by County: CETA Fund 'Misused" by Cerro Gordo Firm." *Eugene Register-Guard* (April 21, 1979): 1A-2A.

Urhammer, Jerry. "SEC Found Cerro Gordo Methods Illegal: But Canfield's Recruiting Errors Called Inadvertent." *Eugene Register-Guard* (April 16, 1979): 1C.

Urhammer, Jerry. "Securities Law Breach Claimed: Cerro Gordo Project." *Eugene Register-Guard* (December 18, 1974): 11B.
Urhammer, Jerry, and Doug Bates. "Cerro Gordo Teeters on Brink of Collapse." *Eugene Register-Guard* (April 14, 1979): 1A-2A.
Urhammer, Jerry, and Doug Bates. "Dream of Utopian Village Shaky From Start." *Eugene Register-Guard* (April 15, 1979): 1C-2C.
Vanneman, Brian Robert. "Searching For Paradise in the Rain: Oregon's Communes and Intentional Communities of the 1960s and 1970s." (Honors thesis, University of Oregon, 1997): 23-25.
Walker, Dorothy, ed. *The Cerro Gordo Experiment: A Land Planning Package.* [Cottage, Grove, OR]: The Town Forum, 1974.
Wilkins, Lee. "Planned Community May Win County's OK." *Eugene Register-Guard* (June 3, 1977): 1E.
Wilner, Joseph Bear. "All My Sisters and Brothers: Redefinitions of Family in Oregon Intentional Communities During the Late Twentieth Century." (M. A. thesis, University of Oregon, 2000): 50-51.

## Children of the Valley of Life

Place:       Eugene
Formed:      1973
Directories: Miller, *The 60s Communes*: 258.

## Christ Brotherhood

Place:       Eugene
Formed:      1969
Directories: Miller, *The 60s Communes*: 258.

Bellamy, Ron, and Joe Mosley. "Gentle Christians or Dangerous Cult?" *Eugene Register-Guard* (November 6, 1981): 1E-2E.
Miller, Timothy. *The 60s Communes: Hippies and Beyond* (Syracuse, NY: Syracuse University Press, 1999): 100.
Wilner, Joseph Bear. "All My Sisters and Brothers: Redefinitions of Family in Oregon Intentional Communities During the Late Twentieth Century." (M. A. thesis, University of Oregon, 2000): 98.

## Christian Farm

Place:       Brownsville
Formed:      1970

Bates, Doug. "Lane County's Rural Areas Nurture Communal Lifestyle." *Eugene Register-Guard* (August 29, 1971): B1.
Thoele, Mike. "Hippie-style 'Christian farm' praised for youth work." *Eugene Register-Guard* (November 30, 1970): B1.
Wilner, Joseph Bear. "All My Sisters and Brothers: Redefinitions of Family in Oregon Intentional Communities During the Late Twentieth Century." (M. A. thesis, University of Oregon, 2000): 98.

221

## Church of the Creative

Place:       Creswell
Formed:      1970s
Directories: Miller, *The 60s Communes*: 258.

Bates, Doug. "Lane County's Rural Areas Nurture Communal Lifestyle." *Eugene Register-Guard* (August 29, 1971): B1.

Miller, Timothy. [Gordon Adams interview]. *The 60s Communes: Hippies and Beyond* (Syracuse, NY: Syracuse University Press, 1999): 196, 200.

## Citizens Micro Economy

| | |
|---|---|
| Place: | Portland |
| Forming: | 2005 |
| Directories: | Community Directory (online) |
| | *Communities Directory*, 2007: 308-9. |

## Coagulators

| | |
|---|---|
| Place: | Eugene |
| Formed: | Mid-1970s |
| Directories: | Miller, *The 60s Communes*: 259. |

## CoHo Ecovillage (Cohousing)

| | |
|---|---|
| Place: | Corvallis |
| Formed: | 2002 |
| Directories: | Communities Directory (online) |
| | *Communities Directory*, 2005: 119. |
| | *Communities Directory*, 2007: 310. |
| | Cohousing Directory (online) |
| Web: | www.cohoecovillage.org |
| | www.cohousing-corvallis.com |

## Columbia Cooperative Colony

| | |
|---|---|
| Place: | Mist |
| Dates: | 1886-1888 |
| Note: | Succeeded by Nehalem Valley Cooperative Colony |

Albertson, Ralph. *A Survey of Mutualistic Communities in America*. Reprinted from *Iowa Journal of History and Politics*, 34 (1936) (New York: AMS Press, 1973): 419-20.

Bushee, Frederick A. "Communistic Societies in the United States." *Political Science Quarterly* 20 (December 1905): 664.

Eaton, Joseph W., and Saul M. Katz. *Research Guide on Cooperative Group Farming*. (New York: H. W. Wilson Company, 1942): 37.

Kopp, James J. "Documenting Utopia in Oregon: The Challenges of Tracking the Quest for Perfection," *Oregon Historical Quarterly* 105 (2004): 308-19.

Kopp, James J. "Looking Backward at Edward Bellamy's Impact in Oregon." *Oregon Historical Quarterly* 104 (Spring 2003): 62-95.

Okugawa, Otohiko. "Appendix A: Annotated List of Communal and Utopian Societies, 1787-1919." In Robert S. Fogarty. *Dictionary of American Communal and Utopian History* (Westport, CT: Greenwood Press, 1980): 214.

Pitzer, Donald E., ed. *America's Communal Utopias* (Chapel Hill: University of North Carolina Press, 1997): 458.

Stephan, Karen H., and G. Edward Stephan. "Religion and the Survival of Utopian Communities." *Journal of the Scientific Study of Religion* 12 (March 1973): 89-100[96].

Walker, Lisa. "A Selected Bibliography of Sources on Communal Societies in Oregon and Washington Available at the Oregon Historical Society" (March 15, 1992): 26.

Williams, Julia Elizabeth. "An Analytical Tabulation of the North American Utopian Communities By Type, Longevity and Location." (M. A. thesis, Department of Sociology, University of South Dakota, 1939): 9.

## Columbia Ecovillage

Place:        Portland
Formed:       2007
Directories:  Communities Directory (online)
Web:          columbiaecovillage.net

[Ad – Columbia Ecovillage]. *Communities* 138 (Spring 2008): 7.
[Ad – Columbia Ecovillage]. *Communities* 139 (Summer 2008): 7.
[Classifieds – Ecovillage Forming]. *The Permaculture Activist* 67 (February 2008): 61.
[Communities with Openings]. *Communities* 138 (Spring 2008): 63.
[Communities with Openings]. *Communities* 139 (Summer 2008): 69.

## The Community in Ashland

Place:        Ashland
Formed:       2004
Directories:  Communities Directory (online)
              *Communities Directory*, 2007: 153.
Note:         Affiliated with Twelve Tribe communities (est. 1972)

## Community Association

Place:        Lake Dorena
Formed:       1972
Directories:  Miller, *The 60s Communes*: 259.
              "1975 Community Directory" (*Communities* 12): 26.
Note:         Precursor to Cerro Gordo

[Reach – Communes Being Formed]. *Communities* 10 (November 1974): 59-60.

## Conscious Life Community

Place:        Lakeview
Formed:       2000?
Directories:  Communities Directory (online)

## Co-Operative Christian Federation

*Appleton's Annual Cyclopædia and Register of Important Events of the Year 1899.* Third Series, Vol. IV (New York: D. Appleton and Company, 1900): 686.
"Bonds Issued for Federation: Promoters of Christian Co-Operative Colony Sanguine of Success." *The Oregonian* (March 1, 1906): 10.
*Constitution, By-Laws and Prospectus of the Co-Operative Christian Federation Incorporated Under the Laws of the State of Oregon. Christadelphia, Oregon, Benton County. Post Office Address, Portland, Oregon.* [1902] William A. Hinds American Community Collection. Syracuse University Library Department of Special Collections.
*Co-Operative Christian Federation.* [Portland, 1906]. Associations, Institutions— Cooperative Christian Federation, MSS 1511, Oregon Historical Society Research Library.
"Co-Operative Federation." *The Oregonian* (June 28, 1905): 8.
*The Co-operator* III(11) (February 23, 1901): 2.

223

*Detailed Prospectus No. 2 of the Co-Operative Christian Federation: The Garden City—Industries and Homes.* Portland: Dunham Printing Co., 1906. Associations, Institutions—Cooperative Christian Federation, MSS 1511, Oregon Historical Society Research Library.

"Floats Bond Issue: Christian Federation Scheme Prospers, Says Wallace." *The Oregonian* (February 16, 1906): 9.

"For Christian Colony Work: Rev. H. S. Wallace Explains Co-Operative Federation Methods." *The Oregonian* (July 31, 1905): 9.

"French-Glenn Ranch Bought: Christian Federation Gets It for Colonization Purposes." *The Oregonian* (August 1, 1905): 11.

"Its Affairs Taking Shape: Rev. R. S. Wallace Tells of Plans of Christian Federation." *The Oregonian* (December 6, 1906): 10.

"Must Change Its Plans: Co-operative Christian Federation Foiled by Sale of C. & E." *The Oregonian* (March 2, 1907): 10.

"Nash Reports Plan's Success: Project of Christian Co-Operative Federation, He Says, Is Near Fruition." *The Oregonian* (July 3, 1906): 10.

Nash, Wallis. "The Co-operative Christian Federation: A Remedy for Various Industrial Evils." *The Oregonian* (November 3, 1907): 8.

"Oregon to be Home of World's Greatest Cooperative Scheme. " *Oregon Daily Journal* (June 26, 1905): 1.

Pitzer, Donald E., ed. *America's Communal Utopias* (Chapel Hill: University of North Carolina Press, 1997): 458.

"Plan Model Settlements: Project of the Co-Operative Christian Federation Outlined." *The Oregonian* (June 27, 1905): 18.

"Plan of Wallace: Christian Co-Operative Colony Seems Assured." *The Oregonian* (July 16, 1905): 9.

"Plans Are Ready: Co-operative Christian Federation About to Begin Work." *The Oregonian* (December 22, 1906): 10.

"Plans Model City: Rev. H. S. Wallace Discusses His Project." *The Oregonian* (February 19, 1906): 13.

"Plans to Succeed: Christian Federation Project Commands Attention." *The Oregonian* (November 13, 1905): 12.

"Pledge Good Sums: Southeastern Oregon Will Aid Co-operative Federation." *The Oregonian* (January 6, 1907): 8.

Scott, Leslie M. "The Yaquina Railroad: The Tale of the Great Fiasco." *Quarterly of the Oregon Historical Society* 16 (September 1915): 228-45.

"To Build Railways: Plans of Co-Operative Christian Federation." *The Oregonian* (August 6, 1905): 11.

"Vale Take $50,000 of Bonds: Co-operative Christian Federation Meets With Favor in That City." *The Oregonian* (January 7, 1907): 4.

"Work for 50,000 People: Christian Federation Will Need Great Many Settlers." *The Oregonian* (August 5, 1905): 11.

## Cooperative Farm

Place:       Eugene
Dates:       1931-1933
Publication: *Bulletin*. Mimeographed Monthly.

Craft, Roy. "Co-operative Farm Found Serious Effort to Work Out Solution of Economic Life." *Eugene Register-Guard* (January 22, 1933): 1, 2.

[Craft, Roy]. "Definite Assignments Mark Work Division At Co-op Farm." *Eugene Register-Guard* (January 23, 1933): 1, 3.

[Craft, Roy]. "Prediction of Failure At Farm Fall As Idea Develops." *Eugene Register-Guard* (January 24, 1933): 1, 3.

Hendricks, Robert J. *Bethel and Aurora: An Experiment in Communism As Practical Christianity with Some Account of Past and Present Ventures in Collective Living* (New York: Press of the Pioneers, 1933): 266-68, 271.

Miller, Timothy. "Co-operative Farm" in *American Communes, 1860-1960: A Bibliography* (New York and London: Garland Publishing, 1990): 92. (This entry incorrectly gives the starting date as 1951 instead of 1931.)

Miller, Timothy. "The Cooperative Farm" in *The Quest for Utopia in Twentieth-Century America. Volume I: 1900-1960.* (Syracuse, NY: Syracuse University Press, 1998): 139.

Pitzer, Donald E., ed. *America's Communal Utopias* (Chapel Hill: University of North Carolina Press, 1997): 458. (This entry incorrectly gives the starting date as 1951 instead of 1931.)

## Cooperative Subsistence Colony

Place:     Dallas
Date:      1933-?

Albertson, Ralph. "A Survey of Mutualistic Communities in America," *Iowa Journal of History and Politics* 34 (1936): 421.

Bercaw, Louise O., A. M. Hannay, and Esther M. Colvin, comps., *Bibliography on Land Settlement with Particular Reference to Small Holdings and Subsistance Homesteads* (Washington: United States Department of Agriculture, 1934): 171.

"Coöperative Subsistence Colony Formed by Jobless Oregon Workers." *Christian Science Monitor* (December 7, 1937): 1.

Eaton, Joseph W., and Saul M. Katz. *Research Guide on Cooperative Group Farming* (New York: H. W. Wilson Company, 1942): 37.

Williams, Julia Elizabeth. "An Analytical Tabulation of the North American Utopian Communities By Type, Longevity and Location." (M. A. thesis, Department of Sociology, University of South Dakota, 1939): 7.

## Copperland

Place:          Grants Pass
Formed:         1990s
Archives/
Manuscripts:
                SO CLAP! (Southern Oregon Country Lesbian Archival Project) Collection, 1974-1999, Special Collections & University Archives, University of Oregon Libraries, Series IV

Association of Lesbian Intentional Communities. "Come to Oregon Women's Lands." http://alicinfo.com/pages/oregon.htm

Summerhawk, Barbara, and La Verne Gagehabib. *Circles of Power: Shifting Dynamics in a Lesbian-Centered Community* (Norwich, VT: New Victoria Publishers, 2000): 62-63.

225

## Cornucopia

Place:          Coos Bay, 90 Commercial Way
Formed:         1972
Also see:       Living Love
Directories:    "1983 Directory" (*Communities* 56): 62.

## Corvallis Cohousing

Place:        Corvallis
Forming:      2003
Directories:  [Directories Update – New]. (*Communities* 117): 66.
              *Communities* 120 (Special 2003): 8.

## Cougar Mountain Land Coop

Place:        Cottage Grove
Formed:       1985
Directories:  *Directory of Collectives*, 1985: 71.

## Crabapple

Place:        Florence/Eugene
Formed:       1975
Directories:  Miller, *The 60s Communes*: 260.
              *A Guide to Cooperative Alternatives*, 1979 (*Communities* 38): 167.
              "1981 Directory of Intentional Communities and Resources"
              (*Communities* 46): 36.
              "1983 Directory" (*Communities* 56): 62.
              Mercer, *Communes: A Social History and Guide*: 131.

[Directory]. *Utopian Eyes* 2 (Autumn 1976):[33].
[Directory]. *Utopian Eyes* 3 (Winter 1977):[42].
[Reach -- Groups Looking for People – Crabapple]. *Communities* 20 (May/June 1976): 47.
[Reach – Groups Looking for People – Crabapple]. *Communities* 21 (July/August 1976): 45.
Email: David Harrington to Jim Kopp, 7/23/05

## Crack of Dawn

Place:        Ashland, 15797 Hwy 66
Formed:       1977
Directories:  "1981 Directory of Intentional Communities and Resources"
              (*Communities* 46): 36-37.
              "1983 Directory" (*Communities* 56): 62.
              Mercer, *Communes: A Social History and Guide*: 131.

## Creekland

Place:        Wolf Creek
Formed:       1974
Directories:  *Communities Directory*, 1996: 322.
Publications: *The RadDish*
Note:         Changed to Nomenus Sanctuary in 1986

Wilner, Joseph Bear. "All My Sisters and Brothers: Redefinitions of Family in Oregon Intentional Communities During the Late Twentieth Century." (M. A. thesis, University of Oregon, 2000): 73.

## Crook's Creek

Place:        Sunny Valley
Formed:       1969
Directories:  Miller, *The 60s Communes*: 260.

Gardner, Hugh. "Son of Sociology: Crook's Creek." In *The Children of Prosperity: Thirteen Modern American Communes* (New York: St. Martin's Press, 1978): 182-93.

Roskind, Robert. *Memoirs of an Ex-Hippie: Seven Years in the Counterculture* (Blowing Rock, NC: One Love Press, 2001): 120.

Wilner, Joseph Bear. "All My Sisters and Brothers: Redefinitions of Family in Oregon Intentional Communities During the Late Twentieth Century." (M. A. thesis, University of Oregon, 2000): 38-39.

## CRO(W) Research Organization (CRO(W) Farm)

Place:       Veneta
Formed:      1968
Directories: Ayd, *The Youth Communes*: 166.
             Miller, *The 60s Communes*: 260.
             "Commune Directory" (*Communities* 1): 32.
             "Commune Directory" (*Communities* 7): 31.
Publications: Directory
             Newsletter

"Conversation ... with Cindi Smith." *Eugene Register-Guard Emerald Empire* (April 29, 1973): 13.

"CRO Farm: A Cultural Alternative." *Augur* 1:10 (March 3, 1970).

Estellachild, Vivian. "Hippie Communes." *W♀men: A Journal of Liberation* 2(2) (Winter 1971): 40-43.

[Fairfield, Richard]. "C.R.O. Farm." *Modern Utopian* 5 ["Communes U.S.A."] (1971): 143-45.

Fairfield, Richard. "The CRO Research Organization" in *Communes USA: A Personal Tour* (Baltimore,MD: Penguin Books, 1972): 304-14.

Goodwin, Michael. "The Ken Kesey Movie." *The Rolling Stone* (March 7, 1970).

Hartzell, Hal, Jr. *Birth of a Cooperative: Hoedads, Inc., A Worker Owned Forest Labor Co-op* (Eugene: Hulogos'I Communications, 1987): 88-89.

Houriet, Robert. *Getting Back Together* (New York: Coward, McCann & Geoghegan, 1971): 106-9.

Miller, Timothy. *The 60s Communes: Hippies and Beyond* (Syracuse, NY: Syracuse University Press, 1999): 137.

[Reach – Land]. *Communities* 11 (December 1974): 60.

Sellard, Dan. "In Search of Utopia." *Eugene Register-Guard* (Oct. 20, 1968): 3EE.

Teeters, Kay. "Communal Utopias of the Pacific Northwest." (Honors thesis, University of Oregon, 1970): 55-58.

Vanneman, Brian Robert. "Searching For Paradise in the Rain: Oregon's Communes and Intentional Communities of the 1960s and 1970s." (Honors thesis, University of Oregon, 1997): 18.

Wilner, Joseph Bear. "All My Sisters and Brothers: Redefinitions of Family in Oregon Intentional Communities During the Late Twentieth Century." (M. A. thesis, University of Oregon, 2000): 33-36.

227

## Daybreak Cohousing

Place:       Portland
Formed:      2005
Directories: Cohousing Directory (online)
             Communities Directory (online)
             *Communities Directory*, 2007: 317.

Web:         daybreakcohousing.org
Formerly:   Sunrise Cohousing

## Dragon Spirit

Place:        Portland area
Forming:    2007
Directories: Communities Directory (online)

## Dulusum Farm

Place:        Salwaka Valley area
Formed:     1970s
Directories: Miller, *The 60s Communes*: 261.

## Du-Má

Place:        Eugene, 2244 Alder St.
Formed:     1988
Directories: [Fall 1992 Update to the Directory of Intentional Communities]
             (*Communities* 79): 19.
             *Communities Directory*, 1996: 241-42.
             *Communities Directory*, 2000: 236.
             *Communities Directory*, 2005: 130.
             *Communities Directory*, 2007: 161.
             *Communities Directory* (online)
Web:         www.efn.org/~dlamp/

[Communities with Openings]. *Communities* 85 (Winter 1994): 70.
[Communities with Openings]. *Communities* 86 (Spring 1995): 71.
[Communities with Openings]. *Communities* 92 (Fall 1996): 70.
[Communities with Openings]. *Communities* 93 (Winter 1996): 71.
[Communities with Openings]. *Communities* 94 (Spring 1997): 70.
[Community Grapevine]. *Communities* 118 (Summer 2003): 8.
Wilner, Joseph Bear. "All My Sisters and Brothers: Redefinitions of Family in
    Oregon Intentional Communities During the Late Twentieth Century." (M. A.
    thesis, University of Oregon, 2000): 42.

## Earth Home

Formed:     1970s
Directories: Miller, *The 60s Communes*: 261.

## Earth's Rising Coop

Place:        Monroe, 25358 Cherry Creek Road
Formed:     1970
Directories: Miller, *The 60s Communes*: 261.
             *Directory of Intentional Communities*, 1991: 183.

Bates, Doug. "Lane County's Rural Areas Nurture Communal Lifestyle." *Eugene
    Register-Guard* (August 29, 1971): B1.
Johnson, David. "Greener Grass: A Short History of Oregon's Utopia Tradition,"
    *Oregon Heritage* 1 (Winter/Spring 1995): 17.

## Earthsky Tribe

Place:        Independence
Forming:    2005
Directories: *Communities Directory*, 2005: 133.

## Earthswell Farm

Place:        McMinnville
Forming:    2005
Directories:   Communities Directory (online)

## East Blair Housing Cooperative

Place:        Eugene
Formed:    1981
Web:          www.geocities.com/eastblair/eastblair.htm

Omogrosso, Michael. "The Flowering of Art at East Blair: 'Hot, Intimate, & Wildly Reveling'." *Communities* 93 (Winter 1996): 44-46.

## East Portland Cohousing

Place:        Portland
Forming:    2007
Directories:   Cohousing Directory (online)
              Communities Directory (online)
Web:          www.eastportlandcohousing.org

## The Eater Family

Place:        Coquille
Formed:    1970
Directories:   Miller, *The 60s Communes*: 261.
              "Commune Directory" (*Communities* 1): 33.
              "Commune Directory" (*Communities* 7): 31.
Note:         Former theater group

## ECOS

Place:        Cave Junction
Forming:    1977

[Community Living Directory – Northwest]. *Utopian Eyes* 3 (Winter 1977): [34].

## Eduen

Place:        Gresham
Forming:    2002
Web:          http://www.eduen.net/

"Farm Plans Arch Gresham Eyebrows." *The Oregonian* (November 12, 2004).

## The 80 Acres

Place:        Elephant Rock
Formed:    Early 1970s

229

## Eloin Community

Place:        Ashland
Formed:    1990
Directories:   [Communities Directory: Updates & Additions to the Third
                 Printing] (*Communities* 79): 33.
              [Directory Update Spring/Summer '93 Update – New Listings, North
                 America] (*Communities* 80/81): 84-85.
              *Communities Directory*, 1996: 245.

## End of the Road House and Aprovecho Research Center

Place:         Cottage Grove, 80574 Hazelton Road
Formed:        1981
Directories:   *Directory of Collectives*, 1985: 72.
               *Directory of Intentional Communities*, 1991: 185.
Note:          See Aprovecho Research Center

## Essene Cooperative

Place:         La Grande, 62460 Halley Rd
Forming:       2004
Directories:   Communities Directory (online)
Web:           http://bcn.boulder.co.us/community/essene/
Note:          Formerly in Boulder, Colorado

## Eugene Cohousing

Place:         Eugene, 711 West 11th
Forming:       1993
Directories:   [Directory Update Spring/Summer '93 Update – New Listings, North
                  America] (*Communities* 80/81): 85.
               *Communities Directory*, 1996: 246.
               [Communities Directory Winter '96 Update – North American
                  Updates] (*Communities* 93): 67.
               *Communities Directory*, 2005: 143.

## Eugene Downtown Cohousing

Place:         Eugene, NW Corner of 11th and Lincoln
Forming:       2003
Directories:   Cohousing Directory (online)
               *Communities Directory*, 2007: 328.
Web:           www.eugenecohousing.com

David Wann, ed., *Reinventing Community: Stories from the Walkways of
   Cohousing* (Golden, CO: Fulcrum Publishing, 2005): 46.

## Evenstar

Place:         Oregon coast
Formed:        1970s
Directories:   Miller, *The 60s Communes*: 260.
               [Directory Updates] (*Communities* 123): 65.

## Fairview Cooperative

Place:         Hood River, 5348 Binns Hill Dr.
Formed:        1998 (in Port Orchard, WA)
Directories:   [Directory Update – Changes] (*Communities* 120): 20.

## Family of the Living Arts

Place:         Sunny Valley
Formed:        1970
Formerly:      Family of the Mystic Arts
Directories:   Miller, *The 60s Communes*: 262.

Miller, Timothy. *The 60s Communes: Hippies and Beyond* (Syracuse, NY: Syracuse
   University Press, 1999): 240.

## Family of the Mystic Arts

Place:         Sunny Valley
Formed:        1968
Directories:   Ayd, *The Youth Communes*: 166.
               Miller, *The 60s Communes*: 262.

"Bob Carey and the Family: Getting It Together in the Woods [Interview by
    Edmund Helminsky]" in *Communes USA: A Personal Tour* (Baltimore, MD:
    Penguin Books, 1972): 106-13.
[Fairfield, Richard]. "Family of Mystic Arts." *Modern Utopian* 5 ["Communes
    U.S.A."] (1971): 8-10.
Fairfield, Richard. "The Oregon Family" in *Communes USA: A Personal Tour*
    (Baltimore, MD: Penguin Books, 1972): 102-6.
Houriet, Robert. *Getting Back Together* (New York: Coward, McCann &
    Geoghegan, 1971): 91-106.
"Interview with Bob Carey, Member, Family of Mystic Arts." *Modern Utopian* 5
    ["Communes U.S.A."] (1971): 10-13.
Miller, Timothy. *The 60s Communes: Hippies and Beyond* (Syracuse, NY: Syracuse
    University Press, 1999): 15, 77, 173, 240.
Roskind, Robert. *Memoirs of an Ex-Hippie: Seven Years in the Counterculture*
    (Blowing Rock, NC: One Love Press, 2001): 120.
Snickley, John. "The Youth Communes: New Way of Living Confronts the U.S."
    *Life* 67 (3) (July 18, 1969): 16B-[23].
Teeters, Kay. "Communal Utopias of the Pacific Northwest." (Honors thesis,
    University of Oregon, 1970): 60. [Commune is referred to as "Sunny Valley."]
Vanneman, Brian Robert. "Searching For Paradise in the Rain: Oregon's
    Communes and Intentional Communities of the 1960s and 1970s." (Honors
    thesis, University of Oregon, 1997): 22.

## The Fanatic Family

Place:         Cave Junction
Formed:        1970s
Directories:   Miller, *The 60s Communes*: 262.

Wilner, Joseph Bear. "All My Sisters and Brothers: Redefinitions of Family in
    Oregon Intentional Communities During the Late Twentieth Century." (M. A.
    thesis, University of Oregon, 2000): 31.

## The Farm

Place:         Takilma
Formed:        1970s
Directories:   Miller, *The 60s Communes*: 262.

## Ferry Sisters (Ferry Street Home)

Place:         Eugene
Formed:        1969
Directories:   Miller, *The 60s Communes*: 263.

231

## Fish Pond

Place:         Grants Pass
Formed:        1970s

Sandia Bear, "Lesbians on Land: A Tribe of Womyn." In Lynn Witt, Sherry
    Thomas, and Eric Marcus, eds. *Out in All Directions: The Almanac of Gay and
    Lesbian America* (New York: Warner Books, 1995): 323-26.

Summerhawk, Barbara, and La Verne Gagehabib. *Circles of Power: Shifting Dynamics in a Lesbian-Centered Community* (Norwich, VT: New Victoria Publishers, 2000): 62-63.

## Fly Away Home

Place:          Myrtle Creek
Formed:        1976
Directories:   Miller, *The 60s Communes*: 263.
                    Association of Lesbian Intentional Communities (online)
                    *Shewolf's Directory of Wimmin's Land*. Fifth Edition
**Archives/Manuscripts:**
                    Ruth Mountaingrove Papers. Special Collections & University
                         Archives, University of Oregon Libraries.
                    SO CLAP! (Southern Oregon Country Lesbian Archival Project)
                         Collection, 1974-1999, Special Collections & University
                         Archives, University of Oregon Libraries
                    Tee A. Corinne Papers, 1966-2003. Special Collections & University
                         Archives, University of Oregon Libraries.

Association of Lesbian Intentional Communities. "Come to Oregon Women's Lands." http://alicinfo.com/pages/oregon.htm

Bethroot. "Fly Away Home." *Rough Road* 2 (1982): 5-6.

"Fly Away Home [advertisement[." *Woman's Place Newsletter* (July 1981): 6.

"Fly Away Home [Announcements]." *Women's Press* (May/June 1981): 19.

Kleiner, Catherine B. "Doin' It For Themselves: Lesbian Land Communities in Southern Oregon, 1970-1995." (Ph.D. dissertation, University of New Mexico, 2003): 117-25.

Madrone, Hawk. *Weeding at Dawn: A Lesbian Country Life*. New York: Harrington Park Press, 2000.

Madrone, Hawk. "Fly Away Home." *WomanSpirit* vol. 3, no. 11 (Spring Equinox 1977): 13-16.

Ní Aódagaín, H. "Empowerment through Community: From Separatism to Sanctuary." Paper presented at the 26th Annual Gender Studies Symposium, Lewis & Clark College, March 8, 2007.

Sandia Bear, "Lesbians on Land: A Tribe of Womyn." In Lynn Witt, Sherry Thomas, and Eric Marcus, eds. *Out in All Directions: The Almanac of Gay and Lesbian America* (New York: Warner Books, 1995): 323-26.

Sandilands, Catriona. "Lesbian Separatist Communities and the Experience of Nature: A Queer Ecology." *Organization & Environment* 15 (June 2002): 131-63.

Sandilands, Catriona. "Rainbow's End? Lesbian Separatism and the Ongoing Politics of Ecotopia." In Margrit Eichler, June Larkin, and Sheila Neysmith, eds. *Feminist Utopias: Re-Visioning Our Future* (Toronto, Canada: Inanna Publications and Education, 2002): 37-50.

Summerhawk, Barbara, and La Verne Gagehabib. *Circles of Power: Shifting Dynamics in a Lesbian-Centered Community* (Norwich, VT: New Victoria Publishers, 2000): 54-57.

Wilner, Joseph Bear. "All My Sisters and Brothers: Redefinitions of Family in Oregon Intentional Communities During the Late Twentieth Century." (M. A. thesis, University of Oregon, 2000): 70.

## Folly Farm
Place:       Grande Ronde, 9380 Hebo Rd
Formed:      Mid 1970s
Directories: Miller, *The 60s Communes*: 263.
             "1983 Directory" (*Communities* 56): 64.

[Reach – Groups Looking]. *Communities* 52 (February/March 1982): 55.
[Reach – Groups Looking]. *Communities* 57 (February/March 1983): 53.

## Footbridge Farm
Place:       Swisshome
Formed:      1970s
Directories: Miller, *The 60s Communes*: 263.

Bates, Doug. "Lane County's Rural Areas Nurture Communal Lifestyle." *Eugene Register-Guard* (August 29, 1971): B1.
Miller, Timothy. *The 60s Communes: Hippies and Beyond* (Syracuse, NY: Syracuse University Press, 1999): 11, 200, 237.

## Fordyce Street Cohousing
Place:       Ashland, 1338 Seena Ln
Forming:     2005
Directories: Communities Directory (online)
             *Communities Directory*, 2005: 146.
             *Communities Directory*, 2007: 332.

## Forgotten Works
Place:       Wolf Creek
Formed:      1970s
Directories: Miller, *The 60s Communes*: 263.

Roskind, Robert. "Forgotten Works" in *Memoirs of an Ex-Hippie: Seven Years in the Counterculture* (Blowing Rock, NC: One Love Press, 2001): 119, 125-30.

## Fort Mudge
Place:       Dexter
Formed:      1967
Directories: Miller, *The 60s Communes*: 263.

## 40th Avenue Cohousing
Place:       Eugene, 550 E. 40th Ave.
Formed:      2002
Directories: Communities Directory (online)

## Four Winds Farm
Place:       Hood River
Formed:      1974
Directories: Miller, *The 60s Communes*: 263.

Miller, Timothy. *The 60s Communes: Hippies and Beyond* (Syracuse, NY: Syracuse University Press, 1999): 77.

233

## Free Ashland

Place:       Ashland
Formed:      1970

Johnson, David. "Greener Grass: A Short History of Oregon's Utopia Tradition." *Oregon Heritage* 1 (Winter/Spring 1995):16.

## Friends and Neighbors

Place:       Several locations
Forming:     2004
Directories: Communities Directory (online)
             *Communities Directory*, 2007: 333.

## Galilee

Place:       Portland, 6215 SE 53rd St.
Formed:      1990
Directories: *Directory of Intentional Communities*, 1990: 177.
             [Fall 1992 Update to the Directory of Intentional Communities] (*Communities* 79): 19.
             [Communities Directory Summer '95 Update – North American Community Updates] (*Communities* 87): 65.
             [Communities Directory Fall '95 Update – North American New Listings] (*Communities* 88): 67.

## Gathering Light . . . a retreat

Place:       Chiloquin
Forming:     2006?
Directories: Communities Directory (online) (as Nature Retreat)
             *Communities Directory*, 2007: 217 (as Nature Retreat)
Web:         www.gatheringlight.com

## Goat Farm

Place:       Eugene
Formed:      Early 1970s
Directories: Miller, *The 60s Communes*: 264.

## Golden

Place:       Wolf Creek
Formed:      1974
**Archives/Manuscripts:**
             Ruth Mountaingrove Papers, Special Collections & University Archives, University of Oregon Libraries
             Ruth Mountaingrove Videotape Autobiography Collection, 1988-1997. Special Collections & University Archives, University of Oregon Libraries.
             SO CLAP! (Southern Oregon Country Lesbian Archival Project) Collection, 1974-1999, Special Collections & University Archives, University of Oregon Libraries

"Golden" in Joyce Cheney, ed., *Lesbian Land* (Minneapolis: Word Weavers, 1985): 50-54.
Klein, Rena. "Golden." *Rough Road* 2 (1982): 13.

Sandilands, Catriona. "Lesbian Separatist Communities and the Experience of Nature: A Queer Ecology." *Organization & Environment* 15 (June 2002): 131-63.

Shugar, Dana R. *Separatism and Women's Community* (Lincoln and London: University of Nebraska Press, 1995): 100, 103-4.

Summerhawk, Barbara, and La Verne Gagehabib. *Circles of Power: Shifting Dynamics in a Lesbian-Centered Community* (Norwich, VT: New Victoria Publishers, 2000): 40-44; 117-20.

Valentine, Gill. "Making Space: Lesbian Separatist Communities in the United States." In Paul Cloke and Jo Little, eds. *Contested Countryside Cultures: Otherness, Marginalisation and Rurality* (London and New York: Routledge, 1997): 109-22.

Wilner, Joseph Bear. "All My Sisters and Brothers: Redefinitions of Family in Oregon Intentional Communities During the Late Twentieth Century." (M. A. thesis, University of Oregon, 2000): 61-63.

## Golden Heart Village

Forming:        2007
Directories:   Community Directory (online)

## Good Earth Commune

Place:          Southern Oregon
Formed:        1971
Directories:   Miller, *The 60s Communes*: 264.

## Gospel Outreach – Grants Pass

Place:          Grants Pass, 611 N.W. "A" Street
Formed:        1976
Directories:   Jackson, Dave. *Coming Together*: 185-86.
Note:           Part of Gospel Outreach ministries.

Peterson, Joe V. "Jesus People: Christ, Communes, and the Counterculture of the Late Twentieth Century in the Pacific Northwest and a Brief Review of the Shiloh Youth Revival Centers, Inc., The Highway Missionary Society/Servant Community, and the House of Elijah." (M.A. thesis, Northwest Christian College, 1990): 31.

## Gospel Outreach – Silverton

Place:          Silverton, 602 Oak Street
Formed:        1974
Directories:   Jackson, Dave. *Coming Together* (Minneapolis: Bethany Fellowship, 1978): 185-86.
Note:           Part of Gospel Outreach ministries.

## Great Pumpkin Commune

Place:          Tillamook
Formed:        1967

Vanneman, Brian Robert. "Searching For Paradise in the Rain: Oregon's Communes and Intentional Communities of the 1960s and 1970s." (Honors thesis, University of Oregon, 1997): 18.

# Groundworks
Place:        Murphy
Archives/Manuscripts:
        SO CLAP! (Southern Oregon Country Lesbian Archival Project)
        Collection, 1974-1999, Special Collections & University
        Archives, University of Oregon Libraries, Series VI

[Calendar – June 1-8 – 1st Women's Natural Building Symposium]. *The Permaculture Activist* 34 (June 1996): 68.
[Natural Building Calendar – June 19-26 – The Second Women's Natural Building Symposium]. *The Permaculture Activist* 36 (March 1997): 41.

# Haney (pseudonym)
Place:        Northwestern Oregon
Formed:       1969

Zicklin, Gilbert. *Countercultural Communes: A Sociological Perspective*. Westport, CT, and London: Greenwood Press, 1983.

# Harmony Heart Community
Place:        Williams
Formed:       Mid-1970s
Directories:  Miller, *The 60s Communes*: 265.

# Heart On Farm
Place:        Eugene, 88470 Fisher Road
Forming:      2005
Directories:  Community Directory (online)

# Hearthome Northwest
Place:        Portland
Forming:      1998

[Communities Directory Winter '98 Update – North American New Listings]. *Communities* 101 (Winter 1998): 68.

# Heartsong
Place:        Applegate
Forming:      1986

[Reach – Groups Looking]. *Communities* 70 (Spring 1986): 58.

# Heartwind Community
Forming:      1986

236

[Classifieds – Real Estate – 300 acres of former Heartwind Community]. *Communities* 69 (Winter 1986): 46.

# High Ridge Farm
Place:        Southern Oregon
Formed:       1968
Directories:  Miller, *The 60s Communes*: 266.
Note:         Identified as Saddle Ridge Farm and Magic Farm in many works.

Fairfield, Richard. "Magic Farm" in *Communes USA: A Personal Tour* (Baltimore, MD: Penguin Books, 1972): 220-24, 226-33.

Gardner, Hugh. "Forever Choice, Forever Changes: Saddle Ridge Farm" in *The Children of Prosperity; Thirteen Modern American Communes* (New York: St. Martin's Press, 1978): 194-217, also passim.

Houriet, Robert. "Oregon: High Ridge Farm" in *Getting Back Together* (New York: Coward, McCann & Geoghegan, 1971): 29-87.

Sundancer, Elaine. *Celery Wine: Story of a Country Commune.* Yellow Springs, OH: Community Publications Cooperative, 1973.

Sundancer, Elaine. "Life on a Country Commune." From the *Los Angeles Free Press*, Dec. 17, 1971. *Communitas* 2 (September 1972): 5-11.

Sundancer, Elaine. "Saddle Ridge Farm." *Communities* 4 ([1973]): 5-8.

Sutton, Robert P. "High Ridge Farm" in *Communal Utopias and the American Experience: Secular Communities, 1824-2000* (Westport, CT, and London: Praeger, 2004): 139-41.

Sutton, Robert P. "High Ridge Farm" in *Modern American Communes: A Dictionary* (Westport, CT, and London: Greenwood Press, 2005): 73.

## Higher Ground Cohousing

Place:        Bend, 1911 NE Higher Ground Ave.
Formed:       1992
Directories:  Cohousing Directory (online)
              *Communities Directory*, 2005: 160.
              *Communities Directory*, 2007: 184.
              Community Directory (online)

[Communities with Openings – Cohousing Community, Bend, Oregon]. *Communities* 96 (Fall 1997): 69.

[Communities with Openings – Cohousing Community, Bend, Oregon]. *Communities* 97 (Winter 1997): 78.

[Communities with Openings – Cohousing Community, Bend, Oregon]. *Communities* 98 (Spring 1998): 67.

[Communities with Openings – Cohousing Community, Bend, Oregon]. *Communities* 99 (Summer 1998): 72.

[Communities with Openings – Cohousing Community, Bend, Oregon]. *Communities* 100 (Fall 1998): 72.

[Community Houses for Sale]. *Communities* 111 (Summer 2001): 75.

[Community Houses for Sale]. *Communities* 112 (Fall 2001): 66-67.

## Highway Missionary Society/Servant Community

Place:     Southern Oregon
Formed:    1970s

Peterson, Joe V. "Jesus People: Christ, Communes, and the Counterculture of the Late Twentieth Century in the Pacific Northwest and a Brief Review of the Shiloh Youth Revival Centers, Inc., The Highway Missionary Society/Servant Community, and the House of Elijah." M.A. thesis, Northwest Christian College, 1990.

Warner, Keith. "Responding to Sexual Misconduct in Christian Community." *Communities* 92 (Fall 1996): 56-59.

# Hoedads

Place:          Eugene/Mobile
Formed:         1971
Directories:    Miller, *The 60s Communes*: 266.
                *Directory of Collectives*, 1985: 71.
Publication:    *Together*

Baker, Loraine. "Half & Half Hoedads." [West by Northwest 2000-2002]. (http://www.westbynorthwest.org/summerlate01/Loraine.shtml
"Cooperative Forestry Work [Cull Crew]." *Woman's Place Newsletter* (January 1981): 12.
Freundlich, Paul. "Introducing This Issue." *Communities* 29 (November/December 1977): inside front cover.
"Full Moon Rising Quits Hoedads." *Women's Press* (August/September 1979): 1.
Gunn, Christopher Eaton, "Hoedads" in *Workers' Self-Management in the United States* (Ithaca, NY, and London: Cornell University Press, 1984): 75-80.
Gunn, Christopher E. "Hoedads Co-op: Democracy and Cooperation at Work." In Robert Jackall and Henry M. Levin, eds. *Worker Cooperatives in America* (Berkeley: University of California Press, 1984): 141-70.
Hartzell, Hal, Jr. *Birth of a Cooperative: Hoedads, Inc., A Worker Owned Forest Labor Co-op*. Eugene: Hulogos'i Communications, 1987.
"Hoedads." *Whole Eugene Catalog* (1975/76): 37.
*Hoedads Together Again, 2001: Legends in Our Own Minds* [video]. Eugene: Moving Image Productions, 2001.
Mackie, Gerry. "The Rise and Fall of the Forest Workers' Cooperatives of the Pacific Northwest." M.A. thesis, University of Oregon, 1990.
Mackie, Gerry. "Success and Failure in an American Workers' Cooperative Movement." *Politics & Society* 22 (June 1994): 215-35.
Miller, Timothy. *The 60s Communes: Hippies and Beyond* (Syracuse, NY: Syracuse University Press, 1999): xxii.
Nagle, Greg. "Hoedads" in *A Guide to Cooperative Alternatives* (New Haven, CT, and Louisa, VA: Community Publications Cooperative, 1979): 33-36.
[Reach – Services Offered]. *Communities* 10 (November 1974): 63.
Sutton, Robert P. "Hoedads" in *Modern American Communes: A Dictionary* (Westport, CT: Greenwood Press, 2005): 75.
Trahair, Richard C. S. "Hoedads" in *Utopias and Utopians: An Historical Dictionary* (Westport, CT: Greenwood Press, 1999): 183.
Wadsworth, Lois. "Tree Planters: The Mighty Hoedads, Back for a 30-year Reunion, Recall Their Grand Experiment." *Eugene Weekly* (August 2, 2001).

# Hog Farm

Place:      Marcola
Formed:     1971

Bates, Doug. "Lane County's Rural Areas Nurture Communal Lifestyle." *Eugene Register-Guard* (August 29, 1971): B1.

# Hopeland

Kopp, James J. "To the Editor [letter]." *Oregon Historical Quarterly* 106 (Winter 2005): 691-2.
Lockley, Fred. "Impressions and Observations of the Journal Man." *Oregon Journal* (June 7, 1936): 10.

Nyden, Evangeline. "Panama Riot Helped Establish Sellwood." *The [Sellwood] Bee* (May 15, 1975).

Plumb, Dale. "Christian Utopia." *Oregon City Enterprise-Courier* Magazine Section (November 22, 1953).

[Sellwood, John]. "Rules to be Observed by All the Residents of Hopeland, Oregon." Library of Congress' American Memory web site at http://memory.loc.gov/ammem/rbpehtml/pehome.html.

Stoy, William H. *A Sermon. In Memoriam – Rev. John Sellwood, B.D. Born May 6, 1806. Died August 27, 1892* (Portland, 1892).

Walker, Lisa. "A Selected Bibliography of Sources on Communal Societies in Oregon and Washington Available at the Oregon Historical Society" (March 15, 1992): 27.

## Hosanna House

| | |
|---|---|
| **Place:** | Eugene |
| **Formed:** | Early 1970s |
| **Directories:** | Miller, *The 60s Communes*: 266. |

Ward, Hiley H. *The Far-Out Saints of the Jesus Community: A Firsthand Report and Interpretation of the Jesus People Movement* (New York: Association Press, 1972): 28.

## House Alive Homestead

| | |
|---|---|
| **Place:** | Jacksonville, 7540 Griffin Lane |
| **Forming:** | 2007 |
| **Directories:** | Community Directory (online) |
| **Web:** | www.housealive.org |

## House of Elijah

| | |
|---|---|
| **Place:** | Grants Pass (initially in Yakima, Washington) |
| **Formed:** | Late 1970s |

Peterson, Joe V. "Jesus People: Christ, Communes, and the Counterculture of the Late Twentieth Century in the Pacific Northwest and a Brief Review of the Shiloh Youth Revival Centers, Inc., The Highway Missionary Society/Servant Community, and the House of Elijah." M.A. thesis, Northwest Christian College, 1990.

## House of Joy

| | |
|---|---|
| **Place:** | Portland |
| **Formed:** | Early 1970s |
| **Directories:** | Miller, *The 60s Communes*: 267. |

Ward, Hiley H. *The Far-Out Saints of the Jesus Community: A Firsthand Report and Interpretation of the Jesus People Movement* (New York: Association Press, 1972): 18-19; 48; 87-88; 96.

239

## House of the Risen Son

| | |
|---|---|
| **Place:** | Eugene |
| **Formed:** | Late 1960s |
| **Directories:** | Miller, *The 60s Communes*: 267. |

## The Human Dancing Company

Place:       Ashland, 159 N. Laurel
Formed:      1967
Directories: Miller, *The 60s Communes*: 267.
             "1975 Community Directory" (*Communities* 12): 28.
             "Directory 1977" (*Communities* 24): 51-52.
             Mercer, *Communes: A Social History and Guide*: 135.
Publication: *For Humans Only* (newsletter)

Carpenter, Andre. "Human Dancing Company." *Communities* 17 (November/
    December 1975): 2-7.
[Communes Looking for People]. *Communities* 10 (November 1974): 57.
[Grapevine -- Human Dancing Company]. *Communities* 11 (December 1974): 51.
[Reach – Groups Looking]. *Communities* 25 (March/April 1977): 46.

## Hungry Hill

Place:       Creswell
Formed:      Ca. 1970
Directories: Miller, *The 60s Communes*: 267.

Bates, Doug. "Lane County's Rural Areas Nurture Communal Lifestyle." *Eugene
    Register-Guard* (August 29, 1971): B1.

## Indian Creek

Place:       Swisshome
Formed:      1971

Bates, Doug. "Lane County's Rural Areas Nurture Communal Lifestyle." *Eugene
    Register-Guard* (August 29, 1971): B1.

## Indigo

Place:       Grants Pass
Formed:      1994

Summerhawk, Barbara, and La Verne Gagehabib. *Circles of Power: Shifting
    Dynamics in a Lesbian-Centered Community* (Norwich, VT: New Victoria
    Publishers, 2000): 62-63.

## International Puppydogs Movement

Place:       Portland, 2208 SE 26th Avenue
Formed:      1993
Directories: [Directory of Intentional Communities – Summer '94 Update]
                 (*Communities* 83): 52.
             *Communities Directory*, 1996: 262.
             *Communities Directory*, 2000: 269.
             [Community Updates – Changes] (*Communities* 120): 21.
             *Communities Directory*, 2005: 166-67.
             Communities Directory (online)
             *Communities Directory*, 2007: 345.

240

## Iona Colony

Kopp, James J. "Documenting Utopia in Oregon: The Challenges of Tracking the
    Quest for Perfection." *Oregon Historical Quarterly* 105 (2004): 308-19.

St. Romain, Monica. "What Is Mystery of Old Religious Colony?" *Newport News-Times* (May 29, 1969).

## Ithilien
Place:       Sheridan
Formed:      1969
Directories: Miller, *The 60s Communes*: 268.
             "1975 Community Directory" (*Communities* 12): 29.

Alexander, Geoff. E-mail to Jim Kopp, September 6, 2007.
Berg, Rudy. E-mail to Jim Kopp, September 2, 2007.
Bergel, Peter Bergel. E-mail to Jim Kopp, August 17, 2007.
*Communities* 12 (January/February 1975): 29.
*Kaliflower* 1:21 (September 11, 1969).
*Kalifower*, 1:47 (March 12, 1970).
Seal, Herb. *Alternatives Life Styles* (Singapore: Printed for CCS, Inc. by FEP International, 1974): 88.

## Jawbone Flats (The Mines)
Place:       Mehama
Formed:      1970s
Directories: Miller, *The 60s Communes*: 268.

## Jeshua Ben Josef School of the Heart
Place:       Eugene
Formed:      1985
Directories: *The New Consciousness Sourcebook: Spiritual Community Guide. Sixth Edition* (Pomona, CA: Arcline Publications, 1985): 77, 171.

## Jesuit Volunteer Corps: Northwest
Place:       Portland
Formed:      1950
Directories: "Directory of Intentional Communities 1978" (*Communities* 30): 38.
             *Directory of Intentional Communities*, 1991: 195.
             *Communities Directory*, 1996: 262-63.
             *Communities Directory*, 2005: 279.

[Community Grapevine]. *Communities* 95 (Summer 1997): 8.
Wilner, Joseph Bear. "All My Sisters and Brothers: Redefinitions of Family in Oregon Intentional Communities During the Late Twentieth Century." (M. A. thesis, University of Oregon, 2000): 101-2.

## Jubilee House
Formed:      1970s
Directories: Miller, *The 60s Communes*: 268.

241

Duin, Julia. "Authority & Submission in Christian Community." *Communities* 92 (Fall 1996): 51.

## Jump Off Joe
Place:       Sunny Valley
Directories: Miller, *The 60s Communes*: 268.

Roskind, Robert. *Memoirs of an Ex-Hippie: Seven Years in the Counterculture* (Blowing Rock, NC: One Love Press, 2001): 120.

## Kiya Alternative Relationship Center

Place:      Eugene
Formed:   1982

[Reach – Groups Looking]. *Communities* 55 (October/November 1982): 61-62.

## Landlovers

Place:         Portland (land in Coast Range), 9220 SE Pardee
Formed:      1975
Directories:   Miller, *The 60s Communes*: 269.
               "1975 Community Directory" (*Communities* 12): 30.
               Mercer, *Communes: A Social History and Guide*: 136.

## Lane County Catholic Worker

Place:         Eugene, 4488 Knoop Ave.
Formed:      1998
Directories:   Communities Directory (online)
               *Communities Directory*, 2007: 201.

"About Catholic Worker and Camphill Communities." *Communities* 124 (Fall 2004): 53.

## L'Arche Nehalem

Place:      Portland, 8501 SE Stephens
Formed:   1983
Web:        http://www.larche-portland.org/

Janzen, David. *Fire, Salt, and Peace: Intentional Christian Communities Alive in North America* (Evanston, IL: Shalom Mission Communities, 1996): 196.

## LeisureLand!

Place:         Mapleton
Formed:      1999
Directories:   Communities Directory (online)
               *Communities Directory*, 2007: 202-3.

## Liberty Cluster

Place:         Eugene
Formed:      1985?
Directories:   "1985 Directory of Intentional Communities." *Communities* 66 (Spring 1985): 56.

[Classifieds – Books/Publications – Polyfidelitous Educational Productions, Eugene, Oregon]. *Communities* 68 (Winter 1985): 59.
[Communities – Group Marriage – PEP [Polyfidelitous Educational Productions], Eugene, Oregon]. *Communities* 71/72 (Summer/Fall 1986): 71.

## Lichen

Place:      Wolf Creek, 3050 Coyote Creek Rd.
Formed:   1971

Directories:   Miller, *The 60s Communes*: 270.
"Directory of Intentional Communities 1978" (*Communities* 30): 40.
*A Guide to Cooperative Alternatives*, 1979 (*Communities* 38): 172.
"1983 Directory" (*Communities* 56): 70.
Mercer, *Communes: A Social History and Guide*: 136.
*Directory of Intentional Communities*, 1990: 199.
*Communities Directory*, 1995: 269.
*Communities Directory*, 1996: 268.
*Communities Directory*, 2000: 282.
*Communities Directory*, 2005: 280.
*Communities Directory*, 2007: 203.

[Community Grapevine]. *Communities* 112 (Fall 2001): 11.
[Community Living Directory – Northwest]. *Utopian Eyes* 3 (Winter 1977): [34].
[Reach – Groups Seeking People – Lichen]. *Communities* 21 (July/August 1976): 46.
[Reach]. *Communities* 22 (September/October [1976]): 49.
Kelly, Marcia, and Jack Kelly. *The Whole Heaven Catalog: A Resource Guide to Products, Services, Arts, Crafts, and Festivals of Religious, Spiritual, and Cooperative Communities* (New York: Bell Tower/One Spirit, 1998): 215.
Wilner, Joseph Bear. "All My Sisters and Brothers: Redefinitions of Family in Oregon Intentional Communities During the Late Twentieth Century." (M. A. thesis, University of Oregon, 2000): 48-49.

## Lighthouse Intentional Community
Place:     Portland, 2111 S. E. Madison St.
Formed:   2004
Directories:   Communities Directory (online)

## Lilac Ridge
Place:     Wolf Creek

Wilner, Joseph Bear. "All My Sisters and Brothers: Redefinitions of Family in Oregon Intentional Communities During the Late Twentieth Century." (M. A. thesis, University of Oregon, 2000): 62.

## Little Funky Egg Company
Place:     Takilma
Formed:   Mid-1970s
Notes:     Became New Land

Plagge, Dick. "Takilma – Communal Valley." *Willamette Week* 4:12 (Jan. 24, 1978): 5, 7.
Wilner, Joseph Bear. "All My Sisters and Brothers: Redefinitions of Family in Oregon Intentional Communities During the Late Twentieth Century." (M. A. thesis, University of Oregon, 2000): 30.

## Live Wood Farm
Place:     Lane County
Formed:   1971

Bates, Doug. "Lane County's Rural Areas Nurture Communal Lifestyle." *Eugene Register-Guard* (August 29, 1971): B1.

## Living Love Community

Place:     Coos Bay, 790 Commercial Ave.
Formed:   1972

McLaughlin, Corinne, and Gordon Davidson. "Living Love Community (The Ken
   Keyes Center): Reprogramming the Human Bio-computer" in *Builders of the
   Dawn: Community Lifestyles in a Changing World* (Walpole, NH: Stillpoint
   Pub., 1985): 207-11, also 47 and 356.

## Living Springs

Place:        Southern Oregon
Formed:      Ca. 1970
Directories:  Miller, *The 60s Communes*: 270.

Seal, Herb. *Alternatives Life Styles*. (Singapore: Printed for CCS, Inc. by FEP
   International, 1974): 108.
Vanneman, Brian Robert. "Searching For Paradise in the Rain: Oregon's
   Communes and Intentional Communities of the 1960s and 1970s." (Honors
   thesis, University of Oregon, 1997): 22.
*Year of the Commune* [videorecording]. Narrated by Rod Steiger. Rawlings-
   Chickering Productions. Released by McGraw-Hill, 1971.

## Lorien

Place:     Eagle Point
Formed:   1977

Davies, Karen. Email to Jim Kopp, June 8, 2006

## Lost Valley Educational Center

Place:        Dexter, 81868 Lost Valley Ln.
Formed:      1989
Directories:  *Directory of Intentional Communities*, 1990: 200.
             [Communities Directory Fall '97 Update – North American Updates]
                (*Communities* 96): 65.
             *Communities Directory*, 1996: 270.
             *Communities Directory*, 2000: 287.
             [Community Updates – Changes] (*Communities* 120): 21.
             Communities Directory (online)
             *Communities Directory*, 2005: 181-82.
             *Communities Directory*, 2007: 205-6.
Publications: *Talking Leaves*
Web:          www.lostvalley.org
             www.talkingleaves.org

[Ad – Ecovillage and Permaculture Certificate Program]. *The Permaculture Activist*
   59 (March 2006): 22.
[Ad – Ecovillage and Permaculture Certificate Program]. *The Permaculture Activist*
   60 (May 2006): 53.
[Ad – Ecovillage & Permaculture Certificate Programs]. *Communities Directory*,
   2007: 204.
[Ad – Ecovillage & Permaculture Certificate Programs]. *Communities* 138 (Spring
   2008): 65.
[Ad – Ecovillage & Permaculture Certificate Program]. *The Permaculture Activist*
   67 (February 2008): 47.

[Ad – Ecovillage and Permaculture Institute]. *Communities* 139 (Summer 2008): 17.

[Ad – Immerse yourself in Permaculture and community living]. *The Permaculture Activist* 39 (July 1998): 65.

[Ad – Lost Valley Educational Center]. *Communities* 96 (Fall 1997): 13.

[Ad – Lost Valley Educational Center]. *Communities* 97 (Winter 1997): 13.

[Ad – Lost Valley Educational Center]. *Communities* 98 (Spring 1998): 55.

[Ad – Lost Valley Educational Center]. *Communities* 99 (Summer 1998): 56.

[Ad – Lost Valley Educational Center]. *Communities* 100 (Fall 1998): 57.

[Ad – Lost Valley Educational Center]. *Communities* 101 (Winter 1998): 60.

[Ad – Lost Valley Educational Center]. *Communities* 102 (Spring 1999): 62.

[Ad – Lost Valley Educational Center]. *Communities* 103 (Summer 1999): 15.

[Ad – Lost Valley Educational Center]. *Communities* 104 (Fall 1999): 18.

[Ad – Lost Valley Educational Center]. *Communities* 105 (Winter 1999): 63.

[Ad – Lost Valley Educational Center]. *Communities* 106 (Spring 2000): 14.

[Ad – Lost Valley Educational Center]. *Communities* 107 (Summer 2000): 14.

[Ad – Lost Valley Educational Center]. *Communities* 108 (Fall 2000): 64.

[Ad – Lost Valley Educational Center]. *Communities* 109 (Winter 2000): 63.

[Ad – Lost Valley Educational Center]. *Communities* 110 (Spring 2001): 16.

[Ad – Lost Valley Educational Center]. *Communities* 111 (Summer 2001): 14.

[Ad – Lost Valley Educational Center]. *Communities* 112 (Fall 2001): 64.

[Ad – Lost Valley Educational Center]. *Communities* 113 (Winter 2001): 7.

[Ad – Lost Valley Educational Center]. *Communities* 114 (Spring 2002): 7.

[Ad – Lost Valley Educational Center]. *Communities* 115 (Summer 2002): 7.

[Ad – Lost Valley Educational Center]. *Communities* 116 (Fall 2002): 7.

[Ad – Lost Valley Educational Center]. *Communities* 117 (Spring 2003): 7.

[Ad – Lost Valley Educational Center]. *Communities* 118 (Summer 2003): 12.

[Ad – Lost Valley Educational Center]. *Communities* 119 (Fall 2003): 12.

[Ad – Lost Valley Educational Center]. *Communities* 121 (Winter 2003): 12.

[Ad – Lost Valley Educational Center]. *Communities* 122 (Spring 2004): 63.

[Ad – Lost Valley Educational Center]. *Communities* 123 (Summer 2004): 13.

[Ad – Lost Valley Educational Center]. *Communities* 124 (Fall 2004): 17.

[Ad – Lost Valley Educational Center]. *Communities* 125 (Winter 2004): 12.

[Ad – Lost Valley Educational Center]. *Communities* 126 (Spring 2005): 17.

[Ad – Lost Valley Educational Center]. *Communities* 127 (Summer 2005): 19.

[Ad – Lost Valley Educational Center]. *Communities* 128 (Fall 2005): 52.

[Ad – Lost Valley Educational Center]. *Communities Directory*, 2005: 181.

[Ad – Ecovillage & Permaculture Certificate Programs]. *Communities* 125 (Winter 2004): 71.

[Ad – Ecovillage & Permaculture Certificate Programs]. *Communities* 126 (Spring 2005): 69.

[Ad – Ecovillage & Permaculture Certificate Programs]. *Communities* 134 (Spring 2007): 65.

[Ad – Ecovillage & Permaculture Certificate Programs]. *Communities* 135 (Summer 2007): 65.

[Ad – *Talking Leaves*]. *The Permaculture Activist* 38 (February 1998): 9.

[Ad – *Talking Leaves*]. *The Permaculture Activist* 39 (June 1998): 36.

[Ad – *Talking Leaves*]. *The Permaculture Activist* 41 (May 1999): 12.

[Ad – *Talking Leaves*]. *The Permaculture Activist* 43 (June 2000): 21.

[Ad – *Talking Leaves*]. *The Permaculture Activist* 45 (March 2001): 10.

[Ad – *Talking Leaves*]. *The Permaculture Activist* 46 (July 2001): 19.

[Ad – *Talking Leaves*]. *The Permaculture Activist* 47 (May 2002): 12.

[Ad – *Talking Leaves*]. *The Permaculture Activist* 48 (September 2002): 5.

[Ad – *Talking Leaves*]. *The Permaculture Activist* 49 (December 2002): 12.

[Ad – *Talking Leaves*]. *The Permaculture Activist* 50 (May 2003): 18.

[Ad – *Talking Leaves*]. *The Permaculture Activist* 51 (February 2004): 19.

[Ad – *Talking Leaves*]. *The Permaculture Activist* 52 (May 2004): 27.

[Ad – *Talking Leaves*]. *The Permaculture Activist* 53 (August 2004): 5.

[Ad – *Talking Leaves*]. *The Permaculture Activist* 54 (February 2005): 6.

[Ad – *Talking Leaves*]. *The Permaculture Activist* 56 (May 2005): 14.

[Ad – *Talking Leaves*]. *The Permaculture Activist* 57 (August 2005): 32.

[Ad – *Talking Leaves*]. *The Permaculture Activist* 58 (November 2005): 35.

Beaty, Frank. "The Dilettante's Journey – Part 1." *Communities* 132 (Fall 2006): 24-29.

[Calendar – August 1-6 – Advanced Permaculture Design Course]. *The Permaculture Activist* 31 (May 1994): 52.

[Calendar – February 4-16 – Advanced Permaculture Design/Teacher Training Course]. *The Permaculture Activist* V(4) (November 1989): 24.

[Calendar – February 4-16, 1990 – Advanced Permaculture Design/Teacher Training Course]. *The Permaculture Activist* VI(1) (Spring 1990): 32.

[Calendar – July 31-August 5 – Advanced Permaculture Design: "Water in the Landscape"]. *The Permaculture Activist* 32 (April 1995): 52.

[Calendar – August 7-12 – Advanced Permaculture Teaching Course]. *The Permaculture Activist* 32 (April 1995): 52.

[Calendar – January 8-15, 2003 – Advanced Permaculture Teaching Training Course]. *The Permaculture Activist* 49 (December 2002): 65.

[Calendar – August 24-29 – Community Experience Week]. *The Permaculture Activist* 53 (August 2004): [68].

[Calendar – November 14-18 – Community Experience Week]. *The Permaculture Activist* 53 (August 2004): [68].

[Calendar – November 14-18 – Community Experience Week]. *The Permaculture Activist* 54 (November 2004):[68].

[Calendar – June 1-August 29 – Deep Agroecology Apprenticeship Program]. *The Permaculture Activist* 36 (March 1997): 52.

[Calendar – June 15-August 21 – Deep Agroecology Apprenticeship Program]. *The Permaculture Activist* 38 (February 1998): 60.

[Calendar – June 26-August 18 – Ecovillage & Permaculture Certificate Program]. *The Permaculture Activist* 60 (May 2006): 65.

[Calendar – October 2-27 – Ecovillage & Permaculture Certificate Program]. *The Permaculture Activist* 60 (May 2006): 66.

[Calendar – October 2-27 – Ecovillage & Permaculture Certificate Program]. *The Permaculture Activist* 61 (August 2006): 65.

[Calendar – June 18-August 10 – Ecovillage & Permaculture Certificate Program]. *The Permaculture Activist* 63 (February 2007): 65.

[Calendar – May 11-13 – Ecovillage & Permaculture Certificate Program]. *The Permaculture Activist* 64 (May 2007): 57.

[Calendar – December 2-15 – 11th Annual Permaculture Design Course]. *The Permaculture Activist* 46 (July 2001): 68.

[Calendar – June 20-August 13 – Ecovillage and Permaculture Certificate Program]. *The Permaculture Activist* 56 (May 2005): 63.

[Calendar – Sept. 21-23 – 5th Annual Regional Permaculture Gathering]. *The Permaculture Activist* 46 (July 2001): 68.

[Calendar – October 10-13 – 1st Annual Lost Valley Permaculture Reunion]. *The Permaculture Activist* 36 (March 1997): 52.

[Calendar – October 10-13 – 1st Annual Lost Valley Permaculture Reunion]. *The Permaculture Activist* 37 (September 1997): 68.

[Calendar – August 13-14 – Intro to Permaculture]. *The Permaculture Activist* 57 (August 2005): 64.

[Calendar – December 1-14, 1990 – Maritime West Coast Permaculture Design Course]. *The Permaculture Activist* VI(4) (Winter 1990): 48.

[Calendar – May 11-13 – Native Plants and Permaculture: A Gathering of Plant Enthusiasts]. *The Permaculture Activist* 63 (February 2007): 65.

[Calendar – June 18-August 10 – Native Plants and Permaculture: A Gathering of Plant Enthusiasts]. *The Permaculture Activist* 64 (May 2007): 57.

[Calendar – September 24-26 – Northwest Permaculture Gathering]. *The Permaculture Activist* 41 (May 1999): 84.

[Calendar – February 16-March 1, 1992 – Permaculture Design Course]. *The Permaculture Activist* VII(2) (Autumn 1991): 40.

[Calendar – November 28-December 12 – Permaculture Design Course]. *The Permaculture Activist* 29-30 (July 1993): 68.

[Calendar – December 1-14 – Permaculture Design Course]. *The Permaculture Activist* 35 (November 1996): 52.

[Calendar – November 29-December 12 – Permaculture Design Course]. *The Permaculture Activist* 38 (February 1998): 60.

[Calendar – November 29-December 12 – Permaculture Design Course]. *The Permaculture Activist* 39 (July 1998): 68.

[Calendar – November 29-December 12 – Permaculture Design Course]. *The Permaculture Activist* 40 (December 1998): 68.

[Calendar – November 28-December 11, 1999 – Permaculture Design Course]. *The Permaculture Activist* 42 (December 1999): 60.

[Calendar – December 1-14 – Permaculture Design Course]. *The Permaculture Activist* 48 (September 2002): 65.

[Calendar – November 27-December 11 – Permaculture Design Course]. *The Permaculture Activist* 56 (May 2005): 64.

[Calendar – November 27-December 11 – Permaculture Design Course]. *The Permaculture Activist* 57 (August 2005): 65.

[Calendar – November 27-December 11 – Permaculture Design Course]. *The Permaculture Activist* 58 (November 2005): 65.

[Calendar – November 30-December 13 – Permaculture Design Course]. *The Permaculture Activist* 62 (November 2006): 65.

[Calendar – August 1-14 – Permaculture Design for Women]. *The Permaculture Activist* 29-30 (July 1993): 68.

[Calendar – August 12-14 – Permaculture Design for Women]. *The Permaculture Activist* 31 (May 1994): 52.

[Calendar – February 9-11 – Permaculture Design for Women]. *The Permaculture Activist* 44 (November 2000): 60.

[Calendar – September 7-October 23 – Permaculture/Self-Awareness Apprenticeship]. *The Permaculture Activist* 38 (February 1998): 60.

247

[Calendar – September 7-October 23 – Permaculture/Self-Awareness Apprenticeship]. *The Permaculture Activist* 39 (July 1998): 68.

[Calendar – August 8-13 – Permaculture Teachers Training]. *The Permaculture Activist* 31 (May 1994): 52.

[Calendar – June 9-11 – Pond Construction Workshop]. *The Permaculture Activist* 43 (June 2000): 84.

[Calendar – November 9-11, 1990 – Restoration Forestry Conference]. *The Permaculture Activist* VI(3) (Autumn 1990): 40.

[Calendar – December 1-13 – 7th Annual 2-Week Permaculture Design Course]. *The Permaculture Activist* 36 (March 1997): 52.

[Calendar – December 1-13 – 7th Annual Permaculture Design Course]. *The Permaculture Activist* 37 (September 1997): 68.

[Calendar – December 3-15 – 10th Annual Permaculture Design Course]. *The Permaculture Activist* 44 (November 2000): 60.

[Calendar – December 3-17 – Two-Week Intensive Design Course]. *The Permaculture Activist* 33 (December 1995): 52.

[Calendar – March 7-9, 2003 – A Women's Retreat: Introduction to Permaculture]. *The Permaculture Activist* 49 (December 2002): 65.

[Calendar – June 16-August 18 – Ecovillage and Permaculture Program]. *The Permaculture Activist* 67 (February 2008): 63.

[Calendar – June 16-August 18 – Ecovillage and Permaculture Program]. *The Permaculture Activist* 68 (May 2008): 63.

Christian, Diana Leafe. *Creating A Life Together: Practical Tools to Grow Ecovillages and Intentional Communities*. Gabriola Island, BC, Canada: New Society Publishers, 2003.

[Christian, Diana Leafe]. "How Country Communities Pay the Bills." *Communities* 116 (Fall 2002): 26-27.

Christian, Diane Leafe. "An Intern's-Eye View." *Communities* 108 (Fall 2000): 34-35.

Christian, Diana Leafe. "No Funds? How One Community Did It." *Communities* 116 (Fall 2002): 44.

[Christian, Diana Leafe]. "Sample Income Sources in Rural Communities." *Communities* 116 (Fall 2002): 29.

[Classifieds – Help Wanted – Grower Wanted Immediately]. *The Permaculture Activist* 36 (March 1997): 50-51.

[Classifieds – Help Wanted – Position Open for Land Steward at Lost Valley Educational Center]. *The Permaculture Activist* 49 (December 2002): 66.

[Community Calendar – Aug 15-18 – Appropriate Technology Intensive: Tools for Sustainable and Self-Reliant Living]. *Communities* 91 (Summer 1996): 70.

[Community Calendar – Ongoing – Apprenticeships in Permaculture and Organic Gardening]. *Communities* 107 (Summer 2000): 64.

[Community Calendar – Oct 14-16 – Bioneers' "Sustainability Package"]. *Communities* 128 (Fall 2005): 60.

[Community Calendar – May 11-18 – Community Experience Week]. *Communities* 117 (Spring 2003): 63.

[Community Calendar – Sep 14-21 – Community Experience Week]. *Communities* 118 (Summer 2003): 61.

[Community Calendar – Sep 18-22 – Community Experience Week, also Nov 13-17]. *Communities* 127 (Summer 2005): 70, 71.

[Community Calendar – Nov 13-17 – Community Experience Week]. *Communities* 128 (Fall 2005): 60.

[Community Calendar – Aug 16-20 – Earthstewards Gathering]. *Communities* 107 (Summer 2000): 64.

[Community Calendar – Aug 30-Sep 3 – EcoArts Gathering]. *Communities* 91 (Summer 1996): 71.

[Community Calendar – June 20-Aug 13 – Ecovillage and Permaculture Certificate Program; Integrating Land, Building, and Social Sustainability]. *Communities* 126 (Spring 2005): 66.

[Community Calendar – June 20-Aug 13 – Ecovillage and Permaculture Certificate Program; Integrating Land, Building, and Social Sustainability w/David Holgrem]. *Communities* 127 (Summer 2005): 66.

[Community Calendar – Oct 2-27 – Ecovillage & Permaculture Certificate Program]. *Communities* 132 (Fall 2006): 75.

[Community Calendar – Sep 28-30 – Fall Harvest Celebration]. *Communities* 112 (Fall 2001): 60.

[Community Calendar – Sep 22-24 – 4th Annual Northwest Regional Permaculture Gathering]. *Communities* 107 (Summer 2000): 65.

[Community Calendar – Apr 8-11 – Heart of Now: The Basics, also May 6-9, Jul 15-18, Aug 12-15]. *Communities* 126 (Spring 2005): 65, 66, 67.

[Community Calendar – Jul 15-18 – Heart of Now: The Basics; also Aug 12-15, Sep 2-5, Sep 23-26, Oct 21-24, Nov 18-21, Dec 9-12]. *Communities* 127 (Summer 2005): 66, 68, 69, 70, 71.

[Community Calendar – Sep 23-26 – Heart of Now: The Basics; also Oct 21-24, Nov 18-21, Dec 9-12]. *Communities* 128 (Fall 2005): 59-60, 61, 62.

[Community Calendar – Sep 15-18 – Heart of Now: The Basics, also Jun 8-11, Oct.6-9]. *Communities* 132 (Fall 2006): 74, 76.

[Community Calendar – Apr 20-23 – Heart of Now: The Basics, also Jun 8-11]. *Communities* 134 (Spring 2007): 62, 63.

[Community Calendar – Jul 20-23 – Heart of Now: The Basics, also Sep 28-Oct 1 and Oct. 19-22]. *Communities* 135 (Summer 2007): 63, 65.

[Community Calendar – Heart of Now: The Basics, Sep 28-Oct1, also Oct 19-22]. *Communities* 136 (Fall 2007): 63.

[Community Calendar – Aug 16-20 – Heart of Now: Dancing on the Edge]. *Communities* 134 (Spring 2007): 62.

[Community Calendar – Aug 16-20 – Heart of Now: Dancing on the Edge]. *Communities* 135 (Summer 2007): 64.

[Community Calendar – Apr 21-25 – Heart of Now 2, also Aug 25-29]. *Communities* 126 (Spring 2005): 65, 67.

[Community Calendar – Aug 25-29 – Heart of Now 2, also Nov 3-17]. *Communities* 127 (Summer 2005): 68, 71.

[Community Calendar – Nov 3-7 – Heart of Now 2]. *Communities* 128 (Fall 2005): 60.

[Community Calendar – May 26-28 – Heart of Passion: Unleashing the Sacred Erotic]. *Communities* 134 (Spring 2007): 63.

[Community Calendar – Ongoing – Internships & Apprenticeships in Sustainable Living]. *Communities* 102 (Spring 1999): 70.

[Community Calendar – Ongoing – Internships & Apprenticeships in Sustainable Living]. *Communities* 103 (Summer 1999): 68.

[Community Calendar – Ongoing – Internships & Apprenticeships in Sustainable Living]. *Communities* 104 (Fall 1999): 69.

[Community Calendar – Sep 19-24 – Lost Valley Community Experience Week]. *Communities* 132 (Fall 2006): 75.

[Community Calendar – June 24-29 – Lost Valley Community Experience Week]. *Communities* 134 (Spring 2007): 64.

[Community Calendar – June 24-29 – Lost Valley Community Experience Week, also Oct. 23-28]. *Communities* 135 (Summer 2007): 62, 64.

[Community Calendar – Oct 23-28 – Lost Valley Community Experience Week]. *Communities* 136 (Fall 2007): 63.

[Community Calendar – Sep 1-Oct 10 – Lost Valley Fall Apprenticeship Program]. *Communities* 118 (Summer 2003): 61.

[Community Calendar – Jun 21-23 – Lost Valley Summer Solstice Celebration]. *Communities* 114 (Spring 2002): 67.

[Community Calendar – Apr 18-20 – Naka-Ima, also May 16-18]. *Communities* 98 (Spring 1998): 66.

249

[Community Calendar – Sep 19-21 – Naka-Ima]. *Communities* 99 (Summer 1998): 68.

[Community Calendar – Jul 21-24 – Naka-Ima, also Sept 8-11]. *Communities* 107 (Summer 2000): 64, 65.

[Community Calendar – Oct 20-23 – Naka-Ima]. *Communities* 108 (Fall 2000): 66.

[Community Calendar – Apr 6-9 – Naka-Ima, also May 18-21, Jun 8-11, Jul 20-23]. *Communities* 110 (Spring 2001): 69, 70.

[Community Calendar – Jul 20-23 – Naka-Ima]. *Communities* 111 (Summer 2001): 65.

[Community Calendar – Oct 12-15 – Naka-Ima, also Nov 9-12]. *Communities* 112 (Fall 2001): 61.

[Community Calendar – May 17-20 – Naka-Ima, also Jun 14-17]. *Communities* 114 (Spring 2002): 66, 67.

[Community Calendar – Oct 11-14 – Naka-Ima, also Nov 8-11]. *Communities* 115 (Summer 2002): 66.

[Community Calendar – June 6-9 – Naka-Ima]. *Communities* 117 (Spring 2003): 64.

[Community Calendar – Jul 18-21 – Naka-Ima]. *Communities* 118 (Summer 2003): 60.

[Community Calendar – Sep 1-4 – Naka-Ima Summer Arts Camp]. *Communities* 107 (Summer 2000): 65.

[Community Calendar – Apr 2-5 – Naka-Ima 1: The Basics, also May 7-10, May 21-24, Jun 11-14, Jul 2-5]. *Communities* 122 (Spring 2004): 63, 65, 66, 67.

[Community Calendar – Sep 24-27 – Naka-Ima 1: The Basics, also Oct 22-25, Nov 19-22, Dec 10-13]. *Communities* 124 (Fall 2004): 62, 63.

[Community Calendar – Jul 2-5 – Naka-Ima 1: The Basics, also Aug 20-23, Sep 3-6, Sep 24-27]. *Communities* 123 (Summer 2004): 66, 68, 69.

[Community Calendar – Apr 15-19– Naka-Ima 2: The Practice, also Jul 29-Aug 2]. *Communities* 122 (Spring 2004): 63, 69.

[Community Calendar – Nov 4-8 – Naka-Ima 2: The Practice]. *Communities* 124 (Fall 2004): 63.

[Community Calendar – Jul 29-Aug 2 – Naka-Ima: The Practice]. *Communities* 123 (Summer 2004): 68.

[Community Calendar – Aug 19-21 – Natural Building for the Real World with Rob Bolman]. *Communities* 127 (Summer 2005): 68.

[Community Calendar – Summer/Fall 2001 – Organic Gardening Apprenticeship]. *Communities* 111 (Summer 2001): 65.

[Community Calendar – Summer/Fall 2001 – Organic Gardening in Community Apprenticeship]. *Communities* 112 (Fall 2001): 60.

[Community Calendar – Jun 2-Aug 1 – Organic Gardening in Community Apprenticeship]. *Communities* 117 (Spring 2003): 64.

[Community Calendar – Jul 9-Aug 3 – Organic Gardening, Permaculture and Community: An Experience in Sustainable Living]. *Communities* 111 (Summer 2001): 65.

[Community Calendar – Mar-Oct – Organic Gardening, Permaculture, and Community—An Experience in Sustainable Living]. *Communities* 114 (Spring 2002): 66.

[Community Calendar – Jun 20-22 – Papercrete Building Workshop]. *Communities* 117 (Spring 117): 65.

[Community Calendar – Jun 20-22 – Papercrete Building Workshop]. *Communities* 118 (Summer 2003): 61.

[Community Calendar – Sep 11-12 – Papercrete Construction]. *Communities* 123 (Summer 2004): 69.

[Community Calendar – Jun 2-Jul 11 – Permaculture in Community Apprenticeship]. *Communities* 117 (Spring 2003): 64.

[Community Calendar – Sep 7-Oct 23 – Permaculture & Self Awareness Apprenticeship]. *Communities* 99 (Summer 1998): 68.

[Community Calendar – Nov 16-20 – The Practice]. *Communities* 112 (Fall 2001): 61.

[Community Calendar – Nov 21-25 – The Practice: Creating Intimacy and Community Through the Practice of Honesty]. *Communities* 115 (Summer 2002): 67.

[Community Calendar – Sep 25-26 – Reduce Your Urban Environmental Footprint]. *Communities* 123 (Summer 2004): 69.

[Community Calendar – Sep 25-26 – Reduce Your Urban Environmental Footprint]. *Communities* 124 (Fall 2004): 62.

[Community Calendar – Sep 5-7 – 6th Annual Northwest Permaculture Gathering]. *Communities* 118 (Summer 2003): 61.

[Community Calendar – Apr 12-25 – Spring Ecological Living Mini-Apprenticeships, also May 10-23]. *Communities* 98 (Spring 1998): 66.

[Community Calendar – Jun 15-Aug 21 – Summer Apprenticeship Program]. *Communities* 98 (Spring 1998): 66.

[Community Calendar – Jun 21-Aug 13 – Sustainability Education Program at Lost Valley]. *Communities* 122 (Spring 2004): 67.

[Community Calendar – Jun 21-Aug 13 – Sustainability Education Program at Lost Valley]. *Communities* 123 (Summer 2004): 66.

[Community Calendar – Jul 14-27 – Wild at Art]. *Communities* 118 (Summer 2003): 60.

[Community Calendar – Nov 27-Dec 11 – Winter Permaculture Design Course]. *Communities* 127 (Summer 2005): 71.

[Community Calendar – Nov 27-Dec 11—Winter Permaculture Design Course]. *Communities* 128 (Fall 2005): 61.

[Community Calendar – July 13-19 – Women's Earth-Home Building Workshop]. *Communities* 91 (Summer 1996): 70.

[Community Calendar – Jul 20-Aug 2 – YES! Sustainable Living Skills Retreat]. *Communities* 94 (Spring 1997): 69.

[Community Calendar – Jul 20-Aug 2 – YES! Sustainable Living Skills Retreat]. *Communities* 95 (Summer 1997): 68.

[Community Calendar – Aug 2-22 – YES! Sustainable Living Skills Retreat]. *Communities* 99 (Summer 1998): 67.

[Community Calendar – July 5-11 – YES! (Youth for Environmental Sanity) Summer Camp for Youth]. *Communities* 91 (Summer 1996): 70.

[Community Grapevine]. *Communities* 96 (Fall 1997): 8.

[Community Grapevine]. *Communities* 100 (Fall 1998): 8.

[Community Grapevine]. *Communities* 106 (Spring 2000): 11.

[Community Grapevine]. *Communities* 117 (Spring 2003): 9.

[Community Grapevine]. *Communities* 118 (Summer 2003): 8-9.

[Events – Ecovillage and Permaculture Certificate Program]. *The Permaculture Activist* 56 (May 2005): 58.

[Events – Ecovillage & Permaculture Certificate Program]. *The Permaculture Activist* 64 (May 2007): 51.

[Events – Ecovillage & Permaculture Certificate Program]. *The Permaculture Activist* 63 (February 2007): 61.

251

[Events – Ecovillage and Permaculture Program.] *The Permaculture Activist* 67 (February 2008): 58.

[Events – Ecovillage and Permaculture Program]. *The Permaculture Activist* 68 (May 2008): 58.

[Events – 8th Annual Permaculture Design Course]. *The Permaculture Activist* 38 (February 1998): 50.

[Events – 8th Annual Permaculture Design Course]. *The Permaculture Activist* 39 (July 1998): 59.

[Events – 8th Annual Permaculture Design Course]. *The Permaculture Activist* 40 (December 1998): 58.

[Events –11th Annual Permaculture Design Course]. *The Permaculture Activist* 46 (July 2001): 59.

[Events – 11th Annual Permaculture Design Course]. *The Permaculture Activist* 48 (September 2002): 68.

[Events – 15th Annual Permaculture Design Course]. *The Permaculture Activist* 62 (November 2006): 61.

[Events – 4th Annual Oregon Permaculture Gathering]. *The Permaculture Activist* 43 (June 2000): 76.

[Events – Lost Valley Educational Ctr.]. *The Permaculture Activist* 36 (March 1997): 46.

[Events – Lost Valley Educational Ctr.]. *The Permaculture Activist* 49 (December 2002): 62.

[Events – 9th Annual Permaculture Design Course]. *The Permaculture Activist* 41 (May 1999): 73.

[Events – 9th Annual Permaculture Design Course]. *The Permaculture Activist* 42 (December 1999): 52.

[Events – 1999 Northwest Permaculture Gathering]. *The Permaculture Activist* 41 (May 1999): 73.

[Events – Permaculture & Self-Awareness Apprenticeship]. *The Permaculture Activist* 38 (July 1998): 58.

[Events – Permaculture & Self-Awareness Apprenticeship]. *The Permaculture Activist* 39 (February 1998): 50.

[Events – Permaculture at Lost Valley Educational Center]. *The Permaculture Activist* 43 (June 2000): 77.

[Events – Permaculture Design Course]. *The Permaculture Activist* 33 (December 1995): 45.

[Events – Permaculture Design Course]. *The Permaculture Activist* 37 (September 1997): 60.

[Events – Permaculture Design Course]. *The Permaculture Activist* 44 (November 2000): 56.

[Events – Permaculture Design Course]. *The Permaculture Activist* 57 (August 2005): 60.

[Events – Permaculture Design Course]. *The Permaculture Activist* 58 (November 2005): 64.

[Events – Permaculture for Women]. *The Permaculture Activist* 44 (November 2000): 56.

[Events – 7th Annual Women's Permaculture Design Workshop]. *The Permaculture Activist* 42 (December 1999): 52.

Fenger, Darin. "What Interns and Work Exchanges Say About Us." *Communities* 134 (Spring 2007): 34-39.

Greenberg, Daniel. "Communities Where You Can Learn." *Communities* 108 (Fall 2000): 49-52.

Greenberg, Daniel. "Let's Go. Learning Opportunities About Community." *Communities* 108 Fall 2000): 26-29.

[Interns and Work Opportunities – Lost Valley Educational Center, Dexter, Oregon]. *Communities* 110 (Spring 2001): 77.

Kaplowitz, Larry. "Community on a 'Bad Day'." *Communities* 107 (Summer 2000): 76, 75.

Kaplowitz, Larry. "The Dark Side of Lost Valley." *The Permaculture Activist* 42 (December 1999): 39.

Kaplowitz, Larry. "The Dark Side of Lost Valley," *Talking Leaves* (Spring/Summer 1999): 38.

Kaplowitz, Larry. "Living 'Naka-Ima' at Lost Valley." *Communities* 104 (Fall 1999): 22-27.

Kaplowitz, Larry. "Living Outside the Box." *Communities* 118 (Summer 2003): 36-39, 50-51.

Kaplowitz, Larry. "Lost Valley: Building Design That Fosters Community." *Communities* 99 (Summer 1998): 28-30.

Kunkle, Stuart. [Letter]. *Communities* 132 (Fall 2006): 5.

Lakeman, Mark. "The Village Blooms in the City: Portland's Natural Building Convergence." *Communities* 115 (Summer 2002): 26-29.

[Learning Permaculture – Permaculture Design, Advanced Design & Teachers Training Courses in Oregon]. *The Permaculture Activist* 31 (May 1994): 47.

[Learning Permaculture – Permaculture Design for Women]. *The Permaculture Activist* 31 (May 1994): 47.

Mare, Chris. "Designing My Own Education for the 'Ecovillage Millennium'." *Communities* 108 (Fall 2000): 46-48.

Moussalli, Guy, "Report from Oregon Advanced Permaculture Design and Teaching Course." *The Permaculture Activist* VI(2) (Summer 1990): 21.

[Networks & Resources – Lost Valley Now Publishes *Talking Leaves*]. *The Permaculture Activist* 39 (July 1998): 62.

[Permaculture Educational Programs – Restoration Forestry Conference, November 9-11, 1990]. *The Permaculture Activist* VI(3) (Autumn 1990): 31.

[Permaculture Educational Programs – Maritime West Coast Permaculture Design Course]. *The Permaculture Activist* VI(3) (Autumn 1990): 35.

[Permaculture Educational Programs – Oregon Permaculture Design Course]. *The Permaculture Activist* VII(2) (Autumn 1991): 33.

[Permaculture Learning – Design Course in Oregon]. *The Permaculture Activist* 29-30 (July 1993): 62.

[Permaculture Learning – Permaculture Design for Women]. *The Permaculture Activist* 29-30 (July 1993): 62.

Riggs, Teryani. "Creating a Permanent Culture at Lost Valley." *The Permaculture Activist* 42 (December 1999): 36-38.

Roth, Chris. "But Not Without Tears: Our Toughest Membership Decision Ever." *Communities* 128 (Fall 2005): 26-31.

Roth, Chris. "A Day in the Life at Lost Valley." *Talking Leaves* (Late Summer/Fall 2004 Web Extra)

Roth, Chris. "The Haybox Cooker: Why Every Community Needs One." *Communities* 115 (Summer 2002): 48-50.

Roth, Chris. "In Deep Forest and Meadow." *Communities* 123 (Summer 2004): 50-54.

[6th Annual Intensive Permaculture Design Course]. *The Permaculture Activist* 35 (November 1996): 47.

Sternfeld, Joel. "Lost Valley Educational Center, Dexter, Oregon, April 2004" in *Sweet Earth: Experimental Utopias in America* (Göttingen, Germany: Steidl, 2006): 58-59.

Valley, Rick. "Goose Praise [letter]." *The Permaculture Activist* 57 (August 2005): 67.

Wilner, Joseph Bear. "All My Sisters and Brothers: Redefinitions of Family in Oregon Intentional Communities During the Late Twentieth Century." (M. A. thesis, University of Oregon, 2000): 52-53.

## Lunasa

Place:          Portland
Forming:        2006
Directories:    Communities Directory (online)

## Lynx Hollow Farm

Place:          Cottage Grove
Formed:         1971

Bates, Doug. "Lane County's Rural Areas Nurture Communal Lifestyle." *Eugene Register-Guard* (August 29, 1971): B1.

## Madison Street House

Place:          Portland, 8130 SE Madison St.
Formed:         1999
Directories:    *Communities Directory*, 2000: 290.

## Maggie's Farm

Place:          Portland
Formed:         Ca. 1968
Directories:    Miller, *The 60s Communes*: 271.

## Magic Farm – see High Ridge Farm

## Magic Mountain Farm/Magic Forest?

Place:          Cave Junction
Formed:         1970
Directories:    Ayd, *The Youth Communes*: 166.
                Miller, *The 60s Communes*: 271.

[Fairfield, Richard.] "Magic Forest Farm." *Modern Utopian* 5 ["Communes U.S.A."] (1971): 100-106.

Plagge, Dick. "Takilma – Communal Valley." *Willamette Week* 4:12 (Jan. 24, 1978): 5, 7.

Vanneman, Brian Robert. "Magic Farm: A Country Commune" in "Searching For Paradise in the Rain: Oregon's Communes and Intentional Communities of the 1960s and 1970s." (Honors thesis, University of Oregon, 1997): 27-38.

Wilner, Joseph Bear. "All My Sisters and Brothers: Redefinitions of Family in Oregon Intentional Communities During the Late Twentieth Century." (M. A. thesis, University of Oregon, 2000): 30.

## Main Street Gathering

Place:          Portland, 4012 SE Main
Formed:         1972

Directories: Miller, *The 60s Communes*: 271.
"Commune Directory" (*Communities* 7): 35.
"1975 Community Directory" (*Communities* 12): 30.

## Maitreya Ecovillage
Place:      Eugene
Formed:     2002
Web:        www.maitreyaecovillage.org/

[Ad – Live in an Ecovillage in Eugene, Oregon]. *The Permaculture Activist* 59 (March 2006): 25.
[Community Grapevine]. *Communities* 118 (Summer 2003): 8.
Lakeman, Mark. "The Village Blooms in the City: Portland's Natural Building Convergence." *Communities* 115 (Summer 2002): 26-29.

## Mama Keefer's Boarding House
Place:      Eugene
Formed:     1970s
Directories: Miller, *The 60s Communes*: 271.

## Manifest Sons
Place:      Portland
Formed:     Early 1970s
Directories: Miller, *The 60s Communes*: 271.

Ward, Hiley H. *The Far-Out Saints of the Jesus Community*: *A Firsthand Report and Interpretation of the Jesus People Movement* (New York: Association Press, 1972): 37.

## Maranatha Church
Place:      Portland
Formed:     Early 1970s

Ward, Hiley H. *The Far-Out Saints of the Jesus Community*: *A Firsthand Report and Interpretation of the Jesus People Movement* (New York: Association Press, 1972): 87.

## The Meadows
Place:      Takilma
Formed:     1970s
Directories: Miller, *The 60s Communes*: 272.

Plagge, Dick. "Takilma – Communal Valley." *Willamette Week* 4:12 (Jan. 24, 1978): 5, 7.
Wilner, Joseph Bear. "All My Sisters and Brothers: Redefinitions of Family in Oregon Intentional Communities During the Late Twentieth Century." (M. A. thesis, University of Oregon, 2000): 30.

255

## Merry Pranksters
Place:      Pleasant Hill
Formed:     1963 (1967 in Oregon)
Directories: Ayd, *The Youth Communes*: 166.

Goodwin, Michael. "The Ken Kesey Movie," *Rolling Stone* (March 7, 1970): 24.
Miller, Timothy. *The 60s Communes: Hippies and Beyond* (Syracuse, NY: Syracuse University Press, 1999): 19-20, 272.
Sutton, Robert P. "Kesey, Ken" in *Modern American Communes: A Dictionary* (Westport, CT: Greenwood Press, 2005): 90-91.
Sutton, Robert P. "Merry Pranksters" in *Modern American Communes: A Dictionary* (Westport, CT: Greenwood Press, 2005): 111-12.

## The Mining Claim

Place:     Southern Oregon
Formed:    1970s
Directories:  Miller, *The 60s Communes*: 272.

## Mirage Garage

Place:     Takilma
Formed:    1970s

Plagge, Dick. "Takilma – Communal Valley." *Willamette Week* 4:12 (Jan. 24, 1978): 5, 7.
Wilner, Joseph Bear. "All My Sisters and Brothers: Redefinitions of Family in Oregon Intentional Communities During the Late Twentieth Century." (M. A. thesis, University of Oregon, 2000): 30.

## Mirkwood

Place:     West of Eugene
Formed:    Ca. 1970
Directories:  Miller, *The 60s Communes*: 272.

## Mist Mountain Farm

Place:     Mist
Formed:    Mid-1970s
Directories:  Miller, *The 60s Communes*: 272.

## Mizpah

Place:     Woodburn
Formed:    1984

[Reach – Groups Looking]. *Communities* 64 (Fall 1984): 61.

## Moon Garden

Formed:    Early 1970s
Directories:  Miller, *The 60s Communes*: 272.

## The Motherlode

Formed:    1970s
Directories:  Miller, *The 60s Communes*: 273.

## Mountain Grove

Place:     Glendale
Formed:    1966
Directories:  Miller, *The 60s Communes*: 273.
            "1975 Community Directory" (*Communities* 12): 31.
            *A Guide to Cooperative Alternatives*, 1979 (*Communities* 38): 173.

"1981 Directory of Intentional Communities and Resources" (*Communities* 461): 44.
"1983 Directory" (*Communities* 56): 71.
Mercer, *Communes: A Social History and Guide*: 138.
*Directory of Intentional Communities*, 1990: 204.
*Communities Directory*, 1996: 388-89.
**Manuscripts:** Ruth Mountaingrove Papers. Special Collections & University Archives, University of Oregon Libraries.
Ruth Mountaingrove Videotape Autobiography Collection, 1988-1997. Special Collections & University Archives, University of Oregon Libraries.

[Grapevine – Mountain Grove]. *Communities* 12 (January/February 1975): 56.
Johnson, David. "Greener Grass: A Short History of Oregon's Utopia Tradition." *Oregon Heritage* 1 (Winter/Spring 1995): 17.
[Reach – Communes Looking for People]. *Communities* 14 (May-June 1975): 56.
[Reach – Groups Looking]. *Communities* 75 (Summer 1988): 54.
[Reach – Services Offered]. *Communities* 8 (May-June 1974): 59.
Wilner, Joseph Bear. "All My Sisters and Brothers: Redefinitions of Family in Oregon Intentional Communities During the Late Twentieth Century." (M. A. thesis, University of Oregon, 2000): 63-64.

## Mountain Home/Homestead
**Place:** Coquille, 95245 Rink Creek Ln.
**Formed:** 1989
**Directories:** *Communities Directory*, 2000: 298.
[Community Updates – Changes] (*Communities* 120): 23.
*Communities Directory*, 2005: 191.
Communities Directory (online)
*Communities Directory*, 2007: 215.

[Events – Permaculture Design Course]. *The Permaculture Activist* 69 (August 2008): 56.
[Interns and Residencies – Mountain Home, Coquille, Oregon]. *Communities* 118 (Summer 2003): 70-71.
[Interns and Residencies – Mountain Home, Coquille, Oregon]. *Communities* 119 (Fall 2003): 62-63.
[Interns and Residencies – Mountain Home, Coquille, Oregon]. *Communities* 122 (Spring 2004): 75.
[Interns and Residencies – Mountain Home, Coquille, Oregon]. *Communities* 123 (Summer 2004): 75.

## Mountainlight

Sandilands, Catriona. "Rainbow's End? Lesbian Separatism and the Ongoing Politics of Ecotopia." In Margrit Eichler, June Larkin, and Sheila Neysmith, eds. *Feminist Utopias: Re-Visioning Our Future* (Toronto, Canada: Inanna Publications and Education, 2002): 37-50.

## Mu Farm
**Place:** Yoncalla
**Formed:** 1971
**Directories:** Miller, *The 60s Communes*: 273.
"Commune Directory," (*Communities* 1): 34.

[More Grapevine]. *Communitas* 1 (July 1972): 51.
Miller, Timothy. *The 60s Communes: Hippies and Beyond* (Syracuse, NY: Syracuse University Press, 1999): 77.

## Mud Farm

Place:        Eugene
Formed:       1974
Directories:  Miller, *The 60s Communes*: 273.

## Mulleinsong

Place:        Applegate
Formed:       1982

"Mulleinsong." By Julie. *Rough Road* 2 (1982): 4.

## Nanish Shontie

Place:        Blachly
Formed:       2002
Formerly:     Center for Experimental Cultural Design
Directories:  Communities Directory (online)
              *Communities Directory*, 2005: 193.

## Nature Retreat

Place:        Chiloquin
Forming:      2006?
See:          Gathering Light

## Nehalem Valley Cooperative Colony

Place: Mist
Dates: 1888-1892

Albertson, Ralph. *A Survey of Mutualistic Communities in America*. Reprinted from *Iowa Journal of History and Politics* 34 (1936) (New York: AMS Press, 1973): 419

Bushbee, Frederick A. "Communistic Societies in the United States." *Political Science Quarterly* 20 (December 1905): 646.

Eaton, Joseph W., and Saul M. Katz. *Research Guide on Cooperative Group Farming* (New York: H. W. Wilson Company, 1942): 37.

Gaylord, A. J. "Duties of Members [letter]." *The Co-operator* III(3) (December 29, 1900): 1.

Girard, H. E. "From Nehalem Colony [letter]." *The Kaweah Commonwealth* 1(33) (August 1890): 3.

Girard, H. E. "Nehalem. A New Co-operative Colony in Oregon [letter]." *The Kaweah Commonwealth* 1(8) (March 1890): 1.

Haycox, Ernest, Jr. "To the Editor[letter]." *Oregon Historical Quarterly* 105 (Winter 2004): 659-60.

Kent, Alexander. "Nehalem Valley Cooperative Colony" in "Cooperative Communities in the United States." *Bulletin of the Department of Labor* 6 (July 1901): 642.

Kopp, James J. "Documenting Utopia in Oregon: The Challenges of Tracking the Quest for Perfection." *Oregon Historical Quarterly* 105 (2004): 308-19.

Kopp, James J. "Looking Backward at Edward Bellamy's Impact in Oregon." *Oregon Historical Quarterly* 104 (Spring 2003): 84.

258

Kopp, James J. "To the Editor [letter]." *Oregon Historical Quarterly* 104 (Winter 2003): 616-17.

Lockley, Fred. "Fred Lockley's Impressions." *Oregon Journal* (August 17, 1947).

Miller, Timothy. "Nehalem Valley Cooperative Colony" in *American Communes, 1860-1960: A Bibliography* (New York & London: Garland Publishing, 1990): 421.

Neketin, Peter. "To the Editor [letter]." *Oregon Historical Quarterly* 106 (Summer 2005): 334.

Okugawa, Otohiko. "Appendix A: Annotated List of Communal and Utopian Societies, 1787-1919." In Robert S. Fogarty. *Dictionary of American Communal and Utopian History* (Westport, CT: Greenwood Press, 1980): 214.

*Oregon Mist* (September 4, 1891; September 25, 1891).

Oved, Yaacov. *Two Hundred Years of American Communes* (New Brunswick, NJ: Transactions Books, 1988): 489.

Pitzer, Donald E., ed. *America's Communal Utopias* (Chapel Hill: University of North Carolina Press, 1997): 478.

Stephan, Karen H. and G. Edward Stephan. "Religion and the Survival of Utopian Communities." *Journal of the Scientific Study of Religion* 12 (March 1973): 89-100[97].

Stockwell, Foster. "Nehalem Valley Cooperative Colony" in *Encyclopedia of American Communes, 1663-1963* (Jefferson, NC: McFarland & Co., 1998): 143.

Walker, Lisa. "A Selected Bibliography of Sources on Communal Societies in Oregon and Washington Available at the Oregon Historical Society" (March 15, 1992): 26.

Williams, Julia Elizabeth. "An Analytical Tabulation of the North American Utopian Communities By Type, Longevity and Location." (M. A. thesis, Department of Sociology, University of South Dakota, 1939): 10.

## Network for a New Culture (NFNC)

Place:          Eugene
Formed:         1994
Formerly:       Center for Experimental Cultural Design (AZ)
Directories:    *Communities Directory*, 1996: 277.
                [Communities Directory Summer '96 Update – North American Updates] (*Communities* 91): 68.
                [Communities Directory Summer '98 Update – North American Updates] (Communities 99): 65.
                [Community Updates – Changes] (*Communities* 120): 23.
                *Communities Directory*, 2007: 218-19.
                Communities Directory (online)

[Community Calendar – Aug 11-23 – Network for a New Culture's Summer Camp '98]. *Communities* 99 (Summer 1998): 67.

[Community Calendar – Aug 8-20 – Network for a New Culture Summer Camp 2000]. *Communities* 107 (Summer 2000): 64.

[Community Calendar – Aug 14-26 – NFNC's 7th Annual Summer Camp]. *Communities* 111 (Summer 2001): 65.

[Community Calendar – Aug 6-20 – Network for a New Culture Summer Camp West]. *Communities* 126 (Spring 2005): 67.

[Community Calendar – Aug 8-17 – Summer Camp '97, Network for a New Culture]. *Communities* 95 (Summer 1997): 68.

Kozeny, Geoph. "Community as Performance Art." *Communities* 93 (Winter 1996): 8.

## Networking for Peace Multicultural Cohousing Resource Neighborhood

| | |
|---|---|
| Place: | Portland |
| Forming: | 2005 |
| Directories: | Communities Directory (online) |
| | *Communities Directory*, 2007: 360. |
| Web: | http://www.freewebs.com/abwwrpeace/ |
| | networkingforpeacemulticulturalcohousing.html |
| Publication: | *The Peace & The Press* |

## Newberry House

| | |
|---|---|
| Place: | Portland, 14845 NW Newberry Road |
| Formed: | 2005 |
| Directories: | *Communities Directory* (online) |
| | *Communities Directory*, 2007: 361. |
| Web: | http://homepage.mac.com/carlvz/newberryhouse/Personal47.html |

## New Era

Florin, Lambert. "New Era, Oregon" in *Ghost Towns of the West* (New York: Promontory Press, 1993): 754-55.

Johnson, David. "Greener Grass: A Short History of Oregon's Utopia Tradition." *Oregon Heritage* 1 (Winter/Spring 1995):16.

Kopp, James J. "Documenting Utopia in Oregon: The Challenges of Tracking the Quest for Perfection." *Oregon Historical Quarterly* 105 (2004): 308-19.

Lawton, George. *The Drama of Life After Death: A Study of the Spiritualist Religion.* (New York: Henry Holt and Company, 1932): 600.

*Oregon, End of the Trail. Compiled by Workers of the Writers' Program of the Work Projects Administration in the State of Oregon.* Revised Edition with added material by Howard McKinley Corning. (Portland: Binford & Mort,[1951]): 306.

## New Jamestown – See Open Gate

## New Land

| | |
|---|---|
| Place: | Takilma |
| Formed: | Mid-1970s |
| Formerly: | Little Funky Egg Company |

Plagge, Dick. "Takilma – Communal Valley." *Willamette Week* 4:12 (Jan. 24, 1978): 5, 7.

Wilner, Joseph Bear. "All My Sisters and Brothers: Redefinitions of Family in Oregon Intentional Communities During the Late Twentieth Century." (M. A. thesis, University of Oregon, 2000): 30.

## New Odessa

| | |
|---|---|
| Place: | Near Glendale |
| Dates: | 1882-1886 |

### Archives/Manuscripts

New Odessa Colony. Oregon Historical Society Research Library Manuscripts.
New Odessa Colony. Oregon Historical Society Research Library Vertical File.
William Frey Papers. New York Public Library Manuscripts & Archives.

Abdill, George B. "New Odessa: Douglas County's Russian Communal Colony." *Umpqua Trapper* 1 (Winter 1965): 10-14; and 2 (Spring 1966): 16-21.

Amsden, Elizabeth. "Communes Rooted in Oregon History." *The Oregonian* (October 11, 1984): C6.

Bartelt, Pearl W. "American Jewish Agricultural Colonies" in Pitzer, Donald E., ed. *America's Communal Utopias* (Chapel Hill: University of North Carolina Press, 1997): 352-74.

Blumenthal, Helen E. "New Odessa Colony of Oregon, 1882-1886." *Western States Jewish Historical Quarterly* 14 (July 1982): 321-32.

Blumenthal, Helen E. "New Odessa 1882-1887: United We Stand, Divided We Fall." M.A. thesis, Portland State University, 1975.

Blumenthal, Helen E. "Pioneer Jewish History: 'New Odessa.'" *Historical Scribe* (Summer 1977): 1-2.

Brandes, Joseph. "Jewish Gauchos Had Counterparts in U.S. [letter]." *New York Times* (May 7, 1996): A22.

Bushee, Frederick A. "Communistic Societies in the United States." *Political Science Quarterly* 20 (December 1905): 663.

Cowen, Philip. *Memories of An American Jew* (New York: International Press, 1932): 98-99.

Eaton, Joseph W., and Saul M. Katz. *Research Guide on Cooperative Group Farming* (New York: H. W. Wilson Company, 1942): 40.

Davidson, Gabriel, and Edward A. Goodwin. "Unique Agricultural Colony." *Reflex* 2 (May 1928): 80-86. Reprinted in *Our Jewish Farmers*. New York: L. B. Fischer, 1943.

Epstein, Melech. *Jewish Labor in U.S.A.: An Industrial, Political and Cultural History of the Jewish Labor Movement, 1882-1914* ([New York]: KTAV Publishing House, 1969): 226-30.

Feldstein, Stanley. *The Land That I Show You: Three Centuries of Jewish Life in America* (Garden City, NY: Anchor Press/Doubleday, 1978): 147, 150-51, 157.

Fogarty, Robert S. "American Communes, 1865-1914." *Journal of American Studies* 9 (August 1975): 157-58.

Fogarty, Robert S. *Dictionary of American Communal and Utopian History* (Westport, CT.: Greenwood Press, 1980): 49-50, 154-55.

Frankel, Jonathan. *Prophecy and Politics: Socialism, Nationalism, and the Russian Jews, 1862-1917* (Cambridge, UK: Cambridge University Press, 1981): 67, 94, 121.

Glanz, Rudolf. *The Jewish Woman in America: Two Female Immigrant Generations, 1820-1929. Volume 1: The Eastern European Jewish Woman* ([New York]: KTAV Publishing House and National Council of Jewish Women, 1976): 13-14.

Goering, Violet, and Orlando J. Goering. "The Agricultural Communes of the *Am Olam*." *Communal Societies* 4 (1984): 74-86.

"Grigorij Machtet: Frey's Community" in Olga Peters Hasty and Susanne Fusso, eds. *America Through Russian Eyes, 1874-1926* (New Haven, CT: Yale University Press, 1988): 54-82.

Herscher, Uri D. "New Odessa, Oregon" in *Jewish Agricultural Utopias in America, 1880-1910* (Detroit, MI: Wayne State University Press, 1981): 37-48.

Johnson, David. "Greener Grass: A Short History of Oregon's Utopia Tradition." *Oregon Heritage* 1 (Winter/Spring 1995): 16.

Kopp, James J. "Am Olam." The Oregon Encyclopedia (http://www.oregonencyclopedia.org/entry/view/am_olam/).

Kopp, James J. "Documenting Utopia in Oregon: The Challenges of Tracking the Quest for Perfection." *Oregon Historical Quarterly* 105 (2004): 308-19.

261

Levin, Nora. *While Messiah Tarried: Jewish Socialist Movements, 1871-1917.* (New York: Schocken, 1977): 49-53.

Lowenstein, Steven. *The Jews of Oregon, 1850-1950.* (Portland: Jewish Historical Society of Oregon, 1987): 77, 89-91.

Menes, Abraham. "Am Olyom Movement." *YIVO Annual of Jewish Social Science* 4 (1949): 9-33.

Miller, Timothy. "Oregon: New Odessa" in *American Communes, 1860-1960: A Bibliography* (New York & London: Garland Publishing, 1990): 293-96.

Moskowitz, Henry. "Paul Kaplan: An East Side Portrait." *Outlook* 118 (January 16, 1918): 108-9.

Okugawa, Otohiko. "Appendix A: Annotated List of Communal and Utopian Societies, 1787-1919." In Robert S. Fogarty. *Dictionary of American Communal and Utopian History* (Westport, CT: Greenwood Press, 1980): 212.

Oved, Yaacov. "New Odessa: A Jewish Commune of the Am Olam Group" in *Two Hundred Years of American Communes* (New Brunswick, NJ, and Oxford: Transactions Books, 1988): 223-31.

Parry, Albert. "Russian Names for American Towns." *Russian Review* 3 (Spring 1944): 30-43 [40].

Pitzer, Donald E., ed. *America's Communal Utopias* (Chapel Hill: University of North Carolina Press, 1997): 473, 480.

Pollak, Gustav. *Michael Heilprin and His Sons: A Biography.* New York: Dodd, Mead and Company, 1912.

Price, George M. "Russian Jews in America." *Publication of the American Jewish Historical Society* 48 (December 1958): 78-133. Reprinted in *The Jewish Experience in America.* Edited by Abraham J. Karp. Volume 4 (New York: KTAV Publishing House, 1969): 300-55.

Reizenstein, Milton. "Agricultural Colonies in the United States" in *The Jewish Encyclopedia*, edited by Isidore Singer. Volume 1 (New York and London: Funk and Wagnalls Company, 1901): 256-62.

Rischin, Moses. "The Jewish Experience in America: A View from the West." In Moses Rischin and John Livingston, eds. *Jews of the American West* (Detroit, MI: Wayne State University Press, 1991): 26-47.

Rosenthal, Herman. "Chronicles of the Communist Settlement Known by the Name 'New Odessa'" Translated by Gary P. Zola. Cincinnati, 1979. Typescript. 31pp. American Jewish Archives.

Rosenbluth, Robert. "The Many Lives of Robert Rosenbluth: Excerpts from His Autobiography." *Forest History* 8 (1-2) (1964): 17-21.

"Russian Colonies to be Founded." *New York Times* (May 8, 1884): 8.

Seldes, Marian. "Tell Me, Grandfather." *New York Times* (August 18, 1985): NJ1.

Shaw, Albert. *Icaria: A Chapter in the History of Communism* (New York & London: G. P. Putnam's Sons, 1884): 182-85.

Shpall, Leo. "Jewish Agricultural Colonies in the United States." *Agricultural History* 24 (July 1950): 120-46.

Singer, Richard E. "New Odessa," pp. 535-38 in *American Jews in Agriculture, Past History and Present Condition.* Prize essay, 1941, in manuscript at American Jewish Archives. Also on microfilm. V. 1, 358pp; v. 2, pp. 359-707.

Solis, Miguel J. "New Odessa Community" in *American Utopias (1683-1900): Evolution versus Revolution: A Descriptive and Bibliographic Dictionary* (Bloomington, IN: The Author, 1984): 139.

Sorin, Gerald. *A Time for Building: The Third Migration, 1880-1920* (Baltimore, MD, and London: Johns Hopkins University Press, 1992): 66-67, 155.

Stockwell, Foster. "New Odessa" in *Encyclopedia of American Communes, 1663-1963* (Jefferson, NC: McFarland & Co., 1998): 110-12.

262

Stephan, Karen H., and G. Edward Stephan. "Religion and the Survival of Utopian Communities." *Journal of the Scientific Study of Religion* 12 (March 1973): 89-100[97].

Sutton, Robert P. "New Odessa" in *Communal Utopias and the American Experience: Religious Communities, 1732-2000* (Westport, CT: Praeger, 2003): 46-48.

Suwol, Samuel M. *Jewish History of Oregon* (Portland: S. M. Suwol, 1958): 4.

Walker, Lisa. "A Selected Bibliography of Sources on Communal Societies in Oregon and Washington Available at the Oregon Historical Society" (March 15, 1992): 18-21.

"Wedding Among the Communistic Jews in Oregon." *Overland Monthly* 6 (second series) (December 1885): 606-11.

Williams, Julia Elizabeth. "An Analytical Tabulation of the North American Utopian Communities By Type, Longevity and Location." M. A. thesis, Department of Sociology, University of South Dakota, 1939, 13.

Wischnitzer, Mark. "The Am Olam Movement: Hopes and Failures" in *To Dwell in Safety: The Story of Jewish Migration Since 1800* (Philadelphia, PA: The Jewish Publications Society of America, 1948): 60-64.

Yarmolinsky, Avrahm. *A Russian's American Dream: A Memoir of William Frey.* Lawrence: University of Kansas Press, 1965.

## Nomenus Radical Faerie Sanctuary

| | |
|---|---|
| Place: | Wolf Creek |
| Formed: | 1987 |
| Directories: | *Communities Directory*, 2000: 304-5. |
| | *Communities Directory*, 2005: 198-99. |
| | *Communities Directory*, 2007: 223. |
| | Communities Directory (online) |
| Publications: | *The RadDish* |
| Formerly: | Creekland |
| Also see: | Wolf Creek Radical Faerie Sanctuary |

"Gay Men's Communities [letter]." *Communities* 85 (Winter 1994): 4-5.

Wilner, Joseph Bear. "All My Sisters and Brothers: Redefinitions of Family in Oregon Intentional Communities During the Late Twentieth Century." (M. A. thesis, University of Oregon, 2000): 77-85.

## Northern Lights

| | |
|---|---|
| Formed: | 1970s |
| Directories: | Miller, *The 60s Communes*: 274. |

## Oahspe Foundation

| | |
|---|---|
| Place: | Phoenix/Ashland |
| Formed: | 1975/1992 |
| Directories: | [Communities Directory: Updates & Additions to the Third Printing] (*Communities* 79): 33. |

[Reach – Communes Forming]. *Communities* 13 (March/April 1975): 56.

## Older Women Network (OWN)

| | |
|---|---|
| Place: | Wolf Creek, 3502 Coyote Creek Rd. |
| Formed: | 1977 |
| Directories: | "Directory of Intentional Communities 1978" (*Communities* 30): 42. |

"1981 Directory of Intentional Communities and Resources"
(*Communities* 46): 35.
**Publications:** *Older Women's Newsletter*
**Manuscripts:** Ruth Mountaingrove Papers. Special Collections & University
Archives, University of Oregon Libraries.

Elana. "Women's Communities: A Letter to Older Women." *Women's Press*
(August 1975): 19.
"[Grapevine – Older Women's Network]." *Communities* 33 (July/August 1978):
56.
"Ideas for the Older Women's Community." *Older Women's Newsletter*, Vol. 1,
No. 1 (March 1977): 2:
Raimy, Eric. "National Organization and Publications." *Shared Houses, Shared
Lives: The New Extended Families and How They Work* (Los Angeles: J. P.
Tarcher, 1979): 165.
[Reach – Conferences – Older Women's Network Workshop – July 12-16].
*Communities* 33 (July/August 1978): 52.
[Reach – Groups Forming – Older Women's Rural Community]. *Communities* 28
(September-October 1977): 57.
[Resources – Older Women's Network] in *A Guide to Cooperative Alternatives*
(New Haven, CT, and Louisa, VA: Community Publications Cooperative,
1979): 76.
[Resources – Older Women's Network]. *Communities* 56 (December 1982/January
1983): 87.
Wilner, Joseph Bear. "All My Sisters and Brothers: Redefinitions of Family in
Oregon Intentional Communities During the Late Twentieth Century." (M. A.
thesis, University of Oregon, 2000): 65-66.

## One By One
**Place:** Eugene, 3920 East 17th.
**Formed:** 1991
**Directories:** *Communities Directory*, 1996: 393.

## Ongoing [Concerns] Cohousing Community
**Place:** Portland, 1905 NE Going St.
**Formed:** 1991
**Directories:** *Communities Directory*, 2000: 308.

[Community Grapevine]. *Communities* 98 (Spring 1998): 8.
Meisenhelter, Diane. "Building Community in the City." *Communities* 82 (Spring
1994): 10-11.

## Onion Farm
**Formed:** Ca. 1970
**Directories:** Miller, *The 60s Communes*: 275.

Houriet, Robert. *Getting Back Together* (New York: Coward, McCann &
Geoghegan, 1971): 75-77.

## Open Forum Network [Cerro Gordo]
**Place:** Portland, 5567 Multnomah Blvd.
**Directories:** *Communities Directory*, 1996: 394.
**Note:** Information resource for Cerro Gordo.

## Open Gate

Place:       McMinnville
Formed:     1972

[Community Clearinghouse]. *Communitas* 2 (September 1972): 54.
"Open Gate." *Communities* 2 (February 1973): 23-25.

## Orchard Street Church

Place:       Eugene, 1598 Orchard Street
Formed:     1970
Directories:  Jackson, Dave. *Coming Together*: 185-86.

## Oregon Extension

Place:       Lincoln (?)
Formed:     1975
Directories:  Miller, *The 60s Communes*: 275.

## Oregon Family – See Family of Mystic (Living) Arts

## Oregon Woman's[Womon's] Land (OWL) Trust

Place:       Eugene, 1821 Jefferson St.
             Grants Pass, 1501 Grays Creek Road
Formed:     1974
Directories:  Miller, *The 60s Communes*: 275.
             *A Guide to Cooperative Alternatives*, 1979 (*Communities* 38): 174.
             "1981 Directory of Intentional Communities and Resources"
                (*Communities* 46): 45-46.
             "1983 Directory" (*Communities* 56): 73.
             "1985 Directory of Intentional Communities" (*Communities* 66): 59.
             *Directory of Intentional Communities*, 1990: 281.
             *Communities Directory*, 1996: 394

**Archives/Manuscripts:**
             Ruth Mountaingrove Papers. Special Collections & University
                Archives, University of Oregon Libraries.
             SO CLAP! (Southern Oregon Country Lesbian Archival Project)
                Collection, 1974-1999, Special Collections & University
                Archives, University of Oregon Libraries, Series II.

Dee. "[Oregon Women's Land Trust – letter]." *Women's Press* (March/April 1977):
    2.
"[Grapevine – Land Trusts – Oregon Women's Land]." *Communities* 28
    (September-October 1977): 48.
Guthrie and Roz. "Notes on a Land Trust." *WomanSpirit* vol. 3, no. 11 (Spring
    Equinox 1977): 34-35.
"The Gypsy Caravan." *WomanSpirit* vol. 3, no. 11 (Spring Equinox 1977): 36.
"A Herstory of the Oregon Women's Land Trust." *WomanSpirit* vol. 3, no. 11
    (Spring Equinox 1977): 10-12.
"Land Trust." *WomanSpirit* vol. 2, no. 5 (Fall Equinox 1975): 35.
"Land Trust." *WomanSpirit* vol. 5, no. 21 (Fall Equinox 1979): 41-43.
"News from Oregon Women's Land Trust." *Women's Press* (August/September
    1980): 4.
"Oregon ♀'s Land Trust." *Whole Eugene Catalog* (1975/76): 9.
"Oregon Women's Land Trust News." *Woman's Place Newsletter* (October 1978):
    16.

265

"Oregon Womens Land Trust Report." *Women's Press* (July/August 1976): 16.

[Resources – Land Trusts] in *A Guide to Cooperative Alternatives* (New Haven, CT, and Louisa, VA: Community Publications Cooperative, 1979): 67.

Sandilands, Catriona. "Lesbian Separatist Communities and the Experience of Nature: A Queer Ecology." *Organization & Environment* 15 (June 2002): 131-63.

Summerhawk, Barbara, and La Verne Gagehabib. *Circles of Power: Shifting Dynamics in a Lesbian-Centered Community* (Norwich, VT: New Victoria Publishers, 2000): 49-54; 123-27.

Sunlight. "Wimmin's Open Land." *WomanSpirit* vol. 5, no. 21 (Fall 1979): 36.

Traveller, Helen. "A Traveller's Tale." *WomanSpirit* vol. 3, no. 11 (Spring Equinox 1977): 28-30.

"A Women's Land Trust is being formed …[Ms.Ellaneous]." *Women's Press* (Septmber 1975): 20.

## Oregon Working Group 2006

Place:         Eastern Oregon
Forming:       2006
Directories:   Communities Directory (online)
               *Communities Directory*, 2007: 369.

## Organic Mud Farm

Place:         Lane County
Formed:        1971

Bates, Doug. "Lane County's Rural Areas Nurture Communal Lifestyle." *Eugene Register-Guard* (August 29, 1971): B1.

## Osho Ansu Meditation Center

Place:         Lake Oswego
Forming:       1992
Directories:   [Fall 1992 Update to the Directory of Intentional Communities] (*Communities* 79): 24.

## OWL Farm/Oregon's [Open Womyn's] Woman Land

Place:         Days Creek
Formed:        1976
Directories:   Miller, *The 60s Communes*: 275.
               *A Guide to Cooperative Alternatives*, 1979 (*Communities* 38): 174.
               "1981 Directory of Intentional Communities and Resources" (*Communities* 46): 46.
               "1983 Directory" (*Communities* 56): 73.
               "1985 Directory of Intentional Communities" (*Communities* 66): 59.
               *Directory of Intentional Communities*, 1990: 208.
               *Communities Directory*, 1996: 282.
               *Communities Directory*, 2000: 310.
               [Community Updates – Lost/Disbanded] (*Communities* 120): 29.
               Communities Directory (online)
               Association of Lesbian Intentional Communities online
               *Shewolf's Directory of Wimmin's Land*. Fifth Edition

**Archives/Manuscripts:**
> Ruth Mountaingrove Papers. Special Collections & University Archives, University of Oregon Libraries.
> SO CLAP! (Southern Oregon Country Lesbian Archival Project) Collection, 1974-1999, Special Collections & University Archives, University of Oregon Libraries

Arnica. "Access to Land: The Realization of a Dream." *WomanSpirit* v. 3, no.11 (Spring Equinox 1977): 22-23.

Association of Lesbian Intentional Communities. "Come to Oregon Women's Lands." http://alicinfo.com/pages/oregon.htm

"Celebrating Long-Lived Communities." *Communities* 93 (Winter 1996): 12.

"Community Events [OWL Farm]." *Rag Times* (March 1983): 6.

Félicé Ana and kaseja O. "Special Animals at OWL Farm." *Womyn's Press* (August/September 1990): 7.

Johnson, David. "Greener Grass: A Short History of Oregon's Utopia Tradition." *Oregon Heritage* 1 (Winter/Spring 1995): 17.

kaseja O. "Country Dykes." *Womyn's Press* (October/November 1989): 3.

kaseja O. "Country Dykes." *Womyn's Press* (February/March 1990): 6.

kaseja O. "Country Dykes." *Womyn's Press* (April/May 1990): 2.

kaseja O. "Country Dykes." *Womyn's Press* (June/July 1990): 4.

Kleiner, Catherine B. "Doin' It For Themselves: Lesbian Land Communities in Southern Oregon, 1970-1995." (Ph.D. dissertation, University of New Mexico, 2003): 105-8.

Lee, Pelican. "Owl Farm: The Oregon Women's Land Trust: The Early Years" in Tee Corinne, ed., "Resources: Southwestern Oregon Women on the Land." SO CLAP! Files, Special Collections & University Archives, University of Oregon.

Ní Aódagaín, H. "Empowerment through Community: From Separatism to Sanctuary." Paper presented at the 26th Annual Gender Studies Symposium, Lewis & Clark College, March 8, 2007.

"Open Country Land." *Women's Press* (April/May 1979): 11.

"[OWL Farm – advertisement]." *Rag Times* (May 1982): 5.

"Owl Farm." *Women's Press* (March/April 1981): 18.

"Owl Farm." *Rag Times* (May 1982): 6.

"OWL Farm." *Rag Times* (July 1982): 6.

"OWL Farm to Celebrate 10th Year." *Rag Times* (July 1986): 7.

"Owl I Sing to Yr Magic." *Women's Press* (January/February 1981): 14.

"Owl Farm [photo by Elizabeth Freeman]." *Women's Press* (August/September 1980): 5.

"Owl Farm: Tightening Up." *Women's Press* (November/December 1980): 2.

"OWL Farm News, 1980." *Woman's Place Newsletter* (March 1980): 9.

"OWL Update." *Women's Press* (May/June 1981): 2.

Pelican. "Notes from the Journal of a Womon Living on Open Land." *WomanSpirit* v. 3, no. 11 (Spring Equinox 1977): 24-25.

Sandia Bear, "Lesbians on Land: A Tribe of Womyn." In Lynn Witt, Sherry Thomas, and Eric Marcus, eds. *Out in All Directions: The Almanac of Gay and Lesbian America* (New York: Warner Books, 1995): 323-26.

Sandilands, Catriona. "Lesbian Separatist Communities and the Experience of Nature: A Queer Ecology." *Organization & Environment* 15 (June 2002): 131-63.

Sandilands, Catriona. "Rainbow's End? Lesbian Separatism and the Ongoing Politics of Ecotopia." In Margrit Eichler, June Larkin, and Sheila Neysmith, eds. *Feminist Utopias: Re-Visioning Our Future* (Toronto, Canada: Inanna Publications and Education, 2002): 37-50.

Sprecher, Katharine Matthaei. "Lesbian Intentional Communities in Rural Southwestern Oregon: Discussions on Separatism, Environmentalism, and Community Conflict." (M. A. thesis, California Institute of Integral Studies, 1997): 73-81.

Summerhawk, Barbara, and La Verne Gagehabib. *Circles of Power: Shifting Dynamics in a Lesbian-Centered Community* (Norwich, VT: New Victoria Publishers, 2000: 49-54; 123-27.

Thyme & Seagull. "[Letter – OWL Farm]." *Woman's Place Newsletter* (June 1981): 5.

Wilner, Joseph Bear. "All My Sisters and Brothers: Redefinitions of Family in Oregon Intentional Communities During the Late Twentieth Century." (M. A. thesis, University of Oregon, 2000): 66-67.

"Work Week at OWL Farm [Announcements]." *Women's Press* (November/December 1980): 23.

Yael. "Owl Farm." *Women's Press* (November/December 1984): 12.

Yael. "Visit to OWL Farm." *Women's Press* (December 1982/January 1983): 12.

## Pahana Town Forum

| | |
|---|---|
| **Place:** | Lake Dorena |
| **Formed:** | 1972 |
| **Directories:** | Miller, *The 60s Communes*: 275. |
| | "Commune Directory" (*Communities* 7): 36. |
| **Note:** | Precursor to Cerro Gordo. |

[Grapevine]. *Communities* 5 (October/November 1973): 42.
[Grapevine]. *Communities* 6 (December 1973/January 1974): 54-55.
"The New New Towns." *Communities* 7 (March/April 1974): 2-10.

## Peninsula Park Commons

| | |
|---|---|
| **Place:** | Portland, 6325 N. Albina Ave. #6 |
| **Formed:** | 2004 |
| **Directories:** | Cohousing Directory (online) |
| | Communities Directory (online) |
| | *Communities Directory*, 2005: 206-7. |
| | *Communities Directory*, 2007: 229. |
| **Web:** | www.penparkcommons.org |

## Poppyseed

| | |
|---|---|
| **Place:** | Sunny Valley |
| **Formed:** | 1990s |

Sandilands, Catriona. "Lesbian Separatist Communities and the Experience of Nature: A Queer Ecology." *Organization & Environment* 15 (June 2002): 161n12.

Summerhawk, Barbara, and La Verne Gagehabib. *Circles of Power: Shifting Dynamics in a Lesbian-Centered Community* (Norwich, VT: New Victoria Publishers, 2000) 12, 38, 184.

Wilner, Joseph Bear. "All My Sisters and Brothers: Redefinitions of Family in Oregon Intentional Communities During the Late Twentieth Century." (M. A. thesis, University of Oregon, 2000): 70.

## Portable Village (PVR)

Place:      Philomath
Forming:    1983

[Reach – Groups Looking]. *Communities* 59 (July/August 1983): 43.

## Portland Eastside Cohousing

Place:        Portland
Forming:      2003
Directories:  [Directories Update – New] (*Communities* 117): 67.
              [Directory Updates – New] (*Communities* 120): 13.
              [Directory Updates] (*Communities* 123): 65.
See:          East Portland Cohousing

## Portland Group

Place:        Portland (acreage in Washington)
Formed:       Early 1970s
Directories:  Miller, *The 60s Communes*: 272.
              "Commune Directory" (*Communities* 1): 35.

## Possum Place

Place:    Eugene
Formed:   2004
Web:      www.possumplace.com

[Communities Forming and Reforming – Intentional Artists Community/
   Permaculture Project/Evolving Urban Eco-village, Eugene, Oregon].
   *Communities* 132 (Fall 2006): 81-82.
[Communities Forming and Reforming – Intentional Artists Community/
   Permaculture Project/Evolving Urban Eco-village, Eugene, Oregon].
   *Communities* 133 (Winter 2006): 70.
[Communities Forming and Reforming – Intentional Artists Community/
   Permaculture Project/Evolving Urban Eco-village, Eugene, Oregon].
   *Communities* 134 (Spring 2007): 68.

## Prince of Peace

Place:    Portland
Formed:   1970s

Peterson, Joe V. "Jesus People: Christ, Communes, and the Counterculture of the
   Late Twentieth Century in the Pacific Northwest and a Brief Review of the
   Shiloh Youth Revival Centers, Inc., The Highway Missionary Society/Servant
   Community, and the House of Elijah." (M.A. thesis, Northwest Christian
   College, 1990): 31.

269

## Rainbow Family

Place:        Dunes City/Eugene
Formed:       1971
Directories:  "Commune Directory" (*Communities* 1): 35.
              "Commune Directory" (*Communities* 7): 31.
              "Directory of Intentional Communities 1978" (*Communities* 30): 29.
              Mercer, *Communes: A Social History and Guide*: 140.

Bacon, Larry. "Rainbow Family to Leave Coast for Eugene." *Eugene Register-Guard* (February 14, 1975): 1B.

Bacon, Larry. "Unwelcome Rainbow: A Tiny Coastal Community Finds Itself Uneasy over the Arrival of a Growing Spiritual 'Family'." *Eugene Register-Guard* (December 22, 1974): 1F.

"[Classified Ad] Rainbow Family needs and can use all your old rakes, shovels, picks, hoes, pressure cookers, wheelbarrows, valentines and the like. Bring tools to 1674 Washington Ave." *Augur*, v. 2, no. 10 (February 26, 1971).

Keller, Bill. "Children Mature in Rainbow Family." *The Oregonian* (November 28, 1971).

Vanneman, Brian Robert. "Searching For Paradise in the Rain: Oregon's Communes and Intentional Communities of the 1960s and 1970s." (Honors thesis, University of Oregon, 1997): 19.

Wilner, Joseph Bear. "All My Sisters and Brothers: Redefinitions of Family in Oregon Intentional Communities During the Late Twentieth Century." (M. A. thesis, University of Oregon, 2000): 36-37.

## Rainbow Farm

Place:          Drain
Formed:         1970
Directories:    Miller, *The 60s Communes*: 277.

Bates, Doug. "Lane County's Rural Areas Nurture Communal Lifestyle." *Eugene Register-Guard* (August 29, 1971): B1.

"A Day in the Life of a Commune Dweller: 17-year-old Ty of Rainbow Farm." *Eugene Register-Guard* (August 29, 1971): B1.

[Grapevine]. *Communities* 1 (December 1972): 47.

[Grapevine]. *Communities* 3 (1973): 50.

John, Michael, comp. *The Rainbow Nation 1982 Cooperative Community Guide V. A Peoples Guide to the Liberation of Earth* (McCall, ID:[Rainbow Nation], 1982): 61.

Johnson, David. "Greener Grass: A Short History of Oregon's Utopia Tradition." *Oregon Heritage* 1 (Winter/Spring 1995): 16-17.

## Rainbow Mist

Place:          Five Rivers
Formed:         1970s
Directories:    Miller, *The 60s Communes*: 277.

## Rainbow's End

Place:          Roseburg, 886 Raven Lane
Formed:         1976
Directories:    Association of Lesbian Intentional Communities online
                *Shewolf's Directory of Wimmin's Land*. Fifth Edition
Archives/Manuscripts:
                Ruth Mountaingrove Papers. Special Collections & University
                     Archives, University of Oregon Libraries.
                SO CLAP! (Southern Oregon Country Lesbian Archival Project)
                     Collection, 1974-1999, Special Collections & University
                     Archives, University of Oregon Libraries

Association of Lesbian Intentional Communities. "Come to Oregon Women's
Lands." http://alicinfo.com/pages/oregon.htm
Kleiner, Catherine B. "Doin' It For Themselves: Lesbian Land Communities in
Southern Oregon, 1970-1995." (Ph.D. dissertation, University of New Mexico,
2003): 115-16.
"Rainbow's End: Douglas County Planning Department Threatens Women's
Collective." *Women's Press* (January/February 1982): 11.
Sandia Bear, "Lesbians on Land: A Tribe of Womyn." In Lynn Witt, Sherry
Thomas, and Eric Marcus, eds. *Out in All Directions: The Almanac of Gay and
Lesbian America* (New York: Warner Books, 1995): 323-26.
Sandilands, Catriona. "Lesbian Separatist Communities and the Experience of
Nature: A Queer Ecology." *Organization & Environment* 15 (June 2002): 131-
63.
Sandilands, Catriona. "Rainbow's End? Lesbian Separatism and the Ongoing
Politics of Ecotopia." In Margrit Eichler, June Larkin, and Sheila Neysmith,
eds. *Feminist Utopias: Re-Visioning Our Future* (Toronto, Canada: Inanna
Publications and Education, 2002): 37-50.
Sonnenberg, Valerie. [Poem]. *Rough Road* 2 (1982): 16-17.
Sprecher, Katharine Matthaei. "Lesbian Intentional Communities in Rural
Southwestern Oregon: Discussions on Separatism, Environmentalism, and
Community Conflict." (M. A. thesis, California Institute of Integral Studies,
1997): 63-66.
Star. "How I Came to Rainbow's End" in Tee Corinne, ed., "Community Histories:
Living in Southern Oregon." SO CLAP! Files, Special Collections & University
Archives, University of Oregon.
Star. "[Rainbow's End]." *WomanSpirit* vol. 3, no.11 (Spring Equinox 1977): 19.
Summerhawk, Barbara, and La Verne Gagehabib. *Circles of Power: Shifting
Dynamics in a Lesbian-Centered Community* (Norwich, VT: New Victoria
Publishers, 2000) 57-59; 122-23.
Wilner, Joseph Bear. "All My Sisters and Brothers: Redefinitions of Family in
Oregon Intentional Communities During the Late Twentieth Century." (M. A.
thesis, University of Oregon, 2000): 70-71.

## Rainbow's Other End

Place:        Roseburg, 925 Raven Lane
Formed:       1977
Directories:  Association of Lesbian Intentional Communities online
              *Shewolf's Directory of Wimmin's Land.* Fifth Edition

Association of Lesbian Intentional Communities. "Come to Oregon Women's
Lands." http://alicinfo.com/pages/oregon.htm
Sandia Bear, "Lesbians on Land: A Tribe of Womyn." In Lynn Witt, Sherry
Thomas, and Eric Marcus, eds. *Out in All Directions: The Almanac of Gay and
Lesbian America* (New York: Warner Books, 1995): 323-26.
Sandilands, Catriona. "Lesbian Separatist Communities and the Experience of
Nature." *Organization & Environment* 15 (June 2002): 131-63.
Sandilands, Catriona. "Rainbow's End? Lesbian Separatism and the Ongoing
Politics of Ecotopia." In Margrit Eichler, June Larkin, and Sheila Neysmith,
eds. *Feminist Utopias: Re-Visioning Our Future* (Toronto, Canada: Inanna
Publications and Education, 2002): 37-50.
Sonnenberg, Valerie. [Poem]. *Rough Road* 2 (1982): 16-17.

# Rajneeshpuram

Place:      Antelope
Dates:     1981-86

**Archives and Manuscripts:**
Rajneesh Artifacts and Ephemere Collection, 1981-2004. Special Collections & University Archives, University of Oregon Libraries.

**Dissertations and Theses**
Dolch, Jessie. "Press Coverage and the Image of the Rajneeshees in Four Oregon Newspapers: August 1981 to August 1982." M. S. thesis, University of Oregon, 1985.

Latkin, Carl Asher. "Rajneeshpuram, Oregon—An Exploration of Gender and Work Roles, Self-Concept, and Psychological Well-Being in an Experimental Community." Ph.D. dissertation, University of Oregon, 1987.

Price, Mary Daly. "Rajneeshpuram and the American Utopian Tradition." M.A. thesis, University of California, Berkeley, 1984.

Puttick, Elizabeth. "Gender, Discipleship and Charismatic Authority in the Rajneesh Movement." Ph.D. dissertation, University of London, 1984.

Vanneman, Brian Robert. "Searching For Paradise in the Rain: Oregon's Communes and Intentional Communities of the 1960s and 1970s." (Honors thesis, University of Oregon, 1997): 25.

Welsh, Thomas Lawrence. "Dreams to Redeem: Utopian Ideals and Outcomes at Rajneeshpuram and Wildhorse Canyon." Honors thesis, University of Oregon, 2002.

Wilner, Joseph Bear. "All My Sisters and Brothers: Redefinitions of Family in Oregon Intentional Communities During the Late Twentieth Century." (M. A. thesis, University of Oregon, 2000): 106-25.

**Monographs**
Appleton, Sue. *Bhagwan Shree Rajneesh, The Most Dangerous Man Since Jesus Christ.* [Cologne, Germany]: Rebel Publishing House, 1987.

Appleton, Sue. *Was Bhagwan Shree Rajneesh Poisoned by Ronald Reagan's America?* Cologne, Germany: Rebel Publishing House, [1989].

Braun, Kirk. *Rajneeshpuram: The Unwelcome Society.* West Linn, OR: Scout Creek Press, 1984.

Carter, Lewis F. *Charisma and Control in Rajneeshpuram : The Role of Shared Values in the Creation of a Community.* Cambridge, UK: Cambridge University Press, 1990.

Floether, Eckart. *Bhagwan Shree Rajneesh and His New Religious Movement in America.* Downers Grove, IL: InterVarsity Press, 1983.

Forman, Juliet. *Bhagwan: Twelve Days That Shook The World.* Cologne, Germany: Rebel Publishing House [1989].

Franklin, Satya Bharti. *The Promise of Paradise: A Woman's Intimate Story of the Perils of Life with Rajneesh.* New York: Station Hill Press, 1992.

Goldman, Marion S. *Passionate Journeys: Why Successful Women Joined A Cult.* Ann Arbor: University of Michigan Press, 1999.

Gordon, James S. *The Golden Guru: The Strange Journey of the Bhagwan Shree Rajneesh.* Lexington, MA: S. Greene Press, 1987.

Gunther, Bernard. *Neo-Tantra: Bhagwan Shree Rajneesh on Sex, Love, Prayer, and Transcendence.* New York: Harper & Row, 1980.

Hamilton, Rosemary. *Hellbent for Enlightenment: Unmasking Sex, Power, and Death with a Notorious Master.* Ashland, OR: White Cloud Press, 1998.

Mann, W. E. *The Quest for Total Bliss: A Psycho-Sociological Perspective on the Rajneeshee Movement*. Toronto: Canadians' Scholars Press, 1991.

McCormack, Win, ed. *The Rajneesh Files, 1981-86*. Portland: New Oregon Publishers, 1985.

McCormack, Win, ed. *The Rajneesh Chronicles*. Portland: New Oregon Publishers, 1987.

Meredith, George. *Bhagwan: The Most Godless Yet the Most Godly Man*. Poona, India: Rebel Publishing House, 1988.

Milne, Hugh. *Bhagwan: The God That Failed*. New York: St. Martin's Press, 1986.

Mullan, Bob. *Life As Laughter: Following Bhagwan Shree Rajneesh*. London: Routledge & Kegan Paul, 1983.

Palmer, Susan J. *Moon Sisters, Krishna Mothers, Rajneesh Lovers: Women's Roles in New Religions*. Syracuse, NY: Syracuse University Press, 1993.

Palmer, Susan J., and Arvind Sharma, eds. *The Rajneesh Papers: Studies in a New Religious Movement*. Delhi, India: Motilal Banarsidass, 1993.

Price, Marie Daly. *Rajneeshpuram and the American Utopian Tradition*. Syracuse, NY: Dept. of Geography, Syracuse University, 1985.

Quick, Donna. *A Place Called Antelope: The Rajneesh Story*. Ryderwood, WA: August Press, 1995.

*Rajneeshpuram: A Blueprint for Man's Future*. Antelope, OR: Rajneesh Neo-Sannyas International Commune, 1982.

*Rajneeshpuram: An Oasis*. Antelope, OR: Rajneesh Neo-Sannyas International Commune, 1982.

Rajneeshpuram City Council. *City of Rajneeshpuram Comprehensive Plan*. [Rajneeshpuram, OR: Rajneeshpuram City Council, 1982].

Satya Bharti, Ma. *Death Comes Dancing: Celebrating Life with Bhagwan Shree Rajneesh*. London & Boston: Routledge & Kegan Paul, 1981.

Satya Vedant, Swami (Vasant Joshi). *The Awakened One: The Life and Work of Bhagwan Shree Rajneesh*. San Francisco: Harper & Row, 1982.

Shay, T. L. *Rajneeshpuram and the Abuse of Power*. West Linn, OR: Scout Creek Press, 1985.

Strelley, Kate, with Robert D. Dan Souci. *The Ultimate Game: The Rise and Fall of Bhagwan Shree Rajneesh*. San Francisco: Harper & Row, 1987.

Thompson, Judith and Paul Heelas. *The Way of the Heart: The Rajneesh Movement*. Wellinborough, Northamptonshire, UK: Aquarian Press, 1986.

Webber, Bert. *Rajneeshpuram: Who Were Its People?* [Medford, OR]: Webb Research Group, 1989.

Webber, Bert. *The Rajneesh and the U. S. Postal Service: Includes, From Wasteland to An Oasis, The Building and Operation of A City*. Medford, OR: Webb Research Group, 1988.

Wright, Charles. *Oranges & Lemmings: The Story Behind Bhagwan Shree Rajneesh*. Richmond, Victoria, Canada: Greenhouse Publications, 1985.

**Sections in Monographs**

Bird, Frederick, and Rooshikumar Pandya. "Therapeutic Aspects of New Religious Movements." In Susan J. Palmer and Arvind Sharma, eds. *The Rajneesh Papers: Studies in a New Religious Movement* (Delhi, India: Motilal Banarsidass, 1993): 57-83.

FitzGerald, Frances. "Rajneeshpuram" in *Cities on a Hill: A Journey Through Contemporary American Cultures* (New York: Simon and Schuster, 1986): 247-381.

Goldman, Marion S. "Avoiding Mass Violence at Rajneeshpuram." In James K. Wellman, Jr., ed. *Belief and Bloodshed: Religion and Violence Across Time and Tradition* (Lanham, MD: Rowman & Littlefield, 2007): 165-77.

Goldman, Marion S. "From Promiscuity to Celibacy: Women and Sexual Regulation at Rajneeshpuram." In Mary Jo Neitz and Marion S. Goldman, eds. *Sex, Lies, and Sanctity: Religion and Deviance in Contemporary North America. Volume 5: Religion and the Social Order* (Greenwich, CT: JAI Press, 1995): 203-19.

Goldman, Marion S. "When Leaders Dissolve: Considering Controversy and Stagnation in the Osho Rajneesh Movement." In James R. Lewis and Jesper Aagaard Petersen, eds. *Controversial New Religions* (New York: Oxford University Press, 2005): 119-37.

Gordon, James S. "A Letter from Poona, November 1989." In Susan J. Palmer and Arvind Sharma, eds. *The Rajneesh Papers: Studies in a New Religious Movement* (Delhi, India: Motilal Banarsidass, 1993): 138-54.

Gussner, Robert (Swami Anand Jina). "The Work of Osho Rajneesh: A Thematic Overview." In Susan J. Palmer and Arvind Sharma, eds. *The Rajneesh Papers: Studies in a New Religious Movement* (Delhi, India: Motilal Banarsidass, 1993): 47-55.

Mann, Ted. "The Crazies—Who Follows Rajneesh and Why." In Susan J. Palmer and Arvind Sharma, eds. *The Rajneesh Papers: Studies in a New Religious Movement* (Delhi, India: Motilal Banarsidass, 1993): 17-45.

"The Meaning of Discipleship: Interview with a Rajneesh Therapist, Swami Veet Atito (Dr. Jack Rains)—Interview Conducted by Susan J. Palmer." In Susan J. Palmer and Arvind Sharma, eds. *The Rajneesh Papers: Studies in a New Religious Movement* (Delhi, India: Motilal Banarsidass, 1993): 85-101.

Palmer, Susan J. "Rajneesh Women: Lovers and Leaders in a Utopian Commune." In Susan J. Palmer and Arvind Sharma, eds. *The Rajneesh Papers: Studies in a New Religious Movement* (Delhi, India: Motilal Banarsidass, 1993): 103-35.

"Rancho Rajneesh" in Robert P. Sutton, *Modern American Communes: A Dictionary* (Westport, CT, and London: Greenwood Press, 2005): 139-40.

Sharma, Arvind. "Rajneesh and the Guru Tradition in India." In Susan J. Palmer and Arvind Sharma, eds. *The Rajneesh Papers: Studies in a New Religious Movement* (Delhi, India: Motilal Banarsidass, 1993): 1-16.

Shay, Roshani, and Ted Shay. "Better Dead Than Red: Local Letters and the Rajneesh Movement." In Mary Jo Neitz and Marion S. Goldman, eds. *Sex, Lies, and Sanctity: Religion and Deviance in Contemporary North America. Volume 5: Religion and the Social Order* (Greenwich, CT: JAI Press, 1995): 131-51.

Sutton, Robert P. "Rancho Rajneesh" in *Modern American Communes: A Dictionary* (Westport, CT: Greenwood Press, 2005): 139-40.

Wallis, Roy. "Religion as Fun? The Rajneesh Movement" in Roy Wallis and Steve Bruce, *Sociological Theory, Religion and Collective Action* (Belfast, Northern Ireland: Queen's University Press, 1986): 191-224.

**Journal/Magazine Articles**

Abbott, Carl. "Utopia and Bureaucracy: The Fall of Rajneeshpuram, Oregon." *Pacific Historical Review* 59:1 (1990): 77-103.

Amitabh, S.P. "Shree Rajneesh Ashram: A Provocative Community." *Journal of Humanistic Psychology* 22:1 (Winter 1982): 19-42.

Androes, Louis C. "Cultures in Collision: The Rajneesh Search for Community." *Communities* 71/72 (Summer/Fall 1986): 49-54.

Androes, Louis C. "The Rajneesh Experience: A Report." *Communal Societies* 6 (1986): 101-17.

"As the Bhagwan Turns." *Newsweek* (October 14, 1985): 43.

"Betraying the Bhagwan." *Newsweek* (September 30, 1985): 35.

"The Bhagwan Bows Out." *The Christian Century* 102:38 (December 4, 1985): 1112-13.

"Bhagwan Shree Rajneesh: Worldly Guru in the Western Wild." *U. S. News & World Report* (October 14, 1985): 15.

"Bhagwan Woes." *The Christian Century* 102:30 (October 9, 1985): 889.

Bruning, Fred. "Holy Cities in the Oregon Hills." *Macleans* (January 14, 1985): 7.

Buckwalter, Doyle W., and J. Ivan Legler. "Antelope and Rajneeshpuram, Oregon—Cities in Turmoil: A Case Study." *Urbanism Past and Present* 8:2 (1983): 1-13.

Carter, Lewis F. "The New 'Renunciates' of the Bhagwan Shree Rajneesh: Observations and Identification of Problems of Interpreting New Religious Movements." *Journal for the Scientific Study of Religion* 26:2 (June 1987): 148-72.

Christensen, Mark. "Rancho Rajneesh." *Penthouse: The International Magazine for Men* 16 (July 1985): 40-44, 72-74, and 106.

Clarke, Ronald O. "The Teachings of Bhagwan Shree Rajneesh." *Sweet Reason: A Journal of Ideas, History, and Culture* 4 (1985): 27-44.

Clarke, Ronald O. "The Narcissistic Guru: A Profile of Bhagwan Shree Rajneesh." *Free Inquiry* 8 (1988): 33-45; 9: 41-48.

Cooper, Marc. "A Guru's Ghost Town." *Macleans* (October 20, 1986): t1.

"Cults: Rattlesnake-heaven." *The Economist* 323(7754) (April 11, 1992): 29.

Davisson, Sven. "The Rise & Fall of Rajneeshpuram." *Ashé: Journal of Experimental Spirituality* 2(1) (Spring Equinox 2003): 47-66.

Drennen, William T. "Rajneeshpuram: Hound Dogs with Scent." *Journal of Humanistic Psychology* 23:3 (Summer 1983): 28-100.

Duin, J. "The Guru Down the Road." *Christianity Today* 26 (April 23, 1982): 38-40.

Ebon, Martin. "The Decline and Fall of Rajneesh." *Fate* 39:3 (March 1986): 32-41.

FitzGerald, Frances. "Rajneeshpuram-I." *New Yorker* 62:31 (September 22, 1986): 46-60.

FitzGerald, Frances. "Rajneeshpuram-II." *New Yorker* 62:32 (September 29, 1986): 83-125.

Goldman, Marion S. "The Women of Rajneeshpuram." *CSWS Review* 2 (1988): 18-21.

Goldman, Marion S., and Lynne Isaacson. "Enduring Affiliation and Gender Doctrine for Shiloh Sisters and Rajneesh Sannyasins." *Journal for the Scientific Study of Religion* 38:3 (September 1999): 411-22.

"Goodbye, Guru." *Newsweek* (November 25, 1985): 50.

Gordon, James S. "The Cult Leader: How Absolute Power Corrupts [excerpt from *The Golden Guru*]." *Utne Reader* (March/April 1989): 136-37.

Grossman, Lawrence K. "The Story of a Truly Contaminated Election." *Columbia Journalism Review* 39:5 (January/February 2001): 65.

Guilliatt, Richard. "'It Was a Time of Madness'." *The Australian Magazine* (June 17, 2006): 22.

"Guru Arrested." *The Christian Century* 102:35 (November 13, 1985): 1025.

"Guru in Cowboy Country." *Asiaweek* 9(30) (July 29, 1983).

"Guru on the Range." *Newsweek* (March 22, 1982): 37.

Howard, Lucy. "C'mon Down." *Newsweek* (May 12, 1986): 5.

"Illegal City." *The Christian Century* 100:31 (October 26, 1983): 960.

"Indian Guru Rajneesh Ordered to Leave U.S." *Christianity Today* 27 (February 4, 1983): 47-48.

275

Ingle, S. "The Natives Are Restless." *Maclean's* 96 (September 26, 1983): 12-13.

Johnson, David. "Greener Grass: A Short History of Oregon's Utopia Tradition." *Oregon Heritage* 1 (Winter/Spring 1995): 17.

Karlen, Neal, with Mark Kirchmeier. "The Homeless and the Guru." *Newsweek* (September 24, 1984): 35.

Karlen, Neal, with Pamela Abramson. "Bhagwan's Realm." *Newsweek* (December 3, 1984): 34.

Karlen, Neal, with Pamela Abramson. "Rajneeshpuram: Final Days." *Newsweek* (December 9, 1985): 30.

Karlen, Neal, with Vern E. Smith, Debbie Seward, Suzie Boss, and Pamela Abramson. "Busting the Bhagwan." *Newsweek* (November 11, 1985): 26.

Keerdoja, Eileen, with Mark Kirchmeier. "The Guru Who Came to Stay in Oregon." *Newsweek* (April 11, 1983): 13.

Latkin, Carl A. "Coping After the Fall: The Mental Health of Former Members of the Rajneeshpuram Commune." *The International Journal for the Psychology of Religion* 3:2 (1993): 97-109.

Latkin, Carl A. "From Device to Vice: Social Control and Intergroup Conflict at Rajneeshpuram." *Sociological Analysis* 52:4 (Winter 1991): 363-78.

Latkin, Carl A. "Gender Roles in the Experimental Community: Rajneespuram." *Sex Roles* 21:9/10 (November 1989): 629-52.

Latkin, Carl Asher. "Seeing Red: A Social-Psychological Analysis of the Rajneeshpuram Conflict." *Sociological Analysis* 53:3 (Fall 1992): 257-71.

Latkin, Carl Asher. "The Self-Concept of Rajneeshpuram Commune Members. *Journal for the Scientific Study of Religion*." 29:1 (March 1990): 91-98.

Latkin, Carl A. "The Self-Consciousness in Members of a New Religious Movement: The Rajneeshees." *Journal of Social Psychology* 130:4 (August 1990): 557-58.

Latkin, Carl A., Richard A. Littman, Norman D. Sundberg, and Richard A. Hagan. "Pitfalls and Pratfalls in Research on an Experimental Community: Lessons in Integrating Theory and Practice from the Rajneeshpuram Research Project." *Journal of Community Psychology* 21:1 (January 1993): 35-48.

Latkin, Carl A., Norman D. Sundberg, Richard A. Littman, Melissa G. Katsiskis, and Richard A. Hagan. "Feelings After the Fall: Former Rajneeshpuram Commune Members' Perceptions of and Affiliation with the Rajneeshee Movement." *Sociology of Religion* 55:1 (Spring 1994): 65-73.

Latkin, Carl A., Richard A. Hagan, Richard A. Littman, and Norman D. Sundberg. "Who Lives in Utopia? A Brief Report on the Rajneeshpuram Research Project." *Sociological Analysis* 48:1 (1987): 73-81.

Magnuson, Ed. "Whose Home Is This?" *Time* (October 22, 1984): 42.

McCall, C. "To Keep a Cult From Taking Over, An Oregon Town Wants to Go Out of Business." *People Weekly* 17 (April 19, 1982): 123-24, 126.

Moore, Art. "From Cult Site to Teen Camp." *Christianity Today* 43:13 (November 15, 1999): 22-23.

O'Hara, Jane. "Trouble in the Blessed One's Paradise." *Maclean's* 98:46 (October 14, 1985): 74.

Pace, Enzo. "Conversion Time in Religious Movements: The Case of the Rajneeshes." *Religioni e Societa* 2:3 (January-June 1987): 96-114.

Palmer, Susan J. "Charisma and Abdication: A Study of Leadership of Bhagwan Shree Rajneesh." *Sociological Analysis* 49:2 (Summer 1988): 119-35.

Palmer, Susan J. "Purity and Danger in the Rajneesh Foundation." *Update* 10:3 (1986): 18-29.

Palmer, Susan J., and Frederick Bird. "Therapy, Charisma and Social Control in the Rajneesh Movement." *Sociological Analysis* 51 (1992 Supplement): S71-S85.

276

Plummer, W. "Rumors of Plots and Scandals Abound as the Bhagwan's Closest Aides Flee His Eden in Oregon." *People Weekly* 24 (October 7, 1985): 96-98, 100.

"Prison Sentences." *The Christian Century* 103:25 (August 27-September 3, 1986): 738.

Puttick, Elizabeth. "Sexuality, Gender and the Abuse of Power in the Master-Disciple Relationship: The Case of the Rajneesh Movement." *Journal of Contemporary Religion* 10(1) (1995): 29-40.

Raine, George. "A Disciple's Surprise Sentence." *Newsweek* (December 8, 1986): 14.

"Rajneeshpuram Ceases to Exist." *Newsweek* 106:24 (December 9, 1985): 30.

"Rajneeshpuram: To Be, Or Not To Be." *Christianity Today* 29:16 (November 8, 1985): 58.

"Rajneeshpuram: Trouble at t'commune." *The Economist* 297(7414) (October 5, 1985): 27.

"Rattlesnake-heaven." *The Economist* 323(7754) (April 11, 1992): 29.

Rein, Richard K. "The Daughter of Jonestown Victim Leo Ryan Argues That Her Guru's Sect Is Not A Cult." *People Weekly* (February 16, 1981): 36-38.

Rosen, Mark D. "The Outer Limits of Community Self-Governance in Residential Associations, Municipalities, and Indian Country: A Liberal Theory." *Virginia Law Review* 84:6 (September 1998): 1053-1144.

Sandhill, Laird. "Snapshop of a Moving Target: The Communities Movement." *Communities* 97 (Winter 1997): 5-7.

Sarasohn, David. "Sagebrush Gothic." *Oregon Magazine* (May 1982): 24-31, 65.

Seyl, Susan. "Images Through Time: The OHS Photographic Archives." *Oregon Historical Quarterly* 99:2 (1998): 164-88.

"Sheela Strikes Back." *Newsweek* (October 7, 1985): 35.

Sperow, Janice L. "Rajneeshpuram—Religion Incorporated." *Hastings Law Journal* 36:6 (July 1985): 917-68.

Sternberg, David E. "Church Control of a Municipality: Establishing a First Amendment Institutional Suit." *Stanford Law Review* 38:5 (May 1986): 1363-1409.

Sundberg, Norman D., Marion Goldman, Nathan Rotter, and Douglas Smythe. "Personality and Spirituality: Comparative TAT's of High Achieving Rajneeshees." *Journal of Personality Assessment* 59:3 (1992): 326-39.

Sundberg, Norman D., Carl Latkin, Richard Lattman, and Richard Hagan. "Personality in a Religious Commune: CPI's in Rajneeshpuram." *Journal of Personality Assessment* 55:7 (1990): 7-17.

Swaine, Lucas A. "How Ought Liberal Democracies to Treat Theocratic Communities?" *Ethics* 111:2 (January 2001): 302-43.

"This is the place." *The Economist* 292(7361) (September 29, 1984): 28.

Trippett, Frank. "Blown Bliss." *Time* (September 30, 1985): 32.

Urban, Hugh B. "The Cult of Ecstasy: Tantrism, the New Age, and the Spiritual Logic of Late Capitalism." *History of Religions* 39:3 (2000): 268-304.

Urban, Hugh B. "Zorba the Buddha; Capitalism, Charisma and the Cult of Bhagwan Shree Rajneesh." *Religion* 26 (1996): 161-82.

Van Driel, Barry, and Jacob Van Belzen. "The Downfall of Rajneeshpuram in the Print Media: A Cross-National Study." *Journal for the Scientific Study of Religion* 29:1 (March 1990): 76-90.

"Wanted: A Few More Rock Stars to Buy the Bhagwan's Rolls-Royces." *Business Week* (March 3, 1986): 40.

**Unpublished Works**

Clarke, Ronald O. "The Teachings of Bhagwan Shree Rajneesh; and Their Social, Ethical and Environmental Implications." Report to the Oregon Committee for the Humanities, 1983 Summer Research Project. [Corvallis]: Oregon State University, Department of Religious Studies, September 27, 1983.

Price, Mary Daly. "Rajneeshpuram and the American Utopian Tradition." Discussion Paper. Syracuse, NY: Department of Geography, Syracuse University, 1985.

Schafer, Walter E. "Utopia Gone Awry: Social Dynamics in the Demise of Rajneeshpuram." Discussion Paper Series. Chico: California State University, Chico, College of Behavioral and Social Sciences, 1987.

Walker, Lisa. "A Selected Bibliography of Sources on Communal Societies in Oregon and Washington Available at the Oregon Historical Society" (March 15, 1992): 22-25.

**Newspaper Articles**

Rajneeshpuram was included in newspaper reports throughout the world, from local newspapers in Oregon to international publications. An exhaustive compilation of these citations is beyond the scope of this directory but presented here are a portion of such reports. Some specific newspapers have been the source of study. See, for instance, Paul Ryan Myers, "A Study of Attitudes Toward the Rajneeshees Through Content Analysis of Newspapers" (Honors thesis, University of Oregon, 1986) and Barry Van Driel and Jacob Van Belzen. "The Downfall of Rajneeshpuram in the Print Media: A Cross-National Study." *Journal for the Scientific Study of Religion* 29:1 (March 1990): 76-90.

"Around the Nation; Commune's New Policy Stirs Fears in Oregon." *The New York Times* (September 29, 1984): 6.

"Around the Nation; Daughter of Rep. Ryan Married at Guru's Ranch." *The New York Times* (December 28, 1982): A14.

"Around the Nation; Oregon Commune Stops Recruiting the Homeless." *The New York Times* (October 19, 1984): A12.

"Around the Nation; 7,000 Followers of Guru Gather in Oregon Hills." *The New York Times* (July 6, 1982): A10.

"Bacteria Samples 'Identical' at Ranch, The Dalles." *The Oregonian* (March 28, 1986): C1.

Bennett, Will. "'Free Love' Guru Dies of Heart Attack, Aged 58." *The Independent* (London) (January 20, 1990).

"Bhagwan Followers on Conspiracy-To-Kill Counts." *Sunday Herald* (September 16, 1990).

"Bhagwan On His Way!" *Telegraph* (November 15, 1985).

"Bhagwan Shree Rahneesh, 58, Was Guru at Oregon Commune." *The Toronto Star* (January 20, 1990): A6.

"Bhagwhan's 'Secretary' in Court." *Sunday Mail* (QLD) (February 9, 1986).

"Blast Hurt 2 at Oregon Hotel; A Victim Is Arrested." *The New York Times* (July 30, 1983): 28.

Bone, James. "Free-love Guru Dies of Heart Failure in Poona; Bhagwan Sri Rajneesh." *The Times* (London) (January 20, 1990).

Boyd, G. "Bhagwan Quits the Guru Business." *Telegraph* (October 1, 1985).

Buckley, D. "Aussie Held in Sect Round-Up." *Telegraph* (October 30, 1985).

Bumiller, Elisabeth. "The Guru's Himalayan Repose; Bhagwan Rajneesh, Looking Back in Anger And Ahead to Life in the Indian Motherland." *The Washington Post* (December 17, 1985): B1.

278

Chandler, Russell. "Sect Recalled as 'Bad Dream': Bhagwan's Deserted Buildings in Oregon Sold to Another Church." *The Washingon Post* (June 27, 1987): D12.

"Church, State and the Bhagwan. Rajneeshpuram Is A Religious Group, Not A Real City, And Should Not Receive the Government Funds That Cities Get [Editorial]." *Willamette Week* (May 17, 1983): 3.

Cohen, Nick. "On A Hippy Mission to Murder?" *The Independent* (London) (December 20, 1992): 6.

Coster, P. "I Will Bring Turmoil, Guru Warns Australia." *Courier-Mail* (July 22, 1985).

Coster, P. "Orange People Face A Battle for Big Muddy." *Courier-Mail* (April 29, 1985).

Coster, P. "A Pistol-Packin' Sheela with a Tongue to Match." *Courier-Mail* (May 10, 1985).

Coster, P. "Sheela 'Turns Against' Guru." *Telegraph* (Queensland) (September 17, 1985).

Coster, P. "Trouble in Paradise." *Telegraph* (October 29, 1985).

Cramer, John. "Oregon Suffered Largest Bioterrorism Attach in U. S. History, 20 Years Ago." *The (Bend) Bulletin* (October 14, 2001).

"Cult Britons 'Knew of Murder Plot From Outset.'" *The Herald* (Glasgow) (July 8, 1995): 6.

"Cult Mayor Sickened US Town, Court Told." *The Herald* (Glasgow) (July 7, 1995): 8.

Cummings, Judith. "Guru of Big Oregon Commune Facing Deportation." *The New York Times* (March 18, 1983): A14.

Cummings, Judith. "Political Storm Swirls Around Newcomers to the Guru's Fold." *The New York Times* (November 3, 1984): 8.

Dammann, Peter. "All the News Rajneesh Sees Fit." *Willamette Week* (November 2, 1982): 7.

Dammann, Peter. "Bhagwan's Agents of Orange. Buying the Ranch That Became Rajneeshpuram." *Willamette Week* (December 8, 1981): 1.

Dammann, Peter. "Bhagwan's Rancho Deluxe: All's Quiet At Rajneeshpuram, But Stories Continue to Circulate About Bhagwan's Indian Days." *Willamette Week* (January 19, 1982): 1.

Dammann, Peter. "LA Reporter's Story on Rajneeshpuram and Oregon Takes A Hatchet to Everyone Involved." *Willamette Week* (October 18, 1983): 3.

Dammann, Peter and Carlton Smith. "Ranch of the Rising Sun: Two Reporters Visit Rajneeshpuram, Opiate of the Elite." *Willamette Week* (July 13, 1982): 1.

"Disciples Try to Build New Image for Commune." *The Oregonian* (September 24, 1985): A1.

Driver, Bill. "Bhagwan and the Bombs: In the Wake of the Hotel Rajneesh Bombings, Many Are [Looking At] Explosions Which Rocked the Bhagwan's Ashram in India." *Willamette Week* (August 30, 1983): 1.

Dunn, Katherine. "Bhagwan Babe: Not Necessarily the Last Words from Ma Anand Sheela." *Willamette Week* (November 29, 1988): 4.

Egan, Timothy. "Antelope Journal: Oregon Ranch With a Troubled Past Faces a Dubious Future." *The New York Times* (October 20, 1995): A14.

"84 Rolls-Royces Bought As Liquidation of Guru's Oregon Commune Continues." *Christian Science Monitor* (December 2, 1985): 12.

"The End of a Guru's Paradise." *Courier-Mail* (October 30, 1985).

"Evangelists Try to Bring Christian Message to Rajneeshpuram." *The Oregonian* (October 7, 1985): B1.

Falk, Susan Hauser. "A Red Renaissance." *Wall Street Journal* (October 28, 1986): 32.

"Few Followers of Guru Vote." *The New York Times* (November 9, 1984): A29.

Fishlock, Trevor. "Bermuda-bound Guru Held; Bhagwan Shree Rajneesh Charged With Violating US Immigration Laws." *The Times* (London) (October 29, 1985).

Fishlock, Trevor. "The Magic Kingdom Which Became a Paradise Lost; Bhagwan Shree Rajneesh's Rajneeshpuram Community in Oregon Begins to Close." *The Times* (London) (December 2, 1985).

Fitzherbert, V. "Devoted Still in Rajneesh Fight." *Sunday Herald Sun* (April 18, 1993).

"5 Rajneeshees Plead Guilty to Immigration Fraud." *The Oregonian* (December 14, 1985): F6.

"505 File Claims in Rajneeshees Poisoning Scheme." *The Oregonian* (December 2, 1986): B2.

Fleming, Richard. "Paradise Now: What Life Is Really Like at Rancho Rajneesh. (Part 1 of a Two-Part Story)." *Willamette Week* (November 19, 1984): 1.

Fleming, Richard. "Paradise Now II: The Conclusion of Our Look at Life at Rancho Rajneesh." *Willamette Week* (November 26, 1984): 1.

"Follow-up on the News; Rajneesh haven: A Legacy of Debts." *The New York Times* (April 24, 1988): 41.

"Former Aids to Guru in Oregon Plead Guilty to Numerous Crimes." *The New York Times* (July 23, 1986): B9.

"Former Wasco County Judge Defends 1981 Sale of Cattle to Rajneeshees." *The Oregonian* (December 19, 1985): C3.

"Forum Focuses on Rajneeshees." *La Grande Observer* (April 8, 2002): 1a.

"'Germ War' Inquiry." *Courier-Mail* (September 30, 1985).

Gilliam, Dorothy. "Suspicions." *The Washington Post* (October 4, 1984): C1.

"Golden Guru: Obituary of Bhagwan Shree Rajneesh." *The Guardian* (London) (January 20, 1990).

Gross, Jane. "Seattle Journal; With Guru Deported, Disciples Struggle On." *The New York Times* (January 25, 1989): A12.

"Guru Accuses Disciples of Bugging." *The Globe and Mail* (Canada) (September 18, 1985).

"Guru Returning to Face Charges." *The New York Times* (November 5, 1985): A12.

"Guru's Aides Quit Commune." *The New York Times* (September 17, 1985): A15.

"Guru's Book Is Burned at Oregon Commune." *The New York Times* (October 1, 1985): A15.

"Guru's City Found Unconstitutional." *The New York Times* (October 7, 1983): A28.

"Guru's City in Desert Sits Nearly Empty." *The New York Times* (August 9, 1987): 18.

"Guru's Commune-City Held Unconstitutional." *The New York Times* (December 12, 1985): A23.

"Guru's Commune in Oregon Votes to Restore Town Name." *The New York Times* (November 7, 1985): A32.

"Guru's Departure Forcing Commune to Disband, Mayor Says." *The New York Times* (November 24, 1985): 27.

"Guru's Disciples Taking Over in Oregon Town." *The New York Times* (December 19, 1982): 32.

"Guru Followers Go Home." *The Washington Post* (October 14, 1984): A6.

"Guru's Followers in Oregon Vote on Restoring Old Name to Town." *The New York Times* (November 6, 1985): A19.

"Guru's Former Aide Denies She Tried to Kill Him." *The New York Times* (September 29, 1985): 39.

Hale, Sally Carpenter. "Guru's Spirit Still Haunts Oregon Hills." *Chicago Tribune* (December 18, 1995): 8:1.

Horst, Shannon. "Chronicle of Guru's Trouble and Flight." *Christian Science Monitor* (November 1, 1985): 4.

Hyer, Marjorie. "Bomb Plot Is Alleged." *The Washington Post* (February 27, 1988): D14.

"I'm Just Ordinary, Says Bhagwan." *Courier-Mail* (October 3, 1985).

"Japanese Rajneeshee Drowns in Commune Lake." *The Oregonian* (July 4, 1985): B5.

Katz, Ian. "The Mystic and the Mayhem." *The Guardian* (London) (August 1, 1994): T2.

Katz, Ian. "Oregon Shows No Sympathy For Britons in Death Plot." *The Guardian* (London) (July 29, 1995): 8.

King, Wayne. "Red-Clad Disciples of an Indian Guru Build a Farm Community in Oregon." *The New York Times* (September 26, 1981): 6.

[Kirchmeier, Mark]. "Frohnmayer Pulls Strings: Lawrence Tribe Joins Forces. Renowned Constitutional Scholar Aids Oregon in Legal Fight Against Rajneeshpuram." *Willamette Week* (March 26, 1984): 4.

Klages, P. "In Rajneespuram, Followers Chant for Bhagwan's Return." *Courier-Mail* (October 31, 1985).

"Lab Reputedly Used in Germ Experiments." *The Oregonian* (September 28, 1985): A1.

LaFollette, Cameron. "Bhagwan's Rural City Raise Some Questions. LCDC and 1000 Friends of Oregon Are Watching." *Willamette Week* (December 15, 1981): 7.

"Lawsuits Filed in Oregon Ask for Share of Commune's Assets." *The New York Times* (December 6, 1985): B10.

Levine, Richard. "Ideas & Trends; Ballot Battle in Wasco County." *The New York Times* (October 28, 1984): 4:7.

"Limit on Voters By Oregon County Is Upheld." *The New York Times* (October 23, 1984): A14.

Marriott, Michel. "D.C.'s Homeless Line Up for Oregon Commune Bus." *The Washington Post* (September 21, 1984): B1.

Marriott, Michel. "Homeless Taken to Commune of Indian Mystic." *The Washington Post* (September 15, 1984): A1.

Martin, Douglas. "Guru's Commune Roiled as Key Leader Departs." *The New York Times* (September 22, 1985): 26.

Mathews, Jay. "Rajneeshees' Prospects Are Cloudy; Guru Gone, Commune Seeks New Sustenance." *The Washington Post* (November 22, 1985): A3.

Mead, James S. "Other Voices: A Little Bigotry in Our Righteousness. Oregonians Are Not Blameless in Rajneeshpuram Debacle." *Willamette Week* (November 28, 1985): 4.

"Meanwhile, Back at the Rancho Rajneesh . . . ." *Sydney Morning Herald* (August 11, 1987): 9.

Molle, Chris and Peter Popham. "What A Long, Strange Trip It's Been." *The Independent* (London) (May 10, 1998): 6-7.

Mulgrew, Ian. "There's Trouble in Guru Country." *The Globe and Mail* (Canada) (May 11, 1982).

"Mum, Me and A Childhood with the Bhagwan." *Canberra Times* (Australia) (April 17, 2004): 12.

"Murder Manuals in Rajneesh Home." *Courier-Mail* (September 19, 1985).

281

Neustatter, Angela. "For the Love of a Strange God." *The Guardian* (London) (March 10, 1993): 9.

"Orange People Face a Battle for Big Muddy." *Courier-Mail* (April 29, 1985).

"Oregon Bill Would Halt Aid to Rajneesh School." *The Washington Post* (March 23, 1985): C6.

"Oregon Guru Burns Work of Cult Rival." *The Globe and Mail* (Canada) (October 2, 1985).

"Oregon Guru Rebuffed in Bid on Permanent U.S. Residency." *The New York Times* (December 24, 1982): B4.

Pace, Eric. "Bhagwan Shree Rajneesh, Indian Guru, Dies at 58." *The New York Times* (January 20, 1990): A30.

Pederson, Mary Catherine, and Rick Rubin. "Ma Mary's Song: A Former Portland Activist Tells of Her Conversion to the Ways of Rajneeshpuram." *Willamette Week* (December 28, 1982): 1, 9, 21, 24.

Puttick, Elizabeth. "First-Hand: People Didn't Just Come Looking for Orgies." *The Independent* (London) (July 31, 1994): 21.

"Rajneesh Group Is Absolved of Election Charge." *The Washington Post* (August 2, 1985): A10.

"Rajneeshee Editor Recalls Difficult Times." *The Oregonian* (December 1, 1985): E3.

"Rajneeshee Real Estate Goes on Sale." *The Oregonian* (October 16, 1985): B2.

"Rajneeshees Converging for Festival." *The Oregonian* (June 20, 1985): B6.

"Rajneeshs' Impact on Oregon Begins to Fade." *The Oregonian* (November 17, 1986): B1.

"Rajneeshees Isolate Two in AIDS Test." *The Oregonian* (September 4, 1985): B2.

"Rajneeshees To Close Ranch." *The Oregonian* (November 23, 1985): 1.

"Rajneeshees To Pay Millions for Poisonings." *The Oregonian* (August 16, 1986): A1.

"Rajneeshism Renounced by Rajneesh!" *Sunday Mail* (QLD) (September 29, 1985).

"Rajneeshpuram Dispute to Go Before State Land Use Board." *The Oregonian* (October 26, 1985): D7.

Raspberry, William. "Bus to Rajneeshpuram." *The Washington Post* (September 24, 1984): A19.

Reed, Christopher. "The Guru, The Girls and Me." *The Guardian* (London) (August 1, 1994): T3.

Reed, Christopher. "Oregon's Rolls-Royce Guru Devotees Provide Spiritual Leader with the Trappings of the Good Life." *The Globe and Mail* (Canada) (August 10, 1985).

Rucci, Michelangelo. "Bizarre Episode in Religious Fervor." *The Advertiser* (January 23, 1990).

"Sale: Steal This Ranch for $28 Million." *The Oregonian* (July 24, 1986): D3.

Schmidt, William H. "U.S. Indicts Oregon Guru and Says He Tried to Flee Country." *The New York Times* (October 29, 1985): A16.

Schwarz, Walter. "Face to Faith: Rolling in the New Religion." *The Guardian* (London) (January 22, 1990).

"Sect Recruits Street People." *The Washington Post* (September 6, 1984): A13.

Senior, Jeanie. "Guru's Commune Faces Hostile Community, Internal Problems." *Christian Science Monitor* (November 1, 1985): 3.

Senior, Jeanie. "Rajneeshees Plan Reunion at Central Oregon Ranch." *The Oregonian* (September 9, 1988): 3C.

"Sheela Caused Anguish, Foreman's Wife Testifies." *The Oregonian* (November 27, 1985): B8.

"Sheela, Others Quit Commune." *The Oregonian* (September 17, 1985): A1.

"6 Agencies to Probe Guru Claims." *The Oregonian* (September 19, 1985): A1.

"Street People Deny Political Role." *The Washington Post* (September 19, 1984): A28.

"Swami Back at Commune." *The Washington Post* (October 6, 1985): A16.

"Tension Building Over Oregon Sect." *The New York Times* (September 16, 1984): 38.

"Therapy, Sex and a 64,000-Acre Ranch." *The Independent* (London) (August 28, 1993): 27.

Thornton, Mary. "Guru's Followers Keep the Faith; Rajneesh Commune in Oregon Transcending Local Opposition." *The Washington Post* (April 28, 1985): A4.

Thornton, Mary. "Oregon Guru Disavows Rajneeshism, Vows to Survive Investigations." *The Washington Post* (October 20, 1985): A7.

Thornton, Mary. "Rajneesh Arrest in N. Carolina; Guru, 7 Other Face Immigration Charges." *The Washington Post* (October 29, 1985): A3.

"Time Finally Runs Out for Rolex-Laden Guru." *Sydney Morning Herald* (January 22, 1990): 11.

"Town May Abolish Itself to Bar Sect's Takeover." *The New York Times* (March 12, 1982): B8.

Turner, G. "Bhagwan Hits Out As Commune Chiefs Flee." *Courier-Mail* (September 18, 1985).

Turner, Wallace. "Oregonians See Vindication in Troubles of Guru." *The New York Times* (November 3, 1985): 34.

Turner, Wallace. "Shock Sets in As Guru's Followers in Oregon Leave to Face Outside World." *The New York Times* (November 27, 1985): A18.

Usborne, David. "Strange Days When the Guru Came to Town." *The Independent* (London) (July 27, 1995): 2.

"Use of Electronic 'Bugs' Traced at Rancho Rajneesh." *The Oregonian* (September 23, 1985): B2.

"Voter Registration Halted As Guru Is Picketed." *The New York Times* (October 11, 1984): A25.

Whittell, Giles. "British Cult Pair Plotted Murder to Save Commune." *The Times* (July 29, 1995).

Whittell, Giles. "Oregon Cult Leader 'Tried to Hire Killer Gunmen'." *The Times* (July 7, 1995).

"Why Didn't I Understand What Was Happening? [Editorial]." *The Oregonian* (September 22, 1985): B1.

Wilson, George. "Sue's Love Among the Orange People." *The Sun Herald* (Sydney) (January 22, 1989): 15.

"Witness Puts Rajneeshpuram Mayor At Salad Bar." *The Oregonian* (December 7, 1985): C1.

Yates, Skye. "Charming money-Bhag." *The Daily Telegraph* (Sydney, Australia) (May 25, 2000): 53.

Zusman, Mark L. "Bhagwan's 'Homeless' Program: Rajneeshee Rules and Regulations. Not All Homeless Who Visit the Commune Are Grateful." *Willamette Week* (September 17, 1984): 5.

283

### Sound Recordings

Goldman, Marion S. *The Women of Rajneeshpuram: Achievement, Ambivalence and Religious Seeking.* Eugene, OR: University of Oregon Center for the Study of Women in Society, 1988.

*Rajneeshpuram, What Price Paradise?* [Eugene, OR]: D. Roberts, 1986.

## Rat Creek

Place:          Cottage Grove
Formed:       1970 or 1971
Directories:  Miller, *The 60s Communes*: 272.

## Repose

Formed:       Ca. early 1970s
Directories:  Miller, *The 60s Communes*: 272.

## RFD Collective

Place:          Wolf Creek, 4525 Lower Wolf Creek Rd.
Formed:       1976
Directories:  "Directory of Intentional Communities 1978" (*Communities* 30): 43.
                   Mercer, *Communes: A Social History and Guide*: 141.
Publications: *RFD Quarterly*

[Advertisement – RFD, a magazine for country faggots]. *Communities* 22 (September/October [1976]): 50.

Hale-Wehmann, Kenneth. "RFD: A Look at the Turbulent Life of 'A Country Journal for Gay Men Everywhere'." *Gay Community News* 10:33 (March 12, 1983): 8-9.

[Resources – Men – R.F.D., Wolf Creek] in *A Guide to Cooperative Alternatives* (New Haven, CT, and Louisa, VA: Community Publications Cooperative, 1979): 147.

## Rivendell (Rivendale)

Place:          Eugene
Formed:       1968
Formerly:     Yellow Submarine

Bates, Doug. "Lane County's Rural Areas Nurture Communal Lifestyle." *Eugene Register-Guard* (August 29, 1971): B1.

Johnson, Dave, and Aragorn. "Rivendale: A Communal Experience." *The Augur* 1:1 (October 14, 1969): 6-7.

Johnson, Dale, and Aragorn. "Rivendale." *Mother Earth News* 4 (July/August 1970).

Teeters, Kay. "Communal Utopias of the Pacific Northwest." (Honors thesis, University of Oregon, 1970): 52-54.

Wilner, Joseph Bear. "All My Sisters and Brothers: Redefinitions of Family in Oregon Intentional Communities During the Late Twentieth Century." M. A. thesis, University of Oregon, 2000.

## Riverland

Place:          Near Portland

Sandia Bear, "Wimmin's Land." In Lynn Witt, Sherry Thomas, and Eric Marcus, eds. *Out in All Directions: The Almanac of Gay and Lesbian America* (New York: Warner Books, 1995): 327.

## Rock Creek

Place:          Deadwood
Formed:       Early 1970s
Directories:  Miller, *The 60s Communes*: 278.

## Rootworks

Place: Sunny Valley, 2000 King Mountain Trail
Formed: 1970s
Directories: Miller, *The 60s Communes*: 278.
Directory of Intentional Communities, 1990: 213.
Association of Lesbian Intentional Communities online
*Shewolf's Directory of Wimmin's Land*. Fifth Edition
Manuscripts: Ruth Mountaingrove Papers. Special Collections & University
Archives, University of Oregon Libraries.
Ruth Mountaingrove Videotape Autobiography Collection, 1988-
1997. Special Collections & University Archives, University of
Oregon Libraries.

Association of Lesbian Intentional Communities. "Come to Oregon Women's
Lands." http://alicinfo.com/pages/oregon.htm
Johnson, David. "Greener Grass: A Short History of Oregon's Utopia Tradition."
*Oregon Heritage* 1 (Winter/Spring 1995): 17.
Kleiner, Catherine B. "Doin' It For Themselves: Lesbian Land Communities in
Southern Oregon, 1970-1995." (Ph.D. dissertation, University of New Mexico,
2003): 111-14.
Miller, Timothy. *The 60s Communes: Hippies and Beyond* (Syracuse, NY: Syracuse
University Press, 1999): 139.
Mountaingrove, Jean. "A Dream for Rootworks." *WomanSpirit* vol. 5, no. 21 (Fall
1979): 35.
Mountaingrove, Jean. "'Women in Community' include Lesbian Communities"
[letter]. *Communities* 83 (Summer 1994): 6.
Mountaingrove, Ruth, and Jean Mountaingrove. "Rootworks" in Joyce Cheney,
ed., *Lesbian Land* (Minneapolis, MN: Word Weavers, 1985): 125-28.
Roskind, Robert. *Memoirs of an Ex-Hippie: Seven Years in the Counterculture*
(Blowing Rock, NC: One Love Press, 2001): 120.
Sandilands, Catriona. "Lesbian Separatist Communities and the Experience of
Nature: A Queer Ecology." *Organization & Environment* 15 (June 2002): 131-
63.
Sandilands, Catriona. "Rainbow's End? Lesbian Separatism and the Ongoing
Politics of Ecotopia." In Margrit Eichler, June Larkin, and Sheila Neysmith,
eds. *Feminist Utopias: Re-Visioning Our Future* (Toronto, Canada: Inanna
Publications and Education, 2002): 37-50.
Sprecher, Katharine Matthaei. "Lesbian Intentional Communities in Rural
Southwestern Oregon: Discussions on Separatism, Environmentalism, and
Community Conflict." (M. A. thesis, California Institute of Integral Studies,
1997): 57-63.
Summerhawk, Barbara, and La Verne Gagehabib. *Circles of Power: Shifting
Dynamics in a Lesbian-Centered Community* (Norwich, VT: New Victoria
Publishers, 2000): 60-62, 127-29.
Vanneman, Brian Robert. "Searching For Paradise in the Rain: Oregon's
Communes and Intentional Communities of the 1960s and 1970s." (Honors
thesis, University of Oregon, 1997): 18.
"We Experience – Our Intuition." *WomanSpirit* vol. 8, no. 31 (Spring 1982): 20-
26.
Wilner, Joseph Bear. "All My Sisters and Brothers: Redefinitions of Family in
Oregon Intentional Communities During the Late Twentieth Century." (M. A.
thesis, University of Oregon, 2000): 68-69.

285

## Sabin Green

Place:    Portland

Lakeman, Mark. "Urban Ecovillages: Micro-Infill Cohousing Without Cars." *Communities* 139 (Summer 2008): 41-44.

## Sacred Oak Community

Place:    Selma, 129 Warren Rd
Formed:    1999
Directories:    *Communities Directory*, 2000: 324.
    [Community Updates – Lost/Disbanded] (*Communities* 120): 29.

## Saddle Ridge Farm – See High Ridge Farm

## Second Growth

Place:    Eugene
Formed:    1980s?
Directories:    *Directory of Collectives*, 1985: 72.

## Seed Company

Place:    Takilma
Formed:    1970s

Plagge, Dick. "Takilma – Communal Valley." *Willamette Week* 4:12 (Jan. 24, 1978): 5, 7.
Wilner, Joseph Bear. "All My Sisters and Brothers: Redefinitions of Family in Oregon Intentional Communities During the Late Twentieth Century." (M. A. thesis, University of Oregon, 2000): 30.

## Seven C's

Place:    Medford/Central Point
Formed:    1989
Directories:    *Directory of Intentional Communities*, 1990: 216.
    [Communities Directory: Updates & Additions to the Third Printing] (*Communities* 79): 32.
Note:    CrippleCreekCrossCircleCedarCityCo-Camp

## Seven Springs Community

Place:    Dillard
Formed:    Ca. 1971
Directories:    Miller, *The 60s Communes*: 279.
    "1981 Directory of Intentional Communities and Resources" (*Communities* 46): 37.
    "1983 Directory" (*Communities* 56): 74.
    Mercer, *Communes: A Social History and Guide*: 141.

## Seven Waves

Place:    Central Point
Formed:    1990s
Directories:    *Communities Directory*, 1996: 296.
    [Communities Directory Summer '96 Update – North American Updates] (*Communities* 91): 68.

**Formerly:**     Seven C's InterNetworking Cohousing Estate

## Shekinah

**Place:**       Logsden
**Formed:**      1970s
**Directories:** Jackson, Dave. *Coming Together*: 186.
                 Mercer, *Communes: A Social History and Guide*: 142.
                 Miller, *The 60s Communes*: 272.

## Shiloh Youth Revival Centers

**Place:**       Eugene (and others)
**Formed:**      1969
**Directories:** Miller, *The 60s Communes*: 280.

Bodenhausen, Nancy. "The Shiloh Experience." *Willamette Valley Observer* 4:5 (February 3, 1978): 10-11.

Bolt, Greg. "Shiloh Won't Fight $1.7 Million Tax Lien." *The Springfield News* (February 6, 1988).

Di Sabatino, David. *The Jesus People Movement: An Annotated Bibliography and General Resource*. Westport, CT: Greenwood Press, 1999.

Duin, Julia. "Authority & Submission in Christian Community." *Communities* 92 (Fall 1996): 52.

Esteve, Harry. "County Recalls Offer to Obtain Shiloh Retreat."*Eugene Register-Guard* (July 2, 1987): 1A, 4A.

Esteve, Harry. "Shiloh Work Camp Proposal Booed."*Eugene Register-Guard* (July 1, 1987): 1A, 4A.

Goldman, Marion S. "Continuity in Collapse: Departures from Shiloh." *Journal for the Scientific Study of Religion* 34 (1995): 342-53.

Goldman, Marion S., and Lynne Isaacson. "Enduring Affiliation and Gender Doctrine for Shiloh Sisters and Rajneesh Sannyasins." *Journal for the Scientific Study of Religion* 38:3 (September 1999): 411-22.

Isaacson, Lynne M. "Delicate Balance: Rearticulating Gender Ideology and Rules for Sexuality in a Jesus People Communal Movement." Ph.D. dissertation, University of Oregon, 1996.

Isaacson, Lynne. "Marriage, Ideology, and Gender in a Jesus People Communal Movement." In Joanne M. Greer and David O. Moberg, eds., *Research in the Social Scientific Study of Religion*, Vol. 8. (Greenwich, CT: JAI Press, 1997): 141-62.

Isaacson, Lynne. "Rule Making and Rule Breaking in a Jesus Community." In Mary Jo Neitz and Marion S. Goldman, eds. *Sex, Lies, and Sanctity: Religion and Deviance in Contemporary North America. Volume 5: Religion and the Social Order* (Greenwich, CT: JAI Press, 1995): 181-201.

Jackson, Dave, and Neta Jackson. *Living Together in a World Falling Apart: A Handbook on Christian Community*. Carol Stream, IL: Creation House, 1974.

Kaplowitz, Larry. "Lost Valley: Building Design That Fosters Community." *Communities* 99 (Summer 1998): 28.

McChesney, Jim. "Shiloh: The Coup, the IRS Battle, and the Future." *The Springfield News* (January 15, 1983): 5A.

McChesney, Jim. "Shiloh: The Road from Idealism to Organization." *The Springfield News* (January 8, 1983): 5A.

Miller, Timothy. *The 60s Communes: Hippies and Beyond* (Syracuse, NY: Syracuse University Press, 1999): 95-96.

287

Miller, Timothy. "The Sixties-Era Communes" in Peter Braunstein and Michael William Doyle, eds. *Imagine Nation: The American Counterculture of the 1960s and '70s* (New York & London: Routledge, 2002): 338.

Murphy, Jeanie. "A Shiloh's Sister Story." *Communities* 92 (Fall 1996): 29-32.

Peterson, Joe V. "Jesus People: Christ, Communes, and the Counterculture of the Late Twentieth Century in the Pacific Northwest and a Brief Review of the Shiloh Youth Revival Centers, Inc., The Highway Missionary Society/Servant Community, and the House of Elijah." M.A. thesis, Northwest Christian College, 1990.

Peterson Joe V. "The Rise and Fall of Shiloh." *Communities* 92 (Fall 1996): 60-65.

Peterson, Joe. "'You've Gotta Be a Baby'—The Power of Spirit" [interview]. *Communities* 84 (Fall 1994): 44-48.

Richardson, James T., Mary White Stewart, and Robert B. Simmonds. *Organized Miracles: A Study of a Contemporary Youth, Communal, Fundamentalist Organization.* New Brunswick, NJ: Transaction, 1979.

"Shiloh Youth Revival Centers" in Robert P. Sutton, *Modern American Communes: A Dictionary* (Westport, CT, and London: Greenwood Press, 2005): 153-54.

Stewart, David T. "A Survey of Shiloh Arts." *Communal Societies* 12 (1992): 40-67.

Sutton, Robert P. "Shiloh Youth Revival Centers" in *Modern American Communes: A Dictionary* (Westport, CT: Greenwood Press, 2005): 153-54.

Taslimi, Cheryl. "A Follow-up Study of Former Shiloh Commune Members: The Adjective Check List Seventeen Years Later." M. S. thesis, University of Tennessee at Chattanooga, 1989.

Taslimi, Cheryl, Ralph Hood, and P. J. Watson. "Assessment of Former Members of Shiloh." *Journal of the Scientific Study of Religion* 30:3 (September 1991): 308-11.

Vanneman, Brian Robert. "Searching For Paradise in the Rain: Oregon's Communes and Intentional Communities of the 1960s and 1970s." (Honors thesis, University of Oregon, 1997): 21.

Ward, Hiley H. *The Far-Out Saints of the Jesus Community: A Firsthand Report and Interpretation of the Jesus People Movement* (New York: Association Press, 1972): 37, 152.

Wilner, Joseph Bear. "All My Sisters and Brothers: Redefinitions of Family in Oregon Intentional Communities During the Late Twentieth Century." (M. A. thesis, University of Oregon, 2000): 91-93, 99-101.

## Southern Oregon Women's Network

Place:         Sunny Valley, 2000 King Mountain Trail
Formed:        1972
Directories:   *Communities Directory*, 1996: 401.
               *Communities Directory*, 2000: 335.
               *Communities Directory*, 2005: 284.
               Communities Directory (online)

*I Know You Know.* Indianapolis, IN: Gernan, Ltd., March 1985.

Madrone, Hawk. *Weeding at Dawn: A Lesbian Country Life.* New York: Harrington Park Press, 2000.

Madrone, Hawk. "The Canyon." *WomanSpirit* Vol. 3, No. 11 (1977).

Summerhawk, Barbara, and La Verne Gagehabib. *Circles of Power: Shifting Dynamics in a Lesbian-Centered Community.* Norwich, VT: New Victoria Publishers, 2000.

## Spirit Journey

Place: Ashland
Formed: 1999
Directories: *Communities Directory*, 2000: 337.

## Steppingwoods

Place: Roseburg, 6012 Coos Bay Wagon Road
Formed: 1992
Directories: [Communities Directory: Updates & Additions to the Third
 Printing] (*Communities* 79): 34.
 [Directory Update Spring/Summer '93 Update – New Listings, North
 America] (*Communities* 80/81): 88.
 *Communities Directory*, 1996: 307.
 Association of Lesbian Intentional Communities online
 *Shewolf's Directory of Wimmin's Land*. Fifth Edition

Association of Lesbian Intentional Communities. "Come to Oregon Women's
 Lands." http://alicinfo.com/pages/oregon.htm
Sandilands, Catriona. "Lesbian Separatist Communities and the Experience of
 Nature: A Queer Ecology." *Organization & Environment* 15 (June 2002): 131-
 63.
Sandilands, Catriona. "Rainbow's End? Lesbian Separatism and the Ongoing
 Politics of Ecotopia." In Margrit Eichler, June Larkin, and Sheila Neysmith,
 eds. *Feminist Utopias: Re-Visioning Our Future* (Toronto, Canada: Inanna
 Publications and Education, 2002): 37-50.
Summerhawk, Barbara and La Verne Gagehabib. *Circles of Power: Shifting
 Dynamics in a Lesbian-Centered Community* (Norwich, VT: New Victoria
 Publishers, 2000): 59-60.
Wilner, Joseph Bear. "All My Sisters and Brothers: Redefinitions of Family in
 Oregon Intentional Communities During the Late Twentieth Century." (M. A.
 thesis, University of Oregon, 2000): 70.

## Stillmeadow Farm

Place: Clackamas County, 16561 SE Marna Road
Formed: 1976
Directories: "1983 Directory" (*Communities* 56): 76.
 *Directory of Intentional Communities*, 1990: 221.
Web: stillmeadowcommunity.com

Sandhill, Laird. "Snapshop of a Moving Target: The Communities Movement."
 *Communities* 97 (Winter 1997): 5-7.

## Stillstone

Place: Eugene
Formed: 1975
Directories: Miller, *The 60s Communes*: 281.

289

## Students' Cooperative Association

Place: Eugene
Formed: 1935
Directories: *Communities Directory*, 2000: 342.
 *Communities Directory*, 2005: 234.
 *Communities Directory*, 2007: 253

Communities Directory (online)
Web:          www.uoregon.edu/~asuosch/

## SunnyRidge

Place:        Cave Junction
Formed:       1970s
Directories:  Miller, *The 60s Communes*: 281.
Web:          http://www.sunnyridge.net/

Kahn, Stan. Email to Jim Kopp, August 16, 2008
Miller, Timothy. *The 60s Communes: Hippies and Beyond* (Syracuse, NY: Syracuse University Press, 1999): 234 [Shannon Perry interview].

## Sunny Valley

Place:        Grants Pass/Medford
Formed:       1968
Directories:  Miller, *The 60s Communes*: 281.

*Year of the Communes* [videorecording]. Narrated by Rod Steiger. Rawlings-Chickering Productions. Released by McGraw-Hill, 1971.
"*Year of the Communes* [review]." *American Anthropologist* 76 (September 1974): 724-25.

## Sunrise Cohousing (see Daybreak Cohousing)

## Sunstar

Place:        Cave Junction
Formed:       Ca. 1971
Directories:  Miller, *The 60s Communes*: 282.

## Takilma

Place:        Southern Oregon
Formed:       Early 1970s
Directories:  Mercer, *Communes: A Social History and Guide*: 143.
              Miller, *The 60s Communes*: 282.

Plagge, Dick. "Takilma – Communal Valley." *Willamette Week* 4:12 (Jan. 24, 1978): 5, 7.

## Talsalsan Farm

Place:        Takilma
Formed:       1968
Directories:  Miller, *The 60s Communes*: 282.
              "Commune Directory," (*Communities* 1): 36.

290

Fairfield, Richard. "A Digression About Talsen [sic]" in *Communes USA: A Personal Tour* (Baltimore, MD: Penguin Books, 1972): 225.
Gardner, Hugh. "A Question of Trust: Talsalsan." In *The Children of Prosperity: Thirteen Modern American Communes* (New York: St. Martin's Press, 1978): 170-181.
Miller, Timothy. *The 60s Communes: Hippies and Beyond* (Syracuse, NY: Syracuse University Press, 1999): 137-38.
Vanneman, Brian Robert. "Searching For Paradise in the Rain: Oregon's Communes and Intentional Communities of the 1960s and 1970s." (Honors thesis, University of Oregon, 1997): 18.

## Talsen – See Talsalsan Farm

## Temple Tribe

Place:        Portland
Formed:       Late 1960s
Directories:  Miller, *The 60s Communes*: 282.

## Terra Firma

Formed:       1970s
Directories:  Miller, *The 60s Communes*: 282.

## Terrasquirma

Place:        Portland
Formed:       1972
Directories:  Miller, *The 60s Communes*: 282.

Patterson, Alexander. "Terrasquirma and the Engines of Social Change in 1970s
   Portland." *Oregon Historical Quarterly* 101 (Summer 2000): 162-91, reprinted
   in John Trombold and Peter Donahue, eds. *Reading Portland: The City in Prose*
   (Seattle: University of Washington Press, 2007): 358-66.
Renken, Patricia. "Lifestyle of the Main Street Gathering: Planted Firmly in
   Terrasquirma." *Oregon Times* (July 1973): 21.

## This is It! Cohousing

Place:        Ashland
Forming:      2003
Directories:  [Directory Updates - New] (*Communities* 120): 15.

## Threshold

Place:        Portland
Formed:       Ca. 1971
Directories:  Miller, *The 60s Communes*: 282.

## Thunder River

Place:        Trail
Formed:       Mid-1970s
Directories:  Miller, *The 60s Communes*: 282.

## Thunderhawk

Place:        Portland
Formed:       Mid-1970s
Directories:  Miller, *The 60s Communes*: 282.

## Tiara Intentional Neighborhood

Place:        Eugene
Formed:       1999

[Community Grapevine]. *Communities* 118 (Summer 2003): 8.
[Community Houses and Property for Sale or Rent, Tiarra Intentional
   Neighborhood, Eugene, Oregon]. *Communities* 119 (Fall 2003): 60.
[Community House for Sale – Eugene, Oregon]. *Communities* 103 (Summer 1999):
   74.
[Community Houses for Sale – Intentional Neighborhood, Eugene, Oregon].
   *Communities* 105 (Winter 1999): 74.

[Community Houses for Sale – Intentional Neighborhood, Eugene, Oregon].
*Communities* 106 (Spring 2000): 82.
[Community Houses for Sale – Intentional Neighborhood, Eugene, Oregon].
*Communities* 107 (Summer 2000): 71.
[Community Property for Sale – Home for sale in intentional neighborhood, Eugene, Oregon]. *Communities* 101 (Winter 1998): 70.
[Community Property for Sale – Home for sale in intentional neighborhood, Eugene, Oregon]. *Communities* 102 (Spring 1999): 68.

## Titanic Lifeboat Academy

Place:        Astoria
Formed:       2004
Directories:  Communities Directory (online)
Web:          www.lifeboat.postcarbon.org/

## Town Forum

Place:   Corvallis
Formed:  1974
Note:    Precursor to Cerro Gordo

[Reach – Communes Looking for People]. *Communities* 8 (May/June 1974): 53.

## Tree House Commune

Formed:       1970s
Directories:  Miller, *The 60s Communes*: 283.

## The Trestle

Place:   Wolf Creek
Formed:  1970s

Roskind, Robert. *Memoirs of an Ex-Hippie: Seven Years in the Counterculture* (Blowing Rock, NC: One Love Press, 2001): 120.

## Trillium Farm Community (Land Trust/Farm)

Place:        Jacksonsville
Formed:       1976
Web:          www.deepwild.org
Formerly:     Trillium Trout Farm
Directories:  *Communities Directory*, 2000: 349.
              [Directory Updates] (*Communities* 123): 65.
              *Communities Directory*, 2005: 243-44.
              *Communities Directory*, 2007: 261.
              Communities Directory (online)

292   [Ad – Trillium Community Land Trust]. *Communities* 109 (Winter 2000): 64.
[Ad – Trillium Community Land Trust]. *Communities* 110 (Spring 2001): 62.
[Ad – Trillium Community Land Trust]. *Communities* 111 (Summer 2001): 21.
[Communities Forming and Reforming – Trillium Farm, Jacksonville, Oregon].
*Communities* 127 (Summer 2005): 74-5.
[Communities Forming and Reforming – Trillium Farm, Jacksonville, Oregon].
*Communities* 128 (Fall 2005): 66.
[Communities with Openings]. *Communities* 98 (Spring 1998): 68-69.
[Communities with Openings]. *Communities* 102 (Spring 1999): 74.

[Communities with Openings]. *Communities* 123 (Summer 2004): 72.
[Communities with Openings]. *Communities* 133 (Winter 2006): 67.
[Communities with Openings]. *Communities* 134 (Spring 2007): 67.
[Communities with Openings]. *Communities* 135 (Summer 2007): 68.
Greenberg, Daniel. "Communities Where You Can Learn." *Communities* 108 (Fall 2000): 49-52.
[Interns Wanted]. *Communities* 102 (Spring 1999): 77.
Thomas, Chant. "'Wilderness is our Classroom ...': Growing Education—and Community—at Trillium Farm." *Communities* 108 (Fall 2000): 36-40.
"Trillium Community Land Trust." *Radical @ Magazine* 5 (Millennium Edition): 17.
Wilner, Joseph Bear. "All My Sisters and Brothers: Redefinitions of Family in Oregon Intentional Communities During the Late Twentieth Century." (M. A. thesis, University of Oregon, 2000): 70.

## Trillium Hollow

Place:        Portland, 9601 NW Leahy Rd.
Formed:      1991
Established:    1998
Directories:    Cohousing Directory (online)
                Communities Directory (online)
                *Communities Directory*, 2005: 244.
                *Communities Directory*, 2007: 261.
Web:          www.trilliumhollow.org

[Ad – Trillium Hollow Cohousing]. *Communities* 123 (Summer 2004): 76.
/Ad – Trillium Hollow Cohousing]. *Communities* 124 (Fall 2004): 13.
[Ad – Trillium Hollow Cohousing]. *Communities* 125 (Winter 2004): 4.
[Ad – Trillium Hollow Cohousing]. *Communities* 126 (Spring 2005): 75.
[Ad – Trillium Hollow Cohousing]. *Communities* 127 (Summer 2005): 60.
[Ad – Trillium Hollow Cohousing]. *Communities* 128 (Fall 2005): 67.
[Communities Directory Summer '99 Update] (*Communities* 103): 67.

Maclean, Charles B. "What I Learned from Children about Giving and Receiving" in David Wann, ed., *Reinventing Community: Stories from the Walkways of Cohousing* (Golden, CO: Fulcrum Publishing, 2005): 41-42.
Margolis, Diane R. "On the Cohousing Trail in the Pacific Northwest." *Communities* 109 (Winter 2000): 16-19.

## Trillium Trout Farm

Place:        Ashland
Formed:      1970s
Directories:    Miller, *The 60s Communes*: 283.

## Try/on Life Community

Place:        Portland
Formed:      1991
Web:          tryonfarm.org/share/

Dvorak, Laura, and J. Brush. "Let's Do Greywater First! Could the City of Portland Become ... Ecotopia?" *Communities* 137 (Winter 2007): 44-47.
[Events – 2007 Earth Activist Trainings – EAT Intensive – May 4-18]. *The Permaculture Activist* 64 (May 2007): 52.

"It May Take a Village to Save The Farm." *The Oregonian* (October 27, 2005).

## 21st Family

Directories:   Miller, *The 60s Communes*: 283.

## Two Rivers Farm

Place:          Aurora
Formed:        1974
Directories:   Miller, *The 60s Communes*: 283.

Kherdian, David. *The Farm* [poems]. Aurora, Oregon: Two Rivers Press, 1978.
Kheridan, David. *On a Spaceship With Beelzebub*. By a Grandson of Gurdjieff.
    New York: Globe Press Books, 1991.
Miller, Timothy. *The 60s Communes: Hippies and Beyond* (Syracuse, NY: Syracuse
    University Press, 1999): 116.

## Union Mill Company

Place:          Nehalem
Dates:          1892-1896

Bushee, Frederick A. "Communistic Societies in the United States." *Political
    Science Quarterly* 20 (December 1905): 664.
Eaton, Joseph W., and Saul M. Katz. *Research Guide on Cooperative Group
    Farming* (New York: H. W. Wilson Company, 1942): 38.
Gaylord, A. J. "Duties of Members [letter]." *The Co-operator* III(3) (December 29,
    1900): 1.
Kent, Alexander. "Nehalem Valley Cooperative Colony" in "Cooperative
    Communities in the United States." *Bulletin of the Department of Labor* 6 (July
    1901): 642.
Kopp, James J. "Documenting Utopia in Oregon: The Challenges of Tracking the
    Quest for Perfection." *Oregon Historical Quarterly* 105 (2004): 308-19.
Okugawa, Otohiko. "Appendix A: Annotated List of Communal and Utopian
    Societies, 1787-1919." In Robert S. Fogarty. *Dictionary of American
    Communal and Utopian History* (Westport, CT: Greenwood Press, 1980): 214.
Stephan, Karen H., and G. Edward Stephan. "Religion and the Survival of Utopian
    Communities." *Journal of the Scientific Study of Religion* 12 (March 1973):
    89-100[98].
Stockwell, Foster. "Union Mills Company" in *Encyclopedia of American
    Communes, 1663-1963* (Jefferson, NC: McFarland & Co., 1998): 210.
Walker, Lisa. "A Selected Bibliography of Sources on Communal Societies in
    Oregon and Washington Available at the Oregon Historical Society" (March
    15, 1992): 28.
Williams, Julia Elizabeth. "An Analytical Tabulation of the North American
    Utopian Communities By Type, Longevity and Location." (M. A. thesis,
    Department of Sociology, University of South Dakota, 1939): 10.

## Universing Center

Place:          Cottage Grove
Formed:        1973
Directories:   Miller, *The 60s Communes*: 283.

## Varsity House

| | |
|---|---|
| Place: | Corvallis, 119 NW 9th St. |
| Formed: | 1964 |
| Directories: | *Communities Directory*, 2000: 362. |
| | *Communities Directory*, 2005: 286. |
| | Communities Directory (online) |
| Web: | varsityhouse.org |

## Vision Foundation

| | |
|---|---|
| Place: | Coos Bay |
| Formed: | 1972 |
| Directories: | Miller, *The 60s Communes*: 284. |
| | [Directory of Intentional Communities – Summer '94 Update] (*Communities 83*): 55. |
| | [Communities Director Winter '95 Update – Groups That Have Folded] (*Communities 89*): 66. |
| | [Communities Directory Summer '96 Update – Index of Listings] (*Communities 91*): 67. |

## Vonu Life

| | |
|---|---|
| Place: | Cave Junction |
| Formed: | 1972 |
| Directories: | Miller, *The 60s Communes*: 284. |
| | "Commune Directory" (*Communities 1*): 36. |

## WAHOO!

| | |
|---|---|
| Place: | Portland, 4510 NE Holman St.; Eugene, 2560 Alder St. |
| Forming: | 1998 |
| Directories: | *Communities Directory*, 2000: 363. |
| | [Community Updates – Changes] (*Communities 120*): 27. |
| Web: | www.WahooCommunity.com/ |

## Walnut St. Co-op

| | |
|---|---|
| Place: | Eugene, 1680 Walnut St. |
| Formed: | 2000 |
| Directories: | [Directories Update] (*Communities 118*): 64. |
| | [Directory Updates – New] (*Communities 120*): 16. |
| | Communities Directory (online) |
| | *Communities Directory*, 2005: 262. |
| | *Communities Directory*, 2007: 280. |
| Web: | walnutstreetco-op.org |

Bressen, Tree. "The Quest for Community: A Personal Journey into the Grey Zone." *Communities* 139 (Summer 2008): 18-22.

Bressen, Tree. "Radical Resource-Sharing." *Communities* 122 (Spring 2004): 11-13.

Bressen, Tree. [Letter]. *Communities* 125 (Winter 2004): 5.

Bressen, Tree. "Our Community Revolving Loan Fund: How Walnut Street Co-op Financed Its Property." *Communities* 128 (Fall 2005): 14-16.

[Communities with Openings – Coop House, Eugene, Oregon]. *Communities* 111 (Summer 2001): 73.

[Communities with Openings – Coop House, Eugene, Oregon]. *Communities* 112 (Fall 2001): 65.

[Communities with Openings]. *Communities* 113 (Winter 2001): 74.
[Communities with Openings]. *Communities* 114 (Spring 2002): 72.
[Communities with Openings]. *Communities* 115 (Summer 2002): 72.
[Communities with Openings]. *Communities* 116 (Fall 2002): 73.
[Communities with Openings]. *Communities* 117 (Spring 2003): 72.
[Communities with Openings]. *Communities* 118 (Summer 2003): 68.
[Community Grapevine]. *Communities* 118 (Summer 2003): 8.
[Community Grapevine]. *Communities* 119 (Fall 2003): 11.
Daniell, Alex. [Letter]. *Communities* 132 (Fall 2006): 5.
Franklin, David. "Why Does Anyone Do This?" *Communities* 125 (Winter 2004):
    26-28.

## We'Moon

**Place:**      Estacada
**Formed:**     1973
**Note:**       See also We'Moon Healing Ground, We'Moon Land, and WHO
                Farm

[Ad – *We'Moon '97*]. *Communities* 93 (Winter 1996): 25.
[Community Calendar – Jul 6-12 – Syster Moon Mud Camp]. *Communities* 99
    (Summer 1998): 67.
[Community Openings, Live-in Employment Opportunities – Mother Tongue Ink].
    *Communities* 103 (Summer 1999): 70.
[Interns and Work Opportunities – Mother Tongue Ink]. *Communities* 103
    (Summer 1999): 76.
Musawa. "A 'Feast of Art' at We'Moon." *Communities* 93 (Winter 1996): 62-64.
[Reviews – *We'Moon '97: Gaia Rhythms for Womyn—Womyn in Community*].
    *Communities* 93 (Winter 1996): 21.
Schutzer, Amy. "Musings on a Summer Day at We'Moon." *Communities* 93
    (Winter 1996): 64.
Wilner, Joseph Bear. "All My Sisters and Brothers: Redefinitions of Family in
    Oregon Intentional Communities During the Late Twentieth Century." (M. A.
    thesis, University of Oregon, 2000): 72.
[Work Opportunities – Job Openings in Womyn's Publishing]. *Communities* 114
    (Spring 2002): 76.
[Work Opportunities – Job Openings at We'Moon]. *Communities* 115 (Summer
    2002): 76.
[Work Opportunities – We'Moon, Estacada, Oregon]. *Communities* 116 (Fall
    2002): 77.
[Work Opportunities – Job and Resident Openings at We'Moon]. *Communities*
    119 (Fall 2003): 64.

## We'Moon Healing Ground

**Place:**        Estacada
**Formerly:**     WHO Farm
**Directories:**  [Directory Update Spring/Summer '93 Update – New Listings, North
                  America] (*Communities* 80/81): 85.
                  *Communities Directory*, 1996: 318.
Sandia Bear, "Lesbians on Land: A Tribe of Womyn." In Lynn Witt, Sherry
    Thomas, and Eric Marcus, eds. *Out in All Directions: The Almanac of Gay and
    Lesbian America* (New York: Warner Books, 1995): 323-26.

## We'Moon Land

Place:      Estacada
Formed:      1973
Formerly:      WHO Farm; We'Moon Healing Ground
Directories:      *Communities Directory*, 2000: 365.
     *Communities Directory*, 2005: 286.
     Communities Directory (online)
     Association of Lesbian Intentional Communities online
     *Shewolf's Directory of Wimmin's Land*. Fifth Edition
Web:      http://www.wemoon.ws/land.html
Archives/Manuscripts:
     SO CLAP! (Southern Oregon Country Lesbian Archival Project) Collection, 1974-1999, Special Collections & University Archives, University of Oregon Libraries, Series IX

Association of Lesbian Intentional Communities. "Come to Oregon Women's Lands." http://alicinfo.com/pages/oregon.htm

"Community Business Seeks Members/Workers." *Communities* 116 (Fall 2002): 10.

[Community Grapevine]. *Communities* 111 (Summer 2001): 8.

[Community Grapevine]. *Communities* 117 (Spring 2003): 11.

Green, Oriana. "Chop Wood, Carry Water and Publish: Hidden Away in the Hills, A Determined Group of Dykes Perpetuate Their Unique Way of Life." *just out* 17:1 (November 5, 1999): 43.

Sandilands, Catriona. "Lesbian Separatist Communities and the Experience of Nature: A Queer Ecology." *Organization & Environment* 15 (June 2002): 131-63.

## West Hills Cohousing

Place:      Portland, 7415 SW Virginia Avenue
Formed:      1995
Directories:      [Communities Directory Winter '95 Update – North American New Listings] (*Communities* 89): 66.

## Whispering Oaks

Place:      Winston

Summerhawk, Barbara, and La Verne Gagehabib. *Circles of Power: Shifting Dynamics in a Lesbian-Centered Community* (Norwich, VT: New Victoria Publishers, 2000): 38.

## White Oak Farm

Place:      Williams
Formed:      2002
Web:      www.whiteoakfarmcsa.org/

297

[Communities Forming – White Oak Farm, Williams, Oregon]. *Communities* 126 (Spring 2005): 71.

[Communities Forming and Reforming – White Oak Farm, Williams, Oregon]. *Communities* 127 (Summer 2005): 75.

[Communities Forming and Reforming – White Oak Farm, Williams, Oregon]. *Communities* 128 (Fall 2005): 66.

[Communities Forming and Reforming – White Oak Farm, Williams, Oregon]. *Communities* 132 (Fall 2006): 83.

[Communities Forming and Reforming – White Oak Farm, Williams, Oregon]. *Communities* 133 (Winter 2006): 71.

[Communities Forming and Reforming – White Oak Farm, Williams, Oregon]. *Communities* 134 (Spring 2007): 69.

## WHO Farm

**Place:** Estacada, 37010 S.E. Snuffin Road
**Formed:** 1973
**Manuscripts:** Ruth Mountaingrove Papers. Special Collections & University Archives, University of Oregon Libraries.

"Dear women's community." *Woman's Place Newsletter* (January 1981): 13.

"From WHO Farm to Sierra and the Women's Community." *Woman's Place Newsletter* (1981): 6.

"Growing [WHO Farm]." *Rag Times* (October 1982): 8.

"[Letters]." *Woman's Place Newsletter* (February 1981): 2.

"[Letters]." *Woman's Place Newsletter* (May 1981): 2-3.

"[Letters]." *Woman's Place Newsletter* (June 1981): 3.

"News Flash – WHO Farm." *Woman's Place Newsletter* (July 1981): 3.

Sandia Bear, "Lesbians on Land: A Tribe of Womyn." In Lynn Witt, Sherry Thomas, and Eric Marcus, eds. *Out in All Directions: The Almanac of Gay and Lesbian America* (New York: Warner Books, 1995): 323-26.

Vanderburgh, Nancy. "WHO Farm: A Chronology." *Woman's Place Newsletter* (August 1981): 8-9, 13, 15.

"WHO Farm [Announcements]." *Women's Press* (November/December 1980): 23.

"[WHO Farm] Community Bulletin Board." *Rag Times* (May 1982): 11.

"[WHO Farm] Community Bulletin Board." *Rag Times* (June 1982): 8.

"[WHO Farm] Community Events." *Rag Times* (October 1982): 7.

"[WHO Farm] Community Events." *Rag Times* (November 1982): 4.

"WHO Farm Events." *Rag Times* (February 1983): 5.

"[WHO Farm events] Calendar." *Rag Times* (November 1982):[12].

"[WHO Farm events] Calendar." *Rag Times* (July 1982):[12].

"WHO Farm Evolves Into Retreat." *Rag Times* (March 1986): 10.

"WHO Farm Is Changing!!!!!" *Woman's Place Newsletter* (November 1980): 22.

"WHO Farm is having a work week May 9-17." *Woman's Place Newsletter* (May 1981): 19.

"[WHO Farm meeting]." *Rag Times* (April 1983): 7.

"WHO Farm News." *Woman's Place Newsletter* (May 1979): 12-13.

"WHO Farm News." *Woman's Place Newsletter* (July 1981): 4.

"WHO Farm News." *Rag Times* (March 1982): 15.

"WHO Farm News." *Rag Times* (May 1982): 6.

"WHO Farm News." *Rag Times* (July 1982): 6.

"WHO Farm Note." *Woman's Place Newsletter* (March 1980): 9.

298

"WHO Farm Presents." *Rag Times* (April 1982): 9.

"WHO Farm Presents." *Rag Times* (May 1982): 7.

## Wholesome House

**Place:** Portland, 2137 SE Taylor St.
**Formed:** 2005
**Directories:** Communities Directory (online)
    *Communities Directory*, 2007: 402.
**Web:** www.wholesome-house.net/

## Wicca
Place:         Eugene
Directories:   Association of Lesbian Intentional Communities online map
               *Shewolf's Directory of Wimmin's Land*. Fifth Edition
Note:          Women in Conscious Creative Action

## Wilsonville Cohousing
Place:     Wilsonville
Forming:   2003

[Communities Forming – Wilsonville Cohousing, Oregon]. *Communities* 118
   (Summer 2003): 70.
[Communities Forming – Wilsonville Cohousing, Oregon]. *Communities* 119 (Fall
   2003): 62.

## Wolf Creek Sanctuary
Place:         Wolf Creek
Formed:        1985
Directories:   *Directory of Intentional Communities*, 1990: 230.

"Celebrating Long-Lived Communities." *Communities* 93 (Winter 1996): 12.

## Wolf Creek Radical Faerie Sanctuary –
## see Nomenus Radical Faerie Sanctuary

## WomanShare Feminist Women's Land
Place:         Grants Pass, 1531 Grays Creek Rd
Formed:        1974
Directories:   Miller, *The 60s Communes*: 285.
               *Directory of Intentional Communities*, 1991: 230.
               *Communities Directory*, 1996: 322.
               *Communities Directory*, 2000: 369.
               *Communities Directory*, 2005: 287.
               *Communities Directory*, 2007: 284-85.
               Communities Directory (online)
               Association of Lesbian Intentional Communities online
               *Shewolf's Directory of Wimmin's Land*. Fifth Edition
Publications:  *Womanshare Newsletter*
               *Rough Road*
Archives/Manuscripts:
               Ruth Mountaingrove Papers. Special Collections & University
                  Archives, University of Oregon Libraries.
               Ruth Mountaingrove Videotape Autobiography Collection, 1988-
                  1997. Special Collections & University Archives, University of
                  Oregon Libraries.
               SO CLAP! (Southern Oregon Country Lesbian Archival Project)
                  Collection, 1974-1999, Special Collections & University
                  Archives, University of Oregon Libraries

Association of Lesbian Intentional Communities. "Come to Oregon Women's
   Lands." http://alicinfo.com/pages/oregon.htm
"Celebrating Long-Lived Communities." *Communities* 85 (Winter 1994): 14.
[Communities Directory Summer '99 Update]. *Communities* 103 (Summer 1999):
   67.

299

[Communities with Openings]. *Communities 95* (Summer 1997): 71.

*Country Lesbians: The Story of the WomanShare Collective.* By Sue, Nelly, Dian, Carol, Billie. Grants Pass: WomanShare Books, 1976.

Kleiner, Catherine B. "Doin' It For Themselves: Lesbian Land Communities in Southern Oregon, 1970-1995." (Ph.D. dissertation, University of New Mexico, 2003): 109-10.

Miller, Timothy. *The 60s Communes: Hippies and Beyond* (Syracuse, NY: Syracuse University Press, 1999): 138-39.

Miller, Timothy. "The Sixties-Era Communes" in Peter Braunstein and Michael William Doyle, eds. *Imagine Nation: The American Counterculture of the 1960s and '70s* (New York & London: Routledge, 2002): 340-41.

Miracle, Billie. "Womanshare" in Joyce Cheney, ed. *Lesbian Land* (Minneapolis, MN: Word Weavers, 1985): 146-50.

Ní Aódagaín, H. "Empowerment through Community: From Separatism to Sanctuary." Paper presented at the 26th Annual Gender Studies Symposium, Lewis & Clark College, March 8, 2007.

Olszewska, Jo. "Womanshare Fall 1984" in Joyce Cheney, ed. *Lesbian Land* (Minneapolis, MN: Word Weavers, 1985): 150.

Sandia Bear, "Lesbians on Land: A Tribe of Womyn." In Lynn Witt, Sherry Thomas, and Eric Marcus, eds. *Out in All Directions: The Almanac of Gay and Lesbian America* (New York: Warner Books, 1995): 323-26.

Sandilands, Catriona. "Lesbian Separatist Communities and the Experience of Nature: Toward A Queer Ecology." *Organization & Environment* 15 (June 2002): 131-63.

Sandilands, Catriona. "Rainbow's End? Lesbian Separatism and the Ongoing Politics of Ecotopia." In Margrit Eichler, June Larkin, and Sheila Neysmith, eds. *Feminist Utopias: Re-Visioning Our Future* (Toronto, Canada: Inanna Publications and Education, 2002): 37-50.

Sprecher, Katharine Matthaei. "Lesbian Intentional Communities in Rural Southwestern Oregon: Discussions on Separatism, Environmentalism, and Community Conflict." (M. A. thesis, California Institute of Integral Studies, 1997): 66-73.

Summerhawk, Barbara, and La Verne Gagehabib. *Circles of Power: Shifting Dynamics in a Lesbian-Centered Community* (Norwich, VT: New Victoria Publishers, 2000): 45-49; 120-22.

Sutton, Robert P. "Womanshare Feminist Women's Land" in *Modern American Communes: A Dictionary* (Westport, CT: Greenwood Press, 2005): 177-78.

Traveller, Helen. "*Country Lesbians*: A Review." *WomanSpirit* vol. 3, no. 11 (Spring Equinox 1977): 26-27.

Vanneman, Brian Robert. "Searching For Paradise in the Rain: Oregon's Communes and Intentional Communities of the 1960s and 1970s." (Honors thesis, University of Oregon, 1997): 18.

Weston, Jennifer. "Womanshare Winter 1985" in Joyce Cheney, ed., *Lesbian Land* (Minneapolis, MN: Word Weavers, 1985): 150-51.

Wilner, Joseph Bear. "All My Sisters and Brothers: Redefinitions of Family in Oregon Intentional Communities During the Late Twentieth Century." (M. A. thesis, University of Oregon, 2000): 60-61.

"Womanshare Feminist Women's Land" in Robert P. Sutton, *Modern American Communes: A Dictionary* (Westport, CT, and London: Greenwood Press, 2005): 177-78.

# Yellow Submarine
Place:       Eugene, 2449 Flora Hill Drive
Formed:      1968
Directories: Ayd, *The Youth Communes*: 166.
             Miller, *The 60s Communes*, 285.
             "Commune Directory" (*Communities* 1): 36.

Bates, Doug. "Lane County's Rural Areas Nurture Communal Lifestyle." *Eugene Register-Guard* (August 29, 1971): B1.
[Fairfield, Richard]. "Yellow Submarine." *Modern Utopian* 5 ["Communes U.S.A."] (1971): 132-33.
Fairfield, Richard. "Yellow Submarine" in *Communes USA: A Personal Tour* (Baltimore, MD: Penguin Books, 1972): 348-53.
Teeters, Kay. "Communal Utopias of the Pacific Northwest" (Honors thesis, University of Oregon, 1970):): 52.
Vanneman, Brian Robert. "Searching For Paradise in the Rain: Oregon's Communes and Intentional Communities of the 1960s and 1970s." (Honors thesis, University of Oregon, 1997): 20.

# Yew Wood Healing Center
Place:       Deadwood
Forming:     1995
Directories: [Communities Directory Winter '95 Update – North American New Listings] (*Communities* 89): 66.

# The Zoo
Place:       Newport
Formed:      1965
Directories: Miller, *The 60s Communes*: 285.

Miller, Timothy. *The 60s Communes: Hippies and Beyond* (Syracuse, NY: Syracuse University Press, 1999): 65.

# Miscellaneous
Many publications include ads and other announcements for possible communal groups or others interested in joining for forming such groups. There are also ads and announcements for publications and products that might provide information on other communal groups in Oregon. Such items are often leads to other information and so are included here for that purpose. Some of the items listed may relate to a community noted above but, as no specific reference was included, these are included separately here.

[Ad – *Community ConneXion*[Portland]]. *Communities* 94 (Spring 1997): 75.
[Ad – *Community ConneXion*[Portland]]. *Communities* 95 (Summer 1997): 67.
[Ad – *Community ConneXion*[Portland]]. *Communities* 96 (Fall 1997): 18.          301
[Ad – *Community ConneXion*[Portland]]. *Communities* 97 (Winter 1997): 65.
[Ad – *Community ConneXion*[Portland]]. *Communities* 98 (Spring 1998): 71.
[Ad – *Community ConneXion*[Portland]]. *Communities* 99 (Summer 1998): 73.
[Ad – *Seriatim, Journal of Ecotopia*, McMinnville, Oregon]. *Communities* 18 (January/February 1976): 64, inside back cover, back cover.
[Ad – *Seriatim, Journal of Ecotopia*, McMinnville, Oregon]. *Communities* 19 (March/April 1976): 80.

[Ad – *Seriatim, Journal of Ecotopia*, McMinnville, Oregon]. *Communities* 21 (July/August 1976): 35.

Cerf, William. "Toward a New American Dream [letter]. *Communities* 127 (Summer 2005): 5.

Christian, Diana Leafe. "Can We Make a Difference?"[City Repair]. *Communities* 137 (Winter 2007): 34-38.

[Classifieds – Communities – Spirited woman needed to be and buy into a beautiful community in Veneta, Oregon]. *Communities* 66 (Spring 1985): 87.

[Classifieds – Communities – Who can help us with establishing a PEACE COMMUNITY? Yachats, Oregon]. *Communities* 66 (Spring 1985): 87.

[Classifieds – Land – Opportunity to live in beautiful 360 acre forest in exchange for help on homesteading projects. Coquille]. *The Permaculture Activist* VI(3) (Autumn 1990): 39.

[Communities Forming – Portland, Oregon. Seeking one or two individuals or couple, for shared household potential community in Portland Metro-area]. *Communities* 93 (Winter 1996): 74.

[Communities Forming – Portland, Oregon. Seeking one or two individuals or couple, for shared household potential community in Portland Metro-area]. *Communities* 94 (Spring 1997): 73.

[Communities Forming – Portland, Oregon. Seeking one or two individuals or couple, for shared household potential community in Portland Metro-area]. *Communities* 95 (Summer 1997): 73.

[Communities Forming – Portland, Oregon. Seeking one or two individuals or couple, for shared household potential community in Portland Metro-area]. *Communities* 96 (Fall 1997): 72.

[Communities Forming – Portland, Oregon. Seeking one or two individuals or couple, for shared household potential community in Portland Metro-area]. *Communities* 97 (Winter 1997): 80.

[Communities Forming – Portland, Oregon. Seeking one or two individuals or couple, for shared household potential community in Portland Metro-area]. *Communities* 98 (Spring 1998): 71.

[Communities Forming – Portland, Oregon. Seeking one or two individuals or couple, for shared household potential community in Portland Metro-area]. *Communities* 99 (Summer 1998): 76.

[Communities Forming – Portland, Oregon. Seeking one or two individuals or couple, for shared household potential community in Portland Metro-area]. *Communities* 100 (Fall 1998): 75.

[Communities Forming – Portland, Oregon. Seeking one or two individuals or couple, for shared household potential community in Portland Metro-area]. *Communities* 101 (Winter 1998): 75.

[Communities Forming – Retreat Center, Oregon Coast]. *Communities* 113 (Winter 2001): 76.

[Communities Forming – Community Homestead Available, Central Point, Oregon]. *Communities* 119 (Fall 2003): 61.

[Communities Forming – Community Homestead Available, Central Point, Oregon]. *Communities* 121 (Winter 2003): 65.

[Community Calendar – Apr 28-29 – Cooportunities Portland!]. *Communities* 110 (Spring 2001): 69.

[Community Calendar – Apr 20-22 – NASCO West Coast Conference "Hands on Co-ops," Eugene, Oregon]. *Communities* 110 (Spring 2001): 69.

[Community Clearinghouse – Mike, Tripper and I are a unit of an extended family. We are planning to move to Oregon sometime in the next year. Los Angeles]. *Communitas* 2 (September 1972): 54.

[Community Land for Sale, Rentals – Sunny Southern Oregon]. *Communities* 91 (Summer 1996): 69.

[Community Living Directory – Northwest – We are a conscientious vegetarian family living on a large mountain ranch, seeking adoptable or foster children over three years old. Visitors are also welcome. Black Mt. Ranch, Box 51, Sumpter State, Baker, OR 97814]. *Utopian Eyes* 3:1 (Winter 1977): [34].

[Community Living Directory – Northwest – We live on 80 acres in forest area, grow our own food, and seek merger with hard-working vegetarians devoted to God. Want to start school. Long or short term mergers. Bob and Susan Binzler, 59814 Deer Creek Road, Selma, OR 97538.] *Utopian Eyes* 3:1 (Winter 1977): [34].

[Community Living Directory – Late Entries – Seeks others to live in a polyfidelitous closed group of enlightened peasants on a self-sufficient homestead. Would like to exchange ideas of utopian visions. Interests in gardening, animal husbandry, building, construction. Phil Hyre, 3566 Elmira Rd., Eugene, OR 94702, 689-3700]. *Utopian Eyes* 3:1 (Winter 1977): [44].

[Community Property for Sale – House for Sale, perfect for intentional community or cohousing [Portland]]. *Communities* 99 (Summer 1998): 70.

[Communities with Openings – Land Share, Newburg, Oregon, Arcadian Vision at Yamhill County Co-op]. *Communities* 134 (Spring 2007): 67.

[Directory of Intentional Communities – Summer '94 Update – Sandra Moilanen – Clatskanie]. *Communities* 83 (Summer 1994): 54.

Douglas, Claire, and Jim Scott. "Siuslaw Rural Health Center" in *A Guide to Cooperative Alternatives* (New Haven, CT, and Louisa, VA: Community Publications Cooperative, 1979): 21-24. (Originally published in *Win* Magazine, July 27, 1978).

[Eugene Community Sustaining Fund]. *Communities* 19 (March/April 1976): 60-61.

Freifelder, Rachel, Gina Baker, and Steve Lafer. "Planning and Zoning for Ecovillages—Encouraging News." *Communities* 91 (Summer 1996): 62-65.

"Gay Women's Communities." *Communities* 87 (Summer 1995): 45.

[Grapevine – Oregon Farm]. *Communities* 4 (1973): 51.

[Grapevine – WomanSpirit]. *Communities* 17 (November/December 1975): 57.

Lakeman, Mark. "The Village Blooms in the City: Portland's Natural Building Convergence." *Communities* 115 (Summer 2002): 26-29.

Lone-Wolf-Circling [Oregon State Penitentiary]. "Prisoners Struggle – Where Are We?" *Communities* 7 (March/April 1974): 14-17.

"Oregon Country Fair." *Communities* 34 (September/October 1978): 44.

"Our Oregon Community." *Communities* 3 (1973): 11-12.

[People Looking – My partner and I are looking for collective/communal living situation]. *Communities* 55 (October/November 1982): 63.

[People Looking – Interested in Eco-Forestry, Permaculture, Organic Gardening? – 29 acres in Yamhill County]. *Communities* 126 (Spring 2005): 72.

[People Looking – Interested in Eco-Forestry, Permaculture, Organic Gardening? – 29 acres in Yamhill County]. *Communities* 128 (Fall 2005): 68.

[People Looking – Looking for Non-Hierarchical, Sustainable, non-dogmatic rural community in Northwest U.S.]. *Communities* 91 (Summer 1996): 76.

[Periodicals – *Community Connexion*]. *Communities* 94 (Spring 1997): 67.

[Reach – Commune to Commune – We are a worker-owned and managed feminist collective which wholesales and distributes natural foods. Starflower Co., Eugene]. *Communities* 7 (March/April 1974): 56.

[Reach – Communes Being Formed – Carl and I are moving to Oregon, near Roseburg, in the spring. We are interested in the formation of a diverse spiritual community, and would like to extend a welcome to anyone who is also interested, and would like to drop by next summer and see us. La Canada, CA]. *Communities* 11 (December 1974): 60.

[Reach – Communes Forming – We are starting a healing arts community in Oregon. My work is in reflexology or zone therapy, Swedish massage, polarity, and Shiatsu. Portland]. *Communities* 12 (January /February 1975): 37.

[Reach – Co-op Contact. Portland]. *Communities* 9 (July/August 1974): 54.

[Reach – Group Forming – Dividing a beautiful old church into four extra-large "apartments" – Portland]. *Communities* 50 (October/November 1981): 55.

[Reach – Help Wanted – Siuslaw Rural Health Center]. *Communities* 46 (October/November 1980): 58.

[Reach – Land – We are a group of small communities and individuals interested in combining our energies to get a large piece of land. Veneta]. *Communities* 39 (August/September 1979): 47.

[Reach – We have 62 acres of beautiful forest and tillable land, abundant pure spring water, marvelous varied wildlife, a comfortable home, tranquil views of the Columbia River and New Columbia River Gorge Scenic Area ...]. *Communities* 76 (May 1990): 50.

[Reach – Oregon Coast. To help people in their search for responsible living and friendship, we are forming a cooperative on 400 acres in the Grants Pass area of the Oregon Pacific Coast.] *Communities* 79 (Fall 1992): 39.

[Reach – People Looking – Any group searching for new members, please contact me and explain in detail about your group. I'm a woman with former communal experience, a lot of energy and love to share. Corvallis]. *Communities* 39 (August/September 1979): 45.

[Reach – People Looking for People – Healthy family of six want to help build a stable, organic farm cooperative where family privacy is coupled with community spirit and resources to achieve simple self-sufficiency. Portland]. *Communities* 21 (July/August 1976): 47.

[Reach – People Looking – Woman, man, child (8 mo. girl) looking for community. Into theatre, dance, song, spiritual awareness, political awareness, child rearing awareness. Eugene]. *Communities* 39 (August/September 1979): 46.

[Reach – People Looking – I am a 30 year old male looking for a West Coast community that is rural, agriculturally-oriented (organic): and economically self-sufficient, Florence, Oregon]. *Communities* 41 (December 1979/January 1980): 58.

[Reach – People Looking – We, Sheila, Jack, and Kevin (age 4) are looking for two other families with children under six to share finances, work and friendship on our Southern Oregon farm. Cave Junction]. *Communities* 25 (March/April 1977): 54.

[Reach – People Looking – I'm looking for an established community needing new members or other like-minded individuals to form a group with. Eugene]. *Communities* 25 (March/April 1977): 54.

304

[Reach – People Looking – We are looking for homestead acreage in a community or back-to-the-land area where folks live simply, organically, and in harmony with nature while sharing skills and experience, La Grande, Oregon]. *Communities* 32 (May/June 1978): 58.

[Reach – People Looking – We have bought 80 acres in Southern Oregon and are looking for people to help us homestead and pay off the land contract.] *Communities* 42 (February/March 1980): 51-52.

[Reach – People Looking for Groups – Musical Community? I am looking to study music intensively, in a community or school setting? Is there a group around that's geared to this? Birkenfeld, Oregon]. *Communities* 27 (July/August 1977): 53.

[Reach – People Looking for Groups – We are presently living a fairly straight lifestyle but would like to change. Portland]. *Communities* 28 (September/October 1977): 58.

[Reach – People Looking for Groups or People – We have set out to learn what our christian fathers should have learned long ago before the Indians. That is walking balance with nature. ... Oregon seems to be the place we are headed but we are open to suggestions. Portland]. *Communities* 15 (July/August 1975): 41.

[Reach – People Looking for People – We're four people from 1 year to 33 years old who plan to live on the land in a non-monogamous extended communal family. Eugene]. *Communities* 13 (March/April 1975): 61.

[Reach – People Looking for People – We are a conscientious vegetarian family of five, are financially stable, and are seeking one or two adoptable or foster children over the age of three. Baker, Oregon]. *Communities* 21 (July/August 1976): 48.

[Reach – People seeking community on a small and personal scale may be able to locate others thru our matching service. Send 2 stamps to 10th House, PO Box 1903, Eugene, Oregon 97401 and you will receive a "response form" to fill out and return.] *Communities* 15 (July/August 1975): 49.

[Reach – People Who Need Help – A group of people in the Klamath Falls area about 30 mi. from Chiloquin, Oregon will be starting the first of what we see as several intentional communities this spring. Chiloquin]. *Communities* 7 (March/April 1974): 58.

[Reach – People Who Need Help – I'm writing out of my personal needs, but certain feedback I may get will be passed on to my brothers here in the penetentiary [sic]. Eugene]. *Communities* 7 (March/April 1974): 58.

[Reach – We are Christina (24): Paul (32): Sundance (3): and Isaac Sparrow (3 weeks). We're seeking to meet people who would like to become part of an extended family with us. Eugene]. *Communities* 9 (July/August 1974): 55.

[Reach – We are seeking to join in community with our spiritual family. We live on 80 acres in the forest of southern Oregon. Selma, Oregon]. *Communities* 22 (September/October[1976]): 48.

[Reach – We're looking into the possibilities of forming a community business and/or a cooperative living arrangement somewhat similar to "Middle Class Commune" reported on in Communities. Portland]. *Communities* 3 (1973): 59.

[Readback – Ford, Margaret [letter] – "I am 73, I am daughter of American pioneers. I lived at the beginning of this century in a community. They tell me that the idea has never quite been lost and the people of Oregon where I live are still aware of it."] *Communities* 3 (1973): 64.

[Reports from Regional Groups – Permaculture in the Oregon Coast Range, Chip and Clara Boggs, Coquille]. *The Permaculture Activist* VI(4) (Winter 1990): 38.

[Resources – *Cascade: Journal of the Northwest*, Eugene]. *Communities* 44 (June/July 1980): 62.

[Resources – Cooperative Living – Skillsbank, Ashland]. *Communities* 49 (June/July 1981): 55.

[Resources – Community Connexion]. *Communities* 84 (Fall 1994): 71.

[Resources – Community Referral Service: Getting People Together, Eugene, Oregon]. *Communities* 66 (Spring 1985): 76.

[Resources – Farmstead Workshops. Junction City]. *Communities* 7 (March/April 1974): 61.

305

[Resources – Health – Alternatives in Health Care is published four times a year and covers a variety of issues around the main area of health. Deadwood]. *Communities* 39 (August/September 1979): 51.

[Resources – Men – The Men's Resource Center/*Changing Men*, Portland] in *A Guide to Cooperative Alternatives* (New Haven, CT and Louisa, VA: Community Publications Cooperative, 1979): 146-47.

[Resources – Publications – *Edcentric: A Journal of Educational Change*, Eugene]. *Communities* 43 (April/May 1980): 60.

[Resources – Publications – *WomanSpirit*, Wolf Creek] in *A Guide to Cooperative Alternatives* (New Haven, CT, and Louisa, VA: Community Publications Cooperative, 1979): 21-24.

[Resources – Regional Networking – Cascadia Regional Library, Cascade: Journal of the Northwest, Eugene] in *A Guide to Cooperative Alternatives* (New Haven, CT, and Louisa, VA: Community Publications Cooperative, 1979): 78.

Roe, Gerald Walden [McMinnville, Oregon]. "An open loveletter to Kat Kinkade" [Instant Read-Back]. *Communities* 18 (January/February 1976): 59-63.

# Notes

## Preface

1. James J. Kopp, "Documenting Utopia in Oregon: The Challenges of Tracking the Quest for Perfection." *Oregon Historical Quarterly* 105:2 (Summer 2004): 308-19.

## Introduction

1. Abigail Scott Duniway, *Oregon: Land of Promise* (Portland: Claiborne H. Rhodes, 1907). The poem first appeared as "West and West" in her *David and Anna Matson* (New York: S. R. Wells & Co., 1876), 172-87. Thanks to Jean Ward for providing this connection. *The Promised Land* also is the title of a statue in the courtyard of the Oregon Historical Center and represents the Edenic draw of Oregon. Jeffrey Lloyd Uecker explores this and other aspects of "utopian imagery" in "From *Promised Land* to *Promised Landfill*: The Iconography of Oregon's Twentieth-Century Utopian Myth" (M.A. Thesis, Portland State University, 1995).
2. Abigail Scott Duniway, *From the West to the West: Across the Plains to Oregon* (Chicago: A. C. McClurg & Co., 1905), 223.
3. Ibid., 226.
4. S. A. Clarke, *Pioneer Days of Oregon History. Volume I.* (Portland: J. K. Gill Company, 1905), 338.
5. Malcolm Clark, Jr., *Eden Seekers: The Settlement of Oregon, 1818-1862* (Boston: Houghton Mifflin,1981), 2.
6. Ibid., 3.
7. William G. Robbins, "Willamette Eden: The Ambiguous Legacy," *Oregon Historical Quarterly* 99 (Summer 1998): 190. Reprinted in Dale D. Goble and Paul W. Hirt, eds., *Northwest Lands, Northwest Peoples: Readings in Environmental History* (Seattle: Univeresity of Washington Press, 1999), 95-110.
8. Frederick Merk, *Albert Gallatin and the Oregon Problem: A Study in Anglo-American Diplomacy* (Cambridge: Harvard University Press, 1950), 15. The "journal" cited was the New York *Gazette* of March 16, 1822.
9. Clarke, *Pioneer Days of Oregon History*, 630.
10. William L. Lang, "An Eden of Expectations: Oregon Settlers and the Environment They Created," *Oregon Humanities* (Winter 1992): 26. This was one of several articles in a Special Oregon Trail issue on the theme 'Seeking Eden: The Challenge of Oregon'."
11. Julia Veazie Glen, "John Lyle and Lyle Farm," *The Quarterly of the Oregon Historical Society* 26 (June 1925): 143.
12. See, for example, the Oregon Land Company advertisement on the back cover of *The West Shore* (February 1889).
13. Robbins, "Willamette Eden," 190. Many of Robbins' works touch on the Eden-like elements in one manner or another. See, for instance, his *Hard Times in Paradise: Coos Bay, Oregon, 1850-1986* (Seattle: University of Washington Press, 1988), *Landscape of Promise: The Oregon Story, 1800-1940* (Seattle: University of Washington Press, 1997), and *Landscapes of Conflict: The Oregon Story, 1940-2000* (Seattle: University of Washington Press, 2004). William Cronon addresses this aspect of Robbins' work in the "Foreword" to *Landscape of Conflict*: "Still Searching for Eden at the End of the Oregon Trail" (p. xi-xvi). The Trail Band also used "The Land At Eden's Gate" as the

lead song in their 2000 release, *Voices from the Oregon Trail*. And a 2008 publication, *Looking Back: The Land at Eden's Gate,* uses this phrase for a historical photograph collection of pioneering communities in the upper Willamette Valley, including Aurora, Butteville, Canby, Champoeg, St. Paul, and Wilsonville.

14. Oregon Historical Society Web site: http://www.ohs.org/exhibitions/ Willamette%20Valley/ (accessed 10/27/03).

15. Lewis A. McArthur, *Oregon Geographic Names.* 7th Edition. Revised and enlarged by Lewis L. McArthur (Portland: Oregon Historical Society, 2003), 317-18.

16. Ibid., 317. The entry also states, "About the time of World War I, John Eden filed a coal-mining claim in the area. This may be just a curious coincidence."

17. Ibid. The Paradise post office was established in 1889 and remained in operation until 1942. Promise was settled in the early 1890s and initially was called Promised Land and Land of Promise. The post office served the area from 1896 to 1944. Joy was supposedly "named because of the joy settlers expressed about the possibility of mail service." (520) That joy was short-lived, however, as the post office existed only from 1888 to 1895. Arcadia in Wallowa County served as post office from 1887 to 1896; there also was an Arcadia in Malheur County, a few miles north of Nyssa, that served as post office from 1896 to 1898.

18. Ibid., 986. Sir Thomas More and his influential book, *Utopia,* will be discussed in the next chapter.

19. City of Enterprise. http//:www.enterpriseoregon.org/city/index.htm (accessed 5/27/2007).

20. Robert V. Hine's *California Utopianism: Contemplations of Eden* (San Francisco: Boyd & Fraser, 1981), for example, examines the broad nature of utopianism in California.

21. Lang, "An Eden of Expectations," 26.

22. Brent Walth, *Fire at Eden's Gate: Tom McCall and the Oregon Story* (Portland: Oregon Historical Society Press, 1994), 2. A multi-week series in the *Statesman Journal* of Salem in the mid-1990s reexamined the Edenic aspects of McCall's era in "Paradise Lost? Searching for Tom McCall's Oregon." The initial article by John Henrikson appeared under the banner headline, "A cloud over Eden."

23. Craig Wollner, *Electrifying Eden: Portland General Electric 1889-1965* (Portland: Oregon Historical Society, 1990). Patricia Brandt and Lillian A. Pereya, *Adapting in Eden: Oregon's Catholic Minority 1838-1986* (Portland: Oregon Historical Society, 2002).

24. Amy Jo Woodruff, "Cooking in Eden: Inventing Regional Cuisine in the Pacific Northwest," (M.A. thesis, Portland State University, 2000). Derek R. Larson, "Preserving Eden: The Culture on Conservation in Oregon, 1960-1980," (Ph.D. dissertation, Indiana University, 2001).

25. Cobie de Lespinasse, *Second Eden: A Romance* (Boston: Christopher Publishing House, 1951); Richard S. Wheeler, *The Fields of Eden* (New York: Forge/Tom Doherty Associates Book, 2001.

26. Robert V. Hine, *California's Utopian Colonies* (San Marino, CA: Huntington Library, 1953).

27. Charles Pierce LeWarne, *Utopias on Puget Sound 1885-1915* (Seattle: University of Washington Press, 1975).

28. Justine Brown, *All Possible Worlds: Utopian Experiments in British Columbia* (Vancouver: New Star Books, 1995); Andrew Scott, *Promise of Paradise: Utopian Communities in B. C.* (Vancouver: Whitecap Books, 1997).

29. I explore some aspects of the challenges of documenting these experiences in Oregon and the opportunities for further research in James J. Kopp, "Documenting Utopia: The Challenges of Tracking the Quest for Perfection," *Oregon Historical Quarterly* 105 (Summer 2004): 308-19.

## *Chapter 1*

1. This information is based on an informal exercise undertaken as part of my public presentation on Oregon's utopian heritage given over thirty times throughout Oregon from 2003 to 2006, most sponsored by the Oregon Council for the Humanities.
2. *The New Interpreter's Dictionary of the Bible*, Volume 2 (Nashville: Abingdon Press, 2007), 186. The entry for "Eden" also states rather simplistically, "The etymology of Eden has been the subject of considerable discussion." It also should be noted that Eden is mentioned elsewhere in the Old Testament: Isaiah 51:3; Ezekiel 31:9, 16, 18; 36:35; and Joel 2:3.
3. Translations noted here are from the New Revised Standard Edition (New York: American Bible Society, 1989).
4. Most sources attribute the name Adam to either the Hebrew for "man" or "ground," from which God formed him in Genesis 2:8.
5. See Jean Delumeau, *History of Paradise: The Garden of Eden in Myth and Tradition.* Translated by Matthew O'Connell (New York: Continuum, 1995).
6. Frank E. Manuel and Fritzie P. Manuel, *Utopian Thought in the Western World* (Cambridge, MA: Belknap Press of Harvard University Press, 1979), 43.
7. See Joseph E. Duncan, *Milton's Earthly Paradise: A Historical Study of Eden* (Minneapolis: University of Minnesota Press, 1972).
8. Ibid., 59, 81-84.
9. See, for instance, Diane Kelsey McColley, *A Gust for Paradise: Milton's Eden and the Visual Arts* (Urbana and Chicago: University of Illinois Press, 1993).
10. Although it is the Western concept of Eden that is core to this examination of Oregon's utopian heritage, it is important to note that there were comparable, if not exactly parallel, stories or myths of paradise in other cultures, including Sumerian, Babylonian, and Assyrian counterparts. Some of these, such as the story of Gilgamesh, predate the accepted time of the composition of Genesis. See Duncan, 10-11.
11. Joyce Oramel Hertzler, *The History of Utopian Thought* (New York: Macmillan, 1923), 7-8, 99-120. Hertzler includes Amos, Hosea, Isaiah, Jeremiah, and Ezekiel among those who left in writing a utopian tradition that previously had been an oral one.
12. Manuel and Manuel, *Utopian Thought in the Western World*, 64.
13. Ibid.
14. Lewis Mumford, *The Story of Utopias* (New York: Boni and Liveright, 1922), 59.
15. See Manuel and Manuel, *Utopian Thought in the Western World*, 46-48.
16. See Hertzler, *History of Utopian Thought*, 50-66. Several of these millennial groups are discussed later.
17. On backgrounds to utopian thought prior to Thomas More, including information on Cokayne and excerpts from Amerigo Vespucci's report of his first voyage, see Thomas More, *Utopia. A Revised Translation, Backgrounds, Criticism.* Second Edition. Translated and edited by Robert M. Adams (New York and London: W. W. Norton & Company, 1992), 87-107. Also see Introduction in Mark Holloway, *Heavens on Earth: Utopian Communities in America, 1680-1880* (New York; Liberty Publishers, 1951), 17-30. On

Cockayne (also spelled Cockaigne and Cockaygne), see Pamela Neville-Sington and David Sington, *Paradise Dreamed: How Utopian Thinkers Have Changed the Modern World* (London: Bloomsbury, 1993), 3-14.

18. The full title of More's book is *Libellus vere aureus nec minus salutaris quam festivus de optimo reip. statu, deq; nova insula Utopia.*

19. See Peter R. Allen, "*Utopia* and European Humanism: The Function of the Prefatory Letters and Verses," *Studies in the Renaissance* 10 (1963): 91-107. Also see "The Humanist Circles: Letters" in More, *Utopia. A Revised Translation*, 108-33.

20. Some scholars have suggested that *Utopia* was an attempt to describe actual civilizations in the Americas. See Arthur E. Morgan's *Nowhere Was Somewhere: How History Makes Utopias and How Utopias Make History* (Chapel Hill: University of North Carolina Press, 1946), in which Morgan suggests that *Utopia* may be based on the Inca empire. Lorainne Stobbart makes a similar argument that More may have been using the Mayan civilization as the model for *Utopia* in her *Utopia, Fact or Fiction? The Evidence from the Americas* (Stroud, Gloucestershire: Sutton Publishing Ltd., 1992).

21. See Jaspar Ridley, *Statesman and Saint: Cardinal Wolsey, Sir Thomas More, and the Politics of Henry VIII* (New York: Viking Press, 1982), 263-84. The first English translation was undertaken by Ralph Robynson, and it served as the basis for many later translations. The work had been translated into Italian in 1548 and French in 1550. See Reed Edwin Peggram, "The First French and English Translations of Sir Thomas More's 'Utopia'," *The Modern Language Review* 35 (July 1940): 330-40. For a bibliography of editions of *Utopia* to 1750, see R. W. Gibson and J. Max Patrick, comp., *St. Thomas More: A Preliminary Bibliography of His Works and Moreana to the Year 1750. With a Bibliography of Utopiana* (New Haven, CT: Yale University Press, 1961).

22. See, for example, Lyman Tower Sargent, *British and American Utopian Literature, 1516-1985: An Annotated, Chronological Bibliography* (New York & London: Garland Publishing, 1988).

23. Robert M. Adams, "Preface to the Second Edition" in Thomas More, *Utopia. A Revised Translation, Backgrounds, Criticism*, viii.

24. Ibid.

25. Alessandro Scafi. *Mapping Paradise: A History of Heaven on Earth* (Chicago: University of Chicago Press, 2006), 84.

26. Oscar Wilde, *The Soul of Man under Socialism* (Boston: John W. Luce and Company, 1910), [27]. Often left off in this quote from Wilde are the following two sentences that complete his thought: "And when Humanity lands there, it looks out, and, seeing a better country, sets sail. Progress is the realisation of Utopias."

27. Interestingly, Carol Weisbrod used the phrase *The Boundaries of Utopia* in her 1980 study on the legal perspective of several nineteenth-century American communal groups, suggesting that even in contractual areas the schemes of utopia can be cloudy. Her work "focuses on controversies between former members of the societies and the societies themselves, and treats in detail a number of lawsuits involving four of the most famous of the nineteenth-century American utopian communities: the Shakers, the Harmony Society, Oneida, and Zoar." Carol Weisbrod, *The Boundaries of Utopia* (New York: Pantheon Books, 1980), xi.

28. James H. Sweetland, "Federal Sources for the Study of Collective Communities," *Government Publications Review* 7A (1980): 129. I examine some of these issues in "Documenting Utopia in Oregon: The Challenges of Tracking the Quest for Perfection," *Oregon Historical Quarterly* 105 (2004): 308-19.

29. Mary Hennell, *An Outline of the Various Social Systems & Communities Which Have Been Founded on the Principle of Co-operation* (London: Brown, Green, and Longmans, 1844), 6.

30. The Oneida Community is examined in Chapter Two.

31. John Humphrey Noyes, *History of American Socialisms* (Philadelphia: J. B. Lippincott, 1870), iii. Noyes developed his study using the "collections of observations made by others" (iv), in particular those of A. J. Macdonald, who had visited the communities and taken copious notes. Macdonald died in 1854 before his work was published. *History of American Socialisms* does not include any communities in Oregon.

32. See John Humphrey Noyes, *History of American Socialisms*, With a New Introduction by Mark Holloway (New York: Dover, 1966) and John Humphrey Noyes, *Strange Cults and Utopias of 19th Century America*, With a New Introduction by Mark Holloway (New York: Dover, 1966). Mark Holloway's own study, *Heavens On Earth: Utopian Communities in America, 1680-1880* (New York: Library Publishers, 1951), is core in communal histories. It is interesting to note that Holloway's book also had a change in title in later printings when "Heavens on Earth" was dropped and the book was just titled *Utopian Communities in America 1680-1880*. Perhaps the religious overtones, like the socialist ones, were too restrictive for sales.

33. The full title is *The Communistic Societies of the United States From Personal Visit and Observation: Including Detailed Accounts of the Economists, Zoarites, Shakers, The Amana, Oneida, Bethel, Aurora, Icarian, and Other Existing Societies, Their Religious Creeds, Social Practices, Numbers, Industries, and Present Condition* (New York: Harper & Brothers, 1875).

34. Quoted in Henry T. Finck, *My Adventures in the Golden Age of Music* (New York and London: Funk & Wagnalls Company, 1926), 40. Ben Holladay, known as the "Stagecoach King," dominated the stagecoach and express business in the West in the mid-nineteenth century and later led the building of the Oregon and California Railroad. His mansions and other financial holdings were the antithesis of communism.

35. Franklin H. Littell, "Prefatory Essay" in Charles Nordhoff, *The Communistic Societies of the United States* (New York: Schocken Books, 1965), ix-x.

36. Ted Carlson, "How Communism Came to Oregon," *Eugene Register-Guard, Emerald Empire* (February 27, 1966).

37. Stewart H. Holbrook, "Aurora Communists," *American Mercury* 67 (July 1948): 54-59; John E. Simon, "William Keil and Communist Societies," *Oregon Historical Quarterly* 36 (1935): 119-38. Charles Carey notes in his *A General History of Oregon Prior to 1961*. Volume II (Portland: Metropolitan Press, 1935), 664, "The single communist experiment associated with the early growth of neighborhood settlements, in Oregon, is suggested by the name of Aurora." Robert J. Hendricks, whose *Bethel and Aurora: An Experiment in Communism As Practical Christianity with Some Account of Past and Present Ventures in Collective Living* (New York: Press of the Pioneers, 1933) is the standard work on the Aurora Colony, uses "communism: in his subtitle. The *Oregon Statesman* carried an article titled "Communism Was A Success at Aurora" (March 28, 1926) and Bethel was described as "A German Communistic Society in Missouri," William Godfrey Bek, *Missouri Historical Review* 3 (1908): 52-74, 99-125.

38. Eugene Edmund Snyder, *Aurora, Their Last Utopia: Oregon's Christian Commune, 1856-1883* (Portland, OR: Binford & Mort, 1993), 3.

39. Stewart H. Holbrook, *Far Corner: A Personal View of the Pacific Northwest* (New York: Macmillan, 1952), 61.

311

40. Littell, ix. Also see William A. Hinds, *American Communities* (Oneida, NY: American Socialist, 1878), 139.

41. See William Alfred Hinds, *American Communities: Brief Sketches of Economy, Zoar, Bethel, Aurora, Amana, Icaria, The Shakers, Oneida, Wallingford, and the Brotherhood of the New Life* (Oneida, NY: Office of the American Socialist, 1878), and his *American Communities. Revised Edition. Enlarged to Include Additional Societies, New and Old, Communistic, Semi-Communistic and Co-operative* (Chicago: Charles H. Kerr & Company, 1902), and *American Communities and Co-operative Colonies. Second Revision.* (Chicago: Charles H. Kerr & Company, 1908). Hinds will be discussed further in Chapter Six as his work relates to one of the attempts at a communal settlement in Oregon.

42. William Graham, *Socialism: New and Old* (New York: D. Appleton and Company, 1893), 2.

43. Ibid.

44. Ibid., 2-3.

45. Ibid., 3, 6.

46. Morris Hillquit, *Socialism In Theory and Practice* (New York: Macmillan and Company, 1909), 320.

47. Ibid., 321. This essay of Hillquit on "The History of Socialism" also appeared in William D. P. Bliss, ed., *The New Encyclopedia of Social Reform. New Edition* (New York and London: Funk & Wagnalls, 1908), 1137-47. Also see Howard H. Quint, *The Forging of American Socialism: Origins of the Modern Movement* (Columbia: University of South Carolina Press, 1953), 5-6. Quint states:"To establish a direct organizational relationship between the earlier utopian societies and the socialist political movement of the latter decades of the nineteenth century would be difficult if not impossible. Yet the two should not necessarily be sharply divided one from the other, since the utopian spirit and in particular its ethical ideals were to permeate American reform, labor, and radical movements for many years to come." (6)

48. See, for instance, Lawrence J. McCrank, "Religious Orders and Monastic Communalism in America," in Donald E. Pitzer, ed., *America's Communal Utopias* (Chapel Hill and London: University of North Carolina Press, 1997), 204-52.

49. Hillquit, *Socialism in Theory and Practice*, 12.

50. Alexander Kent, "Cooperative Communities in the United States," *Bulletin of the Department of Labor* 35 (July 1901): 563.

51. Robert Fogarty observes, "The problems of defining a communal settlement have perplexed writers so much that a standard may be difficult to arrive at." Robert S. Fogarty, "American Communes, 1865-1914," *Journal of American Studies* 9 (1975): 148n17. He explores this further in the Introduction to his *Dictionary of American Communal and Utopian History* (Westport, CT: Greenwood Press, 1980). Timothy Miller goes even further: "No generally accepted system of terms describing communalism exists. What to one author is 'communal' is to another perhaps 'cooperative' or 'collective'." Timothy Miller, *The Quest for Utopia in Twentieth-Century America. Volume I: 1900-1960* (Syracuse: Syracuse University Press, 1998), xxii.

52. Fogarty, "American Communes," 148-50.

53. Lisa Walker, "A Selected Bibliography of Sources on Communal Societies in Oregon and Washington Available at the Oregon Historical Society" ([Portland]: The Author, 1992), [2]. She goes on to note, "Such groups include the Russian Old Believers of the Woodburn area, the Basques of Eastern Oregon, and the Japanese of Takota City, a pre-World War II Japanese enclave near Salem."

54. Miller, *The Quest for Utopia in America*, xiv-xviii.
55. Ibid., xx-xxii. Also see Timothy Miller, *The 60s Communes: Hippies and Beyond* (Syracuse: Syracuse University Press, 1999), xxii-xxiv.

## Chapter 2

1. Louis B. Wright, *The Dream of Prosperity in Colonial America* (New York: New York University Press, 1965), 5. In this initial lecture, "American Cornucopia for All the World"—one of four delivered as part of the Anson G. Phelps Lectureship on Early American History at New York University— Wright continues: "In a letter describing this portion of his exploration, sent to their majesties King Ferdinand and Queen Isabella, Columbus elaborated his views of the site of Eden. He cited authorities from the past who discussed the problem—St. Isidore, the Venerable Bede, Strabo, St. Ambrose, and Duns Scotus—all of whom agreed that the earthly paradise lay in the East, where Columbus thought he was."
2. As Wright also suggests, "For nearly five hundred years Europeans have looked across the Atlantic and dreamed of an infinite variety of benefits that might accrue to them from the wealth of the new world." Ibid., 1.
3. For examinations of various aspects of the broad utopian heritage in the American experience, see Kenneth M. Roemer, ed., *America as Utopia* (New York: Burt Franklin & Company, 1981).
4. Wright examines several of these in the other lectures included in *The Dream of Prosperity in Colonial America*— "The Lure of Fish, Furs, Wine, and Silk," "Cures for All the Ills of Mankind," and "The Continuing Dream of an Economic Utopia." The literature on El Dorado is extensive. See, for example, the identically titled Walter Chapman, *The Golden Dream: Seekers of El Dorado* (Indianapolis: Bobbs-Merrill, 1967) and Robert Silverberg, *The Golden Dream: Seekers of El Dorado* (Athens: Ohio University Press, 1996). Also see Victor W. von Hagen, *The Golden Man: A Quest for El Dorado* (London: Book Club Associates, 1974). El Dorado also became linked with Oregon, as suggested by Thomas Bulfinch's 1866 book, *Oregon and Eldorado, or, Romance of the Rivers*. Bulfinch treats Oregon and Eldorado separately in this volume but it is interesting that he brings the two together.
5. Harold V. Rhodes, *Utopia in American Political Thought* (Tucson: University of Arizona Press, 1967), 17-18.
6. Ray Allen Billington, *The American Frontier* (Washington: Service Center for Teachers of History, 1958), 23, as quoted in Rhodes, *Utopia in American Political Thought*, 19.
7. Joel Nydahl, "From Millennium to Utopia Americana," in Roemer, ed., *America as Utopia*, 238.
8. Rhodes, *Utopia in American Political Thought*, 16.
9. Nydahl, "From Millennium to Utopia Americana," 241.
10. Ibid., 237.
11. Glenn Negley in his *Utopian Literature: A Bibliography with A Supplementary Listing of Works Influential in Utopian Thought* (Lawrence: Regents Press of Kansas, 1977) identifies twenty-two other utopian works published after 1516 through the sixteenth century. He lists sixty-two such works published in the seventeenth century.
12. E. Sparks, "Seeking Utopia in America" (Chapter XXX of The Expansion of the American People), *The Chautauquan* 31 (May 1900): 151.
13. V. F. Calverton, *Where Angels Dared to Tread* (Indianapolis and New York: Bobbs-Merrill Company, 1941), 15-16.
14. See Lyman Tower Sargent, *British and American Utopian Literature, 1516-1985: An Annotated, Chronological Bibliography* (New York & London:

Garland Publishing, 1988), 3-4. Also see Glenn Negley and J. Max Patrick, eds., *The Quest for Utopia: An Anthology of Imaginary Societies* (New York: Henry Schuman, 1952), 297-303, 313-47, 359-78, and Mary Ellen Snodgrass, *Encyclopedia of Utopian Literature* (Santa Barbara, CA: ABC-Clio, 1995), 113-19, 501-3.

15. H. F. Russell Smith, *Harrington and His Oceana: A Study of a 17th Century Utopia and Its Influence in America* (Cambridge: The University Press, 1914), 152. Harrington's "Oceana" should not be confused with George Orwell's "Oceania," the setting of his 1949 dystopian novel, *1984*.

16. Ibid., 195. Smith does point out that "We can hardly say that there was a cult of Harrington in New England, but his name was held in peculiar veneration" and he offers quotes from sermons and from the writings of John Quincy Adams to support his claims.

17. See Wilfried Nippel, "Ancient and Modern Republicanism: 'Mixed Constitution' and 'Ephors'," in Biancamaria Fontana, *The Invention of the Modern Republic* (Cambridge: Cambridge University Press, 1994), 6-26.

18. Pamela Neville-Sington and David Sington, *Paradise Dreamed: How Utopian Thinkers Have Changed the Modern World* (London: Bloomsbury, 1993), 193, 195. And they continue: "The Founding Fathers were not content simply to shake off the shackles of British rule. They were about the task of creating an ideal republic to be a model for all nations."

19. Mark Holloway, *Heavens on Earth: Utopian Communities in America, 1680-1880* (New York: Library Publishers, 1951).

20. Donald F. Durnbaugh, "Communitarian Societies in Colonial America," in Donald E. Pitzer, ed., *America's Communal Utopias* (Chapel Hill and London: University of North Carolina Press, 1997), 15-17; Foster Stockwell, *Encyclopedia of American Communes, 1663-1963* (Jefferson, NC, and London: McFarland & Company, 1998), 201-2. Also see James M. Morris and Andrea L. Kross, *Historical Dictionary of Utopianism* (Lanham, MD: Scarecrow Press, 2004), 243-44. Zwaanendael/Horekill is not always included in surveys of early American communal groups, most likely because of its short duration.

21. Calverton, *Where Angels Dared to Tread*, 18-42. Also see Durnbaugh, "Communitarian Societies in Colonial America," 17-19; Stockwell, *Encyclopedia of American Communes*, 34-35; Holloway, *Heavens on Earth*, 31-36.

22. Calverton, *Where Angels Dared to Tread*, 43-53. Also see Durnbaugh, "Communitarian Societies in Colonial America," 19-22; Stockwell, , *Encyclopedia of American Communes*, 111, 22-24; Holloway, *Heavens on Earth*, 36-43; Robert S. Fogarty, *Dictionary of American Communal and Utopian History* (Westport, CT, and London: Greenwood Press, 1980), 62-63. Stockwell and others use the name The Woman of the Wilderness.

23. On the Moravian Brethren, see Durnbaugh, "Communitarian Societies in Colonial America," 27-30.

24. Colonies spun off from Ephrata include Antietam, Bermudian Creek, and Snow Hill in Pennsylvania as well as settlements in Virginia and the Carolinas. Durnbaugh, "Communitarian Societies in Colonial America," 26-27. Also see Robert P. Sutton, *Communal Utopias and the American Experience: Religious Communities, 1732-2000* (Westport, CT and London: Praeger, 2003), 13. On the religious aspects of Ephrata, see Jeff Bach, *Voices of the Turtledoves: The Sacred World of Ephrata* (University Park: Pennsylvania State University Press, 2003).

25. Calverton, *Where Angels Dared to Tread*, 54-68; Durnbaugh, "Communitarian Societies in Colonial America," 22-27. Stockwell, *Encyclopedia of American*

*Communes*, 67-71; Holloway, *Heavens on Earth*, 43-52; Sutton, *Communal Utopias and the American Experience: Religious Communities*, 1-16.. Also see Julius Friedrich Sachse, *The German Sectarians of Pennsylvania, 1708-1800: A Critical and Legendary History of the Ephrata Cloister and the Dunkers* (Philadelphia: Printed for the Author, 1899-1900; reprint AMS Press, 1971) and Walter C. Klein, *Johann Conrad Beissel: Mystic and Martinet, 1690-1768* (Philadelphia: University of Pennsylvania Press, 1942).

26. See Richard Francis, *Ann the Word: The Story of Ann Lee, Female Messiah, Mother of the Shakers, The Woman Clothed With the Sun* (New York: Arcade, 2001) and Stephen J. Stein, *The Shaker Experience in America: A History of the United Society of Believers* (New Haven: Yale University Press, 1992). Also see Holloway, *Heavens on Earth*, 53-79, and Calverton, *Where Angels Dared to Tread*, 97-110.

27. On one aspect of this revival, see J. P. MacLean, *The Kentucky Revival and Its Influence on the Miami Valley* (Columbus, OH: s.n., 1903).

28. See, for example, Mary L. Richmond, comp., *Shaker Literature: A Bibliography*. In two volumes (Hancock, MA: Shaker Community, 1977).

29. One of the standard studies of Shaker music is Edward D. Andrews, *The Gift to be Simple: Songs, Dances, and Rituals of the American Shakers* (New York: J. J. Augustin, 1940, reprinted in 1962 by Dover Publications).

30. See Edward Deming Andrews and Faith Andrews, *Work and Worship: The Economic Order of the Shakers* (Greenwich, CT: New York Graphic Society, 1974), reprinted as *Work and Worship Among the Shakers: Their Craftsmanship and Economic Order* (New York: Dover Publications, 1984).

31. Rhodes, *Utopia in American Political Thought*, 20.

32. Sutton, *Communal Utopias and the American Experience*, 26-27.

33. Otohiko Okugama, "Appendix A: Annotated list of communal and utopian societies, 1787-1919," in Fogarty, *Dictionary of American Communal and Utopian History*, 175-76; Stockwell, *Encyclopedia of American Communes*, 64, 208.

34. Donald E. Pitzer, "The New Moral World of Robert Owen and New Harmony," in Pitzer, ed., *America's Communal Utopias*, 125n1.

35. Sutton, *Communal Utopias and the American Experience: Secular Communities*, 19. The literature on Robert Owen, New Harmony and the Owenites is vast. Two of the standard works are Arthur Bestor, Jr., *Backwoods Utopias: The Sectarian Origins and the Owenite Phase of Communitarian Socialism in America, 1663-1829* (Philadelphia: University of Pennsylvania Press, 1950) and John F. C. Harrison, *Quest for the New Moral World: Robert Owen and the Owenites in Britain and America* (New York: Scribner's, 1969). Also see Donald E. Pitzer, ed., *Robert Owen's American Legacy* (Indianapolis: Indiana Historical Society, 1972).

36. See, for instance, Calverton, *Where Angels Dared to Tread*, 127-67, and Dean L. May, "One Heart and Mind: Communal Life and Values Among the Mormons," in Pitzer, ed., *American Communal Utopias*, 135-58. Also see Leonard J. Arrington, Feramorz Y. Fox, and Dean L. May, *Building the City of God: Community and Cooperation among the Mormons* (Urbana: University of Illinois Press, 1992). Lawrence Foster includes the Mormons among the utopian societies he examines in *Religion and Sexuality: The Shakers, the Mormons, and the Oneida Community* (Urbana, University of Illinois Press, 1984) and *Women, Faith, and Utopia: Communal Experiments of the Shakers, the Oneida Community, and the Mormons* (Syracuse: Syracuse University Press, 1991). Not all studies of utopian communities include the Mormons, which again suggests the variance in definition and intent of such groups.

315

37. Although Equity lasted less than two years, Warren later established Utopia in Ohio in 1847 and, with Stephen Pearl Andrews, the Modern Times community on Long Island, New York, in 1851.Warren was one of many reformers to spend time at New Harmony. On Warren, see Bowman N. Hall, "The Economic Ideas of Josiah Warren," *History of Political Economy* 6 (1974): 95-108, Ann Caldwell Butler, "Josiah Warren and the Sovereignty of the Individual," *The Journal of Libertarian Studies* 4 (Fall 1980): 433-48, and James J. Kopp, "Josiah Warren" in Hester Lee Furey, ed., *American Radical and reform Writers* Second Series. *Dictionary of Literary Biography,* Vol. 345. (Detroit: Gale, 2009), 334-40.

38. See Carl J. Guarneri, "Brook Farm and the Fourierist Phalanxes: Immediatism, Gradualism, and American Utopian Socialism," in Pitzer, ed., *American Communal Utopias*, 159-80. Also see Carl J. Guarneri, *The Utopian Alternative: Fourierism in Nineteenth-Century America* (Ithaca, NY: Cornell University Press, 1991) and Edith Roelker Curtis, *A Season in Utopia: The Story of Brook Farm* (New York: Thomas Nelson & Sons, 1961).

39. Lawrence Foster, "Free Love and Community: John Humphrey Noyes and the Oneida Perfectionists," in Pitzer, ed., *American Communal Utopias*, 256.

40. Writings on the Oneida Community are abundant, including works by John Humphrey Noyes and several publications of the Community itself and reflections by former members as well as by some of Noyes' descendants. Some of the standard historical studies of Oneida include Maren Lockwood Carden, *Oneida: Utopian Community to Modern Corporation* (Baltimore: Johns Hopkins University, 1969); Robert David Thomas, *The Man Who Would Be Perfect: John Humphrey Noyes and the Utopian Impulse* (Philadelphia: University of Pennsylvania Press, 1977); and Spencer Klaw, *Without Sin: The Life and Death of the Oneida Community* (New York: Allen Lane, Penguin, 1993). The sexual and marriage aspects of Oneida have also been examined in a number of studies, often in comparison to the Shakers and Mormons. See, for example, Louis J. Kern, *An Ordered Love: Sex Roles and Sexuality in Victorian Utopias—the Shakers, the Mormons, and the Oneida Community* (Chapel Hill: University of North Carolina Press, 1981); Lawrence Foster, *Religion and Sexuality: The Shakers, the Mormons, and the Oneida Community* (earlier published as *Religion and Sexuality: Three American Communal Experiments of the Nineteenth Century* (1981)); and Robert S. Fogarty, ed., *Special Love/ Special Sex: An Oneida Community Diary* (Syracuse: Syracuse University Press, 1994).

41. Karl J. R. Arndt, "George Rapp's Harmony Society," in Pitzer, *America's Communal Utopias*, 57. Arndt was the leading scholar on George Rapp and the American communal settlements he led. Robert Sutton lists Arndt's ten monographs and other works in *Communal Utopias and the American Experience, Religious Communities, 1732-2000*, 60n1. Particularly noteworthy are Arndt's efforts in compiling and editing documents of the Harmony Society, including the two-volume *A Documentary History of the Indiana Decade of the Harmony Society, 1814-1824* (Indianapolis: Indiana Historical Society, 1975).

42. Arndt, "George Rapp's Harmony Society," 59-61; Sutton, *Communal Utopias and the American Experience, Religious Communities*, 37-38.

43. Arndt, "George Rapp's Harmony Society," 62-63.

44. In addition to the works of Karl J. R. Arndt, other important sources include John Archibold Bole, *The Harmony Society: A Chapter in German American Culture History* (Philadelphia: Americana Germanica, 1904), Christiana F. Knoedler, *The Harmony Society: A 19th Century American Utopia* (New York: Vantage Press, 1954), and Donald Pitzer and Josephine

Elliott, "New Harmony's First Utopians, 1814-1824," *Indiana Magazine of History* 75 (September 1979): 225-300. The Harmonists are also included in the nineteenth-century studies of John Humphrey Noyes, Charles Nordoff, and William Hinds, as well as in Calverton's *Where Angels Dared to Tread*, Holloway's *Heavens on Earth*, and other surveys of American communal history.

45. On the role of music in the Harmony Society, see Richard D. Wetzel, *Frontier Musicians on the Connoquesnessing, Wabash, and Ohio: A History of the Music and Musicians of George Rapp's Harmony Society, 1805-1906* (Athens: Ohio University Press, 1976).

## Chapter 3

1. A. T. Hawley, "A Picturesque Tour," *The West Shore* 6 (June 1888): 319. Aurora was not yet incorporated as a town, which would occur in 1893.

2. Charles Nordhoff, *The Communistic Societies of the United States; From Personal Visit and Observation: Including Detailed Accounts of the Economists, Zoarites, Shakers, The Amana, Oneida, Bethel, Aurora, Icarian, and Other Existing Societies, Their Religious Creeds, Social Practices, Numbers, Industries, and Present Condition* (New York: Harper & Brothers, 1875), 305.

3. John E. Simon, "Wilhelm Keil: Founder of Aurora," (M.A. thesis, University of Oregon, 1935), [1]. Also see John E. Simon, "Wilhelm Keil and Communist Colonies," *Oregon Historical Quarterly* 36 (June 1935): 119-53.

4. My own personal experience, based largely on living in Aurora, is that many individuals even in Portland or Salem are not aware of Aurora, except perhaps for a sign on the interstate between those two cities. That Aurora has not achieved a greater identity is curious also as the Aurora Colony Historical Society has been in existence since 1963 and the museum complex established a few years later draws tourists to the town, as do the numerous antique stores.

5. See Victor Peters, "The German Pietists: Spiritual Mentors of the German Communal Settlements in America," *Communal Societies* 1 (Autumn 1981): 55-66.

6. Among many discrepancies related to the life of Keil are his birth date and place. Possibly the earliest recorded information on Keil's birth is presented in Carl Koch's *Lebenserfahrungen von Carl G. Koch, Prediger des Evangeliums* (Cleveland: Verlagshaus der Evangelischen Gemeinschaft, 1871). Koch writes that Keil was born March 6, 1811, at Erfurt, Prussia. Several others use this date, including Nordhoff, although he provides only the year. John Simon in his "Wilhelm Keil and Communist Colonies" also uses the 1811 date but he notes that "Nordhausen is also given as his birthplace," apparently following the information included in William Hinds' report (119). William G. Bek, often considered one of the more reliable sources, agrees with the date of birth and places it at Bleicherode, which is in the district of Erfurt, but in a footnote offers that "The statement of Hinde [sic], in his 'American Communities,' p. 287, in which he states that Keil was born in Nordhausen, Germany, is according to the best sources, fallacious." William G. Bek, "The Community at Bethel, Missouri, and its Offspring at Aurora, Oregon," *The German American Annals*, n. s. 7 (1909). However, a remembrance of Keil printed in the January 5, 1878, *Oregonian*, a week after his death, states he "was born at Bleicherode, in the kingdom of Prussia, on the 6th day of March, A.D. 1812." "The Late Dr. Keil," *The Oregonian* (January 5, 1878): 1. Robert Hendricks uses this date in his *Bethel and Aurora* (1933), as do others, including Patrick Harris and Eugene Snyder. See Patrick Harris, "William Keil and the Aurora Colony: A Communal

Society Crosses the Oregon Trail" in Carl Guarnieri and David Alvarez, eds., *Religion and Society in the American West: Historical Essays* (Lanham, MD: University Press of America, 1987): 425-47, and Eugene Snyder, *Aurora, Their Last Utopia: Oregon's Christian Commune, 1856-1883* (Portland: Binford & Mort Publishing, 1993), 7. I have used the 1812 date here.

7. Like his birth date, the year in which Keil arrived in the United States is a point of contention, ranging from 1831 to 1836. Charles Nordhoff does not mention a date of arrival but Koch provides the date as 1831. The remembrance in the January 5, 1878, *Oregonian* states Keil emigrated to the U.S. "in the spring of 1836." William Bek, who uses Koch as one of his primary sources, states: "The exact date of Keil's coming to America is not positively fixed. It is very probable, however, that it was in 1835 or 1836." Bek does not provide a source for this, but others followed his lead, including John Simon in the 1930s, while Robert Hendricks does not address the issue in his *Bethel and Aurora*. In a letter from A. Roebling to Clark Moor Will of May 18, 1924, Roebling notes that he has the diary of his father, John A. Roebling, and included are the names of several passengers who sailed from Bremen for Baltimore in May 1831 aboard the "August Edward, a small American built Bark." Among the names were "Dr. Keil, Wm., and his wife from Würtzburg, Bavaria," according to Roebling. However, the versions of the diary published present conflicting information, as the English translation published in 1931 states it was "Dr. Kling from Wuertzburg" who was on the ship. Johan August Roebling, *Diary of My Journal from Muehlhausen in Thuringia via Bremen to the United States of North America In the Year 1931*. Translated with occasional notes, from the original German, by Edward Underwood. With a Foreword by Hamilton Schuyler (Trenton, NJ: Privately Printed by the Roebling Press, 1931), 10, 93. A German edition of the diary published in 2006, *Tagebuch meiner Reise von Mühlhausen in Thüringen über Bremen nach den Vereinigten Staaten im Jahre 1831*, however, only specifies "Dr. K.," thus adding to the mystery. In the entry for Keil in the *Dictionary of American Communal and Utopian History* (1980), Robert S. Fogarty states, "Keil arrived in the United States in 1831 on the same ship as John A. Roebling, the builder of the Brooklyn Bridge," but the source of this statement is unclear.

8. William G. Bek, "The Community of Bethel, Missouri, and Its Offspring at Aurora, Oregon," *German American Annals* n.s. 7:5 (September/October 1909): 260-63. Also see: David Nelson Duke, "A Profile of Religion in the Bethel-Aurora Colonies," *Oregon Historical Society* 92 (Winter 1992): 346-59; David Nelson Duke, "The Evolution of Religion in William Keil's Community: A New Reading of Old Testament," *Communal Societies* 13 (1993): 84-98; and Adolf E. Schroeder and David N. Duke, *Bethel German Colony, 1844-1879: Religious Beliefs and Practices* (Bethel, MO: Historical Bethel German Colony, 1990).

9. On Boehme (1575-1624) and his influences, see Andrew Weeks, *Boehme: An Intellectual Biography of the Seventeenth-Century Philosophy and Mystic* (Albany: State University of New York, 1991). It is curious to note that one of Boehme's earliest writings was titled *Aurora*.

10. Bek, "The Community of Bethel, Missouri, and Its Offspring at Aurora, Oregon," 260. Bek's full assessment of Keil is "a man with broad and high forehead, rather thick nose and a square chin—in other words, the type of a strong animal with indomitable will and bull-dog tenacity."

11. Regarding the debate over this connection, Stanton wrote, "Much misinformation has been perpetuated by loose statements and counter-statements regarding a connection between William Keil's followers and the

Harmony Society of George Rapp." Coralie Cassell Stanton, "The Aurora Colony, Oregon" (M.A. thesis, Oregon State University, 1963), 8.

12. Eileen Acker, *1833 Residents of Phillipsburg (Now Monaca), Pennsylvania: An Historic Register, Transcribed from German Script and Supplemented With Notes: With a Directory of the New Philadelphia Society, Dating From Its Inception on March 21, 1832* (Eight Four, PA: Skeeter Hill Press, 2004).

13. Stanton, "The Aurora Colony, Oregon," 7.

14. John Friesen and Virginia Friesen include Bethel and Aurora in their chapter on "The Harmonists" and refer to Bethel as a "model Harmony-like settlement minus the celibacy principle." This most likely is an overstatement on the Harmonist influence on Keil. John W. Friesen and Virginia Lyons Friesen, *The Palgrave Companion to North American Utopias* (New York: Palgrave Macmillan, 2004): 162. Probably more accurate is the inclusion of Bethel and Aurora under the heading of "Separatist Colonies," such as that in Robert P. Sutton's *Communal Utopias and the American Experience: Religious Communities, 1732-2000* (Westport, CT and London: Praeger, 2003), 46-48.

15. Robert J. Hendricks, *Bethel and Aurora: An Experiment in Communism As Practical Christianity With Some Account of Past and Present Ventures in Collective Living* (New York: Press of the Pioneers, 1933), 12. Hendricks notes that besides individuals from Pennsylvania others came from Ohio, Iowa, Missouri, and Germany. He also states, "There was at least one Jewish family." Also see Bek, "The Community at Bethel, Missouri, and Its Offspring at Aurora, Oregon" (September/October 1909): 270-71, and Snyder, *Aurora, Their Last Utopia*, 33.

16. Bek, "The Community at Bethel, Missouri, and Its Offspring at Aurora, Oregon," (November/December 1909): 306.

17. Ibid., 306-10; Snyder, *Aurora, Their Last Utopia*, 41-45; Stanton, "The Aurora Colony," 11-12. Keil and his family lived in a residence called "Elim," which sometimes is noted as a satellite community to Bethel.

18. On the importance of music at Bethel, see David N. Duke, Adolf E. Schroeder, and Julie Youmans, *The Musical Life of Bethel Germany Colony, 1844-1879* (Bethel, MO: Historical Bethel German Colony, 1990).

19. Harris, "William Keil and the Aurora Colony," 428.

20. The Donation Land Claim Act of 1850 was influenced by the efforts of the Oregon Territorial delegate, Samuel R. Thurston, and addressed the increased demand for land in the Pacific Northwest.

21. Harris, "William Keil and the Aurora Colony," 435-36. Details of the journey from Missouri to Washington Territory are not presented here but among the documentation available are letters Keil wrote to colonists back in Bethel. Bek includes many of these in his "The Community at Bethel, Missouri, and Its Offspring at Aurora, Oregon," and they are also included in William G. Bek, "From Bethel, Missouri to Aurora, Oregon: Letters of William Keil, 1855-1870," *Missouri Historical Review* 48 (1953): 23-41 and 48 (1954): 141-53. Accounts of Willie's death and burial are many, with several in *The Sou'Wester*, the publication of the Pacific County (Washington) Historical Society. An index to *The Sou'Wester* is available at http://www.pacificcohistory.org/sw_index.htm

22. "The Late Dr. Keil," *The Oregonian*, January 5, 1878.

23. Snyder, *Aurora, Their Last Utopia*, 73.

24. One of those Keil sent to Bethel to assist in overseeing the community was his son, August, but he was ill prepared to manage the business side of things, let alone his own life—he was too fond of the alcohol produced by the colony. He died of exposure in a barn at Bethel supposedly after consuming too much alcohol.

25. Bek, "The Community at Bethel, Missouri, and Its Offspring at Aurora, Oregon," n.s. 8:1 (January/February 1910): 26-44. Bethel did not have a comparable "constitution" but it did have some documents describing the nature of the community. The lack of formal agreements between the two colonies would come into play in their eventual dissolution.
26. Hendricks, *Bethel and Aurora*, 226-27.
27. See, for example, Philip Dole, "Aurora Colony Architecture: Building in a Nineteenth-Century Cooperative Society," *Oregon Historical Quarterly* 92 (Winter 1992): 337-416; Deborah M. Olson and Clark M. Will, "Musical Heritage of the Aurora Colony," *Oregon Historical Quarterly* 79 (Fall 1978): 233-67; and Betty Keeler, "The Cultural Landscape of Aurora, A German Communal Society Settlement, 1856-1881" (Paper prepared for Geog 493, Oregon State University, June 21, 1974. Clark Moor Will Papers, University of Oregon Special Collections). The Appendix includes an extensive list of resources on Aurora.
28. On the role of quilts and crafts in the Aurora Colony, see Jane Kirkpatrick, *Aurora: An American Experience in Quilt, Community and Craft* (Colorado Springs, CO: Waterbrook Multnomah Publishing Group, a Division of Random House, 2008).
29. Duke, "The Evolution of Religion in Wilhelm Keil's Community," 85, 86.
30. [H. S. Lyman], "The Aurora Community," *The Quarterly of the Oregon Historical Society* 2 (March 1901): 79. In an effort to attest to the validity and merit of Lyman's work, which overall is a useful study, there is a note appended at the end of the article from one of William Keil's sons:
    Aurora, Oregon
    March 16, 1901
    To Prof. F. G. Young, University of Oregon:
    Having examined the manuscript prepared by Mr. H. S. Lyman, in regard to the Aurora Colony, founded by my father, Dr. William Keil, I find it correct, so far as my information extends.
    EMANUEL KEIL
    Even here, Emanuel Keil provides the caveat "as far as my information extends," suggesting that he was cautious about claiming to know all there was about his father.
31. Simon, "Wilhelm Keil and Communist Colonies," 146n58.
32. Bek, "The Community at Bethel, Missouri, and Its Offspring at Aurora, Oregon," (September-October 1909): 259.
33. Mark Holloway, "Introduction to the Dover Edition" in Charles Nordhoff, *The Communistic Societies of the United States From Personal Visit and Observation* (New York: Dover Publications, 1966), ix.
34. Elizabeth Sill, trans., "A Visit to the King of Aurora (from the German of Theodore Kirschoff [sic])," *Lippincott's Magazine of Popular Literature and Science* 11 (January 1873): 80-86. Also see Frederic Trautmann, ed., *Oregon East, Oregon West: Travels and Memoirs by Theodor Kirchhoff, 1863-1872* (Portland, OR: Oregon Historical Society Press, 1987), 179n12.
35. Trautmann, *Oregon East, Oregon West*, 177n1.
36. Ibid., 124, 125.
37. Ibid., 125
38. Ibid., 179n12.
39. Harris, "William Keil and the Aurora Colony," 425-26.
40. On the Bethel Constitution, see Hendricks, *Bethel and Aurora*, 16-17, and Stanton, "The Aurora Colony, Oregon," 68-69. The Aurora Constitution and Articles of Agreement are presented in Stanton, 64-67.

41. Nordhoff, *Communistic Societies in the United States*, 320, 321.
42. Stanton, "The Aurora Colony, Oregon," [i].
43. Cobie de Lespinasse, *Second Eden: A Romance* (Boston: Christopher Publishing House, 1951). Jane Kirkpatrick, *A Clearing in the Wild* (2006), *A Tendering in the Storm* (2007), and *A Mending at the Edge* (2008) (Colorado Springs: WaterBrook Multnomah Publishing Group).

## *Chapter 4*

1. Otohiko Okugawa lists sixty communities established in the United States in the 1840s, dropping to twenty-two in the 1850s, and twelve in the 1860s. There is an increase in the 1870s, with twenty-five communities, then a slight drop in the 1880s (twenty-three) before an upswing again in the 1890s to thirty-five. In the "Annotated list of communal and utopian societies, 1787-1919" included in Robert S. Fogarty's *Dictionary of American Communal and Utopian History* (Westport, CT: Greenwood Press, 1980), 173-233. Many of the late-twentieth-century compilations rely on the same historical sources, but since definitions of communities can vary substantially and dates of establishment are difficult to pinpoint accurately, there are often variations in the number of communal groups in a given time frame. In his tabulation of "American Communes 1663-1984," Yaacov Oved lists the same number for the 1840s (sixty) as Okugawa and just small variances for the following decades: twenty-six (1850s), thirteen (1860s), twenty-two (1870s), twenty-one (1880s), and thirty-one (1890s). Yaacov Oved, *Two Hundred Years of American Communes* (New Brunswick and Oxford: Transaction Books, 1988), 493. Foster Stockwell in his *Encyclopedia of American Communes, 1663-1963* (Jefferson, NC: MacFarland & Company, 1998) has comparable numbers for the 1840s (sixty-seven), 1850s (twenty-four), and 1860s (fifteen), but substantially more groups in the 1870s (sixty-four) as well as larger figures for the 1880s (thirty-four) and 1890s (forty-six). Here, as with all such compilations, this likely represents only a portion of such communities undertaken or planned.
2. Abraham Menes, "The Am Oylom Movement," *Yivo Annual of Jewish Social Science* 4 (1949): 9-11. Also see Nora Levin, *While Messiah Tarried: Jewish Socialist Movements, 1871-1917* (New York: Schocken Books, 1977), 47-49; Helen E. Blumenthal, "New Odessa, 1882-1887: United We Stand – Divided We Fall" (M.A. thesis, Portland State University, 1975), 12-27; and George B. Adbdill, "New Odessa: Douglas County's Russian Communal Colony," *The Umpqua Trapper* 1 (Winter 1965): 10. The name of the movement appears in several ways – Am Olam, Am Oylom, and Am Olem. The most common use is Am Olam, which is used here.
3. Menes, "The Am Oylom Movement," 11.
4. See "Agriculture Colonies in the United States," in Isidore Singer, ed., *The Jewish Encyclopedia* (New York: Funk and Wagnalls, 1901): 258-62. Also see Leo Shpall, "Jewish Agricultural Colonies in the United States," *Agricultural History* 24 (July 1950): 120-46; Elbert Sapinsley, "Jewish Agricultural Colonies in the West: The Kansas Example," *Western States Jewish Historical Quarterly* 3 (April 1971): 157-69; Uri D. Herscher, *Jewish Agricultural Utopias in America, 1880-1910* (Detroit: Wayne State University Press, 1981) and George M. Price "The Russian Jews in America," *Publications of the American Jewish Historical Society* 48 (September 1958): 28-62, also published in Abraham J. Karp, *The Jewish Experience in America: Selected Studies from the Publications of the American Jewish Historical Society*. IV (New York: KTAV Publishing, 1969): 300-355.

5. Heilprin (1823-1888) is noted for his study of *The Historical Poetry of the Ancient Hebrews*, as associate editor of the second edition of the *American Cyclopœdia*, and as a frequent contributor to the *Nation*. See Gustav Pollak, *Michael Heilprin and His Sons: A Biography* (New York: Dodd, Mead and Company, 1912).

6. Blumenthal, "The New Odessa Colony of Oregon," 322-23. Villard was involved in various activities related to promoting settlement. See James Blaine Hedges, *Henry Villard and the Railways of the Northwest* (New York: Russell & Russell, 1930), 112-32.

7. Blumenthal, "The New Odessa Colony of Oregon," 323.

8. See Avraham Yarmolinsky, *A Russian's American Dream: A Memoir on William Frey* (Lawrence: University of Kansas Press, 1965).

9. Ibid., 3-9. Also see Robert Fogarty, *Dictionary of American Communal and Utopian History*, 37-8.

10. See Lloyd David Harris, "Sod Jerusalems: Jewish Agricultural Communities in Frontier Kansas" (M.A. thesis, University of Oklahoma, 1984).

11. Edward Spencer Beesly, *The Life and Death of William Frey, An Address Delivered at Newton Hall, Sunday, November 11th, 1888* (London: Reeves and Turner, 1888), 4.

12. Yarmolinsky, *A Russian's American Dream*, 16-22.

13. Ibid., 23-60.

14. Ibid., 70-81.

15. Ibid., 82-97.

16. Pollak, *Michael Heilprin and His Sons*, 205-7. Also see Shpall, "Jewish Agricultural Colonies in the United States," 127-29.

17. Pollak, *Michael Heilprin and His Sons*, 213.

18. Menes quotes a correspondent who would later go to Oregon as saying there were twenty-one men and five women in this first group. He does not name the correspondent but the letter goes on to state, "The other members have taken jobs in New York, Boston, and St, Louis, whence I write. In the spring we, too, shall leave for Oregon." Menes, "The Am Oylom Movement," 29. Some members of the Am Olamites who wished to settle in Oregon were sent to other colonies. See, for example, Marian Seldes, "Tell Me, Grandfather," *New York Times* (August 18, 1885): NJ1, who recounts her grandfather's experience in the Alliance community in New Jersey although he (Sergius Seldes) had hoped to go to Oregon.

19. *The Douglas Independent* (September 9, 1882). Also see Blumenthal, "The New Odessa Colony of Oregon," 323-24. The reason for the discrepancy in the number of colonists is unclear.

20. There were several towns named Odessa in the United States, including New Odessa, which Albert Parry explores in "Russian Names for American Towns," *Russian Review* 3 (Spring 1944): 30-43. He briefly mentions New Odessa, Oregon, on page 40 and states erroneously, as many others did, that New Odessa was "near Portland."

21. See Gabriel Davison, *Our Jewish Farmers and The Story of the Jewish Agricultural Society* (New York: L. B. Fischer, 1943), 230.

22. Yarmolinsky, *A Russian's American Dream*, 100.

23. George B. Abdill, "New Odessa: Douglas County's Russian Communal Colony [Part I]," *The Umpqua Trapper*, 12. Abdill also states, "It is interesting to note that the real estate transfers were notarized by Sol Abraham, long a prominent pioneer Jewish merchant in Douglas County. Samuel and Asher Marks were also of Jewish ancestry, coming to the West Coast from Poland in 1852-1853." He adds, "In a document recorded in October 1884, Simon Krimont transferred

the title to Peter Fireman, Moses Free, and Abraham Heardman, Trustees of the New Odessa Community, a corporation." Steven Lowenstein also notes that Solomon Abraham was a right-of-way agent for the Oregon and California Railroad and he founded Glendale, near the colony site, in early 1883, first naming it Julia after his wife. See Steven Lowenstein, *The Jews of Oregon, 1850-1950* (Portland: Jewish Historical Society of Oregon, 1987), 90. Also see Lewis A. McArthur, *Oregon Geographic Names*. 7th Edition. Revised and enlarged by Lewis L. McArthur (Portland: Oregon Historical Society, 2003), 406, where it is noted that the named was changed to Glendale in August 1883.

24. Quoted in Menes, "The Am Oylom Movement," 29-30. Menes does not provide the name of the correspondent for this or the subsequent letter.

25. Ibid, 30-31.

26. Ibid., 30. Also see Price, "The Russian Jews in America," 313.

27. Quoted in Menes, "The Am Oylom Movement," 31.

28. Shpall, "Jewish Agricultural Colonies in the United States," 135.

29. Gabriel Davidson and Edward A. Goodwin, "A Unique Agricultural Colony," *The Reflex* 2 (May 1928): 85.

30. The *New York Times* includes this brief report in its May 8, 1884 edition: A large number of the Russian Hebrews of this city met at No. 264 Broadway Tuesday evening, to tender a reception to Mr. Paul Caplan [sic], the representative in this city of the Russian colony at New-Odessa, Douglass [sic] County, Oregon, who is about to return to that place. An address in the Russian language, eulogistic of Mr. Caplan's services in behalf of the colony, was made, and that gentleman responded in the same language. Other addresses were delivered in English and Russian by Edward Kind and others. The meeting resolved to encourage further emigration from Russia to this country, and to plant new colonies in Kansas and Dakota. An address signed by those present was tendered to Michael Heilpren, of this city, thanking him for assistance rendered to the Russian immigrants in this country. "Russian Colonies to be Founded," *New York Times* (May 8, 1884): 8.

31. Menes, "The Am Oylom Movement," 31.

32. His report on the colony appeared in the October 3, 1884 issue of the *American Israelite*. Quoted in Shpall, "Jewish Agricultural Colonies in the United States," 135.

33. Menes, "The Am Oylom Movement," 33.

34. Henry L. Feingold, *Zion in America: The Jewish Experience from Colonial Times to the Present* (Mineola, NY: Dover, 2002), 156.

35. Abraham Cahan, *The Education of Abraham Cahan*. Translated by Leon Stein, Abraham P. Conan, and Lynn Davison from the Yiddish autobiography, *Bleter Fun Mein Leben* by A. Cahan, Volumes I and II (Philadelphia: Jewish Publication Society of America, 1969), 339, 340, 341.

36. Robert Rosenbluth to Thomas Vaughan [1963], Oregon Historical Society Research Library Manuscripts. Rosenbluth also offers this general assessment of communal life: "I have visited many other communes in this country and I think that the lesson to be learned from all of them is that they do not fit the facts of life, but I suppose this has to be proved over and over again." 323

37. "The Many Lives of Robert Rosenbluth: Excerpts from His Autobiography," *Forest History* 8 (1964): 17.

38. Philip Cowen, *Memories of An American Jew* (New York: International Press, 1932): 99.

39. "Wedding Among the Communistic Jews in Oregon." *Overland Monthly* 36 (second series) (December 1885): 608. The reference to "Graham" is for Sylvester Graham (1794-1851), a health reformer and strong advocate of

vegetarianism. The "hard baked biscuits of unbolted flour" were known as Graham Bread and the Graham Cracker is also a legacy.

40. Yarmolinsky, *A Russian's American Dream*, 104.
41. Abraham Cahan offers this assessment of Frey's efforts on positivism: "Few of the colonists actually subscribed to positivism. One of them was the brother of the famous Jewish actress Sarah Adler. But the others had no heart to refuse Frey. He was so friendly, so tolerant, so saintly, so respected, so well-educated, so much older than most of the members. Besides, he was a gentile and an aristocrat. While his influence surpassed Kaplan's, his positivism grew more burdensome. Between that and Kaplan's bitter smiles, peace diminished." *The Education of Abraham Caplan*, 342.
42. Yarmolisky, *A Russian's American Dream*, 106. Yarmolinsky also notes that following their departure from New Odessa William and Mary achieved a relationship that they had lacked up to that time.
43. Blumenthal, "United We Stand—Divided We Fall," 71.
44. Davidson and Goodwin, "A Unique Agricultural Colony," 85.
45. Blumenthal, "United We Stand—Divided We Fall," 73. Blumenthal also notes, "It was not until December 31, 1945, by action of the Corporation Commission of the State of Oregon that the community of New Odessa was officially dissolved."
46. Shpall, "Jewish Agricultural Colonies in the United States," 135.
47. Davidson, *Our Jewish Farmers*, 233.
48. Alexander Kent, "Cooperative Communities in the United States," *Bulletin of the Department of Labor* 35 (July 1901): 642. Also see James J. Kopp, "To the Editor [letter]," *Oregon Historical Quarterly* 104 (Winter 2003): 616-17.
49. See, for example, Frederick A. Bushee, "Communistic Societies in the United States," *Political Science Quarterly* (December 1905): 646. Also see Ralph Albertson, "A Survey of Mutualistic Communities in America," *Iowa Journal of History and Politics* 34 (1936): 419; Oved, *Two Hundred Years of American Communes*, 489; Timothy Miller, *American Communes 1860-1960: A Bibliography* (New York & London: Garland Publishing, 1990): 421; Stockwell, *Encyclopedia of American Communes, 1663-1963*, 143. The Columbia Co-operative Colony is listed in the compilation by Otohiko Okugawa in Fogarty's *Dictionary of American Communal and Utopian History* (214) where it is noted that it was later renamed Nehalem Valley Co-operative Colony. This entry suggests that a constitution for the colony was available, which I have not been able to track down.
50. My very special thanks to Stacy Kozakavich for bringing these documents to my attention. See her "The Center of Civilization: Archaeology and History of the Kaweah Co-operative Commonwealth" (Ph.D. dissertation, University of California, Berkeley, 2007).
51. On Kaweah, see Jay O'Connell, *Co-Operative Dreams: A History of the Kaweah Colony* (Van Nuys, CA: Raven River Press, 1999). Also see Robert V. Hine, *California Utopian Colonies* (San Merino, CA: The Huntington Library, 1953), 78-100.
52. H. E. Girard, "NEHALEM. A New Co-operative Colony in Oregon [letter]." *Kaweah Commonwealth* 1(8) (March 1890): 1.
53. Ibid.
54. Ibid.
55. Ibid.
56. Ibid.
57. Ibid.

58. On Bellamy's influence in Oregon, see James J. Kopp, "Looking Backward at Edward Bellamy's Influence in Oregon, 1888-1936," *Oregon Historical Quarterly* 104 (Spring 2003): 62-95.

59. See, for example, *The Weekly Nationalist* 1 (May 17, 1890). In an interesting side note, an ad for the Kaweah Colony appeared in the December 1888 issue of *World Advance Thought*, a spiritualist publication published at that time in Portland.

60. As Jay O'Connell notes in his study of the California community, "It wasn't long before Haskell was claiming that the Kaweah Colony was Bellamy's model realized." O'Donnell, *Co-operative Dreams*, 89. And Robert Hine in his study of *California Utopian Colonies* notes, "The Bellamy movement directed a steady stream of members to Kaweah, even from as far away as England." Hine, *California Utopian Colonies*, 85.

61. *The Weekly Nationalist* 1 (May 17, 1890).

62. *The Nationalist* 3 (1) (August 1890) and *The Nationalist* 3 (2) (September 1890). Also see Kopp, "Looking Backward at Edward Bellamy's Influence in Oregon, 1888-1936," 80.

63. Egbert S. Oliver, *Homes in the Oregon Forest: Settling Columbia County 1870-1920* (Brownsville, OR: Calapooia Publications, 1983), 85.

64. H. E. Girard, "From Nehalem Colony [letter]." *The Kaweah Commonwealth* 1 (33) (August 30, 1890): 3.

65. Ibid.

66. Ibid.

67. *Oregon Mist* (September 4, 1891), under "Clatskanie News."

68. *Oregon Mist* (September 25, 1891).

69. On the Burley Colony, see Charles Pierce LeWarne, *Utopias on Puget Sound, 1885-1915* (Seattle: University of Washington Press, 1975), 129-67.

70. A. J. Gaylord, "Duties of Members," *The Co-operator* III (3) (December 29, 1900): 1. My thanks to Charles LeWarne for bringing this to my attention.

71. Ibid.

72. In support of his argument, Gaylord invokes Edward Bellamy into the discussion:

> I have no doubt that most of the members of the Brotherhood have read *Looking Backward*, and it is altogether likely that it was the idea of soon being able to realize the benefits and pleasures of such a condition as Bellamy portrays that induced many to join the Brotherhood. I think, however, it would be well to suggest that the members read the book again, and as they read count the names that are used by the author in describing his ideal of correct social condition, and then try to find out what made it possible for the masses to arrive at their condition of wonderful prosperity. I think they will find that it was by correlating their energies, and not simply by putting their names together, that brought about their desirable condition.

Ibid., 1-2.                                                                    325

73. "A Timely Letter," *The Co-operator* III (11) (February 23, 1901): 2. Gaylord's reference to the boy in Manila likely is to the impact of the Spanish American War in The Philippines but it may also reflect a broader concern about imperialistic intents of the United States.

74. Oregon State Archives. File No. 3319. Thanks to Peter Neketin for bringing this information to light. See Peter Neketin, "To the Editor [letter]," *Oregon Historical Quarterly* 106 (Summer 2005): 334. I have discovered no additional information on Botts.

75. Fred Lockley, "Fred Lockley's Impressions," *Oregon Journal* (August 17, 1947). Also see Ernest Haycox, Jr., "To the Editor [letter]," *Oregon Historical Quarterly* 105 (Winter 2004): 659-60.
76. Ogukawa, "Annotated list of communal and utopian societies," 214.
77. Kent, "Cooperative Communities in the United States," 642. Again, Kent uses a quoted statement suggesting his information came from a source close to the colony.
78. Haycox, 658-60.
79. Kent, "Cooperative Communities in the United States," 642. The name of this colony is spelled inconsistently in the various compilations of communities. Frederick Bushee (1905) and Foster Stockwell (1998) use Union Mills. Okugawa (1980) and Oved (1988) list it as Union Mill. Given that A. J. Gaylord, the only member of the colony who has provided information on its name, uses no "s," although calling it the Nehalem Bay Union Mill Co., I have used the form Union Mill Company.
80. Okugawa, "Annotated list of communal and utopian societies," 214.
81. H. E. Girard, "From Nehalem Colony," 3.
82. A. J. Gaylord, "Duties of Members," 1.
83. Kent even notes in his entry that "No information has been received as to the number of members or the amounts invested," which once more suggests he was receiving information from a source close to the colony. Kent, "Cooperative Communities in the United States," 642.
84. Ibid.
85. Okugawa, "Annotated list of communal and utopian societies," 214.
86. LeWarne, *Utopias on Puget Sound*, 7.
87. See Monica St. Romain, "What Is Mystery of Old Religious Colony?" *Lincoln County Leader* (May 29, 1969). Most of this report appears verbatim in the online edition of *Sovereigns of Themselves: A Liberating History of Oregon and Its Coast*, compiled by M. Constance Guardino III and Rev. Marilyn A. Riedel (2006). Available at http://ftp.wi.net/~census/lesson36.html (accessed 8/2/07).
88. Noel V. Bourasaw, "Alice Elinor Lambert and Elizabeth Poehlman and their quest for history and a special guest – painter Tom Thomson." *Skagit River Journal of History & Folklore* (2005). Available at http://www. stumpranchonline.com/skagitjournal/Washington/Snohomish/Monte/Alice1-Bio1.html (accessed 8/2/07).
89. St. Romain, "What Is Mystery of Old Religious Colony?"; Bourasaw, "Alice Elinor Lambert and Elizabeth Poehlman ..."
90. The Bourasaw article quotes this as "Ona."
91. On the island of Iona, see, for example, Thomas P. Rausch, *Radical Christian Communities* (Collegeville, MN: Liturgical Press, 1990), 154.
92. St. Romain, "What Is Mystery of Old Religious Colony?".
93. Ibid.
94. *The Oregonian* (February 18, 1894): 8. The national administration was that of Grover Cleveland, a Democrat, who had been reelected to the White House in 1892. Confronting an economic depression, Cleveland focused on securing the U.S. Treasury by championing the repeal of the Silver Purchase Act, an action seen by his critics as kicking the ordinary people who already were down on their financial luck. On the impact of the Panic of 1893, as well as other economic panics of this era, see Elmus Wicker, *Banking Panics of the Gilded Age* (Cambridge; Cambridge University Press, 2000). For a variety of essays on the reform activities of the late nineteenth century, see Paul H. Boase, ed., *The Rhetoric of Protest and Reform, 1878-1898* (Athens: Ohio University Press, 1980).

95. *Oregonian* (February 18, 1894): 8.
96. Paula Wild, "Sointula's Free-Love Utopia," *Beautiful British Columbia* 40 (Winter 1998): 15.
97. See Paula Wild, *Sointula: Island Utopia* (Madeira Park, B.C.: Harbour Publishing, 1995), Gordon Fish, *Dreams of Freedom: Bella Coola, Cape Scott, Sointula* (Victoria, BC: Sound and Moving Image Division, Province of British Columbia, 1982), Andrew Scott, *The Promise of Paradise: Utopian Communities in B.C.* (Vancouver and Toronto: Whitecap Books, 1997), and Justine Brown, *All Possible Worlds: Utopian Experiments in British Columbia* (Vancouver: New Star Books, 1995). On the Finnish community in Astoria, see Paul George Hummasti, *Finnish Radicals in Astoria, Oregon, 1904-1940: A Study in Immigrant Socialism* (New York: Arno Press, 1979), a revision of his doctoral dissertation at the University of Oregon, 1975, and Ruby Hammarstrom, "The Finnish Settlement in Astoria, Oregon" (thesis, University of Oregon, 1912).
98. Bernhardt Selvig Jacobsen, "Viking Roots: The Story of the Family of Roy and Sophia [Romtvedt] Jacobsen" (Typescript, 1963), 13. For information on the Bellamy Colony I am most grateful for the work of Rosa Claridge who initiated the study of the colony in the 1960s, and for Carol Ginter who built on that work and added much valuable information. See Rosa Claridge, "Lincoln County's Bellamy Colony." Typescript. (Prepared for the Lincoln County Historical Society and the Sons of Norway, 1965-1966) and Carol Romtvedt Ginter, "Looking Backward ... at The Bellamy Colony," *Bayfront* 9 (June 1999). Also see James J. Kopp and Carol Ginter, "Seeking Prosperity and Freedom on the Oregon Coast: The Bellamy Colony, Lincoln County, Oregon (1897-1899)," *Communal Societies* 25 (2005): 57-74.
99. On Tweitmoe's life, see Lloyd Hustvedt, "O. A. Tveitmoe: Labor Leader," *Norwegian-American Studies*, Vol. 30 (Northfield, MN: Norwegian-American Historical Association, 1985): 3-54.
100. On the Farmers' Alliance, see John D. Hicks, *The Populist Revolt: A History of the Farmers' Alliance and the People's Party* (Minneapolis: The University of Minnesota Press, 1931).
101. An author sympathetic to the Alliance wrote: "Edward Bellamy is the beloved Apostle of Nationalism. His enchanting romance, 'Looking Backward,' is its bible." N. B. Ashby, *The Riddle of the Sphinx* (Des Moines: Industrial Publishing Co., 1890): 237.
102. Edward Bellamy, *Looking Backward (Tilbageblik), 2000-1887* (Boston: Houghton Mifflin, 1893). *Looking Backward* was translated and published in Denmark and Sweden as early as 1889. The Nationalist Movement also caught on in Norway and the other Scandinavian countries. The Norwegian review, *Kringsjaa*, includes various reports on "Det nationalistiske program." See Lars Ahnebrink, "A Contribution to Scandinavian Socialism" in Sylvia Bowman, et al., *Edward Bellamy Abroad: An American Prophet's Influence* (New York: Twayne Publishers, 1962), 261-64. This work continues to be the prime source on Bellamy's influence outside the United States.
103. On the Ruskin Colony, see W. Fitzhugh Brundage, *A Socialist Utopia in the New South: The Ruskin Colonies in Tennessee and Georgia, 1894-1901* (Urbana and Chicago: University of Illinois Press, 1996).
104. Ager based his accusations on an incident in 1893 when Tveitmoe was found guilty of forgery on a promissory note that he had issued to buy a share in the Alliance newspaper in Crookston, Minnesota. He served eight months in 1894 at Stillwater Prison until granted a pardon by the governor in December of that year. See Hustvedt, "O. A. Tveitmoe," 5-7.

105. *Reform* (July 6, 1897, August 24, 1897, September 7, 1897, October 12, 1897).

106. *Lincoln County Leader* (December 14, 1897).

107. Fred Romtvedt, "Fred Romtvedt: His Life and Loves, 1890-[1983]." Typescript prepared by Carol Ginter (1981), 2.

108. Ibid. Rosa Claridge in her study of the Bellamy Colony (2) reports, "The records of the Postoffice [sic] Department in the National Archives show that the site was located in the Northwest quarter of section 32, Township 10 South, Range 10 West, 3½ miles north of Toledo, 10½ miles south of Siletz and 8½ miles northwest of Yaquina."

109. *Lincoln County Leader* (January 4, 1898). The newspaper report states, "Mr. Tveitmoe and family are to be congratulated upon so handsome and appropriate New Year's gift."

110. *Lincoln County Leader* (February 8, 1898).

111. The *Lincoln County Leader* (August 5, 1898), in its obituary of Mrs. Johnson, reports, "The funeral was conducted under the auspices of the Bellamy Co-operative Association last Sunday, July 31." A "Card of Thanks" from Oliver Johnson appeared in the same edition in which he states, "Especially do I wish to thank the brothers and sisters of the Bellamy Co-operative Association for their many kind deeds and loving words."

112. *Lincoln County Leader* (April 8, 1898).

113. *Lincoln County Leader* (June 17, 1898). Olaf Tveitmoe was named postmaster and he later noted the post office had been established on May 24, 1898, just two days after Bellamy's death.

114. *Lincoln County Leader* (December 23, 1898). This report of Allen's age differs from that recalled by Fred Romtvedt but his was an estimate recorded some eighty years later.

115. Charles P. LeWarne, "Equality Colony: The Plan to Socialize Washington," *Pacific Northwest Quarterly* 59 (July 1968): 140. Also see LeWarne, *Utopias on Puget Sound*, 55-113. The first building constructed at Equality was named Fort Bellamy.

116. O. A. Tveitmoe, "Bellamy Beamings," *Industrial Freedom* (February 4, 1899): 2.

117. Ibid.

118. Ibid.

119. Ibid.

120. Ibid.

121. Ibid.

122. *Lincoln County Leader* (January 13, 1899).

123. *Lincoln County Leader* (January 20, 1899).

124. *Lincoln County Leader* (January 27, 1899).

125. Rosa Claridge "Interview with Mr. Fred (Fritjof) Romtvedt at his home, January 27, 1966" included in Claridge, "Lincoln County's Bellamy Colony." Fred Romtvedt was just a small child when he lived at the colony very briefly but his father, Sondre, likely passed along his assessment of Tveitmoe. In the interview, Fred Romtvedt also notes, "Mrs. Tveitmoe was addicted to a pipe and used to hide to smoke, as it was disgraceful for a woman to smoke in those days."

126. *Lincoln County Leader* (February 10, 1899).

127. Ibid. The newspaper specifically mentioned one "Jos. Bergin," presumably one of the new members accepted at the January meeting, who "has departed for La Grand [sic] Monday and if no work be found there he will return to his old home in North Dakota." *Lincoln County Leader* (April 14, 1899).

128. Claridge, "Interview with Fred Romtvedt."

129. See Carol Romtvedt Ginter, "Looking Backward ... at the Bellamy Colony," and Carol Ginter, "Romtvedt Reunion This Weekend," *South Lincoln County News* (July 26, 1995): 4. Carol Ginter also was responsible for corrections to the entry for "Bellamy" in the seventh edition of *Oregon Geographic Names* by noting the connection to Edward Bellamy and the colony established in his name. See McArthur, *Oregon Geographic Names*, 7th edition, 68-69. Rosa Claridge's study of the Bellamy Colony was the basis for an item by Monica St. Romain in the *Lincoln County Leader* for June 26, 1969 under the headline, "County Saw Another Try at Religious Colony Plan."

130. See Hustvedt, "O. A. Tveitmore: Labor Leader," and Claridge, "Lincoln County's Bellamy Colony." Rosa Claridge notes (3) that "A bitter news article in 1912 gives the only available mention of the Bellamy Colony and Tveitmoe's leadership of it."

131. McArthur, *Oregon Geographic Names*, 894. McArthur credits Joyce Boles of Portland for her efforts in tracking down this information. Others, including Michael Munk, have sought to find out more about this community but thus far this has been a utopian quest. Michael Munk does include a brief mention of Socialist Valley, as well as a modern photo of Socialist Valley Road, in his *The Portland Red Guide: Sites & Stories of Our Radical Past* (Portland, OR: Ooligan Press, 2007), 37, 46. Munk also mentions Aurora, Bellamy, New Odessa, and the Nehalem Valley Cooperative Colony in his chapter on "The Nineteenth Century: Utopians & Marxists."

132. McArthur, *Oregon Geographic Names*, 701. Also see "Once-Hopeful Town of New Era Fades As Modern Age Tightens Encirclement," *Oregonian* (July 5, 1964). It is not clear what publication was the source of inspiration for the camp, and in turn, the community.

133. *Oregon, End of the Trail. Compiled by Workers of the Writers' Program of the Work Projects Administration in the State of Oregon.* Revised Edition with added material by Howard McKinley Corning (Portland: Binford & Mort, [1951]), 306. It is not clear how much, if any, of the information for this entry may have come from McArthur.

134. David Johnson, "Greener Grass: A Short History of Oregon's Utopian Tradition," *Oregon Heritage* 1 (1994-95): 16.

135. Martha Anderson, "New Era Spiritualist Camp Opens 94th Annual Session," *The Oregonian* (July 5, 1967).

136. On the earlier publications, see, for example, *Oregon. Facts Regarding Its Climate, Soil, Mineral and Agricultural Resources, Means of Communication, Commerce and Industry, Laws, Etc., for the Use of Immigrants* (Portland: Oregon State Board of Immigration, 1876), and *Oregon As It Is: Solid Facts and Actual Results. For the Use and Information of Immigrants* (Portland: D. C. Ireland & Co., 1885).On later boosterism, see *The New Empire: Oregon, Washington, Idaho. Its Resources, Climate, Present Development, and Its Advantages As a Place of Residence and Field for Investments. The City of Portland. Its Trade, Commerce and Position . . .* (Portland: Ellis & Sons, 1888), and *Portland, the Metropolis of the Pacific Northwest* (Portland: Oregon Immigration Board, 1889).

137. H. N. Maguire, "Colony Matters—The Place for Homes," *The Universal Republic* 2 (1888): 143. *The Universal Republic* and its sister publication, *The World's Advance-Thought*, published in alternate weeks, were two spiritualist organs published in Portland in the 1880s and 1890s.

138. The reports of these groups appeared frequently in *The Oregonian*, including some it calls "Birds of Passage," who move throughout the West looking

329

for a spot good enough for them but repeatedly "expressing disappointment at not finding it this side of heaven." *Oregonian* (April 16, 1893): 4. Other reports include an article on "Forty-one people from Nebraska at The Dalles" (*Oregonian* (March 1, 1896): 7), and one week later a story notes an "advance guard for fifty families has arrived" from Columbus, Ohio, on their way to Roseburg (*Oregonian*, March 12, 1896: 7). In June 1899 a Canadian settlement in Malheur County is reported as "A Colony at Arcadia" (*Oregonian*, June 19, 1899: 9). "Many Danes Are Coming" read the headlines in a May 20, 1900 *Oregonian* article, and two months later the paper reports on a "Big Mormon Colony" in the Grande Ronde Valley (*Oregonian*, July 27, 1900: 4). A September 21, 1904 report notes that "Four carloads of colonists reached Portland yesterday from the East over the O. R. & N., and each train brings an equal number" (*Oregonian*, September 21, 1904: 12). The *East Oregonian* in Pendleton ( (January 15, 1904: 5) reports on a large colonization company from Minnesota looking at Eastern Oregon as a "promising opportunity." In 1905 *The Oregonian* reports that "Swedes Will Form Colony" (*Oregonian*, November 12, 1905: 10) and the following year the paper carried an article on a "Colony of Poles" that "will be established in the City of Portland" (*Oregonian*, June 3, 1906: 30).

## Chapter 5

1. On the challenges of documenting utopian schemes in Oregon, see James J. Kopp, "Documenting Utopia in Oregon: The Challenges of Tracking the Quest for Perfection," *Oregon Historical Quarterly* 105 (Summer 2004): 308-19.
2. Evangeline Nyden, "Panama Riot Helped Establish Sellwood," *The [Sellwood] Bee* (May 15, 1975). Also see Fred Lockley, "Observations and Impressions of the Journal Man," *Oregon Journal* (May 29, 1922).
3. Nyden, "Panama Riot Helped Establish Sellwood"; Dale Plumb, "Christian Utopia," *Oregon City Enterprise-Courier* Magazine Section (November 22, 1953).
4. Plumb, "Christian Utopia."
5. Rev. William H. Stoy. *A Sermon. In Memoriam – Rev. John Sellwood, B.D. Born May 6, 1806, Died August 27, 1892.* (Portland, 1892), 6.
6. My thanks to Richard Engeman who first brought this document to my attention. It can be found on the Library of Congress' American Memory Web site at http://memory.loc.gov/ammem/rbpehtml/pehome.html.
7. Plumb, "Christian Utopia."
8. Stoy, 23. Also see James J. Kopp, [Letter to the Editor], *Oregon Historical Quarterly* 106 (Winter 2005): 691-92.
9. Bolton Brown, "Early Days of Woodstock," *Publications of the Woodstock Historical Society* 13 (Aug-Sept. 1937): 3.
10. John Dixon Hunt, *The Wider Sea: A Life of John Ruskin* (New York: Viking Press, 1982), 324.
11. W. G. Collingwood, *The Life of John Ruskin* (London: Methuen & Co., 1905), 287.
12. Hervey White, "Ralph Radcliffe Whitehead," *Publications of the Woodstock Historical Society* 10 (July 1933): 19. White accompanied Whitehead to visit the carpenter many years later and White notes, "I have never before or since seen Mr. Whitehead in such openly, unreservedly happy temperament."
13. Robert Edwards, "The Utopias of Ralph Radcliffe Whitehead," *The Magazine Antiques* 127 (1985): 260. Edwards suggests that these communes were in Florence and Styria, Austria.

14. Alf Evers, *The Catskills: From Wilderness to Woodstock* ( Garden City, NY: Doubleday & Company, 1972), 604.
15. Nancy E. Green, "The Reality of Beauty: Ralph Whitehead and the Seeds of Utopia in John Ruskin, William Morris, and Victorian England," in Nancy E. Green, ed., *Byrdcliffe: An American Arts and Crafts Colony* (Ithaca, NY: Herbert F. Johnson Museum of Art, 2004), 41-42. Regarding information on Marie, Green notes, "Whitehead's second wife, Jane, is said to have disposed of any references to Marie among the papers left at her husband's death" (41).
16. Quoted in Green, "The Reality of Beauty," 42.
17. White, "Ralph Radcliffe Whitehead," 16.
18. Both essays appear in a collection published the following year titled *Grass of the Desert* (London: Chiswick Press, 1892). The title page of this publication shows his name in the hyphenated form, which does not appear elsewhere. Other essays in the volume include "Tuscany to Venice," "Words," "Dante," and "Modern Painters." Evers, *The Catskills: From Wilderness*, 608.
19. Whitehead, *Grass of the Desert*, 59.
20. Ibid., 61.
21. Ibid., 64-65.
22. Ibid, 64.
23. Ibid., 65-66.
24. Ibid., 73.
25. Heidi Nasstrom Evans, "Jane Byrd McCall Whitehead: Cofounder of the Byrdcliffe Art School," in Green, ed., *Byrdcliffe*, 58.
26. Green, "The Reality of Beauty," 43 and 55n35.
27. Quoted in Evans, 62.
28. White, "Ralph Radcliffe Whitehead," 21.
29. Green, "The Reality of Beauty," 49.
30. [Ralph Radcliffe Whitehead], *Arrows of the Dawn*. The first such essay was titled "The Unemployed" (1895). Subsequent essays were titled "The Power of Hellas" (1896) and "Picture for Schools" (1901).
31. Green, "The Reality of Beauty," 49.
32. Ibid, 50. Stetson had yet to marry George Houghton Gilman at this time and was going by her previous husband's surname. On the Ruskin Colony, see W. Fitzhugh Brundage, *A Socialist Utopia in the New South: The Ruskin Colonies in Tennessee and Georgia, 1894-1901* (Urbana and Chicago: University of Illinois Press, 1996). Summerbrook, founded by Prestonia Mann in 1895, is examined by Richard Plunz in "Chapter Six: Urban Intellectuals in the Valley," in Richard Plunz, ed., *Two Adirondack Hamlets in History: Keene and Keene Valley* (Keene Valley: Keene Valley Library Association, 1999), 222-26. Plunz notes, "Gilman, who was in attendance for several years, wrote the washing song used during the communal laundry work" (223).
33. White and Stetson would later collaborate on a play. See Denise D. Knight, ed. *The Diaries of Charlotte Perkins Gilman. Volume 2: 1890-1935* (Charlottesville: University Press of Virginia, 1994), 609-10, 752-57, and elsewhere. Gilman would continue to interact with both Ralph and Jane Whitehead, including correspondence with Jane (see Knight, p. 700) and visiting with Ralph. A letter from Pasadena on January 14, 1900, notes, "Mr. White, Mr. Whitehead and I walked a bit on the north beach in the glowing sweet color, and Mr. White & I ran and skipped and jumped over stones and were jolly." Mary A. Hill, ed., *A Journey from Within: The Love Letters of Charlotte Perkins Gilman, 1897-1900* (Lewisburg: Bucknell University Press, 1995), 339.
34. Brown, "Early Days at Woodstock," 4. On White, Alf Evers notes, "A native of a small town in Iowa, Hervey White went from there as a boy to a sod

house on the Kansas prairies where he learned to fiddle at dances besides working on his father's farm. He took off for the University of Kansas and to an exploring and scientific expedition in the mountains of Mexico. He left Kansas for Harvard and after graduation made a walking tour of Italy." Alf Evers, *Woodstock: History of an American Town* (Woodstock, NY: Overlook Press, 1987), 409-10.

35. White, "Ralph Radcliffe Whitehead," 14, 15.

36. Ibid, 23.

37. Hervey White, "Hervey White Autobiography," unpublished manuscript, p. 125. (University of Iowa Libraries).

38. White, "Ralph Radcliffe Whitehead," 23.

39. White's recollection of the instrument played by Reed differs from that noted by Alf Evers, who states that Reed played the piano.

40. White, "Autobiography," 127.

41. White, "Ralph Radcliffe Whitehead," 23, 24. Helena Modjeska (1840-1909) was a Polish actress who immigrated to the United States in the 1870s and was involved in the establishment of a utopian colony near Anaheim, California. See "Madame Modjeska and the Polish Colony at Anaheim" in Milton J. Kosberg, "The Polish Colony of California" (M.A. Thesis, University of Southern California, 1952), 18-33.

42. Jane Whitehead did not travel to Oregon as a son, Ralph, Jr., was born in 1899 and she was tending to him and recuperating herself. A second son, Peter, arrived in 1901.

43. Ralph Radcliffe Whitehead (hereafter RRW) to Jane Whitehead (hereafter JW), July 1, 1900. Winterthur Library, Joseph Downs Collection of Manuscripts and Printed Ephemera, Col. 209 (hereafter Downs Collection).

44. RRW to JW, July 3, 1900. Winterthur Library, Downs Collection.

45. RRW to JW, July 4, 1900. Winterthur Library, Downs Collection.

46. White, "Ralph Radcliffe Whitehead," 24.

47. Quoted in "The Reality of Beauty," 51.

48. White, "Autobiography," 127-28.

49. Quoted in Green, "The Reality of Beauty," 51.

50. White, "Autobiography," 129.

51. White, "Ralph Radcliffe Whitehead," 25.

52. Quoted in Green, "The Reality of Beauty," 51.

53. White, "Ralph Radcliffe Whitehead," 25.

54. Byrdcliffe was named by taking Jane's middle name and the second syllable in Ralph's middle name. On the history of Byrdcliffe, see Green, ed., *Byrdcliife: An American Arts and Crafts Colony*.

55. "List of Passengers and Officers of Foundered Steamship Vestris," *New York Times* (November 13, 1928).

## Chapter 6

1. John Curl, *History of Work Cooperation in America: Cooperatives, Cooperative Movements, Collectivity and Communalism from Early America to the Present* (Berkeley: Homeward Press, 1980), 1.

2. Wayne D. Rasmussen, *Farmers, Cooperatives, And USDA: A History of Agricultural Cooperative Service*. Agricultural Information Bulletin 621 ([Washington, D.C.]: U. S. Department of Agriculture, 1991), 21.

3. E. Sparks, "Seeking Utopia in America" (Chapter XXX of The Expansion of the American People), *The Chautauquan* 31 (May 1900): 151.

4. On the Rochdale Pioneers, see George Jacob Holyoake, *Self-Help By the People: A History of Co-operation at Rochdale* (London, 1858), later published as

*Self-Help By the People: The History of the Rochdale Pioneers* in numerous editions. Also see W. Henry Brown, *The Rochdale Pioneers: A Century of Co-operation* (Manchester: Co-operative Wholesale Society, 1944).

5. E. G. Nourse, "The Economic Philosophy of Co-operation," *The American Economic Review* 12 (December 1922): 578. At the outset of his article Nourse declares, "Taken by and large coöperators are long on practice and short on theory" (577). This puts them in a different category than most utopians, who seem to be long on theory and short on practice. Also see Charles P. LeWarne, "Labor and Communitarianism, 1880-1900," *Labor History* 16 (Summer 1975): 393-407.

6. The cooperative movement was not without its dissenters. One of these was Socialist Olive M. Johnson, who wrote the *Cooperative Movement: An Infantile Disorder and an Old-Age Disease* (New York: New York Labor News Company, 1924).

7. Ross E. Paulson, *Radicalism & Reform: The Vrooman Family and American Social Thought, 1837-1937* ([Lexington]: University of Kentucky Press, 1968), 159.

8. "Oregon to Be Home of World's Greatest Cooperative Scheme," *Oregon Daily Journal* (June 26, 1905), 1. My thanks again to Richard Engeman for bringing this article to my attention.

9. Ibid. The article includes a list of incorporators: "E. W. Langdon, president First National bank of Albany; N. W. Blagen, Bucoda Lumber company; Samuel Connell, president Northwestern Door company; J. Frank Watson, president Merchants' National bank; L. O. Ralston, president Oregon Savings bank; Harry L. Corbett, First National bank; C. E. S. Wood, Wallis Nash, and H. S. Wallace."

10. "Plan Model Settlement," *Oregonian* (June 27, 1905): 18. This article also lists Rev. David Leppert [Lippert] of Ontario and Rev. W. E. Randall of Portland as incorporators.

11. "Co-operative Federation," *Oregonian* (June 28, 1905): 8.

12. Ibid.

13. *Appleton's Annual Cyclopædia and Register of Important Events of the Year 1899.* Third Series, Vol. IV (New York: D. Appleton and Company, 1900), 686.

14. *The Co-operator* III (11) (February 23, 1901): 2. *The Co-operator*, has been noted earlier as the source of information on one of the members of the Nehalem Valley Cooperative Colony.

15. H. D. Staley to Wm. A. Hinds, March 7, 1902. William A. Hinds American Community Collection. Syracuse University Library Department of Special Collections. My thanks to Diane L. Cooter of the Special Collections Research Center at the Syracuse University Library for assistance in obtaining a copy of this document. The motto is from St. Paul, derived from "1st Thess., 5-23 and Tim 4-8." There are other quotes from the New Testament under banners for "Christ Jesus Our All in All," "The Holy Spirit Our Leader," and "Love, Our Badge." The address given for the Federation is Room 504 Marquam Bldg, Portland.

16. See Mark F. Weimer, "The William A. Hinds American Community Collection," *Syracuse University Library Associates Courier* 22 (Spring 1987), reprinted on the Syracuse University Library Department of Special Collection Web site at http://library.syr.edu/digital/collections/w/WilliamAHindsAmericanCommunitiesCollection/. The first edition of Hinds' *American Communities* was published in 1878 at Oneida by the Office of the *American Socialist*, the weekly publication of the Oneida Community.

The new edition was "enlarged to include additional societies, new and old, communistic, semi-communistic and co-operative." It was published by C. H. Kerr in Chicago, and included over one hundred forty communities in 435 pages. A second revised edition appeared in 1908, also published by Kerr, 608 pages in length.

17. The McKinley assassination is used by the author to demonstrate one of the key points of the document: "I suppose there is not an informed man in the world that does not know that the sad affair is the direct result of the great agitation going on over the question, the Rich and the Poor." The author also notes, "President Roosevelt emphasizes the great necessity of the immediate enactment of national laws to suppress anarchists; recommends that they be treated as pirates on the high seas." *Constitution, By-Laws and Prospectus of the Co-Operative Christian Federation Incorporated Under the Laws of the State of Oregon* (Christadelphia, Oregon, [1902]), 3.

18. Ibid., 2-3.

19. Ibid., 7-8.

20. Ibid., 26.

21. Ibid., 85. The name change to Christadelphia, along with the focus on the Bible and the spirit of Christian Brotherhood, suggests, though there is no direct evidence, that there may have been some influence by the small Christian denomination founded by John Thomas (1805-1871) in England in 1848, originally called the Thomasites but which adopted the name Christadelphians in 1864. On the Christadelphians, see "The Christadelphians" in Bryan P. Wilson, *Sects and Society: A Sociological Study of the Elim Tabernacle, Christian Science, and Christadelphians* (Berkeley: University of California Press, 1961), 219-314. Also see Charles H. Lippy, *The Christadelphians in North America* (Lewiston, ME: Edwin Mellen Press, 1989).

22. *Constitution*, 27. Capitalization here and elsewhere is as it appears in the document.

23. Ibid., 27-28.

24. Ibid., 29-30.

25. Ibid., 35.

26. Ibid., 40. Some of the inconsistencies in the document can be noted here, as it calls for a board of seven directors but the initial appointments suggest at least nine members, not counting Wallace.

27. Ibid., 46, 51, 52, 57.

28. These include Farm No.1 (G. C. Millet), 850 acres; Tract No. 2, Wilhelm farms, 2300 acres consisting of: Tract No. 1 (Townsite tract), 20 acres, Farm No. 2 (Richardson tract), 43 acres, Farm No. 3 (Dow farm), 40 acres, Farm No. 4 (Harkness farm), 160 acres, Farm No. 5 (Bundy Farm), 250 acres, Farm No. 6, 160 acres, Farm No. 7 (Cox Farm No. 1), 80 acres, Farm No. 8 (Cox Farm No. 2), 240 acres, Farm No. 9 (Huggins farm), 280 acres, Farm No. 10 (Looney farm), 513 acres, Farm No. 11 (Excelsior prune farm), 500 acres.

29. *Constitution*, 73-74. The original source of the letter has not been determined.

30. Ibid., 74. C. C. Hogue was not a known founder of the Federation but he apparently was a strong advocate. This was not Hogue's first involvement in social causes, including those with utopian underpinnings. He was president of the Corvallis Nationalist Club, founded in January 1890 in support of the ideas put forth in Edward Bellamy's utopian novel, *Looking Backward 2000-1887* (1888). He also had written an essay on "The Southern Question" that appeared in the June 1890 issue of *The Nationalist*, the monthly publication of the Nationalist movement sparked by followers of Bellamy's plan for

nationalized industry. What role Hogue played in later developments of the Co-operative Christian Federation, if any, are unclear. See James J. Kopp, "Looking Backward at Edward Bellamy's Influence in Oregon, 1888-1936," *Oregon Historical Quarterly* 104 (Spring 2003): 78, 93n40.

31. *Constitution*, 90-91. The St. Charles on Front and Morrison streets is recommended, where "The management is courteous, prompt and accommodating."
32. Ibid., 78.
33. Ibid., 84.
34. Ibid., 90.
35. Ibid., 91-92. This reads:

> THIS IS TO CERTIFY, That ..................... of ..................... Did on the ......... day of 190..., make application to the Co-operative Christian Federation, No. 1, for the purchase of a membership in said Federation, and that said ..................... made said application to the regular form printed and authorized by the Federation, and that he furnished a certificate of health signed by ..................... M.D., and paid the $20 earnest fee. THIS CERTIFICATE BEING RECEIPT FOR THE SAME; and furnished evidence that he was able to pay the remainder of $180 when the same was ordered into the hands of the trustee. And said Federation appointed and designated .....................
> ... of ....................., trustee to hold $180 on the following conditions, viz.: Said trustee shall hold said $180 and pay the same to the order of the Co-operative Christian Federation when said Federation shall have deeds conveying and vesting the title in the Federation of the lands, hotel, flouring mill, described in the Prospectus, Constitution and By-Laws of the Co-operative Christian Federation.
> In witness of which the Federation has caused the names of the President and Secretary set hereunto and the seal of the Federation affixed hereto.
> ................................................... President
> (Seal).................................................. Secretary

36. "Plan of Wallace," *Oregonian* (July 16, 1905): 9.
37. "For Christian Colony Work," *Oregonian* (July 31, 1905): 9.
38. "French-Glenn Ranch Bought," *Oregonian* (August 1, 1905): 11. Board members reported to have been present were J. Frank Watson, Samuel Connell, N. J. Blagen, R. L. Durham, L. O. Ralston, C. E. S. Wood, Wallis Nash, and H. S. Wallace.
39. "To Build Railways," *Oregonian* (August 6, 1905): 11.
40. "Work for 50,000 People," *Oregonian* (August 5, 1905): 11.
41. "Plans to Succeed," *Oregonian* (November 13, 1905): 12.
42. "Floats Bond Issue," *Oregonian* (February 16, 1906): 9.
43. "Plans Model City," *Oregonian* (February 19,1906): 13.
44 "Bonds Issued for Federation," *Oregonian* (March 1, 1906): 10.
45. In his study of "The Yaquina Railroad," Leslie Scott states, "Wallis Nash and other incorporated the Coöperative Christian Federation February 21, 1906" to build the road into that region, for colonization purposes. Leslie M. Scott, "The Yaquina Railroad: The Tale of a Great Fiasco," *Quarterly of the Oregon Historical Society* 16 (September 1915), 245. Also see "Compiler's Appendix" in Harvey W. Scott, *History of the Oregon Country*. Volume IV. (Cambridge, MA: The Riverside Press, 1924), 341; and M. Constance Hodges, *Lords of Themselves* ([Eddyville, OR]: Delion Historical Publications, 1978), 209, which provides a verbatim statement from Scott.

46. H. S. Wallace, *Co-Operative Christian Federation* (Portland: [The Federation], 1906), [1], 2-7. Associations, Institutions – Cooperative Christian Federation, MSS 1511, Oregon Historical Society Research Library. Other sections of the document include "The Methods and Limits of Control Over Associated Labor," "Character, Capabilities, and Requirements of Active Members," "Social and Personal Advantages of Membership," "Co-operative Stores," "Associate Member and Farmer's Unions," and "Preliminary Application for Membership." The document is "By H. S. Wallace, President" and is dated December 1906.

47. "Its Affairs Taking Shape," *Oregonian* (December 6, 1906): 10; "Plans Are Ready," *Oregonian* (December 22, 1906): 10.

48. "Vale Takes $50,000 of Bonds," *Oregonian* (January 7, 1907): 4.

49. "Must Change Its Plans," *Oregonian* (March 2, 1907): 10.

50 Scott, "Yaquina Railroad," 245. Harriman paid $750,000 for the railroad that was being sold by A. B. Hammond, who had incorporated the Corvallis & Eastern in December 1897. Hammond had intended to extend the railroad to Eastern Oregon but never did. This was the basis of Nash's and the Federation's interest in building a line across the state. Nash was involved in earlier railroad ventures, including that of the Oregon Pacific. See Wallis Nash, *A Lawyer's Life on Two Continents* (Boston: Richard G. Badger, 1919), 171-89.

51. *Detailed Prospectus No. 2 of the Co-Operative Christian Federation – The Garden City—Industries and Homes* (Portland: [The Federation], 1906). Associations, Institutions – Cooperative Christian Federation, MSS 1511, Oregon Historical Society Research Library, 5. Further details of the site are provided:

> The Clackamas River divides the land unequally—the largest part open, easily drained, lying about 75 feet above the river, inviting the placing there of stores, business houses, and of the residences of the citizens. The smaller area, on the west side of the town site, offers several hundred acres of rich bottom land along the river, suitable for fruit and vegetable growing, with beautiful residence sites on the surrounding hills, now covered with well grown fir trees and much native shrubbery.
>
> On the southwest boundary of the land, Clear Creek, a stream of pure mountain water, descending in rapid and cataract from the upper slopes of the Cascades, offers abundant supplies, both for drinking and for all other needs of the city. A smaller, but similar stream on the northeast edge of the tract gives opportunity for creating a "gravity system," the surplus of which can be used for occasional irrigation of the fruit and vegetable lands along the course of the main river.

52. Ibid., 8.

53. Ibid., 11.

54. See Robert Fishman, *Urban Utopias in the Twentieth Century: Ebenezer Howard, Frank Lloyd Wright, and Le Corbusier* (New York: Basic Books, 1977), 32-37, 40

55. Also on Howard, see Kermit C. Parson and David Schuyler, eds., *From Garden City to Green City: The Legacy of Ebenezer Howard* (Baltimore: Johns Hopkins University Press, 2002), and Robert Beevers, *The Garden City Utopia: A Critical Biography of Ebenezer Howard* (London: Macmillan, 1987).

56. *Oregonian* (June 19, 1907): 9.

57. Wallis Nash, "The Co-operative Christian Federation: A Remedy for Various Industrial Evils," *Oregonian* (November 3, 1907): 8.

58. "Co-Workers Will Build Model City," *Oregonian* (December 29, 1906): 14.

59. Included are Frank Parsons, author, lawyer, reformer, and champion of

vocational guidance; Elmer Gates, scientist and psychologist; Benjamin O. Flower, founder and editor of *The Arena* magazine and considered the "father of the muckrakers"; Ralph Albertson, a social worker and author whose "survey of mutualistic communities" has been noted; Bradford Peck, author of a utopian novel, *The World A Department Store*, and president of an organization established to realize the plans put forth in that novel; and several other individuals, including two of Vrooman's brothers, Carl and Harry. Of Hiram Vrooman himself, *The Oregonian* provides this background: "Rev. Hiram Vrooman, of Portland, Or., president. Mr. Vrooman is also vice-president and director of the Washburn Realty Trust, limited [sic], which controls as landlord $4,000,000 of the most central located mercantile business blocks in Boston, Mass.; president the Oregon League for Public Ownership of Railways; general supervisor the Great Department Store; director of the Boston Envelope Company; author. Mr. Vrooman preaches regularly Sunday morning in Knights of Pythias Hall, corner Eleventh and Alder streets, Portland." On Frank Parsons, see Arthur Mann, "Frank Parsons: The Professor as Crusader," *The Mississippi Valley Historical Review* 37 (December 1950): 471-90. Also see Roy P. Fairfield, "Benjamin Orange Flower: Father of the Muckrakers," *American Literature* 22 (November 1950): 272-82.

60. Robert S. Fogarty, *All Things New: American Communes and Utopian Movements, 1860-1914* (Chicago and London: University of Chicago Press, 1990), 172-73. Fogarty's work is one of the few that briefly mentions the attempted colony in Oregon.

61. Paulson, *Radicalism & Reform*, 92-93.

62. Hiram Vrooman, "The Organization of Moral Forces," *The Arena* 9 (February 1894): 348.

63. Bradford Peck, *The World A Department Store: A Twentieth Century Utopia* (Lewiston, Maine: Bradford Peck, 1900). In his Foreword, Peck outlines the intent of his book: "I offer this book to the thinking public as my humble contribution toward some solution of the great evils which, in my thirty-five years of business experience, I have noticed in our present system of life. It is not offered as a full-fledged system, but in the hope that the Coöperative Association of America, in a feasible way, may evolve by continued growth from its present small beginning in the city of Lewiston, Me. It is not intended as a literary effort, but as a word from one business man to others who know the cares of business life, and written so a youth could understand it" (v). On Peck, See Francine C. Cary, "The World A Department Store: Bradford Peck and the Utopian Endeavor," *American Quarterly* 29 (Autumn 1977): 370-84.

64. Wallace Evan Davies, "A Collectivist Experiment down East: Bradford Peck and the Coöperative Association of America," *The New England Quarterly* 20 (December 1947): 479, 480, 482.

65. Ibid., 483. Also see Paulson, *Radicalism & Reform*, 158-72; LeWarne, "Labor and Communitarianism," 406-7.

66. Davies, "A Collectivist Experiment," 484.

67. Vrooman, "The Government Can Employ the Unemployed," *The Arena* 25 (May 1901): 531-32. The influence of both Edward Bellamy and Laurence Grönlund is evident in this plan.

68. Vrooman, "Co-operative Association of America," *The Arena* 26 (December 1901): 578-87.

69. Vrooman, "A National Coöperative Conference," *The Arena* 27 (June 1902): 613. Vrooman provides this rationale for such a conference:

> The opportune time for the first real representative national conference of cooperators in this country is now. The country is dotted with small but

noble cooperative societies and stores struggling against odds to survive and grow. The time is ripe for all these enterprises to seek the mutual advantages of union. The opportunity seems to be open for the first time in this country for a national federation of all cooperative interests.

70. Vrooman, *The Federation of Religions* (Philadelphia and London: The Nunc Licet Press, 1903), 9.

71. Fogarty, *All Things New*, 173. *The Woman's Tribune*, which was published in Portland, Oregon, from October 1904 to May 1906 included a curious notice about Vrooman in its December 24, 1904, issue under the headline, "Scooping Up Gold with Steam Dredger": "The Rev. Hiram Vrooman, of Boston, whose gold and platinum dredging company has been advertised in previous issues of the *Woman's Tribune*, spent last summer in the gold fields of the Yukon Territory in behalf of the company." *The Woman's Tribune* 27 (27) (December 24, 1904): 106.

72. "For a Club of 1000," *Oregonian* (February 18,1907): 8.

73 Davies, "A Collectivist Experiment down East," 489-90.

74. "New Religious Body to Clean Up Corrupt Colorado," *New York Times* (August 18, 1912): SM3.

75."Utopia for Colorado," *New York Times* (May 2, 1915): 1.

## Chapter 7

1. Otohiko Okugawa's compilation shows a drop from thirty-five communities initiated in the United States in the 1890s to twenty each in the first and second decade of the twentieth century, when this study ends its analysis in 1919. Otohiko Okugawa, "Appendix A: Annotated list of communal and utopian societies, 1787-1919," in Robert S. Fogarty *Dictionary of American Communal and Utopian History* (Westport, CT: Greenwood Press, 1980), 173-233. Yaacov Oved's compilation includes twenty-three communities begun in the 1900s with fifteen initiated in the 1910s, and only one begun in the 1920s. Yaacov Oved, *Two Hundred Years of American Communes* (New Brunswick and Oxford: Transaction Books, 1988), 493. Foster Stockwell lists twenty-two societies founded in the first decade of the twentieth century but then thirty-two formed in the 1910s, dropping to seventeen in the 1920s. Some of the increase in Stockwell's count is due to the inclusion of several locations of a religious or ethnic group, many not included in other compilations. Foster Stockwell, *Encyclopedia of American Communes, 1663-1963* (Jefferson, NC: MacFarland & Company, 1998), 237-38. While these numbers vary again, depending on the definition and determination of communal groups, they do suggest a downturn in the number of such experiments.

2. Timothy Miller, *The Quest for Utopia in Twentieth-Century America. Volume I: 1900-1960* (Syracuse: Syracuse University Press, 1998), 1, 42-120. Also see Charles Pierce LeWarne, *Utopias on Puget Sound, 1885-1915* (Seattle and London: University of Washington Press, 1975).

3. Stockwell, *Encyclopedia of American Communes*, 85-86. This Freedom Colony should not be confused with the Freedom Colony in Kansas that lasted from 1897 to 1905.

4. See Michael Barkun, "Communal Societies as Cyclical Phenomena," *Communal Societies* 4 (1984): 35-48.

5. See Frederick Jackson Turner, "The Significance of the Frontier in American History," *Annual Report of the American Historical Association* (1893): 197-227. On the impacts of science, technology, and medicine on utopian thought, see Howard P. Segal, *Future Imperfect: The Mixed Blessings of Technology in*

*America* (Amherst: University of Massachusetts Press, 1994). Also see Joseph J. Corn, ed., *Imaging Tomorrow: History, Technology, and the American Future* (Cambridge, MA: MIT Press, 1986).

6. Steven Kesselman, "The Frontier Thesis and the Great Depression," *Journal of the History of Ideas* 29 (April-June 1968): 253.

7. Such works were published in the nineteenth century, including Ignatius Donnelly's *Caesar's Column* (1890), but more and more works of this type began to appear in the twentieth century, with Jack London's *The Iron Heel* (1907) often viewed as a benchmark. On dystopian literature, see M. Keith Booker, *The Dystopian Impulse in Modern Literature: Fiction As Social Criticism* (Westport, CT: Greenwood Press, 1994) and Paul G. Haschak, *Utopian/Dystopian Literature: A Bibliography of Literary Criticism* (Metuchen, NJ & London: Scarecrow Press, 1994).

8. Chad Walsh, *From Utopia to Nightmare* (New York & Evanston: Harper & Row, 1962), 13.

9. This change in mood led to such influential works as Aldous Huxley's *Brave New World* (1932), Ayn Rand's *Anthem* (1937), George Orwell's *Animal Farm* (1945) and *1984* (1949), and Ray Bradbury's *Fahrenheit 451* (1951), with many other dystopian works published between 1900 and the 1950s.

10. See Iver Willis Masterson, "A History of the Consumer's Cooperatives in Oregon Prior to 1900," M.A. thesis, University of Oregon, 1938.

11. U. S. Department of Labor, Bureau of Labor Statistics, *Cooperative Movement in the United States in 1925 (Other Than Agriculture). Bulletin No. 437* (Washington, D.C.: United States Government Printing Office, 1927), 157, 132. By the 1940s, this number would triple with the 1943 *Directory of Consumers' Cooperatives in the United States,* Bulletin No. 750 of the Bureau of Labor Statistics (Washington: GPO, 1943) listing seventy-three consumer cooperatives in Oregon (71-73).

12. E. G. Nourse, "The Economic Philosophy of Co-operation," *The American Economic Review* 12 (December 1922): 593, 594.

13. Joseph W. Eaton, *Exploring Tomorrow's Agriculture: Co-operative Group Farming—A Practical Program of Rural Rehabilitation* (New York & London: Harper & Brothers, 1943), 207. Eaton defines a co-operative group farm as "an association of a number of farm families who operate jointly a large-scale farming enterprise and who equitably share the returns of their group effort" (xiii).

14. Joseph W. Eaton and Saul M. Katz, *Research Guide on Cooperative Group Farming* (New York: H. W. Wilson Company, 1942), 41.

15. "Why Back to the Land," *World's Work* 23 (1912); 239. A bibliography of books on "back-to-land" was printed in the March 15, 1911 issue of *Country Life* and included titles "of most value to the average person . . . who has decided to take up farming seriously."

16. H. L. Davis, 'Back to the Land—Oregon, 1907," *American Mercury* 16 (1929): 323.

17. Eugene Davenport, "When Johnny Comes Marching Home, Will He Want Such a Farm as Uncle Sam Can Give Him?" *Country Gentleman* 83 (46) (November 16, 1918): 3.

18. "Farms for Our Soldiers," *Oregon Voter* 18 (September 6, 1919): 369-74.

19. R. W. Murchie, *Land Settlement as a Relief Measure* ([Minneapolis]: University of Minnesota Press, 1933), 5, 16.

20. Alvin Johnson, "The Happy Valley," *Yale Review* 22 (1933): 678.

21. A promotional brochure issued by the Resettlement Administration in 1936 explains the nature of greenbelt towns: "A greenbelt town is simply a

community built on raw land, in which every acre is put to its best use, and in which the traditional dividing lines between town and country are broken down. To the city worker, it offers a home in healthful country surroundings, yet within easy reach of his job." *Greenbelt Towns: A Demonstration in Suburban Planning* (Washington, D.C.: Resettlement Administration, 1936), [4]. Four greenbelt projects are identified—Greenbelt in Maryland, Greenbrook in New Jersey, Greenhills in Ohio, and Greendale in Wisconsin. On Greenbelt, Maryland, see George A. Warner, *Greenbelt: The Cooperative Community* (New York; Exposition Press, 1954).

22. One of the most thorough studies of Tugwell during the 1930s remains Bernard Sternsher's *Rexford Tugwell and the New Deal* (New Brunswick, NJ: Rutgers University Press, 1964). Also see Michael V. Namorato, *Rexford G. Tugwell: A Biography* (New York: Praeger, 1988) and his "Rexford G. Tugwell and the Resettlement Administration: An Alternative in Land-Use Planning," *Essays in Economic and Business History; Selected Papers from the Economic and Business Historical Society* 14 (1996): 267-78. For a list of works on FSA Farms, see Timothy Miller, *American Communes, 1860-1960: A Bibliography* (New York & London: Garland Publishing, 1990), 127-31. One of Tugwell's dissenters, Blair Bolles, invoked the negative aspect of utopianism in an article in the November 1936 issue of *American Mercury* titled "Resettling America: Dr. Tugwell's Dream Cities of Utopia," *American Mercury* 39 (November 1936): 337-45.

23. He wrote: "Twisting our hopes backward, sighing for past ages we imagine to have been more pleasant, or vainly straining forward toward the unrealities of Utopia—all this must be modified into a willingness to accept the clay of to-day as the material of to-morrow which may be molded in our hands." Rexford Guy Tugwell, *Industry's Coming of Age* (New York: Harcourt, Brace & Co., 1927), vi. Tugwell repeatedly comes back to the "Utopia" comparison throughout the book. In the penultimate paragraph of the book, he writes, "My own idea is that we might grow away from poverty and the other ugly concomitants of industrialism and toward something better, though not, indeed, like Athens or Florence or any of Mr. Well's Utopias" (266-67). And he concludes that paragraph by stating, "The first condition of achieving such a plan, however, seems to me, as I have implied, the recognition of present trends so that we may have some assurance that we are working for an attainable result and not wasting effort on Utopian aircastles" (267). Tugwell also revealed his interest in utopian thought when he reviewed Joyce O. Hertzler's *The History of Utopian Thought* in the *Political Science Quarterly* 39 (1924): 354-56.

24. Jonathan Mitchell, "Low-Cost Paradise," *The New Republic* (September 18, 1935): 152, 153.

25. Headings to the text speak of the "Birth of Empire," "Trail Blazers," "Cattle Kings and Sheep Barons," "Hey Day of the Homesteader" and "The Golden Decades," but then present "Days of Darkness," "The Stump Ranch," "Dust Blown Acres," and "Slough of Despond." But, as the text reads under the heading, "New Foundations," "The Resettlement Administration in Region XI, Oregon, Washington, and Idaho is launching the first concerted attack on the closely related problems of land use and rural poverty. The outcomes include "Beneficial Land Use," "Forests for the Future," "Rebirth of the Range," "Out of the Red," "Work for the Unemployed," and "Courage Renewed," among other positive developments. *Rehabilitated: Oregon, Washington, Idaho* (Portland: Resettlement Administration, 1936), 5. Another publication, Volume

One of the *Resettlement Administration Program in Oregon, Washington, and Idaho*, published in January 1936, includes some of the same rhetoric as other pamphlets—"Dreams of Empire," "Decades of Exploitation," "Return to Reality," "New Day Dawns," and provides information on two Oregon projects: one in Central Oregon and the other in "second growth timber land in Yamhill, Tillamook, Douglas, Lincoln, and Lane Counties." *Resettlement Administration Program in Oregon, Washington, and Idaho* (Portland, OR: Resettlement Administration Region XI, 1936), 30. The Resettlement Administration's Region XI office in Portland (in the Mayer Building) also published *Suggestions to Prospective Settlers in Idaho, Washington, and Oregon* in August 1936, a pamphlet "issued to assist in accomplishing the fundamental object of the Resettlement Administration – to bring about the best use of our land resources." *Suggestions to Prospective Settlers in Idaho, Washington and Oregon* (Portland: Resettlement Administration, Region 11, 1936), [2]. And the agency also produced land use studies, such as *A Land Use Study of Tillamook County, Oregon*, published in June 1937.

26. John Hyde Preston, "Collective Living," *Harper's Magazine* 176 (May 1938): 603.
27. Edward A. Norman, "Preface" in Eaton and Katz, *Research Guide on Cooperative Group Farming*, 14.
28. In 1941 the Rural Settlement Institute was established, with Edward A. Norman as its initial president. In 1949 its name was changed to the Group Farming Research Institute when it was incorporated in the State of New York. The Institute provided grants-in-aid, including one to Joseph Eaton for a follow-up study of Farm Security Administration group farms, and published a serial publication titled *Cooperative Living* from 1949 to 1957 that periodically included updates to the Eaton and Katz research guide under the title "Cooperative Communities Today," as well as sponsoring a series of books on cooperation including *Cooperative Group Living: An International Symposium on Group Farming and the Sociology of Cooperation*, edited by Henrik F. Infield, Director of the Group Farming Research Institute (New York: Henry Koosis & Company, 1950). See "Current Items," *American Sociological Review* 14 (July 1949): 426.
29. "The Aurora Experiment," *Sunday Oregonian* (February 28, 1932). The item ends with this brief statement on Keil: "Dr. William Keil was a native of Prussia, who came to the United States in 1836. Two years later, while in Pittsburgh, he became interested in Fourierism. He was a good orator and went about winning followers in several states."
30. Robert J. Hendricks. *Bethel and Aurora: An Experiment in Communism As Practical Christianity with Some Account of Past and Present Ventures in Collective Living* (New York: Press of the Pioneers, 1933), 253-73.
31. Roy Craft, "Co-operative Farm Found Serious Effort To Work Out Solution of Economic Life," *The Eugene Register-Guard* (January 22, 1933): 1.
32. Ibid., 2.
33. Ibid. Craft used the term "Native American" to mean native born American, not American Indian as the term later was used.
34. [Roy Craft], "Definite Assignments Mark Work Division At Co-op Farm," *The Eugene Register-Guard* (January 23, 1933), 1, 3. Also see Hendricks, *Bethel and Aurora*, 266.
35. [Roy Craft], "Predictions Of Failure At Farm Fall As Idea Develops," *The Eugene Register-Guard* (January 24, 1933): 1, 3.
36. *Co-operative Farm Bulletin* (August 1932), quoted in Hendricks, *Bethel and Aurora*, 268.

37. In Louise O. Bercaw, A. M. Hannay, and Esther M. Colvin, comps., *Bibliography on Land Settlement with Particular Reference to Small Holdings and Subsistance Homesteads* (Washington: United States Department of Agriculture, 1934), there is a reference (p. 171) to an article in the *Eugene Register-Guard* for November 10, 1933, with the headline "Group Planning for Community Living Project." The entry reads "Arnold Bodtkin explains in detail the proposed plan for a community settlement near Eugene, Oreg., which is 'to be self supporting through various industries working together and [is] to bring together families of the community who can be mutually helped'." It is unclear if there is a connection with this proposed group and the Cooperative Farm. The lack of subsequent information on either group suggests that had there been any connection that nothing further came of it.

38. "Coöperative Subsistence Colony Formed by Jobless Oregon Workers," *Christian Science Monitor* (December 7, 1937): 1. Interestingly, Ralph Albertson included this group in his "Survey of Mutualistic Communities in America," published in 1936, one of the few mentions of this cooperative activity. Ralph Albertson, "A Survey of Mutualistic Communities in America," *Iowa Journal of History and Politics* 34 (1936): 421. An entry for this group also appears in Bercaw, et al., *Bibliography on Land Settlement with Particular Reference to Small Holdings and Subsistance Homesteads*, 171.

39. "Coöperative Subsistence Colony," 1.

40. Florence E. Parker, *The First 125 Years: A History of Distributive and Service Cooperation in the United States, 1829-1954* (Chicago: Cooperative League of the U.S.A., 1956), 294. Florence Parker (1891-1974) is an inductee in the Cooperative Hall of Fame, an honorary organization established by the National Cooperative Business Association. Edwin G. Nourse, cited earlier in this chapter, also is an inductee. See http://heroes.coop/index.html.

41. Campbell's thesis was "undertaken primarily as an investigation of methods of social re-organization as applied by the unemployed in an attempt to meet the current economic crises by the creation of 'depression co-operatives'." Wallace J. Campbell, "'Depression Cooperatives': A Study in Social Reorganization," (M. S thesis, University of Oregon, 1934), 1.

42. See http://www.uoregon.edu/~asuosch/, and http://directory.ic.org/records/?action=view&page=view&record_id=2731. The Cooperative is listed in the *Directory of Intentional Communities.*

43. See http://varsityhouse.org/index.php?n=Main.History, and http://directory.ic.org/records/?action=view&page=view&record_id=5496. It is also listed in the *Directory of Intentional Communities.*

44. Kenneth Holland, *Work Camps for College Students* (Washington, D.C.: American Council on Education, 1941), 2.

45. Parker, *The First 125 Years*, 167.

46. On the Tule Lake Relocation and Segregation Center in northern California, where many Japanese Americans from Oregon were interned, see *A Question of Loyalty: Internment at Tule Lake*, Volume 19, *Journal of the Shaw Historical Library* (2005). Also see Lauren Kessler, *Stubborn Twig: Three Generations of a Japanese-American Family* (reprint: Corvallis: Oregon State University Press, 2008).

47. Parker, *The First 125 Years*, 167. Camps were located in Arizona, Arkansas, California, Colorado, Idaho, Utah, and Wyoming.

48. Parker states (167), "There are known to have been cooperatives in at least nine of the CPS camps: Two in Arkansas, three in California, two in Indiana, and one each in Michigan and Oregon. Most of them were stores, but the residents of Camp Magnolia, Ark., also had a book-buying club." This "book-

buying club" at Camp Magnolia is of interest to Oregon's cultural heritage as it was at this camp that William Stafford, later Poet Laureate of Oregon, served as librarian. For his personal reflections on these experiences, see William Stafford, *Down in My Heart* (Elgin, IL: Brethren Publishing House, 1947, reprinted with an introduction by Stafford's son, Kim Stafford, by Oregon State University Press in its Northwest Reprints series). This was based on his master's thesis with the same title presented at the University of Kansas in 1946.

49. On Oregon's CPS camps, see Joyce Justice, "World War II Civilian Public Service," *Prologue: Quarterly of the National Archives* 23 (Fall 1991): 266-73. Also see Leslie Eisan, *Pathways of Peace: A History of the Civilian Public Service Program, Administered by the Brethren Service Committee* (Elgin, IL: Brethren Publishing House, 1948), and *Camp 56: An Oral History Project: World War II Conscientious Objectors & the Waldport, Oregon Civilian Public Service Camp* (available at http://www.ccrh.org/oral/co.pdf). On the fine arts community at Waldport, see [Paul Merchant], *Glen Coffield, William Everson, & Publishing at Waldport, Oregon* (Portland, OR: Lewis & Clark College Special Collections, 2003).

50. See, for example, Katrine Barber and Eliza Elkins Jones, "'The Utmost Human Consequence': Art and Peace on the Oregon Coast, 1942-1946," *Oregon Historical Quarterly* 107 (Winter 2006): 510-35 and [Doug Erickson, Paul Merchant, and Jeremy Skinner], *Footprints of Pacifism: The Creative Lives of Kemper Nomland & Kermit Sheets* (Portland, OR: Berberis Press, Lewis & Clark College Special Collections, 2007).

51. Edward A. Norman, "Preface" in Eaton and Katz, *Research Guide on Cooperative Group Farming*, 9.

52. See Bennett M. Berger, "Suburbia and the American Dream" in Irving Lewis Allen, ed., *New Towns and the Suburban Dream: Ideology and Utopia in Planning and Development* (Port Washington, NY: Kennikat Press, 1977): 229-40. Other essays in this compilation are also very valuable on this topic.

53. M. Keith Booker explores this theme in *Monsters, Mushroom Clouds, and the Cold War: American Science Fiction and the Roots of Postmodernism, 1946-1964* (Westport, Connecticut: Greenwood Press, 2001).

54. Daniel Bell, *The End of Ideology: On the Exhaustion of Political Ideas in the Fifties* (Glencoe, IL: Free Press, 1960).

## Chapter 8

1. Margaret Ford, "Readback" [letter]. *Communities* 3 (1973): 64. *Communities* first appeared in December 1972 and was the consolidation of three earlier publications devoted to the commune/intentional community movement—*Alternatives* (which itself succeeded *The Modern Utopian*), *Communitarian*, and *Communitas*. All of these publications are vital resources in the study of communal societies in the post-1960s period. *Communities* is still published quarterly by the Fellowship for Intentional Community (see http://communities. ic.org/). For most of its existence it carried the subtitle *The Journal of Cooperative Living* but also appeared briefly as *The Journal of Cooperation*.

2. The same issue of *Communities* includes an article, "Our Oregon Community," about an unnamed community in Lane County early in the twentieth century. Although no author is given for this piece, it may also have been written by Margaret Ford as the author states "It was 1902, the year I was three years old, when my parents and I arrived in Lane County, Oregon." This would be consistent with Ford's age in early 1973 when the letter was written. The spirit and tone of the article are consistent with Ford's letter as well. The author of the article describes the reason for leaving that community:

When I was ill it was found that I could not stand the wet climate. I already had infected sinuses and bronchitis. I had to get to a dry climate or die early. So, we sold out the prosperous farm which we then had and left Eden. I did not know that the rest of the world was different but I was to find out. And I cried my lonely heart out on the wide barren plains of California ever since.

"Our Oregon Community," *Communities* 3 (1973): 12-13.

3. Elinor Lander Horwitz, *Communes in America: The Place Just Right* (Philadelphia: J. B. Lippincott Co., 1972), 157-58.

4. Joseph Stephen Olexa, "Search for Utopia" (Ph.D. Dissertation, University of Oregon, 1972), 61.

5. Timothy Miller, *The 60s Communes: Hippies and Beyond* (Syracuse: Syracuse University Press, 1999), 77, 70-71. The product of a broader study titled the 60s Commune Project, funded by a grant from the National Endowment for the Humanities, Miller's study is based on documentation from communities throughout the United States and numerous interviews of residents of many of the communal groups.

6. [John Stickney], "The Commune Comes to America: Youthful Pioneers Leave Society to Seek, From the Land and One Another, A New Life," *Life* 67:3 (July 18, 1969): 16B-[23]. To place this issue in a broader historical context, the next issue of *Life* (July 25, 1969) has on its cover a photo of Neil Armstrong as he sets out for the launch pad for Apollo 11, the mission that led to the first humans on the moon. The cover of the previous issue (July 11, 1969) reads, "A Choice of Heroes," with illustrations of actors Dustin Hoffman and John Wayne.

7. Ralph Graves, "Two Young Men in a Forest Commune [Editors' Note]," *Life* 67:3 (July 18, 1969): 1.

8. [Richard Fairfield], "Family of Mystic Arts," *Communes U.S.A. [The Modern Utopian*, Vol. 5, #1, 2, 3]. (San Francisco: Alternatives Foundations, 1971), 8. Fairfield was one of the first chroniclers of communes in the United States and elsewhere and as editor of *The Modern Utopian* provided some of the most valuable documentation on communes in the late 1960s and early 1970s. This letter also was published in Richard Fairfield, *Communes USA: A Personal Tour* (Baltimore: Penguin Books, 1972), 102-6, in which Fairfield identifies the communes as "Oregon Family" in respect to this condition of anonymity although he had used the real name in both the earlier version of the article and in the directory in *Alternatives*. Timothy Miller included the "Oregon Family" as a separate commune established in 1972 in his directory appended to *The 60s Communes* (p. 275).

9 Stickney, "The Commune Comes to America," 16B, 21.

10. Ibid., 21.

11. "An Interview with Bob Carey, Member, Family of Mystic Arts," *Communes U.S.A.*, 10. Also published as "Bob Carey and the Family: Getting It Together in the Woods," in Fairfield, *Communes USA: A Personal Tour*, 113.

12. Miller, *The 60s Communes*, 19.

13. Ibid., 20. Also see Michael Goodwin. 'The Ken Kesey Movie," *Rolling Stone* (March 7, 1970): 24.

14. "Interview with Bob Carey," 13.

15. On the international nature of the commune movement, see, for instance, the two compilations by Richard Fairfield, *Communes Europe* (San Francisco: Alternative Foundation, 1972) and *Communes Japan* (San Francisco: Alternative Foundation, 1972).

16. Miller, *The 60s Communes*, 15. Information on the Family was included in Fairfield's compilation. It was also included in Roy Ald, *The Youth Communes* (New York: Tower, 1970), 166, and Abby Hoffman, *Steal This Book* (San Francisco, 1971), 55.

17. Miller, *The 60s Communes*, 240. Interestingly, thirty-five years after the *Life* magazine article, the cover illustration appeared on the dust jacket of a book about the back-to-land movement of the 1970s. See Eleanor Agnew, *Back from the Land: How Young Americans Went to Nature in the 1970s, and Why They Came Back* (Chicago: Ivan P. Dee, 2004).

18. Miller, *The 60s Communes*, 65.

19. *A Guide to Cooperative Alternatives*, 1979 (*Communities* No. 38), 173.

20. Andre Carpenter, "Human Dance Company," *Communities* 17 (November/ December 1975): 3.

21. [Communes Looking for People], *Communities* 10 (November 1974): 57.

22. Miller, in the aptly titled chapter, "Out of the Haight and Back to the Land: Counterculture Communes after the Summer of Love, "*The 60s Commune*, 67.

23. Timothy Miller, "The Sixties-Era Communes" in Peter Braunstein and Michael William Doyle, eds., *Imagine Nation: The American Counterculture of the 1960s and '70s.* (New York & London: Routledge, 2002): 327.

24. Richard Fairfield refers to the commune as "Magic Farm" in *Communes USA: A Personal Tour*, 220-24, 226-33, and Hugh Gardner refers to it as Saddle Ridge Farm in *The Children of Prosperity: Thirteen Modern American Communes* (New York: St. Martin's Press, 1978), 194 and 194n. It was also identified as "Sunny Valley" in other studies. Interestingly, Robert Houriet in one of the earliest reports of the commune calls it High Ridge Farm but he is not specific on its location, which may have been the more critical element of concern. Robert Houriet, *Getting Back Together* (New York: Coward, McCann & Geoghegan, 1971), 28-87.

25. Elaine Sundancer, *Celery Wine: The Story of a Country Commune* (Yellow Springs, OH: Community Publications Cooperative, 1973), 9.

26. Gardner, *The Children of Prosperity*, 170.

27. Ibid., 198.

28. Houriet, *Getting Back Together*, 36.

29. Elaine Sundancer, "Saddle Ridge Farm," *Communities* 4 (1973): 8.

30. Gardner, *The Children of Prosperity*, 171-80. Richard Fairfield briefly mentions Talsalsan in his *Communes USA: A Personal Tour* but he refers to it as "Talsen" (p. 225).

31. Stan Kahn email to Jim Kopp, 8/16/08. Kahn lived on the land for several years and later became involved in environment issues, running for office on the Pacific Green Party in the 1990s. He also wrote a novel, *Y3K* (2007), that presents a story of thirtieth-century communards in the Pacific Northwest largely reflective of values of the late 1960s and early 1970s communal groups in Oregon.

32. Kahn to Jim Kopp, 8/16/08. The former residents of Sunnyridge, and their descendants, have one of the more interesting Web sites devoted to the commune—http://www.sunnyridge.net/. The site includes photos, maps, information on reunions, and a questionnaire with responses that provides some detailed views of the commune.

33. Fairfield, *Communes USA: A Personal Tour*, 305.

34. "CRO Farm: A Cultural Alternative," *The Augur* (March 3, 1970): 8. The reference to *Life* most likely is to the article on the Family of Mystic Arts.

35. Fairfield, *Communes USA: A Personal Tour*, 309.

36. Vivian Estellachild, "Hippie Communes," *W♀men: A Journal of Liberation* 2:2 (Winter 1971): 41, 42.
37. "Conversation ... with Cindi Smith," *Eugene Register-Guard Emerald Empire* (April 29, 1973): 13.
38. Fairfield, *Communes USA: A Personal Tour*, 349. Fairfield still referred to the commune as Yellow Submarine although it supposedly had changed its name in 1969. The original name also would appear in later writings.
39. Kay Teeters, "Communal Utopias of the Pacific Northwest," (Honors thesis, University of Oregon, 1970), 52-53. Teeters' information was based "on interviews and a visit with the commune on February 19, 1970" (52n). This and other theses written on Oregon communes are invaluable sources for information on these groups.
40. Dave Johnson and Aragorn, "Rivendale: A Communal Experience," *The Augur* 1:1 (October 14, 1969): 6. This article was reprinted in *Mother Earth News* 4 (July/August 1970): 23.
41. Kaliflower was a commune in San Francisco but it appears the commune adopted its named from the publication. An index to *Kaliflower* is on the Digger Archives web site at http://www.diggers.org/kaliflower. *Kaliflower* also is discussed below.
42. *Kaliflower* 1:21 (September 11, 1969). The address given was 474 McAuley.
43. Peter Bergel, e-mail to Jim Kopp, August 17, 2007. Bergel continues to be involved in efforts of nonviolent living as Executive Director of Oregon PeaceWorks (see http://www.oregonpeaceworks.org/site/index.php).
44. *Kalifower*, 1:47 (March 12, 1970).
45. Rudy Berg, e-mail to Jim Kopp, September 2, 2007. Among those in the move, according to Berg, was "another cluster of folks including Geoff and Judy Alexander [who were] based south of San Francisco."
46. Herb Seal, *Alternative Life Styles* (Singapore: Printed for CCS, Inc. by FEP International, 1974), 88.
47. *Communities* 12 (January/February 1975): 29.
48. Berg, e-mail to the Jim Kopp, September 2, 2007.
49. Geoff Alexander, e-mail to the Jim Kopp, September 6, 2007. I am grateful to several members of Ithilien for their willingness to share reflections on their experiences and memories of the commune.
50. A review of this film appeared in the *American Anthropologist* 76 (September 1974): 724-25. The film was produced by Rawlings-Chickering Productions and released by McGraw-Hill.
51. Gardner, *The Children of Prosperity*, 182-93.
52. On the House of Joy, see Hiley H. Ward, *The Far-Out Saints of the Jesus Community: A Firsthand Report and Interpretation of the Jesus People Movement* (New York: Association Press, 1972), 18, 48, 87-88, 96. Ron Bellamy and Joe Mosley take a look at Christ Brotherhood in "Gentle Christians or Dangerous Cult?" *Eugene Register-Guard* (November 6, 1981): 1E-2E.
53. Joe V. Peterson, "The Rise and Fall of Shiloh," *Communities* 92 (Fall 1996): 61. Peterson was an administrator at The Land in the 1980s and also wrote of Shiloh and the broader Jesus People movement in his master's thesis.
54. Ibid.
55. See, for example, Lynne M. Isaacson, "Delicate Balance: Rearticulating Gender Ideology and Rules for Sexuality in a Jesus People Communal Movement" (Ph.D. dissertation, University of Oregon, 1996) and Lynne Isaacson, "Rule Making and Rule Breaking in a Jesus Community" in Mary Jo Neitz and

Marion S. Goldman, eds. *Sex, Lies, and Sanctity: Religion and Deviance in Contemporary North America. Volume 5: Religion and the Social Order* (Greenwich, CT: JAI Press, 1995): 181-201.
56. See, for example, James T. Richardson, Mary White Stewart, and Robert B. Simmonds. *Organized Miracles: A Study of a Contemporary Youth, Communal, Fundamentalist Organization* (New Brunswick, NJ: Transaction, 1979) and Marion S. Goldman, "Continuity in Collapse: Departures from Shiloh," *Journal for the Scientific Study of Religion* 34 (1995): 342-53.
57. Peterson, "The Rise and Fall of Shiloh," 64.
58. Miller defines the 1960s era as "1960 to 1975, inclusive," but even in his compilation of communes he uses "mid-1970s" as a time frame, thus further illustrating that not only are the descriptive boundaries of utopia fuzzy but the temporal ones are also.
59. The Appendix lists resources where information can be found on almost all of these communities and, as noted previously, there are likely many others not included in this compilation.

## *Chapter 9*

1. From David Kherdian, *The Farm* (Aurora, OR: Two Rivers Press, 1978), 6. Kherdian was the leader of the Two Rivers Farm near Aurora.
2. Doug Bates, "Lane County's rural areas nurture communal lifestyle," *Eugene Register-Guard* (August 29, 1971): B1. On the same page is an article, "A Day in the Life of a Commune Dweller: 17-year-old Ty of Rainbow Farm."
3. Bates, "Lane County's rural areas nurture communal lifestyle," B1.
4. Herb Seal, *Alternative Life Styles* (Singapore: Printed for CCS, Inc. by FEP International, 1974), 56, 63-81.
5. Timothy Miller, *The 60s Communes: Hippies and Beyond* (Syracuse: Syracuse University Press, 1999), 92, 128-48.
6. Sandia Bear, "Lesbians on Land: A Tribe of Womyn," in Lynn Witt, Sherry Thomas, and Eric Marcus, eds., *Out in All Directions: The Almanac of Gay and Lesbian America* (New York: Warner Books, 1995), 324.
7. Miller, *The 60s Communes*, 138.
8. Association of Lesbian Intentional Communities, http://alicinfo.com/pages/directory.htm (accessed 8/12/07). Brief descriptions of ten of these communities are also included on the A.L.I.C. site—Cabbage Lane, Copperland, Fly Away Home, OWL Farm, Rainbow's End, Rainbow's Other End, Rootworks, Steppingwoods, We'Moon Land, and Womanshare. The A.L.I.C Statement of Intent reads: "A.L.I.C. is a participatory organization, designed to support the Lesbian intentional communities movement by sharing our collective wisdom, experience, and skills. Our intent is to foster solidarity, sisterhood, and community amidst diversity through: networking, energy, and resource sharing, and project funding. Our overall outreach goals is to be a vehicle for Lesbians to discover, participate in, and contribute to Lesbian intentional communities."
9. We'Moon Land has had several name changes in its herstory, first known generally as The Farm, then WHO Farm, We'Moon, and We'Moon Healing Ground. See http://www.wemoon.ws/land.html (accessed 10/01/07). The name of We'Moon Land also suggests the variant forms of words to represent women used in the names of communities and in the writings from and about these groups. These include, but are not limited to, womyn, womoon, womЯen, and wimmin. The general form of "women" is used here but with recognition of the concern and connotations that form brings with it.

10. Ní Aódagaín, "Empowerment through Community: From Separatism to Sanctuary" (Paper presented at the 26th Annual Gender Studies Symposium, Lewis & Clark College, March 8, 2007), 1.

11. See Dana R. Shugar, *Separatism and Women's Community* (Lincoln: University of Nebraska Press, 1995).

12. I have used the term herstory here as this often is the preferred term used by the women in community. The *Oxford English Dictionary* provides this definition of herstory: "In feminist use: history emphasizing the roles of women or told from a woman's point of view; also, a piece of historical writing by or about women." It notes the first usage in Robin Morgan's *Sisterhood Is Power* (1970). Also see June Sochen, *Herstory: A Woman's View of American History* (New York: Alfred Publishing, 1974).

13. Ní Aódagaín, "Living Among the Muses," *Woman of Power* 22 (1992): 76.

14. Several of Corinne's contributions on the herstory of Oregon women's land are unpublished anthologies and compilations, such as "Resources: Southwestern Oregon Women on the Land" and "Community Herstories: Living in Southern Oregon." These are available as part of the SO CLAP! (Southern Oregon Country Lesbian Archival Project) now in Special Collections and University Archives at the University of Oregon Libraries. Other of her writings and works are available at the University of Oregon in the Tee A. Corinne Papers. Finding guides to both of these collections are available on the Northwest Digital Archives web site—SO CLAP! at: http://nwda-db.wsulibs.wsu.edu/findaid/ark:/80444/xv68074, and the Tee A. Corinne Papers at http://nwda-db.wsulibs.wsu.edu/findaid/ark:/80444/xv98508. It is impossible to note these collections and others related to Oregon women's land without recognizing the efforts of Linda Long, Manuscript Librarian at the University of Oregon, who has been responsible for bringing together these important resources. To borrow from an earlier accolade of her contributions – "Linda Long ... has spent many years convincing the communities to deposit their collected papers at the University of Oregon. That she did so successfully is no mean feat, given the separatists' skepticism with patriarchal academic institutions." Catriona Sandilands, "Lesbian Separatist Communities and the Experience of Nature: A Queer Ecology," *Organization & Environment* 15 (June 2002): 160n12. In the years since this statement was made, Long has further enhanced the collections and access to these resources.

15. The compilation of these materials by Jean and Ruth Mountaingrove serve as the basis for The Feminist and Lesbian Periodical Collection in Special Collections at the University of Oregon. Information on this collection, including a list of titles and links to similar collection is available at http://nwda-db.wsulibs.wsu.edu/findaid/ark:/80444/xv94741. Ruth Mountaingrove also donated to the University of Oregon twenty-one autobiographical videotapes that include information on several of the communal groups with which she was involved, including Mountain Grove (from which she and Jean adopted their name), Cabbage Lane, Golden, and Rootworks. A finding guide to the Ruth Mountaingrove Videotape Autobiographical Collection is available at http://nwda-db.wsulibs.wsu.edu/findaid/ark:/80444/xv27369. The Ruth Mountaingrove Papers are also held at the University of Oregon.

16. Sue, Nelly, Dian, Carol, Billie, *Country Lesbians: The Story of the WomanShare Collective* (Grants Pass: WomanShare Books, 1976).

17. Joyce Cheney, ed. *Lesbian Land* (Minneapolis: Word Weavers, 1985). See Billie Miracle, "WomanShare" (p. 146-51); Jo Olszewska, "WomanShare Fall 1984" (p. 150); Jennifer Weston, "WomanShare Winter 1985" (p. 150-51); zana and

Hannah Blue Heron, "Golden" (p. 50-54); Ruth and Jean Mountaingrove, "Rootworks" (p. 125-28).

18. Hawk Madrone, *Weeding at Dawn: A Lesbian Country Life* (New York: Alice Streed Editions, 2000); Barbara Summerhawk and La Verne Gagehabib, *Circles of Power: Shifting Dynamics in a Lesbian-centered Community* (Norwich, VT: New Victoria Publishers, 2000).

19. These include Catherine B. Kleiner's "Doin' It For Themselves: Lesbian Land Communities in Southern Oregon, 1970-1995" (Ph.D. dissertation, University of New Mexico, 2003). Also see Jennifer Marie Almquist, "Incredible Lives: An Ethnography of Southern Oregon Womyn's Lands" (M. A. thesis, Oregon State University, 2004), and Katharine Matthaei Sprecher, "Lesbian Intentional Communities in Rural Southwestern Oregon: Discussions on Separatism, Environmentalism, and Community Conflict" (M. A. thesis, California Institute of Integral Studies, 1997).

20. Ní Aódagaín,"Empowerment through Community," 6.

21. The intent of such a trust was presented in the September 1975 issue of *Women's Press*: "A Woman's Land Trust is being formed in Oregon in order to expand the limited opportunities for women who want to live and work in the country. In order to make the Women's Land Trust a reality, we need women to work with our lawyer toward incorporation and getting tax exempt status, to obtain information on available land, to help set guidelines for the operation of the land trust and the use of the land, developing fund-raising techniques and sponsoring fund raising events, and continue the process of educating and disseminating information." *Women's Press* (September 1975): 20.

22. *WomanSpirit* 5:21 (Fall 1979): 41.

23. "Oregon Women Land Trust Report," *Women's Press* (July/August 1976): 16.

24. "Notes on a Land Trust," *WomanSpirit* 3:11 (Spring 1977): 34.

25. Ibid.

26. "Oregon Women's Land Trust News," *Woman's Place Newsletter* (October 1978): 16.

27. Elana, "Women's Communities: A Letter to Older Women," *Women's Press* (August 1975): 19.

28. *Older Women's Newsletter* 1:1 (March 1977).

29. *Communities* 33 (July/August 1978): 52, 56. Additional information on the Older Women Network is presented later in the same issue.

30. Ní Aódagaín, "Empowerment Through Community," 2-3. Also see Catherine B. Kleiner, "Doin' It For Themselves: Lesbian Land Communities in Southern Oregon, 1970-1995," 100.

31. Summerhawk and Gagehabib, *Circles of Power*, 42. The Wolf Creek area also would become home to communities of gay men, including the Wolf Creek Radical Faerie Sanctuary and the RFD Collective, which for a time in the 1970s published the *RFD Quarterly*.

32. Bethroot Gwynn, "Fly Away Home and Ritual: Some Herstorical Notes," SO CLAP!, Special Collections, University of Oregon.

33. Valerie Sonnenberg, "Rainbow's End," SO CLAP! Special Collections, University of Oregon.

34. Sandilands, "Lesbian Separatist Communities and the Experience of Nature," 139.

35. Teeters, "Communal Utopias of the Pacific Northwest," 51.

36. *Communities* 1 (December 1972): 31. Although only these few Oregon groups were listed in this issue, *Communities* became an important resource for identifying communal activity in Oregon.

37. [Reach – Artopia]. *Communities* 23 (November/December 1976): 51.
38. See Mercer, *Communes: A Social History and Guide*, 131, and Miller, *The 60s Communes*, 77, 116.
39. Alexander Patterson, "Terrasquirma and the Engines of Social Change in 1970s Portland," *Oregon Historical Quarterly* 101 (Summer 2000): 358-66.
40. Miller, *The 60s Communes*, 135.
41. Even Eve (Eve Furchgott) quoted in Ayala Pines and Elliot Aronson, "Polyfidelity: An Alternative Lifestyle Without Jealousy?" *Alternative Lifestyles* 4:3 (August 1981): 373-74.
42. "The History of the Kerista Community," http://kerista.com/herstory.html (from the "Kerista Village Handbook," February 1979).
43. David Harrington e-mail to Jim Kopp, July 23, 2005. The idea that "free love" was a common characteristic of all communes in the late 1960s and early 1970s is reflected in Joseph Olexa's statement, "As someone has stated, humorously, but perceptively, the motto of the new generation is 'Coitus, ergo sum'." Olexa, "Search for Utopia," 79. Others also thought the nuclear family was in crisis. See Michael Gordon, ed., *The Nuclear Family in Crisis: The Search for Alternatives* (New York: Harper and Row, 1972). There is a specific contribution by Larry L. and Joan M. Constantine on "The Group Marriage" (p. 204-22) as well as one by R. M. Kanter on "Communes" (p. 173-79). Interestingly, as will be noted below, the Oneida Community reappears in examinations of group marriage in the 1970s, illustrated in this volume by an essay by W. M. Kephart on "Experimental Family Organization: An Historico-Cultural Report on the Oneida Community" (p. 59-77).
44. As an aside, it can be noted that Oregon figured in the history (and future) of the *Kaliflower* publication and the communes that adopted its name. In a multi-colored "Assified Ad" in issue number 50 (April 2, 1970), there was a plea for input into the future of *Kaliflower*:

> We seem to be drawing inward and are growing involved in moving to Oregon and making a dirty movie. Should we give KF up with #52, should we expand our commune to include new energy sources who can carry on the newspaper, while other members of the commune can go to Oregon to fuck each other silly in a Shanghai vice den circa 1925??? If we have made any difference in your life, then come forward now and tell us what to do. Should we turn the newspaper over to another commune? Take it to Oregon for now then to maintain hand delivery? We hate meetings, otherwise we would call one and invite you all at once to tell us what is in your heart for the future of Kaliflower ...

The next issue, #51 (April 9, 1970), included a report on "Moving to the Country, Part Two, Grants Pass, Oregon." *Kaliflower*, however, continued to be published in San Francisco through 1972 and then revived briefly in 1980 with a compilation of earlier articles.
45. Dues in the Utopian Society were $5 and included a subscription to *Utopian Eyes* magazine, *Storefront Classroom* newspaper, and services offered by the "Utopian Liaison Office." This service "puts members all around the world in touch with other members so that correspondence, personal meetings, local utopian friendships based on shared utopian ideals can begin to happen between all of us." *Utopian Eyes* 2:1 (Winter 1976). The Spring 1976 issue notes that there were "253 paid members in the Utopian Society (8 of these are libraries)."
46. *Utopian Eyes*, 2:3 (Summer 1976): 39.
47. *Utopian Eyes* 2:4 (Fall 1976): 33.

48. "Seeks others to live in a polyfidelitous closed group of enlightened peasants on a self-sufficient homestead. Would like to exchange ideas of utopian visions. Interests in gardening, animal husbandry, building construction. Phil Hyre, 3566 Elmira Rd, Eugene, OR 97402." *Utopian Eyes* 3:1 (Winter 1977): [44].
49. David Harrington, e-mail to Jim Kopp, October 17, 2007.
50. "Polyfidelity Central," *Utopian Eyes* 4:4 (Autumn 1978): 21-22.
51. Ibid, 22. Beginning in the Summer 1977 issue of *Utopian Eyes*, an entry appeared in the "Personal Contacts" section of the magazine that would run in several subsequent issues. The entry read: "Seek others to enter into a long term commitment to build 1) an ecotopian (homeplace) village (Cerro Gordo); 2) a homestead neighborhood within Cerro Gordo; 3) a polyfidelitous family within the neighborhood. Allan Jensen, P. O. Box 831, Cottage Grove, Oregon. 97424." See, for example," *Utopian Eyes* 3:3 (Summer 1977). Cerro Gordo is discussed in more detail below.
52. David Harrington, e-mail to Jim Kopp, July 23, 2005.
53. Miller, *The 60s Communes*, xxii.
54. See Robert P. Sutton, *Modern American Communes: A Dictionary* (Westport, CT: Greenwood Press, 2005), 75, and Richard C. S. Trahair, *Utopias and Utopians: An Historical Dictionary* (Westport, CT: Greenwood Press, 1999), 183.
55. Hal Hartzell, Jr., *Birth of a Cooperative—Hoedads, Inc.: A Worker Owned Forest Co-op* (Eugene, OR: Hulogos'i, 1987), 39-48.
56. See "Full Moon Rising Quits Hoedads," *Woman's Press* (August/September 1979), 1.
57. Christopher Eaton Gunn, *Workers Self-Management in the United States* (Ithaca and London: Cornell University Press, 1984), 75.
58. "Business As Unusual," *Together* 1(2) (July 1974).
59. Hartzell, *Birth of a Cooperative*, 88-89.
60. *Together*, 2 (3) (September 1975).
61. "Full Moon Rising Quits Hoedads," 1. See Loraine Baker, "Half & Half Hoedads," http://www.westbynorthwest.org/summerlate01/Loraine.shtml.
62. Gunn, *Workers' Self-Management in the United States*, 75; Lois Wadsworth, "Tree Plants: The Mighty Hoedads, Back for a 30-year Reunion, Recall Their Grand Experiment," *Eugene Weekly* (August 2, 2001).
63. Gunn, *Workers' Self-Management in the United States*, 79. The Hoedads continued to be included in such studies as "Theoretical and Empirical Studies of Producer Cooperatives: Will Ever the Twain Meet?" in the *Journal of Economic Literature* (1993) and Gerrie Mackie, once president of the Hoedads, examined the Hoedads as part of his master's thesis at the University of Oregon and subsequently in "Success and Failure in an American Workers' Cooperative Movement" in *Politics & Society* (1994). John P. Bonin, Derek C. Jones, and Louis Putterman, "Theoretical and Empirical Studies of Producer Cooperatives: Will Ever the Twain Meet?" *Journal of Economic Literature* 31 (September 1993): 1290-1320; Gerry Mackie, "The Rise and Fall of the Forest Workers' Cooperatives of the Pacific Northwest" (M.A. thesis, University of Oregon, 1990); Gerry Mackie, "Success and Failure in an American Workers' Cooperative Movement," *Politics & Society* 22 (June 1994): 215-35.
64. Joel Sternfeld, *Sweet Earth: Experimental Utopias in America* (Göttingen: Steidl, 2006). The photo along with accompanying text on Alpha Farm appears on p. 10-11. Other Oregon communities included in this work are Lost Valley Educational Center in Dexter (p. 58-59) and Aprovecho Research Center in Cottage Grove (p. 88-89), both founded in the 1980s and discussed below.

65. Janine Altongy, "Alpha Farm, Deadwood Creek, Oregon," *Aperture* 144 (Summer 1996): 60-73. Photos by Eugene Richards.
66. George Howe Colt, "For the Foreseeable Future (The American Family, Part Six)." Photographic Essay by Eugene Richards. *Life* 14 (December 1991): 76-87.
67. Michael Theole, "Alpha Farm," *Communities* 34 (September/October 1978): 14-19.
68. Glenn Hovemann, "Alpha," *Communitas* 1 (July 1972): 20. The entry for "Alpha" in *Oregon Geographic Names* states: "The post office at Alpha was established in 1890 and operated until 1940. It was named for Alpha Lundy, the daughter of the first postmaster, Flora B. Lundy." Lewis A. McArthur, *Oregon Geographic Names.* 7th Edition. (Portland: Oregon Historical Society, 2003), 19.
69. [More Grapevine – Alpha], *Communitas* 1 (July 1972): 51.
70. Hovemann, "Alpha," 22. It is interesting to note this differentiation and concern over the word "commune," something that would become widespread in the 1970s. The adoption of "intentional communities" gradually became common, although its use, like many other aspects of these later communal activities, was not new. The term had been used at least in the 1940s when the Federation of Intentional Communities was established in 1948 in Yellow Springs, Ohio. (See http://fic.ic.org/history.php.) Henrik F. Infield in his study, *The American Intentional Communities: Study on the Sociology of Cooperation*, offered this explanation of the choice of the term in 1955:

> The intentional communities, the latest in a long line of similar attempts that have seen their day in America, represent an interesting variant of communitarian development. The people who found and populate them do so because of needs that apparently even they themselves to not consider to be compelling. Indicative of their attitude is the name by which they want to be known. Of all the possible and available designations, such as 'full community,' 'integral' or 'comprehensive' cooperative, they have decided upon one that is least specific. The term 'intentional' as applied to community sounds vague and empty, as if the people who decided on it were deliberately attempting to evade any definitive commitment. It is, nevertheless, a logical choice. For it suggests better than any other term the peculiar conditions out of which these communities grew.

Henrik F. Infield, *The American Intentional Communities: Study on the Sociology of Cooperation* (Glen Gardner, NJ: Glen Gardner Community Press, 1955), 5-6.
71. The "multigenerational" aspect that Hovemann notes is because Caroline Estes was in her mid-forties when Alpha Farm was started and Jim Estes was fifty. Two other members of the original group were in their fifties.
72. Leah Yanoff, "Communing to Work: Practical Idealism at Alpha Farm, a Back-to-the-Land Intentional Community" (Senior thesis, Lewis & Clark College, 2006), 15. Caroline also has a long involvement with the Fellowship for Intentional Communities.
73. On Alpha-Bit, see Mitch Harkovitch, "Alpha-Bit: Charmingly, Disarmingly Nice," *The Siuslaw News* (Spring 1991): 21-22, and Paula Ross, "Warmth and Caring Guide Alpha-Bit On," *Willamette Valley Observer* (October 9, 1980). Caroline Estes teaches and facilitates the consensus method of decision making and established the Alpha Institute, with Lysbeth Bories, to offer these services. See http://www.pioneer.net/~alpha/presenters.html.

74. http://www.pioneer.net/~alpha/mission.htm

75. Frances Newell, "I Didn't Know You Were A Warrior," *Communities* 45 (October/November 1980): 40. A general history of Breitenbush can be found on their Web site at htpp://www.breitenbush.com/about/history,html.

76. See *Communities* 44 (June/July 1980): 55; Corrine McLoughlin and Gordon Davidson, *Builders of the Dawn: Community Lifestyles in a Changing World* (Summertown, TN: Book Publishing Co., 1985), 47, 351.

77. *Communities Directory: A Comprehensive Guide to Intentional Communities and Cooperative Living. 2007 Edition* (Rutledge, MO: Fellowship for Intentional Community, 2007), 140. Breitenbush has consistently been listed in these directories since the early 1980s. Geoff Kozeny explored the nature of the Breitenbush community, the only Oregon community included, in his 2002 video, *Visions of Utopia: Experiments in Sustainable Culture.*

78. See, for example, [Reach – Communities With Openings], *Communities* 136 (Fall 2007): 65. Similar ads appear frequently in *Communities.*

79. *Communities Directory 2007,* 147.

80. *Communities* 24 (January/February 1977): 47.

81. Louis C. Androes, "Cerro Gordo: A Study in Tenacity," *Communities* 71/72 (Summer/Fall 1986): 18. This article provides a good summary of the background to Cerro Gordo and its challenges in formation. Also see "Pahana Town Forum," *Communities* 5 (October/November 1973): 42; [Grapevine], *Communities* 6 (December 1973/January 1974): 54-55; and, Dorothy Walker, ed. *The Cerro Gordo Experiment: A Land Planning Package* ([Cottage, Grove, OR]: The Town Forum, 1974).

82. "The New New Towns," *Communities* 7 (March/April 1974): 9. Other projects included in this article were Bakavi in Quebec, Communitarian Village, Alternative Community, Fayerweather, Village One, FutureVillage, and Arcosanti. The Commune Directory in that issue also included "Pahana Town Forum" for the first time, with a post office box at Lake Dorena.

83. Marvin Tims, "Planners delay 'utopian' village decision," *Eugene Register-Guard* (April 10, 1974): 2B.

84. Marvin Tims, "Planners delay action on Cerro Gordo," *Eugene Register-Guard* (May 30, 1974): 2B.

85. Don Bishoff, "Cerro Gordo plan rejected; appeal pledged," *Eugene Register-Guard* (June 12, 1974): IC.

86. Jerry Uhrhanner, "Cerro Gordo project: Securities law breach claimed," *Eugene Register-Guard* (December 18, 1974): 11B.

87. "Cerro Gordo Dream Still Alive, but Barely," *Eugene Register-Guard* (February 26, 1976): 1C; Deirdre McNamer, "Building a Dream," *Eugene Register-Guard* (January 16, 1977): 1F-2F; Lee Wilkins, "Planned Community May Win County's OK," *Eugene Register-Guard* (June 3, 1977): 1E.; John Thompson,"Long-delayed Cerro Gordo Project Started," *Eugene Register-Guard* (November 15, 1977): 1A-2A; Jerry Urhammer and Doug Bates, "Cerro Gordo Teeters on Brink of Collapse," *Eugene Register-Guard* (April 14, 1979): 1A-2A; Doug Bates, "Is Chris Canfield a Saint or a Fake?" *Eugene Register-Guard* (April 14, 1979): 2A; Doug Bates, "Developer Blasts R-G Investigation," *Eugene Register-Guard* (April 15, 1979): 2C.

88. Christopher Canfield, "Cerro Gordo: Future Residents Organize to Plan and Build an Ecological Village Community" in Gary J. Coates, ed., *Resettling America: Energy, Ecology, & Community* (Andover, MA: Brick House Publishing Co., 1981): 186-213.

89. Androes, "Cerro Gordo: A Study in Tenacity," 24.

90. [Networks & Resources – Cerro Gordo: A New Eco-Town in Oregon], *The Permaculture Activist* 34 (June 1996): 58; Toby Hemenway, "Cerro Gordo's Long Road to Community," *The Permaculture Activist* 35 (November 1996): 14-16. Bill Bishop, "State Files Lawsuit Against Eco-Village," *Eugene Register-Guard* (June 27, 1997): 1B, 5B.

91. *Communities* 66 (Spring 1985): 56. Also see *Communities* 62 (Spring 1984): 53. A classified ad for PEP appeared in the Winter 1985 issue of *Communities* with the text: "Ever Considered Group Marriage? Profit from our past and ongoing experience in successful, ideals-based polyfidelity." *Communities* 68 (Winter 1985): 59. Another ad ran in the Summer/Fall 1986 issue that read: "Group Marriage—Explore an option which includes deep friendship, shared parenting, enhanced economics, and evolutionary personal growth." *Communities* 71/72 (Summer/Fall 1986); 71.

92. Stephen Mallery and Ianto Evans, "Aprovecho Institute and the End of the Road Community: Pragmatic Idealism and a Living Example," *Communities* 74 (Summer 1987): 35.

93. *Communities Directory* 2007, 131.

94. See Larry Kaplowitz, "Living 'Naka-Ima' at Lost Valley," *Communities* 104 (Fall 1999): 22-27. Kaplowitz has written several articles on Lost Valley in various publications. On Naka-Ima, see http://www.nakaima.org/.

95. *Talking Leaves* is available at http://www.talkingleaves.org/.

96. Larry Kaplowitz wrote of "The Dark Side of Lost Valley" in *Talking Leaves* (Spring/Summer 1999): 38. This also appeared in *The Permaculture Activist* 42 (December 1999): 39. Diana Leafe Christian, former editor of *Communities*, incorporated many examples from Lost Valley in her 2003 book. Diana Leafe Christian, *Creating a Life Together: Practical Tools to Grow: Ecovillages and Intentional Communities* (Gabriola Island, BC: New Society Publishers, 2003).

97. The 2007 *Communities Directory* lists thirty-nine communities in Oregon but fourteen of these are identified as "forming." Some of these same ones have been listed as "forming" in one or more previous editions of the directory. It is important to note that my compilation comes from other sources in addition to the *Communities Directory*.

98. Kathryn McCamant, Charles R. Durrett, and Ellen Hertzman. *Cohousing: Contemporary Approach to Housing Ourselves* (paperback edition, Berkeley: Ten Speed Press, 1993).

99. Cohousing Association of the United States, htpp://www.cohousing.org/overview.aspx.

100. The Cohousing online directory only lists ten communities in Oregon but others are listed in *Communities* and other sources. For an overview of some of the cohousing communities in Oregon, see Diane R. Margolis, "On the Cohousing Trail—in the Pacific Northwest," *Communities* 109 (Winter 2000): 16-19. The theme of the Spring 2000 issue (#106) of *Communities* was "Cohousing: Building Community One Neighborhood at a Time."

101. Titanic Lifeboat Academy, http://www.lifeboat.postcarbon.org.

## *Chapter 10*

1. Tim Miller, "'Cults' and Intentional Communities: Working Through Some Complicated Issues," *Communities Directory: A Guide to Intentional Communities and Cooperative Living* (Rutledge, MO: Fellowship for Intentional Community, 2000), 30, 31. Also see the 2005 edition (p. 30-32) and the 2007 edition (p. 28-30).

2. See William W. Zellner and Marc Petrowsky, eds. *Sects, Cults, and Spiritual Communities: A Sociological Analysis* (Westport, CT: Praeger, 1998). An earlier study also sought to categorize the different types of groups. See Richard R. Mathison, *Faiths, Cults and Sects of America: From Atheism to Zen* (Indianapolis: Bobbs-Merrill, 1960).

3. The literature on these groups is extensive and several documentaries have also been produced. For the relationship of Jonestown to other events noted here, see Catherine Wessinger, *How the Millennium Comes Violently: From Jonestown to Heaven's Gate* (New York: Seven Bridges Press, 2000). On Heaven's Gate, see Janja Lalich, *Bounded Choice: True Believers and Charismatic Cults* (Berkeley: University of California Press, 2004). The Branch Davidian incident is examined in Kenneth G. C. Newport, *The Branch Davidians of Waco: The History and Beliefs of an Apocalyptic Sect* (Oxford and New York: Oxford University Press, 2006.). Also see David G. Bromley and Anson D. Shupe, Jr., *Strange Gods: The Great American Cult Scare* (Boston: Beacon Press, 1981).

4. Tim Miller, "The 'Cult' Scare Is Nothing New," *Communities* 88 (Fall 1995): 37.

5. The English version of the popular web site, Wikipedia, provides a list of groups and organizations listed by the media and elsewhere as cults, including Wikipedia itself. http://en.wikipedia.org/wiki/List_of_groups_referred_to_as_cults. The reference to Wikipedia as a cult comes from an essay by Charles Arthur in *The Guardian* (December 15, 2005), "Log on and join in, but beware of the web cults." http://www.guardian.co.uk/technology/2005/dec/15/wikipedia.web20.

6. Tim Miller, "'Cult' as a Useless Word," *Communities* 88 (Fall 1995): 31.

7. Definitions and usages noted here are from the online *Oxford English Dictionary*.

8. Wiley was one of the regular characters in the comic strip. The strip with this definition appeared on April 30, 1994. Others have also used this definition, which may derive from the comment Dean Kelley (1926-1997), noted advocate of religious liberty, made about the tragedy at Jonestown—"'The trouble is, one man's cult is another man's religion." See Gustav Niebuhr, "Dean Kelley, 70, Advocate for Religion Liberty, Dies," *New York Times* (May 14, 1997). Other quotes on cults frequently cited are those by Tom Wolfe—"A cult is a religion with no political power," and Frank Zappa, "The only difference between a cult and a religion is the amount of real estate they own."

9. Maurice Beam, *Cults of America* (New York: MacFadden-Bartell, 1964), 35-36. Beam, a journalist and free-lance writer, provides no sources for his information on Creffield or any other of the cultists he discusses, including Joseph Smith who he calls the "Hoopskirt Hypnotist." He does acknowledge the assistance of a pastor and a retired special investigator for the Attorney General of California in the preparation of the book so these may have been the source of some of his information. The intent of the work clearly is not historical accuracy but anti-cult rhetoric. Creffield and his followers were not Oregon's first communal "cult," as spiritualists and others in the nineteenth century were viewed in that manner, but it definitely is one that has caught not only the popular imagination but also that of scholars in a wide range of fields, from sociology to law.

10. In their 2002 study, *Holy Rollers*, aptly subtitled *Murder and Madness in Oregon's Love Cult*, T. McCracken and Robert B. Blodgett document several hundred of these newspaper articles in their extensive bibliography with nearly forty newspapers in the Pacific Northwest included, as well as some from San Francisco and Los Angeles. T. McCracken and Robert B. Blodgett, *Holy*

*Rollers: Murder and Madness in Oregon's Love Cult* (Caldwell, ID: Caxton Press, 2002), 279-92.

11. Brian Booth, "Stewart Holbrook," Oregon Cultural Heritage Commission "Oregon Originals"—http://www.ochcom.org/holbrook

12. Stewart H. Holbrook, "Oregon's Secret Love Cult," *American Mercury* 40 (February 1937): 167-74. This was reprinted in Alexander Klein, ed., *Grand Deception: The World's Most Spectacular and Successful Hoaxes, Impostures, Ruses and Frauds* (Philadelphia: Lippincott, 1955), 16-23. Stewart Holbrook, "Death and Times of a Prophet," in *Murder Out Yonder: An Informal History of Certain Classic Crimes in Back-Country America* (New York: Macmillan, 1941), 1-21, 221-22. This was reprinted in *Wildmen, Wobblies and Whistle Punks*, edited by Brian Booth (Corvallis: Oregon State University Press, 1992), 41-60. S. Underwood, pseud. [Stewart H. Holbrook], "Blonde Esther and the Seducing Prophet," *True Detective Mysteries* 27 (March 1937): 10-15, 92-94; and C. K. Stanton, pseud. [Stewart H. Holbrook], "The Enigma of the Sex-Crazed Prophet," *Front Page Detective* (January 1938): 4-9, 108-10.

13. L. Thompson, "Nemesis of the Nudist High Priest," *Startling Detective* 42 (March 1951): 5-11.

14. Several books have been published recently on the events, perhaps related to the centennial anniversary of the episodes. Prior to McCracken and Blodgett's *Holy Rollers*, published in 2002, a fictionalized account by Linda Crew based on newspaper reports appeared—*Brides of Eden: A True Story Imagined* (New York: Harper Collins, 2001). The legal aspects of the incidents, along with background information, are included in Jim Phillips and Rosemary Gartner, *Murdering Holiness: The Trials of Franz Creffield and George Mitchell* (Vancouver, BC: UBC Press, 2003). The press response to the events is examined in Gerald J. Baldasty, *Vigilante Newspapers: A Tale of Sex, Religion, and Murder in the Northwest* (Seattle: University of Washington Press, 2005).

15. Jan Parrot-Holden, "Joshua the Second: The Man Who Put the Hex on San Francisco," *Columbia* 11 (Winter 1997-98): 35-37, and Dick Pintarich and J. Kingston Pierce, "The Strange Saga of Oregon's Other Guru," *Oregonian* (January 7, 1986): C1-C2.

16. These included McMinnville, Grants Pass, Oregon City, The Dalles, Corvallis, and Heppner. Phillips and Gartner, *Murdering Holiness*, 290n15. The spelling of Creffield's surname appeared in various forms—Crefeld, Krofield, and Krafel. See Phillips and Gartner, 250n18. His middle name also has appeared as Edmond. See, for example, Dick Pintarich, 'The Gospel According to Edmond Creffield," *Oregon Magazine* (March 1983): 44-46. This was reprinted in Win McCormack and Dick Pintarich, eds. *Great Moments in Oregon History: A Collection of Articles from the Oregon Magazine* (Portland: New Oregon Publishers, 1987), 5-10. It is interesting that the editors would consider this a "great moment" in Oregon's history.

17. Phillips and Gartner, *Murdering Holiness*, 5-6.

18. Holbrook, "Death and Times," 4-5.

19. Ibid., 5.

20. The island is called Kiger Island by Holbrook while others call it Smith Island.

21. Holbrook, "Death and Times," 5.

22. *The Oregonian* (October 31, 1903): 1.

23. *The Oregonian* (November 24, 1903): 3.

24. Holbrook, "Death and Times," 7. Also see McCracken and Blodgett, *Holy Rollers*, 57-60.

25. Holbrook, "Death and Times," 9.

26. McCracken and Blodgett, *Holy Rollers,* 105-07.
27. Ibid., 110. Also see Parrot-Holden, "Joshua the Second," 35-37.
28. Holbrook, "Death and Times," 11.
29. Dick Pintarich captured some of this in two articles. The first, "The Gospel According to Edmond Creffield" appeared in the March 1983 issue of *Oregon Magazine.* The article notes in a fashion similar to earlier sensational discussions of the events: "Creffield was not your typical turn-of-the-century pastor. He debauched dozens of young women, lived naked underneath a house for two months and may have caused the great San Francisco earthquake. This is the story of his Bride of Christ Church, one of the strangest cults in Oregon's history." Pintarich, "The Gospel According to Edmond Creffield," 44. See also another article by Pintarich, this one with J. Kingston Pierce, that appeared in the January 7, 1986 edition of *The Oregonian.* "The Strange Saga of Oregon's Other Guru," C1.
30. Documentation on Rajneesh and Rajneeshpuram is voluminous, with more studies being published regularly. Basic information presented here is from several sources, including Sven Davisson, "The Rise & Fall of Rajneeshpuram," *Ashé Journal of Experimental Spirituality* 2:2 (2003); Vasant Joshi, *The Awakened One: The Life and Work of Bhagwan Shree Rajneesh* (New York: Harper & Row, 1982); Louis C. Androes, "Cultures in Collision: The Rajneesh Search for Community," *Communities* 71/72 (Summer/Fall 1986): 49-54; Louis C. Androes, "The Rajneesh Experience: A Report," *Communal Societies* 6 (1986): 101-17; James S. Gordon, *The Golden Guru: The Strange Journey of Bhagwan Shree Rajneesh* (Lexington, MA: Stephen Greene Press, 1987); Susan J. Palmer and Arvind Sharma, eds. *The Rajneesh Papers: Studies in a New Religious Movement* (Delhi: Motilal Banarsidass Publishers, 1993); Lewis F. Carter, *Charisma and Control in Rajneeshpuram: The Role of Shared Values in the Creation of Community* (Cambridge: Cambridge University Press, 1990); and Frances FitzGerald, *Cities on a Hill: A Journal Through Contemporary Cultures* (New York: Simon and Schuster, 1986). The University of Oregon has the Rajneesh Artifacts and Ephemera Collection, 1981-2004, which includes many important documents and publications produced at Rajneeshpuram. A finding guide to this collection is at http://nwda-db.wsulibs.wsu.edu/findaid/ark:/80444/xv60199.
31. For a brief biography of Ma Anand Sheela, see the Oregon History Project, http://www.ohs.org/education/oregonhistory/Oregon-Biographies-Ma-Anand-Sheela.cfm
32. This act was considered the largest act of bioterrorism in U. S. history and was brought back to memory in the post-September 11 anthrax scares in 2001. See, for example, John Cramer, "Oregon Suffered Largest Bioterrorist Attack in U. S. History, 20 Years Ago," *The [Bend] Bulletin* (October 14, 2001).
33. Eric Pace, "Bhagwan Shree Rajneesh, Indian Guru, Dies at 58," *New York Times* (January 20, 1990): A30.
34. The story of the Big Muddy Ranch at three stages of its existence—in 1901 as a working ranch; 1984 as the site of Rajneeshuram; and in the late 1990s as it developed into the Young Life's Washington Family Ranch at Wildhorse Canyon—is captured in Jane Kirkpatrick's historical novel, *A Land of Sheltered Promise* (Colorado Springs: Waterbrook Press, 2005).
35. Susan J. Palmer, "Rajneesh Movement," in William H. Swatos, *Encyclopedia of Religion and Society* (Walnut Creek, CA: AltaMira Press, 1998), 402.
36. Kirk Braun, *Rajneeshpuram, the Unwelcome Society: Cultures Collide in a Quest for Utopia* (West Linn: Scout Creek Press, 1984). Also see Louis C.

Androes, "Cultures in Collision: The Rajneesh Search for Community," and "The Rajneesh Experience: A Report."

37. Marie Daly Price, *Rajneeshpuram and the American Utopian Tradition* (Syracuse, NY: Department of Geography, Syracuse University, 1985).

## Conclusion

1. Ellis Lawrence to Mrs. Dorothy Mackenzie, July 16. 1943. Special Collections and University Archives, University of Oregon Libraries. In her response to Lawrence, dated October 4, 1943, Mackenzie wrote: "What tantalizing visions of Utopia you can conjure up! Not only ravishing glimpses of deep forests and majestic mountains and ocean but also mental havens with certain spiritual qualities existing most amicably with traits of human nature not ordinarily compatible. I wish we might have many more incorrigible idealists such as you." On Lawrence, see Michael Shellenbarger, "Ellis F. Lawrence (1879-1946): A Brief Biography" in Michael Shellenbarger, ed., *Harmony in Diversity: The Architecture and Teaching of Ellis F. Lawrence* (Eugene: Museum of Art and the Historic Preservation Program, School of Architecture and Allied Arts, University of Oregon, 1989), 8-24. My thanks to Stephen Dow Beckham for bringing this to my attention.

2. Prior to penning his utopian work, Hayes had written reflections on life in the West. See, for example, Jeff W. Hayes, *Tales of the Sierras* (Portland: F. W.Baltes, 1900) and *Looking Backward at Portland* (Portland: Kilham Stationery & Printing, 1911).

3. Jeff W. Hayes, *Paradise on Earth* (Portland: F. W. Baltes, 1913) and *Portland Oregon A.D. 1999 and Other Sketches* (Portland: F. W.Baltes, 1913). It is not clear why this compilation was published with two different titles. Howard P. Segal has offered the most complete account on Hayes and his venture into the utopian realm. See Howard P. Segal, "Jeff W. Hayes: Reform Boosterism and Urban Utopianism," *Oregon Historical Quarterly* 79 (Winter 1978): 345-57.

4. Hayes, *Portland, Oregon A.D. 1999*, 4, 5. References are given to this version of the publication but pagination is identical in *Paradise on Earth*. It is important to remember that these perceptions of the "death dealing automobile" are being made in 1913 when the automobile was still a very recent addition to the urban landscape.

5. Ibid., 6, 7.

6. Ibid., 8, 9, 12.

7. Ibid., 10, 16.

8. Ibid., 13-14, 16.

9. Ibid., 10, 11, 17.

10. Ibid., 18-19.

11. Ibid., 24, 35.

12. Duniway was working on a revised version of this novel, titled "Margaret Rudson, A Pioneer Story," shortly before she died in 1915.

13. Charles Cole, *Visitors from Mars; A Narrative* (Portland: Beattie & Hofmann, 1901). See Lyman Tower Sargent, *British and American Utopian Literature, 1516-1985: An Annotated Chronological Bibliography* (New York & London: Garland Publishing, 1988), 125.

14. Ira S. Bunker, *A Thousand Years Hence, or, Startling Events in the Year A. D. 3000; A Trip to Mars, Incidents by the Way* (Portland, 1903). See Sargent, *British and American Utopian Literature*, 128.

358

15. Francis H. Clarke, *Morgan Rockefeller's Will: A Romance of 1991-2* (Portland: Clarke-Cree Publishing Company, 1909). See Sargent, *British and American Utopian Literature*, 145.

16. Charles Ellsworth Linton, *The Earthmotor and Other Stories* (Salem: Statesman Publishing Company, 1920). The two stories are titled "The Hermit of Chimaso Island" and "Three Weeks Inside the Earth." See Sargent, *British and American Utopian Literature*, 167.

17. Ursula K. Le Guin, *The Dispossessed: An Ambiguous Utopia* (New York: Harper & Row, 1974) and *Always Coming Home* (New York: Harper & Row, 1975). The latter book was published with an audio tape of "The Music & Poetry of the Kesh." On utopian aspects of Le Guin's writings, see Laurence Davis and Peter Stillman, eds., *The New Utopian Politics of Ursula K. Le Guin's The Dispossessed* (Lanham, MD: Lexington Books, 2005) and Tony Burns, *Political Theory, Science Fiction, and Utopian Literature: Ursula K. Le Guin and The Dispossessed* (Lanham, MD: Lexington Books, 2008). Also see Naomi Jacobs, "Beyond Stasis and Symmetry: Lessing, Le Guin, and the Remodeling of Utopia" in Michael S. Cummings and Nicholas D. Smith, eds., *Utopian Studies II* (Lanham, MD: University Press of America, 1989), 109-17, Eileen M. Mielenhausen, "Comings and Goings: Metaphors and Linear and Cyclical Movement in Le Guin's *Always Coming Home*," Michael S. Cummings and Nicholas D. Smith, eds., *Utopian Studies III* (Lanham, MD: University Press of America, 1991), 99-105, and Werner Christie Mathisen, "The Underestimation of Politics in Green Utopias: The Description of Politics in Huxley's *Island*, Le Guin's *The Dispossessed*, and Callenbach's *Ecotopia*," *Utopian Studies* 12(1) (2001): 56-78.

18. Ernest Callenbach, *Ecotopia: The Notebooks and Reports of William Weston* (Berkeley: Banyan Tree Books, 1975). Portions of the novel appeared in "Ecotopia," *Oregon Times* (October-November 1975): 32-36, 22-23.

19. Jeff Kuechle, "The Way We Were: Portland Evolves from Shady Stumptown into Urban Utopia," *Pacific Northwest* (1989): P-4, P-6.

20. Bradshaw Hovey, "Building the City, Structuring Change: Portland's Implicit Utopian Project," *Utopian Studies* 9:1 (1998): 68.

21. Ibid., 68, 76-77.

22. Jim McChesney explores "Portland: Urban Eden or Sprawling Hell?" in the *Oregon Quarterly* 78 (4) (Summer 1999): 18-23. Also see Alex Marshall, "Portland and Oregon: Taming the Forces That Create the Modern Metropolitan Area" in *How Cities Work: Suburbs, Sprawl, and the Roads Not Taken* (Austin: University of Texas Press, 2000), 157-186.

23. Carolyn Merchant, *Reinventing Eden: The Fate of Nature in Western Culture* (New York & London: Routledge, 2004), 2.

24. See Robert Fishman, *Bourgeois Utopias: Rise and Fall of Suburbia* (New York: Basic Books, 1987).

25. Edward J. Blakely and Mary Gail Snyder, *Fortress America: Gated Communities in the United States* (Washington, D.C.: Brookings Institution Press and Cambridge, MA: Lincoln Institute of Land Policy, 1997). Another perspective on retirement communities is presented in Andrew D. Blechman, *Leisureville: Adventures in America's Retirement Utopias* (New York: Atlantic Monthly Press, 2008).

26. For the text of Ballot Measure 37, see http://www.sos.state.or.us/elections/nov22004/guide/meas/m37_text.html. A measure to modify some aspects of this Measure was passed by the Oregon voters in November 2007 (Ballot Measure 49).

359

# Index

367